STEPS ON THE PATH TO ENLIGHTENMENT

Steps on the Path to Enlightenment

A Commentary on Tsongkhapa's

Lamrim Chenmo

Volume 2: Karma

Geshe Lhundub Sopa

with David Patt

Wisdom Publications • Boston

Wisdom Publications
199 Elm Street
Somerville MA 02144 USA
www.wisdompubs.org

Library of Congress Cataloging-in-Publication Data ***for Volume 1***
Lhundup Sopa, Geshe, 1925-
Steps on the path to enlightenment : a commentary on Tsongkhapa's Lamrim chenmo / Geshe Lhundub Sopa ; David Patt, senior editor ; Beth Newman, editor.
p. cm.
Includes bibliographical references and index.
ISBN 0-86171-303-6 (alk. paper)
1. Tsoṇ-kha-pa Blo-bzaṇ-grags-pa, 1357-1419. Lam rim chen mo. 2. Lam-rim. I. Patt, David. II. Newman, Beth. III. Tsoṇ-kha-pa Blo-bzaṇ-grags-pa, 1357-1419. Lamrim chenmo. IV. Title.
BQ7950.T754L359 2003
294.3'444--dc22
2003017363

ISBN for volume 2: Karma
0-86171-481-4

13 12 11 10 09
5 4 3 2

Cover and interior design by Gopa&Ted2, Inc. Set in Diacritical Garamond 10.5/13.
Frontispiece and jacket photograph by Kalleen Mortensen.

Wisdom Publications' books are printed on acid-free paper and meet the guidelines for permanence and durability set by the Council of Library Resources.

Printed in the United States of America

This book was produced with environmental mindfulness. We have elected to print this title on 30% PCW recycled paper. As a result, we have saved the following resources: xx trees, x million BTUs of energy, x,xxx lbs. of greenhouse gases, x,xxx gallons of water, and x,xxx lbs. of solid waste. For more information, please visit our website, www.wisdompubs.org. This paper is also FSC certified. For more information, please visit www.fscus.org

Table of Contents

Foreword

THE *Great Treatise on the Stages of the Path to Enlightenment (Lamrim Chenmo),* composed by Tsongkhapa and explained here by Geshe Lhundub Sopa, is a commentary on the *Lamp for the Path to Enlightenment* by Atiśa. The primary goal of these teachings is to discipline and transform the mind. These texts have their source in the sutras and the other teachings of the Buddha himself, but their special virtue is that they convey the thought of the Buddha in a format that is easy to apply in actual practice.

The authors of these wonderful texts composed them in order to help all living beings. Since they developed the altruistic attitude to benefit mother sentient beings, we too should follow their example, irrespective of our own weak situation.

The Buddha and the great teachers who followed him gave clear instructions on how to proceed from a state of suffering to a state of peace and happiness. Following such teachings of the great masters of the past, Atiśa summarized them in his famous text, the *Lamp for the Path to Enlightenment.* It is a wonderful text, and Atiśa's disciples such as Dromtonpa and Potowa put what it teaches into practice. It was then transmitted through the Kadam lineages, finally coming down to Tsongkhapa.

He was an unparalleled scholar, who composed the *Great Treatise on the Stages of the Path to Enlightenment,* the marvelous text explained here in the manner of the great masters of Nālandā monastic university. We are indeed fortunate after so much time to have access to such a great work and to be able to read and think about what it contains. With this publication of Geshe Sopa's commentary, Tsongkhapa's words are brought to life and illuminated for a modern audience, continuing the lineages of scripture and realization that the Buddha set in motion more than 2500 years ago.

The two principal aspects of practice described here are a proper understanding of emptiness and the awakening mind of *bodhicitta.* A correct understanding of the view of emptiness is very important, for whether you are taking refuge, or cultivating the awakening mind of *bodhicitta,* all other practices are enhanced by such an understanding. At the same time, it is extremely important that our insight into the ultimate nature of reality is supported by compassion and the awakening mind of *bodhicitta.*

In my own case, regardless of my limited capacity, I try my best to develop these two minds: the wisdom understanding emptiness, and *bodhicitta*—the wish to achieve enlightenment for the sake of all sentient beings. Merely trying to approach and cultivate these two minds brings greater peace and happiness. The development of these two minds is really the heart of Buddhist practice. It is the essential meaning of this *Stages of the Path to Enlightenment.* If we were to examine all the sutras and words of the Buddha, along with the subsequent treatises that are commentaries to them, we would find that they can be summed up in these two practices. Therefore, we should study these teachings motivated by an aspiration to achieve enlightenment for the sake of all sentient beings.

Today, Buddhism is spreading throughout the Western world, encountering new cultures and new languages. During such a period of transition it is very important that the Dharma be transmitted by scholars and practitioners who possess a deep and vast understanding of the teachings, because that is the only way to protect the authenticity and purity of the teachings.

Atiśa exemplified this role by bringing the pure teachings from the great monastic centers of North India and establishing them in Tibet in an authentic and complete form that was, at the same time, suitably adapted to the Tibetan personality. He reestablished monasticism in Tibet and emphasized ethical conduct as the heart of Buddhist training. He dispelled the many misconceptions and erroneous customs that had entered the practice of the Dharma in Tibet. In this way he reestablished the pure Buddhadharma in many places where it had been lost, and enhanced it where it survived.

Requested by Jangchub Ö to give a teaching that would be beneficial to the Tibetan people in general, Atiśa composed the *Lamp for the Path to Enlightenment,* which condensed the essential points of both sutras and tantras into a step-by-step method that would be easy to follow. This text inaugurated the grand tradition of the study and practice of the stages of the path method in Tibet. Atiśa also worked with his Tibetan students on the translation of many texts from Sanskrit into Tibetan and so made a rich contribution to the flourishing of Buddhism in the Land of Snows.

Geshe Sopa, the author of this commentary on the *Lamrim Chenmo,* was one of the several good students of Geshe Lhundrub Tabke and was therefore chosen to debate with me during my final examination. Geshe Lhundrub Tabke, who became the abbot of Sera Je, was in turn one of the several good students of Geshe Tsangpa Lhundrub Tsondru, who was a renowned scholar at the time of the Thirteenth Dalai Lama and later ascended the throne of

Ganden Tripa. Geshe Sopa is therefore the third generation of high-quality scholarship commencing from Geshe Tsangpa Lhundrub Tsondru and he continues the excellent tradition today.

He is an exemplary heir of Atiśa's tradition conveying the pure Dharma to a new world in an authentic and useful way. He has been a pioneer among those bringing Buddhism to the West. He left for America in 1962. In due course, Geshe Sopa was invited to the University of Wisconsin, where he became one of the first Tibetan language instructors at an American university. He later rose to become a tenured faculty member, and his career as a Professor of Buddhist Studies eventually spanned more than thirty years.

All Tibetans should feel honored and proud that Geshe Sopa, a man from far away Tibet, could rise to the highest levels of Western academic attainment largely on the basis of his Tibetan monastic education combined with his own brilliance and personal qualities. Publication of this excellent series of books is a fitting tribute to an illustrious career.

Tenzin Gyatso, the Fourteenth Dalai Lama

Editor's Preface

One of the distinguishing features of Indian religions is a belief in karma and rebirth. In this worldview, the material world is fully integrated with the spiritual or ethical plane, and the key element in this integrated system is karma. In Buddhism, Jainism, and Hinduism, the action of karma is seen to control the process of rebirth and to determine the quality and length of one's life as well as the nature of one's experiences within that life.

The theory of karma pervades every aspect of the Buddhist tradition—the ethics, the metaphysics, the soteriology, the ontology—to such an extent that no comprehensive understanding of Buddhism as a philosophy, as a religion, as a worldview, or as a practical method of self-transformation can be complete without an accurate picture of the Buddhist view of karma. And yet, despite many decades of translation and scholarly studies of the sources, doctrinal development, and philosophical implications of Buddhist karmic theory, there has been no single volume where the reader could find a truly comprehensive picture of karmic theory. Now, here in Geshe Sopa's commentary on Tsongkhapa's encyclopedic *Lamrim Chenmo,* the Buddhist law of karma is laid out with an unprecedented thoroughness.

The word *karma* is derived from the Sanskrit root *kṛ,* "to do," and literally means "action." Understood as a causal principle, the law of karma states that happiness arises from virtuous actions and suffering arises from nonvirtuous actions. This is a completely natural process, immune to error, which is why Buddhists speak of the "law" of karma. In fact, Buddhists *define* virtue as those actions that lead to happiness and nonvirtue as those that lead to disappointment, pain, and suffering. Understanding which actions—which karmic causes—lead to which type of results is essential to any practice of the Buddhist path—the path leading to the ultimate cessation of suffering.

Understanding how the karmic law of cause and effect operates, and gradually developing the confidence that it is, in fact, a natural law that reliably determines the nature of our experience, is the foundation of all Buddhist ethics. Ethical conduct is the necessary condition for the most ordinary forms of happiness in the future, as well as for the realizations that bring about liberation and buddhahood. In other words, from the Buddhist point of view, we can achieve neither temporary nor lasting happiness if we do not come to terms with the cause and effect of karma.

This understanding and confidence in the processes of karma is called *right view,* the first component of the Buddha's noble eightfold path. As Geshe Sopa explains in chapter 1, we can distinguish two kinds of right view: *conventional right view* and *ultimate right view.* "Ultimate right view—the correct view of the ultimate nature of things—is the realization of *emptiness (śūnyatā).* Conventional right view is correct understanding of the cause and effect of karma and its results." Conventional right view, in other words, comprises both the understanding that positive karma will definitely produce happy results and that negative karma will definitely produce suffering, and the confidence that these karmic processes will certainly occur.

The Buddhist theory of karma contains profound implications for the way we view our world, ourselves, and the interconnected web of mind, body, and environment. Understanding those implications must begin with accurate knowledge of what that theory entails. The tools for gaining that knowledge were collected and assembled by Tsongkhapa from the explanations of such great Indian masters as Asaṅga, Vasubandhu, Nāgārjuna, and Śāntideva, and they have been elucidated here in the most accessible, straightforward terms by Geshe Sopa. Understanding the Buddhist teachings on karma that are presented in this volume is the first step for anyone who wishes to practice the Buddhist path, or for anyone who merely seeks to know what the Buddha taught concerning who we are and how we should live our lives.

This book is the second volume of a five-part series that will make available the commentary on Tsongkhapa's *Lamrim Chenmo* that Geshe Lhundub Sopa taught over many years at Deer Park, his Buddhist Center in Madison, Wisconsin. Geshe Sopa himself received the entire commentary on the *Lamrim Chenmo* from his teacher in Tibet, Ganden Trisur Lhundrub Tsondru. All who have contributed to this project have worked from a deep appreciation of the unique combination it represents: Tsongkhapa's unparalleled presentation of the Mahayana Buddhist path to enlightenment, opened up for the modern student, in its entirety by one of the greatest scholars and teachers ever to come out of Tibet. Recently I had the opportunity to offer a copy of volume 1 of *Steps on the Path to Enlightenment* to His Holiness the Dalai Lama. He looked down at the book on the table, tapped it with his fingers and said, "Authentic. Authentic."

Since I first proposed this series, everyone associated with it has grown a good bit older and grayer. Geshe Sopa has retired from his many years as a professor at the University of Wisconsin, traveled the world to give teachings, and lately has focused some energy on plans to build a beautiful new temple at Deer Park—an undertaking for which his students have worked tirelessly to raise funds. I remember so vividly how we built, with our own hands, the current wood-frame temple in 1981 to host the first Kālacakra initiation ever offered by the Dalai Lama outside of Tibet or India. That temple, which is still splendid in its simplicity, has been consecrated by a great many holy teachers, and its walls have absorbed a great many rare and precious teachings. But like all constructed phenomena, it is impermanent; it is doomed to decay and dissolution. The new temple, on the other hand, is a reminder of the optimism, the great possibilities for the future, that lie at the heart of the Buddha's message. Things change, all of us who have turned gray will sooner or later be gone, but the authentic Buddhadharma survives and continues to offer the means to peace and happiness for every being.

No one has done more to make the theoretical possibilities of the Dharma take shape in the world than Lama Zopa Rinpoche. Among his seemingly limitless projects he provides the financial support for this series of books. His faith in the lineage of Tsongkhapa, his respect for Geshe Sopa, and his devotion to carrying out the grand vision of his teacher, Lama Yeshe, have inspired all who have worked on this project.

The staff at Wisdom Publications, headed by Tim McNeill, have created the patient and appreciative context in which this work could be done, and they have done all they could to make these books the best they can be. David Kittelstrom has combined the refined editorial judgment and interpersonal skills that mark every great editor in supervising the editorial process. It has been a special treat and a privilege to work with Jon Landaw as the copyeditor on this volume. He has brought his poet's feel for the language and his vast knowledge of the Dharma to every page in this book, and I learned a great deal from his input. The entire project grew out of discussions I had with Nick Ribush, one of the founders of Wisdom Publications.

Beth Newman's massive editorial effort on volume 1 contributed greatly to determining the style and format for these books. I look forward to volume 3, on bodhicitta and the first four perfections, which she is editing. Volume 4, on the cultivation of single-pointed concentration, will be edited by Jim Blumenthal. Tenzin Dechen Rochard has already been working for a long time on the last volume, dealing with the realization of emptiness, and it is destined to be a major contribution to Madhyamaka literature in English.

A number of old friends in Madison have assisted me in large and small ways over the years. These include John Haggarty, Rod and Karen Stevenson, Sharon Van Sluijs, and Bob Victor. At Deer Park, David Farrell was always available to solve problems with tapes and technology; Geshe Sopa's secretary, Ani Lhundub Jampa, has been supportive and helpful in countless ways; and Venerables Lobsang Thapkey and Lhundrup Sherab have invariably bestowed impeccable Tibetan hospitality and good cheer.

For help during the final stages, I owe a debt of gratitude to Roy Li for invaluable contributions to the footnotes and bibliography; and to Robert Kulik for his proofreading and other editorial assistance. Bill Waldron has always been available to offer helpful suggestions. My own contribution to this endeavor would not have been possible without the unwavering support of my wife, Mary Christine Lauppe.

If there are errors in this book they are certainly mine. The benefit received by those who read it is purely the result of the wisdom and compassion of Geshe Sopa. I speak for everyone connected with this publication, and for many, many others, when I express how deeply grateful I am to have had the opportunity to know Geshe Sopa and to learn from him. May his teachings long abide in this world. *Sarvamangalam!*

Technical Notes

References

All works mentioned are referenced by their titles in English. Although there are many ways to render a particular title, we have employed the versions used in Cutler's translation of the *Lamrim Chenmo—The Great Treatise on the Stages of the Path to Enlightenment*—to make it simple for the reader to use both works.

At the first mention of a particular work we provide the title in its language of composition. Again, although scholars may find some irregularities, for the ease of the general reader we have followed the Sanskrit titles as they appear in *The Great Treatise on the Stages of the Path to Enlightenment.* The bibliography allows readers to find an English title and see the same title in Sanskrit (if applicable) and/or Tibetan.

Pronunciation

Terms from Sanskrit and Tibetan that have become part of the English language appear without diacritic marks or Tibetan spelling.

Tibetan technical terms and names are spelled phonetically for ease of use of non-Tibetan speakers. Sanskrit technical terms that are not commonly used in English appear in this work with diacritic marks. These terms appear in the glossary in English alphabetical order.

The following rough guide to Sanskrit pronunciation is from *The Wonder That Was India,* by A. L. Basham.

The vowels *ā, ī, ū, e, ai, o,* and *au* are long and have approximately the same pronunciation as in Italian, or as the vowels in the English words *calm, machine, rule, prey, time, go,* and *cow,* respectively. The vowels *a, i,* and *u* are short and equivalent to the vowels in the English words *cut, bit,* and *bull. Ṛ* is classed as a short vowel and pronounced *ri* as in *rich.*

The aspirated consonants *th* and *ph* are pronounced as they are in the words *pothole* and *shepherd;* they are never pronounced as the English *thin* or *photo. C* is pronounced *ch* as in *church. Ś* and *ṣ* are both generally pronounced as English *sh* as in *shape.* The distinction between the other subdotted retroflex consonants *(ṭ, ṭh, ḍ, ḍh, ṇ)* and the dentals (without subdots) is not important to the general reader.

Stylistic Note

Steps on the Path to Enlightenment is based on an oral commentary on Tsongkhapa's *Lamrim Chenmo* that Geshe Sopa gave to his students over the course of more than a decade. In turning Geshe-la's presentation into a series of books the editors have chosen to use an informal second-person voice. In contrast, the Tibetan language generally leaves person understood and is often rendered with an abstract third person: "one can do this" or "one should do that." We chose the second-person style in order to preserve something of the oral nature of the original and to create a more intimate bond between the author and the reader. The intent of Tsongkhapa and of Geshe Sopa was to give those who wish to embark on the path to enlightenment advice on how to proceed. This advice is offered here in the direct address of a teacher to his students.

Structure of the Book

The outline of headings in this book is drawn from Tsongkhapa's own outline of the *Lamrim Chenmo.* The chapter breaks and the format of the outline correspond to *The Great Treatise on the Stages of the Path to Enlightenment,* the English translation of the root text. Chapter 1 of this book corresponds to chapter 13 of volume 1 of that root text translation. The full outline for this volume is reproduced in Appendix 1 below, beginning on page 439.

Introduction

IT IS A FUNDAMENTAL TRUTH of life that everyone is searching for some kind of happiness. That is the central purpose in the mind of every being. You can watch people wandering from this experience to that experience, and what they are always looking for is something that will make them feel better. But no sooner is one craving satisfied than another desire arises demanding attention. This is the way beings spend their whole lives: trying to sustain some form of happiness and trying to avoid unpleasant conditions.

Unfortunately, the actions of most beings lead them in the wrong direction, because they do not know how to look for happiness or how to free themselves from misery. Their floundering efforts to find happiness actually become causes for more trouble and misery. Śāntideva says in *Engaging in the Bodhisattva Deeds (Bodhisattva-caryāvatāra):*

> Although their mind wants to be rid of misery,
> They rush straight for misery itself.
> Although they wish for happiness, due to ignorance
> They destroy their own happiness as if it were an enemy.[1]

Beings do not understand the actual root of their troubles; they do not see the ultimate goal; and they have no conception of the method to achieve that goal. Without understanding these essential aspects of the path to happiness they can only seek short-term solutions. These solutions take the form of temporary worldly pleasures, which distract them from their pain for a short time and provide the illusion of happiness. But attachment to these pleasures only leads them deeper and deeper into the cycle of suffering and dissatisfaction. They behave like children, who do all sorts of dangerous things because they seem fun at the time, without understanding the potentially harmful consequences of their actions.

Most beings never think about the cause and effect of their actions. They are unaware that the root cause of the unhappiness at the core of their lives is ignorance of their own true nature. This kind of ignorance is not merely a lack of knowledge: it actually perceives things in the wrong way. Out of that ignorance develops self-centered thinking along with many other afflictions *(kleśa)* such as desire, anger, jealousy, and pride. From these afflictions all kinds of contaminated actions arise. Those actions, called *karma* in Sanskrit, may be virtuous or nonvirtuous, but because they are rooted in the afflictions, they can only lead to further experiences within cyclic existence *(samsara).* Contaminated karma, which is based on afflictions, only leads to samsaric suffering.

Once trapped in this cycle we are subject to many painful diseases, some of which lead to death. But no physical illness can compare to the disease of samsaric life itself. The disease of cyclic existence is a mental disease, a disease caused when the mind is infected by karma and afflictions. It is a disease that has produced incalculable suffering because it has infected numberless beings since beginningless time. No ordinary medicine can cure this kind of deep sickness. The only remedy for the disease of samsaric suffering is the powerful medicine of wisdom, which comes from the study and practice of the *Dharma* teachings. This medicine is dispensed by buddhas, bodhisattvas, and teachers who have already cured themselves of samsaric sickness by their own practice of the teachings.

Because beings are obscured by so many different kinds of afflictions, the Dharma consists of many different antidotes. First we need to determine which mental states need to be eliminated, how they are caused, and how they can be purified. Then we need to learn what the specific methods for purifying them are. Then we need to put them into practice. It is not enough merely to put this knowledge into your head or tell someone else about it. You have to put the teachings into practice by training your mind in the antidotes to the afflictions; only then will you be cured. Apart from that sincere effort there is no way of curing this deep disease.

Of course, these teachings can be very difficult to put into practice because they are antithetical to our usual way of thinking and behaving. Most of the time our perceptions and actions proceed under the power of the afflictions. We align ourselves with the side of ignorance; though ignorance is our most powerful inner enemy, we agree with it because we do not recognize it as the enemy. Instead we look outside ourselves for the source of our troubles and blame all our problems on external conditions. But the truth is that all the causes of our problems are inside ourselves, in the qualities of our own minds. The purpose of the Dharma teachings is to provide the skillful methods to transform those mental qualities. First you have to learn those methods, then practice them with concentrated effort over a long period of time.

Because this disease of samsara is so deep and manifests on so many levels, many different levels of teaching are required to cure it. That is why the teachings in this *lamrim* tradition, these steps on the path to enlightenment, are structured in progressive stages. Each step leads us along a gradual path back to health. The Buddha's original teachings were collected in many different sutras, tantras, and other scriptures. The various remedies for the afflictions were not presented systematically, all in one place. But here, in the *Lamrim Chenmo*, Tsongkhapa has gathered together the methods that were scattered throughout the scriptures and organized them into a format that can be practiced step-by-step. Basing his presentation on the work of Atiśa,[2] he has given us a method to transform our minds that is easy to learn and easy to practice.

The organizing principle into which all of these stages fit is the concept of the three levels of the path, based on three types of practitioners. The path of the being of small scope consists of the trainings that must be practiced by an individual whose main goal is to attain a high rebirth in his or her next life. The path of the being of intermediate scope includes the practices for an individual who seeks complete emancipation from all of cyclic existence, but mainly for himself or herself. The ultimate goal of the lamrim system is perfect buddhahood, or enlightenment. The trainings that can achieve that goal of perfect enlightenment are included on the path of the being of great scope, which is the Mahayana path, the path of the bodhisattva. This is the path for beings who seek complete liberation not merely for themselves, but in order to lead all other sentient beings out of samsaric suffering and to their enlightenment. This is the bodhisattva's motivation: the determination to attain enlightenment for the benefit of all sentient beings. It is called the Mahayana path: *Mahayana* means *great vehicle,* and it is called that because it is a vehicle that can carry *all* beings to liberation. It is the practice of beings of *great scope* because Mahayana practitioners take responsibility for all beings rather than just themselves.

It is important to understand that all the trainings of the being of small scope and the being of intermediate scope are *common* to the being of great scope, the Mahayana practitioner. In order to develop the renunciation and the compassion that are the foundation of Mahayana practice, it is necessary to realize all the teachings that are laid out in the earlier stages of the path. This is the reason the student is led through all three of these levels.[3] Though individually each of these three paths is directed toward a different goal and has a different emphasis, they all fit together in an integrated system that ultimately leads to the Mahayana path.

This second volume in our series emphasizes the practices of the being of intermediate scope. It begins with the cause and effect of karma, which we must understand in order to build a firm foundation of ethical conduct. The training in ethical conduct is the indispensable cause of achieving the goals of the being of small scope, which is to have a higher rebirth in the future, and forms the basis of all future progress on the path. The goal of the being of intermediate scope is to escape from all samsaric suffering by attaining liberation from cyclic existence. To do this a practitioner must realize the four noble truths, and in this volume we focus particularly on the first two truths: *suffering* and the *cause of suffering.* We meditate on the general sufferings of samsara, bringing to mind the reasons why cyclic existence is completely enmeshed in suffering and why only complete emancipation can bring us true happiness. In this section only the sufferings of the higher realms are discussed, because the sufferings of the lower realms were previously treated in the first volume in this series.

We then meditate on the twelve links of dependent origination, which analyze the truths of suffering and the cause of suffering in still more detail. We examine how cyclic existence evolves, and how this process can actually be deconstructed and put into reverse by meditating on these twelve links.

Finally, we turn to the last two noble truths: the truth of *cessation* and the truth of the *path* that can lead us out of suffering. This path is embodied in the three trainings of ethical conduct, meditative stabilization, and wisdom. The latter two are treated at great length in subsequent volumes, but here we focus on ethical conduct, which forms the basis of everything we are trying to build and accomplish in our practice. It is the training of wisdom that finally brings about the cessation of suffering, and in order to achieve that level of realization we must focus the mind with the training of meditative stabilization. But we cannot attain either one of these goals without the firm foundation of ethical conduct. Whether we want to achieve a better rebirth in our next life, personal liberation from cyclic existence, or perfect buddhahood for the sake of all sentient beings, we must begin with the training of ethical conduct. The meditations in this volume will give us the means to build that solid foundation.

Taking the initial steps on a spiritual path

The decision to engage in a spiritual practice begins with an appreciation of the unusual opportunity we hold in our hands at this very moment. Śāntideva says in *Engaging in the Bodhisattva Deeds:*

> Although countless buddhas have passed by
> With the purpose of helping all sentient beings,

> Due to my own faults,
> I was not the object of their curative care.[4]

We have been cycling up and down in samsara since beginningless time. During that time innumerable buddhas and bodhisattvas have appeared in the world and their only purpose has been to help sentient beings, and countless beings have received their aid. Some of them have already achieved their own buddhahood; some have reached the bodhisattva stage; some have attained emancipation from cyclic existence; and many many more beings are still progressing along the path. But if the buddhas have already led so many other beings to higher realizations, it might lead us to wonder, "Why am I still here? The buddhas who came into the world are perfect teachers who help all beings without partiality. I have been in this miserable condition through so many lives, but I have nothing to show for it. Why were all these other beings cured by the buddhas, but I have been left out?"

If you ask yourself these questions, Śāntideva has the answer. It is because of "my own faults" that I have not received their care. We describe the Buddha as the perfectly skillful, compassionate doctor. He administers the perfectly powerful medicine, in the form of his teachings, which definitely cures all sickness and misery. And yet, even though the perfect doctor exists and gives patients what they need, sometimes the patient does not take the medicine. In that case there is no hope of a cure. That is the reason we have not benefited from the Buddha's curative power. We did not pay attention to the teachings that were there; we did not take them seriously or practice them carefully. We have behaved like a sick person who throws his medicine into the garbage. These most useful teachings can definitely cure suffering, but because of our own faults we have not derived benefit from them.

In other words, we have senselessly wasted many lives in the past, accomplishing almost nothing that would free us from suffering. We are still under the power of karma, ignorance, and the other afflictions. Until now we could not see an end to this aimless wandering because we had not found a reliable path to happiness. But now, in this lifetime, we have found the beneficial medicine of the buddhas; we have met their teachings and we have the opportunity to follow their instructions. Therefore, during this lifetime it is most important to at least begin our journey on the path. If we can just reach the beginning of the Mahayana path, we will have grasped the highest purpose of this most distinctive human life; we will have used this life in a meaningful way.

A human life has the power to accomplish many different things. If we use that power in a senseless way, for nonvirtuous activity, we will build up a storehouse of negative karma as vast as the earth. On the other hand, if we use this life properly we can create a vast accumulation of positive potential and develop our inner mental life to perfection. In the Mahayana system you can actually achieve buddhahood in one short lifetime by using the powerful means of tantric practice. Although this is not easy, you certainly can place yourself firmly on the path that will lead to enlightenment in a few lifetimes from now. At the very least, you can assure that in future lives you will be able to progress higher and higher, and in this way you will not waste the potential of the precious life you hold in your hands right now.

So right now we have no excuses. We live in a free country where we can do what we like. Of course, if we go too far with our freedom—if we become wild—that freedom itself can become a fetter. We must use our freedom in a healthy way. When we think about the external conditions that we possess in this life—the general prosperity, personal security, physical condition, diet, opportunity to exercise—these are actually superior to those of many past buddhas and bodhisattvas. When those beings began their spiritual journeys they were not born with special bodies, nor did they live in some special place. We have the same kind of bodies they had, our minds are the same kind of minds. The only difference is the way they used their bodies and minds. They trained and sacrificed and spent their entire lives in a meaningful way. There is nothing to prevent us from doing exactly the same thing. Once we take control of our life and live it in a meaningful way, we can bring our next life—and each of our subsequent lives—into alignment. We can ensure that with each life we progress further and further along the spiritual path.

Not only do we have these exceptional outer conditions, we also have access to innumerable Dharma teachings. The complete teachings of the Buddha, both Sutrayana and Tantrayana, still survive. There are still fully qualified teachers surviving in the world who can explain these teachings. There are still many people all over the world who are seriously practicing the path. If you study and learn from these teachers; if you follow these practitioners by engaging in a sincere practice; if you come to understand the higher purpose of this life—then you will know what you are supposed to do.

In the beginning, the most important thing is to rely on a teacher who can show the way to emancipation and enlightenment. It must be someone who has studied, practiced, and experienced the meaning of the teachings. It must be a person you regard with the highest respect, so that you will take his or her teaching seriously. It should be someone who is not only qualified to teach the Dharma, but who helps you in every respect, even in the small aspects of your life.

In this lamrim tradition of teaching the steps on the path to enlightenment, different teachers use different methods for guiding their students.

Some teachers point directly to the final goal at the beginning. They begin by pointing out the city you are heading toward, the goal you are trying to reach. They then work backward, explaining that in order to reach that glorious city you need to get to this point, and before that you need to reach this point, and so forth, until they get to the very beginning of the path: relying on a fully qualified spiritual teacher.

On the other hand, you can follow the steps from the beginning up to the end, which is what Tsongkhapa has done here in the *Lamrim Chenmo.* You begin with the topic called "relying on a spiritual teacher" because in the beginning you need to find out what needs to be learned and who can teach it to you. From the spiritual point of view, at the beginning you are like a child. Like a child you need to rely on someone who knows the things you need to learn, someone whose primary interest is to guide you carefully and properly.

This is why it is important to know what makes a qualified teacher. Once you have found such a teacher, you need to know what your relationship with that teacher should be, how you should rely on the teacher both mentally and practically. You are not just seeking some pleasant experience for a few days or a few years. You are embarking on a quest for the highest possible goals. You are heading toward unknown destinations, and the journey may take a very long time. For such a journey it is essential that you have a close relationship with your guide.

As Śāntideva indicates, "In the past I was not a suitable disciple, so I did not receive any benefit from the buddhas and bodhisattvas who passed through this world. But now, this time, I have met this kind and wonderful teacher, who has such wonderful teachings! This time I must derive as much benefit as I can in this life; I should become a son or daughter of these buddhas and bodhisattvas." This kind of determined mental attitude is most important at this stage of your practice.

Considering the unstable nature of life

One of the key practices for leading the mind toward the Dharma and a more virtuous way of life is meditation on the impermanence of life and the inevitability of death. It may seem ironic, but by concentrating on the inevitability of death you can finally take control of your life. It will naturally cause you to reduce actions that harm other beings because you will see that there is no benefit in committing negative actions for the petty purposes of this short life. Recollecting death and impermanence is truly one of the most effective types of analytical meditation for beginners.

Most people indulge in all sorts of negative thoughts and harmful actions. They do this out of selfishness and for the sake of this temporary life. They have the feeling that this life will stay forever, so all of their energy goes toward seeking happiness in this life. This is the most common obstacle to spiritual practice. This is why recollecting death is the very first meditation for the being of small scope, the first step on the path to enlightenment. Death is definite. No one escapes.

The second thing to remember about death is that the time of death is uncertain. It may come many years from now, or it could be next month. It could come tomorrow, or even in the next hour. We have all seen how others are taken by sudden, unexpected death. It does not make any difference if people have riches, power, fame, youth, or great erudition—none of these will help when the Lord of Death arrives. The only thing that will make a difference at that moment will be the force of their karma—the causes they created by their past deeds, which will ripen into their future birth.

Great practitioners always consider death to be right in front of them, as if it were there in the next moment. In fact, there is no logical reason why you or I will not die within the next hour. No one can swear, "I will not die today." There is no logical reason to say that. Since death is always close by you need to consider, "If I die, what will happen next?"

Pure Dharma practitioners are mainly concerned with what will happen in the life after this one. We cannot see what that life will be; it is a dark and frightful area. If we fall into an unhappy rebirth, what kind of misery and pain will we face? If we fall into a downward spiral of more and more miserable situations, the great opportunity we now have—with our good health, keen intellect, and the rare chance to practice—will be utterly lost because we did not make the effort to prepare.

Of course we need to eat and drink and protect this body so that we can do the long work of seeking the higher goals of spiritual practice. But we should not be distracted and apply all our energy toward the comforts of this life. We should not behave like an animal who looks for nothing but food, sex, and a comfortable place to sleep. Humans have far greater vision: they can think and learn, study and research, and find methods that lead to much higher goals than the temporary pleasures of this life. Even in this single short life many great things can be achieved. Therefore, we should not waste even one moment, but work constantly for the benefit of the future. If you do this your life will be meaningful and useful. Otherwise, if you waste this life by spending it senselessly, death will come before you know it.

Considering the suffering states of existence

After death, what lies in the future? There is the possibility of a higher rebirth in the blissful worlds of *devas,* or as a human being in a high state. There are also three kinds of lower rebirths: among the animals, hungry ghosts, or the hell beings. Human life can also be extremely painful; we know that many human beings live in misery and deprivation that can be like hell itself.

In order to fully appreciate the importance of the precious opportunity we have right now, we need to give some thought to the kinds of things that may happen to us in the future. For that reason we need to meditate on the sufferings of the lower realms. But when we think about this we should not have the attitude: "Those beings are somewhere else. They live in other realms. Their suffering has nothing to do with me." Thinking like that when you do these meditations will not help. To do this practice properly you have to imagine yourself actually being in these lower rebirths. You must ask yourself, "If I were born in that lowly existence, what would my situation be like?"

You may find this hard to do. You may listen to descriptions of the lower realms and say to yourself, "They are just making this up. And anyway, I am not born there now. I am still human." But that will not resolve the real question: Have you created the cause to be born into one of these miserable conditions in the future? First you have to learn what the causes of suffering rebirths are. Then you need to honestly examine whether you have those causes within yourself. The point is that when you meditate on the sufferings of the lower realms you have to relate it to yourself. That is what leads you in the proper direction, to proper thought, proper action, and proper practice.

Proper practice means realizing that this precious opportunity of a human life is brief and can come to an end at any moment. When death comes, if we are not prepared we will be cast out of this comfortable life to wander helplessly among the desperate beings of the suffering realms. That being the case, there is one overriding question: "Where can I find protection from such a miserable future? Where can I find a refuge from the limitless sufferings of cyclic existence?"

Finding a reliable source of refuge

At this stage of the path we begin to realize the methods that can actually bring happiness in future lives. The first of these methods is taking refuge in the Three Jewels: the Buddha, Dharma, and Sangha. Taking refuge is described as "the sacred gateway for entering the teachings." Once you pass through this door you have put yourself on the path that leads away from perpetual dissatisfaction and toward true happiness in the future.

As the *Lamrim Chenmo* makes clear, there are different levels of spiritual goals with different methods to achieve them. But all of these have their roots in the practice of taking refuge in the Three Jewels. In fact, the entire Buddhist path can be included in the practice of taking refuge.

This practice begins with recognizing the causes for seeking a refuge. The two fundamental causes are *fear* and *faith.* A refuge is a source of protection, and it is obvious that if you are not afraid of something there is no need to seek protection. In other words, you seek a refuge because you have some kind of problem, and that problem is causing you anxiety or fear. There are worldly refuges providing temporary protection from common problems, such as a house or a cave that provides protection from the elements, or a charity that distributes food when people are hungry.

But here we are not concerned with these common, temporary types of refuge. In this case we are concerned with the fear of suffering in cyclic existence. We are seeking a spiritual refuge, an ultimate refuge that can protect us from all forms of samsaric suffering. In this sense, the first motivation for seeking this kind of ultimate refuge is fear of the infinite miseries sentient beings experience within cyclic existence.

Once we recognize the danger we are in, we naturally look for a person or a method that can protect us from it. But first we need to be convinced that that person or method actually has the ability to save us from the suffering that we fear. We need to develop trust that the refuge can solve our problem. This trust—which we often call *faith*—that the object of refuge can protect us from all of the fearful sufferings of cyclic existence is the second cause of going for refuge.

Now we have to consider what kind of object actually has the power to protect us from such all-pervasive problems. First of all, the object of refuge must itself be free of all suffering, all types of faults, and free of fear. It must have the capacity to actually give us the protection we seek. And the object of refuge must also be willing to help; it must be someone who is completely impartial and willing to help anyone who seeks protection. Worldly protectors, like kings or armies, may help you when they think you are on their side, but if you haven't supported them in the past they will have no interest in aiding you. That is not the sort of refuge you can rely on, because you never know if that kind of refuge will help you or not.

Buddhas have all the qualities of a reliable refuge. They possess perfect compassion for all beings without partiality. Buddhas have perfect knowledge: They understand the causes of suffering and they know the best methods to lead us out of our predicament. Together with their perfect knowledge and perfect compassion they have the power and ability to lead each and every being to a state of liberation from all suffering. Because they possess these three qualities of perfect knowledge, compassion, and power, buddhas are the highest possible objects of refuge.

Once we trust in the Buddha based on this understanding, we naturally trust his teachings, the Dharma. The Dharma is, in fact, the very expression of his transcendent knowledge coupled with his impartial compassion. The Dharma emerges from the Buddha's own experience of the path that leads to enlightenment. He offers it as the method that can actually protect us from the fears of cyclic existence. It is by taking the Dharma as a refuge, by practicing what the Buddha teaches us to practice, that we gain actual protection from samsaric suffering.

Based on this understanding of the qualities of the Buddha, together with the direct experience of the benefits of the Dharma, we gradually gain trust in those who are following the Buddha's teachings according to his instructions. This is the Sangha refuge: those followers who become good friends to our practice and accompany us on the path. Without virtuous companions to assist us along the way we could wander off in the wrong direction.

Once we have identified these three as reliable sources of refuge, we must discern how to take them as our refuge. Since each of the Three Jewels plays a different role in protecting us from suffering, there is a difference in the way we take each one as a refuge. The Buddha is the supreme teacher, the guide who leads us to the teaching. The Dharma is the teaching itself, the actual refuge, the spiritual path that was taught by the Buddha. Just as the Buddha is the perfect doctor, the Dharma is the perfect medicine: the direct cure of suffering. The doctor understands our condition and can show us the medicine that will work, but the doctor cannot enter our body and destroy our sickness directly. What actually fights the disease is the medicine he or she prescribes, but in order for the medicine to work we have to take it—we have to actually do the practice, cultivating our own mental development step-by-step. That is what actually fights the disease of samsaric suffering.

Taking refuge in the Sangha means placing trust in a slightly different kind of object. The Sangha is constituted by those people who understand the Dharma and are practicing it seriously. They are the companions of all those who seek to follow the Buddha's path. By virtue of their own practice they are able to support the practice of others and help those who encounter problems. They are like nurses who are able to help in the healing process because they understand the remedy that the doctor has prescribed. Because they are taking the medicine themselves, they are able to show others exactly how to follow the instructions of the perfect doctor, the Buddha. Because they are on the right path, if we follow them and emulate them we will be led toward emancipation. This is why the Sangha, the community of spiritual friends, is a proper refuge.

Once we possess those three types of protection, all of the external conditions necessary to cure samsaric suffering are fulfilled. What do those who are ill with a serious disease require to be cured? First they need a skillful doctor who is familiar with that sickness, who knows how to cure it, and has the compassion to do all he or she can to help. But beyond the willingness to help, that doctor must also have the medicine that can actually produce a cure. Once patients have found the right doctor and have been given effective medicine, they will need friends who can help them to take the treatment and nurse them back to health. No matter how sick people may be, if those three elements are there, they have all the external conditions they need to be cured of their illness. Then all they need to do is to take the treatment as it is prescribed by the doctor. If they do that, they will be cured.

So it is for disciples who go for refuge to the Three Jewels. The Buddha, Dharma, and Sangha provide everything we need to cure the disease of cyclic existence. All we have to do is take the medicine of the Dharma according to the instructions of the Buddha. This is the most important point about taking refuge in the Three Jewels. Taking refuge does not mean seeking protection from something outside, over there. It does not mean looking at some statues on a table and bowing down and saying some special words. That is not enough. We can recite, "I take refuge in the Buddha, Dharma, and Sangha" a million times, but if there is no sincere mental commitment it will not do much good. There may be some small benefit from the words of the recitation, but there will be no actual refuge.

When we take refuge in the Buddha we must feel in our heart, "You are the teacher, the guide who shows me the way. You are like a doctor who gives me the treatment that will cure my pain." When we take refuge in the Dharma we must feel in our heart, "If I take this treatment in accordance with the Buddha's instructions, I will definitely be cured of samsaric suffering." When we take refuge in the Sangha we must feel in our heart, "These are my true friends. If I accompany these spiritual friends and make them my example, I will stay on the path to happiness." If we practice that way everyday, from now until we obtain perfect enlightenment, we are really taking refuge in the Three Jewels. In the end, the whole practice of the Buddhist path is included within taking refuge. You cannot separate taking refuge from the practice of the Dharma. The entire path unfolds from refuge in the Three Jewels.

The famous Gungthangpa said in *The Advice for Meditating on Impermanence (Mi rtag bsgom tshul gyi bslab bya):*

> The Dharma is the guide for those who don't know their way.
> The Dharma is the provisions for a long voyage.
> The Dharma is the leader for an arduous journey.
> So fix your three doors [of body, speech, and mind] on the Dharma from now on.[5]

The pathways of cyclic existence are roads we know only too well. We have been traveling those roads for many millions of lifetimes. But the spiritual path, the journey toward buddhahood, is a path we have never walked before. What is the best guide to lead us down this unfamiliar road? It is the teachings of the Dharma.

Since the city of enlightenment may be a long way off, we have to prepare by gathering the supplies for the long journey. The provisions we need for this journey are not food and warm clothing. They are gathered by practicing the teachings, accumulating virtues, and cultivating inner mental development. The actual Dharma *is* the practice of the teachings, and this practice provides us with everything we need to reach the goal of liberation.

Because the path is hazardous and beset with obstacles, we will require an escort to protect and lead us through the difficulties. The Dharma is the most qualified spiritual escort, the best protection for this hazardous path. The Dharma is an inner companion leading us in the most powerful way, by turning our heart and mind in the right direction.

Since human beings do not have a definite life span, we do not know when death will come. If we lack the provisions of the Dharma, after death our journey will be dark and hopeless, without any guidance or protection. If we do not begin to prepare for that journey now, when the time of death arrives it will be too late. We will have no freedom to choose, no opportunity to change the future. Under the power of karma and afflictions we will be hurled into the unknown in complete darkness. Therefore, Gungthang Rinpoche says that if you want to practice Dharma, you must begin from right now.

Fortunately, right now we have everything we need to accomplish our goal. The Dharma is right here in our hands, and we have the leisure and the opportunity to practice. The kind of body and life we have right now has been compared to a wish-fulfilling jewel, because if you recognize its capacity you can accomplish anything you desire. All the past buddhas, great arhats, and famous bodhisattvas began with exactly the same kind of body, the same kind of mind, the same potential that we have right now. What distinguishes them is that they followed the teachings, they practiced seriously, and so they were able to reach the highest spiritual levels.

If we spend our lives according to the guidance of the Dharma, we can accomplish exactly the same thing. First, we need to learn how to practice—what to engage in and what to leave behind. Then we need to relate what we have learned to our own life and our daily actions of body, speech, and mind. We try to bring our behavior and thoughts into conformity with the guidelines of the teachings. We try to get rid of negative tendencies and cultivate positive qualities.

As Candrakīrti says in his *Commentary on the "Middle Way" (Madhyamakāvatāra):*

> For ordinary individuals, for śrāvakas who arise from the Buddha's teachings, for pratyekabuddhas who will definitely obtain realization on their own, and for the bodhisattvas, the sons of the conquerors, the cause of both higher rebirth and the "definite good" is none other than ethical conduct.[6]

Regardless of the spiritual level we are on now, whether the goal is the temporary benefit of a higher rebirth or the "definite good" of liberation, the singular cause of all happy results is the practice of ethical conduct. This does not mean that there is no other cause, but without the solid foundation of ethical behavior nothing positive can be achieved. Practicing ethical conduct means understanding the law of karma and then directing body, speech, and mind to those actions that will produce happiness in the future.

Nāgārjuna says in his *Friendly Letter (Suhṛl-lekha):*

> You must make faultlessness, open-mindedness, mental clarity,
> And purity the basis of ethical behavior.
> Ethical conduct is said to be the foundation of all good qualities,
> Just as the earth is for the animate and inanimate worlds.[7]

Pure ethical conduct is the most important practice. Without that firm foundation nothing else can be achieved. We must understand the cause and effect of karma so that we know what kind of results our virtuous actions will bring and what results will follow from nonvirtues. We begin by studying the Buddha's teachings on karma, which are laid out in great detail in this volume. Think about the way wholesome actions lead to positive results and unwholesome actions lead to suffering. Meditate on it. Cultivate the mental discipline to control your behavior. Subdue harmful activities and develop beneficial practices. You gradually purify past negative karmic seeds and build up a storehouse of positive potential. As understanding of karma and the practice of virtue deepens, you develop an unshakable confidence that the Buddha's teaching on karma describes the cause and effect of the moral universe just as it is. This faith in the teachings on karma is the root of all future well-being. The conviction that virtue leads to happiness and non-virtue leads only to suffering is the indispensable foundation of all the future benefits you will obtain on the path to enlightenment.

As Śāntideva says in *Engaging in the Bodhisattva Deeds:*

> So when I have found leisure such as this,
> If I do not attune myself to what is wholesome,
> There could be no greater deception
> And there could be no greater folly.[8]

Now is the time. The teachings are in our hands. We have the body, the mind, and the method to transform this life; we only need to grasp the opportunity. To practice the Dharma right now means to begin with those things we can do right now. Some of the steps will be easy, some a little harder, some will be quite difficult. We start with those steps we can apply right away. Gradually we work toward the harder stages, taking on each one as it becomes manageable. For the hardest changes we begin with an aspiration, the prayer that declares, "One day may I be able to engage in these practices." If we aim for those higher goals and build a solid foundation, gradually we will progress until we master them.

Practicing the Dharma does not mean that we have to shut off everything that we usually do. We can engage the practice at so many different levels. Human beings are so intelligent, so powerful, so adaptable. We have so much ability and such a great opportunity; we can accomplish a great deal in a single short life. Therefore Gungthang Rinpoche advises us, "Fix your three doors on the Dharma from now on."

The fact that you are holding this book in your hands means you already have some interest in these teachings. You are trying to learn something, and more than just learning, you may be interested in actually *doing* something to change your life, in taking at least one small initial step. That is the most important thing: at least make a small start before death cuts short all possibilities. There is no way of knowing when that will be; you should expect it any time. If you keep the reality of death in your mind, it will naturally lead you to prepare for the next life. You should think, "If I have done even one small thing today that will serve as a provision for that future journey, that will be helpful."

On the other hand, if the thought of death never crosses your mind, then your only concern will be the aims of this life. From the morning when you rise until you lie down at night your only thoughts will be for the desires of this life. From that state of mind all the mental afflictions and negative actions will spin out of control. When your only concern is the pleasure of this life, even actions that look like Dharma practice become worldly activities. The pure practice of the Dharma requires a pure motivation.

Of course, each day you may have many obligations, many things you need to do to prepare for living today. But you should never completely forget the long journey that lies ahead. Each morning when you wake up you should think, "I have survived another night, but who knows whether I will wake up tomorrow morning. If I die today I will begin a long journey to some unknown destination. Therefore, I must do something to prepare for that journey today." That thought in the morning will draw out a pure motivation to make Dharma practice a part of your day.

Then in the evening, before you go to sleep, it is important to think, "I have survived this day. How have I used this precious life that I possess here and now? What have I done with my life during this day that is now past?" While it is still fresh in your mind, you can weigh the nature of that day by recalling the thoughts and actions you engaged in. If there is nothing you can recall that will prove beneficial for a future life—if no spiritual provisions have been gathered; if there is nothing but selfish, worldly, negative attitudes to be found—then of course you have to worry. There is no way to tell when you go to bed what your life will be like when you wake up in the morning.

Of course, if there is no rebirth—if there is complete nothingness after death—then you have nothing to worry about. It doesn't matter what you do because it will all be past and gone. But that is not the view of the Buddha. The entire structure of his teachings is based on his direct knowledge that there *is* a future life, and that your next life will be either happy and comfortable or immersed in suffering, depending on your actions, on your karma. Because of the energetic force of your previous actions, after you die another body will be created. It is the wholesome or unwholesome nature of your previous karma that will determine the type of existence and the conditions you will meet in your next life.

That is the teaching of the Buddha. If you want to achieve real, stable happiness—if you want to progress at all on the spiritual path—you must understand and practice the cause and effect of karma. You must study, learn, think about, and meditate on the law of karma until you develop an unshakable conviction that this teaching of the Buddha truly describes the world in which we live.

All the tools you need are right here in this volume. This is the gift of the great teacher Tsongkhapa. There is no need for me to praise him. If you take these teachings to heart, try to understand them, make the effort and deal with them in your daily life, you will realize for yourself the greatness of the teacher and the greatness of this teaching. You do not need someone else to tell you this is good; you do not need to rely on the praise of others. If you rely on your own experience, the praise will come from within. You will realize for yourself the nature of the perfect teacher and the truth of the perfect teaching. Slowly, you will also realize their effects in your own life.

1

The General Characteristics of Karma

b' Developing the faith of conviction that is the root of all well-being
- 1' Contemplating karma and its results in general
  - a" The actual method of contemplating karma and its results in general
    - 1" The certainty of karma
    - 2" The magnification of karma
    - 3" If an action is not performed, its results will not be met
    - 4" Actions that are done do not perish

THE ROOT OF ALL VIRTUE, happiness, and bliss within cyclic existence and beyond is trust in the cause and effect of karma, and faith in the Three Jewels based on knowing their perfect qualities. Trust in karma develops from a solid understanding of how it works, knowing what kind of results arise from what kinds of actions. When you develop a clear and deep understanding of these causal relationships, trust in the action of karma naturally grows, and that trust is the main root of all well-being.

Though the way in which karma operates is a profound topic and a difficult one to understand in all its complexity, it is essential to gain a clear picture of how karma works. It does not matter whether you are only seeking higher rebirths within samsara, or whether you are striving for complete emancipation—an understanding and appreciation of karma is absolutely essential. Why? Because if you fail to observe the principles of karma, all the roads leading to a higher rebirth and on to liberation will be blocked. It is the key that opens the door to happiness.

In the previous volume of this *Lamrim Chenmo* commentary we began the discussion of the methods for finding happiness in future lives. The first such method is taking refuge in the Three Jewels: the Buddha, the Dharma, and the Sangha. Going for refuge was described as the sacred gateway for entering the teachings. We discussed the causes for taking refuge, the nature of the objects in which we take refuge, the reason those objects are worthy of refuge, and the ways in which we go to them for refuge.

The topic we will be discussing in this second volume—generating the faith of trusting in karma and its results—is the second of the methods for finding happiness in future lives. According to the way the *Lamrim Chenmo* presents the sequence of the stages that lead to enlightenment, after taking refuge in the Three Jewels come teachings dealing with which practices and behaviors are to be taken up and which are to be rejected. It is not enough to merely say the words, "I take refuge in the Buddha," and so forth. It is engaging in the practices described in the lamrim, and leaving behind the negative actions that are repudiated, that actually constitutes the practice of the Dharma.

If the root of all happiness is faith in the Three Jewels and trust in the cause and effect of karma, how do we produce that trust? This question is taken up in three parts:

1' Contemplating karma and its results in general
2' Contemplating the particulars of karma and its results
3' After contemplating karma, how to engage in virtuous actions and avoid nonvirtuous ones

1' Contemplating karma and its results in general

This discussion is divided into two parts:

a" The actual method of contemplating karma and its results in general
b" Contemplating specific categories of karma and its results

a" The actual method of contemplating karma and its results in general

This subject has four parts:

1" The certainty of karma
2" The magnification of karma
3" If an action is not performed, its results will not be met
4" Actions that are done do not perish

1" The certainty of karma

All happiness is the maturation of virtuous karma. Every pleasant feeling—from a cool breeze passing through the hot hells up to the highest bliss of the *arhat*—all arises from previous virtuous action. There is not even the smallest enjoyable experience that ripens from nonvirtue; there is no way that this can happen. Without previous virtue, happiness cannot arise.

In the same way, whether you look at ordinary individuals or *ārya* beings, all painful or unpleasant feelings are the result of nonvirtuous karma that was previously performed. Although arhats have completely removed all the obscuring afflictions and have achieved liberation from the causes of cyclic existence, they sometimes continue to suffer from small pains and discomforts until they die, because their body was produced by previous karma. Even these subtle forms of suffering can only result from negative karma. There is no way that any kind of unhappiness can ripen from virtuous action.

You may have certain questions about this—for example, special cases in which a certain kind of pain contributes to a pleasurable feeling. But here we are talking about the result of a particular action: when you perform a virtuous or nonvirtuous action it is like planting a seed having a particular kind of potential to ripen into a particular type of result. What is definite is that a virtuous action can only produce a pleasant result, and a nonvirtuous action can only produce an unpleasant or suffering result.

Nāgārjuna says in his *Precious Garland (Rāja-parikathā-ratnāvalī):*

> From nonvirtues come all sufferings,
> And likewise all bad migrations,
> From virtues, all happy migrations
> And the pleasures of all lives.[1]

In other words, happiness and misery do not arise without cause, nor do they arise from causes that are discordant or contradictory with the result. If suffering could arise without a cause, it could arise all the time; there would be no need for particular conditions to enable it to appear. It would just come or not come on a totally arbitrary basis.

Furthermore, the cause must be concordant with the result. For example, light does not arise from darkness. Tsongkhapa refers here to concepts from the Sāṃkhya school of Indian philosophy, which holds that there is a single, permanent cause, called *primal matter,* which is the seed from which everything arises. Some also hold that a supreme creator god, who is permanent, manifests all of creation out of this primal matter, or *fundamental nature.* These are discordant causes, because the great variety of different results—of misery and enjoyment—are all impermanent, and impermanent results cannot arise from a permanent cause. Equally, a permanent result cannot arise from an impermanent cause.

In general, happiness arises from virtuous karma and suffering arises from nonvirtuous karma. The various particular instances of misery or happiness arise from particular instances of virtuous or nonvirtuous action. There is not the slightest inconsistency in this natural process. You should grasp this law of karma and its results clearly and with certainty.

All the buddhas have praised this right view as the basis of all white dharmas, meaning that all positive, happy, and blissful experience arises from that right view. We can distinguish two kinds of right view: conventional right view and ultimate right view. Ultimate right view—the correct view of the ultimate nature of things—is the realization of emptiness *(śūnyatā)*. Conventional right view is correct understanding of the cause and effect of karma and its results. Another way to look at this is in terms of the two truths, phenomenal and absolute truth. The right view of the absolute truth is the realization of emptiness. The right view of phenomenal truth is a proper understanding of karma and its results.

Conventional right view, the correct view of phenomenal truth, is just this understanding that positive karma will definitely produce happy results and negative karma will definitely produce suffering results. When you gain understanding and confidence in the certainty of this process of cause and effect, that is conventional right view.

An illustration of the way in which karma is certain is the story of a monk called Nyanpa Zangdan.[2] He was born with a repulsive appearance because in a previous life he had developed an extremely disrespectful attitude toward a *stupa,* or reliquary monument, he was working on. However, because he rejoiced in the stupa when it was complete, and offered a lovely golden bell to adorn the completed monument, he was also born with an enchanting singing voice. This story illustrates how karma is certain and how its results are never mixed up or inconsistent. Virtuous karma invariably brings happy results; nonvirtuous karma brings only suffering. Each action brings its own definite, distinct result. The details of this topic, with other illustrative examples from the sutras, will come later.

2" The magnification of karma

Karma increases greatly. Even a small virtue can bring a very great blissful result, while a small nonvirtuous action can produce great suffering. Either way, the result can be greatly magnified in terms of size, amount, duration, or intensity from the original action that was the cause.

As an example of this increase you can look at the actual seed of a tree. From that very small seed will grow a huge tree with its fat trunk and its many limbs, branches, and leaves. As the sutra describes it, from that tiny seed grows a tree so large that five hundred horse-drawn wagons could be parked beneath the spread of its limbs. This shows how the cause and effect relationship produces a great result from a small cause in the physical world.

But this amount of increase is small compared to the increase of the results from inner, karmic seeds. The increase of effect that grows from an inner cause is incomparably greater than what you see from an outer cause like the seed of a tree. As an example we have a story from the sutras in which the Buddha was offered a small amount of grain by a woman. He then prophesied that this woman would someday obtain buddhahood. The woman's husband was agitated to hear this and with a negative attitude he demanded to know how such a small gesture as offering a handful of grain could possibly produce such a huge result. The Buddha took that occasion to give a detailed explanation of karma and its results. He explained how a seemingly insignificant act—a small karma—increases and produces a very great result. As it says in the *Collection of Indicative Verses (Udāna-varga):*

> Performing even a small misdeed
> Will bring great terrors and disaster
> In future lives,
> Like poison that has been ingested.
>
> Performing even a small meritorious action
> Will lead to great happiness in the next life,
> And great purposes will be accomplished,
> Just as grain ripens into bounty.

Even a small negative action can produce many unhappy rebirths, and during those lifetimes you will meet many unbearable experiences. It can bring great disaster, like poison that has already reached the stomach. In the same way, a small virtuous action will bring great joy in the future and lead to accomplishing great purposes, just as a single healthy seed can produce a tree full of abundant flowers and fruit.

The details of this relationship between karma and its results is extremely profound and subtle; they are much more difficult to understand fully than emptiness. Until you are freed from all the subtle obstacles to knowledge,[3] you cannot know all these details. Even arhats are not completely free of these obstacles to knowledge. Although they have freed themselves from rebirth in samsara and from experiencing samsaric suffering, they still have obstacles to knowing certain things, so they cannot perceive all the details of karma and its relationships. Therefore, the details of karma are fully known only to the omniscience of a perfect Buddha.

Because we cannot directly see the functioning of karma at this stage of our spiritual development, the Buddha told stories that illustrate the principles of how karma works. After he attained enlightenment at the age of thirty-five, the Buddha spent his life teaching until he passed away at eighty. Since he had such profound knowledge, his disciples liked to ask him questions about various good and bad events that happened to themselves or to others they knew. The questions were often provoked by miraculous deeds or other unusual events that transpired at that time. In such a case, one of the chief disciples would ask the Buddha why this event had happened. The Buddha, with his radiant smile, would reply, "You are welcome to ask this question and I am happy to answer," and he would go on to tell the story of the chain of karmic causation that led up to those events. Some of these stories are long and convoluted, carrying on over the course of many lifetimes, until they result in the events that the questioner had inquired about.

In this way the Buddha taught karma and its results by means of personal stories, which are collected in various sutras and in the *Vinaya,* that section of the Buddha's teachings dealing with rules of monastic discipline. Tsongkhapa mentions three texts which collect many stories relating to the workings of karma: the *Bases of Discipline (Vinaya-vastu),* the *Sutra of the Wise and the Foolish (Dama-mūko-nāma-sūtra),* and the *Hundred Actions Sutra (Karma-śataka-sūtra).*

By reading the stories told by the Buddha which describe how certain events developed from certain causes, skillful people can come to understand how karma works. The *Sutra of the Wise and the Foolish* was given this name because when wise or skillful people read it they can gain a realization of karma and its results. However, when those who are foolish read it nothing happens—they will not realize anything. You could say that reading this sutra is a test of which one you are!

The stories in the *Bases of Discipline* are accounts of how the rules of the Vinaya, which govern the behavior of monks and nuns, came to be made. Each of the Vinaya rules is accompanied by an explanation of the events that led the Buddha to establish that particular rule. This enables the members of the Buddhist order to understand the reasons for all of the commitments that accompany their ordination. These stories recount the place, who was present, who asked the question, what was the purpose, and why that particular rule was made. This is why the *Bases of Discipline* contains so many stories related to karma. By hearing and reading these stories you gain an understanding of how karma works.

Tsongkhapa mentions a few of these stories and it would be too much to go through them all here, but let us look at one of them as an example. It is the story from the *Sutra of the Wise and the Foolish* that tells of a child named Golden Gem.[4] This baby was born with his fist tightly closed, and when his parents opened his fingers they found a golden coin. No matter how many times they took the coin from his hand, another one would appear in its place. Amazed by this miraculous event, the family went to the Buddha and asked what it meant.

The Buddha explained that many millions of years earlier, at the time of the previous Buddha, Kāśyapa, a rich and noble family invited that Buddha and his followers to their home where they wished to honor him with offerings. Living nearby was a young boy from a poor family who had nothing to offer. Every day he walked into the hills to gather a small amount of firewood to sell in the market, and from that hard work he earned a meager living.

When the poor boy heard that this noble family had invited the Buddha, he gathered up his meager savings and went off to watch the grand event. Clutching a few pennies in his hand the boy thought, "I am just a poor woodcutter. It is because I did not create sufficient merit in the past that I am so terribly poor now and have nothing to offer. The people in this great family have such wealth that they are able to invite the Buddha and all his followers, and by their generosity they are creating great meritorious karma. How wonderful it is that they have obtained this precious opportunity!"

Feeling pleased in this way, he rejoiced in the merits of others. And with that attitude he offered his hard-earned pennies to the Buddha. The Buddha accepted his offering with a smile. As a result of that act of generosity toward the Buddha, together with his rejoicing in the virtue of others, that woodcutter was born into human rebirths for many, many subsequent lives, and in all of those lives he was born with a golden coin in his hand and lived a life of wealth. The woodcutter's good karma was still not exhausted, for once again in the present life he was born as this baby with a gold coin in his hand.

When the woodcutter made his gift he also offered a special dedication prayer in which he expressed powerful faith in the Buddha and respect for his disciples, and he rejoiced in all the merits they were creating. As a result of that heartfelt prayer, when the boy with the golden coin in his hand got older he was ordained as a Buddhist monk and eventually attained the highest spiritual result.

This story demonstrates how karma increases, because we see how the small offering of few pennies resulted in obtaining wealth for many subsequent lifetimes until finally he was able to attain arhatship. This is the kind of story we find in these sutras, in which each event is explained by karmic potentials accumulated in previous lifetimes. There are stories of good events caused by virtuous actions and unhappy events caused by nonvirtue. As we discuss this topic of karma other stories like this will come up.

Tsongkhapa identifies four facets of spiritual activity that are important for a religious practitioner: ethical conduct, ritual, livelihood, and view. These four elements should be harmonious and in accordance with the teachings of the Buddha. Here, *view* refers to the correct view of karma and its results. What the following sutra says is that if you have right view concerning the relationships of karma, but you degenerate in one of the other three elements of a pure religious life, the result will be birth as a nāga. But if you hold wrong view concerning karma, you will be born in a far worse lower realm. Being born as a nāga is a lower rebirth, but it is the best of the three lower realms. Nāgas are generally included as part of the animal realm, but their existence is often similar to that of low-level devas. In the *Questions of the Nāga Kings of the Ocean (Sāgara-nāga-rāja-paripṛcchā)*, the leader of the nāgas inquires of the Buddha:

> Bhagavan, in the early stages of this world system, when I resided in the great ocean and the Tathāgata appeared in the form of Buddha Krakucchanda, at that time the nāgas and their sons and daughters were fewer, and my retinue was smaller. But now, Bhagavan, there are so many nāgas with their sons and daughters that you cannot count them—their numbers are inconceivable. Bhagavan, what is the cause of this, what are the conditions that brought this about?
>
> To this the Buddha replied: "Lord of the Nāgas. In the past there were those who took ordination, going forth into the discipline of the well-spoken Dharma, but they did not fulfill their vows of ethical conduct. Their performance of religious rituals deteriorated; their ways of gaining livelihood fell short of the standards of the teachings; their ethical conduct degenerated. In these ways they did not fulfill their commitments. Nevertheless, because their view was correct they were not born into the hell realms, but rather, when they passed away they were born as nāgas."

The period of time in which we live is called a *fortunate eon* because during it a thousand buddhas will appear to set the wheel of Dharma teachings in motion. Each of these buddhas has his own particular religious teachings setting forth different levels of lay and monastic vows. Of those who entered into the teachings of the Buddha Krakucchanda, the first of these one thousand, there were nine hundred and eighty million lay and ordained followers whose ethics, ritual life, and livelihood degenerated, and who were subsequently born into the realm of the nāgas. Of those who entered the teachings of Kanakamuni, the second Buddha of this eon, six hundred and forty million were born into that realm. Of those who entered the teachings of the third Buddha, Kāśyapa, there were eight hundred million. And of those who have entered into the teachings of the fourth and present Buddha, Śākyamuni, nine hundred and ninety million have been or will be born as nāgas because of the degeneration of their ritual practice, their means of livelihood, or their ethical conduct. Even since Śākyamuni Buddha's *parinirvāṇa,* members of the fourfold community—consisting of nuns, monks, laywomen, and laymen—whose ethics have degenerated and who perform nonvirtuous actions will be born as nāgas.

Nevertheless, although their actions were impure, because they never lost faith in the teachings and their view remained correct in that they had trust in the action of karma, following their birth in the world of the nāgas they will take rebirth in higher realms. Eventually they all will attain nirvana by following the teachings of the buddhas of this fortunate eon, with the exception of those who have entered the Mahayana path.[5]

Therefore, you need to gain a firm understanding that even the tiniest karma follows you like a shadow follows the body, and it produces great happiness or great suffering. Once you have confidence in this process, you should pursue virtue even in the smallest deeds that you do, and avoid by all means negative actions. Do the very best you can to behave in this way. This subject of karma is one of the fundamental teachings of Buddhism. It is a cornerstone of all the paths that lead to higher rebirths and to enlightenment. These paths are all based on understanding and practicing karma and its results as established in various sutras and as taught here in the *Lamrim Chenmo.*

As we discuss this subject you may find that certain ideas make you uncomfortable, or are not so easy to follow. Other areas may seem clear and understandable. You should begin by concentrating on those areas that make sense to you, and let yourself be influenced by those teachings, so that your own behavior comes into harmony with what the Buddha is suggesting.

When you come to ideas that are not so comfortable, not easy to understand, or which seem unbelievable and beyond your mental scope, the important thing is that you should not automatically deny them. You should leave your mind open. Think, "I will not flatly reject these ideas. Maybe eventually I will understand them." Even when you find statements that are difficult to accept, it is not good to immediately take a negative view; that can be dangerous. Leave the question open and take it as a basis for further investigation.

Meanwhile, you should base your behavior and your practice on the teachings about karma that make sense to you now.

We have been born as humans, with the capacity to learn from the instructions of others, from our own experience, from our own scientific research. By these means we are able to discern these processes of cause and effect. Once we gain this discriminating understanding of how things work, we must make a great effort to act accordingly. Human effort can have tremendous power and can make a great difference in the path that our life takes in the future.

The action of karma is illustrated by several stanzas from the *Collection of Indicative Verses:*

> Just as their shadows accompany
> Birds who dwell in the sky,
> Good and evil actions
> Follow those who commit them.
>
> Just as travelers with insufficient provisions
> Will meet hardship on the journey,
> Beings who do not perform good karma
> Will go to bad migrations.
>
> Just as those with well-prepared provisions
> Will be happy on their journey,
> Beings who do good karma
> Will go to happy migrations.

To make a long journey through a desolate land you need to gather the necessary provisions. If you do not take along what you need you will face difficulties; you could even die from hunger and thirst. In the same way, if those sentient beings who are wandering up and down in cyclic existence—from the lowest hells up to the highest formless world called the Peak of Existence—are not prepared for this journey, if they have not collected the provisions of good karma, they will meet with the disaster of miserable rebirths.

Another stanza from *Collection of Indicative Verses* says:

> Do not discount even a tiny misdeed,
> Believing it will do no harm.
> By collecting water, drop by drop,
> A large vessel is gradually filled.

Do not think that small unwholesome actions will do no harm or make no difference. Day by day, hour by hour, such small negative karmas accumulate, until you are filled with the potential for unpleasant results.

Another set of stanzas expresses a similar thought:

> Do not think, "The small misdeeds
> Will not follow me later."
> Just as a large pot is filled
> By water falling drop by drop,
> The immature being is completely filled up
> By misdeeds accumulated a bit at a time.
>
> Do not think, "The small virtues I do
> Will not follow me later."
> Just as a large pot is filled
> By water falling drop by drop,
> The stable practitioner is completely filled up
> By virtues accumulated a bit at a time.

This last stanza looks at the positive side of the situation. Do not think that small virtuous actions will not help you because they are too small. Just as dripping water accumulates until it fills a great vase, little by little virtuous karma will fill up a person who is well established and steadfast in his or her practice.

The power of habitual action is addressed in this stanza from the *Garland of Birth Stories (Jātaka-mālā):*

> By performing virtuous or nonvirtuous actions habitually,
> It becomes the nature of a person,
> So that in future lives, without intending it,
> They continue to do them, as if in a dream.

If you continuously behave in a certain way it becomes your habit, your nature, to act that way. When a particular type of action becomes that ingrained, you will just continue to act in the same manner, right on into your future lives. Habits like this are performed helplessly. Without your intending to do so, the actions seem to happen by themselves, the way things happen in a dream. We all know from experience that if you do some activity very intensively during the day, you may continue doing that action at night in your dreams.

Further passages from the *Garland of Birth Stories* point out that when it comes to securing happiness in the future, a high social status and the like are not important:

> No matter how excellent their lineage, their form, or their vigor,
> How great their power or wealth may be,
> No one can gain happiness in the next life
> Without having trained in generosity, ethical conduct, and such.
>
> Though their lineage and such may be lowly, if they are not attached to nonvirtue,
> If they posseses such virtues as generosity and ethical conduct,
> In the next life their happiness will surely increase,
> As the monsoons of summer flow down to fill up the sea.
>
> Those who have gained certainty that the happiness or suffering
> Of future lives depends on virtuous or nonvirtuous karma
> Avoid negative actions and strive energetically for virtue.
> Those who lack faith do whatever they please.

You may possess all sorts of excellent qualities such as noble birth, physical beauty, power, and wealth; all such good qualities come as a result of *previous* virtuous actions. But if you do not create good karma during this *present* life, you certainly will not obtain happiness in the *next* life. Conversely, even if you have been born into a low caste, poor and ugly, as long as you are not attracted to negative actions—as long as you maintain good ethics and a generous heart—in future lives your happiness will definitely grow greater and greater. In short, regardless of who you are now, your experience of happiness or suffering in future lives will depend on whether you do virtuous or nonvirtuous actions during this life. This is something you should clearly understand.

The point of this discussion can be stated as follows: while you have the opportunity of this life you should be preparing yourself for the time of death, and for what lies beyond. Imagine that you had to weigh your positive and negative karma at the time of death: will your positive actions be greater than the negative ones? If you can achieve just that much in this life—if you can be certain that your positive deeds outweigh the negative—that would be a great accomplishment. But if you look back and see that your negative karma is much greater than the positive, you should know that you will feel great fear at the time of death. You will be facing a terrifying darkness and you will go into that darkness with deep sorrow.

Therefore, you should make every effort to produce virtue and to avoid all nonvirtue. You should confess whatever negative actions you have already done and purify them by applying the antidotes, and the way to do this will be discussed in detail later.[6] But if, from the very beginning, you do not have faith in the certainty of karmic cause and effect, how will you be able to experience desirable results?

3" If an action is not performed, its results will not be met

If you do not perform an action, you can never experience the result of that action. If you do not perform an action that serves as the cause of a pleasant or unpleasant experience, then you cannot have that experience. The corollary of this is that you cannot experience the results of karma created by someone else.

Then a question arises: If it is true that you cannot meet the results of karma that you did not perform yourself, how do you explain the case in which the Buddha's enlightenment created great happiness for countless other beings? As a bodhisattva, the Buddha accumulated countless merits for many eons, until he finally attained the highest goal of buddhahood. But when he attained enlightenment he was not the only one who benefited from his actions. Many other sentient beings have experienced many good results by virtue of *his* vast accumulation of merits.

Another example is the case of Buddha Amitābha, who resides in the pure land of Sukhāvatī. When he was a bodhisattva he dedicated all of his virtue to other sentient beings with a powerful vow: until sentient beings were able to be born into his pure land, he would not become a buddha. Because of that bodhisattva's vow—that pure motivation to benefit all other beings—and his creation of virtue over many lives, countless beings have been able to be born into Amitābha's pure land. Is that contradictory to the law of karma that says you cannot experience the results of actions performed by another?

Tsongkhapa says that those who experience good results by virtue of the actions of a buddha or bodhisattva do not need to have accumulated *all* of the merits and virtuous karma performed by those exalted beings, but they do need to have performed *some portion* of those positive deeds themselves. In other words, there must be an appropriate relationship between their own virtuous karma and the results they experience.

Without creating any of the virtuous actions that can act as the cause for such a happy result, you will not be able to meet that experience—you will not be born in that pure land. No matter how much a bodhisattva may pray and dedicate his or her merits, such a being will not be able to place just anyone in that happy state. It is the combination of the bodhisattva's powerful prayer, together with the meritorious actions of the individual being benefited, and the dedication of merits by that individual toward the achievement of what the bodhisattva has prayed for, that creates the relationship and the cause for such a happy result.

The importance of making such expansive dedications explains why Tibetans frequently recite the following verses from the *Prayer of Samantabhadra (Samantabhadra-caryā-praṇidhāna):*

> Just as heroic Mañjuśrī knew how,
> Just as Samantabhadra also knew,
> I dedicate all this virtue so that
> I may learn to follow all their ways.

When you dedicate your merit in this way, you make a connection with the unlimited activities of these two great bodhisattvas, which they have dedicated to the welfare of all sentient beings. The karmic relationships are subtle and difficult to comprehend, but making this connection can bring about very great results. If you don't do anything at all from your own side, and if you don't make any connection to these bodhisattvas, you will not attain the benefit of their actions. This is what Tsongkhapa means when he states that a person must at least create some portion of the merits of a buddha or bodhisattva in order to partake in the benefits of their unlimited merits.

The general point here is that if you do not perform any action that can produce a particular result, you will never experience that result. There are many stories in the sutras that illustrate this point. One such story tells about a group of nobles who went for a walk in the forest. They came upon the hut of an arhat who was in retreat. Not caring who was inside, they burned down the hut, killing the arhat. One particular maidservant objected to this action and refused to have any part in it, but she had no power to stop the others. Many lifetimes later, at the time of the Buddha, a hermitage where Buddha's nuns were residing caught fire. Since most of the nuns there were arhats, they had supernatural powers and were able to fly. They used this power to escape the flames but, as they were rising up in the sky, they saw their previous karma and realized that they had been the nobles who set fire to that hut and caused the death of the hermit. With that realization their miraculous powers failed them and they fell back into the fire, where they all died. However, one simple nun who had no special powers was able to escape the fire through a tunnel, and she was the only one who survived. The Buddha explained that this nun had been the maidservant who objected to burning the hut.

When the time comes for the maturation of karmic causes—when it is time to experience the result of previous actions—there is no way to escape those consequences. This is true even for those nuns who had attained the exalted level of arhatship. But the one simple nun who had not created the cause to be burned in the fire was the one who escaped.

We frequently hear accounts of similar situations: in car accidents, in plane crashes, in house fires, we hear about one or two people who survive in a seemingly impossible way when most of the others are killed. Sometimes, in a seemingly impossible way, most survive but one is killed. These are examples of not meeting results when you have not created the karmic cause. That is the Buddhist way of interpreting these situations.

4" Actions that are done do not perish

Once you create a karma, its potential will never be lost until it ripens and yields fruit. The only thing that can prevent it from ripening is destroying the karmic seed by means of an antidote. Otherwise, even if it takes many, many millions of eons, the result of that karma will eventually occur. It is inevitable that those who perform virtuous actions will experience attractive results and those who perform nonvirtuous actions will experience unattractive results.

In his *Praise of the Exalted One (Viśeṣa-stava),* Udbhaṭasiddhasvāmin[7] says:

> The brahmins say that virtues and misdeeds
> Are transferrable, like giving and receiving gifts.
> You have taught that karma created is never lost,
> And what is not created will not be met.

The author of these praises was himself a brahmin who later became a follower of the Buddha, and after developing tremendous devotion he composed this text of praises for the Buddha and his teaching. Here he is pointing out that in some brahmanical systems it is taught that one person can take on another's karma and experience the results of actions performed by that other person, or that one can give one's virtue to a friend. However, the Buddha teaches that once someone performs a karma it will never be lost and its results must be experienced by the person who created the karma. If you do not create a karma, you can never experience its results.

The *King of Concentrations Sutra (Samādhi-rāja-sūtra)* contains a similar statement:

> And once an action is done, there is no circumstance where the results will not be met.
> When another has done an action, you cannot experience the result.

Illustrating this we have the story of Maudgalyāyana, who was renowned among the Buddha's disciples as the one with the greatest miraculous powers.[8] In one of his previous lives he quarreled with his mother, and in a fit of anger he said to her, "I wish your head was beaten like a piece of clay." Many lifetimes later he became a direct disciple of the Buddha and attained arhatship. At that time he saw with his supernatural knowledge that the teacher of a band of ascetics who were opposed to the Buddha had been born into hell for teaching his students to practice animal sacrifice. Maudgalyāyana went to these ascetics and tried to persuade them not to kill for the sake of performing these sacrifices, but his interference only made them mad. So one day they descended upon him in his meditation hut and beat him to a pulp with clubs. It was, of course, a great shock to the Buddha's disciples that such a great arhat could come to such a violent end. The Buddha explained that Maudgalyāyana met this experience as a result of the harsh words he had spoken to his mother; the karmic result of using those hurtful words was that he was beaten to death by this band of ascetics.

As the *Bases of Discipline* concludes:

> Even in one hundred eons,
> Karma will never be lost.
> When the time comes and they meet the conditions,
> Beings surely will experience the results.

2

The Varieties of Karma

b" Contemplating specific categories of karma
- 1" The principal teaching of the ten karmic paths
- 2" Establishing karma and its results
  - (a) Nonvirtuous karma and its results
    - (i) The actual nonvirtuous karmic paths
    - (ii) Distinguishing heavy and light karma
      - (a') The heaviness and lightness of the ten karmic paths
      - (b') An ancillary presentation of a selection of some of the heaviest karmas
        - (1') Powerful in terms of the field
        - (2') Powerful in terms of the actor
        - (3') Powerful in terms of the substance
        - (4') Powerful in terms of the attitude
    - (iii) A presentation of the results
      - (a') Fruitional results
      - (b') Results corresponding to the cause
      - (c') Environmental results
  - (b) Virtuous karma and its results
    - (i) Virtuous karma
    - (ii) The results of virtuous karma
  - (c) A presentation of other classifications of karma
    - (i) The distinction between projecting and completing karma
    - (ii) Karma whose result will definitely or not definitely be experienced

2' Contemplating karma and its results in detail
- a" The qualities of the eight fruitions
- b" The effects of the eight fruitions
- c" The causes of the eight fruitions

b" Contemplating specific categories of karma

This topic is taught in two parts:

1" The principal teaching of the ten karmic paths
2" Establishing karma and its results

1" The principal teaching of the ten karmic paths

In the previous chapter we established four principles of how karma works: first, that happiness and suffering are invariably the respective results of virtuous and nonvirtuous karma, and there is never any inconsistency in this relationship; second, that karma increases, so that the results may be much greater than the cause; third, that you cannot meet results of karma you have not performed; and fourth, that once karma is created it is never lost, until it yields its result or it is purified by applying the antidote.

The person who understands these four principles will naturally wonder, "How can this knowledge be put into practice? Which actions need to be avoided and which need to be cultivated?" These are the questions we shall address in the following section.

The human mind has countless thoughts, and out of those thoughts arise countless actions. In order to formulate this virtually infinite variety of actions into a system that we can easily understand, learn, and practice, the Buddha condensed all actions into ten general categories. These he taught as the ten virtues to be cultivated, or the ten nonvirtues to be abandoned. If you have a basic understanding of these ten actions and their results, you can begin to practice.

All actions, whether positive or negative, are performed exclusively by the three doors of body, speech, and mind. There is no other way to perform an action. Although all physical, verbal, and mental actions have been condensed into these ten karmic paths, it does not mean that every conceivable action is subsumed by these ten. The Buddha has taken the most important types of actions—the most powerful, the ones that most easily occur, those that bring the heaviest results—and he has established them as the ten karmic paths that need to be considered. In this sense, this grouping is not exhaustive. But in order to practice ethical conduct successfully, we need to recognize these ten, learn the details of their karmic consequences, and then apply this knowledge in our daily lives.

In other words, the Buddha focused on these ten powerful negative karmas as a compassionate and skillful method to teach his disciples. Saying that there are only ten negative actions to be avoided makes it seem possible—

much more so than if he catalogued every detail of every conceivable misdeed. When you hear that there are only ten you think, "Ten is not too hard. I can do that."

The Buddha also explained the opposite of these ten nonvirtuous karmic paths, in their positive aspect, as the ten virtues. If you are able to rid yourself of these ten harmful actions, you will replace those harmful deeds with positive behavior, and that positive karma will lead first of all to temporary good results *within* samsara, and ultimately to the highest result of liberation *from* samsara. Practicing in that way will be enormously effective. The *Treasury of Knowledge (Abhidharma-kośa-kārikā)* says:

> By collecting the most prominent,
> The karmic paths were taught as ten:
> Virtuous and nonvirtuous respectively.

And a Vinaya text, the *Exegesis of the Discipline (Vinaya-vibhaṅga)*, says:

> Guard the speech and control the mind;
> Do not perform nonvirtues with the body.
> When you purify these three karmic paths,
> You will attain the path taught by the Sage.

It is clear that the nonvirtues of body and speech are dependent upon the mind. If you practice by controlling the actions that come from all three of these doors—if you keep them pure and do not let them slip to the negative side; if you purify whatever negative actions you have already done—then you will obtain the path that leads to emancipation and enlightenment. This is the path that the great Sage, the Buddha, himself followed, and this is the path he taught.

You need to begin with a certain level of knowledge. First of all you need to recognize that one type of action is positive and another is negative. You need to understand the cause and effect, as well as the faults and the benefits, of these two types of actions. Then, based on that understanding, you need to take control of your physical and verbal actions. You begin by cultivating your knowledge and understanding because actions of body and speech always have the mind in the background. The Dharma, the teaching of the Buddha, is based on this practice.

The bodhisattva Śāntideva often says that in the past harmful actions have controlled your mind; now your mind must control these actions. In the past your physical and verbal activities have contributed to a wild and heedless attitude. Now, as a spiritual practitioner, you must come to know which actions are harmful to yourself and to others, how cause and effect works, and what the temporary and ultimate results of your actions will be. Once you understand how all of this works, you rely on wisdom and good judgment to take control of your physical, verbal, and mental actions. When you do that seriously you are called a religious practitioner. That effort has the real practice within it.

Of course, this is a difficult area, especially at the beginning, because the cause and effect of karma is so subtle, so far beyond the understanding of ordinary people. The long-term results of our actions, which may ripen many lifetimes in the future, are unknown. Although the detailed workings of karma may be difficult to grasp at the beginning, and you may have to spend a long time studying these teachings on cause and effect, it is worthwhile to learn this account of karma and its results. As your understanding deepens you will gradually develop the confidence that will enable you to incorporate these teachings into your practice and your life. Getting a good grasp of this topic is extremely important because the whole Buddhist structure—from the beginning up to emancipation—is built upon this attitude of trust in the action of karma. If your practice is not built upon that trust, you cannot reach the highest goal.

The subject matter now under discussion concerns what is called the *conventional* right view, and this is the most important view to cultivate right now. Later, when you attain the path of the ārya beings—those who have gained insight into the ultimate right view—you will realize the four noble truths directly, and will therefore have no difficulty in seeing how cause and effect work. But until you reach that level of insight—while you are still an ordinary being—it is very difficult to gain a full appreciation of karmic cause and effect. As with other things you want to learn, in order to understand karma you need to study, to listen to teachings, and to investigate the subject. You need to use the wisdom that arises from hearing, the wisdom that comes from analyzing and examining, and you need to apply your intelligence in the form of inferential understanding.

Nevertheless, when it comes to this topic of karma there are certain aspects which do not lend themselves to inferential knowledge. Many of the details of the action of karma can be known only by an omniscient mind, by a buddha. For the time being there is no way to apply any form of logical reasoning to prove these things; they are simply beyond our ordinary knowledge. The only way to gain access to this kind of information is by means of proper teachings, which you receive from a kind and wise teacher in whom you have placed your trust. It is by means of your trust in the teachings and in your teachers that you begin to establish an understanding of the details and the overall meaning of karma. Once you begin to establish this understanding, you can begin to spend your life pursuing the goals of the Buddhist path, and gradually your knowledge will become deeper and your practice will become easier. In this way, little by little, everything will come naturally.

So don't be discouraged or develop a negative mind if you find that you cannot agree with everything that is taught on the subject of karma. Ordinary beings like ourselves need to struggle to cultivate this conventional right view, but once it has been grasped, we will have placed ourselves firmly on the ground of the Buddhist teaching, and will have set out on the path. The teachings on karma and its results that follow are the foundation of that path.

The important thing is that once you begin to understand this process of karma, and you see the disadvantages of negative actions, you should not leave this understanding as mere intellectual knowledge. You should put it into practice by trying to avoid what you now understand to be harmful. You should not only avoid the harmful actions themselves, but you should resist even the mental temptation to perform them; you should reject even the inclination to engage in the negative side. Of course you cannot change all of your habits overnight. It is, unfortunately, not the case that as soon as you understand the workings of karma all of your actions will suddenly become pure. But you begin trying to correct your behavior, and through these teachings you have the knowledge on which to base your efforts.

For example, there are many ways of using speech in a negative way. You should look into the motivation that lies behind your speech, and try not to mix any of the harmful forms of speech into your daily language. This is not something you can accomplish all at once because ordinarily your speech is completely mixed with negativity. But from this point on you gradually try to reduce your negative use of language until finally you achieve pure speech. It is the same way for physical action. You gradually reduce nonvirtuous actions until finally your behavior is not mixed with any negative deeds at all.

The practice here is to understand the motivation that lies behind your actions of body and speech, and to make the effort to refrain from these ten nonvirtuous karmas. What is most important here is the mental aspect, because the mind controls the body and speech. The determination that grows out of a clear understanding is a form of wisdom, and if your understanding is firm enough to stand up against doubt and confusion, then your body and speech will be easy to control. On the other hand, if your mind is weak—if you have not built stability and confidence through learning and meditation—it will be difficult to gain control over your physical and verbal actions.

That is why it is important to study and then to practice meditation. In order to build the solid foundation that comes from meditation, it is good to stay in a quiet place, to get away from distractions and temptations that entice you to engage in negative actions. The early stages of practice are a time when your resolution is weak and the afflictions of attachment and aversion are always ready to arise. When tempting objects are close by, you will not have much self-control. Therefore, at the beginning, it is often better to go to a place of solitude where you will not have any contact with objects that cause the obscuring afflictions to arise.

Later, when the mind is strong—when your understanding and correct view are well established and can stand by themselves—you can go wherever you need to go. You can have close contact with objects of desire without any danger, because now your actions are controlled by the mind. Your trust in the action of karma governs your mind, and your mind has control over your actions of body and speech.

We say that this is the foundation of the path because without pure ethical conduct there can be no inner spiritual development. All of the three vehicles of the śrāvaka, pratyekabuddha, and the bodhisattva are based on keeping your pure behavior uncontaminated by any of the ten negative actions. This practice is the indispensable basis of accomplishing the two human goals: benefiting oneself and benefiting others. Without this foundation of ethical conduct none of these three vehicles or two goals can be achieved. Therefore, again and again, in many different ways, the Buddha advised those who wanted to follow his path that this practice was fundamental, and he recommended this kind of practice to all.

The *Questions of the Nāga Kings of the Ocean* says:

> What are called the "virtuous elements" are the basic root of all the perfections of devas and humans. They are the basic root of the enlightenment of śrāvakas and pratyekabuddhas. They are the basic root of unsurpassed, perfectly complete enlightenment. What are these basic roots? They are the ten virtuous actions.

And the same text continues, with the Buddha addressing the nāga king Sāgaramati, as follows:

> O Lord of Nāgas: All villages, cities, towns, provinces, countries, and the palaces of kings; all grass, shrubs, medicinal herbs, and trees; all

> worldly endeavors; all the seeds and the growth of all crops, the plowing, harrowing, and production—all are based on the earth, have as their foundation the earth. In the same way, O Lord of Nāgas, these ten virtuous karmic paths are the foundation of birth as a deva or a human; the foundation of the achievement of the fruit of the spiritual life—the stage of "learner" or of "no-more-learning"—of the enlightenment of a pratyekabuddha, of the deeds of a bodhisattva; and they are the foundation of all of the qualities of a buddha.

Here the Buddha tells the nāga king that just as the earth is the foundation of all things that exist upon the earth, practicing the ten virtuous actions is the foundation of all worldly and supermundane goals. Worldly goals are higher rebirths in future lives in the human and deva realms. In terms of spiritual goals these ten virtues are the foundation of the attainment of the āryan path, the direct realization of the nature of reality. This realization is referred to as the "fruit of the spiritual life." By means of this realization the inner afflictions are removed from the root. The cessation of these afflictions, together with the knowledge that arises when you are freed from those obscuring afflictions, are also the fruit of the spiritual life. Specifically, there are four levels of realization on the paths of the śrāvaka and pratyekabuddha that constitute the fruit of the spiritual life: the stream-winner, the once-returner, the nonreturner, and the arhat.

The highest fruit of the spiritual life on the Mahayana path is buddhahood, or enlightenment. In buddhahood there are a great many perfected qualities of body, speech, and mind because a buddha is completely purified of all the afflictions and all the subtle remnants of these afflictions. The details of those perfected qualities of a buddha are explained in the sutras, and we discussed them in the first volume of this series.[1] The point here is that the foundation of *all* of these higher results is the practice of maintaining pure virtuous conduct. Without these ten virtues at the beginning, none of these results can be realized. It would be like trying to build a huge building without first laying down a foundation.

In its discussion of the perfection of ethical conduct, the *Sutra on the Ten Levels (Daśa-bhūmika-sūtra)* extols the practice of eliminating nonvirtue and maintaining pure behavior. This explanation of the benefits of ethical conduct is summarized in the following quotation from Candrakīrti's *Commentary on the "Middle Way"*:

> For ordinary individuals, for śrāvakas born from the Buddha's speech,
> For pratyekabuddhas who will definitely become self-realized,

> And for the sons of the buddhas, the cause of the definite good
> And of higher rebirths is none other than ethical conduct.[2]

This stanza is referring to the practitioners of the three vehicles: those "born from the Buddha's speech" are the *śrāvakas,* which literally means *hearers;* they are speech-born because they achieve their attainment as a result of listening to the Buddha's speech. The next line refers to the *pratyekabuddhas* or *solitary realizers,* who are called that because they retreat to a solitary place where they attain their realizations in isolation. Within one hundred eons they will definitely attain their goal, so it says they will "definitely become self-enlightened." The "sons of the buddhas" are the bodhisattvas.

The "definite good" refers to the higher of two spiritual goals. The first goal is a higher rebirth within cyclic existence; this is the goal of the being of small scope. The second goal, the definite good, includes both emancipation from saṃsāra (the goal of the śrāvaka and the pratyekabuddha) and the complete enlightenment of buddhahood (the goal of the bodhisattva). Once you obtain the definite good you can never lose it; you can never fall back into a lower rebirth. This achievement is definite and cannot be lost; in contrast, a higher rebirth is only a temporary achievement, because you have not eliminated the obscuring afflictions from the root.

The main cause of all of these results, whether temporary or definite, is ethical conduct. This does not mean that ethics is the one and only cause and there are no others; it means that without ethical conduct there is no way to accomplish any of these goals.

Once you understand the nature of ethical conduct, you must develop the mental resolve to consistently restrain your mind. Over and over again you need to resolve that you will not engage in particular negative actions, that you will not repeat unwholesome activities you have done in the past. Without that strong mental resolution you will not have much control over your body and speech. Uncontrolled behavior means that you act under the influence of whatever external conditions you meet, without much regard for future consequences. Either way, the mind is in control, determining which direction you will go, which actions you will take, and which you will avoid. The strongest force is your own inner, mental determination. This determination is extremely powerful and far superior to being restrained by others. And it is something you have to generate by yourself.

It is also important to be consistent and to avoid hypocrisy. The religious practitioner does not need to make great claims or to show off to others. You only need to watch what you are doing in your own mind, quietly and peacefully. When talking to others you watch what you are saying. Watching your behavior in this way, you keep your actions and motivations pure. That is the real practice of the Dharma. From that practice real, pure ethical conduct will follow, and many other good results will follow that.

Here Tsongkhapa berates the hypocrisy of some who fail to make even the slightest effort at mental restraint and the practice of ethical conduct, but who boast, "I am practicing the Mahayana. Philosophically I am much superior to the Hinayana view, so I am a high practitioner." This kind of hypocrisy is a low and dishonorable way to behave, as described in the *Sutra of Kṣitigarbha (Kṣitigarbha-sūtra):*

> By observing these ten virtuous paths you will become a buddha. However, the person who during their whole life does not keep even one virtuous karmic path, but who nevertheless makes claims such as, "I am a Mahayana practitioner; I am seeking unsurpassed perfectly complete enlightenment"—that person is an utter hypocrite, a great liar. In the very presence of all the blessed buddhas they are deceiving the world. This is absolutely wrong. That person goes to his death in a state of stupidity and then falls in the wrong direction.

If you seriously and purely maintain these ten virtuous karmas, you will obtain buddhahood. Here, however, we have a person who shows pretensions to high levels of achievement, but in reality does not observe even a single pure action. This person is actually a great liar. In fact, this is a particular form of lying called *falsely claiming attainments that you do not have,* which is a much heavier negative karma than ordinary lying. It is fine for someone who actually has such superior qualities to claim that he or she has them. But when someone who does not have any qualities above the ordinary claims to have them—that person is a great liar.

Moreover, that person is trying to deceive the world right in front of all the buddhas—a serious negative action. The buddhas know what is going on, and they do not want to see someone deceiving other sentient beings. After all, the goal of the buddhas is to protect sentient beings, to free them from the cycle of misery, to lead them to the highest bliss. Trying to deceive the world about your attainments comes from an attitude that does not respect the action of karma and its results. Since such people are deceiving others and probably deceiving themselves as well, they will go to their deaths ignorantly, stupidly, with the weight of that heavy negative karma, and after death they will "fall in the wrong direction." As Tsongkhapa tells us, this means that they will fall into one of the three lower realms.

Most negative actions are done out of ignorance, out of not knowing why they are wrong or what the disadvantages of doing such actions really are. That problem is solved by studying and listening to teachings. But unfortunately, learning the cause and effect of karma does not automatically eliminate all harmful actions. Even when you know what you are doing, negative actions still frequently arise. It may be because you are not paying attention, or because your habits are too strong. Therefore, these teachings tell us that first you have to pay attention to what you are doing, and then you have to bring your actions into harmony with what the teachings advise.

This practice starts with observing your motivation. All actions start there. It is the intention behind the action that drives the action; it is the intention that makes the karma negative or positive. Of course, the motivation is not always clear, and sometimes you have a mixed motivation. You can have a profound understanding of virtuous and nonvirtuous karma and still be motivated by fear or some other confusing affliction that leads you to act in negative way. This kind of confusion can lead even advanced practitioners into acting in a deceitful manner.

To illustrate these points we have the following story of the Kadampa Geshe Ben Kungyal. He was a thief earlier in his life, but once he began practicing the Dharma he became a very great yogi. Although he lived in retreat in a small hermitage, he became quite famous, and one day he received word that a high government official wanted to visit him. On the day when this important personage was due to arrive, he broke with his usual habit and spent the morning cleaning his little hut, setting out incense and flowers, and making a special effort to beautify the place.

When he was finished with this lengthy effort he sat down and thought about what he had done. "This is not my usual routine. What were all these preparations for?" he thought to himself. He realized that he had been acting purely out of a worldly attitude, wanting to impress his important visitor. He saw that he had been motivated by pride and the desire for worldly esteem. What he had done was a wrong action based on a wrong attitude.

The moment he realized this, he got up, went to his cooking fire, and took out a bowl full of ashes. Then he scattered ashes everywhere around his hut, rubbed ashes on himself, and generally made a big mess. That action was the real offering, the real Dharma, because it was directed against the strong worldly attitude created by his inner obscuring afflictions.

For real practitioners that kind of practice is the real practice—not blaming somebody else for your faults, not keeping an eye on someone else's poor qualities, not worrying about what other people are saying, or doing, or thinking. Nobody knows what is going on in another person's mind. But what are *you* doing? What are *you* thinking? How are *you* dealing with the situation in front of you? Real practitioners are always watching what is going on in *their own* mind, watching how they react to the events they encounter every minute of the day. They are always protecting themselves from creating nonvirtuous karma.

2" Establishing karma and its results

In this section the ten virtuous and nonvirtuous karmic paths will be explained. We begin by looking at the ten nonvirtues. The ten virtuous karmic paths are actions taken to oppose and prevent the ten nonvirtues; they are the antidotes to the ten nonvirtuous karmic paths. For example, in the case of stealing, merely not doing the action is not in itself virtuous. A piece of stone does not lie or kill, but that does not make it a virtuous piece of stone. In order for an action to be virtuous, you must first know what the ten nonvirtues are, what their consequences are, and then based on that knowledge, use your own discriminating wisdom to oppose such nonvirtuous attitudes and refrain from committing those nonvirtuous actions. The actual virtue of a particular action lies in preventing and avoiding what is nonvirtuous. Therefore, we begin by looking at the ten nonvirtues and their results.

(a) Nonvirtuous karma and its results

This is presented in three parts:

- (i) The actual nonvirtuous karmic paths
- (ii) Distinguishing heavy and light karma
- (iii) A presentation of the results

(i) The actual nonvirtuous karmic paths

Killing

The Buddha, in his kind and skillful way, condensed all negative actions into ten in order to make the practice of ethics easier to understand. If you train yourself to keep away from these ten, other negative actions will naturally be avoided. In this sense the Buddha highlighted these ten as the most important. Of course, other religions have similar lists of nonvirtues to be avoided, such as those mentioned in the Ten Commandments.

These ten nonvirtues are classified according to the three doors of body, speech, and mind. There are three physical nonvirtues: killing, stealing, and sexual misconduct. There are four nonvirtues of speech: lying, slander, harsh speech, and senseless speech. And there are three negative mental actions: covetousness, malice, and wrong view.

In his *Compendium of Determinations (Viniścaya-saṃgrahaṇī),* Asaṅga teaches these karmic paths in terms of five categories: basis, discrimination, state of mind, obscuring affliction, and culmination. When we use this format to analyze a particular action, the *basis* is the object of the action; *discrimination* is the unmistaken perception or correct recognition of the object; *state of mind* is the thought, intention, or motivation that lies behind the action; *obscuring affliction* refers to which of the three poisons—desire, hostility, or ignorance—produced that thought; and finally there is the *culmination* of the action.

However, Tsongkhapa will follow another mode of explanation. In this method the three middle categories—discrimination, motivation, and obscuring affliction—are rolled into one category, which we simply call *thought.* And a new category is added called the *actual action,* which covers the effort of performing the action. So in this format of analysis there are four categories: the *basis,* the *thought,* the *actual action,* and the *culmination* of the action. Tsongkhapa will explain each of these four elements for each of the ten karmic paths.

Furthermore, every action can be done in a way that makes its karma complete; that means that all four of the elements are fulfilled and the action is therefore performed in its heaviest form. On the other hand, one or more of the elements may be missing. In that case you can still have the action of killing, for example, but the karma is not complete, so the results will not be quite so heavy. We begin this analysis by examining what needs to occur in order to produce a complete karma of killing.

The basis

The basis of the action of killing must be another living sentient being.[3] And it must be a living being who is not yourself. From the Buddhist point of view, killing *any* sentient being, even the smallest insect, is an act of killing.

But why does it have to be *another* sentient being and not yourself? Killing yourself certainly is a negative action. However, it will always lack the fourth element of a complete karma, the culmination, because the killer—the doer of the action—will already be dead at the time of the completion of the action. In order to have a complete karma, the doer of the action must be alive and acting intentionally from the beginning of making preparations for the action right up through the culmination of the action. When you kill yourself, you are obviously not alive at the end of the action; therefore, the karma will not be complete. The basis or object of the action is there; the thought is there, including the correct perception of who you want to kill, the desire to kill, and an affliction that motivates the killing; the performance of actually killing is also there. But when you kill yourself the culmination of the action is lacking because the actor is not there to complete the action. This is why Asaṅga says in his *Levels of Yogic Deeds (Yoga-caryā-bhūmi)* that the object of killing must be "another living being." If you kill yourself it is still negative karma, but it is not the complete karma of killing.

The thought

As we said, this second element subsumes three mental aspects of an action: the first is the correct *discrimination* of the object; the second is the *motivation;* and the third is the *obscuring affliction.*

For the karma of killing to be complete, at the time of the action the killer must have a correct perception of the object he or she is killing. In other words, the killer must kill the exact same being he intended to kill. There are four possibilities with respect to this correct or incorrect discrimination: (1) when the object is a sentient being, perceiving it to be a sentient being; (2) when the object is a sentient being, perceiving it as not a sentient being; (3) when the object is not a sentient being, perceiving it as not a sentient being; and (4) when the object is not a sentient being, perceiving it to be a sentient being. Of course, the first and third of these perceptions are correct and the other two are mistaken discriminations. In order to have the complete karma of killing, the perception of the object you are killing must be unmistaken in this sense.

Whether or not you need a correct perception of exactly *whom* you are killing depends on which of two types of motivations impel your action. If your motivation is to kill a particular being, you must in fact kill *that* being in order for the karma to be complete. You must kill the actual person or creature that you intended to kill. For example, if you mean to kill only the person named Devadatta, but by mistake you wind up killing Yajñadatta, that action is not a complete karma of killing, though it is still a serious non-virtuous action and will have unhappy results.

In the second case, if you act out of a generalized desire to kill, without intending to kill any particular being, once you have taken the action of killing the karma will be complete. In this case you do not need a correct perception of *whom* you are killing. Your motivation is to kill *someone* and you succeed in carrying out that intention. Of course, the main motivation of killing is wanting to kill. If you do not have the desire to kill—if you kill someone unintentionally—it will not be the complete karma of killing.

You can apply this pattern for understanding the discrimination and the motivation to the remaining nine nonvirtuous actions.

The third aspect of thought we need to analyze is which affliction underlies the action. Any one of the three poisons—desire, hostility, or ignorance—can be the underlying cause of killing. Other afflictions may arise at the time of the action, but one of these three will always be present.

In other methods of analyzing karma the motivation and the obscuring affliction are combined into a single category. Here, they both fall under the general category of *thought;* the *obscuring affliction* refers to one of the three poisons while the *motivation* refers to the intention that directly motivates the action. The motivation always arises from one of the three poisons, the three root afflictions. One of these three is always the root of the motivation that finally sets the action in motion.

We are dealing here with samsaric karma. This action is always impure; it is called *polluted* or *contaminated* action.[4] In addition, there is pure, *uncontaminated* karma, which is action that is included in the fourth noble truth: the path that leads to the cessation of suffering. But here we are dealing exclusively with samsaric, contaminated action. Even when such action is virtuous, it is still contaminated or impure. All such action, virtuous or not, is motivated at the root level by one of the three poisons: desire, hostility, or ignorance.

The actual action

In terms of the agent who performs the action, it does not matter whether you do it yourself or you cause someone else to do it—both of these constitute complete karma. In other words, even if you do not do the killing yourself, if you have the motivation to kill and you cause somebody else to do the killing, that constitutes a complete karma of killing.

As for the nature of the action, it does not matter how the killing was carried out. Whether it was done by using a weapon, with poison, by some kind of mantra or black magic—whatever means were involved, the karma will be complete.

The culmination of the action

The culmination of the action is accomplished when the victim dies because of the action of killing—it may be immediately or at a later time. If your particular victim dies seven months or even seven years after the action as a result of what you have done, you receive the complete karma of killing at the moment he or she finally dies. Even if you are sitting in meditation, performing the most virtuous actions—or sleeping, eating, or doing whatever else you might be doing when your victim dies—*at that moment* you will receive the complete karma of killing. You have already planned the action, made preparations for the action, done the deed yourself or made someone else do it—so it does not matter what you are doing when the victim dies; the actual deed is already done. But the action becomes full and complete the moment the victim dies.

On this point the *Treasury of Knowledge* adds, "If the agent dies before or at the same time as the victim, there is no actual karmic path, because the agent is born into another body." If you commit the action of killing someone, but before the victim dies you die yourself, or if you both die at the same time, then the karma will not be complete. This is because, at the time when the victim dies and the action becomes complete, you have already taken another birth. That new body is not the one that prepared to kill or did the killing.

The action will also be incomplete if your motivation thoroughly and sincerely reverses before the victim dies. For example, if you attack a man with the intention of killing him, but you change your mind before he dies and think, "I do not want to see that person die," the action will not be complete, even if the person eventually does die. When your motivation reverses like this, you can even confess and apply antidotes to purify the action before the victim dies. Of course, the action is still negative karma, but the results will be mitigated because the intention to kill was completely reversed before the action was complete.

This has been a brief explanation of the karma of killing. It is by learning the details of these negative karmas that you will be able to gain control of your actions. You need to understand clearly what constitutes a particular karma, and then you need to be aware of what is going on in your body, speech, and mind. In this way you will know when you are involving yourself in heavy nonvirtuous actions and, based on your understanding of the negative consequences of such actions, you will be able to restrain yourself. Concerning those actions you have already committed, you will know that you should purify them through the practice of confession, as explained below in chapter 3 under the heading "In particular, how to purify by means of the four opponent powers.

Stealing

The basis

The next nonvirtuous action of body is stealing. The basis of stealing is an object that is owned by others—an object they consider to be their own, which they think of as "mine."[5]

The thought

The perception at the time of stealing must be unmistaken. If you intend to steal a particular object that belongs to another, but you confuse it and steal a different object, then the karma will not be complete.

The obscuring affliction can be any of the three poisons: desire, hostility, or ignorance. Other afflictions may be involved, but one of these three will certainly be active. Often people steal out of desire, but you can also steal out of hatred, and in most situations ignorance is also at work.

The motivation is the intention to take something that belongs to someone else without permission. It involves the desire to possess an object for yourself, knowing that it belongs to another and knowing that it was not given to you.

The actual action

As with killing, the agent who steals may be yourself, or you can have someone else do it for you. The nature of the action can be to take away the object directly and forcefully, or you can do it surreptitiously, sneaking in and taking it like a burglar.

There are also other, more subtle forms of stealing. For example, you may borrow money from someone with no intention of returning it; that is also a form of stealing. In other words, any use of deception to separate another person from his or her possessions is included in stealing.

The purpose of stealing may be to help yourself, or it may be to benefit someone else. It is also possible to steal merely because you want to harm the person you are stealing from. Any of these would constitute the complete karma of stealing.

The culmination of the action

The culmination of the action of stealing is the subject of much discussion in the Vinaya and other texts. Asaṅga's *Compendium of Determinations* says that the act of stealing is complete when the object "is moved to another place." If you go to a store, steal something, take the object away and hide it somewhere, that is the completion of the act. Moving it from its original place to the place you want to keep it is the completion of the action.

Some make the argument that the mere moving of the object from one place to another cannot constitute the final action because there are many circumstances in which the stolen property is not moved, such as when stealing land. They say that the act of concealing the object is itself the completion of the action.

Tsongkhapa says that the statement: "moving the object from one place to another is the completion of the action" is only meant as an illustration and is not all there is to the completion of the action. The true completion is the arising of the thought, "Now I have it!" in the mind of the thief. Whatever method you use to steal an object—whether you have moved it or not—if you are not sure whether you have the object fully in your possession, the action is not complete. When you are completely sure, with the thought, "Now it's mine!" then the action is complete.

But if that is the definition of the completion, what about the case in which you induce others to steal something for you? In that case, when the thief feels sure that they have possession of the object, at that same time you have the completion of the action. This is similar to the earlier case of killing: when you order someone else to kill, even though you are not aware of the moment when the victim actually dies, at that moment you will receive the complete karma.

Sexual Misconduct

The basis

The third physical unwholesome karma is sexual misconduct. There are four types of inappropriate sexual acts: using an inappropriate partner, inappropriate parts of the body, inappropriate places, and inappropriate times.

What constitutes an inappropriate partner, or object? First, you should not have sex with someone who is not your own partner. Taking the point of view of a man here, that means you should have sex only with your own wife or partner, but not with other women. The second improper object for a man is all men. The third improper object is hermaphrodites and those of uncertain gender—those who are neither completely male nor female, but appear to be something in between.

In discussing sexual misconduct we should remember that the *Lamrim Chenmo* and most Buddhist scriptures describe these actions from the perspective of a man, so most of the improper objects that are mentioned are various types of women. However, the guidelines concerning sexual misconduct are the same for women, and to understand what they are we only need to transpose the genders.

Concerning the improper object, Asaṅga's *Compendium of Determinations* says:

> Those with whom one should not engage in sexual activity are one's own mother and so forth, and those under the care of one's mother [e.g., those who rely upon her instructions concerning what to do and what not to do], just as it is explained in the sutras.

Aśvaghoṣa elaborates the meaning of this in his *Explanation of the Ten Virtuous Paths of Action (Daśākuśala-karma-patha-nirdeśa):*

> What are called "improper objects of sexual activity"
> Are those held by another, those carrying the banner of the Dharma,
> Those under the protection of their lineage or of the king,
> Prostitutes who are taken by another,
> And those who are relatives.
> These are the ones with whom sex is improper.

"Held by another" means the wife or partner of someone else, someone who does not "belong" to you. "Those carrying the banner of the Dharma" are those who have taken vows of renunciation and who therefore wear religious robes. Since this was written from the point of view of a man, here it refers to nuns, but of course this instruction refers to monks as well.

"Those under the protection of their lineage" means young women who are not yet married and who are under the care of their father or other relatives, their prospective in-laws, or who are watched over by a guard. This also includes those who are not in the care of others but are looking after themselves. "Protected by the king" means someone who is under the care of the king or ruler, or who is looked after by someone appointed by the king.

"Prostitutes who are taken by another" means prostitutes or courtesans who are already obligated to or employed by someone who is paying them a fee. You could say that such a woman "belongs" to that person, so it is improper to have sex with her. Stating it this way indicates that if you are paying the correct fee yourself, then it is not sexual misconduct to have relations with a prostitute.

This explanation accords with the way the great Atiśa explained this topic. Even though you may be householders and involved in relationships, when you are practicing the Dharma you should always try to maintain pure ethical conduct. Here we see that even in the realm of sexual relations there are proper and improper ways of engaging in these activities. By learning these details and eliminating improper behavior, you can maintain pure action in this part of your life as well.

The second type of improper sexual object is, from the man's point of view, men. This refers both to oneself and other men. But even if the object is proper—if it is your own wife or some other appropriate partner—the action can still be unwholesome if an improper part of the body is used. This refers to having sex by any avenue other than the *doorway to the womb,* as the vagina is referred to in Tibetan. The master Aśvaghoṣa says about this:

What are the improper parts of the body?
The mouth, the anus, or squeezing between
The calves or thighs, or rubbing with the hands.

Atiśa is in agreement with this:

> The "improper parts of the body" are the mouth, the anus, the front or rear orifices of a young boy or girl, or one's own hand.

The third aspect of sexual activity to be considered is place. Improper places include near a spiritual teacher, or any other person worthy of respect; in the vicinity of religious objects such as a stupa or temple; in the presence of a crowd of people; or in a place that might be harmful to the person you are having sex with, such as on very rough ground, or in a thicket of thorns. Engaging in sex in such places is considered unwholesome action because it either shows disrespect to holy religious objects or it hurts the other person. The master Aśvaghoṣa says:

Here, "improper places" means
In places of the holy Dharma,
At stupas, in front of images and such,
Near the dwellings of beings such as bodhisattvas,
In the vicinity of a preceptor, an *ācārya,*
Or near one's parents.
You should not do it in these improper places.

Atiśa's instructions are the same on this subject.

The next consideration is improper times. These include when the woman is menstruating, when she is in the latter months of pregnancy, or when she is nursing an infant. Other improper times are when one has taken the eight precepts of the one-day ordination vows,[6] when one has a disease that makes sex unsuitable, or when it is excessive indulgence, exceeding a proper amount. It says here that "exceeding a proper amount" means more than five times in a row. I don't know where they got that number; such a statement may appear somewhere in the sutras or in the Vinaya, but I'm not sure.

Ācārya Aśvaghoṣa says:

Here, "improper time" means
When the woman is menstruating or pregnant,
When she is with an infant, or not inclined,

> When physically suffering, depressed and such,
> Or has taken the eight limbs of the one-day ordination vows.

Atiśa agrees with this explanation, except that he adds that it is also improper to have sex during the daytime.

Since having sex by means of improper parts of the body, in an inappropriate place, and at a wrong time constitute sexual misconduct even when done with one's own wife or partner, there is no need to mention that they are improper when done with someone else.

The thought

Again, we have to analyze the action in terms of the three aspects of thought. First of all, is your discrimination of the object correct at the time of taking the action? Asaṅga's *Compendium of Determinations* says that the perception: "This is who I think it is" should be unmistaken. For example, if you plan to have sexual relations with a particular woman, but at the time you confuse her with someone else, that is a mistaken perception. Because of that mistake you will not accomplish the object of your intention, and therefore the karma of that particular action will be incomplete.

The Vinaya, however, explains this point differently. There it says that when it comes to the transgression of the vow of celibacy—which is a vow to refrain from *all* sexual activity—it does not matter whether the perception was correct or mistaken. The Vinaya rules were established by the Buddha for ordained monks and nuns. Those rules are stricter than the rules for laypeople because they apply to those who have taken higher ordination vows. When you break the vow of celibacy, it does not matter whether the person you are having sexual relations with is who you think it is—the vow is still broken and the karma is complete.

Vasubandhu says in the *Treasury of Knowledge Auto-commentary (Abhidharma-kośa-bhāṣya)* that if you believe that you are having sex with your own partner, but your perception is confused and it is actually the partner of another, the karmic path will not be complete.

In the case where you intend to have sex with the partner of another, yet end up with a person different from the one you had in mind—but it is still someone who belongs to another—there are two opinions. In the first view this is still a complete karma because you planned to have relations with someone else's partner and that is what you did. The contrary view is that the karma is not complete because your perception was mistaken and you did not have sex with the person you had intended.

So there are some superficial differences between Asaṅga's system and that of Vasubandhu, but I think we can follow Vasubandhu's thought here because it is more logical. The principle underlying sexual misconduct and all non-virtuous action is that you are doing harm to others. So if you intentionally choose the partner of another and you undertake to have sex with that person—even if in the end you become a little confused and you have relations with a different person who is someone else's partner—it makes sense that this is still a complete karma; you are still doing the same kind of harm, whether your perception is correct or mistaken.

The obscuring affliction, the underlying motivation for sexual misconduct, can be any of the three poisons. It can be done out of desire, out of hatred, or out of ignorance, and based on any of these three afflictions the action can be a complete karma.

The direct motivation is, of course, wanting to have sexual relations.

The actual action

Concerning the action itself, Asaṅga's *Compendium of Determinations* says that even when you make someone else perform the action, you create the misdeed of sexual misconduct for yourself. Vasubandhu disagrees with this analysis and says in his *Treasury of Knowledge Auto-commentary*[7] that, in the case of sexual misconduct, if you do not do the action yourself it is not a complete karmic path. He maintains that for sexual misconduct the actual action must be done by oneself, because if one induces another to perform it one does not experience the same pleasure.

Tsongkhapa suggests that Asaṅga's intention may have been to say that there is still a fault when you cause someone else to perform the sexual misconduct, but it is not a complete karmic path. This is a question that you can investigate further.

The culmination of the action

The culmination of the action takes place when the man and the woman come together. In the Vinaya it says that the completion of the action takes place "when the two touch and experience sensual pleasure."

We have seen these slight differences between the Vinaya interpretation of the completion of the action and the lineage presented here, which comes mainly from Asaṅga and the Abhidharma. We saw a difference in interpreting when the act of stealing is complete. And in the discussion of lying, which comes next, there is a question whether a lie is complete when it is heard or when it is understood. Though we find differences between these two systems, we do not need to worry about this too much. The overriding point is that we need to avoid these behaviors and these situations.

Of course the biggest difference is that the Vinaya presents the rules for ordained monks and nuns, and in that context pure sexual conduct is complete abstinence, or celibacy—what is called in *brahmacārya* in Sanskrit. For lay people, correct sexual conduct does not mean refraining from *all* sexual activity. Monks and nuns have a higher standard, but for householders sexual misconduct as it is described here is what should be avoided if you are trying to observe the ten virtuous actions.

The enemies that really cause us our problems are inside us; the inner poisons are our true enemies. Here in the desire realm in which we live, desire, or attachment, is the predominant enemy. If this is not tamed and controlled—if it is left to run wild, without restraint—then troubles will surely follow. Unhappiness will arise in this life, and many miseries will follow in future lives. And such unrestrained behavior harms others as well, both mentally and physically.

If you want to behave with pure, wholesome action, you first have to understand what that means; you have to know what is right and what is wrong. Then you need the motivation to avoid the negative actions you tend to do. When certain temptations appear, you must immediately try to restrain your tendency to pursue those objects. Such restraint is itself a wholesome, virtuous action, because it stops actions that harm others.

Proper conduct is to eliminate harmful actions and their suffering results. The most effective method to do this is by taking a vow with a clear understanding that the vow means you will purposely avoid doing improper actions. When you see that certain actions are wrong and you think, "I should not be behaving in that way," and through wisdom you decide to avoid those harmful actions, that itself becomes virtuous activity. On the other hand, if you just happen not to commit a negative action, without any intention to avoid it, that action will be neither virtue nor nonvirtue, but will instead be a neutral action.

We study the details of the ten nonvirtuous karmic paths so that we can recognize what is virtuous action, and then intentionally steer our activity in that direction. When it comes to sexual misconduct, we are given guidance on what is an appropriate object, time, and place for sexual activity. Instead of giving ourselves up to whatever desire consumes us at a particular moment, we have the basis to narrow down the field of our activity to a way of acting that does no harm, and respects the status and concerns of others.

Lying

The basis

Lying is the first of the four nonvirtuous karmas of speech. In the analysis of lying there is, first of all, the direct object: the lie that you tell; then there is the indirect object: the person to whom you tell the lie.

A lie can be told with respect to eight types of objects of knowledge. The first four are: something that has been seen; something that has been heard; something that has been discerned by the nose, tongue, or body; and something that has been cognized by the mind. Then, a lie can be told with respect to the opposite of these four: something that has not been seen, heard, and so forth.

For example, you may say about something that you did not see, "I saw that." You may say about something that you do not know, "I know that." This is the affirmative way of lying. Then you can do the reverse, which is to say about something that you saw, "I didn't see it." In general, lying is a misrepresentation about one of these five sense objects or a mental object.

Then there is the person to whom you tell your lie. You cannot lie to yourself. The complete karma of lying requires another being to understand the meaning of the lie that you tell; that indirect object of your lying must understand what you are saying. If you lie to a dog, who cannot understand what you say, or to a piece of stone, that is not an actual lie.

The thought

The mental state behind the lie is again analyzed in terms of three aspects. In terms of discrimination, lying is to alter or distort a perception. For example, you might take something that you had seen and say that you did not see it. You have the perception that you did see it, but you want to mislead someone, so you distort the facts about what you have perceived. You must first have the perception that you did see something, and then you change that to say that you did not see it. Even if you actually did not see it but you believe that you saw it, and then you lie about what you believe to be true, that too is a lie. It is debatable whether that case is a complete karma, but it is certainly a nonvirtue, a part of lying.

The obscuring affliction, the root source of the action, is any one of the three poisons: desire, hostility, or ignorance. Here ignorance means a special kind of wrong view which holds, "I should lie about that. Although I know this to be true, I should say that it is not true." This is a kind of wrong reason or perverted view.

The direct motivation is wanting to tell a falsehood, wanting to misrepresent the truth, wanting to deceive another person.

The actual action

The actual act of lying can be done by saying words yourself, or by not saying anything when someone else says something you know to be untrue. It can also be done with the body, using a physical gesture to indicate something that is untrue. So in this system lying can occur without speech. And it makes no difference whether you lie for your own purposes or for someone else's benefit.

As we have seen, Tsongkhapa's explanation is mainly following Maitreya's teaching as expressed in Asaṅga's *Compendium of Determinations,* as well as in his *Compendium of Knowledge (Abhidharma-samuccaya).* Here again he points out a slight difference in the explanation found in Vasubandhu's *Treasury of Knowledge.* According to the Mahayana texts by Asaṅga, only three of the four nonvirtues of speech—lying, slander, and harsh speech—will be complete karmic paths whether you do them yourself or you cause someone else to do them. However, the "lower Abhidharma" presentation of Vasubandhu's *Treasury of Knowledge Auto-commentary* says that for all four nonvirtues of speech—lying, slander, harsh speech, and senseless speech—the karma is complete even if you cause someone else to do it.

According to the Vinaya system, for all of the four actions of speech, it is necessary to do them oneself for the downfall to be complete. Again, these Vinaya rules are not talking simply about what is negative or not; they deal with the rules of ordination for monks and nuns, and what is specifically necessary to break those rules.

We need to make a distinction between the two different terms that are used here. A *misdeed*—some people translate this as *sin*—is a nonvirtuous action, which is negative karma regardless of whether the person has taken a vow against performing it or not. A *downfall* is an action that would not necessarily be negative for a layperson who has not taken any vows, but is a negative action because it involves breaking a rule to which one is committed by means of a vow.

If we look more closely at the Vinaya rule, there are four major transgressions of the monastic vows, which are called the *four defeats.* With respect to lying, the defeat or major transgression is not just telling an ordinary lie, but falsely proclaiming extraordinary qualities. It is lying about having supernatural knowledge or other high realizations and achievements, such as claiming to be an arhat or an ārya when that is not true.

This transgression includes all sorts of false claims. If you have no attainment beyond ordinary knowledge, but you falsely claim, "I saw a deity," or that you have eliminated certain afflictions when you have not, or you claim to have attained nirvana when you have not, or you claim to have realized the four noble truths without any true realization—if you lie about such things, that is a major transgression. This is a much heavier type of negative karma than an ordinary lie, and for those who have taken a vow this is a complete downfall. But in the context of the Vinaya, for such an action to be complete you have to say the words yourself.

The culmination of the action

The culmination of the action is when the listener understands what you are communicating. If the listener does not understand you, or is not listening to you, your statement will fall into the category of senseless speech. Slander and harsh speech are the same in this respect: the listener must understand your communication for the karma to be complete, and if that listener does not understand you, your statement becomes senseless speech.

It is important to remember that lying does not require words; it can be a mere physical gesture, or even silence. For example, someone may say, "Oh, you are a great bodhisattva!" though in fact you are not. If you want that person to believe that, you can indicate it is true without saying anything, just by a slight physical gesture. That is lying.

You have to be careful about this, because it is easy for such lies to happen. You may say and do things all the time without watching your own mind, silently accepting others' statements when you know they are not true. If you are aware of this danger and you realize what you are doing, you can protect yourself from this kind of situation.

Slander

The basis

The object of slander is twofold: people who are harmonious with each other, and those who are unfriendly, or not on good terms.

The thought

The discrimination and the obscuring affliction are the same as for lying. The obscuring affliction is any of the three poisons, desire, hostility, or ignorance. The perception should be unmistaken: if the people are friendly, you should perceive that they are; if they are not friendly, you should perceive that. The direct motivation is to foster division between people who are harmonious, desiring to make them unfriendly and to separate them. If they are unfriendly, the motivation is to prevent them from reconciling, and to make them even more unfriendly. When you use speech to sow discord and damage the relationship between people, that is slander.

The actual action

The action is to make statements in order to create this discord and division. Whether what you say is true or false, whether it is pleasant or unpleasant to hear, does not matter. Whether you are acting for your own purposes or for the interests of others does not make any difference. If your purpose is to be divisive and sow discord, the speech is slander. An example would be to to say something critical about person B to person A, and then turn around and tell person B something negative about person A. In this way you foster discord.

The culmination of the action

Asaṅga's *Compendium of Determinations* says, "The culmination is when those you wish to divide understand what you say." According to some interpretations the action is complete when your statements actually cause a division between people—when friendly people become unfriendly, or unfriendly people are made more distant as a result of what you said. Here we have a stricter standard than that: even though the division might not actually happen, when your words are understood, the karma is complete. This is the way to think about it in your daily practice. It does not matter whether the people you are talking to become more unfriendly or not; merely by speaking divisive words you are performing a nonvirtuous action, so you should make every effort to prevent that kind of speech.

This kind of divisive speech or slander is also a common problem among people. However, if you have some entirely different motivation—if there is no intention to cause division between people and what you say is true—then that speech will not be slander.

Harsh Speech

The basis

The object of harsh speech is a sentient being who is a source of hostility in you. It is a person whose heart and mind you want to hurt by saying painful words.

The thought

The discrimination and the obscuring affliction are the same as before. The obscuring affliction can be either desire, hostility, or ignorance; and the perception of what you are saying and who you are talking to should be unmistaken. The direct motivation is the desire to say harsh or abusive words.

The actual action

The actual action is to criticize another person, using hurtful and unpleasant language, in terms of their race or ancestry, physical faults, ethical behavior, or character. Whether the harsh words are true or not does not matter, nor does it matter whether the person you are abusing has the faults you impute to them or whether you are making up a lie; in either case, intentionally using hurtful language is harsh speech.

The culmination of the action

Asaṅga's *Compendium of Determinations* says, "The action is complete when you say the harsh words to the person." By merely saying the words, when those words come from your mouth, the action is complete. But according to the *Treasury of Knowledge Auto-commentary,* the action is complete when the meaning of the words you speak is understood by the person you are talking to.

These nonvirtuous actions of speech are not too difficult to understand. We often experience such negativities or engage in them ourselves. The main thing is to recognize when such actions are arising in your mind and to block them before they occur. Try to avoid them as much as possible.

Senseless Speech

The basis

The object of senseless speech is meaningless or purposeless words. This is a little difficult to separate from the other three nonvirtues of speech, but we will elaborate on it later.

The thought

The discrimination needs to be accurate with regard to what you are talking about, but it is not necessary to have in mind a specific person you are talking to. Among the four nonvirtues of speech, this one does not require the person you are addressing to understand you. Even if no one hears you or understands you, even if you are talking to yourself, uttering senseless words constitutes this karma. All you need is a correct perception of what you want to say.

The obscuring affliction can be any of the three: desire, hostility, or ignorance. The direct motivation is the desire to speak frivolously or carelessly, to say whatever happens to come into your mind without any significant meaning or purpose.

The actual action

The actual action is to begin to speak these meaningless words.

The culmination of the action

The culmination of the action is when the speech is finished. Once you say the words, that is enough. There is no need for someone to hear or understand you; the karma is complete.

There are seven different types of senseless speech described here. The first is quarreling, talking about someone's faults, arguing, or instigating fights. The second is to recite or transmit prayers, mantras, or rituals from non-buddhist or brahmanical texts. Such speech does not have much virtuous purpose behind it. This category also includes reading books that only produce stronger afflictions; the more you read the more desire grows within you, or you become angry or jealous. This kind of activity has no virtuous purpose. If you are trying to keep your three doors pure, you should be careful about what you read. Certain books will only increase or intensify your obscuring emotions, so reading them is considered senseless.

The third type of senseless speech is for those who are very poor and helpless to bewail their fate with mourning, wailing, or complaining about their circumstances. That has no benefit at all; it merely stimulates an inner emotional turmoil. The fourth is playful words spoken only for laughter, for pleasure, for play, or for making a joke. When you gather together with friends and your conversation has no other purpose than to laugh or entertain each other, such use of words is senseless.

The fifth is gossiping and exchanging news about politics, kings, presidents, nations, and so forth, with no other purpose than to pass along stories about what is going on. With this kind of idle gossip you pass around all kinds of useless news, from the coming and going of world leaders down to activities of the lowest thieves and criminals. It serves no purpose other than entertainment and passing the time.

Sixth is when you are drunk or intoxicated and you talk like a mad person. The seventh is the speech you engage in when pursuing a wrong livelihood, using your speech to improperly receive money, food, clothes, and so forth.

These seven are really just a few examples. Other forms of senseless speech are *disconnected* speech, in which what comes before and what comes later is unrelated. There is *speech without Dharma,* which refers to speech that comes out of the obscuring afflictions of desire, attachment, anger and so forth. *Meaningless speech* is speech without a positive purpose; this includes speech used for playing, laughing, joking, listening to music or singing, or in connection with shows or entertainment. For example, when you watch some show on television and then you talk to your friends about it—that is talk that has no special purpose or meaning.

There are two systems of thought on whether the first three nonvirtues of speech are also types of senseless speech. The first says that they are, the second maintains that only the last one qualifies as senseless speech. Tsongkhapa agrees with the first theory, that all four of these nonvirtues are senseless speech of one kind or another. After all, the first three are negative and therefore senseless. Each of those first three types of negative speech has its own distinguishing characteristics and function, therefore it is singled out with its own name. The specific category of sensless speech is applied to all the other forms of purposeless verbal behavior not included in the first three.

Together, these make up the four types of negative karma you can produce by speaking. Though many of the words you say may be pointless, still they have effects. Words can be very powerful, on both the virtuous and nonvirtuous sides. Some forms of nonvirtuous speech, such as lying and harsh speech, can be very painful to others. Sharp words can be like a weapon, leaving a painful wound in someone's mind for a long time. If you examine your life closely, you may find that you are constantly producing this kind of karma. Every day you generate so many words saying things that are not in themselves very harmful but can become heavy karma just by virtue of repetition.

Therefore, one important aspect of maintaining virtuous action is to become less talkative. When you speak you should be watching your motivation, aware of what you are saying and why you are saying it. You should always be helpful in what you say, and speak in a considerate, gentle manner. If you use speech in that way, people will find you more reliable and trustworthy.

The object of this practice is to bring the three doors of body, speech, and mind under the control of wisdom. We do this by placing mindfulness and introspective alertness as guards at each of these doors, watching what is coming in and what is going out. Simply by being careful we can eliminate many of the nonvirtues that pass through the door of speech. Even silence can bring great benefits. You may find that life is just as enjoyable when you live it in a quiet way as it was when you got your pleasure from constant talking.

Covetousness

The basis

The object of covetousness is the wealth or the property of others.

The thought

The discrimination is to recognize correctly the object you covet. The obscuring affliction is any of the three poisons. The direct motivation is the wish to possess the object you covet, the desire to make it your own.

The actual action

The actual action occurs when you move from the mere motivation of wishing to possess the object to the actual endeavor to acquire it.

The culmination of the action

The culmination of the action takes place when you resolve that you will make that object your own. It is the thought, "I definitely want to have that thing for myself." In the beginning the thought is not really definite, but it gradually develops until you get to the point where you firmly resolve to have it for yourself. This is a purely mental resolution; there is no physical action necessary.

The following is a common experience. You see some object you like; you go to look at it, admire it and see how nice it is. You take it in your hands and look it over. Then you put it back down. Then you come back to it and pick it up again. You look it over some more. Back and forth you go. Then you come back again to see it one more time. Finally, you make a decision, "I definitely want to have it."

Of course, if you don't have the money, it could be a problem for you. If there is no way to acquire the thing you want, you will feel frustrated and dissatisfied. The next step may be deciding to steal it, or to do nonvirtuous things to get the money to buy it. All these troubles arise from that thought of covetousness, which is a complete action when you make the decision that you definitely want to have that particular object.

All three of the mental nonvirtues have five aspects that make them complete; they are incomplete if any of these five is lacking. The qualities that produce a complete karma of covetousness are as follows. (1) You must have a very strong attachment to your own possessions. (2) You must have an avaricious craving to accumulate wealth—never being satisfied with what you already have. (3) You must have a mind that sees others' possessions as very fine and longs to enjoy those things. You are so attached to your own things, you want to accumulate more and more. Then you see what others have, and you develop a strong need to experience the pleasure of those things. (4) You must have a greedy mind, thinking that whatever pleasurable objects others have you need to have yourself. (5) As the result of covetousness your mind is overcome by shamelessness and you are oblivious to the need of escaping from this fault.

The covetous mind has no thought of shame; it does not recognize that this avaricious attitude is wrong, so it has no thought of turning away from it.

If all five of these qualities of mind are present, that covetous mind is perfect: it is fully developed and complete. If any of them is lacking, it is not a complete karma of covetousness.

If you go to places where you constantly see beautiful and desirable objects, you are feeding covetousness; you are inviting this kind of complete, perfect covetousness to arise in your mind. What you will buy in such places, I am not sure, but you will definitely bring back a full bag of covetousness. Therefore, the best protection is to keep your distance from desire-producing objects. You may find that it is not so urgent to go shopping and expose yourself to all sorts of attractive things. Keeping your distance from such places will help you to avoid this destructive state of mind.

Tsongkhapa wonders here about the nature of the *actual action* in the case of mental actions. For actions of body and speech, the actual action is evident. With stealing, for example, there is an obvious physical act you can point to. The *Levels of Yogic Deeds* by Asaṅga says that all ten of these nonvirtues have an actual action, but where does that lie for these mental nonvirtues? What is the actual action for covetousness, when there is no physical or verbal action? It is just this process of going over and over your craving for the object until you make that decisive resolution, "I will have it." This resolution, when it includes the five qualities we just discussed, constitutes the actual action of covetousness.

There are also incomplete forms of covetousness. Six examples are given here. First, there is the thought, "Oh, how nice it would be if the master of the house became my servant and did my bidding." Second is thinking, "How nice if his children, his wife, food, and all his possessions became mine." Third is thinking, "How nice it would be if I were known by others as someone with little attachment, who remains in solitude, is diligent, learned, and has a generous nature." Of course if you actually possess these good qualities there is no need to desire to be known to have them. A practitioner who truly has these virtues is free of worldly aspirations. In this thought—craving to be known as a pious person—the greedy, covetous mind is mixed with Dharma. This person wants be known to others as a good person, but he or she is really motivated by attachment, pride, and the worldly goal of having a good reputation.

A fourth form of incomplete covetousness is the thought, "How nice it would be if kings and captains and the fourfold retinue[8] of the Buddha paid their respects to me, and if I had all the food and clothes I desired." Fifth is the thought, "How nice it would be if I was reborn in the future as a deva and

I could enjoy playing with the five sense pleasures. May I be reborn from the world of Śiva and Viṣṇu into the Heaven of Controlling Others' Emanations."[9] The sixth and final example of an incomplete form of covetousness is when the desire arises for the possessions of parents, children, wife, servants, or the spiritual community.

Thoughts such as these are included in the general term *covetousness*. However the complete, fully developed karma of covetousness is what was described previously, and includes the five characteristics mentioned. Also, to be a form of covetousness, each of these thoughts must be motivated by attachment or some other affliction. If your motivation is to be beneficial to others—if it is out of compassion, love, and mercy—such thoughts will not be covetousness.

If you do not recognize the covetous mind when it appears—if you do not appreciate its faults and consider it a target to fight against—then these kinds of thoughts will easily arise. Without the watchfulness of introspective awareness, such thoughts flow constantly like a river. Wherever you go, whomever you associate with—this kind of desire arises all the time. Therefore, you should avoid situations that cause these types of thoughts to arise. If you find yourself in such a situation, you should remain mindful. When you see and you are attracted to something that another person has—when you feel that greedy desire to have it for yourself—be prepared to apply an antidote to those thoughts.

Once you understand the faults of these nonvirtuous thoughts, you will work to prevent them from arising. That is why you need to learn what covetousness is. You come to realize that covetousness only produces more suffering. Not only is there the long-term unhappy result that will ripen in the future; there is the immediate consequence that you get rich only in greediness and disappointment. These are important points for any practitioner to consider.

Malice

The basis and the thought

The basis, or object, as well as the discrimination and obscuring affliction of malice are the same as for harsh speech. The direct motivation is the desire to harm someone. You want to hurt them by some means: by hitting them, by saying hurtful words, by physically assaulting them, killing them, binding them with rope, or imprisoning them. You wish that they experience misfortune and financial ruin as the result of external causes, your own actions, or the actions of others.

The actual action

The actual action is the arising of the malicious wish that harm should come to another person. It is the mental process of indulging in this kind of thought as it develops, increases, and becomes stronger.

The culmination of the action

The action is complete when you resolve to definitely go through with the action of beating, killing, or harming in some way. The way this mental process plays out is that the intention to harm increases more and more, until finally a definite decision to hurt dominates the mind: that is the completion of the karma of malice.

The five qualities that must be present to constitute the complete karma of malice are as follows. (1) You must have a mind of hatred that grasps firmly at a cause or reason why you want to do harm to a particular person. For example, if you feel that someone damaged you in the past, you may harbor an intense resentment toward and hold very firmly to what that person did as a reason why you should give harm in return. (2) You must have a mind which cannot bear the harm that was done to you. (3) You must have a mind of resentment, which comes from recollecting and repeatedly dwelling on the reasons for your anger. Over and over you tell yourself, "This person did this terrible thing to me." You meditate on the harms that you believe your enemy has done to you until this powerful thought of resentment arises. (4) You must have a mind of vengeance with a thought such as, "It would be good if that person were beaten or killed." After you have meditated on the harm you believe someone has done to you, you finally feel the need to hit back, to repay the harm in some fashion. Perhaps you have all experienced such thoughts; maybe this is all very familiar to you.

Finally, (5) you must have a mind that is overcome with malice, oblivious to the disadvantages of such an attitude, without shame, and uninterested in avoiding such faults. When you have no countervailing thought challenging your vengeful desire to harm your enemy—when you feel no regret, no shame, no hesitation or doubt; when you are completely under the power of that thought—that is the fifth and final element for complete and perfect malice.

Other than this complete form of malice, we have *simple malice,* general forms of this thought that do not fulfill all the above requirements. An example of simple malice is when you think, "This person has done harm to me or is doing harm to me" and, based on that, you decide to harm that person in return. All such thoughts directed toward paying back harm that was done to you is simple malice. Similarly, wishing that someone's relatives, wealth, or virtues will degenerate in this lifetime, or wishing that in future lives he or she will be born in lower births—that too is malice.

These are all examples of the many different kinds of malicious thoughts that can arise. You can use these examples to examine the situations you find yourself in and, based on that understanding, keep a watch on your own motivation and attitude. When powerful malicious thoughts arise, you should observe how the process develops; then you will see how nothing but trouble results from dwelling on such harmful attitudes. Based on that understanding, you will be able to turn away from such harm. As soon as a small malicious thought arises—even though you could not prevent it from arising—in the back of your mind you will still have a feeling of shame, a regretful feeling that counteracts that negative intention. In one corner of your mind wisdom says, "This is wrong." With this small antidote, even though a malicious thought arises, it will not become complete karma.

Wrong View

The basis

The object of wrong view must be something that actually exists. Of course, all nonvirtuous thoughts can be a form of wrong view; but here, among the three mental nonvirtues, wrong view means a nihilistic view. Therefore, the object with respect to which this view is wrong must be something that is real, that exists, and the *wrong* view is to deny the existence of that object. This refers to such objects as karma, cause and effect, emancipation, samsara, the four noble truths, and so forth. Wrong view is to deny these things, which in fact do exist.

The thought

The discrimination is to believe that it is correct to deny things that actually exist. The obscuring affliction is, as before, any of the three poisons. The direct motivation is wanting to deny the existence of the object.

The actual action

The actual action is to engage in that wrong view. Again, this involves a process of contemplating and progressively cultivating that kind of thought until you actually hold that wrong view.

Wrong view is generally divided into four types: the denial of cause, result, agency, and the existent object. Wrong view that denies *cause* is the view that there is no such thing as good or bad behavior, wholesome and unwholesome karma. Wrong view that denies *results* is to believe that there is no fruition that arises from good and bad karma. The fruit of wholesome action is happiness and higher rebirth, and the fruit of unwholesome action is suffering and lower rebirths. Wrong view is to believe that these results do not occur.

Wrong view that denies *agency* is threefold. The first is to *deny the existence of the agents who plant and take hold of the seed.* This is believing, for example, that a father and mother do not exist—that the ones who respectively plant and contain the physical seeds of a child do not exist. The wrong view that *denies the activity of going and coming* is to believe that there are no past or future lives. The wrong view that *denies the activity of birth* is to believe that there is no miraculous birth. To say that sentient beings never have any form of miraculous birth is to deny the existence of the intermediate state or *bardo.*[10] Beings are born into the intermediate state by means of miraculous birth, but this is not seen by people in our world, so some hold that the intermediate state does not exist.

Wrong view that denies *existent objects* is to believe that arhats and so forth do not exist. This is to hold that there are no arhats, no āryas, no bodhisattvas, no buddhas, emancipation, or enlightenment.

These four types of wrong view produce powerful negative results. Therefore they are separated out from many other types of incorrect attitudes and categorized separately with the name "wrong view."

The culmination of the action

The culmination of the action is when you definitely decide that this is the true nature of things. You cultivate this attitude of mind until you definitely believe and say that these things do not exist. When you make that definite determination that this is the way things are, that is the culmination of the karma of wrong view.

Here again we have five aspects that constitute a complete, perfect, fully developed wrong view. (1) You must have an ignorant mind that does not understand the way things actually are. You are confused and mistaken about the way in which the object of knowledge actually exists. (2) You must have a mind that enjoys nonvirtue, that delights in performing harmful actions. (3) You must have a mind that continuously engages in wrong thinking as the result of concentrating on incorrect teachings. Such wrong thinking describes a faulty reasoning process that leads to accepting a wrong view. Wrong view is generally described as holding impure things as pure, holding impermanent things as permanent, and holding selfless things as having an essential, unchanging self. The process of reasoning along incorrect lines that produces conviction in these mistaken ideas is the type of mind being described here.

Furthermore, (4) you must have what is called the *completely degenerate mind,* which denies the value of all virtuous actions, including generosity, making offerings, and performing fire offerings. You hold that these spiritual practices have no benefit or no purpose. You even deny that "virtuous activity" itself exists. This is the low point of wrong view, and obviously has the potential of destroying all positive efforts; for this reason it is called the "completely degenerate mind." Once again, the fifth aspect is present when (5) the mind is overcome by this kind of wrong view, convinced and confident, without shame, and uninterested in avoiding such faults. When you possess these five elements of wrong view, it is complete, perfect, and fully developed. If any of these five are lacking, the karma is not complete.

As I explained before, there are many other forms of wrong view. The beliefs that are collected and called wrong view here—such as holding that phenomena are permanent, or holding that there is an unchanging eternal soul or self—are the most powerful forms of wrong view. They are views having the potential to cut the roots of virtue. Holding these sorts of erroneous attitudes is very conducive to performing nonvirtuous, harmful actions. The logic of such beliefs leads to a sense of invulnerability—a sense that you can indulge in whatever actions you like without any consequences.

In India there was a philosophical school called the Cārvākas or Materialists. They held that there was no such thing as past or future lives, no such thing as virtuous action, no pure ethical conduct, no karmic cause and effect. It is said that the founder of this school, Akṣapāda, composed a treatise of 100,000 verses asserting that there are no past or future lives because he wanted to establish a philosophical premise that would allow him to have sex with his own daughter.

If you are under the influence of this strong materialist view, karmic cause and effect will be denied. This denial cuts the motivation to pursue virtuous activity and have your behavior conform to the principles of karma. It leads you toward negative actions willingly, joyfully indulging in them to your heart's content. It is in this sense that the beliefs specifically mentioned as constituting wrong view are very conducive to negative action. That is why these particular ideas are separated out from the many other incorrect attitudes and given the name "wrong view."

Two attitudes are taught to be the most powerful destroyers of merit and virtue: hatred and wrong view. A brush fire, once it begins to burn, can destroy an entire forest. In the same way, wrong view can incinerate all the merits you have already accumulated, and insure that you will not create any more merits in the future.

The Concluding Motivation

In the preceding analysis of the ten karmic paths, we have discussed which obscuring afflictions act as the initial or distant motivation for these actions. We saw that all of these negative actions can be initially motivated by any of the three root obscuring afflictions: desire, hostility, or ignorance. Now we look at what kind of thought is motivating the action during its concluding stage; what kind of motivation is active once the action is underway and as it is brought to conclusion.

For the nonvirtues of killing, harsh speech, and malice, the initial motivation may be any of the three poisons, but the concluding motivation is hatred. This means that once the action has begun the intention is to hurt, harm, or destroy; this harming thought is always the motivation at the conclusion of the action. For example, when you kill an animal, it may be out of desire for the meat. But once you undertake the action the motivation is the intention to do harm; it is a form of hostility. You can set out to kill with many motivations. You can kill out of wrong view—such as believing that killing is good—as when people make animal sacrifices as a form of worship. Other people believe that animals were created to be killed and used for the benefit and comfort of human beings; this is another form of wrong view. Those acts of killing are initiated by ignorance, but the conclusion of the action is motivated by the harmful attitude of hostility: the intention to destroy or take the life of the other being.

For stealing, sexual misconduct, and covetousness, the initial motivation may be any of the three poisons, but they are always brought to completion by desire. We can imagine stealing from others because you hate them, or stealing something because you believe you have the right to take it. But at the concluding stage of the action, the intention is always to take the object away; this is a form of desire. It is the same for sexual misconduct and covetousness—those actions are ultimately dominated by desire.

For lying, slander, and senseless speech, both the initiating motivation and the concluding thought can be any of the three poisons. For wrong view the initiating motivation can be any of the three poisons, but the concluding thought is always wrong view itself.

Now we will try to clarify the difference between *karma* and *karmic paths.* These are terms that appear in the sutras and in the Abhidharma literature, so Tsongkhapa also makes this distinction here. *Karma* is intention: the intentional thought that is driving the action. For example, the karma of killing is the intention to take another's life. If the intention to kill is not present, you will not create the actual karma of killing. Karma is mainly internal; it is a mental act: wanting or intending to kill. In Buddhist psychology *intention* is a mental factor that is present at all times.

The *path of karma* means either the *cause* of an intention, or its *object,* meaning its actualization. The seven nonvirtues of body and speech are karma because they are the intention to commit an action—for example, killing. They are also karmic paths because they are also the object of that intention: the path of action down which that intention travels. The karma of killing is the intention to kill; the karmic path is the object of that thought: the carrying out of killing. So the seven nonvirtues of body and speech are both karma and karmic paths, both the intention and the object, or actualization, of that intention.

The three mental karmas—covetousness, malice, and wrong view—are only karmic paths, but they are not karma. These are karmic paths because they are the cause or the source from which an intention arises. Malice, for example, is not itself an intention, but is the underlying cause from which an intention arises. It is a karmic path because it is a cause of an intentional thought, but it is not karma because it is not itself an intention to act.

This distinction is drawn a little more clearly in the Abhidharma system of Vasubandhu's *Treasury of Knowledge,* where it is made in terms of *karma* and *obscuring afflictions;* intention *(karma)* and obscuring affliction *(kleśa)* are mutually exclusive. The three nonvirtues of mind are obscuring afflictions but they are not karma. An obscuring affliction is the mistaken thought that precedes and gives rise to an intention, which is karma. It is the cause, or source, or creator of karma, but it is not the karma itself.

(ii) Distinguishing heavy and light karma

In the presentation of the different degrees of gravity of different types of karma there are two topics:

(a') The heaviness and lightness of the ten karmic paths
(b') An ancillary presentation of some of the heaviest karmas

(a') The heaviness and lightness of the ten karmic paths

There are five parameters that determine the gravity of an action, and we shall discuss them here one by one.

Karma that is heavy because of the thought

Any action becomes heavier if it is performed under the influence of a powerful form of one of the three poisons. When you act out of intense desire, or intense hatred, that karma will be heavier. Conversely, if the underlying attitude is weak, the karma will be lighter.

Karma that is heavy because of the action

Here we will take killing as the paradigm example and the same type of analysis can be applied to the other nonvirtuous deeds. The following types of actions will make the karma of killing heavier because of the manner in which it is performed:

1. If you kill with an attitude of joy or great satisfaction
2. If you praise an act of killing you have done yourself or caused others to participate in
3. If you do it with an attitude that is happy to see an act of killing, or if you plan the act for a long time and make elaborate preparations for it
4. If you perform the action constantly or repeatedly, do it avidly, and each time you kill numerous beings
5. If you purposely kill in an especially cruel or painful way
6. If you kill after forcing your victim to perform improper actions out of fear
7. If you mercilessly kill a being who is weak and helpless, who is suffering greatly, who is poor, who is pathetically moaning or pitifully wailing in pain

Karma that is heavy because of the absence of an antidote

Although you perform negative activities, there are always antidotes available, countervailing activities you can engage in on a regular basis that will mitigate the strength of the karma. When such antidotes are completely absent, the karma becomes heavier.

A number of different kinds of antidotes are referred to here. First of all, you can take the one-day ordination vows, which include eight precepts. Sometimes people take these one-day vows every day. There are also certain holy days on which it is particularly auspicious to observe these precepts, such as on the new moon, on the eighth, fourteenth, or fifteenth of each lunar month. When you observe these precepts, the gravity of your negative actions is lessened. If you never observe any such precepts, your negative actions become heavier.

The reason these particular days are considered auspicious goes back to the time of the Buddha. It is said that certain devas made a commitment to protect the Dharma by traveling around the continent of Jambudvīpa, where humans live, on certain days. They look for those who are practicing virtues and protect them. They also report back to their fellow devas and tell them all about the wonderful activities that these practitioners are engaged in. This causes many other devas to admire those practitioners, which in turn increases the merits of all those devas who are admiring the virtues of others. As the admiration spreads, the practitioner accumulates greatly increased merits for generating so much virtue in the world. Therefore, it is considered particularly auspicious to perform virtuous activities, such as taking one-day ordination vows, on these special days.

Another form of antidote is to perform meritorious activities from time to time. These activities could include giving gifts and making charitable contributions; praising the buddhas, bodhisattvas, and gurus; making prostrations to the Three Jewels; standing up when in the presence of a holy person or sacred object as a sign of respect; making a simple gesture of respect, such as pressing one's palms together; and feeling an attitude of veneration for holy objects.

These are a few examples of ways you can create merit by means of simple actions. All negative actions are done through the three doors of body, speech, and mind. Therefore, any kind of positive actions that are done through these three doors acts as an antidote. By your performance of these virtuous antidotes from time to time, the negative karmas you create will not be as heavy as they might be.

Another important antidote is to feel ashamed and embarrassed about the negative actions you do. You should be aware of how you are behaving, and when you find yourself performing negative actions, you should have a feeling of shame about your actions. You should also feel embarrassed about the way others will look at your behavior. Think about your spiritual friends such as teachers, the buddhas, and bodhisattvas—they will be unhappy about your actions. Embarrassment means worrying what others think about your actions because you respect them. This mental quality can protect you from nonvirtue because, when you are tempted to do something wrong, you begin to worry about it and think, "If I do this my wise spiritual friends will be displeased." Out of that concern you turn away from nonvirtue.

An essential antidote to actions you have already committed is strong remorse. Even after you have done harmful actions, regret can reduce the weight of that karma.

One powerful antidote to nonvirtue is to temporarily suppress the obscuring afflictions, which instigate negative action, by means of the so-called "mundane path." This requires some explanation. Through the practice of single-pointed concentration and the attainment of a high degree of meditative stabilization, you can temporarily become free of worldly attachment. This is achieved by means of what is called the mundane path, through which you strive to achieve levels of meditative stabilization associated with the four concentrations and the four formless absorptions. Attaining one of these higher meditative states temporarily subdues the obscuring afflictions associated with that level. In this way meditators can temporarily subdue all the afflictions of the desire realm. Then, gradually attaining higher meditative states, they subdue the afflictions of the four concentrations of the form realm, then the four absorptions of the formless realm, right up to what is called the "peak of existence," a level having afflictions that cannot be pacified by the mundane path.

This practice is a powerful antidote to nonvirtue because it suppresses the afflictions motivating negative action. It does not eliminate afflictions from the root; that can only be achieved by the uncommon, supermundane path of the Buddha, which leads to the realization of emptiness and the attainment of the ārya stage. But ordinary individuals (non-āryas), and even non-Buddhists, can practice this mundane path, which temporarily subdues the afflictions by means of single-pointed concentration.

The ultimate antidote to the afflictions is direct realization of the truth of emptiness, or *śunyatā.* This antidote completely eliminates all obscuring afflictions from the root. All of the other antidotes we have mentioned are temporary. They cannot eliminate afflictions from the root, but they can subdue them for a time, lessen their frequency, force, or ability to instigate harmful actions. Once you attain the ārya stage by realizing the true nature of self and of all phenomena, the afflictions will be removed from the root. Then there will no longer be any motivating causes to create negative karma.

If you are unable to apply any of these methods at all, then you have no antidote. Without any antidote even small negative actions will become very heavy. We have the saying, "Even a heavy sin, when committed by a wise person, becomes light. Even a light sin, when committed by a fool, becomes heavy." This is because fools do not have the benefit of antidotes. Their nonvirtue is left unpurified, without shame, regret, or any countervailing forces such as vows or meditative realizations. Their negativity becomes habitual and, left unimpeded, their negative karma accumulates in its most potent form, ready to ripen into terrible results in the future. For the wise person, even if he or she commits a heavy nonvirtue, it will become light because such a person knows how to purify it by means of applying antidotes. In other words, the karma does not become fixed. So here we are being encouraged to "sin like the wise person," by taking advantage of the antidotes that can lighten the effects of these negative actions.

Another analogy we can use here has to so with a small piece of metal. If you hammer it out flat and shape it in a special way, it will float on top of the water. Even a very large piece of metal, like a big ship, will float if it is shaped in the right way. However, if the chunk of metal is not hammered into the right shape, it will sink to the bottom of the ocean. Our negative actions are like a piece of metal: we have the capacity to shape them by means of the antidotes. If we do not make use of these antidotes, our nonvirtues will drag us down to the lower realms.

Karma that is heavy because of adhering to wrong views

The karma of killing will also be made heavier if it is based on perverted views, distorted concepts of spiritual practice leading you to believe that doing harm is actually beneficial. This includes killing out of a belief that it is beneficial to make animal sacrifices. We know that there are those who kill animals as part of the worship of their gods, and they do this out of the belief that this will lead them to some kind of emancipation or heavenly existence. They are killing out of a misconceived desire to pursue a spiritual practice. Though they want to be free from misery and suffering, the methods they use will lead them in the opposite direction.

Some who engage in these practices believe that there is no fault in slaughtering animals because they were all created by the Lord of Creation as mere implements to be used for the comfort and pleasure of humans. Karma is made heavier when this kind of wrong view is held with a strong conviction based on what are believed to be valid reasons.

Karma that is heavy because of the object

The previous four ways in which karma becomes heavy had to do with the way the action was performed by the agent. Now we discuss the ways karma becomes heavy because of the object of the action.

According to our Buddhist precepts, animals from the largest elephant down to the smallest insect should not be harmed. Nevertheless, there is a distinction to be made in terms of the size of the body of the animal you kill. In general, if you kill an animal with a big body, you are creating heavier karma than killing a very small insect. And of course killing a human being will always be much heavier karma than killing an animal. This includes killing a human fetus still in the mother's womb, still in the process of developing a human body and mind.

Other types of killing that are extremely heavy because of the object are: killing your own father or mother; killing relatives such as your brother or sister; killing your own spiritual teacher; killing a dear friend; killing a "learner," someone who has entered the path of the Dharma but has not yet obtained arhatship; and killing a bodhisattva, an arhat, or a pratyekabuddha.

When it comes to tathāgatas, or buddhas, you cannot kill them because they have obtained the freedom of the deathless state. However, if you try to harm a buddha with a hostile motivation, and in the process you draw blood, that too would be extremely heavy karma. In the scriptures this action is called "drawing blood from a buddha with the intent to do harm." In the Hinayana system, buddhas are said to have ordinary blood, but in the Mahayana the body of a buddha is only a manifestation, so no one can actually harm a buddha by shooting or cutting or hitting him. Nevertheless, in terms of the intention to do harm to a buddha and acting on that intention, this is very heavy karma.

These are five ways in which the karma of killing is made heavier. Killing that is done in an opposite manner is killing that is lighter.

Objects that make the other nine karmic paths heavy

We have taken the karma of killing as the paradigm example. In general, the other nine nonvirtuous actions are made heavier or lighter in the same way. However, because the objects of different types of actions differ, we need to look at the way different objects affect the gravity of karma.

Stealing is heavy in terms of its object when you steal a large quantity, or when what you steal is very valuable, fine, or precious. Also, the karma of stealing is heavier when your action betrays the trust of someone who has confidence in you. It is heavier when you steal from people who are in difficult straits and have no protection—the poor, the hungry, or the sick. It is heavier if you steal from someone practicing the Buddhadharma, someone who has taken religious ordination, an arhat, a pratyekabuddha, the Sangha, or when you steal something belonging to a stupa.

Sexual misconduct is made heavier if you have sexual relations with those who are inappropriate objects. These include your mother or her relations, and the wives of men who are your friends. Sexual conduct with those who "belong to someone else" is always a negative action, and it is even heavier when the object is the mate of someone you are close to and who trusts you. Of course the karma will be heavy if you have sex with a fully ordained nun, a probationary nun,[11] or a novice.

We must remember that this description of sexual misconduct is written from the perspective of a man, so the objects mentioned are women. Of course the guidelines are the same for women, and you need only transpose the genders.

In terms of inappropriate "limbs" or body parts, even when the partner is appropriate, the karma is heavier when you have sex using the mouth. The time can also be inappropriate. Even with your own wife you should not have sex when one of you is keeping the one-day ordination vows. And you should not have sex with a pregnant woman who is close to giving birth, or who is sick.

Improper places are in the vicinity of a temple, a stupa, or religious statues; near a place where the Sangha is residing, or a place being used by the Sangha for religious purposes, such as a temple or monastery.

Lying is heavier when it is done with the desire to deceive others; or when you lie in many different ways, elaborating many different points in your lie. It is heavier when you lie to your parents or other people you should respect, such as āryas, arhats, pratyekabuddhas, bodhisattvas, and buddhas. Lying to good people; worthy, wise, or spiritual people; or lying to your own dear friends is also heavier. Lying also becomes heavier when it leads to performing one of the three physical nonvirtues: killing, stealing, or sexual misconduct.

Among all the forms of lying, the heaviest is telling a lie in order to create a schism in the Sangha. The act of causing a schism in the Sangha has a very particular meaning. A Sangha assembly is constituted when you have at least four fully ordained monks or nuns. In order to cause a schism, to split the Sangha apart, there must be at least eight monks or nuns to begin with, and you must cause them to divide into two separate Sanghas with at least four members in each. The heaviest form of this nonvirtue is to intentionally cause such a schism by telling a lie. The *Treasury of Knowledge* by Vasubandhu describes this as the heaviest negative karma among the five automatic transgressions, which are the five most powerful negative karmas one can create.[12]

Slander that is heavier because of its object includes causing a division between people who have been friendly for a long time; dividing a spiritual teacher from his or her disciple, or causing trouble between two teachers; dividing two parents, or parents and their children; or using slander to cause a split in the Sangha. Slander is also heavier if it causes someone to commit one of the three heavy physical nonvirtues: killing, stealing, or sexual misconduct.

Harsh speech is made heavier by many of the same objects as slander. It is heavier when the harsh words are spoken to parents and so forth, or to your spiritual teacher. It is heavier when you speak harsh words that are inaccurate, misrepresentations, or lies. It is, of course, possible to speak harsh words that are truthful, but the karma is heavier if what you say isn't even true. The karma is also heavier if you abuse, scold, ridicule, or rebuke someone directly to their face.

As we mentioned earlier, the previous three nonvirtues of speech are types of senseless speech, and they are made heavier in the ways we have just discussed. Other types of senseless speech that are particularly heavy include gossiping about the strife or disagreements among people, about someone else's faults, or about the disputes of others. These are heavier because they are motivated by hatred, attachment, or jealousy on your part. Also in this category is reading the religious texts of non-Buddhists with attachment. This refers to books which have no real spiritual goal, but only serve to increase your own afflictions. Senseless speech is also heavier when it involves ridiculing, abusing, or using unkind or disrespectful language to your parents, relatives, or such figures as your spiritual teacher.

The forms of covetousness that are heavier because of the object include desiring things that belong to the Sangha, or directing greed toward religious objects; or, due to arrogance about your own good qualities, desiring to receive equal respect from kings, great masters, and eminent spiritual practitioners.

Malice is heavier when it involves wanting to harm parents, relatives, spiritual teachers, those who have done nothing to you, or those who are poor, sick, suffering, or in any pitiable situation that should cause them to be the object of compassion. The karma is also heavier if the object is someone who has done you harm, but who has sincerely confessed the fault and apologized to you.

Wrong view that is heavy in terms of its object includes the nihilistic view that denies in every respect the basis of the teachings. This means denying everything, including the cause and effect of karma, and the existence of positive, attainable goals on the path. It is also very heavy to deny that in the world there are arhats, those who have reached perfect realization, or those who have entered the path of perfect realization. Any form of wrong view that is the opposite of these is lighter karma.

We have been talking about ways in which karma becomes heavier because of one's manner of thinking, manner of acting, or in terms of the object of the action. We have given a few examples of how this works based on discussions of karma found in the sutras and commentaries. This list does not include every possibility, but it illustrates the ways in which our actions can become heavier and lead to far more dangerous consequences.

In his *Levels of Yogic Deeds,* Asaṅga presents six ways in which karma becomes heavy. These six apply to both negative and positive karma:

1. *Motivational force.* Karma is heavier when the action is driven by a very sharp, vivid, strong motivation. These are actions that are motivated by an intense form of one of the three poisons. Actions performed without such a powerful motivation are weaker.

If the three poisons are totally absent, the action will be on the virtuous side. What makes a virtuous karma heavier is a powerful form of the opposite of attachment, the opposite of hatred, or the opposite of wrong view. This means nonattachment, loving compassion, and right view or realization. These are actually the antidotes to the three poisons, and actions that are powerfully motivated by these will be weightier virtuous karma.

2. *Habituation.* Even when the motivation is not strong, karma will be heavier if it is done over a long period of time. When you become accustomed to an action because you do it regularly, repeatedly, for a long time—even when there is no intense motivation driving it—that karma can become very heavy.

3. *Nature.* The heaviness of the karma is influenced by the nature of the action. Taking the three karmas of body—killing, stealing, and sexual misconduct—the first is the heaviest, the second is a little lighter, and the third is lighter still. It is the same for the four actions of speech: the first is heaviest and they diminish in order. When it comes to the three mental karmas, the last, wrong view, is the heaviest, second is malice, and the lightest is covetousness.

4. *Object.* As we have already discussed, karma can be heavier in terms of the object. Objects that make a nonvirtuous or virtuous action heavier are objects such as the three jewels of refuge, the Saṅgha, or your spiritual teacher. Actions that benefit or harm such objects will be heavier.

5. *Single-mindedly adhering to unfavorable factors.* This means doing nonvirtuous actions exclusively. If throughout the course of your lifetime all you do are nonvirtuous actions, if you never do even one virtuous thing, then of course, the karma becomes quite heavy, even if the motivation was not strong.

6. *Clearing away unfavorable factors.* This means eliminating everything on the side of nonvirtue. When you have freed yourself from attachment you will always perform virtuous actions. This will happen later, when you reach the āryan stage. Arhats, and bodhisattvas at certain levels, no longer create negative karma. When you reach those levels you will always adhere to the side of virtue. Such beings, of course, create very heavy virtuous karma.

Nāgārjuna, in his *Friendly Letter* to the king, mentioned five ways in which actions become heavy:

> There are five ways in which virtue or nonvirtue become great: when it arises continually, passionately, without antidote, or when the object has great virtues, or is of primary importance. Among these, strive to engage in the virtuous.

Nāgārjuna is describing five ways in which both negative and virtuous actions become great, and of course he says you should make an effort to practice the virtuous ones. What are those five? First, doing an action persistently, continually, all the time. Second, doing an action with an intense, powerful, sharp motivation. Third is to act without making use of any antidote.

The fourth factor, the object of the action, is divided into two types of objects, which is why the verse speaks of five factors. The first is an object that has great virtues or superior qualities, such as a buddha, bodhisattva, spiritual teacher, the Sangha, or the Dharma. The second type of object is one that is "of primary importance" to you; this refers to your father or mother. Parents are the source of life for their children; they nourish them and care for them from birth until they die. For this reason they are considered a great field of benefit for their children, and any action done in relation to your parents becomes powerful karma.

(b') An ancillary presentation of some of the heaviest karmas

Here we have a discussion of a few particularly heavy karmas which are mentioned in the sutras or in the Abhidharma, and are selected here as examples. This discussion looks at four factors: the object, or "field," of the action; the agent, or "actor," of the action; the material, or "substance," of the action; and the attitude behind the action.

(1') Powerful in terms of the field

Other beings are the field of our actions. Karma becomes more powerful when the action is directed toward a powerful field. Higher, more powerful fields are the Three Jewels, your own spiritual teacher, anyone who has high realizations and is working to lead others to happiness, and your own parents. When your actions are directed toward such weighty objects—even when these actions are not motivated by an intense attitude, and even when they bring about just a small amount of harm or benefit—the karma will become powerful because of the great potential of the field of the action.

The *Treasury of Knowledge* says that actions directed toward these fields are heavier "because they destroy or hurt a field of benefaction, or a field of high qualities." As we discussed, parents first produce a person, then they nourish, care for, and protect that person until the child grows to become independent. In all worldly matters we have no greater benefactor than our own dear parents. Although we know that sometimes a bad relationship develops between parents and their children, we can certainly say that it is the nature of parents, especially mothers, to look after their offspring. Even animals and small insects will protect their young, sometimes even to the point where they will sacrifice their own life to protect their children.

The ultimate protector, the highest field of qualities, is the Three Jewels—the Buddha, Dharma, and Sangha—as well as the spiritual teacher who guides you through the Dharma. They are the ultimate and perfect protectors, leading you to the highest goal of permanent freedom from suffering. These are the ultimate sources of refuge and protection, and therefore the *Treasury of Knowledge* calls them the "field of high qualities." The *Mindfulness of the Excellent Teaching (Sad-dharmānusmṛty-upasthāna)* says:

> Even if you steal something insignificant from the Buddha, the Dharma, or the Sangha, the karma will become great. If you repay the Buddha or the Dharma an amount equivalent to what you stole from them, the action can be purified. However, if you steal from the Sangha there can be no purification without experiencing the result, because the field is so heavy. If you steal items that are required for the sustenance of the Sangha, you will fall into the great hell of sentient beings. If you steal items that are not required for their sustenance, you will be born into a place such as Great Darkness, one of the hells surrounding the Uninterrupted Hell.[13]

To steal from the Dharma means to take something like an image of the Buddha, or to steal scriptures, or to take for yourself some substance that you intended to offer to the Three Jewels. Stealing from the Sangha means stealing from monks and nuns. When you steal from the Buddha or the Dharma you can purify that action by applying the powers of confession and regret, and then offering something similar to what you took. But stealing from the Sangha is heavier, and you cannot purify that karma merely by repaying the thing itself; you will have to experience the result of that action, which will be rebirth in some form of hell.

If you steal articles that are required for the nourishment of the Sangha, you will be born in the deepest hot hell; if you steal other items you will be born into one of the sixteen neighboring hells, a region of great darkness surrounding the hot hells, but with an intensity of suffering that is slightly less.

There is a distinction being made here between making an offering to the Buddha or the Dharma on one hand, and making an offering to the Sangha on the other. Let's say you offer some food, or clothes, or a statue, to the Buddha or the Dharma. There is great benefit for you in the merits that you accumulate by making that offering, but there is no direct benefit to the Buddha or the Dharma, because they do not actually need the substances that you offer. In contrast, offering food to the Sangha brings about two kinds of benefit: there is the benefit to you from making the offering, and then there is the direct benefit to the monks and nuns when they make use of the things that you offer. Traditionally, Buddhist monks and nuns live a very simple life with few possessions, sometimes living only on what they receive as alms. Therefore, if you steal from the Sangha—if you take away the food they require to survive—that will produce a great obstacle to their Dharma practice, and in that way you will actually be harming all sentient beings.

Ordinarily we consider the Buddha and the Dharma to be higher objects than the Sangha. But here we find that you have to be very careful about the way that you handle property belonging to the Sangha, especially items that are required to nourish and sustain the monks and nuns.

You can be born into a great hell even for using items as small as leaves, flowers, or fruit, if they belong to the Sangha. This applies even to monks and nuns who have transgressed their vows—if they use the property of the pure Sangha, the neagtive karma for them will be very heavy. Not only will they be born into one of the great hells and suffer there for a long time, but even when they are finally free of hell, they will be born blind, with no hands or feet, possibly as some kind of animal or a hungry ghost, in a dry, barren wilderness where there is little to eat and it is difficult to survive. For many years they will experience such terrible sufferings. Such are the grave consequences of stealing from the Sangha according to the *Sun Essence Sutra (Sūrya-garbha-sūtra).*

That sutra also teaches that once offerings, such as flowers, are dedicated to the Sangha, or to a particular monk or nun, laypeople should not make use of them, nor should they be given to a layperson for their use. On this subject the *Sun Essence Sutra* says:

> Do not give to householders
> What has already been dedicated to the Sangha.
> It would be better to cut off your own limbs
> With sharp razors.
>
> Those who are not members of the Sangha
> Should not make use of the Sangha's property.
> It would be better to eat a lump of metal
> Blazing with tongues of fire.
>
> A householder should not make use of
> What belongs to the Sangha.
> It would be better to accept and eat
> A fire as vast as Mount Meru.
>
> A householder should not make use of
> What belongs to the Sangha.
> It would be better to be disemboweled
> And impaled on a pointed stake.
>
> A householder should not spend the night
> In the dwelling of a Sangha member.
> It would be better to stay in a house
> That was filled with burning embers.

These verses all deliver the same message. Although the tortures they describe all seem quite horrifying, the experience of them in this life would not last very long. You would suffer for a short while, but soon you would be dead. And after all, you are going to die anyway. But if you are born into hell as a result of using the property of the Sangha, that intense suffering would continue for an inconceivably long period of time.

We said earlier that a Sangha consists of four or more fully ordained monks or nuns. This number refers to a group of ordinary individuals. A Sangha is also constituted by one single person who has attained the ārya stage. Among the various types of Sangha, an ārya who is a bodhisattva is an exceptionally heavy field of action, and virtues or nonvirtues directed toward such a person will have much heavier results.

The *Seal of Engaging in Developing the Power of Faith Sutra (Śraddhā-balādhānāvatāra-mudrā-sūtra)* says that it is much greater negative karma to get angry at a bodhishattva and, turning your back with disrespect, to say, "I will not even look upon this vile person," than to put all the sentient beings in the ten directions into a dingy prison. It also says that it is far worse to abuse any kind of bodhisattva than to steal all the possessions belonging to all the beings in the world. In another example, it says that it is much heavier negative karma to get angry and use unpleasant words to a bodhisattva who has entered the Mahayana path—that is, a bodhisattva who has not yet reached the ārya stage—than to destroy as many stupas as there are grains of sand in the Ganges river.

The *Seal of Engaging in Certain and Uncertain Destinies Sutra (Niyatāniyata-gati-mudrāvatāra-sūtra)* discusses the same issue, but in terms of virtuous actions. It says that a person who looks upon a bodhisattva with faith, and out of admiration wants to see and praise that bodhisattva, gains infinitely greater merit than than you would accumulate if you were moved by deep loving-kindness to restore the sight of all the beings of the ten directions after they had their eyes ripped out. That person would gain more merits than someone who liberated all sentient beings after they were locked away in a dingy prison, and then placed them in the exalted state of a Cakravartin king or the bliss of Brahmā.

These illustrations demonstrate just how powerful a field of merit a bodhisattva is, and how powerful an action is when it is directed toward such a being.

The *Sutra on the Magic of Final Peace (Praśānta-viniścaya-prātihārya-sūtra)* compares the negative karma of someone who steals all the property belonging to all the sentient beings in the world, or the karma of someone who kills all those sentient beings, to the karma of someone interrupting a bodhisattva who is in the process of feeding an animal with a handful of grain. It says that the negative karma of the second action is immeasurably greater. Of course the bodhisattva has taken the bodhicitta vow, promising to lead all beings to enlightenment. When you interfere with an action that is being done with the motivation to benefit all sentient beings, even though it appears to be a small action, you are actually harming all those beings. Interfering with a bodhisattva is like obstructing the possibility of emancipation for numberless beings.

Since actions directed to these potent fields create such powerful karma, Tsongkhapa says that you should guard your behavior with great care. Otherwise, what looks like an insignificant action can turn out to have huge negative consequences because of the power of the field. Conversely, you can create great merits and powerful positive karma by means of small acts of respect, praise, and devotion when they are directed toward these powerful fields of merit.

The real danger here is that you never know who is a bodhisattva. Do they wear some special clothes or have a star on their forehead? No, they don't. You can't always judge people by their appearance. It isn't easy to know what powerful spiritual practices may be going on inside a humble person. If you see a large ditch covered with ashes, you should approach it cautiously. Otherwise, if you mindlessly walk out onto the ashes, you may find yourself falling into a pit of blazing embers.

Since you never know who is a bodhisattva and who is not, the best policy is to treat everyone you meet as if he or she were a bodhisattva. When you strive to do as much benefit as you possibly can for everyone you encounter, and you make a serious effort to avoid doing harm to anyone, then it doesn't matter who is a bodhisattva and who is not. You will always be creating virtue and accumulating merits. If the person you are helping turns out to be a bodhisattva and the merits you gain are hugely increased, so much the better. But at least you will have confidence that your actions are not harming others and, in the long run, harming yourself.

(2') Powerful in terms of the actor

Now we turn to the ways in which karma gains power in terms of the actor, the person who performs the action. Earlier we used the metaphor of a lump of iron: if you put it in the water it will sink to the bottom, but if you fashion it into a vessel it will float. In the same way, when a foolish, unskillful person performs a small negative action, it can lead that person right down to the hell realms, because he or she has no idea how to apply the appropriate antidote; without purification that karma will certainly ripen into unpleasant results. The skillful person, on the other hand, may create a heavy negative karma, but because he knows how to apply the antidote and purify the action, the results will turn out to be light. Thus we can see how the same activity performed by different actors can yield very different results.

The *Great Final Nirvana Sutra (Mahā-parinirvāṇa-sūtra)* describes how a small action becomes heavy karma. The ignorant person is like a little fly who gets himself stuck in a wad of mucus that has been spit onto the road. Here in the West, where the streets are so clean, you may not see this very often, but in some places it is common to spit in the street. Flies are attracted to that spit and they stupidly get themselves stuck in the mucus. In a similar way, ignorant, unskillful people get stuck in the small negative actions they create because they do not know how to purify them and thereby escape from the consequences. They are unable to generate any antidotes to their negative actions because they feel no regret for them. And they feel no regret because they are ignorant of the consequences of their actions. Even when they have created previous virtues, those merits are polluted by the impure action of hiding their own faults.

People like that may create some small karma that would otherwise be experienced as a minor problem in this lifetime. Because of their ignorance, however, that minor negativity is transformed into the cause of a future rebirth in a terrible hell realm. The situation is like that of a small container of clean water: if you pour in a handful of salt, the water becomes undrinkable; its taste is completely dominated by the salt. Or it is like a poor man who borrows a little bit of money. Because he is unable to repay what he owes, the interest on the loan keeps compounding until finally he is completely overwhelmed by a debt he can never repay. The problem starts as a small thing, but because there is no countervailing force, the consequences in the end are great.

The ignorance we are referring to here is not knowing what is virtuous and what it is nonvirtuous karma. It is not knowing what to do when you have performed a nonvirtuous action—not knowing how to purify it, or how to prevent it from happening in the future. Ignorant people not only commit many negative actions because they do not know any better, but the actions they create have grave consequences because they do not know how to apply the antidotes.

There are five ways in which a small karma that should ripen as a light result in this life can be changed into the cause of a rebirth in hell: when the actor is very ignorant; when he or she has accumulated very little positive karma, or none at all; when he has committed powerful, heavy nonvirtues; when he does not regret the actions or purify them with confession and other antidotes; and when he or she does not perform virtuous actions as a countermeasure to the nonvirtue.

For skillful people—those who are wise—negative actions become light, because they feel sincere regret for their nonvirtues, and they resolve that they will restrain those actions in the future. Instead of hiding their faults, they confess them in front of the Sangha in order to purify them, and they perform many kinds of virtuous actions that are the natural antidotes to nonvirtue.

But the person who proudly asserts that he or she is an expert in the Dharma and in the action of karma, but then carelessly disregards these antidotes and knowingly engages in nonvirtuous actions—for that person the nonvirtuous karma will be heavy.

The *Heap of Jewels Sutra (Ratna-rāśi-sūtra)* provides an example of the tremendous difference it makes when you perform a virtuous action based on holding vows. Imagine that all the sentient beings in the universe had "entered the Mahayana path," which means they were motivated by bodhicittta. Then imagine that their wealth was as vast as a Cakravartin king. Finally, imagine that each of them offered a butter lamp to a stupa of the Buddha, and each butter lamp was the size of the ocean and had a wick the size of Mount Meru. That would create a vast amount of merit, wouldn't it?

But compare that to a bodhisattva who had renounced the worldly life and taken vows of ordination as a monk or a nun. Imagine that bodhisattva holding a single little butter lamp with a wick that was just smeared with a little bit of butter, and that this bodhisattva lights that flickering lamp and offers it to a stupa of the Buddha. This sutra states that the merits accumulated by that single bodhisattva would be more than one hundred times greater than the merits created by all the other sentient beings in the universe!

Why is that? All of the beings in the first example were also bodhisattvas. They had entered the Mahayana path, so the thought motivating their actions was the same as that motivating the single bodhisattva—in both cases it was bodhicitta. Furthermore, in both cases the offerings were being made to a stupa of the Buddha, so there was no difference in terms of the field. Although there was a significant difference in the material that was offered—one meager butter lamp compared to innumerable vast lamps—that could not account for the difference in merit.

The difference lies in the nature of the actor. The single bodhisattva possessed not only the bodhisattva vows, but also possessed the prātimokṣa vows of full ordination. It is the difference between one fully ordained bodhisattva and an innumerable number of lay bodhisattvas. That is what makes the monk or nun's merits so much greater.

The point here is that the merits of someone who has a vow will be much greater than those created by the person who does not hold that vow. And the person who holds two vows will create more powerful actions than the person who holds only one. This applies to nonvirtues as well, because the consequences of a negative action by someone who holds a vow will be heavier than those experienced from the same action performed by someone who does not hold that vow.

Holding vows not only affects the power of virtuous and nonvirtuous actions. It also enables you to make more rapid progress on the path. Holding two or three vows makes your practice more effective still. In the example from this sutra we see that holding the prātimokṣa vows in addition to the bodhisattva vows makes your practice much, much stronger. If you hold the tantric vows as well, your actions will be even more powerful.

The language that we use to describe this situation in Tibetan is instructive. We say that by basing your practice on vows you will "cover the ground" more quickly. This refers to the distance you are able to travel on a journey. For example, an airplane travels the farthest in the least amount of time; traveling by plane would therefore be comparable to taking all three sets of vows: the prātimokṣa, bodhisattva, and tantric vows. Holding two sets of vows would be comparable to traveling by car. And holding just the prātimokṣa vows might be comparable to traveling by horseback. And practicing without taking any vows at all would cover the least amount of ground, and would be like going on foot. This analogy illustrates how taking vows makes your practice, and all the actions you do, much, much more powerful.

Of course, as stated already, this applies to nonvirtuous actions as well. If you break the vows you have taken and commit even a small negative action, you will "cover the ground quickly," which in this case means you will quickly go to hell.

The benefits of taking vows applies to lay practitioners as well as ordained monks and nuns. As laypeople you can take the five precepts, which are vows you take for life: not to kill, not to steal, not to commit sexual misconduct, not to lie, and not to become intoxicated.

We also have the practice of taking the one-day ordination vows. This is a very effective way to magnify the power of all the meritorious practices you do—a way to increase the ground that you cover in your practice. Although it may not be possible for you to take monastic ordination for your whole life, you can often find opportunities when you can take these vows and keep them purely for just one single day. During that day you remain alert and conscious that you are protecting those vows. You dedicate that time to your practice: to meditating, listening to teachings, doing prostrations, confessing, and purifying past negative actions. Whatever other practices you do during the time that you are guarding your vows will be tremendously empowered, and the ground you cover on the path will be increased. Then, at the end of the day, you dedicate the merits of your practice to the benefit of all sentient beings. You always focus your goal on the benefit of others. In a sincere Mahayana practice you strive to attain enlightenment yourself in order to benefit others.

It is important to be honest with yourself about your own capabilities and your own situation. If you can take the prātimokṣa, bodhisattva, and tantric vows and keep them purely, then with every action, every moment, you are creating great merits. Some people are ready and able to renounce the worldly life. They think, "Now, for the remainder of my life, I will only practice the Dharma. I will keep my vows purely. No matter what hardship I have to undergo, in my mind I will have the joy of knowing that what I am doing is right." With that attitude, although they may face hunger, cold, or poverty, it doesn't matter, because they are so happy to be working for the benefit of other beings.

But you need to ask yourself, "Am I ready to do this? Or is this still a distant destination, a goal I hope to reach someday?" You don't want to take high vows and make huge promises and then, after a little while, go on to break all the promises that you have taken. That will only bring you a huge mountain of negative karma. You would be like the foolish person we mentioned earlier, one who pretends to be a great upholder of the vows but who is actually ignorant of what is beneficial and what is ultimately harmful.

Therefore, if you are not yet ready for these lifelong vows you can begin with one-day ordination vows. You can think, "Most of my life is spent senselessly engaged in worldly concerns. But today I have the leisure to apply myself to virtuous practice. For this one day I will take these vows and keep them purely." You do this with a motivation to benefit all sentient beings. During that day you remain quiet, not making big plans or engaging in social activities, not mixing your mind with worldly thoughts. During this one day of serious practice you can create great, great merits. This is the kind of practice that can act as an antidote to the many negative karmas you create on a daily basis. This is the way to make the consequences of all your negative karma much lighter.

The *Sutra on Overcoming Faulty Ethical Discipline (Duḥśīla-nigraha-sūtra)* gives us an example of the way the nature of the actor can determine the strength of a negative karma. Consider the accumulation of negative karma of a person who commits all ten nonvirtuous actions uninterruptedly for one hundred years. Compare that to the karma of a fully ordained monk or nun who disdains ethical conduct. Though they "fly the victory banner of the Sage"—which means they wear the robes of the Buddha's order—such ordained beings disregard the promises they have made to uphold the moral standards of that order. When such a person partakes of the sincere offering of food by a faithful donor, the nonvirtue created far exceeds that of the lay person who commits every nonvirtue for one hundred years. Here again we see how karma is made powerful by the actor, depending on whether that person possesses a vow or not. Thus we see that having the vow has both advantages and disadvantages; it magnifies both positive and negative actions. Either way, once you have taken vows you must take care to keep your commitments purely.

The *Exegesis of the Discipline* says:

> For those with corrupted discipline,
> Or those who do not keep their vows correctly,
> It would be better to eat a lump of iron ablaze with fire
> Than to eat the alms offered by the people of the region.

Of course if you eat flaming metal you will burn your throat and you may die. That is all that can happen to you. But when you break all your vows and then you eat the alms that are offered to you by people who put their faith in you, it may be that your throat will not be burned, but eventually you will burn for many eons in the realms of hell. Tsongkhapa says that this refers to those who have completely broken their vows as well as to those who have kept their commitments in a slack or shoddy manner. Both of them need to be careful.

The great sage Dromtonpa, the foremost disciple of Atiśa, also said that compared to taking vows and then breaking them, the ten ordinary non-virtues are just small things. And this seems to be true.

(3') Powerful in terms of the substance

The third element that can make an action more powerful is the substance or material that is used in the action; this is also called the direct object of the action. When you give charity, for example, the *field* is the person you give it to, the *actor* is the person who gives, and the *substance* is the thing that you give. You can take this act of giving as an example and apply your understanding of what kind of substances make an action more powerful to other types of actions.

There are three kinds of substances that you can give as charity or offerings. First there is the gift of material goods, such as food, clothes, or money. These are the types of things you might donate to poor people, for example. Second is the gift of the Dharma, meaning giving Dharma teachings. Third is the gift of protection, saving another being from some form of threat or danger. When it comes to giving something to other sentient beings, the giving of Dharma is superior to the gift of worldly goods. Giving food and shelter of course has great benefit in that it alleviates the temporary physical sufferings of people who are in need. In contrast, however, giving the proper teachings to the proper disciple has the benefit of removing *all* forms of mental and physical suffering forever; it leads to the achievement of the highest happiness.

There are many things you can offer the buddhas and bodhisattvas in order to please them: food, beautiful flowers, money, and so forth. But what they find most pleasing is to see disciples practicing what they have been taught. The main goal of buddhas and bodhisattvas is to lead all beings to freedom from all misery. This is why practicing in accordance with the teachings of the buddhas is far superior to any material offering you can make. The great Tibetan yogi Milarepa said, "Of worldly goods, I have absolutely nothing to offer. But I will repay the kindness of my guru by practicing what he taught me."

The third form of giving, which is not mentioned here by Tsongkhapa, is the giving of protection. On the worldly level, examples of this would be saving someone who has fallen into a river, or protecting a person who has been convicted of a crime from being harshly punished. But far superior to such forms of temporary protection is saving people from falling into the depths of misery in their future rebirths. This is the ultimate form of protection, and you give it by leading people along the path of the Dharma.

(4') Powerful in terms of the attitude

The nature of your attitude while you are performing an action also has a major effect on the strength of that particular karma. As we have already seen, the thought that underlies an action makes a big difference. The *Heap of Jewels Sutra* makes the following comparison. Imagine all the beings in the three billion world systems of the universe. And imagine that all these beings are seeking their own individual liberation, freedom from all suffering. With that motivation each one builds a stupa of the Buddha as large as Mount Meru. And then for ten million eons they worship that stupa with circumambulations, prayers, and so forth. All the vast amount of merits created by such virtuous activity would be less than the merits of one bodhisattva offering one single flower to a stupa with an attitude of wanting to attain omniscience in order to benefit all sentient beings. The reason for this is that the simple action of the bodhisattva is motivated by bodhicitta, the attitude wanting to free *all* beings from misery; such a bodhisattva is not acting merely for his or her own welfare alone. Once you attain bodhicitta, all your actions—no matter how small and seemingly insignificant—are spontaneously directed to the benefit of others, and therefore become very powerful.

When we see people doing all sorts of different religious activities—meditating, making offerings, giving charity, saying prayers—how can we tell which of those people doing which actions are creating truly great virtue and which are creating less? We can't tell anything from the surface, can we? Because the main factor making the difference is the attitude, the mind that lies behind the act. If you have sympathy for other sentient beings—if you are sincerely motivated by wanting to alleviate the suffering of *all* beings and not just to benefit yourself—then even one minute of meditating or five minutes of studying the scriptures can be actions of vast scope.

If two people are performing identical actions—if they are offering the same substance to the same field of merit, and they are the same in terms of the vows they have taken—it is the difference in their intentions that will determine whose actions are greater and more powerful. The difference in their mental attitude—in the purpose they intend to achieve by making that offering—is what is significant. For the person who is acting for the greatest purpose, wanting to obtain enlightenment quickly for the benefit of all other beings, there is no way to measure the merits of those actions.

More specifically, the meritorious strength of an action is affected by a number of distinctions in the attitude or purpose of an action. The goal that you seek can be a higher goal, a lower goal, or something in between. You may be seeking only your own benefit or you may be working for the benefit of others. And even within working for your own benefit there are many possibilities: you may be acting for complete emancipation or arhatship; you may only be seeking a high rebirth in your next life; you may merely want peace and enjoyment during this life; or perhaps all you want is for other people to see you practicing nicely so that they will give you respect. There are many, many levels of motivations and goals. Each produces a different level of merit, but in each case the level of merit is determined by the attitude that motivates the action.

Even within seeking the same goal, there can be a distinction in the strength or weakness of your attitude. For example, you may want to benefit other beings, but that may be a vague and weak kind of feeling, not an unshakable resolve rising from deep within your heart. An action done out of such a vague state of mind will of course be weaker than an action motivated by the full force of the realization of bodhicitta.

If the goal is the same, and the strength of the thought is the same, there may be a difference in the length of time during which you perform the action. An action you do frequently or constantly will of course be more powerful than an action you perform just once.

These distinctions of motivation affect not only virtuous karma but non-virtuous actions as well. Even if you kill another person there can be great differences in the intention that lay behind that action. The goal could have been to actually help someone else, or it could have been purely for your own benefit. You can kill out of a very fierce raging hatred, or with a sincere intention to help someone. What we commonly think of as negative actions of body or speech can become virtuous if the intention is virtuous. By the same token, praiseworthy actions—such as prostrations—can become nonvirtuous if one's intention is selfish. It all depends on the attitude. How wide or narrow is your mental scope? How strong or how weak? There are so many different types and levels of motivation. The important thing is to understand the ways in which your attitude affects the strength of a karma.

In general, the strength of a negative action will be determined by the intensity of the obscuring affliction that motivates it and by the duration of the action. Among the afflictions, hatred is one of the most powerful thoughts; action taken with an intense attitude of ill will creates the most powerful negative karma. It not only plants the seed of unhappy results in the future, it can destroy great amounts of merit that were created in the past. Śāntideva says in *Engaging in the Bodhisattva Deeds:*

> Whatever wholesome deeds,
> Such as venerating the buddhas, and generosity,
> That have been amassed over a thousand eons
> Will all be destroyed in one moment of anger.

As Śāntideva says, a single moment of hatred can destroy the virtuous karma you have accumulated in one thousand eons. Hatred and anger are especially weighty when they are directed at someone who is working toward buddhahood by practicing the Dharma.

The *King of Concentrations Sutra* says:

> When one practitioner feels hatred for another,
> He cannot be protected by ethical conduct or by study.
> Meditation will not protect him, nor retiring to a solitary place.
> Generosity will not protect him, nor worshiping the buddhas.

Powerful hatred toward another practitioner will destroy many merits you have accumulated in the past. All of the virtuous activities you do now cannot protect you from that. You may be accumulating some new merits, but you cannot save what is destroyed by that moment of hatred.

Again, *Engaging in the Bodhisattva Deeds* says:

> The Buddha has said that whoever bears an evil thought
> Against a benefactor such as a bodhisattva
> Will remain in hell for as many eons
> As there were evil thoughts.

In this stanza the bodhisattva is called a benefactor. If someone gives you food, money, or clothes you might call him or her a great benefactor. Yet a bodhisattva is giving not only worldly goods, but every source of happiness, starting from the comforts of the world up to the highest goal of enlightenment—all of this he or she tries to provide for other sentient beings. If you indulge in ill will toward a benefactor like that, the consequences will be severe. Bodhisattvas are such dangerous objects for negative actions because they have taken upon themselves the entire responsibility to rescue all beings. So if you have the impulse to injure or destroy such person, you are practically directing that feeling toward every being in the universe. Just as a forest fire can burn to ashes a huge forest, even a single moment of anger or hatred directed toward a bodhisattva can wipe out a vast collection of merit. Hatred really is like fire, and a hate-filled action directed at such an exalted field as a bodhisattva has extraordinarily destructive power.

We have been looking at the factors that make karma heavy or light. It is important to understand these things because situations like the ones I've described arise all the time. If you know the faults of nonvirtuous actions you will be able to stand up and resist the constant impulses to engage in actions motivated by desire, attachment, anger, and ignorance. That is a truly great practice. If you do not know the faults, or if you do not care, then you will give yourself up to whatever arises. In that case your mind has fallen under the power of your own enemy.

It is so important to be able to discriminate between your enemy and your friend. The friend you should be seeking is not some external benefactor who can offer you temporary wealth and comfort. The true friend is inside; it is an inner attitude. It is your interest in helping others, loving others; it is the determination not to harm others. This kind of attitude operates against the selfish or egoistic impulse to abuse others in order to advance what you believe are your own interests. With the attitude that puts others before yourself, you will always be careful about how your actions affect those around you; you become even more careful of others then you are of yourself. This kind of attitude is the basis of noble action and it brings noble results. This is great practice. Someone who sits in meditation without moving for an hour, or for a day, but then gets up and immediately goes back to treating his or her companions badly, with a mind that is completely unchecked by any antidote—that is a person whose practice has nothing behind it, and it will amount to nothing.

The teachings on karma are based on the Buddha's explanations found in the sutras. You need to rely on the Buddha's knowledge because the relationships between cause and effect are beyond our present life's powers of perception. At the beginning, you have to place some trust in the teacher and in these teachings in order to establish a firm foundation of practice. As you progress—as you gradually remove the impurities and afflictions of the mind and your knowledge advances—your understanding deepens, realization dawns, and you will be able to see connections between cause and effect that you cannot see now. You will eventually be able to know directly what kind of cause produces what kind of results in life after life. But at present, in your ordinary condition, these things are difficult to perceive. You have to depend on trust and faith.

What you need to watch out for is the attitude that declares, "I don't see it, so it must not be true. Therefore I needn't bother about karma." That dangerous attitude can block all progress on the path. The cause and effect of karma falls into the category of *extremely hidden phenomena.* There are three types of objects of knowledge. First, there are phenomena we can know directly through our senses. Then there are things we cannot know directly, but can infer—based on sensory data—through the use of logic. There are certain things, however—like the relationship of karmic cause and effect—that are too subtle for ordinary humans to know directly by sense experience, or indirectly by means of inference. To know these extremely hidden phenomena we must put our trust in the word of the Buddha, at least until we obtain the realizations that enable us to know these things for ourselves.

Therefore, at the beginning you base your study of karma on the sutras, on the teachings of the Buddha. You need to trust in those teachings and act in accordance with them. That becomes the foundation of wholesome, virtuous practice. The small actions you take and the decisions you make throughout your daily life are important to a religious practitioner. What you do with your daily life will be determined by your understanding, by the entire frame of reference provided by your knowledge of karmic cause and effect. If you have in the back of your mind an understanding and trust in the cause and effect of karma, it will influence all your choices and lead you to focus your life on worthwhile goals. Once you are established on the path of the wise, skillful person, all heavy karma can be made light. You finally have control of your future. Like a huge chunk of metal that has been shaped into a fine ship, you can travel across the water without sinking.

(iii) A presentation of the results

Now we turn to the results of karma. There are three types of results: fruitional results, results corresponding to the cause, and environmental results.

(a') Fruitional results

Just as a sprout is the main effect of a rice seed, fruitional results are the main results of the ripening of karmic seeds. When you perform an action—that is, when you create karma—it remains as a seed, a potential, or a propensity until it ripens into its result. Then, when certain appropriate conditions are met, the karmic seed ripens into its main result. What it ripens into is the type of life into which you are born—this is the fruitional result of your action. In the Abhidharma it is sometimes called the "fruition of the type of life." The distinction that is being made here is between this fruitional result, which is the type of rebirth you take, and the variety of experiences you meet while you are within that form of life; those experiences are other types of results, which we shall discuss below.

Each of the ten nonvirtuous karmic paths has three different levels of fruitional results: small, medium, and great. The level of the result depends upon the degree of the affliction that motivated the original cause. As a result of the most powerful forms of nonvirtuous actions, you will experience the result with the greatest degree of suffering, which is birth as a denizen of the hell realms. The intermediate result is birth as a hungry ghost. The smallest result is to be born as an animal.

This is the order of small, medium, and great results according to Asaṅga's *Levels of Yogic Deeds*. The *Sutra on the Ten Levels* reverses the last two. It says that the intermediate level of nonvirtuous karma will result in rebirth as an animal, and the smallest level results in birth as a hungry ghost. There are different ways to think about this because some animals have lives that are much worse than some hungry ghosts. In general, the main result—the fruitional result of a nonvirtuous action—is rebirth in one of the three lower realms.

(b') Results corresponding to the cause

The second type of result is a result that is similar to the cause. This means that you experience a result that is similar to the past actions that brought about that result. For example, let's say that you kill someone. The fruitional result of that heavy karma is to be born into a hell realm. After the experience of that fruitional result has been exhausted, you are freed from that hell and you take rebirth elsewhere, let's say as a human. Although you have already experienced the main result—the fruitional result—of your action during your rebirth in hell, the force of that action still yields this other type of result in that subsequent rebirth as a human.

Each of the ten karmic paths has a result corresponding to the cause. The corresponding result of killing is to have a short life, because the main suffering you inflict when you kill someone is to shorten their life. The corresponding result of stealing is to live in poverty. The corresponding result of sexual misconduct is to live with a very troublesome spouse. Since the main violation involved in sexual misconduct is to take for your own pleasure someone who belongs to another, the corresponding result is to have your own partner be unfaithful, loyal to someone else, or very difficult to get along with in some other way.

The corresponding result of lying is to be subject to slander. You will be defamed and have blame heaped upon you. The corresponding result of slander, or divisive speech, is to be divided from dear friends. The corresponding result of harsh speech is to hear unpleasant words spoken by others. The corresponding result of senseless speech is that other people do not listen to anything you say.

The corresponding result of the three mental karmas—covetousness, malice, and wrong view—is to have attachment, hatred, and ignorance, respectively, as your predominant emotions. For example, some people seem to be naturally angry—they are impatient with others, and if one little thing goes wrong they immediately lose their temper. This type of personality is the corresponding result of previous hatred and anger. Similarly, stupidity—an inability to understand the way things are—is a corresponding result of wrong view.

The *Chapter of the Truth Speaker (Satyaka-parivarta)* and the *Sutra on the Ten Levels* both state that each of the ten nonvirtues has two results that correspond to the cause. They say that even if you are born as a human, you will have a short life and suffer from many sicknesses as a result of killing. You can see how these results are similar to the cause. In killing someone you first injure them physically, and then you cut off their life. The corresponding results are, therefore, to have many physical ailments and to have your life shortened.

The corresponding results of stealing are to be poor, and whatever property you have must be shared with others—nothing is completely your own. The corresponding results of sexual misconduct are that your servants, the people you live with, or those who surround you, have bad character, are crude and untrustworthy. The second result is that your wife, husband, or partner will become a competitor or rival, so you will not have a compatible relationship.

These are the kinds of experiences that result from the three nonvirtues of the body. If you learn and remember what the results of these nonvirtues are, and you trust that this process of cause and effect does take place, you will gain two beneficial effects. The first benefit is that when you find yourself experiencing these negative results, you will not blame them on others. When you meet difficult circumstances you will accept them as a result of your own previous actions, and you will not generate more negative karma by getting angry at others for causing your own problems. In fact, such negative circumstances can actually make you happy, because you know that those karmic causes have yielded their results and are now finished. The second benefit is that you will not repeat the same negative actions in the future. Recognizing that your problems were caused by the actions you performed in the past, you will make a serious effort from now on you to avoid repeating those actions so you will never have to experience these forms of suffering again.

The first corresponding result of lying is that other people denigrate and blame you. Secondly, you will always be deceived by others. The first corresponding result of slander is that those who surround you are not harmonious, but are constantly locked in disagreement. For example, the followers of a political leader, the disciples of a teacher, the employees of a businessperson, your own family and friends, might be argumentative and disruptive. The second result is that the people around you are unreliable, dishonest, or evil. Slander is causing division and animosity between people. The natural, corresponding result of this kind of speech is to have the people around you be hostile and contentious with one another.

The corresponding results of harsh speech are that you constantly hear unpleasant words from others, and what you say is naturally contentious and hurtful. People who are experiencing this karmic result are always being attacked and criticized. And even when they tries to speak nicely to others, their words sound argumentative and unpleasant, so no one wants to listen to them.

The first corresponding result of senseless speech is that your own words are not considered trustworthy. Even when you speak the truth, you are not considered reliable or worthy of respect. Secondly, you lack self-confidence and you are uncertain in your thoughts and deeds.

The corresponding results of covetousness are that you are naturally possessed by strong attachment, and you never feel satisfied. Your greed and desire are so strong that no matter how much wealth you accumulate you never feel that you have enough.

The first corresponding result of malice is that you seek out what is not beneficial, and you do not seek out what it is beneficial. This is the behavior of the kind of person who places great value on silly or senseless concerns, and the things such a person desires and seeks are useless or even harmful. The second result is that you habitually harm others, or others are always doing harm to you.

The corresponding results of wrong view are that you naturally adhere to an incorrect view, and you are constantly deceitful to others.

This is the explanation we find in these two sutras. Tsongkhapa says that previous masters analyzed these corresponding results into two types. The first type consists of the *results corresponding to the behavior.* This means that in subsequent lives you continue to behave in the way you were accustomed to behave in past lives. For example, as a result of killing in the past you will continue to be violent and kill in subsequent lives. Another example would be someone who has plenty of food to eat, a nice house, and fine clothes to wear, but still likes to steal other people's property. In both cases these people behave the way they do as a result of actions they habitually performed in a previous lifetime.

The second type of corresponding results consists of the *results corresponding to the experience.* This means that you undergo an experience that corresponds to the experience you caused by your previous action. Most of the examples given above fall into this category, such as experiencing a shortened life as a result of having killed someone.

We begin to see how every action can have many different kinds of effects. Just as one small seed can produce a huge tree with a trunk, leaves, flowers, and fruit, so one powerful action, such as killing, will produce many types of results. First there will be the fruitional result: rebirth in a suffering realm. After that, even if you are born as a human, you will meet the results that correspond to the cause: a short lifespan filled with all kinds of illness and pain.

(c') Environmental results

The first two types of results we have discussed took the form of individual, personal, inner experiences. Now we turn to results that manifest as your external, surrounding environment, your possessions, and the like.

The environmental result of killing is that the food, drink, and medicine that should ordinarily sustain and prolong life prove weak and ineffective. Medicine has no power to cure and food is not nourishing, or it is difficult to digest. Instead of producing happiness and supporting life, such food makes you sick and shortens your life. Most beings who live in such an environment die before their projected lifespan is exhausted.

When you take rebirth in a new life, your karma projects a certain longevity or life span, and death comes when that karma is exhausted. But you can also die from the exhaustion of the merits that are the karmic causes of the material necessities supporting life. When the merits that are the causes for finding food, shelter, and medicine are exhausted, you will die from hunger, cold, or disease. You die from a lack of material supports, even though your projected lifespan is not yet exhausted. The point here is that one environmental result of killing is that you are born in circumstances where most of the beings die this kind of premature death.

The environmental result of stealing is that your fruit and crops are meager. We can actually see examples of this when two farmers who live near each other and grow the same type of crops experience very different yields: one has abundance while the other does very poorly. As a result of stealing, not only will the yield be small, but the fruit will be blemished, it will rot quickly, and the meat of the fruit will be missing. The area in which you live will be plagued by drought, or by excessive rain. Because of these harsh conditions, the fruit will dry out before it can be harvested, or the plants will produce no fruit at all.

The environmental effects of sexual misconduct are to be born in an unclean place. This is described as a place that is full of excrement and urine, that is littered with filth, mud, and slime, and stinks like a sewer. It would, of course, be very unpleasant to live in such a place, but impure sexual activity causes you to be born into just such an environment.

The environmental result of lying is that things do not turn out well for you, no matter what kind of work you do. You can think of lying as a form of cheating others, and as a result of your own previous cheating, you encounter repeated failure in your efforts to make a livelihood. As an example we can imagine a person who buys a farm that was very productive for the previous owner. The new farmer takes over the land and manages it in the same way, but everything seems to go wrong, the crops fail, and the farmer becomes poor and hungry. People usually attribute that failure to the farmer's lack of intelligence or skill, or to poor management, but sometimes these factors don't actually account for what happens. Tsongkhapa specifically mentions farm work, or working on a boat, because these are mentioned in the sutras, but we can apply this kind of environmental result to any type of work. The point is that whatever effort you undertake, it turns out badly. You will also meet disharmony with the people around you and the people you work with. People will cheat and deceive you, and you will often find yourself in dangerous and frightening situations.

The environmental result of slander is to be born in a place that is unpleasant and difficult to move around in. It is described as a place where the ground is bumpy or uneven, so that if you want to walk on it, or plant a field, it is uncomfortable or even painful. The land is difficult to cross because it is broken up into small sections by rivers, roads, and cliffs, and there are extremes of altitude so that you constantly need to ascend or descend steep slopes. The land contains many dangers and reasons to be fearful. Because slander is the sowing of disharmony among people, the environmental result is to be born into this kind of disagreeable environment.

The environmental result of harsh speech is to be born in a place full of splintered logs, piercing thorns, sharp stones and gravel, and splinters of shattered clay pots and bricks. The description here is like that of a garbage dump, where everything is broken, useless, and thrown away. The place is without streams, waterfalls, lakes, or ponds. The land is very salty and barren. It is dry, rough, drab, and dusty, without the verdant colors of healthy vegetation. In short, it is a horrible place, full of dangerous creatures and many causes to be afraid. We say that harsh speech is almost like a sharp weapon that stabs its victim. Therefore, the environmental result is to be born in this kind of harsh, rough environment, where you suffer many similar discomforts.

Senseless speech is fruitless talk. Its environmental result is of a similar nature: fruit trees do not bear any fruit, or they bear fruit at the wrong time. Sometimes the unripe fruit appears to be ripe, the roots are not sturdy, and the trees do not last very long. Also, the place lacks any beautiful features such as parks, temple gardens, groves, woodlands, lakes, or ponds. In fact it is quite the opposite: unpleasant, impure, barren, and full of many causes of fear.

Now we turn to the mental negative actions. Covetousness is wanting what you do not have, always craving more, always wanting better, and never being satisfied. The environmental result of this kind of greediness is to be born into the opposite of what you wanted. All excellent and desirable things will degenerate or decrease each year, each season, every month, every day, and they will never increase or improve.

Since the action of malice is to harm others, the environmental result will be similar. You will be born in a place that suffers from epidemics and infectious diseases, where there are many people and animals who might harm you, and where there is social strife and war. There will be dangerous animals such as lions, tigers, poisonous snakes, scorpions, and poisonous spiders. You may also be threatened by *yakṣas,* thieves, and other evil beings.

These environmental results can be very specific to one individual's circumstances. For example, we may think of our own situation—living in this comfortable place and time—as being very fortunate. But within that generally favorable environment there are individuals who find themselves in miserable conditions. You may be living in a heavenly city, but somewhere in one corner of that thriving metropolis there may be someone whose living conditions are impoverished, repulsive, and dangerous, just as they are described above. Such are the individual, personal environmental results of negative actions.

Finally, we look at the environmental results of wrong view. Here, wrong view refers to the particular nihilistic view that does not believe in karma and its results, that holds that virtuous and nonvirtuous actions do not ripen into happy and suffering effects, that denies the existence of previous and subsequent lives, and claims there are no such things as buddhas, emancipation, and a path leading to emancipation. Wrong view denies all of these with a firm confidence based on reasoning—reasoning that is flawed, as it turns out.

The environmental result of such wrong views is that in the external world—the world outside of your own mind-body continuum—the sources of all precious and essential resources will deteriorate and disappear. For example, if you had a gold mine that was once productive, it would cease yielding valuable ore and would eventually fail. Impure things will appear to be pure, and things that have a suffering nature will appear to be pleasant. In such a depleted environment you will not be able to find any safe haven. There will be no protection from falling into the misery of lower rebirths, no refuge, no guide to lead you to freedom from ignorance and the other afflictions, the root of all the sufferings of cyclic existence.

Of course, wrong view is the view that holds on to the opposite of what is true, denying the possibility of spiritual emancipation. As a result of holding the view that all these elements of liberation do not exist, in the future they will be lacking in your environment. There will not be any teachings; you will not meet any qualified teachers; and there will be no path that can lead you toward freedom and away from lower rebirths.

These are the environmental results of the ten nonvirtuous karmic paths. When you study and try to gain an understanding of karma, the important thing is to maintain an open mind. If you adhere to an absolutely materialistic attitude—if your mind is tightly closed to the spiritual possibilities mentioned here—then there is no chance to benefit from these teachings. If you are more open and willing to study the teachings of the Buddha, to expose yourself to the various explanations and reasons, then your understanding of this most profound area will deepen, and gradually the doubt and darkness in your mind will change into the light of understanding. If you approach the teachings on karma with an open mind and work with them as if you fully believed them, you will begin to experience the benefit of acting in accord with the Buddha's teachings; then your experience and deepening mental capacity will lead you in the right direction.

The basis of all progress on the path is first to listen and study and understand. Although you may not understand all the details immediately, and not everything the Buddha taught will make sense to you right away, you can build a strong foundation based on a general understanding, and gradually the depth of your insight and confidence will grow.

(b) Virtuous karma and its results

We have completed our consideration of negative karma, and now we turn to an examination of wholesome karma and its results. In general, we can take what we have learned about nonvirtuous karma and reverse it, and that will give us a basic understanding of the ten virtuous karmic paths. This discussion has two parts: first, the ten virtuous karmas; then, a consideration of their results.

(i) Virtuous karma

The three virtuous actions of the body are the reverse of the nonvirtuous actions of killing, stealing, and sexual misconduct. However, merely not doing those things is not virtue. A piece of stone does not kill anyone, or steal, or lie, but it has no virtue. Merely not doing an unwholesome action may be neutral karma, but virtuous action requires something more. First, you must see the faults of the negative action and you must believe it is wrong, and that it will bring unpleasant results. Then, with a virtuous mind—a mind that intentionally wants to avoid that harmful action—you make an affirmative effort to avoid doing it. You complete the virtuous action by actually refraining from doing the nonvirtue, thereby shutting the door to the unwholesome karma.

The virtuous actions of speech and the three mental actions work in the same way. First, you must understand the faults of the particular nonvirtuous action; then, with a virtuous mind, you make an effort to refrain from the action; finally, you do refrain from the action. This presentation, which comes from Asaṅga's *Levels of Yogic Deeds,* is a brief summary of the principles involved in creating virtuous karma.

For a more detailed understanding we can apply the four elements that constitute a complete karma: the basis, the thought, the actual action, and the culmination of the action. We can take as our example the action of avoiding killing. The basis is other sentient beings, just as it is for the negative action of killing. The thought or motivation is wanting to avoid that action because you recognize its faults. The actual action, based on that motivation, is to restrain yourself from performing the action of killing. The culmination of the action is the bodily act of completely accomplishing the restraint of that action. For example, if you are in a situation with the possibility of killing another creature, but you clearly see the faults of that act, and with that motivation you concentrate on controlling your physical actions so that you avoid killing or harming that creature until that restraining action is complete—that constitutes a complete karma of avoiding killing. In the case of killing, the culmination of the action is when the victim finally dies, but here it is your own body that completes the action by refraining from killing.

That is the example of killing. Since we have already analyzed the ten nonvirtuous karmic paths in terms of the above four elements, rather than repeating that analysis for the virtuous actions, Tsongkhapa says that you can simply apply the example of killing to the other virtuous actions.

(ii) The results of virtuous karma

As with nonvirtuous actions, there are three types of results of virtuous actions: the fruitional result, the result corresponding to the cause, and the environmental result. Once again, the virtuous results are essentially the reverse of the nonvirtuous results.

The fruitional result is the main result of an action; it is the type of life into which you are born. There are three levels of fruitional results for each of the ten virtuous actions, depending on whether it was a great, medium, or small virtuous action. The result of a great virtuous action is to be born as a deva in one of the two upper realms of existence: the form or formless realm. As a result of intermediate virtuous karma you will be born as a desire realm deva. The fruitional result of small virtuous karma is to be born in a human life.

The beings of the form and formless realm experience no physical or mental pain or suffering. Because their afflictions are much more subtle than those of the desire realm, their mental life is much more peaceful. Compared to the experience of a desire realm being, life in the form and formless realms is a pure, blissful existence—it is almost like emancipation. In fact, however, it is only a temporary state of peace, because beings born into these realms are still subject to death, and eventually they will fall again into miserable lives.

In the desire realm there are six different levels of devas. These devas have a superior existence to humans: their life is more peaceful and much longer than humans; their environment is more pleasurable; and their bodies are more subtle. Still, they are of the desire realm, which means they are still subject to desire, especially sexual desire, and they engage in sexual activity. However, because they have subtle bodies that are not made of gross flesh and bone, their sexual activity is of a much more subtle nature than that of humans.

Why do we say that the human birth is the lowest of the three types of fruitional results? Of course, in one way human life is a high rebirth, much better than birth in one of the three suffering realms. Humans have relatively powerful intelligence and a capacity to achieve the highest possible spiritual goals. They have the ability to see cause and effect and to understand, through their own experience, the truth of suffering. But the human body is delicate and subject to so many kinds of pain and discomfort. It is an earthly, rough kind of body, full of impurities, with a short life span. It requires a great deal of attention to take care of the human body, and such concerns disturb one's peace of mind. It is in this sense that the human rebirth is inferior to the more subtle and more peaceful lives of the devas.

Tsongkhapa does not give a detailed explanation of the result corresponding to the cause or the environmental result of virtuous karma. He says that these are simply the opposite of the results of nonvirtuous actions. We can take the corresponding results of killing as an example: it is to have a short life and to be killed yourself. For the virtuous karma of avoiding killing, the corresponding result is to have a long life, or to have your life protected by others. An example of this would be someone who found himself in deadly circumstances—such as a famine, an epidemic, or some other kind of disaster where people all around were dying—yet somehow managed to survive. His survival could be the corresponding result of the previous virtuous actions of avoiding killing or saving the lives of others.

Similarly, the corresponding result of stealing is to be destitute and always have difficulty acquiring necessary resources. For the virtuous action of avoiding stealing other's property, the corresponding result will be to naturally have wealth and material comfort, and to always find the necessities of life without difficulty.

As for environmental results, these too are the opposite of the results of nonvirtuous actions. As an example of the environmental result of nonvirtuous action we mentioned the farmer whose fields yielded poor crops compared to those of his neighbors. Here, as a result of virtuous actions, that farmer's fields will yield unusually bountiful crops. In general, the environmental results of virtuous actions are that you will become wealthier and healthier, and all your material endeavors will produce excellent results.

The *Sutra on the Ten Levels* explains that practicing these ten virtuous actions can lead to even higher results, right up to complete buddhahood. It says that if you practice the ten virtues out of fear of taking another samsaric rebirth, but you are not motivated by great compassion for other beings, and you rely on the teachings of others, then you will achieve the fruit of a śrāvaka. Those who practice for the sake of their own emancipation, who are not motivated by great compassion for others, and who meditate alone on the twelve links of dependent origination, on the cause and effect of karma, and on the four noble truths, will finally attain their own emancipation and victory over samsaric suffering in the fruit of a pratyekabuddha.

What is the difference between the śrāvaka and the pratyekabuddha? The core of their practice is the same, but śrāvakas base their practice on listening to the teachings of others. Even in their last worldly life, during which they attain arhatship, or nirvana, they depend on special instructions from other teachers to complete their practice. The nature of pratyekabuddhas is that they like to be alone and they do not rely on outside teachers. In their last life, especially, they stay alone. Even if a buddha appears in the world, they will not leave their solitude to go listen to teachings. They remain in a solitary place, on their own, and through their own meditative effort they obtain emancipation.

Finally, there is the practitioner who has the Mahayana, or bodhisattva, motivation. This is the person who has a broad mental scope, who sees beyond his or her own personal emancipation. Such a person recognizes the misery of all sentient beings and sees that they are all equally in need of relief from suffering. These bodhisattvas feel the same fear for the future suffering of others that they feel for themselves. Based on this broad vision, they seek the emancipation of all beings and practice with the intention of placing all beings in the highest bliss of buddhahood. These are spiritual practitioners of great scope, motivated by great compassion, who practice with skillful means and put their compassion into action through all three doors of body, speech, and mind. Because of their special motivation, all their efforts become truly great practice.

The difference between this Mahayana practice of the bodhisattva and the Hīnayana practice of the śrāvaka and the pratyekabuddha is the motivation. Bodhisattvas are motivated by the great wish to obtain the highest enlightenment for the benefit of all other living beings. Everything they do is dedicated to benefit others, not merely themselves. They practice with skillful methods and vow that they will never abandon even one being in cyclic existence. "Abandoning sentient beings" means giving up the effort to lead them to enlightenment; it is deciding that the job is too difficult and therefore thinking, "I will just obtain liberation from my own sake."

True bodhisattvas see that in order to be of maximum benefit to others, they must first attain their own buddhahood. Buddhahood is omniscience; it is wisdom that is perfect; it means understanding all cause and effect, knowing directly the exact needs and capabilities of every being. It means knowing precisely how best to lead others out of suffering to perfect peace. The Buddha knows exactly what will be most beneficial in every circumstance, and bodhisattvas strive diligently to attain that state so that they too can become the most effective helper possible. With this compassionate motivation, Mahayana practitioners focus on attaining the wisdom of buddhahood. It is for that purpose that they put into practice these ten virtues of body, speech, and mind. By training in the ten perfections they complete the ten levels of the bodhisattva and fully accomplish all the qualities of buddhahood.[14]

Therefore, when we speak of the results of virtuous and nonvirtuous karma, we need to remember that there are two different types of results and they exist on two different levels. There are those temporary results that manifest in happiness or suffering on the ordinary, samsaric level. Then there are the everlasting, highest results of attaining liberation and enlightenment. In every case it is the mind, the attitude, the motivation, that determines which goal will be achieved. It may be the goal of a śrāvaka, of a pratyekabuddha, or the ultimate goal of a bodhisattva; it all depends on the motivation.

If all your actions are governed by the Mahayana motivation, then even the practice of these ten virtuous actions becomes the practice of accomplishing the ten perfections and achieving the ten stages of the bodhisattva path. When these are perfected you have reached the highest goal, buddhahood. So there is nothing that is not included in this practice. The buddhas are so kind and so skillful in the way they teach and lead us to freedom. In the beginning we do not need many different, complicated practices. We just need to recognize and understand the activity of the three doors of body, speech, and mind. Then, simply by maintaining all of our actions on the virtuous side, ultimately we will reach the highest goal.

Sometimes people think, "Observance of karma is just a small, unimportant practice. I want to do high practices." This way of thinking is wrong. This practice is the perfect foundation, and it leads to all beneficial results. It is based on these ten virtues that the fruit of buddhahood develops. This is the real, perfect teaching and the pure practice: to cultivate the correct motivation and to engage in virtuous actions. These teachings show clearly the unlimited results that can be achieved if you train your mind in the proper way.

Tsongkhapa says, "Having thoroughly understood the cause and effect of positive and negative karma, I will rely on properly practicing what is to be engaged in and what should be avoided." Achieving any goal on the path depends on properly taking up those actions that should be engaged in, and avoiding those that are harmful. The goal is to eliminate, as best you can, all nonvirtuous karma, and to accumulate as much positive virtue as you can. This is done by right study, by concentrating on the relationships of karma and its results until you develop a firm understanding, and then cultivating that understanding until you reach a certainty that this is indeed the true path to happiness. Once you have stabilized your confidence in the action of karma, you will be able to practice virtue without hesitating. That is why contemplating karma and its results is most important.

Tsongkhapa concludes by saying that in this section he has explained the ten nonvirtuous and virtuous karmic paths along with their results. This material had been explained in other sources but certain points remained unclear. Here in the *Lamrim Chenmo,* Tsongkhapa has made an effort in particular to clarify these difficult points. He says that his explanation has been based on Asaṅga's *Levels of Yogic Deeds* and *Compendium of Determinations.*

(c) A presentation of other classifications of karma

Now Tsongkhapa examines two other ways of categorizing karma. First we examine the difference between projecting and completing karma. Then we discuss the difference between karma that will definitely be experienced and that which will not necessarily be experienced.

(i) The distinction between projecting and completing karma

There are two types of karma. One is called *projecting,* or *throwing karma,* and the other is called *completing karma.* The Tibetan term used for projecting karma brings to mind the action of planting seeds in the spring, when you throw your seeds onto the ground. This type of action throws, or casts, or projects the main seed that will eventually yield fruit as a particular type of rebirth in the future. It is the main, or material, cause of a particular rebirth.

Projecting karma is distinguished from completing karma. Although you throw seeds on the ground in the spring, that by itself is not enough to bring about the growth of abundant crops. For the final fruit to be produced, other supporting causes and conditions are necessary, such as moisture, warmth, and fertilizer. Those other conditions are analogous to what is known as completing karma or, in some sources, as actualizing karma.

You can think of this entire process as similar to making a painting. First you draw the outline of the image with charcoal, sketching in the size and shape of the body and the basic features of the face; this is analogous to projecting karma. Then you fill in the outline with all the details of color and highlight: this is analogous to completing karma. Projecting karma determines the main result: whether you take birth as a human, an animal, a deva, and so forth. Then the completing karma fills in what kind of situations you will experience during that rebirth: whether your life will be pleasant or unpleasant, beautiful or ugly, long or short, and so forth. The projecting karma is the main cause that brings, for example, a human life, but the qualities of that human life will be determined by completing karma, and each of those qualities has its own individual karmic cause.

Asaṅga's *Compendium of Knowledge* says:

> Understand that virtuous and nonvirtuous karma project and bring to completion birth in the happy and suffering rebirths. Projecting karma is what projects the fruition. Completing karma is what determines the desirable or undesirable nature of experience once one is born.

For projecting karma, virtuous action will always bring rebirth in a higher realm and nonvirtue will always bring rebirth in a lower realm. But for completing karma there is not such a clear correspondence. Positive completing karma does not necessarily ripen in a higher rebirth and negative completing karma does not necessarily ripen in a lower rebirth. Negative completing karma can bring its unpleasant results in a higher rebirth, such as a human life. The nature of that birth as a human was determined by virtuous projecting karma, but the details that determine whether it will be a pleasant or unpleasant human existence are produced by many different completing karmas. For example, you may obtain a human rebirth but have a short life, or your life may be filled with miserable conditions, or you may meet numerous disasters.

Similarly, rebirth as an animal is considered a suffering rebirth and is the result of nonvirtuous projecting karma. But some animals end up with conditions that make their life quite happy and peaceful. A common example is our own pets. The karma that brought them to an animal rebirth was negative projecting karma. But during that life they are well fed and well looked after; they have a cozy place to sleep, the best food is delivered to them without any effort, and even when they get sick their owner spends a lot of money to take them to a highly trained doctor. In fact, some pets are treated better than many humans. Their bad rebirth is the result of nonvirtuous projecting karma, but the fortunate circumstances in that life are due to virtuous completing karma.

This is what it means when we say that there is no certainty regarding the results of completing karma. It does not mean that negative karma can produce good results. It means that negative completing karma can produce unhappy results in a good rebirth, and vice versa. Therefore, there are four possibilities to the interrelationship between these two types of karma: (1) both the projecting karma and the completing karma are nonvirtuous; (2) both the projecting karma and the completing karma are virtuous; (3) the projecting karma is virtuous, but the completing karma is nonvirtuous; and (4) the projecting karma is nonvirtuous, but the completing karma is virtuous.

Let us consider these possibilities one by one. When (1) both the projecting and completing karmas are negative, they produce the very worst kind of life in the hell realms. In that situation there is no experience that results from virtuous karma, no mixing of positive and negative results.

When (2) both the projecting and completing karmas are virtuous, the result is rebirth as a deva in the upper realms—not as a desire realm deva but as a deva of the form or formless realms. All experiences in that life are results of virtuous karma. Of course, those devas are still not free from cyclic existence; once they have used up all that positive karmic potential there is a strong possibility they will fall into a suffering rebirth in their next life. They still have negative karmic potentials accumulated in past lives, but in that particular lifetime their negative karma will not ripen, because that rebirth was projected and completed purely by virtuous karma. During that life, from birth until death, they will not experience any results of negative karma.

The other two possibilities of mixed karma are causes to be reborn in the desire realm. And so (3) virtuous projecting karma brings birth as a human or a deva in the desire realm, but some amount of negative completing karma brings various forms of discomfort and unhappiness in that life. The amount of negative completing karma will determine the level of suffering experienced within that higher realm. Some humans seem to live extremely happy lives, never facing serious adversity, sickness, or pain, while others experience a human life that is a ceaseless ordeal of misery.

The same thing holds true for (4) the causes of a life in one of the lower realms. As we said, you can be born as an animal or a hungry ghost, but still live a relatively comfortable life. Even some beings in the hell realms experience mixed results, from time to time finding a little relief as a result of virtuous completing karma. There are many different degrees of these combinations.

This discussion causes certain questions to arise. Projecting karma is the main seed of a life, but does one karma bring about only one life, or can it bring about many lives? Or is it the case that many different karmas have to come together to bring about one life? There are different views on these questions. The understanding of the lower philosophical schools is expressed in Vasubandhu's *Treasury of Knowledge*, and the Mahayana system is stated by Asaṅga in his *Compendium of Knowledge*.

The *Treasury of Knowledge* says, "By one karma one birth is projected. The karmas that complete that existence are many." That means that one projecting karma will project only one life, but many completing karmas can produce the various conditions of that life. Also, according to that system, many karmas together cannot project one single life. Therefore, each individual action of negative karma such as killing will bring another life in the lower realms. Or, if a person repeats an action many times, one powerful instance of the action may become the projecting karma, and the rest of the actions may become the completing karma.

In contrast, the Mahayana system is expressed in the following quotation from the *Compendium of Knowledge:*

> There is karma in which one action projects one body. There is karma in which one action projects many bodies. There is karma in which many actions project one body. There is karma in which many actions project many bodies.

According to this system there are various possibilities. In some cases one karma projects only one life, while in other circumstances one powerful karma will project many lives. Sometimes many smaller karmas together bring one single life. And of course many karmas may project many lives. The commentary on this text explains this point by saying that "one instant" of an action can produce one or many future lives. This does not mean that each single moment of a longer action becomes a separate karma. One complete karma of killing begins from the initial preparation and continues to the final conclusion of the action, and this can stretch over a long time. The term that is used here—which literally means "one instant" or "one moment"—actually refers to one complete karma.

What the *Compendium of Knowledge* is saying here is that one large, powerful action can become the cause of a succession of many rebirths in the future. It is also possible for a collection of smaller karmas to become cumulative and, acting like one big karma, they can project one single rebirth. This might happen in the case of some habitual action that you performed regularly; although each action was not very powerful by itself, by repeating the action with the same motivation over and over again, the karmic potential accumulates and finally produces the same result as one big powerful karma. In that way many karmas together can result in one life. Of course, we always have to remember that the exact details of the evolution of karmic cause and effect are extremely subtle and difficult to comprehend. At this point in our spiritual development we cannot know in exact detail how karma works, but these teachings give us the general picture and the basis upon which we can build our understanding.

(ii) Karma whose result will definitely or not definitely be experienced

Another way of dividing karma is in terms of whether the action will definitely bring its maturation, or whether this is not definite. Concerning this the *Levels of Yogic Deeds* says:

> Karma whose result you definitely will experience is that which is done intentionally and accumulated. Karma whose result you will not definitely experience is that which is intentionally done but not accumulated.

This raises the question: "What is the difference between karma that is done and karma that is accumulated?" The *Levels of Yogic Deeds* goes on to say:

> What is karma that is done? It is that which you have given thought to or, after having considered, you actually carry out by body or speech.

First there is the thought; you start by thinking about doing an action. Take killing for example. First you think about killing a person and you concentrate your mind on that possibility. Then, after thinking about it, you actually carry out the action with your body. For physical or verbal karma, the action must be consciously performed by the body or speech to be *done.*

The *Levels of Yogic Deeds* explains accumulated karma as everything that is *not* included in the following list of ten types of actions:

> Accumulated karma is all actions with the exception of the following ten types: (1) what is done in a dream; (2) what is done unknowingly; (3) what is done unconsciously; (4) what is done neither with intensity nor continuously; (5) what is done erroneously; (6) what is done forgetfully; (7) what is done unwillingly; (8) actions which are by nature ethically neutral; (9) those that have been cleared away through regret; and (10) those that have been cleared away by means of an antidote. Any other karma—whatever is not included in these ten types—is accumulated karma. Karma that is not accumulated is just what has been presented here.

We can see that most of these ten actions that are not accumulated have in common a lack of intentionality. These are the actions you do without knowing that you are doing them. They include actions done without thinking, paying attention, or intending to do them, such as activities you do habitually without thinking about them. Other unaccumulated karma includes actions that are weak in terms of the motivation, or that are done so briefly that they have no real force. Then of course there are actions that you are forced or coerced to do. Furthermore, there are many activities that are naturally neutral, neither virtuous nor nonvirtuous; these include such things as the ordinary movements of the body, like walking, the production of sounds coming naturally from the mouth, and the simple act of breathing in and out. Other instances of unaccumulated karma include those nonvirtuous actions that have been purified by the countervailing power of regret, or cleared away by an antidote such as meditation or other purifying practices.

The *Compendium of Determinations* by Asaṅga points to the four possible combinations of karma done and karma accumulated. Once again we can taking killing as an example. Killing that is (1) done but not accumulated is killing done unwittingly, without knowing you are doing it. We can say that in this case you are ignorant of what you are doing, but the ignorance being spoken of here is not the same ignorance we are speaking about when discussing wrong view. The ignorance of wrong view is not merely a case of not knowing something, but of actually holding some contradictory, harmful view. In this present discussion of karma that is done but not accumulated, ignorance simply means doing something that you are unaware of or oblivious about.

Other types of killing that are done but not accumulated include: killing done in a dream; killing that is done unintentionally; killing that is done unwillingly because you are forced to do it by someone else; killing that is done only one time and after which you you feel great regret about; and killing whose karmic force has been weakened because you see the fault of the action and therefore vow, "I will never do that again." Karma is also not accumulated if, before it yields its result, you attain the state of freedom from attachment by means of the mundane path. This attainment, though it only temporarily suppresses and does not eliminate the afflictions from the root, weakens the karmic seed so that it does not bear fruit. Finally, there is no accumulation if, by means of the supermundane path, you attain the ārya level with its direct realization of the truth of emptiness. This realization completely destroys those karmic seeds from the root.

When karma is done but not accumulated it means that the karma will not be effective; the seed will not yield fruit because it is weakened or destroyed, and there will be no results or only very minor results. In general, karma that is accumulated is karma done with mental attention, with concentration, with strong motivation, or action done repeatedly. The actions listed here lack that level of attention; they are therefore a lighter form of karma and their results will be much lighter. That is the first of the four possible combinations: karma that is done but not accumulated.

Then there is (2) karma that is accumulated but not done. An example of this would if you contemplated killing someone for a long time, planning the best way to do it. You fulfill all the mental requirements of the act: you have a correct perception of whom you plan to kill, you have a definite intention to kill him, and you make a plan of how you will do it. However, in the end you do not kill that being. In that case, the karma is accumulated but the action is not done. The karmic consequences of this situation will be heavier than the previous case where the karma is done but not accumulated.

The next possibility is (3) the karma is both done and accumulated. This is any act of killing other than the previous two situations. This is the case in which you have the motivation to kill, you have the correct perception of whom you plan to kill, and finally, you go through with the action.

The last possible combination is when (4) the karma of killing is neither done nor accumulated. This is any act not included in the previous three possibilities [i.e., any act, whether virtuous or nonvirtuous, other than an act of killing].

We have used the example of killing to illustrate these four possible combinations, and you can apply this analysis of how karma is done and accumulated to the seven nonvirtuous actions from killing through to senseless speech. The second combination, karma that is accumulated but not done, does not apply to the three mental karmas of covetousness, malice, and wrong view. In the case of physical and verbal actions there is first a mental component and then a physical or verbal action; karma is *accumulated* by completing the mental component of intending, perceiving, and planning the action, and then the action is *done* by the body. But the last three are purely mental actions: they are done *at the same time* they are accumulated. The mental process that causes an action to be accumulated is the very doing of these mental actions.

It is also the case that for mental actions, in the category of karma that is done but not accumulated, there is no such thing as a mental action that is done unintentionally, or done unwillingly because you are forced to do it by someone else. In these respects the three mental karmas are different from the seven physical ones.

In terms of time, there are three divisions of karma whose result is certain to be experienced. First, there is *karma to be experienced in the current life;* in this case the karma is experienced in the same life as the one in which the karma was performed. Then there is *karma to be experienced after rebirth;* this karma will be experienced in the very next life. The third type is *karma to be experienced in subsequent existences;* this is referring to karma that will be experienced in some life subsequent to the next one.

The most powerful karma is karma to be experienced in the current life. But this raises a question: if the result of the most powerful karma—let's say killing your parents or an arhat—will be experienced in this very life, does that mean that in the future you will not fall into lower rebirths? No. The point is that this karma is so powerful that its results *start* in this very life. The main result will still be experienced in the future: being born in a lower rebirth and experiencing great misery. But for these most powerful actions the consequences start in the very life in which they are performed, in the form of various misfortunes, sickness, pain, and all kinds of difficulties.

Karma to be experienced in the next life is karma that is not as powerful, so its results do not start until you are reborn. The third type, karma to be experienced in subsequent existences, is weaker still. Its result will ripen further in the future, in the second rebirth after this one, or at any time in the far distant future, even many thousands of lives later. The point here is that for heavier actions the results will be experienced earlier. In this way stronger karma tends to push the weaker out to a later maturation.

Asaṅga, in the *Levels of Yogic Deeds,* specifies eight types of karma to be experienced in the current life:

1. The first type are actions that are done primarily out of attachment or concern for your own body, your material wealth, or for your own existence, for life itself. These are actions that are motivated by a strong attachment to this present existence, are focused on remaining in this life, and on making this life as comfortable as possible. The results of powerful nonvirtuous karma done with this motivation will be experienced in this life.

2. Virtuous actions or thoughts which are *not* focused on such worldly concerns as your own body, wealth, or preserving your own life, can also be experienced in this life. Of course, any such activity done for the benefit of others will be virtuous karma, and powerful virtuous karma will yield its results quickly.

3. In the same way, nonvirtues done with a strong attitude of malice toward other beings will begin to ripen in this life.

4. Virtuous actions done with your mind focused on compassion, or a strong wish to help other beings, will of course be great virtue, and when they are powerful they will yield their fruition in this life.

5. When the object of an attitude of strong ill will is the Three Jewels, your own spiritual teacher, or some other holy being, such strong negative karma will yield its results in this life.

6. Similarly, powerful actions performed with an attitude of deep faith, admiration, or devotion toward these holy objects will also yield results in this life.

7. When the object is one's own parents, or spiritual teacher, or some other source of benefit to you, and you perform a powerful action out of malice, or with no thought of repaying their kindness, such strong negative karma will ripen in this life.

8. When you act toward these sources of benefit with an attitude that remembers their kindness and seeks to repay them for the benefit they have given you, and when this virtuous karma is done with a powerful thought, that too will ripen in this life.

These are a few examples of actions which are so powerful that their results will start in this very life. We can see from this list that one of the most important factors that determines the strength of an action is the object or field of the action. The *Treasury of Knowledge* says:

> The results of beneficial or harmful actions done to any of these will be experienced immediately: those who have just arisen from the "absorption of cessation," or from the meditative states called Measureless Love or Free of Afflictions, or from the path of seeing, or from the fruit of arhatship.[15]

This is a list of high meditative states, and when you do benefit or harm to a meditator who has just arisen from one of these states the action becomes very powerful and the results ripen in that very life. From the perspective of negative karma, these are dangerous areas. But if you want to create great merits, these are among the most powerful fields of virtuous actions.

Later the *Treasury of Knowledge* describes the fields that are most powerful for making offerings:

> The field is particularly superior due to their realm of rebirth, their level of suffering, due to being a benefactor, or due to excellent qualities. The supreme gift is from one who is liberated to one who is liberated; or a gift from a bodhisattva; or the eighth.

> Even though they are not āryas, offerings made to one's father and mother, to a sick person, to a Dharma teacher, to a bodhisattva in his last life, are without measure.

Although they are not āryans, offerings made to your own father and mother are extremely powerful because in your worldly life they have been the most beneficial; they produced you, they nourished you, and they worked to provide you with every benefit they could. This is the nature of parenthood, and this applies not only to humans; even animals have this way of taking care of their offspring. Therefore, on the mundane level, your parents are the highest field of benefit, and you should always honor them, show them respect, and do beneficial things for them. This will create great merit. If you harm them, of course, it produces powerful negative karma.

Also in this list are people who are sick. Those who are suffering from any painful condition—whether it is sickness, hunger, or severe cold—are powerful fields for performing virtuous actions such as giving charity. And those who teach the Dharma, especially your own spiritual teacher, are always a powerful field for either positive or negative karma.

Last on this list is the bodhisattva, especially the bodhisattva who is in his or her last life before obtaining buddhahood. The merits of doing benefit—or the negative consequences of doing harm—to such a being are beyond measure.

These verses give us an idea of which types of objects produce the most powerful karma, and those most powerful karmic seeds will begin to yield their results in the very life in which the action was performed.

Karma to be experienced in the next life refers to actions that are not as powerful as the ones we have just discussed. And karma to be experienced in subsequent existences refers to actions that are weaker still. These three categories of karma give us a sense of the certainty or uncertainty of experiencing the result of a particular action in terms of the time-frame in which it will yield its results.

Now we look at the order of ripening of the many different karmic seeds that reside in an individual's mental continuum. During one lifetime a person creates so many different karmas. How can one experience all those results, and which ones will ripen first and which ones later?

The karma that is the heaviest will ripen first. If two karmas are of equal weight, whichever karma was created nearest to the time of death will be the first to ripen. If that is also the same, whichever karma is more habitual will ripen first. If that is also the same, whichever karma was created first will ripen first.

To illustrate how the priority of karma is determined, Kadampa Geshe Potowa gave the example of a group of people waiting for a small ferryboat to cross a river near Lhasa. Who will go first? If there is powerful government official in the crowd, he will go first. If they are all equal in status, the person with whom the boatman has the most familiarity will go first. If the customers are all equally familiar to him, then the one who arrived first will go first. The *Treasury of Knowledge Auto-commentary* describes the same order:

> Of the karmas that produce cyclic existence,
> Among those that are heavy, those that are near,
> Those that are habitual, and those that were done first,
> The former will ripen before the latter.[16]

2' Contemplating karma and its results in detail

So far, we have been studying the way to contemplate karma and its results in general, getting the big picture of how karma works. Now we begin to focus on particular points in detail, and on ways in which we can make our practice more effective.

By practicing the ten virtuous actions and avoiding the ten nonvirtues you can certainly attain a happy rebirth in your next lifetime. However, our goal is to obtain the perfect realization of buddhahood, and to accomplish this it is not enough merely being born in a comfortable rebirth. You need a special kind of life that gathers together all the conditions and qualities that are required to accomplish that goal. When you possess that special type of life, you are able to make progress on the path to buddhahood in a more skillful and more powerful way; you are able to cover the ground more quickly. Therefore, you should strive to achieve the special qualities of this kind of life.

Actually, when you look at the life that we have right now, we already possess most of the attributes of a "fully qualified" body and mind, which means we have all we need to attain enlightenment. But even if you cannot achieve perfect enlightenment in this life, at least you can create the causes to be born with all the conditions that will enable you to quickly achieve that ultimate goal in the future. If you don't accomplish at least this much during your current life, all the effort and merits you have accumulated may be wasted, and it may be a very long time before you are able to continue on the path.

The truth is, even if you abandoned all samsaric pleasure and spent this whole life working single-mindedly toward buddhahood, it would still be very difficult to attain enlightenment in this very life. Some can do it, but it is difficult because there are so many obstacles. Even for practitioners who spend ninety-nine percent of their time focused on that goal, it is still very difficult. And here you are, spending perhaps one percent of your time on your practice. This excellent human life has such great power, but if you do not use it properly you will not reach your ultimate goal in this lifetime. But what you certainly *can* achieve in this lifetime is to assemble the very best possible conditions for practice in your next rebirth. That is a situation where, from the earliest age, you will have authentic spiritual teachings, deep faith, and all the necessary outer and inner conditions to pursue the path to its highest end.

Some say, "It is selfish to practice Dharma just to attain a high samsaric life in the future." But it is not selfish to practice virtue in order to attain a good rebirth if your final goal is enlightenment for the benefit all sentient beings. To achieve that final purpose there are many steps along the way. In fact, one of the most beneficial things you can do with this current life is to secure a still better situation for practice in your next rebirth. You can do this by creating the causes to be born with those conditions that are most conducive to completing the path quickly. Any kind of virtuous practice with that motivation is pure Dharma practice, pure Mahayana practice. That is why Tsongkhapa advises us here to strive to achieve the most highly qualified human life—because it will give us the capacity to attain perfect enlightenment quickly and efficiently.

a" The qualities of the eight fruitions

Such an excellent human life is characterized by eight "special qualities of fruition." In the following section we discuss the nature of these special qualities and how they function to benefit our practice. Then we consider the beneficial effects of having each of these qualities. Finally, we look at the causes that will enable us to obtain them.

1. *An excellent lifespan.* Possessing an excellent lifespan means being able to remain in this perfect human rebirth for a long and healthy life. You obtain a long life because of your previous virtuous karma, such as protecting the lives of others and not killing other beings.

2. *An excellent physical appearance.* This means having an appealing physical form: an attractive complexion, shape, and general physical nature. Your organs and limbs are complete, well-formed, and the parts of your body are well-proportioned. These are the qualities which we call "beautiful" or "attractive." When you have a pleasant physical appearance people tend to like you, and this makes it easier to accomplish any goal, including making

friends, finding a proper teacher, and securing a good environment in which to practice.

If you are a teacher, your physical appearance can be even more important, because it helps you to attract students. If you are disfigured or very unpleasant to look at, nobody will want to listen to your teachings. When you have an attractive appearance, people just naturally want to meet you and talk to you. We all know people who make you feel happy as soon as you meet them; you immediately like them and you want to have more contact with them. This attractive quality can be quite an asset when you are working to benefit others.

3. *An excellent lineage.* An excellent lineage or caste originally referred to birth among the higher castes in India. Birth in a low caste was a great obstacle to having any opportunity to pursue a spiritual practice. It may not be so important in our time and place, but throughout history, in most of the world, noble birth has been a great advantage in any endeavor. Today, in this country, everyone may have a chance to overcome the obstacles of their birth, but there are still some benefits to being born into a family with a good reputation and high status.

4. *Excellent power.* Having excellent power means having sufficient wealth so that you do not need to worry about your livelihood. Some people are born with wealth, while others spend their whole life constantly struggling just for food and clothing. Along with having an abundance of resources, excellent power includes being surrounded by many helpers, such as family, friends, followers, and supporters.

5. *Trustworthy words.* This means being a person whose word is trusted, who is honored and respected in all situations. When your words are considered trustworthy, people listen to you, follow you, and are willing to rely on what you say. You become a source of reliable information, and when questions are raised others point to you and say, "Because he said so." You become suitable to act as a witness in judicial proceedings and are sought after as an arbiter of disputes because both sides trust you.

There are also people who have the opposite quality. They say whatever is convenient or self-serving, so that after a while nobody believes anything they say. But when your words are reliable, people naturally want to hear what you have to say, and they feel they can depend on it.

6. *Renowned as being powerful.* This is the quality of being famous for displaying outstanding qualities, such as being indefatigable in practicing generosity.

People with this quality are not *seeking* fame, but are motivated by a fearless determination to benefit others. Their virtuous attributes just naturally become the object of respect, honor, and renown among other people.

7. *Being a male.* This is one you will not like. This is the quality of being born as a man. Maybe we should skip this one! Whether or not this is a special asset really depends on the time, place, and situation. In ancient times it was certainly true that being born a man gave you many more opportunities, because there were so many obstacles and limitations put on women. I think this is still true today in many cultures.

In previous times it was not easy for a woman to give her life over to the spiritual path. For example, if someone wanted to renounce the worldly life and retire to a mountain cave or a hut in the wilderness, it was more dangerous for a woman to do so than for a man. A woman would have more difficulty finding a suitable place, and she might require extra protection. A man faced fewer of these kinds of obstacles to practice. This is a quality that is culturally determined, and perhaps it is not so important now. But we should understand that throughout most human history there were many advantages to being born a man.

This item should not be taken to mean that a woman cannot attain buddhahood. It does not mean that women lack buddha-nature. It simply reflects the reality that at the time of the Buddha there were many restrictions on women that kept them from the spiritual life. That is why the Buddha first established an order of *bhikṣus* or monks, and for a long time he did not give any *bhikṣuṇī* or nun's vows.

8. *Possessing strength.* Because of the power of previous karma, you are naturally hale and hearty and content. You encounter few external sources of harm, very little sickness, and you radiate a joyous enthusiasm for life. You are not depressed, neurotic, or constantly bothered by petty things. Even when you find yourself in circumstances of great hardship, your mind is still peaceful, joyful, and enthusiastic. This is a kind of vitality, inner strength, and optimism that comes from a great accumulation of previous merit.

You can summarize the essence of these eight qualities of fruition in the following way. The quality of an excellent life span means being born in a happy rebirth. The quality of having an excellent physical appearance means gaining a fine body. The quality of an excellent lineage means gaining a fine birth. The quality of excellent power means gaining resources and supportive companionship. The quality of having trustworthy words means becoming an authority in the world. The quality of being renowned as powerful means gaining fame for your reliability. The quality of being a male means being born as a vessel of all good qualities. The quality of possessing strength means having energy for all activities.

b" The effects of the eight fruitions

When you have certain qualities you can achieve certain results. All of these eight qualities have their own individual functions, and when you understand what these functions are, you will understand why you should aspire to obtain them.

1. *An excellent lifespan.* A long life gives you the opportunity to practice virtue and accumulate merits for a long time. Human life is especially powerful because it enables you to work not only for your own benefit, but you can also do many things to benefit others. To obtain buddhahood requires so many causes and such a vast accumulation of merits that it is only by practicing over the course of a very long life span that you can accumulate all of this positive potential.

2. *An excellent physical appearance.* Practicing to attain the Mahayana goal of buddhahood means practicing the six perfections not only for yourself, but to help others and lead them to ultimate emancipation. Those beings who have not yet ripened you try to ripen; those who are already ripened you try to free from various obstacles; even arhats—those who are already freed from cyclic existence—you must lead to the Mahayana goal of perfect buddhahood. This is the practice of a bodhisattva.

When you have an excellent physical appearance other people naturally take a liking to you. As soon as they meet you they want to be close to you and want to listen to you. Having this type of "charisma" has a special function for a spiritual teacher: by merely seeing you people are pleased, they gather around you as disciples, listen to your words, and they begin to practice according to your advice.

It is important to understand that striving for an excellent physical appearance does not mean desiring a beautiful body out of attachment. The purpose of having an attractive form is to inspire others to follow the path to enlightenment. If you want to benefit many sentient beings, you first have to have contact with them. By virtue of this quality you do not need to engage in all kinds of strenuous activities in order to make contact with people—they just naturally gather around you and want to follow you. This attribute functions to make your Mahayana practice more extensive, meaningful, and efficient.

It is not easy to gather disciples, and to inspire them to make such deep changes in the their lives. Therefore, among the practices of the bodhisattva are the four means of assembling disciples. The first is to give others basic material aid, such as food, clothing, and shelter. This brings people to you and establishes a relationship. It is similar to parents giving their child a toy as an incentive to do something. The second means of assembling disciples is to say pleasing words, and the most pleasing words anyone can hear are instructions that bring them freedom from all their problems. The third is to act in accordance with the purpose of the disciples. This means giving them what they truly need to progress on the path, teaching what is appropriate to their capacity, and presenting the path in a way that is meaningful and helpful. The fourth means of assembling disciples is to live in accordance with the meaning of the Dharma. Bodhisattvas must behave in accordance with the advice they are giving to others; their words and behavior have to be consistent with one another.

The point of employing these four means is not to gain some kind of sinister power over people. The bodhisattva only does what is necessary to lead people to the highest goal, and the best way to do this is to give them proper teachings. But at the beginning people do not find it easy to embark on the path. Therefore, it is very helpful for the teacher to present an attractive appearance that brings disciples forward, engages their interest, and gives them the opportunity to follow and listen to the Dharma.

3. *An excellent lineage.* When you have a noble lineage or high status people are more likely to follow your instructions, listen to your commands, and avoid transgressing your advice. This is the main function of an excellent lineage, and although this may be more of an asset in other cultures, it is still useful in gaining the respect and authority to lead others.

4. *Excellent power.* Remember that the first of the bodhisattva's four means of assembling disciples is to give material assistance. In order to do this in an extensive way you need to have sufficient resources. If you are born with wealth you are in a position to help those who are in financial need. You can help provide whatever material assistance they require. However, if you lack resources, then even if you want to help those in need, you have nothing to give.

5. *Trustworthy words.* The function of speaking trustworthy words is to bring beings to the teachings and to ripen them. You do this by using pleasant speech, which means, first of all, avoiding speech that is unpleasant or

deceives others. It means always trying to be helpful and make others happy. Beyond that, pleasant speech means giving voice to these teachings, and doing so in a form that is always appropriate to the level of your audience and agreeable for them to hear.

Furthermore, to be a speaker of trustworthy words means that your own aims are the same as those of your disciples, that you sincerely believe what you say, and you behave in accordance with your own advice. It is excellent qualities such as these that enable you to gather sentient beings and mature them on the spiritual path.

6. *Renowned as being powerful.* This is not just any kind of fame. It means having a reputation for benefiting and giving assistance to others in need. When you are renowned for being indefatigable in helping others, you gain widespread respect, people admire you, listen to what you have to say, and they want to repay your kindness.

7. *Being a male.* By being born a male you will be a vessel of all kinds of good qualities, and you will be strong in whatever you try to do. In general, men are stronger, especially when it comes to physical activities. You will have the capacity of broad wisdom and a mind that can correctly analyze phenomena. In public gatherings you will not be embarrassed or easily frightened.

In ancient times women were expected to be modest and stay in the background. It was difficult for them to be in a crowd or to speak publicly before a large gathering. Men did not have that obstacle. Similarly, public activities such as socializing with different kinds of people, or traveling, was easier for men than for women. We have already discussed how it was much more dangerous for a woman to enter solitary retreat in the wilderness. Nowadays things have gotten better, but many of the activities involved in practice and teaching have traditionally been easier for men, while women have faced more obstacles. Therefore, it says here that being born as a man is a more solid situation for a spiritual practice.

8. *Possessing strength.* When you have the excellent quality of strength you will not be easily upset or physically hurt. You will not be discouraged by whatever hardships you encounter, but will retain a brave, joyful enthusiasm for achieving the goals of yourself and others. Because you are stable in your enthusiasm and energy, you are able to attain the power of realization, and this leads quickly to the attainment of all the supernatural powers.

c" The causes of the eight fruitions

1. *An excellent lifespan.* The cause for attaining a long life is not harming other beings, and cultivating the strong conviction: "I will not do harm to anyone." This attitude of nonharming should be based on a clear understanding of the suffering that results from hurting others. The result of harming others and shortening their lives is to have your own life shortened, to be killed, or to suffer from serious illness. Seeing those disadvantages, and trusting in the cause and effect of karma, you make a decision to avoid that kind of negative action. The following stanzas sketch out some of the causes of a long, healthy life:

> By rescuing beings who are about to be slaughtered,
> By benefiting others by giving life in such ways,
> By turning away from harming any living creature,
> You will attain a long life.
>
> By caring for the seriously ill,
> By giving them medicine as a healer,
> By refraining from harming creatures with stones or sticks,
> You will be free from illness.

The practice of charity and generosity has the power to produce a healthy life in which you will have the strength to pursue the path. By giving to the poor, giving food, clothing, housing, and medicine, and by generally serving the needy, you create the causes for a long, healthy, and comfortable life. Some of these results may ripen in this life; most will be experienced in future lives.

2. *An excellent physical appearance.* The cause of excellent appearance is offering light in the form of butter lamps and so forth, as well as offering fresh new clothes. Such offerings can be made to the Three Jewels, or to those in need.

Concerning this practice, there is the following stanza:

> By not resorting to anger,
> And giving ornaments, you will have an excellent body.
> The result of avoiding jealousy,
> Is said to be good fortune.

The cause of having an unhealthy, uncomfortable, unreliable body is indulgence in hatred and anger toward others. You acquire an excellent and useful body in the future by avoiding harmful thoughts and actions now. When you see someone else who has a healthy, attractive body, instead of feeling jealous you should admire that person and rejoice that they are enjoying the happy results of their previous virtuous actions. Such positive thoughts will bring you, too, a fortunate life in the future.

3. *An excellent lineage.* The cause of being born into an excellent lineage is to subdue your own pride, to show reverence for spiritual teachers, and to treat all beings with the same respect that a servant might show his master. In fact, it is the practice of buddhas and bodhisattvas to always hold others as more important than themselves. They always consider their own welfare as less important and make their highest goal benefiting others. With that attitude you will finally become the benefactor of all living beings.

Those who think that they are better than everyone else, who try to climb to the top over the backs of others, may gain some temporary advantage, but in the long run that approach will not bring them honorable status or pleasant results. We should recall from an earlier section of the *Lamrim Chenmo* that there is a type of respect that a disciple shows his or her teacher that is called "the attitude like a dog." Dogs never make a pretense to being higher than their master, and they have a way of showing respect with how they hold their body. You should keep that kind of humility in mind when you are with your spiritual guides. By conquering pride you should cultivate respect for everyone, just as if you were their servant.

4. *Excellent power.* The cause of having abundant resources is to give to those who are needy whatever they require to have a decent life. You should give food, clothing, and all forms of charity to those who request it, as well as to those who do not ask but are nevertheless in need.

Here, the field in which you plant the seeds of your virtuous actions is those who are suffering from poverty, sickness, and helplessness. With a virtuous attitude you help them by giving whatever they may need. When you plant good seeds in a field of merit like that, the result is that in the future you naturally obtain the resources you need without any difficulty.

We also speak of the higher field of merit, which includes your own parents, your spiritual teacher, and the Three Jewels of refuge. Taking these as the objects of your offerings and devotion will also bring great results in the future.

5. *Trustworthy words.* The cause of having your words trusted is to avoid the four nonvirtues of speech: lying, slander, harsh speech, and senseless speech. When you speak to others, watch your motivation; watch what you are saying and

how you are saying it. If you are aware of your speech, you will recognize when you are about to deceive someone and you can change direction. But if you know you are about to say something that is not true and you still say it, you are planting a fresh seed of future problems. In one way, these practices are easy to do; you only need to develop awareness of how you are using your faculty of speech. Once you begin to pay attention to your speech, you may find that you are talking unnecessarily, talking senselessly, or using deceitful words. The point is to be aware of these four kinds of nonvirtuous speech and make an effort to reduce them as much as you can.

When you fail to guard your speech, you can do a lot of harm and create a lot of negative karma. Events can erupt unexpectedly that make you mad, or frightened, and suddenly you say something that may be totally untrue, or creates a great deal of pain in someone's mind. The pain of hearing harsh words can be even sharper than physical pain, to the point where it can even make people sick.

Sakya Pandita says in his *Treasury of Good Advice (Sa skya'i Legs bshad):*

> If you don't control your flat tongue,
> It will make trouble for your round head.[17]

In other words, watch what you say. When you catch yourself about to use harmful words think, "I shouldn't say this. If I say this, it will hurt the other person." Always remaining aware of your speech in this way will produce great results, and in the future you will be born with the excellence of trustworthy speech.

6. *Renowned as being powerful.* The cause of attaining fame for your good deeds and generosity is to make aspirational prayers to attain the full array of virtuous qualities in the future. This means that whenever you worship or make offerings to your parents, the Three Jewels, śrāvakas, pratyekabuddhas, preceptors, or teachers, you dedicate those merits with the wish that you will achieve a life in the future with all the qualities you need to attain enlightenment for the benefit of other beings. By making this kind of aspirational prayer you will gain renown for your virtuous deeds.

7. *Being a male.* As we have said, the value of being born a man depends on the time and place. It does not imply that women cannot attain buddhahood. The causes of being born male are said to be: appreciating the qualities of being a man; not liking female qualities and seeing birth as a woman as having faults; turning away from the desire to be born with a female body

because you see it as faulty; and rescuing those who are going to be castrated. Of course, many animals are castrated, especially on farms, and this is a completely negative karma that will create tremendous obstacles to being born as a male in future lives.

8. Possessing strength. The causes of having irrepressible strength and determination are: solving problems which no one else is capable of resolving; helping others when you have something to contribute to a common endeavor; and giving others food and drink. In other words, this quality of strength results from doing things that are beneficial to others, especially when you have something unique to contribute. With this attribute you will be able to endure all obstacles on the path to achieving your goal.

These are the eight special *qualities of the fruitions* that constitute the most advantageous type of life for attaining the goal of buddhahood. With these attributes you encounter few obstacles on the path. From birth, you naturally possess all the internal and external necessities, so you don't need to spend time and energy struggling to obtain the supports you need to practice. You are well prepared for the journey to enlightenment, and all the physical and mental requirements come to you with ease. If you do not attain enlightenment in the present life, this is the kind of life you should have in your next rebirth. Of course, assembling all these wonderful qualities requires an extraordinary accumulation of virtuous karma.

The three causes of superlative results

In creating these eight causes there are three aspects to your actions which can make the results superlative. These three causal aspects are pure attitude, pure application, and pure field.

Pure attitude

There are two types of pure attitude: pure attitude with respect to oneself, and pure attitude with respect to others.

Pure attitude with respect to oneself

There are two types of pure attitude with respect to oneself. The first is called "not hoping for fruition," which means that whenever you perform a virtuous activity, you dedicate the roots of that virtuous action toward attaining the highest goal of buddhahood. This means that you are not acting out of worldly concerns, such as desire for material comfort, sensual pleasure, or a good reputation. Whatever virtue you do is dedicated toward enlightenment for the benefit of others, not for the sake of some samsaric result.

The second type of pure attitude with respect to oneself is "intense sincerity," which means that you perform these actions from the depths of your heart. When you understand the cause and effect relationship, you know the kind of beneficial results you are trying to achieve. This makes your motivation very sincere and your determination very intense; your virtuous actions really come from deep in the heart.

Pure attitude with respect to others

There are also two types of pure attitude with respect to others. First of all, when you see others practicing the Dharma, you avoid feeling jealous of those whose practice is more advanced than your own, avoid competitiveness toward those who are equal to you, and avoid any feeling of contempt toward those who are inferior. Whenever you see others engaging in the practice of the Dharma, you should rejoice in their virtue and admire their efforts.

Restraining such negative feelings as jealousy and the like is not easy. These emotions arise out of habit, and they grow out of egotistic thought. When you see someone better than yourself, there is a natural tendency to feel jealous. When someone is on roughly the same level as you are, you feel a certain competitiveness. And contempt easily arises for those who are inferior to you in some respect. But if you want your virtuous actions to be pure and powerful, you need to replace those obscuring attitudes with a feeling of joyful admiration. Remember that those other people are doing exactly what you yourself are striving to do.

The second type of pure attitude with respect to others is to apply analytical wisdom. If you cannot generate a spontaneous feeling of admiration and sincerely rejoice in the merits of others, then you should apply some analytical thought. Ask yourself, "What is the meaning of virtuous action? What are its effects and what are its benefits?" Look at the virtuous actions of the other person. Examine the thoughts arising in your own mind in response to what you see. You have to bring your wisdom to bear on these things. In order to change your spontaneous attitude of jealousy, competitiveness, or disdain, you have to apply your analytical wisdom over and over.

It is very important to do this practice. Because it is through the repeated application of discriminating wisdom that you will be able to transform your negative emotions into sincere admiration and joy in the virtuous practice of others. Eventually, natural, spontaneous admiration will arise. Rejoicing in the virtues of others is one of the best ways to increase your own merits. Tsongkhapa said in his *Spiritual Biography: My Destiny Fulfilled (Rang gi rtogs pa brjod pa mdo tsam du bshad pa),* "For assembling a vast collection of merits with a small amount of effort, rejoicing in virtues is said to be best."[18]

Pure application

Pure application with respect to oneself means practicing virtue over a long period of time, uninterruptedly, intensively, and from the heart. Your practice should not be occasional, or just for a short while. It will not help you very much to practice virtues like crazy one day and then forget about it the next.

Pure application with respect to others means to encourage and help people who are not engaged in virtuous practice, or to encourage those who have not yet taken any religious vows to take them up. For those who are already living virtuously, or have already taken some level of vows, you should praise their activities so that they take pleasure in them. Your praise will cause them to continue their practice without losing enthusiasm or giving up. The strength of their practice will increase, and since that increase in their meritorious actions is caused by you, your merits will also increase.

Praising the virtue of others and encouraging them in their practice is a very effective way to create merits for yourself and others. But the same kind of activity, when directed toward negative actions, can also increase negative karma. When you see someone else harming or killing another being, if you admire and encourage them you will be causing them to rejoice in those actions and increase their commitment to such harmful deeds. This will create more negative karma for both them and yourself.

Pure field

The pure field is not a separate item, but refers to the fact that the pure attitude and pure application yield many excellent fruit, and in that way they are just like a very productive field. Tsongkhapa says that this entire explanation has been based on Asaṅga's *Bodhisattva Levels,* supplemented by various points from the commentary.

Making this life meaningful

In the *Talk That Is Like a Jeweled Receptacle of Good Explanations (Subhāṣita-ratna-karaṇḍaka-kathā)* Āryaśūra said of the person who obtains a human rebirth but does not make good use of it:

> He is like a merchant who travels to the land of jewels
> But returns to his home empty-handed.

If you don't follow the path of the ten virtuous actions,
You will not obtain such a life again.[19]

The human life we have obtained is so precious; it is as if we had landed on an island filled with precious jewels. We must not waste this opportunity and leave here empty-handed. Even if you cannot achieve the highest enlightenment during this lifetime, you should at least strive to arrive at the time of death with a joyful heart, confident that you have put into practice, to the best of your ability, the teachings that lead in the direction of true happiness. Then, as you prepare to die, you will think, "Now there is nothing I have to worry about. I have done all I could do, and now I am well prepared for the future." Your Dharma practice should leave you with that much confidence. You have made your life meaningful. Like the merchant who leaves the land of jewels carrying a rich treasure, that kind of satisfaction is the spiritual wealth that you want to take from this life.

The world, the country, the time in which we live right now are all filled with an amazing variety of teachings that have been left here by previous buddhas and bodhisattvas. And as humans with keen intelligence we have the capacity to find those practices that are just right for ourselves, to understand them, to engage in them, and to realize the wisdom they reveal.

We stand in the middle of this land filled with the jewels of the holy Dharma. But these jewels are not outside somewhere, waiting to be collected; the holy Dharma has to be within yourself. The causes of misery, the afflictions that obstruct realization of the truth, are inside, within each individual. To incorporate the wealth of this life, you must take the Dharma in, like a powerful medicine, and make it part of yourself. Understand it, practice it, realize it, and those realizations will lead to a powerful faith and confidence that you have used this lifetime to its fullest potential.

We have been talking about karma and its results, and we have seen how our future depends entirely on the actions that we take now. If you cannot attain enlightenment in this life, you must at least situate yourself so that you will be able to continue to practice in the future. You want to begin with a strong start, and then build upon the foundation of this excellent current rebirth. You want your next life to have even better conditions, with all the inner and outer qualities that will assist you to quickly reach your ultimate goal. There is no contradiction in trying to create the causes to be born with all these excellent qualities in your next life. You are not seeking to be healthy, wealthy, powerful, and have high status merely for your own gratification. The motivation is purely to benefit others by attaining enlightenment yourself as quickly as possible. The point is to build the perfect conditions for practice, so that you can reach the highest goal and truly be of benefit to others. That is the pure Mahayana practice, the practice of the bodhisattva.

3

Cultivating Ethical Behavior

3' Having contemplated the principles of karma, how to engage in virtue and desist from nonvirtue
- a" A general presentation
- b" In particular, how to purify by means of the four opponent powers
  - 1" The first power: remorse
  - 2" The second power: applying antidotes
  - 3" The third power: turning away from faults
  - 4" The fourth power: reliance

3' Having contemplated the principles of karma, how to engage in virtue and desist from nonvirtue

NOW THAT we have looked into karma and its results in general, and in some of its details, we consider how to engage in those actions that are beneficial and how to turn away from those that are harmful. There are two parts to this discussion:

a" A general presentation
b" In particular, how to purify by means of the four opponent powers

a" A general presentation

In *Engaging in the Bodhisattva Deeds,* Śāntideva says:

> "How can I definitely be freed from suffering,
> Which arises from nonvirtue?"

> Constantly, day and night,
> I should think only of this.

And Śāntideva also says:

> The Sage has said that conviction is the root
> Of every aspect of virtue.
> And the root of that is
> Constantly contemplating fruitional results.

How to be free from all the suffering of cyclic existence is the single concern that should occupy our minds. The Buddha taught that the root of all virtue is the conviction, the confident faith, that virtuous actions are the pathway out of suffering and toward stable happiness. When we have confidence that virtuous action will bring us positive results, we will naturally admire virtue and aspire to do it. In other words, the way out of suffering begins with trust in the cause and effect of karma as we have been studying it. The root of that trust is constant contemplation of the kinds of results that arise from the different types of actions. By analyzing what kind of life you will experience as a result of performing virtuous deeds, and comparing that to the kind of life you will experience from nonvirtuous deeds, you will develop a strong conviction and resolve to do virtue.

To look at it from the negative side, the obstacle to freeing ourselves from suffering is our lack of confidence in the action of karma and its results. If you do not firmly believe that nonvirtue will lead to suffering, you will not have the motivation to turn away from nonvirtuous actions. There is a lack of sureness, of confidence, of trust. Therefore, in order to cultivate that trust and move your mind and action in a wholesome direction, Śāntideva tells us to contemplate fruitional results.

You must first understand what kind of results come from what kinds of actions, and then you must contemplate that over and over again. You need to begin by studying the scriptures and gaining a basic understanding of karma. But that is not enough. To really benefit from that understanding you have to integrate it with your mind by repeatedly contemplating how karma works. You study, analyze, and meditate on karma until your mind is thoroughly accustomed to seeing experience through the lens of that understanding. This kind of constant effort is necessary because the cause and effect of karma is an extremely hidden phenomenon, which makes it very difficult for ordinary people like ourselves to gain certainty about its action.

Remember that in Buddhism we postulate three types of objects of knowledge. The first type is *manifest phenomena.* These are objects we can know by means of direct sense perception—by seeing, hearing, and so forth. Then there are *slightly hidden phenomena.* These are objects which cannot be directly perceived, but can be known through inferential knowledge, by the way things relate to one another, and by the deductive power of logic. For example, when we see smoke rising on a hill, we can infer that there must be a fire there, even though we can not perceive the fire directly with our eyes. The fire is a slightly hidden phenomenon in the sense that it is hidden from our visual perception, but nevertheless can be known to us through the power of logical reasoning. Similarly, we use logic and the scientific method to understand many things about the physical world, such as the way matter consists of molecules and atoms, that disease is caused by microbes, and so forth. Finally, we have *extremely hidden phenomena,* the most hidden objects, and these are the most difficult for ordinary people like us to know.

Extremely hidden phenomena include things like the details of karma and the nature and qualities of the buddhas. Karma is especially hard to know directly when a cause and its effect are not both present in one discernable span of time. For example, during this life you do some activity, and by that action you plant a seed of potential in your mental continuum. Then, at some time in the distant future—possibly many lifetimes from now—that seed comes to fruition and produces a certain result. Unless you have supernatural knowledge, it is impossible to see the connection between that cause and that effect directly, because the process takes place over many lifetimes.

Because it is an extremely hidden phenomenon, it is very difficult to develop complete understanding and certainty about the action of karma. Until you have higher realizations, such things can only be known by depending on scriptures, by trusting in the Buddha's knowledge and words. Speaking of the Buddha's words, the *King of Concentrations Sutra* says:

> Though the moon and stars might fall from their places,
> Though the earth with its mountains and cities might be destroyed,
> Though the realm of the sky might be completely transformed,
> You could never utter a word that was untrue.

Though we cannot say it is impossible for the stars to fall out of the sky, or the earth to be destroyed, we can say that it is impossible for the Buddha to lie, because that would be contrary to the very nature of buddhahood. The buddhas teach only for the benefit of other beings. *Buddha* means one who has perfect knowledge, who is omniscient, who is free from all obstacles and all suffering. Therefore, buddhas have no reason to lie. We can trust in their teachings to reveal the truth about hidden phenomena such as the action of karma.

Actually, the situation we are describing is not so unusual. Even when it comes to worldly concerns, there are many things we do not understand about the items we use every day, and we have to rely on other people who do understand them when we need help. When our car breaks down, or our plumbing does not work, or we want to fly in an airplane, we rely on people who understand these things, and we accept what they say because we do not know enough about these things ourselves. We place our trust in experts because they know things that we do not know ourselves.

When it comes to understanding the cause and effect of karma, we have to trust in the words of the Tathāgata, and practice in accordance with his teachings. If you do not cultivate uncontrived certainty and spontaneous trust in the reliability of his teachings, then you will not achieve the firm understanding and conviction that pleases the buddhas. This is true in any aspect of the Dharma, and it means that you must gain certainty with respect to the cause and effect of karma, because that is the cornerstone of all the Buddha's teachings.

Some people claim to have a realization of emptiness but say that they are not concerned with karma and its results, and have no regard for that teaching. This indicates that they have not properly understood emptiness. When you understand emptiness properly you see that the meaning of emptiness is dependent arising. Emptiness means that all phenomenon lack any absolute, essential, independent nature. When you understand emptiness properly in this way, it actually becomes an aid to gaining certainty about the cause and effect of karma. If you think you understand emptiness but your understanding turns you away from the teachings of the Buddha on karma—if your understanding of emptiness leads you to believe in nothingness, that there is no cause and effect—then you can be sure that your understanding of emptiness is mistaken.

The *King of Concentrations Sutra* says:

> Like illusions, bubbles, mirages, and lightning,
> All phenomena are like the moon reflected in water.
> Though the beings who go to their next life after they die
> Do not ultimately exist,
> The karma they have created is not nonexistent.
> It will yield its results according to its virtuous or nonvirtuous nature.
> This noncontradictory mode of understanding is correct.

Though subtle and difficult to understand,
It is within the scope of the buddhas.

These verses first show how all phenomena are empty of absolute reality, illusory like the moon reflected in a lake. They appear one way, but that is not their ultimate mode of existence. Bubbles shimmering in the water appear to have some kind of solidity, but when you touch them there is nothing substantial there; they are empty. So it is that all phenomena falsely appear to have a fixed and ultimate reality, but when we examine them closely, we find that they lack that ultimately real nature.

In the same way, sentient beings who will die and go on to their next lives also do not ultimately exist. Nevertheless, the karma that they have created is not totally nonexistent. The first part of this stanza shows the emptiness of ultimate reality; but the second part shows how the karma that is created by individuals still functions conventionally. It will ripen according to whether it is virtuous or nonvirtuous, bringing happiness or suffering. This cause and effect relationship of dependent arising is not contradictory to the ultimate nature, or emptiness, of all beings. There is no contradiction between the ultimate emptiness of all phenomenon and their dependent nature of arising due to causes and conditions.

In fact, instead of being contradictory, the nature of emptiness and the nature of dependent arising are perfectly suitable and compatible. If things were absolutely real, then they could not change; they could not be created or destroyed and therefore the cause and effect of karma could not function. It is because things are *not* ultimately real, but have a dependent nature, that they are able to function, to arise and disintegrate due to causes and conditions. This is the correct way to understand the compatibility of emptiness and dependent nature.

The action of karma and its results is so subtle that it is difficult for ordinary people to see and understand. But these hidden phenomena are direct objects of knowledge for the buddhas, and we ordinary beings can understand them by relying on the teachings of the Victorious Ones.

The Buddha often explained the details of karma when answering questions from disciples seeking an explanation of some extraordinary event. The Buddha would tell them a story of how actions taken by someone a long time ago—even many eons previously—brought about the results that were being seen at that time. Many such stories are collected in the *Sutra of the Wise and the Foolish*. Where does this title come from? Those who read this sutra and then gain a good understanding of karma are wise. But the person who reads it and thinks that these stories are nothing but amusing entertainment is a stupid fool.

The correct understanding of karma is what we call the *worldly right view* or the *ordinary right view.* In brief, this view recognizes that virtuous actions result in happy experiences and nonvirtue results in suffering. To illustrate this connection there is the following Dharma formula: "From generosity comes wealth, from ethical conduct comes a happy rebirth, from patience comes beauty, from persevering effort comes determination, and from meditative stabilization comes peace." Some people are naturally born with wealth, or with beauty, or with a determination to complete whatever they begin. The Buddha teaches us the types of causes that lead to these results. Though we cannot directly see the actions in a previous lifetime that led a person to be born wealthy and so forth, we can understand the karmic cause that led to that result by means of the Buddha's teachings. He does see all of these causes and results, and he has taught these details to us in order to benefit sentient beings.

Therefore, Tsongkhapa says that you should produce a confident understanding of the dependent nature of things—of virtuous and nonvirtuous karma and the kinds of results they bring. If you base your practice on this certainty, and then day and night keep watch on your three doors of body, speech, and mind, evaluating each thought and deed according to whether it will bring you happiness or suffering in the future, then you can prevent rebirth in a lower realm. However, if you set out with no expertise in the concepts of cause and effect—if you have just a smattering of knowledge but you treat the whole matter carelessly, allowing your physical, verbal, and mental actions to run free—then you are surely opening the door to the lower rebirths.

The *Questions of the Nāga Kings of the Ocean* says:

> Lord of the Nāgas, with a single practice the bodhisattvas completely prevent falling into a rebirth among the bad migrations. What is that one practice? It is analyzing what is virtuous by considering, "How am I living? How am I spending my days and nights?"

That is the single Dharma that will cut off lower rebirths. The true religious practitioner is always thinking that way. When you examine your mind like that, what will happen? What will it bring? Previous teachers in our tradition have said that when you consider your behavior without relating it to any standard, it may seem okay. But when you compare it to the standards found in these teachings on karma and ask yourself, "How much is my action in harmony with the Dharma?" you find that your behavior is almost totally out of line. You have made big mistakes and have gone in a completely wrong direction. Because of that, you never break free from all of your troubles. That means that from beginningless time up to now you have been constantly confused, wandering through cyclic existence with no end in sight, experiencing limitless pain, misery, and trouble.

In this way, when you examine your own mental continuum and your own actions in light of these teachings, it is wise to be honest with yourself. You should recognize that your actions are rarely in accord with the teachings, and, in fact, are the opposite of what you should be doing. These earlier masters say that the truly wise person is the one who realizes and acknowledges this. The *Collection of Indicative Verses* puts it this way:

> Those who are immature and recognize they are immature
> Are here considered the wise ones.
> Those who are immature but think they are wise
> Are the ones who should be called immature.

"Immature" or childish people are those who are not concerned with the long-range future. Like children, they only care about the things that are right in front of them. They need immediate gratification. When something attractive appears before them, they have to have it, even though it will bring many problems in the long term. Like a child, they can't see that far ahead, or are blinded by their present desire. The truly wise person is the one who sees that immature quality in himself or herself and recognizes it for what it is.

This point is made in the Vinaya, in the story of a wayward bhikṣu who is constantly breaking his vows and doing things that monks are not supposed to do. Finally he looks at himself and sees what he has been doing. He feels regret and says, "I was behaving like a child." When the Buddha hears that he responds, "Now that you recognize that, you are seeing things correctly. Now you are a wise man."

When you check to see whether your thoughts and behavior are in harmony with the teachings, you may find that they are "facing in opposite directions, like a corpse on the back of an undertaker." This is an image from Tibetan culture. In Tibet, when someone dies the body is dealt with by a special group of people who are like our undertakers. They fold the body up into a tight little package and carry it away on their back, with the back of the corpse up against the back of the undertaker, and the corpse facing backward. Like that, when you look into your own behavior you may find that it has been totally incompatible with the Dharma, facing the opposite direction, like a corpse on the back of an undertaker.

Nevertheless, some people still envision themselves as high Dharma practitioners or great masters. These people are really the worst sort of immature beings. Therefore, at the very least, you should strive to understand the

Dharma, and investigate whether your own mind and your own behavior are harmonious with the teachings.

The famous Kadampa Geshe Potowa[1] quoted the following passage from the *Garland of Birth Stories*, and advised his students to examine their own minds.

> It is a long way from the sky down to the earth.
> It is also a long way from the far shore to the near shore of the sea.
> It is farther still from the mountains of the east to the mountains of the west.
> But the distance is still farther from ordinary behavior to the holy Dharma.

For ordinary people like us, there is a great gap between the way we normally behave and the way the Dharma advises us to behave. If you let your thoughts and action do whatever they will without examination, without studying the Dharma and trying to conform your life to the teachings, then that gap will grow wider and wiser.

This stanza quoted above is from the story of Prince Sutasoma, in which the future Buddha, as Prince Sutasoma the bodhisattva, pays one thousand gold coins per verse to the brahman Subhāṣita for a Dharma teaching. When his father criticizes him for paying so much for mere words, he explains that teachings such as those found in this verse are actually priceless, because they have the power to give a person wisdom and peace.[2]

Another Kadampa, Geshe Tölungba, said:

> If someone who knew how were to examine our mind and actions, he would find that we had drifted farther and farther from the Dharma, like a ball of string rolling downhill.

The important thing is to realize that this is happening, to admit it to yourself, and then to do something to change it. It is natural for ordinary, immature beings to engage in nonvirtuous actions because they are not free of the obscuring afflictions. The point of this practice is to learn from the teachings and recognize how your own actions are departing from that standard. You are trying to build a new attitude and that attitude cannot rise by itself. You need to hear, study, and learn the teachings on karma, just as we are studying them here; then you must look toward your own daily actions and thoughts, with the intention of bringing them into harmony with those teachings. Once you do that, you can begin to make progress on the path.

When you are practicing this karma section of the *Lamrim Chenmo*, you practice by means of analytical meditation. Meditation does not mean sitting the whole day doing nothing, thinking nothing. Meditation has many different purposes and there are different types of meditation to achieve those purposes. Sometimes you need to bring the mind to a single-pointed focus, and for this, discursive thinking has to stop. But to break through the mind's habitual patterns, and to weaken the grip of powerful afflictions, you have to develop new ways of thinking. You do this by concentrated meditation on the deeper understanding you gain from the teachings. You focus repeatedly on the reasons for changing your mind and your behavior. By means of this type of analytical meditation, gradually your habitual ways of thinking and acting come under the power of your Dharma understanding.

Once your attitude and motivation are brought under the power of wisdom, you begin to see how your thoughts and deeds are not in harmony with the teachings, which are the true path to happiness. When that realization arises strongly, the pure practice of the teachings begins. You become more attentive to what you are doing and you make the effort to correct your own actions. Slowly your life comes closer and closer to the Dharma.

Without meditating on these points change will be difficult. These new concepts must be pushed to the front of the mind where they have the force to affect the way you think and act in your daily life. Otherwise, you hear or read some explanation of karma and you think, "Yes, I have heard about that," and it settles somewhere in the back of your mind. But if you do not focus on this explanation in meditation, it will not have the necessary reinforcement to bring about change. If you do not meditate on karma and its results in this way, your habitual behavior will just go on and on, rolling downhill like a ball of string.

How to actually turn away from unwholesome action is mentioned in a quotation from the *Chapter of the Truth Speaker*, where the Buddha is advising a king as follows:

> O King, do not kill.
> Life is extremely precious to all living beings.
> Therefore, those who desire to live a long life
> Should not think about killing, even in their deepest thoughts.

In this passage killing is used as an example, and you should apply the same principles to all of the ten negative actions. You must contemplate the results of those actions. If you want to reap positive results—such as good health, long life, wealth, and loving friends—you should refrain from those actions. You should not only refrain physically, you should aim to prevent even the thought of harming another being from coming to your mind. Try to accustom your mind to the virtuous way of thinking, which is rooted in empathy and compassion for other beings.

If you fail to do this—if you do not turn away from negative karma—you will have to experience misery, even though you do not want it. Once you have created the complete causes and conditions for suffering results there is no escaping the fruit of your actions, no matter how hard you try to run away. Even the Buddha would be powerless to change that fruition; even if he appeared right in front of you and wanted to help, at that point it would be too late.

The power of the buddhas and bodhisattvas, and the power of one's own karma, are equal. How do the buddhas, bodhisattvas, and the Dharma have the power to destroy suffering? They have the ability to lead you to stop creating new causes of suffering. For the incomplete negative causes you have already created, they teach antidotes that can reduce the results that will ripen from that karma. They show you how to produce powerful positive causes that will create conditions in which negative karmic seeds will not ripen. It is by teaching such methods that the buddhas and bodhisattvas lead you out of suffering.

It makes no sense to pursue actions that appear attractive because they bring you some temporary, minor pleasure, but trap you in an experience that covers your face in tears when the long-term results of these actions ripen. Little children may want to play with fire, or drink a bottle of poison, because on the surface it looks like fun. But their parents, the mature beings, can see the long-term consequences of such childish acts. In the same way, in this life you may indulge in all kinds of sensual pleasure, or harmful actions, which seem so appealing on the surface, but have grave consequences when the results of those actions ripen.

Unwholesome karma always has this quality of cheating our perceptions, of confusing us. When we create such karma we act out of a feeling or a belief that this will bring something good; after all, the purpose of all negative actions is to benefit oneself. But the true results do not come right away, so we are not thinking about them. When they do come, the suffering can be deep and intense, and it brings great regret for the deeds we thought would help us.

On the other hand, it makes perfect sense to engage in those actions that will bring joy and happiness when their seeds ripen. As the *Collection of Indicative Verses* says:

If you are afraid of suffering,
If you find suffering unattractive,
Do not perform nonvirtuous action
Openly or even in secret.

Whether you have performed nonvirtuous actions,
Or whether you are performing them now,
Even if you try to run away,
You will not escape from suffering.

Wherever you go, there is no place
Where you cannot be touched by the karma you have created.
Not out in space, not in the oceans,
Not even in the midst of the mountains.

Of course we are always trying to avoid suffering and looking for pleasurable experiences. Our whole life is spent pursuing good things and trying to escape bad situations. So the fear of future unhappiness is always, directly or indirectly, part of our motivation. As these verses say, if you really want to avoid suffering you should avoid doing harmful actions, because even if you commit unwholesome deeds in secret, or try to run away from the results of your actions, there is no escape from experiencing the fruition of your deeds.

In the sutras we find an account of the time when the powerful Prince Virūdaka was preparing to slaughter the Śākya clan in a war. The Buddha's disciple, Maudgalyāyana, tried to use his magical powers to prevent the war, but because of the karma of the world situation at that time, he was powerless to stop it. The Buddha used his supernatural powers to hide some of the children in magical ways—some in his begging bowl, some in a distant cave—but when the war was over even those children were found dead. When you have planted certain karmic seeds, and when the conditions arise for those seeds to ripen, there is no place in heaven or earth where you can hide from those results.

A little further on the *Collection of Indicative Verses* says:

Immature beings with little wisdom,
Behaving as enemies to themselves,
Perform those nonvirtuous actions
Whose fruits will be painful.

It is better not to engage in those actions
That bring the individual
A fruition of torment, and crying,
Covers the face with tears.

It is better to engage in those actions
That bring the individual a fruition
Without pain, with joy,
And with a happy mind.

I will be crying when I experience
The results of my nonvirtuous actions,
Committed heedlessly,
Because I craved happiness.

Finally, we have three more stanzas from the *Collection of Indicative Verses:*

Nonvirtuous action does not necessarily bring its result
Immediately, as when you are cut by a weapon.
The results of nonvirtuous action will manifest
In rebirths taken in future lives.

Beings who create nonvirtuous karma,
Will experience in future lives
Results that are as painful
As the nonvirtuous acts that caused them.

Rust, which has arisen from iron,
Eats away at that very source.
Like that, those who act without consideration
Go to bad migrations by their own actions.

Whatever happens to you, you cannot blame somebody else. It was done by yourself. You are beaten, cut, and tormented in the lower rebirths because of your own actions. Those who act without examination, without questioning, "What am I doing? What should I be doing? What should I not be doing?" send themselves into the lower rebirths. By contemplating and investigating the meaning of these verses, you can deepen your understanding of karma.

Another Kadampa, Geshe Khamlungba, said to the Geshe Puchungwa: "Geshe Dromtonpa always said that the most important thing is to think about karma and its results. But nowadays people place no value on explaining, listening to, or meditating on it. I think this is because it is singularly difficult to practice." To which Puchungwa replied, "That's right."

Of course, if you do not have any trust in karma and its results, then the whole structure of Buddhism has no base, no ground. Without the theory of karma, you are acting only for the enjoyment of this temporary life and there is nothing beyond that. If you do not study karma, and develop understanding, trust, and faith in it, then all the goals of buddhist practice, whether Hinayana or Mahayana, will remain beyond your reach.

Geshe Dromtonpa was the father of the Kadampa tradition, a direct disciple and the main lineage holder of Atiśa. While most of the other Kadampas were monks, Geshe Dromtonpa remained a layman. He said, "Followers of Lord Atiśa, you should not be too brash. This dependent arising is subtle." By this he meant, "Don't be foolhardy or reckless in thinking that you can behave any way you like. Don't be so presumptuous as to think you understand all the consequences of your actions, because the details of the cause and effect relationships of karma and dependent arising are so subtle."

Geshe Puchungwa said, "In my old age I have steered toward the *Sutra of the Wise and the Foolish*." He is saying that as he grows old and approaches the end of his spiritual career, he has turned his mind and his effort toward studying this sutra, which is one of the main sources of teachings on karma.

And Geshe Sharawa said, "The Buddha said that whatever faults or miserable conditions you experience should not be blamed on an inauspicious place or on the construction of some building; rather, it is simply that by doing a certain action you were born into these circumstances." People are always looking for some external cause to blame when things go badly for them. It never occurs to them that they are experiencing the results of their own previous actions. The Buddha never puts the blame anywhere else: he always explains that by doing certain kinds of actions in the past you were born here and you have to go through this kind of experience. He never explains a person's experience any other way than by referring to their karma.

If you have created powerful karma that has to be experienced, it does not matter where you go. Even though they live in the same place and drink the same water, different people have different experiences. If you have created the cause to be poor and sickly, even if you go to a very healthy and rich country you will be singled out among all the healthy and happy people, and you will experience the sickness, pain, and destitution that is the ripening of your previous karma.

The worst condition is to be dominated by ignorance, with no awareness and no confidence in cause and effect; that will produce a meaningless life.

The point of all these quotations and of this entire section of the *Lamrim Chenmo* is to stress the importance of studying and understanding karma. Based upon that understanding you will develop trust in the cause and effect of karma. With that foundation you will begin to recognize how much negative karma you have created in the past, and how much you continue to create—even in this excellent rebirth in which you have the intelligence and capacity to distinguish between good and bad. You will realize how this negative karma will continue to harm you for a long time. Once you understand this you will try to free yourself from those miserable results. You will try to purify past actions, and turning in a new direction, you will strongly resist creating additional negative actions in the future. The strong wish to eliminate past negative karma so that you will not have to meet its results leads us to the next section: the way to purify previous negative actions.

b" In particular, how to purify by means of the four opponent powers

When you have strong faith in karma, you naturally try to eliminate nonvirtue. But even when you make an effort to avoid being tarnished by unwholesome behavior, you may still create some negative karma out of carelessness, or as the result of intense afflictions such as hatred or attachment. Most beings are continuously creating negative actions because of the power of karma and the afflictions. Even when you are sincerely practicing the spiritual path, your mind is not completely purified until the end of the journey. When such faults arise you should not disregard them as if they did not matter, or leave them to ripen without any attempt to purify that negative potential. As soon as such downfalls occur, you should try to cleanse or destroy these negative karmas by applying the appropriate remedies. For that purpose the kind Buddha taught many different methods to purify negative actions.

Just as there are different levels of virtuous and nonvirtuous actions, there are different levels of antidotes to nonvirtue. First of all, we have three levels of vows, which are themselves powerful countermeasures to nonvirtue: prātimokṣa vows, bodhisattva vows, and tantric vows. Just in terms of the prātimokṣa vows, there are eight levels of vows, including lay vows, one-day vows, novice vows, and vows of a fully ordained monk or nun.[3] All of these are methods to counter faults, to restrain yourself from committing harmful deeds in the future. Taking a vow means that you recognize that certain attitudes and actions are harmful, and you commit yourself to cleaning up and preventing those actions in the future.

In the Mahayana teaching we also have the bodhisattva path and the tantric path. Here too we have sets of vows that steer us away from actions that obstruct our progress on those paths and guide us in a positive direction. All of these vows and precepts at the different levels of practice are methods of counteracting and preventing negative karma.

When a person who has taken a vow violates the promise he or she has made, we call this a *downfall.* We use this image of falling down because by violating your precepts you cause yourself to fall into a bad situation in the future. Each level of vows includes methods to remedy such downfalls; just as one falls to the ground, so there is also a method to get back up. It is because of our own actions that we fall into disastrous situations, and it is by our own actions that we can pull ourselves out of those circumstances. In other words, the negative karmic seeds we have planted are not permanent. They are not something that cannot be removed. All of them can be purified if you use the proper method and make the proper effort.

For those who have taken a vow and then violated their commitments, the method of purifying that downfall is explained within the context of the vow itself. Each of the three systems of vows has its own methods for rectifying downfalls. Usually these remedies are centered around special rituals. When you take one of the three levels of vows you should learn these methods and then apply them whenever it is necessary.

There are also nonvirtuous actions performed by those who have not taken vows. How do you purify these? The method for purifying general nonvirtuous actions is to apply the four powers. These four are explained in the *Sutra Giving the Four Teachings (Catur-dharma-nirdeśa-sūtra).* Here the Buddha is speaking directly to Maitreya, and he tells him that if you make use of these four powers, all the negative karma that you have accumulated can be subdued, mitigated, and completely destroyed:

> Maitreya, when a bodhisattva, a great being, possesses these four teachings, nonvirtuous actions that are performed and accumulated will be overcome. What are these four? They are the power of remorse, the power of the antidote, the power of turning away from faults, and the power of the basis.

The first of these four is the power of remorse. This is regret directed toward negative karmas you have created in the past. The second is the power of the antidote. If you realize that you have inadvertantly eaten poison, first you feel great regret that you have put yourself in serious danger. Then you immediately apply an antidote to counteract the effects of the poison. The antidotes to nonvirtuous actions are meritorious practices such as meditation, prostrations, and the recitation of mantras and prayers.

Third is the power of restraint, the power of turning away from committing those same misdeeds in the future. If you survive eating poisoned food you will naturally make a firm resolve, "I will never eat that again."

Fourth is the power of the foundation, or basis; this is also known as the power of reliance. Since you have created a negative cause that may have very severe consequences, you look for a basis of protection, someone you can rely on to protect you from the results of your negative actions. The most reliable source of refuge and protection is the Three Jewels.

If you practice these four powers to counteract negative karma, there is no nonvirtuous action that cannot be purified. Even if you have commited great negative actions, if you have enough time and energy to apply these opponent powers seriously and intensively, even those grave negative potentials can be destroyed completely. And even if you are not able to destroy a karmic potential from the root, you can at least suppress it so that it is not able to bring its result in the near future, or you can mitigate it so that its result is very mild. As you can see, there are many different levels at which this practice can be effective, but the point is to interrupt the ripening of harmful results.

Remember that karma that is both done and accumulated is called *definite karma*.[4] Its results are certain to be experienced because it was motivated by a strong intention and fully carried out with a concentrated effort. We say that such actions are definite karma because in general there is no way of avoiding their consequences. They will definitely bring their results. However, if you properly and sincerely apply these four powers, you will be able to subdue or destroy even definite karma: those actions which were both done and accumulated. Since this is true of definite karma, obviously it is also true of *indefinite karma,* which is much weaker.

1" The first power: remorse

The first power is generating profound regret for the negative actions you have performed. When you analyze your current situation based on an understanding of samsaric causality and its beginningless nature, you can infer that you must have already created a mountain of nonvirtuous karma. First, focus on your present life and analyze what kinds of actions with what kinds of motivations you perform every day. Ask yourself, "From the time I woke up until the time I went to bed, what kind of actions have I done today?" When you look into the situation carefully, you will see that your time is filled with negative actions. If you don't check up, you will not recognize this problem.

Then realize that so far you have considered only one day of your present life. Even now, while you are trying to practice the Dharma and are making every effort to act intelligently and beneficially, all kinds of afflictions still drive you to act in harmful ways. This is because your mind is so habituated to acting out of attachment, malice, and a basic misunderstanding of your true nature. Your present life is one in which you are practicing Dharma; you know the difference between right and wrong and you are at least trying to live a virtuous life. Nevertheless, every day you are accumulating more and more nonvirtue. Now imagine the wealth of misdeeds you must have collected during those innumerable lives when you totally lacked this level of intelligence or understanding. Consider how all the negative karma produced since beginningless time must be virtually limitless.

In order to produce a heartfelt sense of remorse, you should think about and meditate on the painful consequences that this mountain of negative potential will produce. Contemplate how this vast accumulation of negative potential will bring forth the three types of suffering results: fruitional results, results corresponding to their cause, and environmental results. These contemplations will lead you to a profound regret for all of these actions. That sincere remorse is the first of the four powers of purification.

Tsongkhapa tells us that when you are actually putting these four powers into practice, you can cultivate remorse through two different confession rituals. The *Sutra of the Golden Light (Suvarṇa-prabhāsa-sūtra)* is a tantric text that lays out various methods and procedures for confession. Then there is the short ritual we call the *Confession to the Thirty-five Buddhas*—from the *Sutra of the Three Aggregates (Ārya-tri-skandha-nāma-mahāyāna-sūtra)*—which was the ritual of confession that Tsongkhapa himself used.

In the *Confession to the Thirty-five Buddhas* you invoke the thirty-five tathāgatas and in front of them you confess and purify your negative actions. You clearly imagine them in front of you and then recite their names. In their presence you confess each of the negative actions you have done in the past, are doing in the present, and will do in the future. With your body you bow down to these buddhas, demonstrating your reverence, and remembering the unsurpassed qualities of the body, speech, and mind of the buddhas. Then, you mentally generate a strong sense of remorse for all of the harmful deeds you have done. You generate a countervailing force of positive potential by admiring the vast amount of beneficial actions that have been created by the buddhas, bodhisattvas, śrāvakas, pratyekabuddhas, and all other ordinary individuals who are performing virtuous activity. You rejoice in their merits and aspire to follow in their footsteps. Finally you dedicate the merits of your confession to the benefit of all sentient beings.

Remember that, unlike in many other religions, the Buddha is not a god who decides on the nature of sin and sits in judgment of your actions. The Buddha cannot take away your negative karma in the same way that someone can pull a thorn out of your foot. But during his career as a bodhisattva, the future Buddha made a special dedication of his vast merit with the prayer, "In the future, when I become a buddha, may all beings who call my name be purified of their negative karma, and by this blessing may all good things come to them." By the power of this dedication you can receive those blessings by reciting, with faith, the names of these thirty-five buddhas in order to purify your negative actions.

If you cannot do such an elaborate visualization, with all the thirty-five buddhas arrayed in front of you, you can do this purification practice in a simplified form. Imagine Śākyamuni Buddha alone, as a representative of all these buddhas, with all their power united in him, and then continue with the confession practice.

The key point in this purification practice is to generate the four powers sincerely in your own mind; that is the most important thing. Whether or not you imagine all these thirty-five buddhas in the space before you is not so important. The buddhas have perfect omniscience so wherever they may be, when someone invites them and seeks their help, they will be there.

On the sutra path, this kind of powerful practice can purify many negative actions. We also have certain tantric practices, such as the recitation of the mantra of Vajrasattva, that are very powerful methods of purification. But for any of these methods to be effective, these four powers must be produced in the mind. You must begin by seeing the fault of a harmful action, and based on that you must produce genuine remorse. Out of that sincere sense of regret you must resolve that you will not repeat that action in the future, and then you have to apply a strong antidote. These powers must be based on a foundation of trust and confidence in the Three Jewels of refuge. Without these four powers, which actually transform your mind, merely inviting the buddhas and asking them to do something to help you will not work. The buddhas did not create your negative karma and they cannot purify it for you. It is up to you to do the work of turning your mind in the right direction.

To summarize, the power of remorse is a strong attitude of aversion, renunciation, and opposition to the negative action you have committed. It is the same feeling of regret you would have if you realized you had just eaten poison. Once you see the dangerous consequences of what you have done, you feel profound regret and you resolve never to do that again. But until you see the faults and disadvantages of an action, you will not regret it. Therefore, producing sincere remorse depends on the study of karma and its results. The better you understand the cause and effect of karma, the more effective will be your application of the four powers of purification. If you lack this first power of remorse, the remaining three powers will be weak and ineffective.

2" The second power: applying antidotes

Those people who have just discovered that they have eaten poison and feel the toxins beginning to work in their stomach naturally think, "How can I remove this great danger?" They are ready to do whatever it takes to save themselves from the consequences of their foolish action. They will look for a good doctor with an effective antidote and when they find such an antidote they will be ready to take it.

When this same kind of powerful remorse arises with regard to your own past negative deeds, you are ready to seek out the antidote and to apply it when you find it. The power of applying the antidote offers various methods that can counteract the poison of our past nonvirtuous deeds. In this section six types of antidotes are introduced, but this is not an exhaustive list; there can be many other methods. These are six examples presented according to the sutras and according to Śāntideva's *Compendium of Trainings (Śikṣā-samuccaya).*

1. *Relying on the profound sutras.* The first type of antidote relies on scriptures such as the *Perfection of Wisdom Sutras.* By reading, memorizing, listening to teachings, or explaining to others these sutras, you can purify negative karma. The main subject of these sutras is emptiness, the ultimate nature of reality. Therefore, praising, reading, or hearing these texts has the power to purify negative karma.

In Tibet, even among lay people, this kind of practice was common. Many families would keep the twelve volumes of the *Perfection of Wisdom Sutras* in their house and they would try to recite the text out loud once a year. If they could not read it themselves, they would invite monks from the local monastery to visit their house and recite the texts while the family sat respectfully and listened. This would take several days, during which the family would feed the monks and make offerings. This kind of practice is recommended in the sutras themselves: reading such holy texts—the words of the Buddha—or listening while someone else recites them, plants positive karmic seeds on your mental continuum, and it has a special power to purify negative seeds.

2. *Having an interest in emptiness.* The subject of the *Perfection of Wisdom Sutras*

is the wisdom that realizes emptiness, the ultimate nature of phenomena. Of course the realization of emptiness is the supreme weapon cutting out all negativities, like the axe which cuts the poisonous tree from the root. Ultimately, all negative mental states and actions arise from ignorance, which is not knowing the truth. Realization of the truth severs the root of ignorance, which thereby severs all the negative karma that stems from that ignorance. This is why we say that the best antidote, the direct antidote, the ultimate weapon against negative karmic seeds, is the realization of emptiness.

"Having an interest in emptiness" means having confidence and conviction that emptiness is indeed the ultimate mode of being of the self and of phenomena. You gain this conviction by studying the *Perfection of Wisdom* and other sutras, the commentaries of the great masters such as Nāgārjuna and Candrakīrti, and by applying your own analytical wisdom to comprehend the meaning of emptiness. Then you meditate on that meaning until you gain a direct realization of it. Even if you do not yet understand the meaning of emptiness, you should try to have faith that this teaching of the Buddha is not mistaken. You should aspire to understand it in the future, and expect that you will eventually gain the full realization. "Having an interest in emptiness" means approaching this profound teaching with that kind of positive attitude, rather than thinking, "This does not make sense."

Of course emptiness, *śūnyatā* in Sanskrit, is essentially pure, primordially pure. Therefore, the afflictions, the obscurations within the mind, have a dependent nature—they are temporary, adventitious, created by causes and conditions. They are not intrinsic or inseparable aspects of mind, but are like clouds that pass over and temporarily obscure the mind. In its ultimate nature, one's own mental continuum is naturally, primordially pure from the beginning. Contemplating and meditating on that empty and luminous nature of ultimate reality and relying on the primordially pure nature of mind is also one of the methods of purification.

Āryadeva says:[5]

> Those of little merit would not even
> Entertain doubts that things are ultimately empty.
> Even suspicion that objects are empty
> Wrecks the seeds of cyclic existence.

The mere *suspicion* that ultimately things are empty of inherent existence has the power to shake the foundations of cyclic existence. It is the first glimpse of the truth, and it opens the way to the direct realization of emptiness, which destroys the karmic seeds that cause our suffering. Only the fortunate ones, those with a great accumulation of merit, will be able to produce this doubt about the ultimate mode of being, this suspicion that things lack inherent existence. Those with little merit will never even think about this.

But those fortunate ones who study, think about, analyze, and meditate on emptiness will begin to suspect, "Maybe things are not as solid as they seem. Perhaps, ultimately things are empty of inherent existence." Even this much suspicion that the teaching on emptiness may be true can lead to the complete purification of all negative karmic seeds and the obstacles to liberation.

3. *Relying on recitation.* This refers to purification by means of reciting certain mantras in the context of special rituals. The most common mantra of purification in tantric practice is the one hundred–syllable mantra of Vajrasattva. Those who have received an initiation into the practice of Vajrasattva can use this method. Vajrasattva is invited from his divine abode in a pure land. He comes to the top of your head, and after you pay him respect and make offerings, you confess your misdeeds and request him to purify your negative karma. Then you recite the mantra, with the one hundred syllables circling at the heart of Vajrasattva, and as you repeat the mantra a stream of light and nectar flows down from the mantra at Vajrasattva's heart. This stream enters your heart, and as it fills your body it pushes out all negativities and obscurations in the form of black filth, and replaces it with the white nectar of bliss and emptiness. This is one example of the special kind of ritual taught in the tantric scriptures that can be utilized as a method of purification.

The purifying power of recitation is praised in the *Tantra Requested by Subāhu (Subāhu-paripṛcchā-tantra):*

> Just as the flames of a fire spreading through a spring forest,
> Raging out of control, incinerate all the underbrush,
> The winds of ethical conduct fan the fire of recitation,
> And the flames of great effort burn up seeds of nonvirtue.
>
> Just as the rays of the sun striking the snow
> Melt it with irresistible brilliance,
> The snow of nonvirtuous action melts away when struck
> By the rays of the sun of ethical conduct and recitation.
>
> Just as lighting a lamp in pitch blackness
> Clears away every last bit of the darkness,
> So the darkness of nonvirtue accumulated in thousands of lifetimes,
> Is quickly cleared away by the lamp of recitation.

The first stanza says that the combination of pure conduct and the recitation of mantras and special prayers, intensified by diligent effort, burns up the seeds of negative karma in the same way that a raging forest fire turns an entire forest to ash. In the context of this tantric text, ethical discipline refers particularly to taking and keeping the tantric vows. When these are kept purely, it intensifies the power of your tantric recitations, just as a strong wind whips up the flames of a fire. Persevering effort spreads the purifying power of the recitation to all the seeds of negative karma, just as the tongues of flame effortlessly leap from tree to tree, spreading the fire in every direction.

The imagery of this scripture indicates just how important this method of recitation is for the practice of purifying nonvirtue. Whether you recite the *Confession to the Thirty-five Buddhas,* or use the tantric method of the one hundred–syllable mantra of Vajrasattva, the important thing is to practice these rituals in the manner in which they were taught, and to apply them diligently and from the heart. When you practice recitation properly and sincerely, it has the power to purify all the powerful negative potential you have amassed over many lifetimes.

How long do you have to recite such mantras and prayers? Until you see a certain kind of sign or indication that your negative karma has been purified. Before you enter onto the tantric path, or undertake any grand virtuous endeavor such as a meditation retreat, you should prepare by purifying negative karma. You do this by entering a special preparatory retreat to practice a purification ritual, such as that of Vajrasattva. For how long do you have to do this preparatory purification practice? Until there is some sign of success.

What are some of the signs that your purification practice is working? The text called the *Formula of Exhortation (sKul byed kyi gzungs)* lists the following images that you might see in a dream. Your purification is having some success if you dream any of the following: vomiting bad food; drinking such foods as milk or yoghurt; again, vomiting; seeing the sun and moon; walking in space; seeing a blazing fire; being able to subdue a water buffalo; being able to subdue a dark or demonic person (although the text says "black man" here, it is not a racial description, but refers to the utterly black countenance of a demonic figure); seeing a Sangha consisting of bhikṣus or bhikṣuṇīs; seeing a plant which produces a milk-like substance—perhaps milkweed—sometimes used in tantric rituals; riding on an elephant; climbing to the top of a mountain or a high throne supported by lions; or listening to Dharma teachings.

The point is not to get attached to these auspicious signs and feel superior if you happen to have a dream like this. These signs have meaning only if you are engaged in an intensive purification practice, and if the signs begin to appear with some frequency. Until that happens you should continue to work energetically to purify past negative karma.

4. *Relying on images.* Once you have generated sincere faith in the perfected qualities of the Buddha, you naturally want to show respect to the Buddha's body, speech, and mind. Since you too want to attain perfect buddhahood, you need to purify nonvirtues and accumulate merits. One method to do that is to create images of the buddhas in the form of statues, thangkas, *tsa-tsas,* and other representations of their body, speech, and mind. When it is done out of faith, the physical activity of creating such images is an effective method of purification, especially of bodily negative karma.

In Tibet it was common before embarking on a major tantric practice, such as a three-year retreat, to make many tsa-tsas—small clay images of a meditational deity—as a means of purification. Usually a practitioner would make one hundred thousand of them, using a mold to stamp them out.

5. *Relying on worship.* This includes a variety of spiritual activities through which we honor and demonstrate our respect for the buddhas. The central practice is making offerings of various substances to the buddhas, and to images that represent the buddhas. For example, you can offer clothing to a statue of the Buddha; in Tibet we traditionally offered special brocade garments. Or you can offer the gold leaf to gild a statue, or pure water, as when we offer water bowls on the altar every day, or you can offer just one flower. What you offer does not matter as much as the attitude with which you offer it, because the statue does not need any of these things. The purpose is to advance your own spiritual development by purifying past negative actions and accumulating the positive potential of merit.

6. *Relying on names.* This is related to the third method, "relying on recitation," and it refers to reciting, hearing, and remembering the names of the buddhas and great bodhisattvas. In Tibetan culture there were many examples of this practice, such as carving the mantra of Avalokiteśvara, *Oṃ māṇi padme hūṃ,* on stones all over the country, or setting out prayer flags imprinted with prayers and mantras. These spiritual artifacts would constantly remind people of the buddhas, and bring to their minds the names of Avalokiteśvara or Mañjuśrī. Even illiterate people would see an image painted on a stone by a roadside and it would bring to their mind Avalokiteśvara, the bodhisattva of compassion.

In Tibet the butchers were a special caste, something like the outcastes of India. They had faith in the Dharma, they believed in karma and rebirth, and they understood that they were doing the worst kind of job and committing serious nonvirtue. They did not enjoy killing, but their livelihood depended on it, and they really didn't have much choice. They were born into that caste and that was the only way they could feed their children and their parents. So when they were going to kill an animal, let's say a sheep, they would chant the one hundred–syllable mantra of Vajrasattva out loud, so that they themselves would hear it and the sheep who was about to die would hear it also. Then they killed the animal. In this way they mitigated the strength of that karma of killing; they made it an incomplete karma of killing because they lacked a strong motivation to kill. Their action had no enjoyment or satisfaction in the result because they didn't really want to kill those animals. On the contrary, there was a reluctance to kill, but they were forced to do it by their circumstances.

Not only did they lack the motivation to kill, but by bringing to mind the name of Vajrasattva as they did the act, they were already applying a strong antidote to their action. This is a good example of relying on the name of a buddha as a powerful antidote to negative action.

Many people recite mantras out loud to their pets, or when they encounter other animals. It is believed that when the animal hears these powerful sounds having connection to the buddhas, seeds of positive potential are planted in its mind. Therefore, people think, "Maybe this will help them. Maybe they will not be born again in a lower realm."

The practice of reciting *Oṃ māṇi padme hūṃ,* the mantra of Avalokiteśvara, was practically universal in Tibet. The effectiveness of these syllables to purify negative karma comes from the dedication that Avalokiteśvara himself made. He empowered his own name by praying that whoever recited it with sincere faith would receive blessings.

All six of these practices are effective methods of purifying past karma when they are based on a deep understanding of the perfected qualities of buddhahood. You need to know the nature of a buddha's activity—its wisdom, compassion, and power—and how all of a buddha's actions are for the sake of other beings. When your practice is based on that understanding, then building images or reciting the names of the buddhas can be of great benefit to yourself and others. Tsongkhapa emphasizes that these are the purification practices that are specifically mentioned in Śāntideva's *Compendium of Trainings,* but there are many others as well.

3" The third power: turning away from faults

The third power is the resolve to avoid performing unwholesome actions in the future. Having understood the disadvantages of collecting negative karma, you make a decisive commitment to restrain yourself from doing any of the ten nonvirtuous actions. This resolve is rooted in your understanding of the consequences of each of these harmful actions, and it leads to a very concentrated determination to avoid them in the future. Sometimes this resolution is even expressed out loud, in words.

If you see the faults of your previous bad actions and you feel sincere regret, and based upon that you resolve that you will not repeat those actions, that resolve, that turning away, has the power to destroy many nonvirtuous karmic seeds. The *Sun Essence Sutra* teaches that such well-grounded restraint can destroy whatever unwholesome karma you have created, as well as the afflictions, and obstacles to the Dharma. Whether you did these actions yourself, caused others to do them, or merely rejoiced in seeing them done—all these previously created nonvirtues can be destroyed by this power of turning away from nonvirtue.

However, if the resolution to refrain from nonvirtue in the future is not made with sincerity, it becomes mere words. For example, according to the prātimokṣa vows of bhikṣus like myself, we have a ritual of confession twice each month. All the Sangha members at a monastic institution gather together to reflect on what negative actions they have done during that month. In the course of the ritual they confess to each other the downfalls they have committed. During the ritual each monk or nun responds to a set of questions: "Have you seen your own misdeeds?" To which one responds, "Yes, I have seen them." Then comes the question, "In the future will you refrain from them?" Response: "Yes, I will refrain."

When you are making this kind of confession, if the words come from deep in the heart—if you are thinking with sincere regret about your actions and genuinely committing to avoid them in the future—*that* is the real confession. However, if you respond by saying the right things, but in your heart there is no real remorse and no genuine resolve, then your confession is nothing but words.

Therefore, in the Vinaya we are taught to reflect on our past deeds. At the end of every day you should recall your actions: which ones were on the unwholesome side, which ones were beneficial, even examining what kind of dreams you had that night. This was a famous practice of the great Kadampa masters. You can sit at the end of the day with a pile of stones and recall your activities for that day. When you see a virtuous action, you put a white stone on the table. When you see a nonvirtue, put a black stone. When you are done, check to see which of the two piles of stones is bigger. If the black stones make a bigger pile, you have something to worry about. If the white stones are more numerous, maybe you can relax a little bit. If there are no black stones at all you may feel quite pleasant.

If you are a serious practitioner, you will keep your body, speech, and mind pure and clean. Since afflictions like attachment, hatred, jealousy, and pride are so deeply ingrained in your mind-stream, and are always ready to rise out of habit, it is difficult to put a stop to negative behavior all at once. But even if you cannot completely stop a bad habit, you can at least resolve to diminish its frequency, to lessen it as much as you can. For example, at the time of confessing and applying the antidotes you can resolve, "Instead of getting angry ten times a day, I will not do so more than nine times, or eight times." Later, you can reduce the number even more. The point is to make a decision that you will improve in the future, and then follow through with that resolve. In this way you reduce negative actions and the positive antidotes are strengthened.

You should look into your own situation and make a judgment about which behaviors you can stop completely and which you can only gradually reduce. But making the decision that you will eventually stop is the most important thing. The arising of this kind of strong resolve depends on the first power: remorse. It requires you to see that activity as a fault, and to regret doing it. The strength of your resolve to turn away from an action will ultimately depend on the strength of the regret you feel for having done it. And all of these four powers of purification depend on a lucid understanding of the cause and effect of karma. You can recite the *Sutra of Confession* a thousand times each day, but without an understanding of the benefit and harm of virtue and nonvirtue you will merely be saying the words.

4" The fourth power: reliance

In order to succeed in this practice of purifying past negative karma and refraining from it in the future, you need to base your efforts on a source of reliance and reinforce it with other supports. The basis of reliance is taking refuge in the Three Jewels: the Buddha, Dharma, and Sangha. In fact, merely taking refuge in them with heartfelt trust and a willingness to rely on the Three Jewels will itself purify many negative karmas.

Of course the Buddha's teaching is always pure and free of any causes of unwholesome action. When you take refuge and place your trust in the Dharma, the way of the Buddha, you are placing yourself in reliable hands, and you will be following a path that leads only to virtuous actions and happy results. By trusting in the Sangha you choose as your companions those who share in your aspirations. Your central relationships and friendships are with people who are also striving to perform virtue and purify nonvirtue, and this too has a powerful influence on how you lead your life.

So the Three Jewels of refuge are the first support of your practice of purification. The second is meditation on bodhicitta. Bodhicitta means wanting to attain the highest goal of buddhahood in order to help other sentient beings. You want to help them because you see how they are trapped in a seemingly endless cycle of misery, which is perpetuated by their own misunderstanding, attachment, and hatred. You see how these mental afflictions produce wrong action, and how this cycle of afflictions and harmful action causes their lives of misery to go on and on.

You empathize with these suffering sentient beings and you want to help them. In order to rescue them from the mire of cyclic existence, you want to lead them to perfect buddhahood. In order to do that, you know that you yourself must first obtain enlightenment. This is what bodhicitta means: wanting to save all other living beings, and in order to do that, wanting to quickly become a perfect being oneself, wanting to attain the perfect wisdom, perfect compassion, and perfect power of a buddha. Once you have completed these qualities of a buddha, you can of course be of immeasurable benefit to all beings. Until then, the help you can offer will be quite limited.

This altruistic mind of bodhicitta is itself a powerful tool to remove negative karma. Describing the power of bodhicitta, Śāntideva says in *Engaging in the Bodhisattva Deeds:*

> Just like the fire at the end of an age,
> It instantly consumes all great nonvirtue.[6]

Once bodhicitta arises, in every moment many negative karmas can be destroyed. Bodhicitta has that kind of power because negative karma comes from harming other beings and taking pleasure in their suffering. Bodhicitta is precisely the opposite attitude. It is the wish for all living beings to have the highest happiness. It is the wish to lead all beings to freedom from all misery. It is the wish to quickly obtain enlightenment for that purpose. Such an attitude of course has great power. Therefore, meditating on bodhicitta, together with taking refuge in the Three Jewels, constitute the power of reliance.

The Buddha taught many ways to purify negative karma in general. Among these, the complete antidote requires that all four of these powers are fully accomplished; all four must be working in harmony. Under those circumstances, with these four fully actualized, you can destroy many mountains of negative karma.

There are several mechanisms by means of which the purification of negative karma can take place. The first way in which nonvirtues are purified is that powerful negative karmic seeds, which have the potential to create a horrible rebirth, are transformed into causes of a birth that is not so bad. In other words, the harshness of the negative results can be lessened. A second possibility is that you are born in a lower realm, but you do not experience the pain and suffering of that realm. And the third mechanism by which purification can work is that the karma to be born in a suffering rebirth ripens into nothing more than a headache in this life. In other words, heavy karma that could have had disastrous results is so attenuated that it yields only a small discomfort. Finally, the need to experience suffering for a long time can be reduced to a very brief encounter with that suffering.

There is no absolute rule or way to know for sure how the process of purification will operate, because it depends on a variety of factors: whether the purification was done with all four powers complete, how intensively it was done, and for how long it was done. The essential point is that whatever unwholesome action you have done can definitely be purified. There is no negative karma that cannot be purified. There is no such thing as a permanent, absolute sin. All unwholesome actions are temporary events, created by one's own mind and body. If you apply the proper antidote they can be removed. Some of them can be destroyed from the root. Others may be pushed into the far distant future. Still others will not meet the conditions to bring forth their results. And some will be attenuated, so the results will be less intense, shorter in duration, or reduced to insignificance.

But if that is true, a question arises. It says in the sutras and in the Vinaya that "karma can never be lost, even in one hundred eons." In other words, karma will not fade away and ultimately you have to experience the result. How is it that the purification of karma by this use of antidotes does not contradict the scriptures?

The answer is that the sutra is talking about karma to which you have not applied an antidote. If you have not purified a karma to any degree by means of the four powers, then that karmic seed will certainly yield its result, no matter how long it takes. But if you have cultivated the four powers as an antidote, you can destroy the seeds and prevent any negative results. This is true even of so-called *definite* karma.

This is the view of the Mahayana system: no matter how powerful a negative karma may be, if the proper antidote is applied, it can be purified. The Vaibhāṣika and some other Hinayana schools disagree with this and say that the most powerful negative karma, such as the five automatic transgressions, cannot be purified during the life in which they are committed.[7] These points are explained by Haribhadra in his *Long Explanation of the Perfection of Wisdom Sutra in Eight Thousand Lines (Abhisamayālaṃkārāloka):*

> Thus, whatever has the nature of diminishing when it is brought into the proximity of the antidotes can be permanently extinguished by the antidotes. An example of this is the tarnish on gold. According to that logic, downfalls that occur out of arrogance, even such powerful negative actions as wrong view, which are obstructions to the holy Dharma, can be utterly extinguished.
>
> You should understand such statements from scripture as, "no karma at all will be lost, even in one hundred eons," as referring to karma for which the antidotes have not been cultivated. If that were not the case, it would contradict reason and contradict many sutras.
>
> And you should understand the statement that "there is karma that will definitely be experienced" as also referring to karma for which you have not cultivated the antidotes. "Karma that is not definite" should be distinguished as karma that only sometimes yields results, even when you have not cultivated any antidotes.

The argument here is that nonvirtuous karmic seeds are to the antidotes as water is to heat: as water gets closer and more exposed to the source of heat it gradually evaporates and diminishes. That is the *nature* of water: to diminish in proportion to its exposure to a source of heat. Like that, the nature of nonvirtuous karmic seeds is to diminish in proportion to their exposure to correct antidotes like the four powers. Whatever has that nature can be completely eliminated. If you apply enough heat, water can be completely evaporated. If you apply the antidotes with sufficient intensity for a long enough time, the seeds of nonvirtue can be totally expunged. That is their nature.

I used the example of water and heat. The example Haribhadra uses is the tarnish on gold. The tarnish is an impurity that can be removed gradually, in proportion to the effort you put into the cleaning process. Its nature is that ultimately it can be completely removed. Similarly, the nature of one's own negative karma is that it can be removed gradually, in proportion to the effort you put into cultivating the antidotes. Ultimately, it can be completely eliminated.

This is the same logical argument that Dharmakīrti uses in his *Commentary on the "Compendium of Valid Cognition" (Pramāṇa-vārttika-kārikā)* to prove that enlightenment is possible. Liberation, the complete exhaustion of suffering, is possible. The reason is that the cause of suffering is karma, and the cause of karma is *kleśa,* the obscuring afflictions, which are themselves rooted in ignorance. Is that root destroyable or not? Does that root have an antidote or not?

The answer is yes. It is the *nature* of ignorance and all the afflictions that arise from ignorance that they naturally diminish as they come into proximity with, or are affected by, their antidotes. The more and more the antidotes are cultivated and applied, the weaker and weaker the afflictions become. That is their nature. And whatever has that nature can ultimately be completely removed. Therefore, there can be the total cessation of ignorance, of the obscuring afflictions, and thereby of suffering. That cessation is emancipation.[8]

By this reasoning it is clear that when the Buddha speaks of "karma that cannot be destroyed" he means karma that has not been touched by correct antidotes. When the Buddha speaks of "karma that will definitely be experienced" because it is complete in both motivation and action, he means only that the results of such karma will definitely be experienced if the karmic seeds have not been touched by antidotes. And "karma that is not definite" is karma that is itself weak because it was originally performed in an incomplete way. It may or may not yield results, regardless of whether or not it is affected by antidotes. In short, karma that cannot be purified does not exist. Even karma that is called "definite" in the scriptures can be purified when a sufficient countervailing antidote is applied.

We can see that confession, remorse, restraint, resolve, and the practice of countervailing meritorious practices weaken the capacity of nonvirtuous karmic seeds to bring forth their results. Once karma has been damaged by these antidotes it will not be able to yield fruit, even if it meets the necessary conditions. This is the same as what happens when you plant a seed in the ground. If the seed rots, is burned, or eaten by birds, then no matter how much water, fertilizer, or sunlight there is, a sprout will not be produced.

Just as virtuous practice can destroy negative karma, certain negative actions can destroy the results of virtues you have created. One powerful destroyer of virtuous seeds is the wrong view that denies the cause and effect of karma. This view denies that virtue leads to happiness and nonvirtue leads to suffering, and holds that there is no experience after this life, so any kind of practice for the sake of future lives is therefore nonsense. As the Abhidharma says, this kind of wrong view cuts the roots of virtue.

The other powerful destroyer of virtue is anger and hatred toward other sentient beings. Even one moment of anger or hatred directed toward a bodhisattva will destroy the merits you have generated during many eons of virtuous practice. Śāntideva says in *Engaging in the Bodhisattva Deeds:*

> Whatever wonderful practice
> You have accumulated over thousands of eons,
> Such as practicing generosity and worshiping the buddhas,
> Will all be destroyed in one moment of anger.

In Bhāvaviveka's *Blaze of Reasons (Tarka-jvālā)* it says:

> Wrong view and malice weaken virtuous karma. Antidotes such as regret, restraint, and confession weaken the force of nonvirtuous karma. In such cases, even when the conditions are met, since the capacity of the virtuous or nonvirtuous seeds has been damaged, how could they bring forth results? Since all the necessary conditions have not come together, the time to maturation is changed [i.e. is made longer]. How can one say they have not been thoroughly pulled out from the root?
>
> As it is said, "By adhering to the holy Dharma, nonvirtuous karma that is certain to be experienced as a suffering rebirth will instead be experienced in this very life as an inconsequential result." And, "Moreover, due to these antidotes, the karma to be born in a lower rebirth will become a mere headache."
>
> If the question is raised: "If there is a result of a small headache, how can you say that the seed has been pulled out from the root?" the response is: "The fully complete results of such nonvirtuous karmas would be to experience the sufferings of the hell realms. However, [because of the antidotes] one does not even have to experience the most subtle pains of hell. In light of that, how can one say it has not been pulled out by the root? But since such minor results as a headache in this life do arise, how can one say that this karma is utterly without any results?"

Bhāvaviveka is saying that when karmic seeds are damaged by effective antidotes, their full results cannot arise, even when the other necessary conditions are met. Although you have not yet found the antidote that completely destroys the seeds of the afflictions, your practice of the antidotes has weakened the power of negative karmic seeds to bring results. Even when the other conditions come together, that karma cannot bring its full result. The central point here is that by applying the antidotes you can essentially destroy the ability of negative karmic seeds to ripen into their full, potential, negative consequences. You have not yet pulled out the seeds from the root—that is done only by realizations on the path of seeing and the path of meditation.[9] But you have weakened those seeds so that they will only yield very minor results, or their results have been put off to the far distant future.

We can see examples of this kind of karmic ripening in the lives of people around us. For example, in Tibet we would come across a very serious religious practitioner who spent his whole life practicing virtue, and yet his life seemed to be one continual mishap. His property would get stolen or destroyed in a fire, he would be plagued by chronic medical problems, and his life seemed to be one misfortune after another.

People would always ask, "How can so many bad things happen to such a pious and virtuous person?" Once you understand the dynamics of karma, you see that that person may have committed some very heavy negative karma—karma with the potential to ripen as rebirth in a terrible suffering realm. But he had prevented that severe result from coming about through the practice of purification. The small problems he meets in this life are insignificant compared to what he would have experienced if that negative karma had not been purified. In our Mahayana practice we even say prayers that our nonvirtuous seeds may ripen quickly as a result of our practice. And when they do, we are happy to meet adversity because we see it as an auspicious sign that our practice of purification is working.

Then there is the opposite case: people who spend their whole lives acting in evil ways and harming others, but during that lifetime they encounter nothing but success and good fortune. That is not a good sign! Right now, in this life, they are enjoying the results of some small merits. But when all that is finished—when they come to the end of this life—they will meet the results of the karma they have created.

Therefore, even if you make a great effort to accumulate merits, if you do not guard against the great destroyers of virtue such as hatred and wrong view, the virtuous seeds you have collected will not be able to bring their results. You must create merits. But you also must protect those virtuous seeds by avoiding destructive forces such as hatred, and by repairing nonvirtues you have already accumulated by applying antidotes such as the four opponent powers, confession, and so forth.

Another question is raised: "If it is possible to completely purify even the most powerful karma, why did the Buddha say in the sutras, 'except for the fruition of previous karma'?" This question is coming from the point of view of certain Hinayana schools that hold that the most powerful nonvirtuous actions—called *automatic transgressions,* which include killing your father, mother, or an arhat—cannot be purified in this life, so that the full results will definitely ripen. In the Mahayana system, even these automatic transgressions *can* be purified.

The questioner is implying that the words quoted from the sutra—"except for the fruition of previous karma"—mean that you cannot do anything about this previous heavy karma, such as purifying it by applying antidotes. That is a misunderstanding. In this passage, the intent of the Buddha is that you cannot do anything about karma that *has already ripened.* If you are born blind, or you suffer from some other disability because of some previous unwholesome action, that karma has already ripened in the form of your blindness. The Buddha was saying that it is extremely difficult to have any influence on that outcome by applying antidotes once that outcome has already occurred. It is too late. The karmic process has played itself out and the result has already ripened.

Interestingly, it does not say that it is *completely impossible,* but only that it is *very difficult* to purify or overcome that previous karma by applying an antidote. We can imagine a rare circumstance in which a person was born blind but later, as a result of virtuous practice, recovered his or her sight. In general, however, it is obviously quite difficult to change a result once it has ripened. However, *before* the result ripens, it is easy to prevent it from happening. The method to prevent unpleasant results from ripening is what we are talking about here. When that method is applied properly, you can purify any karma, no matter how heavy. That is what the Buddha meant by this statement.

Once again this point is supported by Bhāvaviveka in his *Blaze of Reasons:*

> Question: If it is the case that nonvirtuous karma can be totally eliminated, why does it say in the sutras, "with the exception of the fruition of previous karma."
>
> Response: In that teaching the Buddha intended to refer to karma in which the results have already been experienced in the form of such things as being born blind, one-eyed, crippled, lame, dumb, deaf, and so forth—in which case there is no ability to completely eliminate the results of such karma, which has already ripened.
>
> The intention that was the cause that created the negative karma *can* be completely eliminated when one acquires certain other intentions. This is illustrated by such teachings as the stories of Angulimāla, Ajātaśatru, Aśoka, Svaka, those who killed their fathers, and others.

> Question: If Ajātaśatru and those who killed their mothers had produced other, virtuous minds by the time they died, why was it that they did not eliminate that nonvirtuous karma and had to be born in Avīci hell?
>
> Response: It is taught that those beings were born in Avīci hell and so forth in order for them to develop confidence in karma and its results. It is not that they did not totally eliminate the remaining karma. They were born in the lowest hell and then were freed from there like a ball of silk that is dropped and then bounces right back up again. They were not touched by the strings of fire and everything else in hell. This shows, on the one hand, that it is possible to remove such nonvirtue completely from the root; and, on the other hand, that there is no karma that has no results whatsoever.

Bhāvaviveka agrees that it is difficult if not impossible to alter a karmic result once it has ripened, and that is what the Buddha meant when he said "with the exception of the fruition of previous karma." However, *before* the result comes to fruition you *can* damage or eliminate the cause, and therefore the karma *can* be purified. He says that, at the time of the cause, there was a certain negative intention that lay behind the negative action. Subsequently, if the actor acquires certain virtuous intentions, they can act as antidotes that destroy those previous karmas. These "certain virtuous intentions" are such things as practicing Dharma, meditating on bodhicitta, and other motivations that act as purifying antidotes.

Then Bhāvaviveka gives us a list of some individuals from the sutras who created the most powerful types of nonvirtue, but later in life adopted Buddhism and were able to purify those actions. Angulimāla killed 999 people because he was told by his teacher that if he killed one thousand he would be liberated. Then he met the Buddha—his one thousandth intended victim—received teachings from him, became a monk, and through his special practice of purification and cultivating wisdom, he actually attained arhatship.

Ajātaśatru was a prince who killed his father, King Bimbisāra. He later became a devoted practitioner of the Dharma. Although he was born in a hell realm when he died, he was there only briefly—like a ball that is dropped and then bounces right back up—and did not experience extreme suffering while he was there. Aśoka of course was the great Buddhist king who unified India in the third century B.C.E. He turned to Buddhism out of remorse after his army had slaughtered many thousands in a battle against the kingdom of Kaliṅga. As one of the greatest propagators of Buddhism in history, he accumulated great merits and was also able to purify his previous evil karma.

The message of all these stories is that if you have a sincere wish to purify past karma, and you apply yourself with diligent effort, through the combination of this capable human life and these wonderful teachings even those giant, most powerful karmas can be purified. Not only can you free yourself from falling into lower realms in the next rebirth, you can actually attain arhatship in this very life.

The questioner wants to know why, if they had truly purified their karma, Ajātaśatru and the others still had to be born in the hell realms. Karma and its results are extremely subtle and complex. Although he was born there, his body was not even touched by the fires of hell. The suffering experience of the hell realms—the main potential fruit of his evil actions—was destroyed. After a brief visit to hell he was again reborn in a high rebirth, similar to the way in which a ball thrown onto the ground bounces right back up. Nonetheless, although the antidotes destroyed the main fruit of his actions, the fact that he still had to be born in hell shows that it is not the case that karma does not have any result at all. It shows that there is still some misfortune that arises as a consequence of that negative karma, but the experience of severe suffering has been completely eliminated.

Because of the complexities of karma, every situation is different. In the above cases powerful negative karma was successfully purified. But for some people it does not work that way. In the *King of Concentrations Sutra* we have the example of King Śūradatta, who killed the future Buddha in one of his previous lives, when he was the bodhisattva Supuṣpacandra. It is taught that killing a bodhisattva is heavier negative karma than killing one hundred thousand ordinary sentient beings. This is because a bodhisattva has taken responsibility for the emancipation of all the beings in the universe, so when you kill a bodhisattva you are actually harming infinite beings.

When King Śūradatta realized his crime he felt profound remorse and set out to purify it. He built a grand stupa and worshiped it with offerings and all kinds of virtuous activities. Every day he confessed his action three times, and continued this for 950 billion years. During that time he maintained irreproachable ethical conduct. But even after doing all this, he was still born into Avīci hell. Of course in Buddhism the hells are not a permanent condition. You stay there until the result of your actions are exhausted. For King Śūradatta it meant he had to suffer for a vast amount of time, ten or twenty billion eons, having his eyes squeezed out, his bones crushed, and so forth.

Then the question arises: if you can practice confession intensely for millions of years and maintain perfectly pure ethical conduct, and still end up in Avīci hell for eons, doesn't this imply that confession is meaningless? No, it is not meaningless. If you did not do those purifying practices, the results would be still worse! King Śūradatta's practice actually cut down the length and severity of his suffering.

So there are many different factors that interact to determine how a purification practice will affect the ripening of karma. In general, by the combination of confession and restraint, by making a firm resolve, "From now on I will never do this again," negative karmas can be purified without any painful result remaining to be experienced.

However, this does not mean that you should think, "Okay, I will go ahead and do a little bit of this unwholesome action, because later I can apply the four powers and purify it." That way of thinking is no good. Even when negative karma is purified without remainder, there is a great difference between creating negative karma and then purifying it, and maintaining pure action from the beginning.

What is the difference? The *Bodhisattva Levels (Bodhisattva-bhūmi)* by Asaṅga says:

> When a root downfall occurs, by taking the bodhisattva vows it is possible to repair the infraction. However, it will not be possible to attain the first bodhisattva level in that lifetime.

If you break a vow with a root downfall, you can recover that vow by means of purification; you will not experience the suffering result of that downfall, such as being born into an inferior life. That part can be remedied by purification. But during that life you will not be able to obtain the first bodhisattva level, the first bodhisattva *bhūmi*. Even though the main result of your downfall will not have to be experienced, still there is a residual bad effect: achieving the first stage of an ārya bodhisattva will be pushed off into the future, which of course also pushes buddhahood into the distant future as well.

The *Sutra Gathering All the Threads (Sarva-vaidalya-saṃgraha-sūtra)* says:

> Mañjuśrī asked the Buddha: "Bhagavan, if someone, under the influence of a nonvirtuous friend, were to do something such as abandon the Dharma, how, Bhagavan, could such a person be liberated in this lifetime?"
>
> The Buddha responded to youthful Mañjuśrī this way: "Mañjuśrī, if you confessed your misdeeds three times a day, every day for seven years, it would be purified. Thereafter, it will take at least ten eons to attain the path of patience."

Here the Buddha is saying that even though you are able to purify the main result of that heavy karma, it will take a very long time to attain a higher realization. For example, it will take at least ten eons to attain the stage of "patience," which is a name for the third of the four levels of the path of preparation.

Therefore, the meaning of complete purification is that the negative karma is totally purified of its capacity to ripen into suffering results. However, the creation of hindrances to the development of the higher realizations is not purified. Performing negative actions will push such high realizations into the distant future, so it is very important not to create negative karma in the first place. Thinking, "It does not matter because I can purify it later" is incorrect.

For this reason, noble beings do not intentionally engage in even the slightest misdeeds, even at the risk of losing their lives. In any case, holding onto this life is not such a big concern for ārya beings. Life is bound to end sooner or later, so losing one's life is not a big deal. But they would never do anything to delay the attainment of realizations on the path. If there were not this difference between being pure from the beginning and purifying negativities by means of confession, then āryas would not need to act in this way.

We can see analogous situations in the world: hands, legs, or eyes that have never been injured are better and stronger than those that have been broken or damaged and then restored through medical treatment. No one ever has the thought, "Okay, I will do this very dangerous trick and break my leg, because with medical treatment I can recover." Limbs that have been broken are never quite the same as they were before; there is always some residual fault. Based on this understanding, you should make a strong effort not to commit negative actions. You should understand karma and its results, be aware of what you are doing, and maintain pure conduct from the beginning. Of course, if something bad happens that you can't help, then you should apply this method of purification.

As the *Collection of Indicative Verses* says:

> People who practice nonvirtue and do not gain merits,
> Who stray from the Dharma and hold to sacrilegious ways,
> Who possess nonvirtuous karma—they will fear death,
> Like someone setting out on a great river in a rotting boat.
>
> People who practice merits and avoid nonvirtue,
> Who practice the Dharma, the system of the holy ones,
> They will never fear death,
> Like sailing to the far shore in a sturdy boat.

This body can be an excellent boat to cross the river of cyclic existence, or it can be a leaky boat, which will fall apart as soon as it sets sail. If you do not use this body for virtuous, meritorious action, then it will be like the boat that breaks apart. And once it breaks up, it will sink into the deepest realms of suffering. That is why those who turn their body into a rotten boat have every reason to fear death. But those who accumulate merits by following the teachings of holy beings know that they can safely sail to the far shore of samsara, so at the time of death they have nothing to fear. Therefore, do not turn this precious body into a rotten, sinking boat. Do all that you can to develop the excellent qualities that can carry you to freedom.

There are people who speak sensible, virtuous-sounding words, but who display ethical conduct that is quite shameless. Even if you know very little Dharma, you should exercise what you know; you should put your knowledge into practice by casting off unwholesome behavior and taking up virtuous practice. That has far more meaning and purpose than speaking eloquently like a great pandit but hypocritically behaving without scruples.

We find this point in the *Collection of Indicative Verses:*

> Although they speak at length, making reasonable arguments,
> Careless people do not behave accordingly.
> Like a shepherd who counts other people's sheep,
> They do not attain the fortune of virtuous practice.
>
> Although of logical arguments they don't have much to say,
> Those who practice the Dharma, following what it says,
> Who eliminate attachment, hatred, and ignorance,
> Attain the fortune of virtuous practice.
>
> Those monks who enjoy being conscientious,
> And view carelessness with fear,
> Draw themselves out of bad rebirths,
> Like an elephant pulls itself out of the mud.
>
> Those monks who enjoy being conscientious,
> And view carelessness with fear,
> Shake off all nonvirtuous actions,
> Like the wind shakes leaves off the trees.

Nāgārjuna says in his *Friendly Letter:*

If you yearn for higher realms or emancipation,
Then please become accustomed to the right view.
For those people with wrong views, though they practice well,
All their results will include unbearable suffering.

Here Nāgārjuna is advising his friend, the king. He says that whether you wish to attain a higher rebirth in your next life, or you seek final liberation, you must cultivate the right view. As I have mentioned before, there are two kinds of right view. The first is the *ultimate* right view: realizing the emptiness of inherent existence. But here we are talking about *conventional* right view, which refers to trusting in the cause and effect of karma, realizing that virtuous karma brings happiness and nonvirtuous karma brings suffering. Nāgārjuna urges the king to cultivate his understanding of karma and to develop complete trust in the cause and effect relationship.

For those people who fail to do that—who hold stubbornly to the wrong view that there is no karma, no life after this one, and no such thing as liberation—they will create karma that will only result in suffering in future lives. They may appear to be doing some positive actions here and there, but their purpose, intention, and view is going completely in the wrong the direction, so even those actions will not be wholesome. The root of good results is this right view.

What Nāgārjuna is saying here is that it is indispensable, absolutely fundamental, to base your practice on this proper view of dependent arising and the cause and effect of karma. You must begin with an accurate understanding of wholesome and unwholesome karma as it is explained in the buddhist teachings; you must understand the natures of the two types of karma, how they arise from obscuring afflictions, and what kind of results they bring. Developing confidence and faith in this view of karma is indispensable for achieving any of the attainments of the three Buddhist vehicles. And all the goals that beings aspire to—happiness and pleasure in this life, a high rebirth in the next life, liberation from cyclic existence, or the highest enlightenment of buddhahood—all depend from the very beginning on this view of causality.

You should base your understanding first of all on the explanations that Tsongkhapa has given us here. Then you can extend your research to other scriptural sources that discuss the relationship of karma and its results. Some of these texts are the *Mindfulness of the Excellent Teaching*, the *Sutra of the Wise and the Foolish*, the *Hundred Actions Sutra*, the *Hundred Bodhisattva Stories (Bodhisattvāvadāna-kalpalatā)*, and certain sections of the Vinaya that also have stories explaining various details of karma. These are the main texts that explain these topics, and there are many other scriptures and commentaries that can deepen your understanding. Studying these, meditating on what they teach, listening to teachings, and learning from others will all contribute to your understanding, and finally you will achieve a stable, enduring certainty in these teachings on karma.

Once you have that stable certainty, which does not fade in and out under the influence of others, it will change your actions. You will not be distracted or bothered by what other people say, because you know that you are going in the proper direction. This is something that you should hold as having the greatest importance, because all of your future practice depends on this.

4

The Attitude of a Person of Small Scope

b) The measure of the attitude of a person of small spiritual scope
c) Clearing up misconceptions concerning the attitude of a person of small spiritual scope

b) The measure of the attitude of a person of small spiritual scope

In volume 1 we established that there are three levels of spiritual beings: the person of small scope, the person of intermediate scope, and the person of great scope. Everything we have discussed so far is part of training the mind in the stages of the path shared with persons of small capacity.[1] This training begins with seeing that this precious human rebirth has great potential, and if we use it properly we can achieve virtually any goal we seek. Then we contemplate that although this life is wonderful, it is impermanent—we are sure to die, and that death can come at any time. If we do not use this life wisely and create positive causes for a happy rebirth in the future, this great opportunity we have in our hands will have been wasted.

We meditate on the various sufferings that beings have to experience in the lower realms in order to generate concern, and even fear, that we might be born there. When that fear arises, the question we must ask is: "What can I do to protect myself from birth in those suffering realms?" The answer is to take refuge in the Three Jewels, because they have the power to protect us from such a suffering future. Once we have taken refuge and turned to the Buddha and his teaching for safe direction, we need to follow his instructions concerning karma and its results. That is the practice that will save us from falling into a lower rebirth, and avoiding a lower rebirth is the main goal of the being of small scope.

All of these stages of the path are taught in the context of the being of small scope, but they are integral to the paths of the two higher types of spiritual beings as well. That is why they are called the steps of the path *shared with* persons of small scope. As Nāgārjuna emphasized at the end of the previous chapter, gaining the correct understanding of karma, and living our lives in accordance with that understanding, is the indispensable foundation of all progress on the path. With that discussion we concluded the actual training to develop the attitude of the person of small spiritual scope.[2]

Now we ask, "How do you determine when you have actually acquired the attitude of the being of small scope? What is your attitude like at this point?" This topic serves as a kind of test to measure whether you have attained this attitude or not. You may discover that you have not even reached the level of the inferior being yet, because you find that the required thought has not yet arisen in your mind.

In the past you always had an interest in *this* life. You didn't need to make any effort or do any special practices to acquire an interest in living a long and happy life—acquiring wealth, fame, pleasure, and praise. The desire for these goals arose naturally, spontaneously, without any need to study or meditate. Any concern you had for future lives or higher rebirth—any interest you showed in the teachings, spiritual friends, and virtuous practice—was merely a weak, vague interest that was temporarily aroused by hearing the words of others or from reading books. It was not a spontaneous, uncontrived interest that arose from deep in your heart.

You have achieved the attitude of the person of small scope when these priorities are reversed—when your highest concern is acquiring a good rebirth in your next life, and your interest in the affairs of this life become secondary. When concern for what will happen in your next life spontaneously and naturally dominates your thoughts and actions, then you are on the path of the person of small scope.

At that point your attitude is similar to that of a man who has arrived in a city he is merely visiting; he plans to remain in that city for only about a year and then move on to a more permanent location elsewhere. Although that person will deal with the basic concerns of living in that city, his mind and energy will be focused mainly on the place he is going to *next,* because he is planning on staying there for a long time.

You were brought to this life by previous karma, and now that karma has ripened; there isn't very much you can do to change it. This is the time to turn your attention to your future life, because that is something you really can control. If you do not take the right steps now, you could wind up residing in a very unpleasant place for a long time.

Once your priorities are reversed like this, all activities done for the benefit of this life become incidental; your main job is to prepare for the future. When that reversal of concerns becomes the spontaneous nature of your mind, the actual attitude of the being of small scope has arisen. That is the measure of the being of small scope. Until then you are not even on the level of the inferior spiritual being; you are lower than inferior.

Yet even when that initial spiritual attitude does take hold in your mind, it is not enough; you have to stabilize that attitude. You have to continuously apply yourself to diligent practice in order to maintain this thought; otherwise you may lose it again. All of the details of the *Lamrim Chenmo* we have discussed so far—all of the meditations, reasonings, and exhortations—lead to this goal, this transformation of our attitude from concern for this life to focusing our energy on preparing for the future. You have reached this first plateau on the path to enlightenment when this change in your scope rises from deep in the heart—when it is not superficial or mere words, but becomes the fundamental motivating force in your life.

Tsongkhapa leads us through so many arguments, so many different points of view, so many quotations from the scriptures, in order to awaken this attitude in our hearts. Everything so far has been building toward this: the first major step that will lead us to the highest path.

c) Clearing up misconceptions concerning the attitude of a person of small spiritual scope

Now we have to clear up some misconceptions and misunderstandings about the topics we've been discussing so far. In general, the scriptures urge us to turn away from the so-called "glories" of cyclic existence: the various desirable objects of samsaric life such as wealth, fame, physical beauty, and so forth. This teaching can become the basis of the following misunderstanding. Someone may think that it is improper to strive for a higher rebirth with an excellent body and abundant resources because such a rebirth is still within cyclic existence and these attainments are therefore merely worldly goals.

The response to this misunderstanding is as follows. There are two types of goals to be pursued: temporary and ultimate. You can strive for certain objects because you require them temporarily, while your ultimate goal may be something quite different.

Although your ultimate goal is freedom from cyclic existence, you still must strive for an excellent body, wealth, intelligence, and so forth, because it is only by means of a succession of excellent rebirths, with the opportunities they afford to pursue the Dharma, that you can finally attain your ultimate goal. Emancipation or highest enlightenment will not come in one moment. You have to spend many lifetimes training the mind, accumulating virtuous causes, and eliminating obstacles. In each of those lives it is important to have good conditions for practice. Without the temporary opportunities you gain from having an excellent body, resources, companionship, surroundings, and so forth, you will not succeed in your ultimate purpose, which is to attain the *definite good* of liberation. Therefore, it is actually essential to seek these samsaric glories. In order to obtain emancipation you have to train your mind, and the body is the support of the mind. For example, wealth enables you to sustain your body and pursue your practice without being distracted by other worldly concerns. So these worldly advantages actually enable you to pursue the path with more freedom and diligence.

The *Ornament for the Mahayana Sutras (Mahāyāna-sūtrālaṃkāra)* says,

> Excellent resources and body,
> And excellent retinue and activity—high status.

"High status" is a phrase that usually refers to birth as a human or deva, but the point here is that the excellent qualities constituting high status are also qualities of buddhahood. From the ultimate point of view, the qualities commonly associated with the high status of a favorable worldly rebirth—such as an excellent body, resources, and companionship—are not necessarily objects to be abandoned; they need not be classified as belonging solely to samsaric existence. The reason for this is that all these glorious qualities are not lost when you attain buddhahood, but are in fact realized in their purest and most perfected forms.[3] When you gain full and completely perfected buddhahood, you obtain the apotheosis of those qualities. Therefore, the excellent qualities of a life of high status are not merely samsaric attachments, but in their perfected forms are the attributes of the *form body (rūpakāya)* of a buddha. Buddhahood endows you with bodily perfection and the splendid environment of a buddha's pure land, and this buddha-field naturally produces all the resources associated with vast wealth and so forth. The companions and retinue of a buddha—in his *saṃbhogakāya,* or *enjoyment body,* aspect—are similarly of the highest quality: a host of ārya bodhisattvas.

We summarize the practices that make up the core of the Mahayana path as the *six perfections,* which will be explained in detail in the latter volumes of this series. The first four of these perfections *(pāramitā)* are the cause for attaining a buddha's *rūpakāya,* or *body of form.* The first is the perfection of giving, which becomes the cause of attaining the unlimited resources of the buddha-field. The second is the perfection of ethical conduct, which becomes the cause of the buddha's perfect body. The third, the perfection of patience, becomes the cause of the buddha's perfect retinue. The fourth perfection is persevering effort, which becomes the cause of a buddha's perfect activity; this means that buddhas act spontaneously in the most meaningful way, and whatever activity a buddha undertakes is brought to the best possible completion. (The last two perfections, concentration and wisdom, result in the *dharmakāya* or *truth body* of a buddha, whose nature is perfect knowledge, or omniscience, and freedom from all obscurations.)

What the *Ornament for the Mahayana Sutras* and other scriptures are saying is that these first four perfections accomplish the qualities of *high status,* but these qualities are not necessarily aspects of cyclic existence; in their perfected forms they are in fact attributes of a buddha. Those who strive for the omniscience of perfect enlightenment practice these four perfections intensively, for a very long time, and in an extraordinary manner. They are aspiring to the fruit of these practices: the extraordinary qualities of high status, which are the buddha's perfect body and its attributes. Even the great bodhisattvas, who practice the perfections in the most powerful way for many eons, are striving for these exceptional qualities, and they achieve these glories as the fruit of that practice.

Therefore, you should not understand these qualities of high status as being purely samsaric ideals that should always be abandoned by the sincere spiritual pracitioner. They are not like that. From the point of view of making temporary progress on the path, or from the ultimate point of view as the attributes of buddhahood, these qualities are tremendously beneficial.

Concerning the achievement of the ultimate goal, the *definite good,* Śāntideva says in *Engaging in the Bodhisattva Deeds:*

> Relying on the boat of a human body,
> Free yourself from the great river of suffering.

In order to reach the far shore, beyond the ocean of suffering we call samsara, you have to rely on the boat of a human body; you require the vehicle of a human life. And not just one. You will require an unbroken succession of many lives that are conducive to this practice of striving for enlightenment. You have to achieve this kind of body in life after life. Therefore, you have to continuously accumulate the causes to obtain this kind of excellent vehicle in the future.

In order to possess such a body in your next life, you have to create the causes for it right now, during this lifetime. The preeminent cause for such an excellent body is pure ethical conduct. Therefore, ethical conduct is the root of the path. It is said that ethical conduct is the foundation of all good qualities, just as the earth is the basis of all animate and inanimate existence. That is why it is so important to practice virtuous behavior. Once you have achieved another high rebirth, you can continue to practice toward the highest goal. But the basic cause, the foundation, is ethical conduct. You should take vows to the extent you are able and protect those vows as best you can.

Not only do you need to be born in a higher rebirth, you also need to obtain all the necessary qualifications. If you have some but lack others, your progress will be impeded. To the extent that you lack any essential qualities, to that extent your practice will be less fruitful. To make rapid progress on the path, all the conducive conditions must be assembled.

In order to obtain such a *fully* qualified body, it will not be sufficient to take and keep the precepts of the novice monk or nun, which are themselves incomplete. You must enter into and observe faithfully the bhikṣu vows: the prātimokṣa vows of the fully ordained monk or nun. In addition to this, you may want to take the bodhisattva vows. And in order to complete the path much more rapidly, you can add the tantric vows. But to obtain all the qualities you need, you must at least observe the complete prātimokṣa vows and make those precepts the foundation of your training.

Some have objections to this and argue as follows: if you are maintaining ethical conduct in order to obtain a higher rebirth, you can achieve that simply by taking the eight precepts of the one-day ordination vows for a layman. Since these are sufficient to obtain a human life, why bother with the complication and difficulty of full bhikṣu vows?

Another objection is this: since the ultimate purpose of the prātimokṣa vows is to obtain arhatship, and you cannot even take the bhikṣu vow until you are twenty years old—and further, since you can also become an arhat as a layperson, on the basis of having taken the *upāsaka,* or lay, vows—aren't the lay vows better? Why bother with the bhikṣu vows, which are so much more difficult to maintain but have no special purpose?

To clarify what is being said here we need to recall that within what we call the prātimokṣa vows—the vows of *individual liberation*—there are eight different levels you can take. There are lay vows for men and women, novice vows for monks and nuns, vows for probationary nuns, full ordination vows for monks and nuns, and one-day ordination vows for laypeople. The arguments here are that you can achieve the temporary and the ultimate goals of the prātimokṣa vows—obtaining a higher rebirth and attaining arhatship—by basing your practice solely on the lower sets of vows, which are easier to keep. Therefore, why bother to take the vows of full ordination, which are the most difficult to maintain?

These may have been arguments Tsongkhapa heard in his day from people who thought that the life of monks and nuns was too difficult and wanted to advance the practice of laymen and laywomen as being equal to or better than ordained life.

Tsongkhapa replies that you should understand such arguments to be the senseless babble of people who have no insight whatever into the key points of the Buddha's teachings. The different levels of the prātimokṣa vows are like stepping stones, with each lower set leading to the next higher set, and this progression culminates in the full ordination of monks and nuns. The lower sets of vows, the one-day vows or the layperson's vows, are not the complete fulfillment of the vows of individual liberation; they are stages one passes through on the way to that completion, which is full ordination.

The lower vows form the foundation for a progressive practice. For example, once you become confident in maintaining the eight precepts of the one-day vows, you may feel ready to take on the ten precepts of the novice monk for life. In that way you progress higher and higher. The important thing is that you make every effort to keep all the precepts of whatever level of vows you have taken. You should not take a lower set of vows and then observe them only partially. You take the complete set of vows, and you guard all the vows you have taken as carefully as you can. Then, gradually, building upon each level, you can reach the culmination of this practice by taking the full ordination of a monk or nun.

Now we have completed the presentation of how to train the mind in the path that is common to the being of small scope. You should try to integrate with your own mind each of the topics we have covered. That is the point of this teaching. The *Lamrim Chenmo* is laid out in a step-by-step method that enables you to study, think about, analyze, and meditate on each of the points progressively. If you do this properly, this method has the power to transform your mind, to change your attitude toward your life, and to purify the misunderstanding that has led to so much confusion and suffering.

Therefore, you should try as hard as you can to contemplate and meditate on these points. This will create a solid foundation for all other practices, and will be very useful to you in this life and throughout all future lives. If you put your effort into this, it will make your time here much more meaningful and beneficial.

5

The Eight Types of Suffering

2) Training the mind in the stages of the path shared with persons of intermediate capacity
    a) The actual training to develop the attitude of the person of intermediate spiritual scope
        i) Identifying the mind that strives for emancipation
        ii) The method for producing the mind that strives for emancipation
            a' Contemplating suffering and the cause of suffering
                1' Contemplating the truth of suffering: the faults of cyclic existence
                    a" Explaining the significance of the Buddha's having taught the truth of suffering first among the four noble truths
                    b" The actual meditation on suffering
                        1" Contemplating the general sufferings of cyclic existence
                            (a) Contemplating the eight types of suffering
                                (i) The suffering of birth
                                (ii) The suffering of aging
                                (iii) The suffering of sickness
                                (iv) The suffering of death
                                (v) The suffering of encountering the unpleasant
                                (vi) The suffering of separating from the pleasant
                                (vii) The suffering of not getting what you want
                                (viii) The suffering of the appropriating aggregates

All of the trainings we have studied thus far have been directed toward turning the mind away from its pursuit of the pleasures of this life, and making a good rebirth in the next life the central concern of our mental and physical activity. We meditate on these practices common to the being of small scope in order to effect this reversal of our ordinary priorities. Based on trust in the cause and effect of karma, we redirect our actions to the virtuous side, purify previous nonvirtue, and accumulate the causes for happy rebirths in the future. If we succeed in this practice, at the time of death we will have confidence that this precious opportunity of a human life has not been wasted.

If you can succeed at even that much, your life has been greatly successful; it has been made meaningful. But still, that is not the final goal. Śāntideva says in *Engaging in the Bodhisattva Deeds:*

> Even though they repeatedly come to a happy existence,
> And experience much pleasure there,
> Upon dying they fall for a long time
> Into the unbearable sufferings of lower realms.

Even if you succeed completely, and secure a comfortable rebirth in a happy realm, that life too will eventually come to an end, and once again you will face the possibility of falling into one of the many levels of misery. Being born as a rich and powerful human, or among the highest worldly gods, offers no security about what will happen in the future. For every samsaric rebirth, no matter how high, there is always the possibility of falling back into a suffering realm, because you remain under the power of karma and afflictions. In every such rebirth you will have to make energetic efforts to prevent the possibility of a lower rebirth.

Therefore, you have to look further. You need to start thinking about the next steps on the path. These are the trainings common to the person of intermediate scope. Their goal is complete emancipation from cyclic existence. This type of practitioner is striving for freedom from *all* future rebirth, regardless of whether it is high or low. He or she wants to cut off all rebirth conditioned by karma and afflictions, because such rebirths offer no certainty about what will happen in the future. The person who strives for complete emancipation from cyclic existence is the being of intermediate scope.

Tsongkhapa says in his poem, *Foundations of All Good Qualities (Yon tan gzhir gyur ma):*

> The splendors of cyclic existence cannot be trusted:
> They are the opening to all sufferings; when indulged in they never satisfy.
> Realizing these faults, I request blessings
> To produce the highest aspiration for the bliss of liberation.[1]

When you examine them closely, the attractive, desirable pleasures of the world never bring any final satisfaction. That is the very nature of any experience conditioned by karma and the afflictions; it cannot deliver any kind of ultimate contentment or peace of mind. Trying to find satisfaction among the pleasures of a samsaric birth is like drinking saltwater to quench your thirst: no matter how much you drink your thirst will only grow greater and greater. When it comes to worldly pleasures, you can never get enough because you are never satisfied. Once you begin to pursue them you only crave more and more. This pattern of behavior opens the door to innumerable troubles. All the dazzling attractions of cyclic existence can never bring stable happiness, and in this sense they are completely unreliable and not to be trusted.

You may enjoy the greatest fame and widespread admiration, but if circumstances change you will be despised by the world. You may have gathered vast wealth, but if circumstances change you will be reduced to abject poverty. You may bask in perfect health, but then suddenly find yourself in pain and close to death. You may delight in the bliss of birth among the gods, but at the end of that life you will fall into the agony of the lower realms.

All favorable circumstances arise in dependence upon causes and conditions. Conditioned by the power of ignorance and the other afflictions, you create karma. The results of that karma are the experiences you meet in your lifetime. Some of those experiences are pleasurable. You are attracted to and get attached to those pleasant feelings. You come to believe, or to hope, that certain of these pleasures can be stabilized; you expect them to bring permanent satisfaction and relief from your underlying anguish. But you are always deceived. There is no such permanent satisfaction. Why? Because these worldly pleasures are by their very nature dependent arisings, impermanent and unstable. They are completely unreliable.

Once you understand that this is the true nature of all worldly pleasures, you recognize that what you really should be striving for is the truly stable, reliable happiness that comes only with emancipation. The only really worthwhile goal is freedom from conditioned, karmically determined experience; that is the only route to happiness that cannot be destroyed. In this prayer by Tsongkhapa you ask the buddhas and the Three Jewels to inspire in your heart the attitude that strives, with unfailing energy, for that freedom of emancipation.

That is the attitude of the being of intermediate scope. These are the trainings that we now begin to study in the middle section of the *Lamrim Chenmo.* The main goal of these meditations is to recognize the faults that are intrinsic to all cyclic existence, including the attractive pleasures of the higher realms. When you see that even the pleasures of cyclic existence are merely gateways to more suffering, it will naturally awaken a strong desire to be free from all samsara. When you see the unfailing benefits of liberation, you will naturally be inspired to strive toward that goal. You will be ready to exchange your ordinary concern for pleasure, fame, praise, wealth, and beauty—which are all temporary and deceitful—for a focused determination to be free of conditioned existence.

The first goal is to generate the desire for emancipation. Without that you will not find the proper method nor make the necessary effort to achieve this liberation. If you lack any of the three—the desire, the method, or the effort—you will continue to be trapped in the cycle of birth and death. Once you see the faults of cyclic existence and the benefits of emancipation, however, a powerful, constant desire to achieve liberation will arise. Then your whole body, mind, and behavior will change. All your activity will work against the causal cycle of samsara and will create the causes of emancipation. This is the main training of the being of intermediate scope.

Once you have firmly established this as your spiritual goal, and you have decisively turned away from any interest in the pleasures of cyclic existence, then you will have the ability to move on to the last step: training in the path of the bodhisattva, the being of great scope. Then you will be working not only for yourself but to help others.

But before you can effectively embark on that path, you must realize deeply and sincerely that there is nothing within cyclic existence that can offer any reliable happiness. Until then, whatever Mahayana path of great compassion that you might profess will be mere words. Until you generate the genuine mind intent on liberation, merely saying "I am practicing bodhicitta; I am practicing the Mahayana path; I am meditating on compassion and love," will be nothing but words.

2) Training the mind in the stages of the path shared with persons of intermediate capacity

To begin the path of the intermediate being, Tsongkhapa offers a dedication to the teachers of the lineage: "I bow down with respect to the revered holy teachers who possess great compassion."

By the time you reach this stage, your practice should be based on a recollection of death and an awareness of the misery you will experience if you have not prepared properly for that inevitable event. Contemplating this, you should produce an attitude that reverses ordinary concerns by decisively turning away from the affairs of this life and aspires to a happy rebirth in the future. The method of avoiding bad rebirths and obtaining good ones is taking refuge in the Three Jewels and gaining certainty about the cause and effect of karma. These are the practices of the being of small scope. If you engage in these trainings you will be able to secure a higher rebirth in your next lifetime.

Here, on the path of the intermediate being, you should not be satisfied with that goal. The intermediate spiritual being sees that not only lower rebirths, but all forms of samsaric birth, are subject to disappointment and suffering—none offers hope of everlasting happiness. Seeing that, you turn away from any desire whatsoever for life within cyclic existence, no matter how blissful. This is the thought of total renunciation of samsara.

It is based on that level of renunciation, reached by means of these trainings of the intermediate being, that you are able to produce the supreme thought of enlightenment, bodhicitta. At that point you step onto the final path of these lamrim teachings, the trainings of the being of great scope, which lead to perfect buddhahood, the great spiritual goal of the Mahayana. It is in order to reach that path of the being of great scope that you must first train on this path of the being of intermediate scope.

The reason is that even if you are born in a splendid human life, or as a deva, you still have not passed beyond the pervasive suffering of having all your experience conditioned by karma and afflictions. You will still be subject to being born again and again, with no control over when you die, where you are reborn, or what unpleasant conditions you meet in future lives. As long as you continue to be conditioned by karma and afflictions you will not find any stable, reliable form of happiness. This pervasive suffering, the suffering of being conditioned, is a subject we will discuss later, when we examine the three types of suffering.[2]

Even if you are born into a lifetime of blissful experience, holding on to that as some kind of ultimate happiness is a big mistake. It is merely a temporary respite within an endless cycle of uncontrolled rebirths. It is happiness that cannot last. It is happiness whose nature is to turn into disappointment and suffering. It is happiness that is certain to come to a bad end.

It is as if a man who was falling from a high precipice were to think, "Ah, this is quite comfortable. I don't feel any pain at all. I am enjoying this pleasurable sensation of flying." Of course, within a short amount of time this person is going to crash. So he has made a mistake: that is not pleasure; it is only a moment of respite before a bad end. In the same way, a comfortable rebirth is nothing more than a brief intermission in the constant cycling through miserable, uncontrolled existence. As I quoted at the beginning of this chapter, Śāntideva says in *Engaging in the Bodhisattva Deeds:*

> Even though they repeatedly come to a happy existence
> And experience much pleasure there,
> Upon dying they fall for a long time
> Into the unbearable sufferings of lower realms.

Similarly, Candragomin's *Letter to a Student (Śiṣya-lekha)* says:

> Those born into the tumbling, incessant change of cyclic existence,
> Clutch on to a simple moment of repose as real happiness.
> They will surely wander helplessly through hundreds of rebirths—
> Some similar to this, some different—one after another.

Once you are caught in the wheel of samsara, your future is like a feather blown helplessly about by the wind. Unable to control your destiny, you grasp at the slightest joyful moment and imagine that this is real happiness. You create all kinds of actions out of attachment and aversion, trying desperately to cling on to that fleeting moment of peace. By those actions you only produce more and more unhappiness in the future. Therefore, you need to reconsider the true nature of "happy" migrations, recognize their fundamental faults, see that they are just as unsatisfactory as suffering rebirths, and become thoroughly disenchanted with their attractions.

Āryadeva says in his *Four Hundred Stanzas (Catuḥ-śataka-śāstra-kārikā):*

> The wise feel the same fear
> For a high rebirth as for the hells.
> It is rare indeed for a worldly state
> Not to produce fear in them.

The stanza says that it is rare to find a realm within cyclic existence that does not produce fear in the heart of a wise practitioner. But the term "rare" here really means "never." Why? Because there is, in reality, no state whatsoever that is not a fearful realm of suffering once you understand the true nature of things. From the lowest hells up to the highest heaven—the so-called "peak of existence"—there is no state that a wise person finds attractive. Equally disenchanted with all of samsara, he or she produces a fervent desire to get out of this cycle of misery altogether. For, as the *Verse Summary of the "Perfection of Wisdom in Eight Thousand Lines" (Ārya-prajñāpāramitā-ratna-guṇa-sañcaya-gāthā)* says, "Those whose minds are attached to cyclic existence will cycle there unceasingly."

In his *Letter to a Student,* Candragomin points out how our perception of experience as happy and pleasant is the source of delusion and attachment:

> To the extent you perceive all beings as happy,
> To that extent the darkness of your ignorance will thicken.
> To the extent you perceive all beings as suffering,
> To that extent the darkness of your ignorance will disperse.
> The more you fixate on attractive objects,
> The more the flames of attachment will spread.
> The more you meditate on unattractive objects,
> The more the flames of attachment will be extinguished.

Since beginningless time you have been grasping at the "glories" of cyclic existence as the sources of real happiness. You have perceived worldly goals such as material possessions, fame, and sensual pleasure to be some kind of ultimate satisfaction and bliss. You have become accustomed to imputing a nature of attractiveness upon those samsaric delights; you invest them with an ability to deliver bliss and contentment. Most human beings are so attached to these splendors that they sacrifice their whole life to attain them. This hopeless pursuit of happiness in the wrong places—this habitual projection of unreal expectations on worldly objects—is the real problem.

The antidote to that habitual, mistaken way of thinking is to meditate on suffering. You must cultivate a correct perception of the nature of these worldly delights by meditating on the many ways in which they bring only disappointment and sorrow. You must concentrate on their faults. When you practice the antidote by meditating on the faulty nature of samsaric attractions, you are concentrating on their real nature—there is no imputation of false qualities. This is the reversal of the ordinary mode of perception. Ordinarily you see impure things as pure, impermanent things as permanent, and objects whose nature is to bring suffering as sources of happiness. For a very long time—beginninglessly, in fact—you have been accustomed to seeing only the falsely imputed "attractive" nature of these objects.

The antidote is to use discriminating wisdom to analyze their true nature, and by means of meditation to accustom your mind to perceiving that truth: their nature of being impure, impermanent, and causes of suffering. Once your perceptions are cleansed and your mind is accustomed to this truth, you will naturally turn away from these false attractions, and in doing so you will eliminate the causes of suffering.

If you do not meditate in this way on the suffering nature of worldly splendors, you will continue to impute attractive qualities onto impure objects, your attachment will increase, ignorance will thicken, and you will go on perpetually turning the wheel of samsaric life. Therefore, it is vitally important to meditate on the faults of cyclic existence. That is the practice of the being of intermediate scope. And that will be the emphasis of the practices we find in the following sections. They are methods to loosen your attachment to cyclic existence and to inspire you to seek complete freedom from it. These methods are explained under the following four headings:

a) The actual training to develop the attitude of the person of intermediate spiritual scope
b) The measure of having produced the attitude of a person of intermediate scope
c) Clarifying misconceptions
d) Establishing the nature of the path that leads to emancipation

a) The actual training to develop the attitude of the person of intermediate spiritual scope

This topic has two parts:

i) Identifying the mind that strives for emancipation
ii) The method for producing the mind that strives for emancipation

i) Identifying the mind that strives for emancipation

If you want to understand the mind that strives for emancipation, you must first identify emancipation. "Emancipation" means freedom from bondage. But what is it that binds you, that ties you up? It is karma and the afflictions that bind you to cyclic existence. By the power of these two you exist in samsara. By their power you are born into one of the three realms: in the desire, form, or formless realm. By their power you are born among one of six types of sentient beings: hell denizens, hungry ghosts, animals, humans, demigods, and devas. By their power you take birth by means of one of the four birth sources: from a womb, from an egg, from moist heat, and by miraculous birth.[3]

Being bound by karma and afflictions means that your five aggregates are compelled to be reborn, over and over again, into these experiences. Emancipation means total release from that cycle of birth and death, which is totally beyond your control. It means cutting the chain of karmic causality that binds you to that endless cycle. The desire to obtain that freedom is identified here as the mind that strives for emancipation. This is an attitude that first understands the causes of bondage in cyclic existence, recognizes the means of gaining freedom from that bondage, and then decisively sets out to achieve that goal.

It is the very nature of phenomena dependent upon causes and conditions that they arise in one moment and then, in the second moment, they change and are destroyed. Every moment there is arisal, change, and destruction. "All conditioned things are impermanent" means that nothing that arises from causes and conditions is ever able to stay exactly the same, because every moment it changes. For example, in the first moment you are born, and then with each passing moment you become older and older. We are all constantly changing, although we do not recognize the change. Suddenly you are not a baby anymore; you are a big, strange person. It appears to happen slowly, gradually, but in every moment everything is constantly in a state of transformation.

But this moment-to-moment destruction of the world produced by karma and afflictions is not what is meant here by "emancipation." That kind of destruction does not require an antidote. It is just like a tree that grows from a small seed: every moment it is changing and growing into something else. If the moment-by-moment destruction of produced phenomena *were* emancipation, then everybody would be automatically liberated without any effort.

The emancipation we are concerned with here is a type of cessation which is based on the application of an antidote, and which destroys its object permanently, from the root. It is like a tree that is intentionally dug up from the root: that tree is permanently destroyed.

If you do not give rise to the antidote, rebirth from one life to the next will just go on and on. Some of these rebirths will be high, some will be low, but they will just keep coming, one after the other. It is by the power of cultivating the antidote that the process of rebirth is finally, permanently, brought to an end. The poison tree of samsaric birth and death can only be destroyed by pulling out its roots of karma and affliction, which can only be done by applying the antidote of meditation.

When, by the power of the antidote, the continuity of rebirth is stopped—that is emancipation. This is what you must comprehend if you are going to "identify the mind that strives for emancipation." Once you know what emancipation is, you can strive for that with energy and determination.

ii) The method for producing the mind that strives for emancipation

If you do not see the faults of a particular type of experience, you will not recognize it as suffering and you will not feel any special desire to be rid of it. The basis of a strong wish to be free of thirst is to recognize the discomfort of that experience, to know its faults, and perceive it as undesirable.

It is the same with the desire to obtain emancipation. Emancipation is freedom from the suffering of the aggregates appropriated by karma and afflictions. The desire to obtain emancipation depends on seeing what is wrong with those aggregates, which is that they have the very nature of suffering. Samsaric life manifests in the body-mind continuum of your aggregates, and if you don't see samsaric life as faulty you will not feel any need to be emancipated from it.

Therefore, you have to meditate on the faults of cyclic existence in order to see, from many points of view, how its very nature is suffering. Once you see that, you will not want to be there anymore. You will want freedom from that condition. The mind intent on emancipation will rise. The great Āryadeva in his *Four Hundred Stanzas* wrote:

> How can anyone who has no aversion
> To this existence take an interest in pacification?
> Like leaving home, it is also hard
> To leave worldly existence behind.

Even if you are in prison, if you don't perceive your life in prison as a problem—if you don't have any objection to the food, or to the way you have to spend your time, or to the people you are imprisoned with—then you won't have any incentive to get out of there. You may want to stay there forever. In a similar way, we think of this prison of cyclic existence as our home. People don't look for the faults of their home; they are comfortable there. In general, everyone thinks that his or her own home is the best place in the world. That is why we say, "There's no place like home." And that is why beings find it so difficult to get out of cyclic existence. It feels like home. We are used to it, deeply attached to it. We want to stay here forever, not think about getting out of it.

That is why we need this method to inspire the interest and desire for emancipation. The method for generating the mind that strives for emancipation is twofold:

a' Contemplating suffering and the cause of suffering
b' Contemplating the twelve links of dependent origination

a' Contemplating suffering and the cause of suffering

This subject has two parts:

1' Contemplating the truth of suffering: the faults of cyclic existence
2' Contemplating the cause of suffering: the stages of involvement in cyclic existence

In this method, you first meditate on suffering *as a result,* and then you proceed to contemplate the *causes* of that suffering—karma and the various afflictions—and how these causes produce their effects, entangling beings in the miseries of cyclic existence.

1' Contemplating the truth of suffering: the faults of cyclic existence

This topic also has two divisions:

a" Explaining the significance of the Buddha's having taught the truth of suffering first among the four noble truths
b" The actual meditation on suffering

a" Explaining the significance of the Buddha's having taught the truth of suffering first among the four noble truths

Why did the Buddha teach the truth of suffering as the first of the four noble truths? When you think about it, you would expect the *cause* of suffering to come first, because a cause always comes before an effect. But as we all know, in his presentation of the four noble truths the Buddha taught the truth of suffering first, then the cause of suffering, then the cessation, then the path. This way of presenting it appears to be backward, doesn't it? The question is this: "Since causes precede effects, why did the Buddha not follow that order when he said, 'Monks, this is the noble truth of suffering. This is the noble truth of the cause'?"

Tsongkhapa says that the Buddha did not make a mistake when he reversed the order. By inverting cause and effect in this way he was making a crucial point about practice. What was this special point?

From the point of view of his disciples, if they did not first produce the desire to obtain emancipation from cyclic existence, how could he lead them to liberation? In teaching this way the Buddha was pointing to the essential method: first the trainees must generate a sincere desire for liberation. If they lack that interest there will be no basis for any further practice. The Buddha saw that his disciples, like most sentient beings, were deceived by the mistaken view that apprehends the attractions of samsara as sources of pleasure and happiness, when in fact they produce only dissatisfaction and suffering. In this way their minds were enshrouded in the darkness of ignorance.

All beings entrapped in cyclic existence suffer, from the very beginning, from this misapprehension. They are deceived by the attractive appearance of objects of desire, which are, in reality, causes of suffering. That attitude has to change. That cloud of misunderstanding must lift, so that you can see that the splendors of cyclic existence are in the nature of suffering, and are not at all true causes of happiness and joy.

Āryadeva's *Four Hundred Stanzas* says:

> When there is no end at all
> To this ocean of suffering,
> Why are you childish people
> Not afraid of drowning in it?

He says to us: you immature people, you are like children who have no concept of how big and how deep the ocean is. You are so ignorant of the dangers that even though you are sinking into the turbulent waters, you don't know enough to be afraid. Worldly beings are deceived; like children, they see only the attractive sparkle of the great ocean of samsara, without realizing that it is an ocean full of misery, and that they are drowning in it.

The truth of the matter is that the splendors of the world are not objects whose true nature is to bestow happiness. Their true nature is to produce all kinds of problems and misery. This is what the Buddha was pointing out when he taught the various aspects of the suffering of cyclic existence. And he did this in order to produce in his disciples disenchantment with cyclic existence, and the thought of renunciation. This is just like parents who warn their children, "Don't touch that stove because it is very hot and you will burn yourself." They do this to stop their children being attracted to an object that looks enticing but is actually very dangerous. Because awakening this awareness in his disciples was so essential to the rest of the path, the Buddha taught the truth of suffering first.

Once you realize that you have plunged into this great ocean of suffering cyclic existence, a powerful desire to get out of it arises, and you realize that to escape you must turn away from the objects that cause it. This sets you to looking for the sources of samsaric suffering. What is the cause of samsara? Where did it come from? How did it happen? It was to answer these questions that the Buddha taught the second noble truth: the truth of the cause of cyclic existence.

When you analyze these questions you discover that samsaric suffering is created by the many forms of contaminated karma, and that karma itself is produced by the inner obscuring afflictions. The root of those afflictions is the ignorance of grasping at a false conception of self; this is the ignorance that holds the self as something permanent, essential, and real. First, you impute upon the ever-changing aggregates a permanent sense of self—an egoistic, central "I"—and then you become attached to that I. That I becomes the center of your attention, so that everything you do is to serve the I. All of your actions—including helping friends, harming enemies, loving some, hating others—are created from this self-grasping. By means of this analysis you come to realize the second noble truth, the cause of suffering: karma and the afflictions.

Is that self-grasping ignorance intrinsic and immoveable, or is there a powerful antidote that can destroy it? Upon analysis you find that this ignorance is not only a wrong, perverted, baseless view of reality, but it is adventitious—the very opposite of intrinsic—and therefore can be eliminated by an effective antidote. Once you see that—once you realize that you actually can get rid of the very root of all unhappiness so that it will never reappear—you will be inspired to achieve that cessation of suffering. You will think, "I must become completely freed from all of this sorrow by rooting out its cause." This intention is based on realizing that you actually have the power to bring about the cessation of suffering. Therefore, the third noble truth, the truth of cessation, was taught third.

A question arises: if it is the case that by realizing the truth of suffering people immediately generate a desire for liberation, why didn't the Buddha teach the truth of cessation second, so that people would pursue liberation right after they realize the truth of suffering? That seems like a reasonable question, doesn't it?

There is no fault in the sequence of the four truths. After you realize the truth of suffering, a general desire to be free of cyclic existence does arise. But you still have not understood the causes of that suffering, and you have not yet ascertained that it is *possible* to achieve the goal of freedom from all sorrow. Without those two interconnected realizations, there is no way to produce a firm and confident resolve: "I will definitely attain the cessation of suffering." It is only after the cause has been analyzed and you determine that emancipation is obtainable that the sincere desire to pursue emancipation will arise. Therefore, the truth of cessation was taught third.

At that point the question becomes: "What is the method to achieve that goal?" Therefore, as the fourth noble truth the Buddha taught the truth of the path that leads to the cessation of suffering. This fourth truth presents the many different paths you can follow to reach the desired destination.

Maitreya's *Sublime Continuum* (*Uttara-tantra)* sums up all four truths this way:

> The illness should be recognized, its cause removed,
> Health should be attained, the remedy should be applied.
> Like that, suffering, its cause, its cessation, and the path
> Should be recognized, eliminated, attained, and practiced.

In this quotation Maitreya is comparing spiritual development to the process of ridding yourself of sickness. First you have to realize that you are sick. You have to recognize that you have an undesirable condition and that you need to get free of it. How do you do that? You need to understand the cause of the sickness. Where does it come from? Is it possible to get rid of it? Or is it something that can never be cured? Once you realize the cause of the sickness, and that it can be cured with a certain medical treatment, you naturally decide to do what needs to be done to get rid of that sickness, and that is what you do. You rely on the appropriate remedy, and although it may be hard at times, you pursue the treatment until the disease is cured from the root.

This metaphor points to the special significance of the order of the four noble truths. The Buddha was not merely teaching the cause and effect of the arising and pacification of suffering. He was laying out a method of practice for us, the practitioners, in a format that would be most effective in actually leading us to that pacification of suffering. It is a process of analysis. First, you recognize the result, suffering, as your problem. That leads you to investigate the cause, and to determine that suffering can actually be overcome. You determine that a different result, the cessation of suffering, is possible, so you decide to pursue that much happier result. Then you investigate the cause of that happy result, which is the path, and you practice that path until you reach your desired goal. That is why the Buddha presented the four noble truths in the way that he did.

The Buddha taught these four noble truths many times throughout the Hinayana and Mahayana scriptures. In his teaching of the four noble truths he summarized the key points of the two causal processes: the cause and effect of entering into cyclic existence, and the cause and effect of how to get out of it. This teaching is extremely important for those who wish to attain emancipation, because it distills all the essential elements of the practice in a format designed especially to lead the disciple directly to the goal. You can think of the four noble truths as the high road into which all the subsidiary paths, lanes, and avenues eventually flow. No matter which direction you come from, everyone must finally travel down this high road; it is the only route to the city of liberation. In order to follow that road, it is essential that students are led along the path of the four noble truths in the order in which they were presented.

By contemplating the truth of suffering from many different points of view, your mind will eventually come around to a feeling of utter revulsion toward the attractions of cyclic existence. This attitude is precisely the reverse of your ordinary attachment to samsara, and it arises naturally, authentically, because you have come to see the splendors of the world for what they are—sources of endless suffering. Until you have produced this authentic attitude of renunciation, your interest in obtaining emancipation will be nothing but words, and everything that you do will only become further causes of suffering.

You can generate that feeling of revulsion for the splendors of cyclic existence, but then what are you going to do about it? How will you get out of that cycle of suffering? In order to know the methods that can lead you out of samsara, you must first identify and understand its root causes: karma and the afflictions. You do this by concentrating on the second noble truth, the cause of suffering. Trying to find your way out of cyclic existence without a clear comprehension of its causes is like an archer hoping for a bull's-eye without even seeing the target. If you do not properly understand the causes of bondage in cyclic existence, you will miss the essential points of the path. You will head off in the wrong direction, mistaking for the path to liberation activities that only lead to more suffering. Running down the wrong roads, trying to reach the wrong goals, you will only exhaust yourself, and in the end you will have achieved nothing.

If you do not comprehend suffering, the cause of suffering, and how they are to be eliminated, you will not be able to identify liberation, which brings final pacification to that suffering. If you do not recognize actual liberation, your interest and efforts to attain it will be nothing but a fanciful notion, a self-deception. You may think that you are striving to obtain emancipation, but in actuality you are not.

As Tsongkhapa told us earlier, these four noble truths contain the essence of all the vital points of the path to liberation. The Buddha taught them in a particular order as a special means for leading his disciples along that path. A disciple who is not led according to the method laid out by the Buddha can go astray, follow the wrong path, and then all his or her efforts will become fruitless. You should keep in mind the significance of the format in which the Buddha taught the four truths, and meditate on them accordingly.

b" The actual meditation on suffering

This is explained in two parts:

1" Contemplating the general sufferings of cyclic existence
2" Contemplating specific sufferings

In the first part we concentrate on the ways in which cyclic existence is, in general, a suffering experience. Later we look at the individual forms of suffering encountered in the six realms of sentient beings.

1" Contemplating the general sufferings of cyclic existence

There are a number of different ways of meditating on the general sufferings of cyclic existence. They can be presented in three sets:

(a) Contemplating the eight types of suffering
(b) Contemplating the six types of suffering
(c) Contemplating the three types of suffering

Although we are immersed in the miseries of cyclic existence, we don't know how to think about them, how to recognize them, how to analyze them. Therefore, the *lamrim* system arranges these topics in a way that is easy to access and put to use. This presentation is based on the sutras and commentaries, where various approaches are introduced. It is useful to have several different presentations because different methods will work for people of different inclinations and capabilities.

Again, the general method we are using to integrate these ideas with our mental continuum is analytical meditation, which directs the mind to logical reasons from many points of view, in order to produce sharp and powerful insights into the true nature of our condition. As with most things in life, the more reasons we have for thinking in a certain way, and the more convinced we are of those reasons, the more forceful our conviction will be and the more energy it will have in motivating our actions.

When you like something, the more reasons you devise for why that object is attractive, the stronger your attachment will become. When you dislike something, the more you concentrate on why that object is disagreeable, the more you will come to hate it. In short, the more reasons you have for a feeling, the stronger it will become. That is the nature of the mind. If you want to generate the energy to escape from cyclic existence, you need to meditate, from many different points of view, on the reasons why cyclic existence is something to get out of. This is what we do in the following sections.

(a) Contemplating the eight types of suffering

Tsongkhapa introduces the eight types of suffering with a quotation from Nāgārjuna's *Friendly Letter:*

> My Lord, be disenchanted with cyclic existence, which is the source of many sufferings: not getting what you want, death, disease, old age, and the others.

Nāgārjuna is addressing his friend the king, and advising him on how to train on the spiritual path. Cultivating disenchantment with cyclic existence means bringing to mind the faults of samsara. Nāgārjuna explicitly mentions four types of suffering: not getting what you want, death, sickness, and old age. These are four of the eight types of suffering, and when Nāgārjuna says "and the others," he is implicitly referring to the remaining four. These eight sufferings were taught by the Buddha in many sutras when he explained the truth of suffering.

In the following pages we will be analyzing from many different angles the faulty qualities of cyclic existence. It is important to approach these trainings with a clear understanding of how you are going to meditate on these points. First of all, you should remember the explanations of samsaric suffering that we have already discussed as part of the trainings of the being of small scope, and incorporate that understanding where it is relevant here.[4]

But now we are going beyond the discussion of the sufferings of the *lower* realms, and exploring the faulty nature of *all* samsaric existence. This introduces practices which are *not* common to the person of small scope. If you have the capacity and mental acuity to follow all the details, explanations, and quotations that are included here in the *Lamrim Chenmo,* you should practice these points just as they are presented here. If such a full presentation is too much for you, you can streamline your approach by focusing on the points that Tsongkhapa himself makes, and leave out the quotations from scripture. This will simplify the material and give you a more accessible outline to follow. Tsongkhapa includes a large number of many scriptural passages from the Buddha and the great Indian masters in the *Lamrim Chenmo*, and he does this to support and elucidate his explanations. If you can, you should include these in your practice because doing so will expand and deepen your understanding. But if your mind only gets confused by so many names and difficult passages, then focus your meditation on the flow of argument that Tsongkhapa himself is making.

Of the two general types of meditation—stabilizing and analytical—what we are doing here here is called analytical meditation. Nevertheless, it is very important that you maintain a stable concentration on the particular topic you are focused on. For example, if you are meditating on the truth of suffering by way of the eight divisions and its various details, your mind may wander to other topics, such as the truth of cessation. Of course there are all sorts of distractions; some may be virtuous, some nonvirtuous, some neutral. But instead of letting your attention be diverted by any of these distractions, you should maintain single-pointed concentration on the topic at hand.

In the practice of *stabilizing* meditation there are two extremes that must be avoided: one is letting the mind get too excited so that it runs after all kinds of extraneous thoughts; the other danger is mental dullness or drowsiness. Even here, in the context of *analytical* meditation, it is essential to avoid these two hindrances. You should maintain your consciousness in a relaxed state of lucid clarity, continuously focused on the subject of meditation.[5]

Śāntideva says in *Engaging in the Bodhisattva Deeds* that whatever virtuous activities you do, if they are done with a distracted mind, their benefits will be diminished:

> The knower of reality has said
> That even if recitation and physical hardships
> Are practiced for long periods of time,
> They will be meaningless if the mind is distracted elsewhere.[6]

In addition, the *Sutra of Cultivating Faith in the Mahayana (Mahāyāna-prasāda-prabhāvanā-sūtra)* says:

> Child of good lineage: You should understand from this enumeration that whatever emerges from the Mahayana, including faith of the bodhisattvas in the Mahayana path, comes from correctly contemplating the meaning and the teachings with an undistracted mind.

This means the Mahayana practitioner gains results from two aspects of practice: from a mind that is focused and not distracted; and from applying that concentrated mind to analyzing the words and meaning of the teachings. These two together produce the fruit of the Mahayana.

Tsongkhapa's commentary provides very specific definitions for the terms and phrases appearing in this sutra quotation. He says that "an undistracted mind" refers to a mind that is directed to certain virtuous objects and that does not wander off to anything else. The phrase "the meaning and teachings" refers to the words of the teachings and their meanings. And "correctly contemplating" these words and their meanings means analyzing and reflecting with discriminating awareness.

The point of this passage is that in order to accomplish any of the spiritual virtues of the Hinayana or Mahayana, you must have both undistracted focus and analytical discrimination. The achievement of all the higher qualities on the paths of the bodhisattva, śrāvaka, or pratyekabuddha depends on a mind that has both of these attributes. First, you must be able to remain single-pointed and not waver from the object you are focused upon. For your mind to have this attribute, you must have attained either actual single-pointed concentration, called *śamatha* in Sanskrit, or at least a state that is similar to it. Second, you must be able to discern the ultimate or conventional nature of phenomena by means of applying analysis to the virtuous object. The ability to distinguish the ultimate nature of the object is called "highest insight," or *vipaśyanā* in Sanskrit, and you must have either actual highest insight or a state that is similar to that.

The *Sutra Unravelling the Intended Meaning (Saṃdhi-nirmocana-sūtra)* makes this point explicitly:

> Maitreya, you should know that all the virtuous qualities, whether mundane or supermundane, belonging to śrāvakas, bodhisattvas, or tathāgatas, are the result of single-pointed concentration and highest insight.

You have to have a combination of both of these, but you do not have to fully accomplish them before you can make progress on the path. Tsongkhapa says that although this sutra literally says that you need both single-pointed concentration and highest insight, it should be understood that it is sufficient if your mind has reached a level that is similar or close to those realizations. As long as you have a high degree of both undistracted focus and analytical wisdom, you can achieve good results on the path.

In general, the emphasis here is on the union of stabilizing and analytical meditation, the union of single-pointed concentration and highest insight. When these two modes of meditation are actualized, joined together, and applied to the analysis of phenomena, meditation becomes very powerful and will be successful.

If you do not unite these two in your practice, when you try to do analytical meditation your mind will tend to wander all over the place. If you try to stabilize the mind by not thinking anything at all, you will not make any progress and you will just end up falling asleep. For meditation to bear the fruit of realization on the path, you need a union of *śamatha* and *vipaśyanā,* or at least a mind that has been developed to a level close to that.

(i) The suffering of birth

When you meditate on the truth of suffering in terms of eight types, the first is the suffering of birth. This topic has five points to consider:

1. Birth is suffering because there is pain at the time of birth itself

In four types of birth, the birth process itself is painful: these are birth into the hell realms, birth among the hungry ghosts, birth from a mother's womb, and birth from an egg. Beings born in these four ways experience various forms of severe pain at the time of birth. In general, beings born into the desire realm—especially beings born from a womb or from an egg—have a painful birth. The exception to this are the devas who are born into the form and formless realms; they do not experience any special suffering when they are born. More detail on these sufferings will follow.

2. Birth is suffering because it possesses the negative tendencies

This means that when you take a rebirth in cyclic existence, you already possess the causes and conditions for suffering in the form of karma and afflictions. Sometimes the term "negative tendencies"[7] refers to the source or cause of obscuring afflictions. Here it refers to the potential you carry with you, even at the moment of birth, to experience undesirable circumstances. The fact that you possess these negative tendencies means that you have no control over your own future experience. You are completely at the mercy of the karmic seeds and obscuring afflictions—the negative tendencies—that are with you even as you are born. Though you desire happiness and do not want suffering, you have no power to bring this about because you possess these tendencies.

All produced phenomena in the three realms of cyclic existence grow out of and are conducive to the obscuring afflictions. The karma that produces both our individual and shared experience is all an outgrowth of these afflictions—it is all compatible with the afflictions and is incompatible with wisdom.

Once you are born into these samsaric realms possessing these negative tendencies, all of the elements of that lifetime become unsuitable for the virtuous actions leading to happiness and liberation, because they are all outgrowths of the afflictions and incompatible with wisdom. It is like trying to make a gold ornament when the gold itself is adulterated with impurities—that gold will be unworkable.

When you are born possessing the impurities of the negative tendencies, your aspirations to achieve happiness by means of virtuous actions will meet with all kinds of hindrances. These difficulties are the results of the very condition in which you were born. You bring with you into this life this unsuitability for directing the actions of your body and mind to the virtuous side. Even if you have the interest to dedicate yourself to a spiritual path, you cannot do whatever you wish because you do not really have full control over yourself. You are under the power of your previous karma and afflictions, and you are limited by the environment into which you were born.

All of the produced phenomena of the external inanimate world—including the earth and the infinite world systems—as well as the inner world of individual sentient beings—their bodies and their minds—are all an outgrowth of karma and afflictions. They are all compatible with and driven by the negative tendencies. You have created your own experience by your own previous karma, and now that world of experience channels your behavior and sets limits on what you can do in this life. In this sense, your control over yourself is quite limited.

You could say that the karmic seeds—the potentials you bring with you into this life—are like the fuel that feeds the birth, survival, and increase of the afflictions. Because all the factors of your being and of your world are associated with these karmic potentials, their natural tendency is to produce, sustain, and increase afflictions. Because all of the factors that constitute existence within samsara are associated with seeds that produce, sustain, and increase the afflictions, your body-mind continuum and all the conditions of this life are unsuitable to perform in the service of virtue. Even if you try to practice virtue, hindrances will arise because of these circumstances.

This is why it is difficult to direct your behavior onto a virtuous course. You lack the freedom or self-control to do whatever you wish. Your options are limited by the power of these negative tendencies. Once you understand this, you recognize that birth is suffering because it possesses the negative tendencies.

3. Birth is suffering because it is the source of suffering

By taking birth in these three realms of cyclic existence under the power of karma and afflictions, you undergo such sufferings as aging, sickness, and finally death. Birth in this world is the very basis or source of these miserable experiences. If you attain emancipation and thereby cut off this cycle, then these various types of suffering will not happen. But as long as you are born by karma and afflictions into this world, such suffering will be the result.

4. Birth is suffering because birth is the source of obscuring afflictions

Birth is not only the source of suffering, it is also the source of the *cause* of suffering. You are born into this world with sense faculties through which you make contact with objects that you find attractive, unattractive, or neutral. Meeting these objects gives rise to desire, aversion, or ignorance—the three poisons—which are the main roots of samsaric suffering. These unsettle the mind and body, disturbing any sense of peace or satisfaction. Agitated by desire or aversion, you take action that is rooted in ignorance of the true methods to find happiness. That karmic action brings only more unpleasant results, which in turn produce more afflictions. This is the chain of the arising of suffering due to karma and affliction, and it begins, in this life, at the time of birth. In this way suffering is a self-perpetuating cycle: birth is the *result* of the afflictions, but then, once you are born into this body, birth becomes the *source* of even more afflictions. It is these afflictions that make you suffer; they are the real enemy.

Of course, when you are immersed in this cycle you are not aware of the process. You don't think about it; you just react to desire and aversion with more craving or hatred. But once you investigate this process by means of meditation, you discover what is actually happening. You see how birth is itself the source of afflictions in this life.

5. Birth is suffering because it is an undesired separation

It is the very nature of taking birth in cyclic existence that eventually you have to separate from that life. In general, beings want to cling on to the life that they have. They do not want to die; they are terrified of dying. But the inevitable end of all birth is death, separation from all the things you love and desire in this life.

From the ordinary perspective—the perspective of the obscured mind—you may look around at all the pleasures available in this life and think, "What is wrong with this? I am surrounded by all these beautiful things. This is wonderful!" Until you look into your situation with analysis, you don't see anything wrong. This is why you have to practice meditation on the true nature of samsaric birth: to see how it is conditioned by suffering and creates the conditions for more suffering; to recognize its many defects from the point of view of its causes, its effects, and its nature. These meditations remind you that you are born into suffering and the causes of suffering, the negative tendencies.

When you meditate on these faults of taking birth in cyclic existence, the decision will finally arise to get out of samsara, to bring an end to what has been, up to this point, an endless round of rebirth. Then you will begin to work toward that and engage in the real yogic work, the inner spiritual work, that leads to liberation.

The sutras describe many sufferings that you undergo while a fetus in your mother's womb and during childbirth. Candragomin's *Letter to a Student* sums them up:

> Having entered into the hellish womb,
> Closed in with unbearable, foul-smelling filth,
> Confined in the narrow, pitch-black space,
> Your constricted body must endure great pain.

These are elaborated in the *Descent into the Womb Sutra (Garbhāvakrānti-sūtra):*

> The womb is located above the intestines and below the stomach. It is filled with many types of impurities and is the home of innumerable kinds of bacteria; there are two foul-smelling openings, holes and channels in the bone, and various filthy substances such as urine, brain-like matter, and marrow. The fetus faces the spine with its back to the stomach membrane. Month by month it is enriched by the menstrual secretions. The various foods the mother eats are ground up by her two rows of teeth and swallowed; then it is moistened from below by smelly digestive fluids and from above by saliva. The fetus is nourished through the opening of the umbilical cord by the remains of that vomit-like food, through the five stages of fetal development: the meeting of semen and egg, the thickening into a quivering mass, the growing into an oblong, the lengthening into a more defined shape, the hardening into a more solid body.[8] Then, with the development of the limbs, it transforms into a complete body. The arms, legs, and cheeks are wrapped up in the amniotic sac where it stinks unbearably like a snot-rag. There the fetus moves up and down.
>
> The various tastes of food eaten by the mother—such as bitter, sour, pungent, salty, spicy, and astringent—affect it like hot sparks. Like an intestinal worm, it is nourished by these filthy fluids. It has arrived in

> a swamp that is oozing with unclean, putrefying substances. The strength of its life force is unstable. The inner heat of the mother's body constantly and thoroughly torments, heats, and burns, so that it experiences a powerful, intense, violent, and unbearable sense of suffering.
>
> To the extent that its mother moves more or less forcefully, it is bounced around, with the head and limbs confined, so that it experiences a sense of suffering that is powerful, intense, violent, unbearable, and hard to imagine. It is like being thrown into a pit of burning coals.

That is the way this sutra describes life in the womb. In other sources it is said that the fetus is harmed when the mother eats either too much or too little food, food that is too greasy, too pungent, too cold, too hot, too salty, too sour, too sweet, too bitter, too spicy, or too astringent. It is also hurt when the mother engages in sexual intercourse, runs too fast or too far, jumps, or swims. When the mother moves in these ways, the child inside has many strange experiences. Some commentaries say that when the mother has sexual intercourse the fetus feels like it is being buried under a mountain of rock, and when she runs it feels like it is falling a long way down. Even certain sitting positions, such as squatting in front of a fire, cause discomfort to the child. The experience of having the mother's bones poking into it is described as being covered over by the stomach, supported by the intestines, bound by the head and four limbs, then being impaled on a stake.

After experiencing such pains in the womb for many months, the infant passes into the birth canal to be born. At that time it undergoes another set of intense pains. This process is again described in Candragomin's *Letter to a Student:*

> It is gradually squeezed the way sesame oil is squeezed from a press,
> Then somehow it is born.
> However, those whose lives are not lost in that process
> Must endure the assault of pain.
>
> The body that rolled about in that filthy place
> Is smeared with slime from the womb and stinks unbearably.
> Memory is lost due to such torment,
> Which is like the culmination of an inflamed wound, or like being
> ready to vomit.

The process of birth is compared here to being squeezed in an oil press. Of course the baby needs to pass down a very narrow passage between bones and through a very small hole. There is barely enough room for the head to get through and the baby is squeezed and stretched in the process. Though the birth process may be extremely painful and difficult, because of strong karma, most children, amazingly enough, are born alive. Of course some children do die in childbirth, and mothers die as well. These verses make the point that even though one survives birth, everyone experiences great pain during the process. For the infant it is as if its whole body were an open wound, and going through birth is the culmination of that painful experience. During the last stage in the womb, the infant realizes how disgusting the environment is, and with a feeling that is almost like wanting to vomit, it feels a strong urge to escape from that confined space.

There are two levels of meaning in the phrase, "memory is lost." It is said in the Kālacakra system and in certain other texts that for the first seven months in the womb the baby has no memories, but at seven months it begins to remember its previous life. It retains these memories until it undergoes the trauma of birth, at which time these memories are once again lost. Another interpretation is that the trauma is so severe as you go through childbirth that the memory of it is blacked out; it is just too difficult to remember so much pain.

The meaning of Candragomin's verses are elaborated in the *Descent into the Womb Sutra:*

> Then, when all the small and large limbs are fully developed, the fetus—which is floating in a place of urine, flowing with rotten substances, having an unbearable stench, pitch-black and terrifying if you could see it—turns toward the orifice, which is smeared with urine and excrement and constantly dripping with stinking filth, blood, and pus. Because of the ripening of previous karma, the winds of karma cause its feet to turn up and its head to face downward, toward the opening. With its two arms folded up, it is squeezed to a greater or lesser degree between two mechanisms of bone. The powerful, intense, violent, and unbearable feeling of pain causes all the limbs of the body, as painful as fresh wounds, to turn blue. All the organs of the body become hot. As the slimy residue from the womb disappears, the surface of the body dries out and the lips, throat, and heart become parched.
>
> By the power of causes and conditions, pushed by the karmic winds of the ripening of previous karma, the infant is born—however difficult it may be—from that confined and overwhelmingly terrifying condition. As soon as it is born, the air outside feels like a harsh

> substance rubbing an open wound. When touched with a hand or cloth, it feels as if it were being cut with a sword. This is the kind of powerful, intense, violent, and unbearable feeling of pain that the newborn endures.

As soon as the baby emerges from the womb it cries, because its body hurts so much. The skin is so sensitive that even the mother's hand feels rough. It is said that, for a newborn baby, being lifted onto the lap or being touched by hot or cold objects feels like the pain of a flayed cow being devoured by insects, or a leper being whipped on his open sores. When the infant was in the womb, it was floating in liquid, but as soon as it emerges its skin is so tender that any contact feels rough and painful.

When you are meditating on these eight types of suffering, it is especially important to focus on this first one, the suffering of birth, and the last one, the suffering of the appropriating aggregates. These two should be given special emphasis and should be considered in detail. When you meditate on the suffering of birth, you should not be thinking about how terrible it is for that baby over there in someone else's womb. The way to do this meditation is to connect these descriptions with your own birth. You should imagine this terrifying experience happening to you, just as it has in the past and as it will be experienced again and again until you achieve liberation from samsaric rebirth. Even if you are born into the highest, most comfortable human life, your life will start with this misery of birth. You meditate by imagining how it will feel. You should bring your own discriminating wisdom to bear on this meditation and practice it over and over.

(ii) The suffering of aging

Once you are born into your new life, you develop through the various stages of growth. You begin in childhood with a new body and mind, like a fresh lotus flower. You enjoy the strength, vigor, and adaptability of youth, and you don't want to lose any of the shining, energetic qualities that you have at that time. But you have no control over such things, and that youthful vigor quickly passes away. With every moment you are aging, losing the brightness of youth, and getting closer to the aches and pains and losses of old age.

In fact, aging starts in the first moment after birth. In the second moment after birth you are older than you were one moment ago. Day and night, moment by moment, you are getting older and older and older, and there is no way to stop the progression of aging. There are five ways of thinking about this process of aging:

1. The excellent body deteriorates

When you are young your body feels fresh and looks beautiful. People may admire your attractive body. But then you get a little older, and a little older, and then one day you find that people just call you "the old man" or "that old woman." You look in the mirror and you find that your back is bent like a bow. The hair on your head has become completely white, like some kind of white flower. Your forehead is covered in wrinkles, like a row of rafters in the ceiling. (This image refers to houses in Tibet, where the ceiling was marked by a series of lines made by the rafters.)

As you age, the fresh, flexible, youthful vitality of your body is gradually destroyed. You become ugly and undesirable. You have no way to control this process; it happens as a result of the action of karma. Although you desperately want to remain attractive, the opposite happens. That itself is suffering. You don't want to get old. You don't want to get weak, and sick, and die. But it definitely will happen, and there is nothing you can do to stop it.

2. Strength and vigor deteriorate

Aging brings with it a loss of physical strength, as well as the deterioration of the mental and physical faculties. Old men and women who have lost the strength in their muscles can't sit down gracefully. They say that an old person sits down like a heavy sack of dirt that has slipped from a rope; they fall into a chair—thud! And when they try to stand up again, it is not a smooth, relaxed movement; it takes as much effort as trying to raise up the fallen trunk of a large tree. When you walk you teeter and stumble, so that it looks like you are going to fall down. Speech also deteriorates, and eventually your words become unintelligible.

The great yogi Milarepa composed a beautiful song about this. He met an angry old woman who berated him for asking for alms. He sang these verses to her to get her to see her own situation and to turn her mind to the Dharma:

> To lift you from a chair is like pulling out a tent peg;
> With feeble legs
> You waddle like a thieving goose;
> Earth and stone seem to shatter
> When you drop into a seat;
> Senile and clumsy is your body.
> Grandmother, you have no choice but to obey.
> Question your own thought and your mind examine.
> You should practice the Buddha's teaching.

What you require is a qualified and dependable guru,
And from that you may find out how you have changed.

Your skin is creased with wrinkles;
Your bones stand out sharply from your shrunken flesh;
You are deaf, dumb, imbecilic, eccentric, and tottering;
You are thrice deformed.
Grandmother, your ugly face is wrapped in wrinkles.
Question your own thought and your mind examine.
You should practice the Buddha's teaching,
You need a qualified and dependable guru,
And then things may be different for you.[9]

Although you often see elderly people in this condition, it never occurs to you, "Soon I will be like this. What will it be like when this happens?" Some people even laugh when they see old people having a hard time. That certainly does not help. When you see what life is like for an old person, you should meditate that the same thing is coming to yourself. While you have the mental and physical ability, you should realize that soon you will lose it. Once you realize that you will decide, "Right now, while I have the opportunity, I am going to make preparations for the future. Because once old age gets a hold of me, I will not be able to do anything."

This kind of resolve, based on analytical reason, is the purpose of meditation. Otherwise, what is the point of thinking about such things? It just makes you miserable. But when you meditate on these sufferings by applying them to yourself and your own condition—when you see that they are coming to you—that brings good results; that is the purpose.

3. The sense faculties deteriorate

Every day, all the time, the sense faculties are degenerating. Gradually, you do not see or hear as well as you used to. Mentally, the mind begins to forget. Slowly these capacities weaken and disappear. You learn some new name or fact, but soon you can't remember it. Even things you used to know well, you can't remember anymore. Little by little, all the physical and mental faculties deteriorate and some are totally lost.

4. The ability to enjoy sense objects deteriorates

When you get older, sense objects such as food no longer bring the pleasure they once did. Hunger wanes, the ability to taste fades. Even when you desire some food you have always loved, you can't eat it anymore because it makes you physically uncomfortable. The same is true for other sense objects: you can no longer hear beautiful music; you can no longer see beautiful pictures or scenery clearly; even sexual enjoyment and the pleasures of touch no longer have any attraction—and even if they do, you lack the capacity to indulge those desires.

5. The suffering of the diminishment of life

This is the misery of realizing that most of your life has ended and now you are approaching death. The arc of your life, like the setting sun, is slipping below the western horizon, and soon you will pass into darkness. Seeing this brings great sorrow and regret.

These miseries of aging are not far from yourself; they *are* yourself. They are sitting on your shoulder. You have to contemplate this over and over, and that is what will push you into meaningful practice. Otherwise, practice will be just an interest you have on the side, while your main concern will be worldly sensual pleasure. Then, suddenly, the things just described will happen to you without your realizing it.

Old age comes quietly, in a most deceitful manner. It is always there, every day, every moment, working its changes, although you never notice it. In fact, if these changes happened all at once, it would probably make you crazy. If you went to bed one night a healthy, vibrant fifteen-year old, then woke up the next morning and you were eighty-nine, how would you feel? You would be really miserable. Fortunately, it does not happen like that. But it is happening, slowly, in a sneaky way, without your noticing. Therefore, while this sneaky thing is coming, and while you still have the mental and physical energy, you should use your time to make preparations.

The *Extensive Sport Sutra (Lalita-vistara-sūtra)* offers vivid images of the aging process:

> By the process of aging, once youth has passed,
> We are like a lush tree that has been struck by lightning,
> Made decrepit by old age, like a frightening house on the verge
> of collapse.
> O Sage, tell us quickly how to escape old age.
>
> Old age desiccates the multitude of vigorous women and men,
> Like the branches of a grove of *sal* trees blasted by a hot wind.
> Age steals away our effort, skill, and strength,
> Renders us helpless, like a person stuck in mud.

Aging makes a beautiful form unappealing,
Aging steals our splendor and robs our strength,
Aging steals all enjoyment and subjects us to ridicule,
Aging robs vitality and finally brings us death.

These verses were spoken by the Buddha when he was the young Prince Siddhārtha, confined by his father to the palace grounds so that he would not awaken to the sufferings of the world. But the prince visited the eastern, southern, and western gates of his compound where he witnessed an old man, a sick man, and a corpse. He inquired of his servants whether these sorrows of old age, sickness, and death happened only to the three people he had seen, but was informed that these sufferings happen to everyone. Finally he arrived at the northern gate where he found a monk who had renounced the worldly life and who appeared wise. With these verses he described the sufferings of old age that he had seen, and he inquired of the monk, "O Sage, tell us quickly how to escape old age."

One of the great Kadampa teachers, Geshe Chenngawa, said, "The misery of death is frightful, but it is brief. But how frightful is old age!" Though death is a horrible fate, at least it doesn't last too long. But aging goes on and on, unwanted, progressively getting worse and worse, and in that sense it is actually worse than death itself. Kamapa said, "It is a good thing that aging takes place little by little. If it came all at once we could hardly bear it."

(iii) The suffering of sickness

There are also five ways of contemplating the suffering of sickness:

1. Sickness changes the nature of the body

The suffering of sickness is easy to understand because it is so common. When you have a disease, it changes the qualities of the body. First of all, you usually lose weight. Perhaps here in America people want to get sick because they like to lose weight! But of course being sick is really not pleasant: you lose the strength in your body, your skin becomes dry and loses its luster, and as your flesh gradually wastes away your whole body becomes thinner and weaker. The body can be completely transformed by disease, so that you don't even recognize the person you used to know.

2. Pain and despair increase and are present most of the time

As sickness increases, physical discomfort also increases and anguish tends to take over your mind.

We say that the body is constituted of four elements: water, earth, fire, and air. When these elements become unbalanced, disease results. You spend your whole life trying to nourish this body, protect it, and keep it healthy. Nevertheless, the elements occasionally fall out of equilibrium and you become sick. Once you slip into the pain of disease, the mind soon follows and falls into a state of unhappiness, depression, and despair. Of course the mind and the body affect each other in many ways, and with prolonged ill health you can spend many days and nights in physical pain and mental anguish. Even healthy people will experience the suffering of sickness many times in the course of a lifetime.

3. There is no desire for attractive objects

When you are sick, you lose your interest in the things you usually enjoy; food, drink, and companionship all lose their appeal. Often, the very things you most enjoyed while healthy become objects of aversion and even nausea when you get sick. Even when you still want them, you are told that you shouldn't eat this, or you shouldn't do that, because it will make your condition worse. And even when you don't have restrictions imposed from the outside, you physically lose the ability to do the things you would like to do.

4. You are forced to make use of undesirable objects, although you don't like to do so

When you are sick, not only are you unable to enjoy attractive objects, you have to do things you really do not like. You have to take all kinds of unpleasant medicines. Your food is restricted and often you have to eat and drink things you do not want. Even when these medicines and foods are so horrible you don't want to take them, they are forced upon you by your doctors and family.

Nowadays, when you go to the hospital you are subjected to many uncomfortable, painful, and invasive procedures. In traditional medicine they sometimes used burning with fire as a remedy. Today we have things like chemotherapy, which can make you feel worse than the disease. You will almost certainly be pricked with injections, poked with I.V.s, and jabbed to take blood. And if you require surgery, you will be cut open with sharp blades and sewn up with needles, and your recovery will be long and painful. You don't usually think about these things, but this is what happens when you become ill.

5. You will be separated from this life

The ultimate result of sickness is that you have to separate from this life. All of the harsh treatments you undergo may help for some time. You may live a few more months, or even many years. But you do not have any freedom to determine when you are going to die because you are under the power of karma and afflictions. In the end, if you do not die from other causes, sickness will cause you to separate from this life. When that time comes—when you see that you are not going to recover from your illness, that there is no hope, that now you have to die—your inner mental anguish will increase.

In meditating on the suffering of sickness you should contemplate these points in detail. The *Extensive Sport Sutra* describes the suffering of illness this way:

> Hundreds of different diseases threaten sentient beings
> with a cloud of suffering,
>
> Just as human hunters threaten wild animals.
> Observe these beings overwhelmed by old age and sickness,
> And quickly explain how to escape from this suffering.
>
> Just as the bitter winds and heavy snows of late winter
> Steal the vitality from the grasses, tree limbs, and forest herbs,
> In the same way sickness steals the vitality of living beings
> As it weakens their faculties, decays their appearance, and diminishes
> their strength.
>
> In the end it will exhaust a fortune in money or grain.
> Disease always humbles living beings.
> It harms them and is enemy to all that they desire,
> Torturing them like the sun burning down from the sky.

(iv) The suffering of death

There are also five points to contemplate in the meditation on the suffering of death:

1. You are separated from objects that are attractive and wonderful

At the time of death, you of course have to separate from everything. All the things you valued during life must be left behind: all the wealth you have accumulated, all the land, clothes, food, and things you have enjoyed. Even if you owned all the wealth in the universe, you have to leave it behind when you die. You cannot take even a single penny with you. During your life you took so much trouble to accumulate that wealth. You thought it would bring you some kind of special pleasure, some degree of safety, and many other benefits. But at the time of death, it is of no use at all. That itself is a miserable truth to face.

As Śāntideva says in *Engaging in the Bodhisattva Deeds:*

> Leaving all I must depart alone.
> But through not having understood this
> I committed various kinds of evil
> For the sake of my friends and foes.[10]

2. You are separated from many close relatives

Though you may have many loving relatives who nurse you and stand by you in your last days, none of them can travel with you when you die. Your spouse who was with you through all the ups and downs of your life, your children whom you supported, nurtured, and protected—as much as they might love you and want to help you, there is nothing they can do. You die alone, and alone you go to your next life.

3. You are separated from many close companions

You will leave behind not only your close family, but also your friends, students, teachers, co-workers, and all the people you enjoyed spending time with while you were alive. Even if you were a powerful ruler with millions of subjects, not one of them can follow you at the time of death. Even if every sentient being was your good friend, at the time of death you would have to leave them all behind.

4. You are separated from an attractive and wonderful body

At the time of death you not only leave behind all the external things that brought you joy, you must leave behind your own body. The body you had from the time you were in your mother's womb—the body that has been with you every moment of this lifetime—has to be left behind.

5. At the time of death you experience terrible pain and unhappiness

At the actual time of death you go through so many powerful experiences. Your family and close friends gather around you. They are crying, trying to ease your pain, to hold you and comfort you, but nothing they do can help. You feel them slipping away. All the people, the familiar faces, the familiar objects, are all slipping away. Now you are facing the unknown, a future that is completely black and uncertain. "Where will I go? Am I going to hell? Am I heading to painful horrors in my next life?"

These kinds of fears fill your mind, but there is no reassurance to be found anywhere. You have no perception of what lies in store in the future. Physically, your organs are failing. Mentally, you are getting weaker and fear is overwhelming your thoughts. Perhaps you wish to do a little virtuous practice to prepare yourself for what lies ahead, but it is too late. Everything is completely too late. Śāntideva says in *Engaging in the Bodhisattva Deeds:*

> When seized by the messengers of death,
> What benefit will friends and relatives afford?
> My merit alone shall protect me then,
> But upon that I have never relied.[11]

You should meditate on these points over and over again until you produce a genuine and heartfelt sense of sorrow and disenchantment with the worldly concerns that have occupied you up until now. When that happens, hold on to that feeling and use it to propel your practice. Continue to do these meditations until you have generated the genuine spontaneous thought of renunciation.

The *Extensive Sport Sutra* says:

> At the time you die and pass on to another life,
> You must separate forever from esteemed and beloved people.
> You will not return, nor ever meet again,
> Like a leaf fallen from a tree or a waterfall that never flows backward.
>
> Death makes the powerful powerless.
> Death sweeps you away like a flood carries off a log.
> People go alone, with no one else, without friends;
> Possessing karma that must ripen, they have no control.
>
> Death seizes innumerable living beings—
> As a sea monster consumes swarms of creatures,
> As the *garuḍa* grasps a snake or a lion takes an elephant,
> Just as fire wipes out the grass, trees, and all the living creatures.

In these verses, the "sea monster" is a beast called a *makara* in Sanskrit, which looks like a giant crocodile with an elephant's trunk. The makara lies sleeping on the ocean floor for a long time with its huge jaws open. Many fish and other sea creatures settle and make their home in its mouth. They produce children, and the population grows and grows until one day the makara wakes up, closes its mouth, and swallows them all at once. That is the way death lies in wait to gobble up the multitude of creatures in the world.

The garuḍa is a type of bird famous for its ability to capture and eat serpents. Most animals avoid poisonous snakes because it is so hard to grab them in a way that keeps them from turning around and biting. But the garuḍa has a special technique of grasping the snake in its talons and then holding the middle of the snake with its teeth. In this way the giant eagle-like creature controls the snake so that it cannot bite or get away. In the same way, when you are grasped by death you will be powerless to escape.

Though these images from the sutras may appear to be mythological, the points that they illustrate are undeniable facts. When you meditate on these points, you should not think that these are just fantastic tales, but analyze your situation until you realize that the fundamental process that is being described here is real life and death.

(v) The suffering of encountering the unpleasant

Once again there are five points to contemplate:

1. By merely encountering your enemies, you suffer and are made unhappy

Once you have decided that someone is your enemy, all you have to do is meet him on the street, or see her across the room, and immediately you feel angry and disturbed.

2. You fear that you will be punished by them

When you have enemies, you are always fearful of what they might do to you. At work, at school, or in your relationships, you feel that you must always be on your guard against their actions and schemes. This causes great anxiety and stress and can make life quite difficult at times.

3. You fear that they will spread malicious rumors about you

You not only worry about the actions of your enemies, but sometimes their words can do even more damage. They may be talking behind your back, spreading rumors, true or false, that will damage your reputation. With this kind of malicious gossip going on, you never know what people are thinking about you.

4. You dread dying

Of course, the most unpleasant thing you have to meet with is death itself. Though you may not spend much time thinking about it when you are young, as you get closer and closer to the end of your life the prospect of death can become a real source of anguish. Especially if you have not used your life meaningfully by preparing for death. If you know you have wasted your life, having created all sorts of nonvirtuous karmic potentials, then you will really have something to dread.

5. You fear that, because of your non-Dharmic actions, you are destined for a lower rebirth

All nonvirtuous actions are contrary to the Dharma teachings. If you know that you have committed many such actions, you will certainly worry about your next rebirth. Knowing that you are likely to go to a miserable realm, your suffering will actually begin in this life, because you will be possessed by fear, sorrow, and regret.

(vi) The suffering of separating from the pleasant

This point is illustrated by five manifestations of the pain of being separated from cherished friends or relatives:

1. When you are separated from your loved ones, grief arises in your mind

You may have family, friends, or a spouse whom you love so much that you don't want to be separated from them for even one moment. But you have no control over that. The day will certainly come when you have to leave them forever, and when that time arrives you will be overwhelmed with grief.

2. When you are separated from your loved ones, you mourn audibly

Often these feelings of loss are so powerful that people express their grief with sobbing, wailing, screaming and other verbal expressions of sorrow.

3. When you are separated from your loved ones, it causes you to harm your own body

In some cases the grief is so unbearable that people actually harm themselves. We speak of "beating your breast" or "tearing out your hair." Sometimes people are so distraught they try to take their own lives.

4. When you recall the qualities of the departed, you yearn for them and feel depressed

You have such fond and treasured memories of the person you have lost, but now you realize that you will never see him or her again. Now the memories themselves become a source of sorrow.

5. You can no longer enjoy those you have lost
If your loved ones were still present, you could enjoy their company and all the pleasure that brought you. But now they are gone and you can never access those good feelings again.

In short, you will have to separate from every single thing that brings you happiness and pleasure in this world. That is the nature of your condition. You can do nothing to prevent that separation and you have no control over when it will happen. You are under the control of karma and afflictions, and that itself is great suffering. You should meditate on these five points until they are integrated with your mind.

(vii) The suffering of not getting what you want

In the course of a lifetime we have so many different desires, and often they end in disappointment. Sometimes we work hard to achieve something we really want—perhaps a special job, or a marriage—but we fail to achieve that goal despite all our efforts. These are examples of the suffering of not getting what you want. This topic has five points, which are similar to the preceding contemplations on separating from what is pleasant. You can do the same meditations, but instead of meditating on things you must separate from, think about things you desire but do not obtain—wealth, fame, honor, love, and so forth. When you have a strong desire for an object but fail to obtain it, you experience the same types of suffering we spoke about in the previous section.

Examples of seeking but not getting what one desires are farmers who work hard to cultivate their fields, but the crop fails; or business people who spend many hours trying to build up their business, but in the end they go bankrupt. You can think of many other situations in which you wanted something very much, worked very hard to achieve that goal, but in the end were disappointed. It is very beneficial to add examples from your own experience, using your own intelligence and insight. The point of all these meditations is to convince your own mind of the truth of the suffering nature of samsaric experience. To plant that insight firmly in your mental continuum, it is very useful to relate these ideas to your own experience, because that is what will make it real for you.

(viii) The suffering of the appropriating aggregates

The Buddha said, "In sum, the five appropriating aggregates are suffering." Here we concentrate on the meaning of that statement. In what way are the *five aggregates* that combine to make up this body-mind continuum the very nature of suffering?

First of all, it is useful to understand why we call these the "appropriating" aggregates. "Appropriating" has the sense of "taking" or "grasping." It means to grasp—out of attachment to things of the present, and out of desire for things of the future—not wanting to lose those things, wanting them to remain forever. It is in this sense that the five aggregates are grasping or appropriating.

This is a case of what we call "applying the name of the cause to the result." The term "appropriating" carries the sense of attachment and desire, which are the cause, and that name is given to the aggregates, which are the result. Think of the term "wood fire." A wood fire is a fire (the result) that arises from wood (the cause); the name of the cause is given to the result and we call it a wood fire. Similarly, we have the five aggregates, and the combination of these five aggregates constitutes this body-mind continuum. The cause of these five aggregates is previous attachment and desire, which created karma, which brought this combination of aggregates into being. Therefore, the name of the cause, appropriating attachment and desire, is given to the result, the five aggregates.

Actually, because of the cyclical nature of samsara, we can also look at this as a case of the "name of the result being given to the cause." From this perspective, we have taken this life with these five aggregates, and during this life our body-mind continuum has continuously created attachment and desire. In this case, the result is the appropriating attachment and desire, and that name is given to the cause, which is the five aggregates. An example of this would be an "apple tree"—a tree that produces apples. The tree is the cause, but the name of the result, apples, is given to the cause and we call it an apple tree.

Why did the Buddha say that the nature of these five appropriating aggregates is suffering? They are suffering in five ways:

1. *They are vessels of future suffering*

What do these five aggregates accomplish? The present aggregates bring future suffering; they are a vessel linking the current body-mind continuum to future misery. By creating karma out of attachment and desire, they construct future unhappiness and perpetuate suffering into future lives. In other words, by merely taking these aggregates in this life you insure future suffering.

2. *The five appropriating aggregates are vessels of suffering that already exists*

As you know, plenty of suffering already exists in this life. It is due to the fact that you have taken this samsaric body that you are subject to sickness, aging, separating from the things you want, meeting the things you don't want, and death.

3. *They are vessels of the suffering of pain*

Having taken this body, you are subject to all the mental and physical ills, discomforts, disappointments, and pain that we commonly call "suffering" in the world. This most obvious form of suffering is called the "suffering of pain" or the "suffering of suffering." This body-mind continuum, made up of this combination of aggregates, is the vessel for all of these miseries. This and the next two types of suffering will be elaborated upon later when we explain "the three types of suffering" in chapter 7.

4. *They are vessels of the suffering of change*

The suffering of change means that all samsaric pleasure transforms into some form of suffering. Happiness switches into misery. Everything changes. It is the nature of these five aggregates that when some happiness or pleasure arises, it cannot be sustained or increased indefinitely, but inevitably changes into dissatisfaction and suffering.

You may recall that previously we discussed how the nature of birth in cyclic existence is suffering because it possesses the "negative tendencies." This means that when you take a samsaric rebirth you already possess the causes and conditions of suffering in the form of karma and afflictions. These negative tendencies mean that from the moment you take birth by appropriating these five aggregates, you carry with you the potential to experience undesirable circumstances.

The five aggregates are vessels of the suffering of pain and the suffering of change because of this inseparable connection with the negative tendencies of karma and afflictions. The negative tendencies make this body-mind continuum like an open wound, always sensitive to contact and ready to create pain. The negative tendencies are the seed or potential, always present, for every experience to turn into suffering. Although, for the time being you may be enjoying yourself, and everything seems quite pleasant, that happiness can easily transform into displeasure or pain at any moment. The conditions for that are always there, because your aggregates are not pure; they are contaminated by the negative tendencies, loaded with the potential for pain.

When you contemplate these points, you need to understand that these descriptions are not mere concepts or flights of imagination; this is actually what is happening. You don't realize it. You hide from it, ignore it, deny it, because you are the disciple of ignorance. Ignorance tells you that there is this huge "I," which is the most important thing. It tells you to do everything to make this "I" feel happy. Ignorance tells you that this "I" will last forever, and if you can make it happy, that happiness will last forever. As the disciple of ignorance, you follow that advice. You use your discriminating wisdom to try to fashion stable happiness out of samsaric objects and conditions. The whole point of these meditations is to redirect your wisdom, to enable you to see things as they truly are, not the way you fantasize them to be.

5. ***They are vessels of the suffering of being conditioned***

As soon as they are born, the five appropriating aggregates have the nature of this suffering of conditionality, because *anything* that is conditioned by karma and afflictions has this nature. Sometimes we call this "pervasive suffering." It is the suffering nature that pervades all conditioned existence because this existence is completely under the power of karma and afflictions. It is "pervasive" because it pervades both external and internal phenomena, the five aggregates themselves. It pervades your body from your toes up to your head. It pervades all the worlds of existence: the desire realm, the form realm, and the formless realm. Even the divine beings who reside in bliss at the peak of worldly existence have this nature of pervasive suffering, because they have not cut the root of cyclic existence, and their blissful life remains conditioned by karma.

When you realize the truth of suffering by means of the union of single-pointed concentration and highest insight, you vividly realize how this whole samsaric situation is pervaded by this subtle nature of suffering. Until then, although you meditate on this as the way things are, it will not be completely believable. You are still what is known as an "immature being." To a small child, everything looks like fun; everything is a toy. Even very dangerous things like a fire, or a bottle of poison, look like sources of pleasure to a child. That is the way objects in the world appear to you until you realize the truth of suffering. Until you transform yourself, through the discipline of practice, from an immature being into an ārya or "noble being" by realizing the conditioned nature of all phenomena, you will not be able to see directly how all those phenomena are the nature of suffering.

Nevertheless, even if you don't yet see this clearly, you have to meditate on the suffering of being conditioned. With effort, contemplating this pervasive nature of suffering from various points of view, your understanding will develop and deepen. As I said, this topic will be explored in more depth later, when we explain the three types of suffering.

In the end you must realize this most subtle level of pervasive suffering—that the whole of cyclic existence is conditioned by karma and afflictions and is therefore in the nature of suffering. It is seeing this deep, inescapable suffering nature of *everything* within cyclic existence that inspires the thought of renunciation. If you have not yet felt this attitude of disenchantment that comes from seeing the faults of this whole situation, then a genuine, uncontrived thought of renunciation will not arise.

Therefore, this meditation is of the utmost importance. Realizing the fundamental faults of cyclic existence, its conditionality, and therefore its nature of suffering, is a prerequisite for engaging in either the Hinayana path of obtaining emancipation for yourself, or the Mahayana path of great compassion for all living beings.

If you haven't produced a sincere thought of renunciation—wanting freedom from cyclic existence for yourself—there will be no way to produce the Mahayana thought of great compassion, which wishes for freedom from samsara for all sentient beings. You may generate some superficial feelings by saying prayers such as, "May all beings be free of suffering," but the uncontrived great compassion will not come without the genuine thought of renunciation.

"Great compassion" does not mean some vague feelings of affection for others. It means compassion which takes on the responsibility of rescuing all beings from their unhappy conditions. Great compassion is the determination to free all these beings from the miserable situation in which they are mired, and which you see vividly. Great compassion is taking responsibility to do that. That is the main gate of the Mahayana path. Once you realize great compassion, any practice you do will be dominated by that motivation, and will become true Mahayana practice. Until then, whatever practice you do will not be the actual Mahayana path.

Therefore, whatever path you plan to engage in, it is essential to produce the thought of renunciation. In order to do this you need to refer to scriptural teachings and authoritative commentaries by great masters who evidence a pure understanding of the Buddha's intent. You need to study those scriptures, and once you find some understanding, you need to meditate on that, using analytical meditation, over and over for a long time.

This means you proceed topic by topic, contemplating each one until you are able to fully convince the mind, to draw the mind in that direction. You apply all the resources at your disposal: textual sources, various reasons, inferential knowledge, and experiential knowledge. You put everything together and then you concentrate, you focus on that. If you practice that way, beginning with an educated understanding, then applying meditation that is able to change your ordinary perception, you will finally reach an unshakable realization.

Tsongkhapa reminds us that what he has presented here is not something he made up by himself. In order to explain the faults of cyclic existence to his disciples, the Buddha presented the truth of suffering in terms of eight types of suffering. Later, Ārya Asaṅga explained the thought of the Buddha by organizing it into an extensive path system, and it is that presentation by Asaṅga that Tsongkhapa has followed here.

The famous Kadampa Geshe Potowa said:

> Wherever we are born among the six types of beings, suffering will arise, such as sickness and death. When there is a cause for sickness, there will be sickness. When the cause of death appears, we will die. These do not arise as some sort of unsuitable or accidental events; it is the very character or nature of cyclic existence. As long as we abide within cyclic existence, there is no escaping it. If we are disgusted by this, we must eliminate birth. For that, we must eliminate its cause.

What Geshe Potowa is saying is that there is nothing strange about the arising of misery in the world in which we live. It is not something that is not supposed to happen. When there is a cause for getting sick—when we have bodies whose nature is that they are prone to get sick—it is not too surprising that we get sick. Aging, sickness, death happen because there are causes for them to happen. It is not as if dying is some amazing miracle that just suddenly fell out of the sky, something "unsuitable or accidental." This is the nature of cyclic existence; this is what defines samsara.

The nature of fire is to burn. If you do not want to get burned you need to get away from the fire. And as long as you remain within cyclic existence, there is no way to escape these suffering outcomes. If you don't like it, the only thing you can do is get out of the whole situation. The only way to do that is to end birth in cyclic existence, and to do that you must eliminate its cause. What is the cause? Karma and the afflictions. They must be eliminated from the root, and you do that by applying the antidotes as they are explained here in the steps of the path to enlightenment.

6

The Six Types of Suffering

(b) Contemplating the six types of suffering
- (i) The fault of uncertainty
- (ii) The fault of insatiability
- (iii) The fault of repeatedly losing one's life
- (iv) The fault of having to take rebirth repeatedly
- (v) The fault of constantly fluctuating from high to low states
- (vi) The fault of having no companions

(b) Contemplating the six types of suffering[1]

(i) The fault of uncertainty

Although you make big plans to insure your current and future pleasure in this world, and you work hard to realize those plans, you can never be certain how things will turn out. To illustrate this you should look at the relationships between yourself and others. As you cycle through samsara, passing from one life to the next, relationships change in totally unpredictable ways. Your close relatives, such as your father and mother in this life, become your enemies in a future life. People who are enemies to you now become your dearly loved parents later on. Every imaginable relationship is possible because you have been cycling through samsara since beginningless time, and you will continue endlessly until you attain emancipation. You have no control over these changes because it is all under the control of your karma.

Since relationships are constantly turning over in this way, there is nothing that you can count on. You cannot establish any relationship that is not destined to change in ways that you cannot foresee. Nāgārjuna said in his *Friendly Letter:*

> The father becomes the son, the mother becomes the wife,
> The enemy becomes a friend.
> Since everything turns around,
> There is nothing certain in cyclic existence.

Out of ignorance your mind perceives someone as an enemy; that person appears to be a definite, absolute, real, permanent enemy. All kinds of negative thoughts about this person arise, and you generate fierce anger and hatred. But in reality, as Nāgārjuna says, there is nothing essential that makes that person your enemy. It is merely a temporary perception or imputation based on transient causes and conditions. It is the same way with those you love. You perceive their closeness to you as their true, ultimate nature, and this brings attachment. But here, too, nothing is permanent. Eventually, "everything turns around."

Once you are under the power of hatred and attachment, you act in innumerable unwholesome ways to destroy those you hate and cling on to those you desire. The negative karma of these unwholesome actions is what drives you through unending, miserable lifetimes. All of this begins with ignorance: not knowing the true nature of cyclic existence. Once you see that this ignorance is the root cause of your suffering, you realize that there is no way to change those conditions without eliminating that cause.

If you had a relationship that was perfectly and unalterably reliable—something like an absolute, unchangeable, permanent friend who was completely favorable toward you and whose nature was completely trustworthy—then no matter what you did, no matter what happened to that person, no matter how long you were in relationship, his or her positive feeling and wish to bring you pleasure would never diminish. The friendship would never end because it was permanent, and it would never change because it was absolutely reliable. The sad thing is that you cannot find anyone like that within cyclic existence. That is the faulty nature of samsara. That is the suffering of uncertainty.

A famous story from the sutras illustrates how relationships change. It is the story of how Śāriputra, one of the Buddha's foremost disciples, saw a family sitting down to dinner. The father of the family had his baby son sitting on his knee and was eating a fish he had caught in a pond behind the house. When he finished, the family dog got hold of the bones and was trying to eat them when the father noticed and began beating the dog.

With his supernatural knowledge, Śāriputra could see the previous lives of all of these beings, and he explained the scene this way. In the past the father had discovered his wife cheating with their neighbor and had killed the neighbor. The father's parents were deceased, but when they had been alive his father had loved fishing in the backyard pond, and his mother had been extremely attached to the family and home.

What Śāriputra saw, and explained to his disciples, was that the dead neighbor, who had been the man's worst enemy, had been reborn as the man's son and was sitting on his knee. The man's father had been reborn as a fish, which he had just caught and eaten. The man's mother, who was so attached to the family, had been reborn as the family dog and, having grabbed the fish bones, was now gnawing on her former husband. When the man beat the dog for taking the fish, he was beating his own mother.

That was the scene as Śāriputra perceived it. Looked at on one level, samsara appears to be a very funny place; Śāriputra even said that looking at this samsaric scene made him laugh. But in reality all the suffering of the world is rooted in the ignorance that misunderstands the nature of our relationships. The afflictions of attachment, hatred, and jealousy instigate a vast amount of harmful action, committed without any understanding of whom you are attacking and whom you are defending. There is no comprehension that the relationships with your worst enemies and your best friends are constantly changing—that there is not a single relationship in cyclic existence that you can establish firmly, rely on, or trust.

Even within this one short life everything changes back and forth. Friends become enemies and enemies become friends and you have no control over it. You are under the power of karma and afflictions. The *Tantra Requested by Subāhu* says:

> In a short span of time an enemy becomes a friend,
> And a friend becomes an enemy.
> Likewise, some become neutral,
> While those who were neutral become enemies,
> Or close friends.
> Knowing this, the wise never become attached.
> Rejecting the notion that they can find happiness in friends,
> They rest their minds in the pleasures of virtue.

Meditating on this, you should prevent the arising of attachment and hostility, which develop from making false distinctions between friends and enemies. You should recognize that there is nothing that is stable in cyclic existence. That will enable you to produce disenchantment with samsara and a sincere thought of renunciation. That is the main thing.

Instead of making these distinctions between friends and enemies, which have no basis in reality, you should direct your mind in the virtuous direction.

This means cultivating a feeling of caring, concern, friendship, and equanimity toward all living beings. Such feelings grow naturally when you realize that all beings are enmeshed in suffering as a result of their sharing this fundamental misunderstanding about how the world is constantly changing, not realizing that all the relationships and objects they rely upon for their happiness are ultimately going to disappoint them. Once you gain a glimpse of this reality you want to free yourself from that situation. You also want to help others because you see that they are stuck in the same condition. That attitude is the basis of virtuous action, and that is the direction in which you should turn your mind.

(ii) The fault of insatiability

Cyclic existence is a suffering condition because no matter where you turn you will not find any lasting satisfaction. Nāgārjuna's *Friendly Letter* says:

> Each one of us has drunk more milk
> Than would fill the four oceans.
> Those in samsara who follow the ways of ordinary beings
> Will seek to drink much more than that in the future.

From the Buddhist point of view, each one of us has been cycling through life after life since beginningless time. Countless times we have been born as humans or as animals suckling at our mother's breast. If you collected all the mother's milk that just one of us has drunk in those numberless lifetimes, it would more than fill all the oceans of the world. Now, consider how much mother's milk you will need to drink in the future if you do not begin to practice the path to emancipation. If you do not find a way out of this endless cycle, you will never drink your fill.

This, of course, is merely one example. Think of all the innumerable sources of pleasure and comfort you look to for satisfaction during one lifetime. Of all the so-called "wonders" of samsara—good food, beautiful clothes, a grand house, a devoted spouse, and so forth—there is not one that you have not experienced some time in the past. And think of the measureless pain, disappointment, and sorrow that you have experienced from beginningless time up to now; there is not one suffering that you have not tasted as well. Nevertheless, after all that experience of pleasures that bring no lasting satisfaction, and all the sufferings that arise from the ignorant quest for those pleasures, you still just want to enjoy yourself. None of these experiences has changed your attitude; you are still thinking about things the same way you have always done. It is as if all that endless experience of pleasure and pain has been completely wasted. It hasn't gotten you anywhere. You are still craving the same things, although by now it might have dawned on you that in the past those things never brought you satisfaction. It is the same routine, always craving more, and it just goes on and on.

When you think this way, you should begin to feel some disenchantment, some sorrow, some sadness. You should wonder, "How can I get out of this situation? How can I renounce this endless trap of cyclic existence?" Such questions will arise when you begin to see that all the wonders of cyclic existence have never brought you satisfaction and are only the basis for trouble.

Nāgārjuna says in the *Friendly Letter:*

> Know that attachment to your desires
> Is just like a leper afflicted with maggots,
> Who resorts to fire in hopes of relief,
> But finds no respite.

If a leper burns himself to relieve the pain of his disease it may help for a short while, but the resulting burn will only make things worse in the end. That is the kind of transient relief you get from indulging in sensual pleasures: it may diminish the pain of cyclic existence for a short while, but in the long term it makes things worse.

The *Compendium of the Perfections (Pāramitā-samāsa)* says:

> When you have obtained your desire,
> And indulged in it every day,
> Piling it up, but still you are not satisfied—
> What pathology is greater than that?

When you think about the sensual pleasures you seek to enjoy—such as food and sexual contact—you are never satisfied by experiencing them just once. You always need to indulge in them over and over again. The problem is that no matter how many times you enjoy these pleasures, you can never get enough of them. You can accumulate vast quantities of food, clothes, or treasure, but you will never be satisfied. Often, the more you get the more you want, so that the craving for satisfaction actually leads to more and more dissatisfaction. Can you think of any sickness that is worse than that?

To a practitioner—one who meditates, who applies discriminating wisdom in order to understand how this process works—this perpetual dissatisfaction will appear to be a very great sickness indeed. Then the question becomes, "How can this sickness be cured?" The only treatment for this disease is the practice of the path.

Candragomin's *Letter to a Student* says:

> What realm of rebirth have we not visited hundreds of times?
> What pleasure have we not enjoyed many times before?
> What luxury have we not obtained, like a splendid white-tail fan?
> Yet, even though we have such things, still our desire increases.
>
> There is no suffering we have not experienced many times in the past.
> There is no desire that provides any being with complete satisfaction.
> There is no sentient being in whose womb we have not lain.
> Then how is it we samsaric beings are not free from attachment?

Today, people are so busy, scurrying around in such a rush—but for what? What is it they spend their whole lives running after? The main thing they are seeking is a source of happiness that will finally bring them a full measure of satisfaction. That is the goal they all have in the back of their minds. But no matter what you do, no matter how hard you try, no matter how many places you look—you never find complete satisfaction. Why? Because all of the actions you take in order to find this satisfaction are actually misleading you. All of these actions are done out of ignorance and bring you further under the power of attachment and hostility. Instead of bringing satisfaction, they only deliver more unhappiness and suffering.

But then, what is the best way to get full satisfaction, perfect satisfaction, everlasting and unchanging happiness? Where is the pure cause of pure satisfaction? That is what you should be looking for. The root of all the sufferings of cyclic existence is ignorance. From there, the obscuring afflictions and karma lead you down the road of endless sorrow. Therefore, to get at the cause of samsara you must remove ignorance from the root, and you do that through the cultivation and realization of wisdom. All of these meditations are designed to reveal the true causality of cyclic existence, and the true causality of emancipation. Is it possible to achieve complete cessation of the cycle of samsara? What is the method to do that? These are the things you need to concentrate on. When these are realized, all of your actions will be turned around and you will begin to behave in ways that ultimately lead to genuine, lasting happiness, instead of endless disappointment and pain.

If you contemplate the following passage from Aśvaghoṣa's *Alleviating Sorrow (Śoka-vinodana),* you will gain a deeper feeling of disenchantment with cyclic existence:

Again and again in hell
You drank boiling molten copper,
In a quantity that would exceed
Even the water in the ocean.

When you were a dog and a pig,
The filth that you ate
Amounted to a great deal more
Than Meru, the king of mountains.

Because of separating from friends and relatives,
You have cried in the realms of cyclic existence.
The ocean would not be a big enough vessel
To contain the tears that have fallen from your eyes.

The heads that have been cut off,
Due to strife between one side and another,
If piled up, would reach so high,
They would surpass the world of Brahmā.

When you were a worm you were so hungry,
You ate so much dirt,
That if you poured it into the milky-white ocean,
It would fill it to the brim.

And the *Array of Stalks Sutra (Gaṇḍa-vyūha-sūtra)* says:

Remember all the bodies which in the past
Were wasted due to your senseless desires.
From now on, with the practice that aims for enlightenment,
You should conquer desire with disciplined practice.

Remember all the bodies which in the past
Were wasted due to your senseless desires.
Though as many buddhas as grains of sand in the Ganges have appeared,
You have not pleased them, nor listened to what they taught.

You should contemplate this and understand it. All of the wonders of cyclic existence that you have experienced were all illusory. You have spent so much mental and physical energy over so many lifetimes, undergone so many hardships, just to enjoy those deceitful pleasures. What a waste! All that effort has done nothing to help you; you remain in the same unhappy situation. Therefore, if you do not make an effort to change direction in this life, you will just continue going around again and again, endlessly wasting life after life. Contemplating this reality, you should generate regret and disenchantment with cyclic existence, and determine that in the future you will turn down a different path.

The famous Kadampa Geshe Chenngawa said:

> Noble teacher,[2] since beginningless time how many different bodies have we taken? But up until now we have not had the experience of practicing the Mahayana teachings. Therefore, we must apply ourselves with diligence.

And Geshe Sangphuwa said:

> You have had to face many ups and downs in this cyclic existence; do not place your hopes on this kind of experience.

You should contemplate these ideas until an attitude of disenchantment with samsaric attractions arises, and even after it arises you should continuously cultivate it in practice. This means that you should survey the scope of your whole life—and then go beyond that to past and future lives—contemplating the cause and effect of the entire samsaric cycle. You need to see clearly how samsara is a state of sorrow and disappointment, in which you have no freedom and no power over your own experience. When you see your true conditions very deeply, with the attitude that finds these miserable circumstances to be totally unsatisfactory, then you need to hold that thought, develop it and deepen it by continuously making it part of your practice. Once you have fully cultivated this attitude, wisdom will naturally lead you to a mode of behavior that will take you in the right direction.

(iii) The fault of repeatedly losing one's life

Once you take birth in a particular life form, in a particular body, you become attached to it, and you apply all your life's energy toward nourishing and protecting it. However, that body cannot be preserved and will not remain as you wish. As you travel through cyclic existence you will have to cast off your beloved body over and over again. As Nāgārjuna says in his *Friendly Letter:*

> Each one of us has left a pile of bones
> That would surpass Mount Meru.

If you piled up all the bones from all the bodies you have had in all your previous lifetimes, they would form a pile much greater than Mount Meru.

(iv) The fault of having to take rebirth repeatedly

Not only do you have to lose your body over and over again, but each time you have to be born again. Even though you may want this to be your last life, the cycle won't stop. Why not? Because you have created the causes and conditions to be reborn out of attachment, hostility, and ignorance. That karma will ripen, whether you wish it to or not. Nāgārjuna says in the *Friendly Letter:*

> If you tried to calculate the limit of mothers by counting
> With pellets the size of juniper berries, the earth would not be big
> enough.

Here Tsongkhapa comments that earlier scholars interpreted this quotation to mean that one single sentient being has been your mother countless times. Although that is also true, it is not the meaning of this particular quotation. Mahāmati's commentary, the *Clear Words: Explanation of the "Friendly Letter" (Vyakta-padā-suhṛl-lekha-ṭīkā),* cites a sutra that says:

> For example, monks, if someone took small pellets the size of juniper berries from this great earth, and set each one aside counting, 'This is my mother; this is the mother of my mother" and so forth—then, O monks, the ground of this great earth would be exhausted long before he reached the end of the lineage of mothers.

This direct quotation from the sutras shows that this image is meant to refer to the lineage of mothers and not to the number of times that one single being has been one person's mother, or how many different mothers one person has had over many lifetimes. Nevertheless, it is also true that since beginningless time we have all been reborn numberless times, so it is possible that all sentient beings have been your mother innumerable times in the past, and this is the way this teaching is often presented.

Contemplating the endless cycles of suffering in this way will lead you to recognize the faults of cyclic existence and to become disenchanted with it. As Āryadeva says in the *Four Hundred Stanzas:*

> When you cannot see the initial cause
> Of even a single result,
> Then you see how vast are the causes of even one result.
> Who would not be frightened?

When you try to isolate the single, initial cause of a particular result—for example, your rebirth in this realm—you discover it cannot be determined. There are so many causes and conditions that contribute to that result. The web of intertwined causes and conditions, and of the causes of those causes, is so vast and deep that, if you could see this network in its entirety, you would certainly feel fear and aversion toward cyclic existence.

The commentary on this passage by Candrakīrti explains the meaning this way:

> It is correct to cultivate a constant disenchantment and to meditate on the true nature of this great lonely wilderness of samsara, in which it is so difficult to make one's way because of the dense thicket whose dimensions are impossible to grasp.

Cyclic existence is compared to a wilderness that seems almost impossible to escape from because it is filled with and surrounded by a multitude of obstacles. It is as if there were mountains, rivers, thorns, fire, and every imaginable obstruction, making it virtually impossible to get through this wilderness to the other side. As soon as you overcome one set of obstacles, you confront a completely new problem. Once you are born into samsara, you are trapped in just such a situation; although you want to get out, it is difficult to move.

But there is a way out. It begins by cultivating disenchantment with those circumstances. This leads to a powerful determination to find a way out. What you discover is that the way out is to "meditate on the true nature" of samsara, which means to reverse the ignorant conceptions that got you into that situation in the first place. Ordinarily, you perceive objects that produce suffering to be sources of pleasure and you become attached to them. You perceive things that are constantly changing to be permanent and reliable. You perceive impure, contaminated objects to be pure and wholesome. From these misconceptions arises the panoply of afflictions: attachment, aversion, pride, jealousy, and all the rest. When you meditate on their true nature, however, you begin to see these things as they really are: in the nature of suffering, impermanent, impure, and empty of any absolute, essential reality. If you meditate on these attributes, you will find your way through the thicket of cyclic existence to the other side.

(v) The fault of constantly fluctuating from high to low states

Not only are you compelled to take birth in cyclic existence over and over again, but you are constantly fluctuating between high and low states in a way that is totally out of your control. Nāgārjuna's *Friendly Letter* says:

> You may become Indra, worshiped by the world,
> But by the power of karma you will fall once more to earth.
> You may become a universal monarch,
> But once again you will become a lowly servant in cyclic existence.

Within the desire realm are a number of different classes of *devas,* or *gods.* The highest of these devas dwell at the peak of Mount Meru in a place known as the Heaven of the Thirty-three. It is given this name because there are thirty-three primary gods residing there. Chief among them is Indra, called the Lord of the Gods. He is said to ride upon a giant elephant that emanates thirty-two heads in order to carry the remaining gods of this realm. In this quotation Nāgārjuna is saying that you may have been born many times as this glorious and lordly Indra, and on those occasions you were worshiped by many beings. But when your life as Indra in the Heaven of the Thirty-three comes to an end, you will "fall once more to earth," meaning that by the power of karma you will take a suffering rebirth, perhaps as a human, or perhaps as an animal or even a hungry ghost.

On a less exalted level, many human beings acquire great fame, wealth, and honor, and live in luxury comparable to that of the gods. All this is the result of their previous good karma. However, when the fruit of that good karma is exhausted, it will be their accumulated negative karma that is then ready to ripen. According to the Buddhist teachings, you may be born in a "heaven" or in a "hell," but these are not permanent conditions. It is your previous karma that causes any particular rebirth; when that karma is exhausted, that lifetime will end. Then you will take a new rebirth, which will depend on whichever karmic potential is strongest at the time. You may be born and live for many thousands of years as a deva in the blissful form or formless realms, where you experience no pain or any other form of gross suffering. But eventually that life will end and your brief respite from samsaric misery will abruptly end with it. Until you cut off karma at the root through the direct realization of the wisdom that cognizes the truth of the self and the truth of phenomena, there is no way to end the misery of fluctuating up and down within cyclic existence.

The *Friendly Letter* continues:

> You may linger long, tasting the joys of caressing
> The breasts and waists of heavenly maidens,
> But then again you will know the unbearable sensation
> Of the grinding, cutting, scraping engines of hell.
>
> You may reside at the peak of Mount Meru,
> Enjoying the feel of cushioned ground beneath your feet,
> But then again, think of the unbearable pain
> Of walking upon hot coals and rotting corpses.

These verses remind us that there is not much distance between the most blissful sensuous pleasures and the most hideous sufferings we can imagine. One night you are in a godly realm where the very ground is as soft as a feather bed and heavenly maidens await your pleasure; then you wake up the next morning sunk to your knees in a bed of hot coals. Between those two experiences there is not much distance; by the power of karma it can happen suddenly, just like that. When you awaken to that sudden, disastrous change, you desperately try to escape from that hellish scene, but there is nowhere to go. You are trapped in the misery of your own experience.

The images in this quotation come from descriptions we find in the scriptures. The "grinding, cutting, scraping engines of hell" refer to machine-like mechanisms that operate in, respectively, the Crushed Together Hell, the Black Line Hell, and the Very Hot Hell.[3] In the god realms it is said that the ground is soft and bouncy, like walking on cushions. The "hot coals and rotting corpses" refer to two of the sixteen subsidiary hells surrounding the eight primary hot hells. The first is called Burning Ash Pit, where you sink up to your knees in hot coals. The second is Putrid Corpse Swamp, where you sink in corpse-filled mud up to the neck while sharp-beaked insects bore into your body.

Again, these hells are not permanent states of existence, but are experienced as a result of the actions that an individual has taken in the past. For example, if you harmed other beings by burning them, that karmic potential might ripen into the experience of walking, for a long, long time, through a wasteland of burning hot coals. That agonizing experience may last a long time, but eventually the karma that produced it will be exhausted.

Nāgārjuna continues:

> You may frolic in beautiful groves,
> Sporting with heavenly maidens,

Then again, you find yourself in the forests of hell,
Where the leaves are like swords slicing off feet, hands, nose, and ears.[4]

With beautiful goddesses
You may enter limpid waters decorated with golden lotuses,
Then again, you will be plunged into the scalding hot waters
Of the unbearable River with No Ford.[5]

You may attain the sensual ecstasy of the desire realm gods,
Or even the detached bliss of Brahmā,
Then again, you will meet unrelenting agony
As fuel for the fires of Avīci Hell.

All the beings of the desire realm crave and indulge in sensual pleasure. There are six levels of desire realm gods, beginning with the Heaven of the Thirty-three, and they all enjoy a very intense and blissful degree of pleasure.

The abodes of the Brahmā-level gods are part of the form realm. One is born there by attaining the meditative absorption of the *first concentration.* Beings in that state of existence still experience physical pleasure, but it is not sexual in nature. It is much more subtle and superior to sexual pleasure because it is a blissful bodily feeling that arises in association with the mental happiness of meditative absorption. In connection with that deep peacefulness of mind, the body also experiences this special kind pleasure. This feeling is called pleasure *free of sensual attachment,* and during that life beings have no experience of pain.

It sometimes happens that practitioners who attain this level of meditative absorption mistake the first concentration for actual emancipation, because they become attached to the blissful mental happiness and concomitant bodily pleasure they experience there. This is the highest physical pleasure one can have in the samsaric world; it is the most subtle, most peaceful, most blissful level of bodily pleasure. Above the level of the first concentration, feelings of physical pleasure do not exist; there is only mental happiness.

And yet, even if you attain that most subtle, blissful feeling, which is free of attachment to sensual experience, it is only a matter of time before you fall again into the agony of burning for millions of years in the fires of Avīci Hell where your body becomes like a burning log or the wick of a lamp. "Avīci" means "unrelenting," and this hell is given that name because from the time you are born there until that karma is exhausted there is not the slightest moment of respite from pain.

The quotations from Nāgārjuna conclude with the following stanza:

> You may attain the status of the sun or the moon,
> The radiance of your body illuminating the entire world,
> Then again, you have to return to the pitch black darkness,
> Where you cannot even see your own outstretched hand.

Though this stanza says that you may attain "the status of the sun or the moon," it does not mean that a being could literally become the sun or moon. This quotation is referring to the ancient Indian myth in which the light of the sun and the moon was thought of as radiating from celestial palaces contained within these heavenly bodies. According to this myth, the sun produces *hot* light because the palace it contains is made of glass whose nature is to produce heat, like a magnifying glass. And the moon produces *cool* light because its celestial palace is made of crystal glass, whose nature is to produce *cool* light.

Tsongkhapa makes the point that the light that illuminates the world is not made by a living being, and one cannot be born as the sun or the moon. However, in Buddhist cosmology there are beings whose bodies naturally emanate light. The devas of the second concentration in the form realm have bodies like that, and the three types of devas there are called Little Light, Limitless Light, and Bright Light. Also, during the *eon of evolution,* when the universe is coalescing and coming back to life, the first humans here in the southern continent of Jambudvīpa have very subtle bodies. They are born by *miraculous birth* and not from wombs; they consume *mental joy* instead of solid food; they have the power to travel in space; they have immeasurably long life spans; and light emanates from their bodies.

But even if you *could* attain a body so powerful it illuminated the whole universe, it would be just a matter of time until you were born into a place of utter and absolute darkness, such as the cold hells, where you cannot even see the end of your own outstretched hand.

This passage from the *Friendly Letter* offers many illustrations of how you are tossed up and down between the various conditions of cyclic existence. In one lifetime you may be enjoying divine bliss, but in the next moment find yourself immersed in agony. So it goes: up and down, up and down. The lowest and poorest become the highest. The highest fall to an in-between state, or to a lowly one. The main point is that there is nothing reliable about any condition in cyclic existence. There is no way to know where you will be in the next moment, and no way to control the process. Within cyclic existence there is nothing stable, permanent, worthy of attachment, worth making the central object of your whole life. No matter how much energy and effort you put into it, there is no worldly purpose that can ever bring everlasting peace and happiness. All of the apparently attractive objects and goals within cyclic existence are, in their very nature, unreliable, ready to collapse at any moment, and therefore in the nature of suffering.

Contemplating these circumstances, you should see the entire range of cyclic existence as one huge jail. You should generate strong disenchantment with the reality that you are trapped within this prison, and make a powerful determination to get out of this situation. That is the main object of these meditations.

In the section of the Vinaya called the *Bases of Discipline,* we find the story of four merchants from Śrāvastī, each of whom had his own special interest. The first was out to amass great wealth. The second wanted to build a fabulous house. The third wanted to make many friends. And the fourth wanted to find a pill for rejuvenation and longevity. The first merchant achieved his goal, became very wealthy, but then had every penny stolen by a powerful king, and finally ended his life as a beggar. The second merchant built a magnificent mansion, but it caught fire and was utterly destroyed. The third merchant became very popular and made many friends, but eventually they all deserted him and left him lonely and miserable. The fourth merchant, who wanted to live a very long time, ended up dead. Commenting on this parable the Buddha said:

> All accumulation in the end is spent.
> The elevated in the end falls down.
> The end of meetings is separation.
> The end of life is death.

Regardless of how rich, splendid, or beloved you may be, it all ends. No matter what you build, it finally deteriorates and declines. All things come to an undesirable end. This is the nature of cyclic existence.

(vi) The fault of having no companions

In the *Friendly Letter* Nāgārjuna tells his friend, the king:

> Thus, please understand that you will come to grief.
> Seize the light of the threefold lamp of merits.
> Otherwise you will be cast alone into endless darkness,
> Which neither sun nor moon can pierce.

He is telling the king that even though you have great wealth, power, and splendor, it is all destined to disintegrate. "You will come to grief" means that you have to die; you have to leave all of this behind. Rather than grasping at these worldly goals, he tells the king, seize the "threefold lamp of merits." This metaphor can refer to maintaining pure ethical conduct of body, speech, and mind, or to the three trainings of pure ethical conduct, meditative stabilization, and the wisdom that realizes the true nature of reality. These latter three are the lights of the lamp clearing away the darkness of cyclic existence. Without such light, even if you own the whole universe, in the end you will go alone into the darkness. Here, "endless darkness" refers not only to the pitch black world of the lower realms, but to the darkness of ignorance, which entraps you in those suffering states.

In *Engaging in the Bodhisattva Deeds,* Śāntideva has this to say about how, in the end, we are alone:

> Although this body arose as one thing,
> The bones and flesh with which it was created
> Will break up and separate.
> How much more so will friends and others?
>
> At birth I was born alone,
> And at death too I shall die alone.
> As this pain cannot be shared by others,
> What use are obstacle-making friends?

At the time of birth you cannot bring friends along as companions. At the time of death you cannot say to your loved ones, "I am going to die now; you must die with me!" You have to go alone. No one can take a share of your misery. Therefore, what use are friends who only create hindrances?

Do not misunderstand what is being said here. Śāntideva is certainly not saying that you should not be friendly to other people, or look at other people as mere hindrances. Cultivating love and compassion for other beings is at the heart of the bodhisattva path. What is being criticized here is one's attachment to friends and loved ones based on the unrealistic expectation that they are the source of stable happiness. That *attachment* is the hindrance; that is the enemy. Out of that attachment you perform all kinds of negative actions, which create all the sufferings and all the obstacles to liberation. That is the point of this stanza.

The object here is to understand the situation of both yourself and others. This leads to developing compassion for others because you recognize how they are suffering just as you are. When you come to understand the nature of cyclic existence, it does not produce aversion to other living beings. Quite the contrary. It produces concern for their welfare and the determination to find liberation not just for yourself, but for all of the beings in the world, who are equally your friends.

The real friend, the best friend in cyclic existence, is virtue—virtuous mental qualities and virtuous actions. This is what leads to a better life, a higher rebirth, and finally to the total cessation of this suffering, samsaric life. That is the kind of friend you can rely on. That is where you should place your trust.

In conclusion, these six types of suffering can be sorted into three categories, which can be stated as follows:

1. There is nothing in cyclic existence that can be trusted or relied upon to provide true and lasting benefit.
2. However much you indulge in the pleasures of cyclic existence, in the end you will never find perfect satisfaction.
3. You have been experiencing this suffering, samsaric nature since beginningless time.

The first of these three can be divided into four parts:

1a. There is no security in obtaining a body. Wherever you are born in cyclic existence, your condition—whether high or low—will eventually change and you will have to take a new body. This corresponds to "the fault of having to take rebirth repeatedly"—the fifth of the six types of suffering.

1b. There is no security in things that benefit or harm you. Relationships with friends and enemies are not static and cannot be trusted. The dearest friend can suddenly change into the most undesirable enemy. This corresponds to "the fault of uncertainty"—the second of the six types of suffering.

1c. There is no security in obtaining the wonders of cyclic existence, because high things eventually become low. This corresponds to "the fault of constantly fluctuating from high to low states"—the fifth of the six types.

1d. There is no security in companions, because when you die, you go without companions. This corresponds to "the fault of having no companions"—the sixth type of suffering.

The second category in this three-part format—"in the end you will never find perfect satisfaction"—corresponds to "the fault of insatiability"—the second of the six types of suffering. And the third category—"You have been experiencing this suffering, samsaric nature since beginningless time" corresponds to "the fault of repeatedly losing one's life"—the third of the six types of suffering.

This condensed presentation gives you another format for meditating on these six unattractive qualities of cyclic existence. We have now considered the disadvantages of samsara in terms of eight types of suffering and the six types of suffering. In the next chapter we learn how to meditate on the nature of cyclic existence in terms of three types of suffering.

7

Further Meditations on Suffering

(c) Contemplating the three types of suffering
- (i) The suffering of change
- (ii) The suffering of suffering
- (iii) The suffering of conditionality

2" Contemplating specific sufferings
- (a) The suffering of human beings
- (b) The suffering of the demigods
- (c) The suffering of the devas
  - (i) The suffering of the devas of the desire realm
    - (a') The suffering of dying and falling
      - (1') The suffering of dying
      - (2') The suffering of falling to a lower state
    - (b') The suffering of being frightened
    - (c') The sufferings of being cut, gashed, killed, and banished
  - (ii) The suffering of the gods of the form and formless realms

(c) Contemplating the three types of suffering

All of the sufferings of cyclic existence can be included within three types: the suffering of change, the suffering of suffering, and the suffering of conditionality.

(i) The suffering of change

The suffering of change is exemplified by the following example. When you have a painful open wound on your skin, the pain can be temporarily relieved by applying cool clean water. That relief from pain is experienced as a pleasant feeling. It is not really pleasure; it is just that the discomfort has lightened up a bit. And that relief, that feeling of pleasure, will not last long; soon it will change again into the suffering of pain.

In the same way, the experiences we ordinarily think of as pleasurable—such as eating, drinking, touching, or lying down—are not inherently, by their very nature, pleasant. There is no real, abiding, reliable pleasure there. What you experience as pleasure is really the temporary relief of a pain or discomfort, such as hunger or thirst. This temporary relief is what we experience as, and label as, pleasure. As soon as that relief stops, the underlying suffering reemerges, just as the pain of a wound returns a few moments after you have applied cool water. This is the meaning of the suffering of change: all feelings of pleasure eventually change into suffering again.

The suffering of change does not only refer to the feeling itself—pleasant and unpleasant sensual feelings—but also includes other mental processes that arise together with those feelings, such as the main mind and the associated mental factors. Furthermore, it includes those contaminated objects that, when experienced, produce those feelings. All of these are included in the suffering of change.

Take, for example, your experience of being hungry. To soothe that discomfort you eat something. There arises as a result the mere feeling that you are experiencing pleasure. Concomitant with that sensory feeling of pleasure are various minds and mental factors. The entire body-mind complex that you experience as pleasure, as well as the food that generates the feeling of pleasure, is the suffering of change. It is the nature of this entire conditioned web of cause and effect that it will eventually change into more suffering. That is the suffering of change. In fact there is no real pleasure there; it is only the degree of suffering that has changed.

(ii) The suffering of suffering

Now consider what would happen to that open wound if you put some irritating substance on it, like salt water. The pain would flare up, becoming sharp and intense. This feeling is what we identify as suffering. Whenever something like this happens, the body or mind experiences an increased level of pain or anguish. That is what constitutes the suffering of suffering.

As we explained for the suffering of change, the suffering of suffering also includes the main mind and the mental factors that arise together with the feeling of suffering, as well as the contaminated objects that produce such a painful feeling.

The Abhidharma speaks of five types of feelings that beings can experience.

There are two types of bodily feeling, which are based on the sense faculties. These are termed: (1) *unpleasant feeling,* a disagreeable bodily experience of pain; and (2) *pleasant feeling,* an agreeable bodily experience. Then there are two types of mental feeling. These are: (3) *mental happiness,* an agreeable mental experience; and (4) *mental unhappiness,* a disagreeable experience. Finally, there is (5) *neutral feeling,* an experience in between agreeable and disagreeable, which can be either physical or mental.

What we have seen in this and the previous section is that (2) pleasant feeling, along with its concomitant (3) mental happiness, are the *suffering of change,* because by their nature they change into suffering. And (1) unpleasant feeling, along with its concomitant (4) mental unhappiness, are the *suffering of suffering;* this is the pain and anguish we ordinarily speak of as "suffering." Now we turn to the *suffering of conditionality,* and as we shall see, this form of pervasive suffering also includes (5) neutral feeling.

(iii) The suffering of conditionality

You have an open wound. We know that if you put cool water on it, the pain will be reduced, and we call that experience a *pleasant feeling.* At the other extreme, if you rub salt into the wound, the pain sharply increases, and we call that *unpleasant feeling.* However, even without either of these two actions, you still have a big open wound. The very nature of that wound—its condition—is suffering. This is the suffering of conditionality, and it pervades all experience within cyclic existence—including *neutral feeling,* when you do not have a strong reaction one way or another to a stimulus. Another name for the suffering of conditionality is *pervasive suffering,* because all of cyclic existence is pervaded by this suffering nature.

The suffering of conditionality encompasses even neutral feelings, because they are inseparably connected to the so-called "negative tendencies." As we explained previously,[1] these negative tendencies refer to the potential you carry with you, in the form of karma and afflictions, to experience undesirable circumstances. Even neutral feelings are produced by karma, which itself was instigated by obscuring afflictions. And, as was the case with the other two types of suffering, the suffering of conditionality does not refer to the feeling alone—whether it be pleasant, unpleasant, or neutral—but includes the entire psycho-physical complex (i.e., the body-mind continuum) that accompanies this feeling.

Every feeling, and the web of experience in which it is embedded, is the product of karma and afflictions. Not only that, this moment of experience carries with it the potential, in the form of afflictions, for future suffering. In this way, *all* experiences, including neutral feelings, are inseparable from the negative tendencies, the afflictions that will produce future suffering. This is why the suffering of conditionality is pervasive: there simply is no experience within cyclic existence, whether pleasant, unpleasant, or neutral, which is not rooted in, and carrying the future potential for, suffering. From the highest formless realms down to the lowest hells, wherever sentient beings are born under the power of karma and afflictions, this is the pervasive condition. Even when the present moment of experience is a neutral feeling, the potential for future suffering is embedded in that moment. The very condition of being born into cyclic existence means that your psycho-physical aggregates are the results of previous karma and afflictions, and are the seedbed of future suffering experience. Until you completely get rid of obscuring afflictions from the root, that will remain your condition.

Because you are entangled with these negative tendencies, when a pleasant feeling arises attachment increases; when a suffering feeling arises hostility increases; and when a neutral feeling arises ignorance increases. This ignorance manifests, for example, in your perceiving impermanent things like the body as permanent; or impure things as pure; or suffering things as truly pleasurable; or perceiving all things—which equally lack any inherent existence—as being ultimately, essentially, real.

Attachment causes rebirth in future lives among the six realms of sentient beings. Whether you are born in the lower realms of the hell beings, hungry ghosts, or animals, or whether you are born in the higher realms of the humans, demigods, or devas—desire and attachment are the precipitating cause of all rebirth within cyclic existence. Hatred and anger give rise to many forms of misery, beginning with sorrow and grief in this life, and leading to rebirth in the terrifying conditions of the lower realms in future lives. Ignorance is the basis of attachment and hostility, the other two root afflictions; it supports them and acts as their foundation. It is due to ignorance that the other afflictions thrive, and ignorance makes it extremely difficult to escape their influence. Therefore, when a pleasant feeling arises, do not become attached to that pleasure, but see it in its true nature: as suffering. This is the way to eliminate attachment. When an unpleasant, suffering feeling arises, instead of reacting with hatred or anger toward some external source, consider how this body itself is like a wound whose very nature is to be a source of pain. If you touch fire, get burned, and the burn hurts, it serves no purpose to get mad at the fire. Instead of surrendering to anger, understand that this is the nature of your body; realize that once you take a body like this, pain will naturally arise. This is the way to eliminate hostility. When neutral feelings arise, recognize that their nature is impermanent and perishable. This is the way to overcome ignorance.

Ordinarily, you allow pleasant, unpleasant, and neutral feelings to become causes of the three poisons: attachment, hostility, and ignorance. This is the powerful engine that drives you through endless cyclic existence. By applying these instructions you transform the way you view these three types of feelings so that, instead of giving rise to the three poisons, they lead to disenchantment with samsara, patience, and the wisdom that realizes the true nature of things. This is the way to gain liberation from cyclic existence. Tsongkhapa says that he has explained these points in accordance with Asaṅga's *Compendium of Determinations* and *Levels of Yogic Deeds.*

When people have to carry a heavy burden, they will not feel comfortable as long as they have that burden on their back. In the same way, as long as you carry the burden of these five *appropriating aggregates*—this combination of body and mind—you will experience suffering and you will not find enduring happiness. As we explained earlier,[2] these aggregates are *appropriating* because they are attached to things of the present and they grasp after things of the future. These aggregates are inextricably bound up with the negative tendencies: that is, (1) karma and afflictions, which are the cause of the aggregates, and (2) the subtle propensities, which are afflictions in their potential form and which will give rise to karma and suffering in the future. In other words, it is the nature of the appropriating aggregates that they have within them the potential to manifest pain and suffering. Although there are times when the overt feeling of pain or discomfort does not manifest, it is always present in a potential form, and at any moment may emerge from any number of causes.

This is the pervasive nature of the suffering of conditionality. The human body is delicate and it is easy to recognize the presence of suffering in human life. Even small stimuli, such as a little too much hot or cold, bring on feelings of pain. But even if you consider the devas—the life forms abiding in the highest heavenly realms where there is no such thing as painful feelings—they still have not removed the subtle propensities that, like seeds, will act as causes of suffering in the future; they are still entwined in the negative tendencies. The devas are enjoying a brief respite in their journey through samsara, and during this respite the gross forms of pain are not manifest. Nevertheless, the conditions for the experience of suffering are still with them. The pervasive conditions of suffering are with *every* being until the causes of suffering are removed from the root. This situation is the suffering of conditionality, and from the perspective of the Dharma practitioner, the blissful life of a deva must be renounced just as much as rebirth in a suffering realm, because they are the same in having this nature of pervasive suffering.

The suffering of conditionality pervades all forms of suffering. It is the root of the suffering of change and the suffering of suffering. When you have a wound you can make it feel better by applying medicine or cold water, or you can make it flair up in pain by applying an irritant like salt. But the wound itself is the base, the root, of those other experiences. It is the fundamental condition enabling the temporary relief of pain (which we call "pleasant") or the intensification of pain (which we call "unpleasant") to arise. The fundamental condition for all of these experiences is your birth into these aggregates, which are inextricably intertwined with karma and afflictions.

Therefore, you need to meditate on this fundamental samsaric condition with intense effort and determination, because the suffering of conditionality is very subtle and extremely hard to see. Beings like us, who are enmeshed in cyclic existence, cannot see it because it is too close to us, because we are right in the middle of it.

The effect of fully realizing the suffering of conditionality is that you actually understand the first noble truth: the truth of suffering. It will not be enough to gain an understanding of a particular occasion of pain, or how the suffering of change works. You must gain a deep insight into the pervasive nature of suffering, the way it encompasses the whole samsaric situation.

Pleasurable feelings in the present—for example, those that arise from eating good food, hearing beautiful music, or making physical contact with another—increase desire and attachment. But there is really nothing in any of these experiences that has an essential nature of pleasure. Most of those pleasant feelings arise from the temporary relief of suffering feelings. This produces a sense of pleasure, a lightening of the burden, which is then labeled "happiness." There is no such thing as a pleasant feeling which is, in its own nature, true pleasure. Pleasure does not exist independent of the occasional relief from suffering. Pleasure is the feeling you get when the pervasive feeling of pain or dissatisfaction stops. Pleasant feeling is actually just a comparison with the previous unpleasant yearning or discomfort, and we label that comparative feeling "pleasure."

Here is an example that makes it very clear. You go for a walk. You enjoy walking and so you walk and walk, until finally you get tired of walking. Your legs are sore; you feel that you've done too much walking. Because of that pain in your legs (the suffering of suffering), you sit down to rest. Ahhh! Sitting there you feel the pleasure of just sitting. That is a pleasant feeling; that is what we call "pleasure," or "happiness."

But is sitting itself a natural cause of pleasure? Is that the nature of sitting? Isn't the pleasure of sitting merely the gradual reduction in the pain from walking? It *appears,* deceptively, to be pleasure, but pleasure is not an intrinsic quality of sitting. Why not? Because if you continued to sit, and sit, and sit, gradually the pleasant feeling would fade and a painful feeling would increase (the suffering of change). Then look what happens: you want to get up and *walk* again! Too much sitting, just like too much walking, leads to pain and trouble. If sitting were intrinsically pleasurable, then as long as you sat the pleasure would continue, or even increase. But it doesn't work that way, does it? Therefore, the pleasant feeling does not reside in the activity, but rather in the relief from suffering that the activity offers. And that relief is invariably short-lived.

You can apply the same analysis to all the activities that give us pleasure: lying down, eating and drinking, sitting in the sun or the shade, and so on. Eating is another good example of what we've been discussing. When you are hungry, eating a good meal gives so much pleasure. But that pleasure will not continue to increase if you keep eating, and eating, and eating. In fact, it will quickly turn into pain and discomfort. Eating is not intrinsically pleasurable and cannot provide everlasting happiness. In fact, the only kind of pleasure it can offer is to end the misery of being hungry. Think of any of the sensory experiences that give you pleasure. Is there even one that will continue to be pleasurable if you continue to do it endlessly? That is not the nature of experience in samsara. The nature of samsaric pleasure is that it will eventually turn into suffering.

The Buddha himself explains this in the *Descent into the Womb Sutra:*

> Nanda, you must understand that physical activities such as walking, sitting, standing up, or lying down are each in the nature of suffering. When meditators examine such activities and their nature, they find that if you pass the entire day walking, and you never stand still, sit down, or lie down, then you will experience that walking purely as suffering. And that suffering experience will be intense, harsh, difficult to bear, and unpleasant. The idea that walking is pleasurable will not arise.

After explaining the other three physical activities in the same terms, the Buddha continues:

> However, Nanda, in order to interrupt that suffering of physical activities, beings engage in other, new activities, and then they conceive those other activities to be pleasure. Nanda, when that feeling of pleasure arises it is only suffering arising. When it stops, it is only this suffering nature that stops. Also, when it arises, it arises in the nature of a produced phenomenon. When it stops, it stops in the nature of a produced phenomenon.

In order to bring an end to the discomfort of the activity you are currently involved in, you try to do something else. That brief respite gives you the perception of pleasure. But that samsaric pleasure is in the nature of suffering. You decrease one kind of suffering only by increasing another. This is the nature of cyclic existence. Whatever samsaric activity stops one pain by providing temporary relief is itself just another form of suffering. While one type of suffering is ceasing, the cause of another, new type of suffering is starting. In this sense, the ceasing of suffering itself, when it is produced by *contaminated* or samsaric activities, is itself in the nature of suffering.

In this passage the Buddha also points out that the feeling of pleasure is not some permanently pleasant state. It is a "produced phenomenon," arising in dependence on causes and conditions, and is therefore impermanent. The new condition, which brings about its cessation, is itself a produced phenomenon, also impermanent, also dependent on karma and afflictions. But because that new condition brings relief from the previous painful feeling, you perceive it as pleasure. But as the cycle continues, that pleasure too will change into suffering, which will persist until another condition arises to relieve that suffering. This is the rising and passing away of all conditioned existence, and with this understanding you can see how suffering pervades it all.

Āryadeva says in his *Four Hundred Stanzas:*

> For pleasure, when it increases,
> Is seen to change into its opposite.
> When pain increases,
> It does not similarly change into its opposite.

If you are doing something pleasurable, and you do more, and more, and more of it, it finally turns into pain and suffering. But when you take something painful and do more of it, does it turn into pleasure? Of course not. Whatever you experience within cyclic existence, when you examine it in this light, you find that its underlying nature is suffering. When you view all of cyclic existence with this perspective, the feeling of disenchantment toward samsaric pleasure begins to develop, and this is the beginning of the thought of renunciation. That is the correct way to view your circumstances, and it will lead you along the pure, right path.

Here, we need to distinguish between this thought and another superficial thought of renunciation. The superficial thought is a reaction to some short-term pain or sorrow, or it can arise out of the fear of death or some other looming misery. This is merely an emotional reaction to some specific, temporary pain you do not want to encounter. This is not a reliable or stable thought of renunciation, because it is not rooted in an encompassing vision of the entire nature of cyclic existence. You are not really renouncing all of cyclic existence, but merely some particular unhappiness that you do not want to experience.

To develop the true thought of renunciation, you need the proper foundation of understanding the whole samsaric situation in its true nature. That is the only way to produce the thought that sees cyclic existence as a big wound, as nothing but a source of suffering, and causes you to renounce all of samsara. That pure thought is what transforms your practice into the true path leading to emancipation, and any virtuous actions you perform with that view as the motivation become the actual path of emancipation.

It is not so easy to produce that thought of renunciation truly and completely. Some people think that they can direct their practice onto the pure path without that genuine thought of renunciation. Some people take high tantric initiations, engage in the most profound Mahayana meditations, and grasp at these methods for gaining liberation without developing sincere renunciation. This kind of practice is really just another form of attachment, and is turning the path of liberation into something else.

But these meditations on the suffering nature of cyclic existence are the foundation for the pure path of emancipation. When you understand your own situation in its totality by means of these trainings, it becomes easy to apply that understanding to the circumstances of others. It becomes easy to see how others are in exactly the same straits you are in, and when you see that deeply, it becomes easy to produce great compassion. Seeing this can produce almost depthless compassion.

Without this broader vision you will only produce some kind of superficial, self-serving kind of compassion. If you just sit peacefully, merely wanting to enjoy a blissful experience, not wanting to engage in any unpleasant thoughts, you may end up with the paradoxical result of creating more unhappiness for yourself instead of true, stable happiness; and you will have no basis for understanding the suffering of others, which is the prerequisite of genuine compassion.

So these practices are important. It may take many years, but this kind of meditation does not require you to sit down somewhere with an unmoving body. You can do it while you are walking, while you are sitting, while you are lying down, even while you are eating. You can do this kind of meditation anytime, all the time. What you see, what you experience every day, all contributes to the development of this understanding. This is the way to put it all together. This is the way to make your unpleasant thoughts very productive. You can think about how the whole samsaric situation is ugly, miserable, full of sorrow and disappointment. When you think about this using the proper methods and reasons, although it is not pleasant, it will bring good results.

2" Contemplating specific sufferings

There are six types of specific sufferings, corresponding to the six realms of cyclic existence. We discussed the details of life in the lower realms in chapter 10 of the first volume of this series. In the context of the trainings of the being of small scope, we discussed the nature of their sufferings, their environment, the length of their lives, and so forth. In this section we will discuss the quality of life in the three higher realms: the realms of human beings, demigods, and devas.

(a) The suffering of human beings

In the discussion of the general sufferings of cyclic existence, which we just completed, we mentioned many of the sufferings that human beings face. We are familiar with such common human miseries as hunger and thirst, heat and cold, searching after goals such as wealth, fame, or friends, and becoming exhausted from the effort. All of the miseries we discussed under the eight types of suffering apply to human life, and you can meditate on the nature of birth as a human by contemplating those eight points as they were explained earlier. Vasubandhu says in his *Discussion of the Requisite Collections (Sambhāra-parikathā):*

> All of the sufferings of the lower realms,
> It seems, are also known to humans.
> They are like the hell beings when afflicted by pain;
> When destitute, like the hungry ghosts in Yama's world.
>
> They have the sufferings of animals;
> As the powerful use force to oppress
> And persecute the powerless,
> The sufferings flow on like a river.

And he further states:

> Some, due to poverty,
> Others, because they are never satisfied,

Suffer unbearably from always seeking more,
And are filled with animosity and murderous thoughts.

Some people can never be satisfied. Even if they owned all the continents, still they would crave more. This unending dissatisfaction and selfishness leads to animosity toward all those who have what they want, or stand in the way of getting what they want. This kind of uncontrolled craving can lead to murder, and even great wars grow out of this dissatisfied mind.

Āryadeva says in the *Four Hundred Stanzas:*

Those with high status have mental suffering,
For low-class people it comes from the body.
Day by day, these two kinds of suffering
Overwhelm people in this world.

Kings, millionaires, the rulers of the world—they do not have to do strenuous physical work like peasants and manual laborers. They may have all the wealth and luxuries anyone could imagine, but these do not bring them any lasting peace of mind. They are still tormented by jealousy, insecurity, dissatisfaction, and every manner of mental unhappiness. In fact, you may find that the poorest beggar, who has to go out into the heat of summer and the cold of winter to beg for a little bit of food, is happier than the man who controls a vast empire but is afflicted with anxiety for his position and a dissatisfied mind.

Wherever you look in the world of humans, everyone is eventually stricken by the physical pains of the body and mental unhappiness of one sort or another. You can meditate on how these two forms of suffering arise in your own life, and then you can extend your meditation out to consider the lives of others. You should contemplate how humans of every social class, race, and religion suffer from these two types of misery. Whether they cover their bodies in rags or wrap themselves in the finest silks and jewels, they are equal in terms of the pain and sorrow they will meet in the end. In fact, you could say that a human being is a pile of suffering wrapped in cloth. As for a king, he is a pile of suffering, wrapped in silk, and wearing a golden crown!

(b) The suffering of the demigods

On the suffering of the demigods, Nāgārjuna's *Friendly Letter* says:

And the demigods, by nature, suffer with intense envy
For the splendor of the devas.

> Due to the afflictions of that realm, even the intelligent ones
> Cannot see the truth on the path of seeing.

Though some explanations count the demigods as a type of animal, Asaṅga's *Levels of Yogic Deeds* includes them in the realm of the devas, and in general they are considered a low level of devas who reside in the desire realm.

These demigods are mentally tormented by their unbearable jealousy toward the wealth, power, and luxury of the superior desire realm devas. Driven by this powerful antipathy, they are constantly attacking the desire realm devas and trying to steal their wealth and their goddesses. This brings them all manner of misery. First of all, in these heavenly wars the demigods always lose. Because of the subtle nature of their bodies, they do not die unless their heads are cut off at the neck, so after they get hacked to pieces in battle the pieces reassemble and heal. Then, under the control of their overpowering envy, they are ready to start fighting all over again, heedless of the misery they will face. Not only that, the demigods also have a kind of supernatural vision that enables them to see their own friends and relatives getting cut up in battle, and this too causes great sorrow.

Because of the particular afflictions of this level of existence, even the most intelligent of these beings cannot attain the realization of the truth that comes on the path of seeing. Although it is possible for demigods to undertake a spiritual practice, their progress on the path would be limited during that lifetime, even if they were to meet the Buddha himself. The devas, on the other hand, *are* capable of attaining the path of seeing.

(c) The suffering of the devas

The devas reside in three different realms: the desire realm, the form realm, and the formless realm. We will discuss them one by one.

(i) The suffering of the devas of the desire realm

The devas who belong to the desire realm have three types of suffering. The first one is:

(a') The sufferings of dying and falling

(1') The suffering of dying

Nāgārjuna says in his *Friendly Letter:*

Though they experience great bliss in the heavenly realms,
When they die the suffering is so much greater.
Considering this, the wise do not crave
The perishable pleasures of a heavenly rebirth.

Beings born in the upper realms, such as desire realm devas, experience what we might call heavenly pleasure. It is a level of mental and physical happiness that is far beyond what we know as humans. They also do not meet the physical hardships and mental challenges that we humans constantly have to face. However, when their time to die approaches they meet with a particularly intense distress. It is a mental anguish that is far more unpleasant than the ordinary sufferings of human beings.

Mental sufferings can be more subtle and, at the same time, more disturbing than physical ones. Sometimes, when physical pain is mentally accepted, or even embraced, it does not bother a person very much. Certain people can be in pain right up to the point of death without experiencing it as great misery. But when the pain is mental—when you don't accept it but resist it with fear and aversion—this kind of suffering can be the most terrible of all. This is the kind of pain that the deities experience at the time of death. Therefore, as Nāgārjuna says, wise people do not covet the sublime-sounding pleasures of the devas, because they know that they are transitory and do not last; furthermore, when these pleasures come to an end, the pain is intense.

As death approaches the devas experience the five signs of death, and this experience causes great suffering to arise. These five signs of death are described in the *Friendly Letter* as follows:

Their complexion turns an unattractive color,
They become unhappy with their abode,
And their flower garlands wither,
Their clothes become soiled, and their bodies
Break out in an unprecedented sweat.
These five signs, which foretell their death,
Appear to the heavenly beings who reside in the god realms,
Just as signs of impending death appear
To humans who are about to die on earth.

Some commentaries speak of ten signs of death: five distant signs and five proximate signs. The five proximate signs are explained in these verses. They begin to appear about one week before the devas are going to die.[3] First of all, the beautiful radiance of their body fades and their complexion turns an unattractive, pale color. Second, their dwelling place, which has been a splendid and luxurious abode up to this point, becomes uncomfortable and unpleasant to them. Because of their excellent previous karma, devas always have beautiful ornaments and flower garlands adorning their bodies, which naturally change and stay fresh without any effort on their part. But as devas approach death their flower ornaments wilt and begin to rot. Their heavenly garments, which previously remained pristine, now become soiled and begin to smell. Finally, they begin to sweat, which has never happened to them before.

The five distant signs of death, found in other sources, are:

1. Devas ordinarily radiate a natural light, which means they do not need to rely on a sun or moon to illuminate their environment. But as death approaches, the light of their body grows dim.
2. Devas bathe in beautiful pools filled with special water, and when they emerge they do not need a towel because the water does not cling to them. But as death approaches, their body stays wet when they emerge from the water.
3. Unpleasant sounds, which they had never heard before, begin to emanate from their clothing and ornaments.
4. Ordinarily, devas never blink; their eyes are always open. As death approaches, they begin to blink.
5. Devas ordinarily do not become attached to any particular location, but as death approaches they desire to be in just one special place.

Humans also experience a series of signs of impending death as the elements of the body dissolve and the coarser minds dissolve into more and more subtle levels. If you have not trained, through meditation practice, to pass through those experiences as you die, they can be extremely frightening. As the body and clothes of dying devas begin to get dirty and smell bad, all of their friends and companions become disgusted and move away, leaving them all alone. Being deserted at their moment of greatest fear is itself a terrible form of suffering. Now they have lost everything: their splendor is gone; they are uncomfortable in their home and in their own body; they feel great fear; and even their best friends and relatives have deserted them. That is the suffering of dying for the devas.

(2') The suffering of falling to a lower state

Nāgārjuna says in the *Friendly Letter:*

> When they have to depart their heavenly worlds,
> If they have no merits left,
> Helplessly they will go wherever they belong:
> To the animals, hungry ghosts, or hells.

When devas die they can be born in any of the six realms of cyclic existence. But the most likely future is rebirth in a life that is far less pleasant than the one they are leaving, because during their long stay in the heavenly realms they have exhausted most of the virtuous karma they had accumulated in past lives. All of that merit has now ripened. What is left is mainly negative karmic potential, which is now ready to ripen into a suffering rebirth.

At that time of death they are powerless to change the course of their next life. Every being has the power to change his or her destiny, but that power comes from applying the antidotes that destroy negative karma while you are still alive and vigorous. The effort must be made long before you are about to die. While they had so much time available to them, the devas did not understand what they needed to do. They just wasted their lives away, using up their vast storehouse of virtuous karma. Finally, at the time of death, they see what lies in store for them, but there is no way for them to do anything about it. All they can do is suffer the unbearable anguish of knowing what is about to happen to them.

When we humans are about to die, we do not see the rebirth we are headed toward. Although this power can be cultivated through yogic practice, in general we don't fear our future rebirth because we cannot see what it will be. Devas, on the other hand, have a natural capacity to see where they are about to go. One epithet for the devas is *three-timers,* which means they have the ability to perceive three lifetimes: the one just past, the present one, and the one about to arise. The power to see where they are going in their next life arises particularly when they near death, and this is the source of the fear they experience at that time. They see that from their current bliss in a splendid heaven they are about to fall into a hideously ugly body in a terrifying place. Even if they are merely headed for an animal realm, the life of a dog or cat is a tremendous fall from the glory of a deva.

This is why devas experience such intense mental anguish when they become aware of their future circumstances. As their body loses its luster and their friends desert them, they see clearly what is going to happen. Of course, they want to do whatever they can to change their fate, but it is too late. They have no chance to apply any antidotes as they move swiftly toward death. Though they do not suffer any physical pain as they die, their mental suffering is unbearable.

(b') The suffering of being frightened

In general, the demigods are the ones described as those who are possessed by jealousy toward beings having better circumstances than they. But this kind of mental unhappiness is found among the devas as well. Between the different classes of devas, and even within one deva world, these beings experience various levels of good fortune based on their individual karmic accumulations. This produces envy among the devas, just as it does among the demigods and among humans.

Of course, this is the nature of the desire realm. It is a place where beings are constantly hankering after sensual objects. We desire beautiful things to see, sweet sounds to hear, delightful fragrances to smell, delicious food to taste, and pleasant things to touch. Among the devas, those with greater accumulations of merit will end up with more, or more pleasant, sensory objects. Those with less merits suffer from dissatisfaction, distress, and jealousy when they see others whose lives appear more wonderful.

(c') The sufferings of being cut, gashed, killed, and banished

This is another way in which the experience of the devas is similar to that of the demigods. As mentioned, demigods attack certain types of devas out of jealousy, and these devas suffer the miseries associated with fighting, such as having their body cut to pieces. Again, devas only die if their heads are cut off. If their limbs are severed or their bodies are cut in two, the parts come back together and regenerate. When there is a battle between devas, the most powerful expel the weaker ones from their dwelling place and push them off to less desirable locales. Speaking of the sufferings of the devas, Vasubandhu says in his *Discussion of the Requisite Collections:*

> Devas who enjoy sensual pleasures,
> Do not possess mental happiness.
> They are burned by the inner fire
> Of the infection of attachment to sensual desire.

> Where is the happiness
> For those whose minds are distracted?
> They do not have the power
> To make their minds undistracted for even one moment.

The minds of beings in the desire realm are always under the power of distraction by the senses. The senses have such a strong effect on the mind. Though the devas are a little better than humans in this regard, they still spend most of their time indulging in their particular objects of attachment, their minds always under the power of these distractions. For them there is not even a moment of undistracted, fully controlled, perfectly peaceful mind. While beings of the upper realms do possess a more concentrated, unwavering mind than humans, they still do not govern their own minds, and they are never truly undistracted.

Vasubandhu continues:

> Their nature is to be agitated by distraction.
> They are never at peace,
> Like a fire spread by a blazing wind,
> When it meets the fuel of the forest.

Their mind is always unsettled, stirred up by this kind of distraction. It is like a forest fire whipped up by the wind. In the desire realm, the winds of karmic propensity and obscuring afflictions whip up the fire of craving and attachment. The available sensory objects are the fuel, ready to feed the flames of desire. All the necessary causes and conditions are there to keep this fire of desire burning in the mind, and it is just as difficult to control as a big forest fire. In that situation, how can the mind find an undistracted state of complete peace?

Another set of verses from the same text says:

> They are like someone recently recovered from an illness,
> Who returns to eating unhealthy food.

The devas are enjoying some relief from the painful aspects of wandering through cyclic existence. They enjoy all kinds of pleasurable feelings and mental happiness. But the very objects they indulge in become the cause of future suffering. They are sick people who recover from a dangerous disease, only to use their good health to indulge in desires that will make them sick again.

When you think of the splendors and pleasures of the upper realms, it is easy to develop great attachment to them. When you first hear about the bliss of the deva realms, you might want to be born there right away. But by practicing these meditations you come to understand their experience in more depth—that it is actually a mixture of happiness and intense suffering. With this understanding you recognize that there is no worldly pleasure worth getting attached to, even in the most enjoyable realms of cyclic existence.

By means of these meditations on the sufferings of samsara, you come to see in a step-by-step fashion how there is no place, no mode of experience in all of cyclic existence, that is totally free of misery—that there is no realm that offers anything like reliable peace and happiness. When you look at all the levels of existence with the wisdom that understands their causes and conditions, you come to see the whole of samsara as a vast ball of suffering. With that realization arises the desire to throw that ball away, because you want something else.

(ii) The suffering of the gods of the form and formless realms

The devas of the form world and the formless world do not have the gross forms of suffering that we have been discussing thus far. They do not suffer from the physical pain of the human realm or the mental unhappiness of the desire realm gods.

Birth as a deva in these upper realms is purely the result of virtuous karma. Although they are still bound by karma and afflictions, and carry innumerable subtle propensities accumulated in past lifetimes, during their life in one of these realms they only experience the result of virtuous karma.

The *Treasury of Knowledge* by Vasubandhu says: "There are three types of karma: meritorious, demeritorious, and immoveable." "Immoveable" is a designation given to virtuous karma that ripens in the form and formless realms. For humans and devas of the desire realm, experience switches back and forth from pleasant to suffering feelings, depending on the ripening of meritorious or demeritorious karma. But in the two upper realms the karma does not "move" in this way; these devas experience purely the ripening of meritorious karma, and from the time they are born until they die they have no unpleasant or unhappy experiences. Their lifetime is very long, with a subtle level of consciousness experiencing only a peaceful state of mental tranquillity.

Nevertheless, they are still within cyclic existence and they still possess afflictions and obstacles to achieving wisdom. They do not possess all the afflictions that desire realm beings have; for example, they do not have hatred or jealousy. But they do retain a certain kind of ignorance, a certain kind of desire, and pride. These afflictions are quite subtle, so they do not produce enough mental agitation to disturb the tranquillity of that lifetime. But they are still there, and they will yield their effects in future lives.

Although they are able to enjoy the fruition of their virtuous karma for the duration of that life without disturbance, these devas do not have the power to remain in that happy state forever. When the result of the virtuous karma that projected that existence is exhausted, they have to die. Still possessing mental afflictions and karmic propensities, they will take birth in accordance with their previous karma. In this sense, just like the beings in all the other realms, they have no freedom. That lack of control over their own destiny is itself a cause of suffering. As with all other beings, the devas of the upper realms do not have control over their own futures because they are under the influence of the negative tendencies, under the power of karma and afflictions. That is the source of their suffering.

In his *Discussion of the Requisite Collections,* Vasubandhu goes on to say:

> Those beings of the form and formless realms
> Are beyond the suffering of suffering and the suffering of change.
> They naturally reside for eons, undistracted,
> In the bliss of meditative equipoise.

Let us recall what we discussed when first speaking about the suffering of suffering: that there are five kinds of feeling. There are two types of bodily feeling based on the sense faculties: an *unpleasant feeling* is a disagreeable bodily feeling of pain; a *pleasant feeling* is an agreeable bodily experience. There are also two types of mental feeling: *mental happiness* is an agreeable mental experience; *mental unhappiness* is a disagreeable one. Finally, there is *neutral feeling,* which is an experience in between agreeable and painful; neutral feelings can be either physical or mental.

All five of these types of feeling are experienced in the desire realm. But in the first concentration of the form realm there are neither unpleasant bodily feelings nor mental unhappiness. Additionally, in the second concentration there is no experience of bodily pleasure. In the fourth concentration there is neither pleasure nor mental happiness, but only neutral feelings. In the formless realm, where beings have no physical faculties, the situation is similar to that in the fourth concentration of the form realm. There is no pleasure or suffering, and there is also neither mental unhappiness nor mental happiness; there are only neutral feelings in the formless realm.

Beings in the formless realm remain in a deep state of meditative equipoise, a very subtle state of mental concentration. Any kind of mental feeling of happiness is actually a coarse and distracted state, but these beings remain in a very even, undistracted, neutral feeling. From our point of view that might appear to be a dull, monotonous type of existence. But you can think of it as similar to a very deep, subtle, undisturbed dream state. The life of a formless realm being passes in that way.

We see that from the first concentration of the form realm on up, all the beings are beyond any form of gross physical suffering or mental unhappiness. For most, their "bliss" is an inner mental experience of meditative concentration. For some of them, when they are first born into that realm, they have some awareness of where they came from, but soon they settle into their meditative trance, and there they remain, undisturbed, for a very long time. They do not need to apply any effort because this state is the ripening of previous karma, the result of previous effort. They spontaneously enter the meditative equipoise of their level, and remain there with nothing to disturb them for their whole life in that realm.

Vasubandhu continues:

> Yet this is most certainly not liberation,
> For they will have to fall again from there,
> Though it appears as if they have escaped
> The waves of suffering in the lower realms.
>
> Though they might try, they cannot stay forever.
> Like a bird soaring across the sky,
> Like an arrow shot with the strength of a child,
> They must come back down in the end.
>
> Just as butter lamps that burn for a long time
> Are perishing with every moment,
> They are afflicted by the suffering
> That all conditioned phenomena are in a state of change.

The main point of these stanzas is that the life of a deva in the upper realms may appear to be ideal, but it is still within cyclic existence and is still caused by karma and afflictions. Such a rebirth is a conditioned phenomenon, possessing all the marks of conditionality: it is subject to change; it is impermanent; and it has a suffering nature. Though they may have risen very high within cyclic existence, their blissful lives will not last forever.

Like birds flying across the sky, eventually they have to come back down to earth. Though their lives may go on for eons, with every moment they get closer and closer to the end, just like a burning candle.

Life in the form and formless realms is so peaceful, the consciousness is so subtle, and the afflictions are operating on such a subtle level that it can seem as though the beings there do not have any faults. Some meditators, practicing at very high levels of meditative concentration, confuse these states for total emancipation. For example, meditators who attain the *absorption of nondiscrimination* experience a cessation of the functioning of the mind and mental factors, which they mistake for liberation. The karmic result of entering this meditative level is to be born in one's next life among the beings of nondiscrimination on the level of the fourth concentration. During that life (which lasts approximately five hundred *great eons*), there is active consciousness only at the moment of birth and at the moment of death. In between those two moments the mind is completely dormant. After that lifetime one is born back into the desire realm. Āryas view this state of nondiscrimination as a pitfall and so they do not enter the absorption of nondiscrimination; it is attained only by ordinary individuals who mistake the state of nondiscrimination for the state of liberation.

In the end we need to realize that even the longest and most blissful lives in cyclic existence are still conditioned phenomena, subject to the causes of suffering: karma and afflictions. Although the devas enjoy a prolonged respite from the gross miseries of lower rebirths, they are still living a conditioned life, dominated by karma and subject to suffering, and it is only a matter of time before they awaken to that sad reality. Therefore, there is nothing to be desired in these higher rebirths. The only sensible goal is to get out of cyclic existence altogether by eliminating its causes from the root.

This is why you need to meditate on the lives of the six types of beings in cyclic existence. You need to learn and contemplate the details of their situation, the conditioned nature of their lives, and the cause and effect relationship that controls their experience. Once you realize this you will become disenchanted by even the most attractive levels of cyclic existence and your mind will become dominated by the thought of renunciation. You will be ready to renounce samsara in its entirety.

Once this thought of renunciation arises spontaneously for yourself, it becomes easy to see how others are trapped in exactly the same cycle of pain and confusion. On that basis it will become easy to generate a powerful feeling of love and compassion for all other beings. But first you must produce this disenchantment with cyclic existence and the determination to attain liberation from it.

The thought of renunciation does not mean having a brief or occasional glimmer of disenchantment with samsara. As Tsongkhapa describes it in his *Three Principal Aspects of the Path (Lam gyi gtsobo rnam gsum):*

> If you contemplate, over and over, karma and its inexorable results,
> And the sufferings of cyclic existence,
> It will counteract the illusory appearances of future lives.
> Meditating this way, when your mind does not entertain even an instant
> Of admiration for the wonders of cyclic existence—
> When day and night your mind is focused on liberation—
> Then the thought of renunciation has arisen.[4]

When you have become utterly disgusted and fed up with the miserable conditions of cyclic existence, which you have recognized in your meditation, and you spontaneously focus your mind, your actions, and your energy on getting out of that trap—that is the real thought of renunciation: the determination to leave cyclic existence. That is the beginning of the path of emancipation. Once that thought arises, you have actually entered the path.

That spontaneous attitude of aversion to cyclic existence, coupled with the single-minded intention to escape from it, naturally leads to one question: what is the cause of this cyclic existence? Therefore, the second noble truth, the truth of the cause of suffering, is the next topic discussed in Tsongkhapa's *Lamrim Chenmo.*

8

The Origin of Suffering

2' Contemplating the process of cyclic existence in terms of its origin
- a" How the obscuring afflictions arise
  - 1" Identifying the obscuring afflictions
  - 2" The process of their production
  - 3" The causes of the obscuring afflictions
  - 4" The faults of the obscuring afflictions
- b" How that causes karma to be accumulated
  - 1" Identifying the karma that is accumulated
    - (a) Karma that is intention
    - (b) Karma that is intended action
  - 2" How karma is accumulated
    - (a) Accumulating karma for pleasant feelings
      - (i) Accumulating karma for the pleasure that comes from enjoying desirable objects: sights, sounds, and the like
      - (ii) Accumulating karma for gaining bliss in meditative concentration, after you have rejected attachments to external sensual pleasures
    - (b) Accumulating karma for neutral feelings
- c" The process of death and rebirth
  - 1" Conditions of death
  - 2" The mind at the time of death
    - (a) Dying with a virtuous mind
    - (b) Dying with a nonvirtuous mind
    - (c) Dying with a neutral mind
  - 3" Where heat gathers
  - 4" How you reach the intermediate state after death
  - 5" How you then take rebirth

2' Contemplating the process of cyclic existence in terms of its origin

This topic has three divisions:

a" How the obscuring afflictions arise
b" How that causes karma to be accumulated
c" The process of death and rebirth

a" How the obscuring afflictions arise

In order for cyclic existence to arise—i.e., in order to produce a samsaric rebirth—karma and afflictions are necessary. Of these two, the afflictions are the principal, most important cause of such a rebirth. Why? Because if there are no obscuring afflictions, then even if you have accumulated incalculable karmic seeds in the past, these karmas will not be able to ripen and yield results. Examples of this are arhats or bodhisattvas, who have taken rebirth in cyclic existence since beginningless time and have created limitless karmic seeds during those infinite numbers of rebirths. However, these karmas cannot ripen because the afflictions—the indispensable cooperating conditions—are absent. Those karmic potentials will be like dry seeds; even though you plant many seeds, if they do not meet necessary conditions such as moisture, they will never produce sprouts. All of the samsaric sufferings we have been describing—birth, aging, and so forth—cannot arise without these special conditions, even when the karmic seed has been planted.

On the other hand, if the afflictions are there, then karma will immediately be created, and from that combination you will take rebirth. This is why we say that the afflictions are the *primary* cause of samsara. Even if the karmic cause for rebirth in cyclic existence has not been created, once the afflictions are present you will create that karma. Then all the conditions necessary for cyclic existence to arise will be present.

Dharmakīrti says in his *Commentary on the "Compendium of Valid Cognition"*:

> The karma of those who have transcended attachment to cyclic existence
> Lacks the power to project another birth,
> Because the cooperating conditions have been extinguished.

And he also says:

> When attachment is there, the aggregates will arise again.

The āryas—those who have gained direct insight into the nature of reality—will still take rebirth in cyclic existence until they obtain arhatship, at which point they completely eliminate their obscuring afflictions. For arhats, although they have accumulated many many karmic seeds in past lifetimes, those seeds become incapable of producing another samsaric rebirth because the primary conditions for them to ripen—the afflictions—have been completely eliminated.

We have been concentrating on the faults of cyclic existence in order to develop a powerful determination to escape from those sufferings. Of course, in order to escape you must get rid of the causes of samsara. As we have just seen, between the two causes, karma and afflictions, afflictions are the primary, most important cause. Therefore, the most important thing is to apply an antidote to those afflictions.

In order to make use of a powerful antidote, you must first identify the target that the antidote is intended to counteract. Once you identify and understand the nature of the afflictions, you will find that some antidotes are useful to weaken them and temporarily suppress them, while others are effective in eliminating them from the root. But it is always necessary to identify the enemy and then, recognizing when it arises, apply an effective antidote. Therefore, in order to master the obscuring afflictions there are four topics to consider:

1" Identifying the obscuring afflictions
2" The process of their production
3" The causes of the obscuring afflictions
4" The faults of the obscuring afflictions

1" Identifying the obscuring afflictions

We begin with a definition that points us to the distinguishing characteristic of obscuring afflictions in general. Then each of the ten main afflictions will be explained. According to Asaṅga's *Compendium of Knowledge:*

> An obscuring affliction is defined as a phenomenon which, when it arises, arises with the characteristic of being unsettling; and due to its arising the mental continuum becomes unsettled.

This is a general definition, which applies to all the obscuring afflictions as a class. It says that an obscuring affliction is an inner mental event whose nature is to disturb or unsettle the mental state. Its action or function is to create a restless, non-tranquil mind. Such is the general characteristic of every affliction, whether it is desire, hatred, jealousy, pride, wrong view, or any of the others. Each one leads to mental disturbance, destroying mental peace and calmness. It always creates some kind of problem—some kind of agitation in one direction or another—and it always brings bad results.

Based on this general definition we have specific details of the ten fundamental afflictions. These details are compiled in the Abhidharma literature, which gathered together and systematized the Buddha's explanations found in the sutras. There are many different divisions of afflictions—for example, the root afflictions and the branch afflictions—but here we are establishing the main, most common, fundamental afflictions. The explanation presented here is from Asaṅga's *Compendium of Knowledge,* which speaks of ten basic obscuring afflictions.

Vasubandhu's *Treasury of Knowledge* presents these basic afflictions slightly differently. It says, "The root of existence is the six polluting tendencies...." "Polluting tendencies" is another term for the afflictions, and five of these six are the same as the first five in the presentation by Asaṅga. The sixth affliction in the *Treasury of Knowledge* is *wrong view,* which can be further divided into five distinct types. When you subdivide wrong view in this way you get Asaṅga's ten afflictions: five which are *views* and five which are *non-views.* And when you condense those five wrong views into one and then add on the initial five, you get Vasubandhu's six polluting tendencies. In the present text Tsongkhapa follows Asaṅga's presentation of ten basic obscuring afflictions, beginning with the *five non-views* as follows:

1. The first is *attachment,* which focuses on an outer or inner object, and seeing it as attractive, wants to have it, pursues it, and attaches to it. When you are attached to an object, if you do not already have it you desire it, if you already possess it you do not want to separate from it. In general, attachment functions a little differently from harsh, explosive afflictions like hatred, in that it arises slowly, then gradually attaches or becomes stuck to its object, almost like glue. Then it tends to seep into its object, going deeper and deeper. Once it becomes attached, it is difficult to separate. It is like a piece of cloth that has been stained with oil: the oil soaks deeply into the cloth, spreads, and becomes very difficult to remove. In the same way, attachment grasps at its desired object and then extends and penetrates deeper and deeper until it is very difficult to separate from that object.

Underlying attachment and the rest of the afflictions is a fundamentally incorrect way of perceiving the object. You see impure objects as pure, or impermanent objects as being permanent, or objects with a suffering nature as pleasurable. Through the force of ignorance you impute characteristics onto the object; you superimpose attractive qualities (or, in the case of hostility, repugnant qualities) that are not truly there. Then, based on this mistaken perception, you grasp at the object and become attached to it. That ignorance, that wrong perception, is the direct cause of your attachment or hostility.

Of course, you can also desire virtuous objects such as compassion, love, bodhicitta, and liberation. In that case, the mind functions in a similar way, in that you see the object, you are attracted to it, you grasp at it, wanting to possess it, and then the mind goes deeper and deeper into the chosen object. This is the same type of consciousness we just described, except for one fundamental difference: instead of being based on a mistaken perception of the object, this attraction to virtue is based on a correct perception of the actual nature of the object. Instead of superimposing qualities that are not there and becoming attached to that distorted view of the object, you are perceiving the object correctly, and aspiring toward a realistic goal. The first case, based on a fundamental misperception, inevitably leads to a bad result; the second case, which accords with reality, brings results that accord with your aspirations.

2. *Hostility* is a mind of ill will, directed toward a source of suffering, wanting to harm or destroy that object. The object of hostility is a source of one's own suffering; it is often another sentient being, but it can also be pain itself, or the immediate cause of pain, such as weapons or thorns. Whatever unhappiness you feel, or whatever causes that unhappiness, can become an object of your anger and hatred. Hostility is your observing one of these objects with a harsh attitude of ill will that desires to damage, harm, and destroy it. When the object of hostility is another sentient being we can say it is an attitude that wants to make that being suffer. This attitude of ill will has different degrees, which we can call "anger" or "hatred," but they all share this hostile thought that wants to damage or destroy its object.

Again, the underlying cause of this affliction is the superimposition, stemming from ignorance, of qualities that are not there. Something extra has been added onto the object so that you see it as unattractive, and you want to harm it or get rid of it. This kind of consciousness is very destructive and harmful to both oneself and others. Anger and hatred have the power to "burn up" many roots of virtue. The merits you have accumulated over many lifetimes can be destroyed in one moment of anger, just as a powerful fire can incinerate all the grass, bushes, and trees in a forest. Anger not only destroys virtues, it completely upsets all inner peace and outer social harmony. The devastating effects of anger and hatred will be discussed later, when we look at the disadvantages of the afflictions.

3. *Pride* is a mind that is puffed up and conceited; it comes from comparing yourself to others and viewing yourself as having superior qualities. This seeing yourself as higher and others as lower is based on the *view of the transitory collections* (see number 6 below), the wrong view that clings to a false, over-inflated sense of self. Pride gives you a puffed up, grander view of yourself by superimposing superior qualities on a self that does not in fact exist the way you perceive it.

With this type of arrogant pride you may compare yourself to others in terms of external qualities, thinking, for example, "I have much greater wealth then they do," or "I have a much nicer body," or "I have much finer clothes." Or you may see yourself as having superior inner qualities, such as intelligence, or spiritual attainment. The main point here is that you are elevating yourself by superimposing a superior value onto your own qualities and superimposing an inferiority on someone else. Once you cling to this image of yourself as superior, many problems and much unhappiness arise, especially when you are confronted with evidence that contradicts this image. Furthermore, such pride becomes an obstacle to increasing your understanding and your virtue. In Tibetan we have the expression, "You can't pour the water of virtues into a balloon filled up with pride." This means that when you are filled up with arrogance—like a balloon filled up with air—it becomes impossible to pour in any new virtuous qualities, with the result that you become an unsuitable vessel for the Dharma.

In his *Treasury of Knowledge* Vasubandhu analyzes pride into seven types. These are the puffed up minds: (1) that, when considering those who are inferior to you in some way, think, "I am superior to them"; (2) that think you are superior to your equals; (3) that think you are superior to your superiors; (4) that when directed at the appropriating aggregates, think "I"; (5) that think you have attained virtues you have not attained; (6) that think you are just a little bit inferior to those who are greatly superior to you; and (7) that think you have acquired virtues, when what you have acquired are not virutes at all, but faults.

We see that pride can take many forms, but it always has this character of over-inflating your image of yourself by attributing qualities that you do not really have.

4. In general, *ignorance* is defined as possessing a mistaken understanding of the four noble truths, the cause and effect of karma, and the nature of the Three Jewels. As a mistaken understanding, ignorance is a kind of mental darkness, because the mind is not clear with regard to the nature and qualities of these things.

On another level, ignorance in connection with ultimate reality takes on a deeper meaning. In that context *knowledge* or *gnosis* is the direct realization of the ultimate nature of self and phenomena. Ignorance, then, means lacking that direct realization of the truth, not seeing reality as it is, not knowing the nature of ultimate truth. This definition emphasizes that ignorance holds to a true, inherently existent, essential self. This ignorance is not merely a *not knowing*, but an actual holding on to a mistaken conception of self; it is a grasping at a wrong view. In that way ignorance is the root of all the obscuring afflictions.

This fundamental ignorance leads to all kinds of incorrect conceptions: grasping impermanent things as permanent, viewing impure things as pure, believing objects whose nature is suffering to have a pleasurable nature. When you grasp at objects through the lens of these misconceptions, desire, attachment, hostility, and all the other afflictions naturally emerge. The ignorance that grasps at a mistaken conception of self is the fundamental root of them all.

5. *Doubt* is an attitude of wondering whether the four noble truths, the cause and effect of karma, and the Three Jewels are true or not. The affliction of doubt implies that one is leaning toward the wrong conclusion, thinking, "This is probably not true" or "This probably does not exist."

As the first Dalai Lama, Gendun Drub, says, doubt damages your ability to find any stable certainty, and in this way it is the great antagonist to the life that leads to liberation. Doubt raises questions in your mind about whether there is such a thing as liberation, or whether there is a path or method that can lead you there. This kind of doubt always undermines the kind of faith, confidence, and certainty that is vital to have if you are to achieve emancipation.

We have now talked briefly about the first five rudimentary afflictions: attachment, hostility, pride, ignorance, and doubt. As we explained, these first five are *nonviews*. In the presentation of six obscuring afflictions, the sixth one is *wrong view*. Here, in the presentation of ten, wrong view is subdivided into five distinct erroneous *views*.

All of these views are described as forms of what is known as "afflictive wisdom." This term (*sherab nyon mong chan* in Tibetan) could also be translated as "incorrect wisdom," or simply "mistaken understanding." The "wisdom" referred to here is the mental factor whose function is to discriminate or distinguish the object before it and thereby to determine its qualities. In terms of this definition, each of these five views is a form of wisdom, but in this case it is mistaken or wrong. Instead of leading to purification and happiness, it leads to further affliction and suffering. Since it leads to further affliction, it is called an "afflictive wisdom." All of the five views are types of afflictive wisdom, and are described as follows:

6. The first is the *view of the transitory collections.* This is an afflictive wisdom that, based on observing the appropriating aggregates, grasps at an inherently existent "I" and "mine." In other words, this discriminating mind takes the aggregates, or some portion of the aggregates, as its object. Then, based on observing that conventional object, it imputes an inherently existent "I"—a self that exists inherently. Grasping at that inherently existent "I," the mind goes on to impute all kinds of other objects, such as the aggregates, which are held to be inherently existent "mine"—inherently belonging to or part of the self.

In realizing the emptiness of inherent existence, there are two kinds of grasping at a self that must be addressed: *grasping at a self of persons* and *grasping at a self of phenomena.* Of these two, the view of the transitory collections is a case of grasping at a self of persons.

Tibetan commentators then raise the issue of whether things that are "mine"—which are phenomena, and apparently *not* the person—can be included in the view of the transitory collections. Sera Jetsunpa, the textbook writer for Sera Je Monastery, solves the problem this way. He says that, of course, in the most basic sense, "mine" refers to phenomena; everything that is produced is a phenomenon. But in the context of the dichotomy in which everything has to be either self or phenomena, "mine" does not indicate phenomena. The nature of the grasping at "mine" is that it can *only* arise together with the grasping at "I." Without the grasping at "I" there is no grasping at "mine" alone. You can only think "mine" by first thinking "me." Without connecting with "me" or "I," there is no way of thinking that something is "mine." If you take "my nose" as an example, then it is true that the nose itself is not a person. But grasping at it as an inherently existent "my nose" can only be done by first thinking "me." Therefore, this type of grasping is grasping at a self of persons.

Afflictive wisdom grasps at "I" and "mine" and experiences them as inherently existent when in fact they are merely imputed by the mind. They only exist as imputations that arise based on observing the aggregates; they are empty of any inherent existence from their own side. The mistaken view that grasps at "I" and "mine" as inherently existent is called the view of the *transitory* collections because the aggregates are constantly perishing, moment by moment. It is a view of transitory *collections* because the aggregates are a combination of many different mental and physical phenomena that come together and are constantly evolving. Thus, the name of this wrong view is pointing directly at the impermanent, perishable nature of the aggregates, and emphasizing that they are not inherently existent things.

In the tenets of many other religions, there *is* a permanent, partless, independent self, soul, or *ātman.* According to those tenets, the self is imperishable and is not an aggregation of many parts; it is a real unity—an ultimate, inherently existing I. What is being asserted here, however, is that *no such self exists.* The self, or I, is nothing but an imputation arising from looking at the aggregates. The view of the transitory collections is the deep-seated, instinctive grasping at a unitary, inherently existent self based on a mistaken view of the aggregates.

That does *not* mean that there is no self at all. Conventionally, the aggregates do arise in dependence upon causes and conditions, and we can conventionally speak of our own particular mind-body continuum as a "self." But this self is an imputation and does not exist the way the view of the transitory collections mistakenly holds that it exists. The self that is projected by the view of the transitory collections is nonexistent. It is the nonexistence of that "inherently existent" self that we try to realize when we meditate on the emptiness of the conventional self.

Once you grasp onto that false conception of self, that self naturally becomes the center of all your concern and attention, your "self-centered view." From there, all the remaining afflictions emerge. You become attached to this self. You become attached to things belonging to this self, which you view as "mine." You imagine a large separation between those things that are "I" and "mine" and all other beings and phenomena. Then anger and hatred arise when the "I" is frustrated and the "mine" is not respected. And so it goes.

7. The *view holding to extremes* is an afflictive wisdom observing the self as perceived by the view of the transitory collections, seeing it either as permanent, or as something that will not take a future rebirth after this life. These are the two extreme views: on the one hand, viewing the self as eternal; on the other hand, not believing that, due to karma, there will be future rebirths.

Many people believe that the physical body dies but the essential self or soul is imperishable and eternal. This is the extreme of permanence. Others believe that the psycho-physical being that is present right here and now is all there is, and once this being dies all traces of it are permanently extinguished. This of course means that there is no rebirth, no cycling through samsara, no going beyond samsara, no nirvana, and no buddhahood. This is the extreme nihilistic view because it holds that after death there is nonexistence.

8. *Esteeming unworthy views* is the afflictive wisdom that observes either the view of the transitory collections, the view holding to extremes, or wrong view (which will be explained below), together with the aggregates upon which these views are based, and holds these mistaken views to be superior and excellent, i.e., to be *right view.*

Of course it is not uncommon to find people who hold that the correct and superior view is the belief in an eternal soul. There are also many who believe that this present life is the only life, and that this view is absolutely correct and unassailable. Pride and attachment arise naturally once you believe that your own view is superior. But when it is also wrong, and leads to further affliction and suffering, esteeming such unworthy views can do a lot of damage.

9. *Esteeming mistaken morality and asceticism* is an afflictive wisdom that holds that various misguided religious practices are superior and lead toward emancipation. There are many practices that people engage in because they believe that to do so will lead them out of suffering and to liberation, but in fact these practices lead in the opposite direction. There are many examples of such misguided practices, such as sacrificing the lives of animals or even committing ritual suicide. Then there are various ascetic practices such as burning the body in the sun in order to purify it, exposing it to fire, standing for a long time on one foot, going naked, or never speaking. One may also attempt to wash one's sins away by bathing in special bodies of water. There are also practices that involve certain types of dress or special implements, such as wearing a human or an elephant skin, or carrying a rosary of human bones.

Sometimes non-Buddhist practitioners attain some level of supernatural knowledge through the common practice of meditative absorption. For example, they may gain the power to see the next rebirth of a particular animal, such as a pig. They see that the pig is going to attain a good rebirth in its next life and they conclude that behaving like a pig is the proper method to attain a higher rebirth. Based on that misunderstanding they encourage pig-like behavior. Or they see a human who has died in a fire and taken rebirth in a deva realm. They conclude that burning the body is the way to a heavenly rebirth. These are examples of the way a limited amount of supernatural knowledge—such as seeing one or two lifetimes ahead—can produce erroneous conclusions. Based on that limited understanding, these practitioners put a high value on practices that will actually lead to more suffering. Many different types of mistaken practices can arise from these misunderstandings. When a practitioner, perceiving the aggregates on which these practices are based, sees these practices as a proper method for purifying negative karma and leading to emancipation, that is what is meant by "esteeming mistaken morality and asceticism."

10. The last afflicted wisdom is known simply as *wrong view.* Of course, all four of the views listed above are wrong views, but here wrong view specifically means the nihilistic view that denies the existence of previous and future lives or the cause and effect of karma. Wrong view can also take the form of holding certain positive assertions about the nature of reality. One example would be holding that a prime deity or divine creator is the cause of cyclic existence and all sentient beings. And another, propounded by the Sāṃkhya school of Indian philosophy, holds that some kind of universal principle is the cause of everything. In general, when we speak of wrong view we are referring to the nihilistic view that holds to the nonexistence of karma and rebirth, because that is the biggest obstacle to practice and progress on the path.

Tsongkhapa concludes this general identification of the ten primary afflictions by saying that his main sources were Asaṅga's *Compendium of Knowledge* and *Levels of Yogic Deeds,* as well as Vasubandhu's *Explanation of the Five Aggregates (Pañca-skandha-prakaraṇa),* and that he has explained this topic in accordance with those texts.

2" The process of their production

Now that we have identified the ten primary afflictions, we look into the sequential process that gives rise to them. After that we will examine the causes of the afflictions, and then their faults.

There are two systems for explaining this process, depending on whether ignorance is taken to be a separate affliction from the view of the transitory collections, or whether they are considered to be identical. The first system represents the understanding found in the Abhidharma system as laid out mainly by Vasubandhu and Asaṅga. They held that ignorance was a generalized mental dullness or darkness, while in contrast, the view of the transitory collections is an afflictive wisdom, a mistaken discrimination. Later, the Yogācārins under Dharmakīrti, as well as the Mādhyamikas, held that ignorance and the view of the transitory collections were one and the same thing.

We begin with the first system, which considers ignorance to be a generalized mental dullness—distinct from the view of the transitory collections—acting as the root of all the other afflictions. As an analogy, consider a dark, gloomy place with a coil of rope lying on the ground. In the darkness it will be unclear whether it is a coil of rope or a snake, and the mistaken thought may arise, "This is a snake." Once you apprehend a snake, other thoughts and emotions naturally follow, such as fear, hatred, and so forth.

In the same way, because of the obscuring darkness of ignorance, we cannot see the true nature of the aggregates clearly. In the darkness we misconstrue that psycho-physical continuum to be a substantial self. From that mistaken view of the aggregates—from misapprehending those changing collections to be a substantial, unitary self—all the other afflictions naturally emerge.

According to the second system of explanation, ignorance and the view of the transitory collections are identical. In that case, the view of the transitory collections is itself the root of the other afflictions. Once you hold the aggregates to be an inherently existent self, that misconception becomes the basis for the self-centered attitude that makes the discrimination between "self" and "other." What is "I" and "mine" is seen as essentially distinct from everything else, which is "other." Once you have made that distinction, you develop *attachment* and feel beneficially inclined toward everything that is on your own side. *Hostility* emerges toward everything that is on the other side. *Pride* develops from grasping at the self and feeling that what is "mine" is superior and more worthy of support than what is "other."

You observe that self, and you come to see it either as eternal and having an indestructible essence, or you believe that it is nothing more than what is immediately present and that it is subject to complete extinction at the time of death. These, of course, are the two views of permanence and annihilation, and grasping at these erroneous views is the *view holding to extremes*. You come to admire the erroneous views of the self that you hold, and at the same time you pursue various harmful practices and behaviors that flow from those views; in this way both *esteeming unworthy views* and *esteeming mistaken morality and asceticism* arise.

In the same way, you develop *wrong view*, denying the Buddha—the teacher who taught selflessness—along with his teachings of karma, rebirth, the four noble truths, and the Three Jewels, including the highest attainment of buddhahood and the path leading to that attainment. When you fall under the influence of nihilistic wrong view, you come to believe that these teachings of the Buddha do not describe reality as it is. Even if you are not absolutely convinced that the Buddha's teachings are not valid, you develop serious doubt about them, and that doubt tends to lean to the negative side, believing that they probably are not valid.

We can see how these various afflictions arise from the fundamental error of holding to a substantial self. Dharmakīrti's *Commentary on the "Compendium of Valid Cognition"* says:

Holding there is a self, you conceive of an other.
Discriminating self and other, attachment and hostility arise.
In connection with these,
All the faults arise.

Among the six rudimentary obscuring afflictions, ignorance, attachment, and hostility are called the "three poisons." This is because it is from these three that all the other afflictions are created. Each affliction can become the motivating thought for actions of the body, speech, or mind. Any action, whether virtuous or nonvirtuous, that is impelled by one of these afflictions is *contaminated action.* The accumulation of that contaminated action, or karma, becomes the potential that ripens into future experience. That karma is what determines the nature of your life in the future; it determines the kind of rebirth you will have and the quality of your experience within that realm of rebirth. Therefore, we can say that all samsaric results arise from those three poisons, and that the ignorance of grasping at an inherently existent self is the root of all cyclic existence. That is what Dharmakīrti is saying here.

The practitioner comes to realize that cyclic existence is not some externally created condition, but is actually an internal process; it arises from the root of ignorance. By looking inward, watching in meditation, you can observe this process, and by so doing the arising of the afflictions and the way they motivate each action become clearer and clearer. You see how each moment emerges out of this nexus of cause and effect. You see how each action—even when you are performing some virtuous deed—has behind it some degree of attachment to self, or perhaps pride, or jealousy—some level of seeking gratification for the self you are clinging to. You act with the expectation that your action will return some benefit for that self. Until you achieve a direct realization of the true nature of the self, every action you perform will have some combination of these afflictions as its cause. In particular, ignorance pervades all the afflictions; it is always there in the background.

Āryadeva says in his *Four Hundred Stanzas:*

Just as the tactile faculty pervades the body,
Ignorance pervades all the afflictions.
Therefore, by vanquishing ignorance,
All the afflictions will be vanquished.[1]

Ignorance is the fundamental, root affliction, pervading all the others. From that mistaken grasping at a self all the others arise. By observing them in meditation you will come to recognize how they perform their destructive functions; you will be observing exactly what the enemy is doing. This is the operation of wisdom. Practitioners do not look outside of themselves for the enemy; they are always attending to the inner enemy, examining who they are and what kind of harm they are doing. If you watch these six inner enemies in this way, you will soon develop the capacity to resist their influence and prevent them from leading you to harmful actions. Even if you cannot immediately resist all negative behaviors, simply developing an awareness of what the afflictions are and how they function will have great long-term benefit.

The Kadampa Geshe Ben Kungyal said, "Standing at the door of the afflictions, holding the spear of the antidotes—other than that I have no other job." All you need to do is guard the door against the afflictions. Your job is to use your wisdom to watch the door of the mind and ask, "What is it doing? What is it planning to do? What is coming in? How is it reacting?" If you are diligent in this, you will be successful. And as you gain control over these inner enemies, you will find that you are naturally controlling the outer enemies—the sufferings you experience in cyclic existence—because they are the results of the inner enemies, the obscuring afflictions.

To destroy the afflictions from the root will ultimately require the direct realization of emptiness. Until you are able to achieve higher realizations, you can utilize the many methods that enable you to temporarily block, suppress, or resist the influence of the afflictions. You can recognize the conditions that give rise to certain afflictions and make an effort to avoid those situations. Realizing that you are mistaking impure objects as pure, you can turn that perception around by meditating on the contaminated nature of all objects of desire. You can use such methods to mitigate the intensity of afflictions such as desire or anger when they arise. This lessens their influence and gives you the mental space to avoid creating strong negative karma. Beyond that, if you cultivate a high degree of meditative stabilization, you can temporarily suppress the afflictions, and this will be very helpful as you progress on the path to the final realization of emptiness, which will eliminate these afflictions from the root.

In order to engage in any of these methods for avoiding or suppressing the afflictions, you need to identify them and understand how they come to arise. For that purpose, in the next section we examine their causes.

3" The causes of the obscuring afflictions

All the afflictions arise from a combination of various causes. Six of the fundamental causes are explained here.

1. The *basis* of the afflictions is their latent status as a *subtle propensity.* This means that whether or not a particular affliction—desire, for example—is active and present in the mind at a particular moment, it is continuously abiding at an unconscious level as a potentiality, a seed, a subtle predisposition or propensity. Until these propensities are eliminated from the root, there remains in every sentient being this readiness for a particular affliction to arise when conducive objects and conditions are met. This potentiality is the basis or support of the obscuring afflictions, and as such it is the first of the six causes.

2. The *object* causing an affliction to arise is the conducive condition that awakens that subtle propensity into a fully active affliction. When you plant a dry seed in the ground, it needs supporting conditions such as moisture, warmth, and nutrients in order to sprout and grow into a flower. In the same way, all sentient beings have within them the seed or subtle propensity for the afflictions to blossom, and when a suitable object is encountered it acts as the supporting condition enabling the affliction to arise in full flower.

In general, we say that an affliction arises when (a) it has not been eliminated from the root, (b) the object is nearby, and (c) you perceive that object erroneously. This means that, to begin with, the affliction is abiding in your continuum as a subtle propensity. Then an object, acting as the suitable condition, comes into proximity. Finally, although that object is impure and has a nature of causing suffering, you view it as pure and a cause of pleasure. Take, for example, the situation in which the affliction of attachment abides in your mental continuum as a subtle propensity. A suitable object then appears, such as another person's body having a particular shape. Finally, you perceive that body as attractive, even though its nature is impure and it is a source of suffering rather than pleasure. Based on that misperception of the proximate object, the active affliction of attachment arises.

Since an object is necessary for an affliction to arise, you can avoid the afflictions by avoiding the objects that give rise to them. It may be a long time before you can eliminate the subtle propensities—the afflictions in their dormant state—from the root, but you can prevent them from awakening into their active forms by keeping your distance from the objects that activate them. You can intentionally avoid situations where you know you will meet those objects. This is a simple method that can be very helpful.

3. *Social distraction* refers to those worldly activities that bring you under the influence of unwholesome acquaintances. When you spend time with people whose minds are completely distracted by drinking, playing games,

and wasting time, this naturally contributes to the development of afflictions such as attachment, hatred, jealousy, pride, and so forth. This kind of social distraction can be very powerful. One day, or even a few hours, of exposure to a stimulating distraction can agitate your mind for days or weeks afterward. It stirs up and excites the afflictions and makes it quite difficult to regain control of your mind.

This is the basic reason why Buddhist monks and nuns isolate themselves from towns and villages and retire to secluded places like monasteries and nunneries. They take vows not to engage in many common social diversions such as drinking, dancing, and watching shows. They change their entire external appearance by shaving their heads and wearing robes that mark them off from lay people who are pursuing worldly concerns. This deliberate change in their appearance not only reminds them of their vows, but actually prevents those who might have a bad influence from even approaching them.

If you are looking for pleasure in this life, the monastic life style will not benefit you. But for those who are seeking inner development, trying to combat and reduce the afflictions, it will be of great benefit. That is the purpose of the austerity of becoming a monk or nun. What does "monastery" mean? It is not supposed to be just another place for social distractions. It is supposed to be a place of solitude, where there is nothing to distract you from the opportunity to develop your inner wisdom.

At a later stage of spiritual development—once you have realized the truth of selflessness to some degree—your inner resolve will not be affected by the external influences of worldly distractions. Like a big, powerful man in the middle of a group of children, you will be unaffected by the influence of harmful companions. In fact, for such a realized being, meeting such "harmful" people—those who are overcome by their own delusions—only reinforces one's realization, and strengthens resistance to the afflictions. At that stage, you can travel freely in the world without fear of losing your vows or giving way to temptations. You will be protected by your own inner wisdom.

But for now, at the beginning of the path, you possess all these inner propensities, like seeds in the spring, just waiting to meet the moisture and warmth that will enliven them and cause them to send out shoots. At that stage of your development, you need the protection of these external precautions.

4. The fourth factor causing afflictions to arise is *explanation.* This refers to listening to various kinds of wrong or harmful teachings, or reading books that lead your mind in the wrong direction. If you listen to teachings that encourage you to commit harmful actions, or read things that stimulate desire

or hatred, that will obviously lead you away from the goal of pacifying and eliminating the afflictions.

5. *Becoming accustomed* means that by repeating certain behaviors over a long time, without applying an antidote, you become habituated to those actions and they become your natural, ordinary, and daily way of life. For example, there are people who get angry all the time, without much provocation; as soon as some little thing does not go their way, they get furious. They have become so accustomed to having this emotion of anger arise, and it has become so natural to them, that they do not even think of trying to stop it.

6. Finally there is *attention.* This refers to incorrect thinking: imputing onto objects qualities that they do not actually have. Prime examples of such incorrect ways of paying attention include imputing: attractiveness onto an object that has an unpleasant character, purity onto the impure, and permanence onto things that are impermanent. For example, if there is a person you do not like, who is unattractive to you, you then proceed to impute all kinds of exaggerated or false attributes onto that person, generating all kinds of false reasons why that person is ugly and horrible. This is the process by which you build up a powerful and very destructive hatred. In the same way, you can produce a powerful attachment by thinking how wonderful, how beautiful, and how good a particular person is. Imputing onto others these "good" and "bad" qualities and then concentrating on them cause attachment and aversion to arise in a very powerful form. The afflictions will increase and strengthen to the extent that you indulge in this kind of deluded attention, or incorrect thinking.

These six points are called the "causes of the obscuring afflictions." In order to eliminate these afflictions from the root, you must directly realize the emptiness of self—the nonexistence of the self as it is held by the view of the transitory collections. That realization is the main antidote to the afflictions. But until you achieve that level of realization, it is very helpful to understand these causes and conditions that give rise to the afflictions. That way you can steer away from these causes and conditions and pacify the afflictions until you are able to eradicate them completely.

4" The faults of the obscuring afflictions

The afflictions always bring bad results; they never have any good effects. As soon as an affliction arises it disturbs your mind and causes you to perceive the object of attention in a distorted manner. It reinforces, solidifies, and perpetuates the subtle propensities that are already present. When an affliction arises, other afflictions of a similar nature are not interrupted but can actually be stimulated and increased. For example, if a desire for some object arises, other, similar types of desire will also be stimulated.

As soon as an affliction arises it harms oneself first, and then it often harms others. For example, when anger arises it immediately harms you by causing mental suffering. Then, when you act on that anger, you will do mental or physical injury to someone else. In the end, both you and the person you are angry with are harmed by the arising of your own inner affliction. Moreover, the negative karma of your aggressive action leaves the propensity for more suffering results to ripen in the future. All the afflictions lead to misdeeds now and in future lives. And all the harmful actions you perform motivated by the afflictions will ripen into unpleasant experiences in this and future lives.

When the afflictions arise they push you far away from nirvana. This is because these deluded thoughts and the harmful actions they give rise to cause you to cycle in samsara for a longer time. Because of the afflictions and negative karma you spend vast periods of time trapped in miserable lives and emancipation is pushed far away.

Even if you have virtuous thoughts within your mind, these afflictions will destroy them and your wholesome actions will degenerate. They will lead to the loss of your wealth and resources and, instead of worldly enjoyments, you will meet loss and misfortune.

When you are dominated by these afflictions you don't function well in front of other people; you feel nervous, hesitant, joyless, and discouraged when you are in public. You lack the fearlessness that comes with a controlled mind, and instead you are overwhelmed by guilt and a loss of self-confidence in public.

When the afflictions are strong your bad reputation spreads far and wide. Even holy beings such as teachers, deities, and protectors see how you are tarnished by these delusions and they denigrate you and will not protect you.

When your time to die arrives you go with great regret and sorrow. You have only your negative actions to recall. And after death you are born into the worst realms of existence. You failed to accomplish any meaningful purpose in this life and have only undesirable fruits to experience in the future. All beings share the desired goals of happiness, peace, and freedom, but you obtain none of them. In fact, because of the afflictions you actually achieve the opposite of all your desired goals. These points are expressed by Maitreya in the *Ornament for the Mahayana Sutras:*

> Because of obscuring afflictions you destroy yourself, destroy other beings, and destroy ethical conduct;
> Your virtues degenerate, your wealth declines, your protectors and teachers revile you;
> Your bad name spreads, in future lives you are born in places devoid of freedom.
> Finally you come to great mental anguish over the decline of virtues you attained or were yet to attain.

Śāntideva also describes the faults of the afflictions in *Engaging in the Bodhisattva Deeds:*

> Though enemies such as hatred and craving
> Have neither arms nor legs,
> And are neither courageous nor wise,
> How have they come to enslave me?
>
> While they dwell within my mind,
> At their pleasure they cause me harm,
> Yet I patiently endure them without anger—
> But patience here is inappropriate and shameful.
>
> Should even all the gods and demigods
> Rise up against me as my enemies,
> They could not lead nor place me
> In the fires of the deepest hell.
>
> But this mighty foe, these obscuring afflictions,
> In one moment can cast me into those flames,
> So hot that if they met Mount Meru,
> Not even its ashes would remain.
>
> The enemy of my obscuring afflictions
> Is long-lasting, with neither beginning nor end.
> Among all other enemies,
> None can remain for so long.
>
> If I agreeably honor and serve anyone,
> They respond with beneficial and pleasing actions.

But if I serve these obscuring afflictions,
They respond with actions that bring harm and pain.

Ordinarily we think of other sentient beings as our enemies, but that is not really where our problem lies. The real enemy is inside; it is these obscuring afflictions. In terms of their power, their insidious manner of doing us harm, and the long period of time over which they operate, these inner enemies are incomparable. In these verses Śāntideva is describing with an amazed tone how powerful, how controlling, this inner enemy is. Although the afflictions have no arms or legs, he says, they have made me their slave; whatever they tell me to do I am compelled to obey.

This enemy is happily harming me all the time. Ordinarily, we speak of patience as an excellent quality. But this is not the place for patience! In fact, you should be trying to damage and destroy this enemy with every weapon at your disposal. If you practice patience with this enemy, it will be more than happy to continue bringing you more and more suffering. This is definitely an inappropriate object for the practice of patience.

Śāntideva makes the point many times in his chapters on "Patience" and "Meditation" that we should never be patient with ignorance, attachment, hostility, and the other afflictions. In fact, we should be applying a kind of "hatred" toward them, with a clear intention to destroy them. Hatred is obviously a negative emotion when it is directed toward other living beings, so we can't really call this attitude "hatred" in the usual sense. But it is analogous to hatred, and it carries the same intense desire to destroy its object—only in this case the destruction of that harmful object is itself a virtuous and liberating act. This is the type of hatred that practitioners need to practice.

That is the point of the meditations we are doing here. We are trying to develop the power to destroy the enemy residing deep inside us. That is the meaning of this practice. First you realize that other beings are not the source of your problems; the real enemy is inside. These afflictions are the real source of danger and all the suffering you experience. Therefore, they must be destroyed. How can you destroy them? What is the method? This attitude of focusing your energy on destroying the afflictions takes on the form of hatred, but it is not hatred in the usual sense; it is the practice of liberating yourself from your own delusion.

Why are these afflictions the proper objects of your hatred? If all the beings of the world rose up against you what is the worst they could do? They could kill you; in other words, they could separate you from this life. But that is not too serious a thing; after all, this separation is going to happen anyway. And the beings of this world cannot do anything to you after you are dead. They cannot put you into the hot fires of hell; they don't have that kind of power.

But the inner enemy, these powerful obscuring afflictions, can cast you right into a fire so intense that it could incinerate the greatest mountain in the world. And this can happen in one brief moment, in the brief instant that lies between this life and the next. If you have created the karma to be born into such a hell, that moment of death is all that separates you from those fires. The distance between you and that suffering experience is not at all great; it is only the distance of a single breath. When the last breath stops you will be born right there. The journey doesn't take many months. One moment will be enjoying your life as a human; in the next moment you will find yourself in hell. That can happen. That is what the powerful inner enemy can do. It is not merely birth in hell, but all the other miseries of this samsaric world—poverty, illness, grief, and the rest—that are brought about by this inner enemy.

From the point of view of time as well, the afflictions surpass all other types of enemy. No external enemy could harm you for longer than the length of this one lifetime. But this inner enemy has been operating since beginningless time, and will continue to bring you endless misery until you are able to uproot it.

In general, with ordinary enemies, if you turn your attitude around—if you treat them with respect and try to benefit them instead of doing them harm—they will often stop being your enemies and will become your friends. It is the nature of things that when you act beneficially toward an external enemy, his or her animosity generally disappears. However, in the case of the inner enemy, the more you cooperate with it—the more you honor it and serve it—the more harm it does to you. As long as you obey it—as long as you give it the opportunity—it will continue to do you harm. These are the faults and disadvantages of the inner enemy, the obscuring afflictions. Until you have successfully applied the antidotes, this is the way they will operate. The more you cooperate with attachment, hostility, jealousy, or pride, the more suffering they will bring you.

But the afflictions do have one favorable characteristic. If you combat the afflictions and succeed in casting them out of your mind, they will never be able to return. If you kick ordinary enemies out of one country, they may find a refuge somewhere else and build themselves up until they are ready to come back for another battle. The situation with the inner enemy is different. Once you eliminate afflictions from the root, there is no way for them to return. When they are eliminated from the mind, there is no other place for them to go. By your application of the inner antidote—the realization of the true nature of self—the obscuring afflictions are permanently terminated.

That is the kind of cessation you need to obtain. That is why practitioners constantly strive to kick these inner enemies out of their mind. Once they are terminated by means of the antidote, their cessation will be permanent. There will be no need to worry about that enemy returning again to cause you trouble.

Once you understand these faults of the afflictions, you must determine to combat them using the methods that are made available here. The famous Kadampa Geshe Gonpawa said:

> In order to eliminate these afflictions you must know their faults, their nature, their antidotes, and what causes their arising. Once you understand their disadvantages, view them as completely faulty, and regard them as enemies. If you do not know their disadvantages, you will not understand how they are enemies. Therefore, you should contemplate this matter as it is explained in the *Ornament for the Mahayana Sutras* and *Engaging in the Bodhisattva Deeds.*

Geshe Gonpawa then goes on to say:

> In order to understand the characteristics of the obscuring afflictions, study the Abhidharma. At least study Vasubandhu's *Explanation of the Five Aggregates.* Once you are familiar with the root afflictions and the subsidiary afflictions, as soon as attachment, hostility, or any of the others appear in your mind, you will be able to identify it with the thought, "This is one of those; now it has arisen," and you will be able to combat it.

Geshe Gonpawa is recommending that you study the Abhidharma texts by Vasubandhu or Asaṅga, where the details of the afflictions are extensively explained. If you cannot go into the subject at such length, at least look at Vasubandhu's shorter text, the *Explanation of the Five Aggregates.* Once you understand the nature of the afflictions and you can identify them, there are many methods to temporarily suppress them, or to try to eliminate them from the root. But first you must know what they are, and be able to recognize them when they arise.

This means more than just knowing these things in your head. There is not much benefit in that. The whole point of identifying the afflictions and learning how they operate is to enable yourself to oppose them more effectively, and eventually to root them out. Just as in a war you need to know the size, disposition, tactics, and strategy of the enemy, you need to know everything about these internal enemies in order to destroy them. This is why we explain this subject in such detail. You first need to educate yourself, equip yourself, and then you can engage in the struggle to oppose and eliminate the forces that do you so much harm.

b" How that causes karma to be accumulated

We have been investigating the process of cyclic existence in terms of its origin, and we began by looking at the way the obscuring afflictions arise. Now we turn to the next stage, which is the way those afflictions cause karma to be accumulated. This has two parts:

1" Identifying the karma that is accumulated
2" How karma is accumulated

1" Identifying the karma that is accumulated

This topic also has two parts:

(a) Karma that is intention
(b) Karma that is intended action

What is the meaning of karma? Karma is explained in two aspects. First comes *karma that is intention,* or *intention karma* for short. This is the mental intention that motivates a physical or verbal action. On the basis of that motivation, an actual physical or verbal action is performed.

The second type of karma is *karma that is intended action,* or *karma-having-intended.* There are two systems of thought regarding the meaning of this type of karma. The lower Abhidharma system, which was held by the Vaibhāṣika school and is elaborated in Vasubandhu's *Treasury of Knowledge,* holds that karma-having-intended is the physical action of body or speech that is motivated by the intention. For these schools this type of karma is a physical action.

In the Mahayana Abhidharma system, presented in Asaṅga's *Compendium of Knowledge,* karma is always mental. Here, karma-having-intended is the thought—the mental action—that accompanies the physical or verbal action motivated by the intention. Although there *is* a physical or verbal act, that does not constitute the karma; instead, karma is the purely mental action that accompanies the physical one. These are the two different interpretations of karma-having-intended, or karma that is the intended action, and they will be discussed shortly.

(a) Karma that is intention

The *Compendium of Knowledge* by Asaṅga says:

> What is intention? It is a function of consciousness that is a mental action initiating the engagement of the mind in virtuous, nonvirtuous, and neutral activities.

Whatever physical or verbal action you perform, there is always a virtuous, nonvirtuous, or neutral motivation that lies behind it, intending it and initiating it. That is *karma that is intention,* or, more simply, *intention karma.*

Here we need to fill in some details about our model of the mind. The general term "mind" is made up of (1) *primary consciousness,* or simply *mind,* and (2) *secondary consciousnesses,* or *mental factors.* In each act of cognition there is a *primary mind*—the primary mental consciousness—and, concomitant with that, various surrounding *mental factors.* Five mental factors accompany *every* primary mind and constitute the aspects of cognition that carry out its fundamental functions. These *five omnipresent mental factors* are *feeling, discrimination, intention, contact,* and *attention.* The karma that we are discussing now is the mental factor of intention.

With this understanding we can paraphrase Asaṅga's definition and say that *intention* is a mental factor whose function is to move and induce the primary mind with which it is concomitant toward an object. In each cognitive act, when consciousness is attending to an object, there is first of all the primary mind. A primary mind apprehends the basic presence or *mere entity* of the object; it is the mere awareness of the data presented to it. But a primary mind never cognizes an object without concomitant mental factors; it is these mental factors that distinguish the specific features of the object. The primary mind is said to be similar to the hand and the mental factors are like the individual fingers. The wholesome or unwholesome nature of the primary mind is determined by the presence or absence of wholesome or unwholesome mental factors. If an unwholesome mental factor is present, the entire mind becomes unwholesome, in the same way that adding a pinch of salt to a glass of water causes a salty flavor to pervade every drop of that water.

In each cognitive act the *primary mind* apprehends the basic presence of the object. The mental factor of *feeling* experiences the object as pleasant, unpleasant, or neutral. The mental factor of *discrimination* identifies the object by discerning its distinguishing characteristic. The mental factor of *intention* (i.e., karma) directs and propels the mind toward the object and moves the mind to become involved with that object. Just as a magnet moves a piece of nearby iron, intention moves the mind toward engagement with beneficial or harmful objects. The mental factor of *contact* acts to connect the three elements of a cognition: the object, the faculty, and the primary mind. This coming together of the three activates the sensory or mental faculty such that it becomes the basis for the feeling of pleasure, pain, or indifference. Lastly, the mental factor of *attention* focuses and stabilizes the mind on its object, not allowing it to move elsewhere. (There are, in addition to these five, many other mental factors that may arise with a particular mental event; some of them are wholesome, some are unwholesome, and some are neutral. These are described in detail in the Abhidharma literature.[2])

The mental factors are said to be "concomitant" with the primary mind because they always share five characteristics with it. They have a similar *basis* in that they are based on the same faculty, whether it is the eye, ear, nose, tongue, body, or mental faculty. They have a similar *duration* in that they arise, abide, and cease simultaneously. They both attend to the same *object*. They have a similar *aspect* in that they both reflect a similar image of the object; for example, when the primary mind observes an object as blue, the mental factors also observe it as blue. Finally, they have a similar *substance* in that there can only be one primary mind at one time, and accompanying that there can only be one of any given type of mental factor at that time. These are the implications when we say that the mental factors are concomitant with the primary mind.

(b) Karma that is intended action

According to the system elaborated upon in Vasubandhu's *Treasury of Knowledge*, *karma that is intended action* (or, more simply, *intended karma*) is any action of body and speech motivated by an intention. As stated above, in this system intended karma is the actual physical or verbal action initiated by intention karma. The *Treasury of Knowledge* says:

> Karma is intention and what it produces.
> Intention is mental karma.
> What it gives rise to is karma of the body and of speech.

According to the Vaibhāṣika school, intention karma is a mental act that motivates a physical action of body or a verbal action of speech, which is the actual karma, the actual action. Karma that is the intended action is not mental but is purely physical; bodily karma is form and verbal karma is speech.

The Vaibhāṣikas also divided this physical and verbal karma into two types: *revealing* and *nonrevealing* karma. A karma is revealing if it enables others to understand one's own motivation. When you act physically, with either your body or speech, you provide information to others concerning the state of mind, the intention, that lies behind and drives that physical act. In this sense physical karma *reveals* or informs others of your inner motivating state.

In this system, physical karma is form in that a particular configuration of color, shape, or gesture of the body—i.e., the form of the body—reveals the motivation that lies behind that gesture. In general, it is difficult to know a person's mental attitude because it is not visible. But certain activities or gestures act as signs that reveal what is inside one's heart. The motivation is revealed by the physical movement. For example, when monks or nuns take a vow, they kneel down with their palms pressed together and follow the ritual in front of their preceptor. These physical gestures reveal the virtuous motivation operating inside the mind of that person. That is revealing karma.

Nonrevealing karma is the ongoing karmic potentiality that is instigated or set in motion by that physical, revealing action of body or speech. It is the form in which the karma persists in the psycho-physical continuum. But once it is set in motion by a physical, revealing action of body or speech, it remains entirely inaccessible to our senses. It reveals nothing. Although it is form—a material substance based on the *four great elements*[3]—it is supremely subtle, invisible, and even non-obstructive.

Once a monk or nun has physically and verbally taken a vow, that vow—that karma—persists in his or her continuum. It is not visible, nor is the intention that motivated the vow visible, but it is always there; whether sleeping, eating, or walking, the vow is always there. That karma is therefore said to be nonrevealing; it is there but it is invisible, and very subtle. I have used the virtuous activity of taking a vow as the example, but both revealing and nonrevealing karma can be either virtuous or nonvirtuous.

This is the Vaibhāṣika view of the way karma persists in the continuum of an individual. Proponents of this view say that both revealing and the nonrevealing karma are form; they are physical. Nonrevealing karma is a very subtle type of form, based on the physical elements of the body that commits the revealing karma. It is so subtle that it is not obstructive to other matter, but it is still considered a type of form.

In his *Treasury of Knowledge* Vasubandhu presents the Vaibhāṣika view of the phenomenal world, but he also interjects objections to that view from his own position, which was in accord with the Sautrāntika school. (In later texts he adopted the Yogācāra viewpoint.) This conception of revealing and nonrevealing karma was one of the key concepts in the Vaibhāṣika karmic system that Vasubandhu criticizes and tries to refute. He rejected the notion that karma was in any way physical. The Sautrāntika, Yogācāra, and Madhyamaka schools maintain that intended karma (i.e., karma that is intended action) is the *thought* that accompanies the action at the time of performing the action. They insist that *the mind is the thing;* physical action is not in and of itself karma.

If we take the act of killing as an example, these upper schools assert that first you have the intention to kill—this is the intention karma—and this sets in motion the act of killing. But the physical action or bodily movement of killing is not itself the intended karma. Rather, the intention to kill sets in motion a second thought, a second intention, that actually moves the body during the action of killing. It is *that thought,* which moves the body at the time of the action, that constitutes the intended karma. In the case of an action of speech, it is the thought that moves the voice at the time of the act that constitutes the karma of speech; it is not the sound, or the physical movement that makes the sound.

Thus, for the upper schools karma is always of a mental nature. The physical configuration of the body is actually a neutral phenomenon; in and of itself it is neither virtuous nor nonvirtuous. For example, you can put your palms together like this and it can be a gesture of paying respect to your spiritual teacher. But you can put your palms together in exactly the same way as a preparation for striking someone with the intention of killing him. It is the same physical gesture, but one is virtuous and the other is nonvirtuous. It all depends on the intention that lies behind the physical action, not on the physical action itself. For this reason the upper schools insist that karma is mental. First there is the *intention karma*—which sets the action in motion—and then there is the *intended karma*—which moves the body or voice at the time of the action.

Now we move on to understand the nature of virtuous and nonvirtuous karma. Karma can be classified as either virtuous, nonvirtuous, or neutral. Here we will be concerned mainly with the first two. Virtuous karma can be subdivided into two kinds: *contaminated virtuous karma* and *uncontaminated virtuous karma.* In general, contaminated phenomena are those that nourish or increase afflictive states of mind—that is, states of mind that lead to suffering and do not lead to liberation. They may increase affliction when they are taken as objects of cognition, or in the case of mental phenomena, they may increase affliction by being concomitant with other states of mind.[4] Contaminated karma is basically action that is motivated by the obscuring afflictions. This is action that is rooted in affliction and, once it is performed, that nourishes future affliction.

Contaminated virtuous karma is also of two types: that which exists in the mind of an ārya being, and that which is present in the mind of an ordinary individual. Since this chapter is discussing the process that brings cyclic existence into being, we will not concern ourselves here with uncontaminated karma, or the contaminated virtuous karma in the mind of an ārya (which we will look at later.) Basically, cyclic existence is produced by contaminated action performed by ordinary individuals, and that is what we will focus on here.

There is also another way of dividing karma: as meritorious, demeritorious, and immoveable. Virtuous karma of the desire realm is called *meritorious.* Nonvirtuous karma in the desire realm is called *demeritorious* karma. (Nonvirtuous karma only occurs in the desire realm; it does not exist in the form and formless realms, so in fact *all* nonvirtuous karma is demeritorious karma.) In other words, meritorious and demeritorious karma are only created by beings of the desire realm. Contaminated virtuous karma of the form and formless realms is called *immoveable* karma. As the *Treasury of Knowledge* states:

> Meritorious karma is virtuous karma of the desire realm.
> Immoveable karma is karma in the upper realms.

Why is virtuous karma of the form and formless realms called "immoveable"? In the desire realm, where we live, both virtuous and nonvirtuous karma are *movable* or *variable.* For example, if you create a virtuous karma that should bear fruit as birth in a deva realm, under certain conditions the result of that karma could vary or change to birth in another realm, perhaps as a human, an animal, or even as a hungry ghost. However, in the upper realms, when you create karma that should ripen in some particular level, it will never ripen in another level—it never varies. For example, if you are on the level of the first concentration in the form realm, and you create karma that is the cause to be born in the second concentration, that is where you will be born; it will not vary or be moved. As the *Treasury of Knowledge* states:

> Why? Because karma that should ripen on one level
> Does not move to another level.

2" How karma is accumulated

First we are going to discuss what types of karma ārya beings can accumulate. Here we have to make a distinction between āryas, or *superior beings,* and *ordinary individuals.* Āryas are those who have attained the direct realization of the truth, which means they have reached the *path of seeing;* they have gained the direct realization of emptiness. Ordinary individuals are all other beings, like ourselves, who have not yet directly realized our true nature. Sometimes āryas are called "those who see the other side." This means that they can directly see the cause and effect of cyclic existence and the cause and effect of emancipation; they have directly realized this cause and effect relationship. Ordinary individuals like us are those who only see this side. We cannot see beyond our own circumstances, beyond what we directly experience.

Āryas *can* accumulate *uncontaminated* karma. For example, ārya bodhisattvas have a *subtle mental body* which is not created by afflictions or contaminated karma, but is produced by the subtle propensities of the obstacles to knowledge[5] that have not yet been purified, together with uncontaminated karma. But what we are talking about here is the cause of cyclic existence, and only *contaminated* karma acts as such a cause. In terms of contaminated karma, āryas only accumulate contaminated *virtuous* karma, which is virtuous karma motivated or dominated by afflictions. It is virtuous, but it is not pure in that it tends to increase affliction rather than lead to emancipation.

This gets even more complicated. There are four levels of ārya beings: stream-enterers, once-returners, non-returners, and arhats. These are the four fruits of the Śrāvaka path. The first two have obtained the ārya state, but they are still capable of accumulating nonvirtuous karma. Both of these can be born back in the desire realm. Once-returners can be reborn back in the desire realm one more time; that is where the name "once-returner" comes from. Though they have eliminated many afflictions, they still retain some subtle afflictions that can act as the cause to be born in the desire realm one more time.

The stream-enterer can be born back in the desire realm more than once. Those stream-enterers with the least capacity can be born a maximum of seven more times in the desire realm. Stream-enterers with sharper faculties will return to the desire realm fewer than seven times; they may return only once. It is even possible for a stream-enterer to attain arhatship in the same lifetime. But in no event will they take rebirth more than seven times in the desire realm.

But the *Treasury of Knowledge* explains that "seven times" has a special meaning here. It refers to the maximum times you, as a stream-enterer, can be born *in the same type of rebirth.* You can be born seven times as a human, seven times as a deva, seven times in the intermediate state as a human, and seven times in the intermediate state as a deva. In total, the stream-enterer with the least capacity can be born up to twenty-eight times in the desire realm before attaining arhatship.

To understand how this works, we need to understand a little bit about how the afflictions for each realm of existence are removed. Arhatship is achieved when you have permanently eliminated all eighty-nine of the obscuring afflictions. These include eight factors to be eliminated on the path of seeing, and eighty-one factors to be eliminated on the path of meditation (that is nine afflictions for each of the nine levels of cyclic existence).[6]

The stream-enterer has removed all of the eight factors to be eliminated on the path of seeing, and by this they have attained the ārya level, so they can no longer be born in the lower realms. But they have not eliminated any of the desire realm factors to be eliminated on the path of meditation. The once-returner, in addition to eliminating the factors on the path of seeing, has temporarily suppressed six of the nine desire realm factors to be eliminated on the path of meditation. The non-returner has temporarily suppressed all nine of the desire realm factors to be eliminated on the path of meditation.

Because they have not eliminated or suppressed any of the nine afflictions of the desire realm, the stream-enterer cannot be born in the upper realms, i.e., the form and formless realms. The practice of suppressing the afflictions of a human rebirth involves meditating on the faults of that type of rebirth and cultivating its antidotes; suppressing the afflictions of a rebirth as a desire realm deva involves meditating on those faults and cultivating antidotes to that type of rebirth. So, for example, if the person attains stream-enterer as a human, he or she will meditate on the faults of a human rebirth and will produce powerful antidotes to being reborn as a human in the next life. Therefore, in the next life this person will be born as a desire realm deva. Then this deva will meditate on the faults of that rebirth and—if arhatship is not attained in that life—will again be born as a human, having cultivated antidotes to rebirth as a deva. Going back and forth, this being will alternate births as a human and as a deva. If he or she is not sharp enough to attain arhatship in one of those lives, it is possible to be born in each life up to seven times. With an intermediate state rebirth preceding each rebirth as a human or a deva, such a being can be reborn a total of twenty-eight times in the desire realm.

Why then does it say in the sutra that the stream-enterer is one who can take rebirth "seven times at the most"? This is analogous to a tree that produces leaves in clusters of seven. That tree might be called the "seven-leaf tree," even though it would have thousands of leaves in total. Similarly, each type of rebirth comes in a bunch of seven. This is the explanation we find in the *Treasury of Knowledge*.

This discussion began with the point that in general, āryas only accumulate contaminated virtuous karma, but that stream-enterers and once-returners can accumulate nonvirtuous karma as well. However, the kind of karma that āryas accumulate is never *projecting* karma—that is, karma that can propel them into a future happy or unhappy rebirth. This is the distinctive difference between the type of karma that āryas can accumulate and the type that ordinary beings accumulate.

Let's review two main types of karma. *Projecting karma* is the strong karma that *projects* or *throws* one into a particular type of rebirth. This is like planting a seed. It is the primary cause of the future rebirth—the cause of being born in a particular realm of existence. The second type is called *completing karma,* or *actualizing karma.*[7] This is what actualizes a projecting karma. When you throw seeds on the ground in the spring, you still require other supporting conditions to produce crops, such as moisture, warmth, and fertilizer. Those supporting conditions are referred to as actualizing karma. Like moisture and fertilizer, actualizing karma must come together with the seed at the right time if the seed is to germinate and bear fruit; when it does, the actualizing karma becomes the direct cause that brings the throwing karma to fruition.

When a person attains the ārya level by means of a direct realization of the truth on the path of seeing, he or she no longer creates any new *projecting* karma. Although some āryas may be born again in the desire realm or the upper realms, the projecting karma for those rebirths was accumulated *before* they attained the ārya state. During all the innumerable lifetimes prior to their realization, they accumulated innumerable causes for all kinds of future rebirths. But once they achieve the ārya level, they do not create any new instances of projecting karma. But they *can* create new actualizing karma, which matures and brings to fruition previously accumulated seeds to be reborn in cyclic existence.

Nāgārjuna says in his *Fundamental Verses of the Middle Way (Mūlamadhyamaka-kārikā):*

> The root of cyclic existence is formative action,
> Therefore, the wise do not act to accumulate karma,
> Therefore, the unwise are those who do.
> The wise do not, because they see reality.

He is saying that the root of cyclic existence is the action that produces the seeds for birth—projecting karma. The "wise" are the āryas, those who do not create projecting karma because they have directly realized the emptiness of the self, the ultimate truth. Because they have achieved that realization, ignorance has no power to lead them to take the kinds of actions that accumulate this kind of karma. It is only the "unwise," ordinary individuals, who produce projecting karma. Vasubandhu makes the same point in his *Explanation of the Divisions of Dependent-Arising (Pratītya-samutpādādi-vibhaṅga-nirdeśa)* when he says: "For those who have seen the truth, there is no projecting karma."

Therefore, Tsongkhapa says, as long as you remain under the influence of ignorance, which grasps at a mistaken conception of self, and as long as this misconception dominates your mind and all your actions, you will continue to create this kind of karma. Once you have directly realized the "suchness of selflessness" directly, although you may still be born in cyclic existence as the result of *previously accumulated* karma and afflictions, you will not create any *new* projecting karma.

As Asaṅga says in his *Levels of Yogic Deeds,* once you have the mental power of the realization of selflessness, it overpowers ignorance and the karma that is created by the inferior force of ignorance, just as a strong man beats a weak one. Thus, stream-enterers and once-returners, who do not assent to grasping at a self but, in fact, have eliminated it, no longer newly accumulate the karma to be born in cyclic existence.

Therefore, those who create the karma to project cyclic existence are those ordinary individuals who remain at a level below the highest level of the *supreme worldly stage* of the Mahayana path of preparation. As mentioned earlier, there are five paths leading to enlightenment: the path of accumulation, the path of preparation, the path of seeing, the path of meditation, and the path of no-more-learning. One becomes an ārya when one attains the path of seeing. Before that, one is on the path of preparation, and the *supreme worldly stage* is the last of the four stages on the path of preparation. This stage can also be divided into three progressive levels, so here reference is made to the highest level of the supreme worldly stage. This is the last moment before the path of seeing. That is why it is called the supreme *worldly* stage, because it is the last step before one directly realizes selflessness, enters the path of seeing, and becomes an ārya.

All the sentient beings at this level or below are ordinary individuals who accumulate projecting karma, the karma that projects samsaric life. They are operating under the power of afflicted ignorance and the view of the transitory collections, holding the I as real, substantial, and permanent. When they perform nonvirtuous actions, such as killing, it creates demeritorious karma, which will cause them to be born in the lower realms. When they perform virtuous actions of the desire realm—such as the practice of giving or keeping ethical conduct—they create meritorious karma. And when they cultivate meditative states such as single-pointed concentration—which are included on the levels of the form or formless realms—they create immoveable karma. All of these are *contaminated* karma. They are actions rooted in ignorance and the impulse to gratify and satisfy the immediate needs of a self that does not exist the way it is conceived to exist.

It appears that until you achieve the ārya stage, every action you take will be a cause of continuing in cyclic existence. Even virtuous actions such as prayer, making offerings, observing vows; even high levels of meditation such as trying to achieve single-pointed concentration or highest insight; even actually attaining the very high subtle states of meditative stabilization such as the four concentrations of the form realm or the formless absorptions of the formless realm—all of these virtuous efforts are being described here as further causes of life in cyclic existence.

All actions—whether virtuous, nonvirtuous, or immoveable karma—are included within the second of the four noble truths; they all belong to the truth of the *cause* of suffering. It appears, then, that until you attain the stage of an ārya, everything you do is wrong, doesn't it? You can't move! Now we have to deal with that question.

The following objection is raised: what about the practitioner who has clearly seen the disadvantages of all worldly wonders, whose only interest is to obtain complete freedom from cyclic existence, and who has accomplished many virtuous actions with that pure motivation? And what about those practitioners who have not yet achieved the ārya stage, but who nevertheless possess a conceptually clear and accurate understanding of the meaning of selflessness. Is the virtuous karma they create—which is similar and close to the wisdom that analyzes selflessness—also included as a cause of cyclic existence?

The answer is as follows. In general, practitioners who are on the first two paths—the path of accumulation and the path of preparation—*do* accumulate ordinary projecting karma. However, virtuous motivations such as those just mentioned, or the virtuous mental karma that is similar to the wisdom that analyzes selflessness, actually constitute a part of the *antidote* to the craving for future samsaric existence. It is clear that seeing the faults of all worldly wonders, or seeking complete emancipation from cyclic existence, or meditating on selflessness, are all antidotes to attachment to samsara, because they are directly opposed to the ignorance of grasping at a self that is the very root of cyclic existence. Since they operate in a manner contradictory to the perpetuation of cyclic existence, these cannot be considered ordinary projecting karma, which is part of the truth of the cause; they are not the actual projecting karma that perpetuates cyclic existence. However, because they are *supportive* of the actual projecting karma producing future rebirth, they *are* included within the truth of the cause.

Right now you do not have the direct realization of emptiness. Until you attain that realization, all of your virtuous actions—even when motivated by the thought of renunciation, or when they involve some level of understanding selflessness—are still contaminated by the subtle influence of the ignorance that grasps at a self. When you are reborn into a samsaric existence, these virtuous actions become the cause of obtaining pleasant conditions, but they are still contaminated by ignorance, and therefore they are included within the truth of the cause of suffering.

Among the four noble truths, the first two—the truth of suffering and the truth of the cause of suffering—are to be abandoned. The third and fourth—the truth of cessation and the truth of the path—are to be implemented. The paradox here is that these contaminated virtuous actions—such as renouncing samsara and meditating on selflessness—are being categorized as part of the truth of the cause, and therefore as practices to be abandoned. Once you attain the direct realization of selflessness, your virtuous actions become part of the truth of the path. At that point the ignorance of self-grasping has been replaced with the wisdom that realizes the true nature of the self, and so your actions become purely, totally contrary to the cause of cyclic existence. But until that point, even your virtuous actions are included within samsaric causality.

This does not mean that you should not be practicing all of these virtuous actions. These are the actions that actually lead directly to the accomplishment of the higher paths. Nāgārjuna has said that even those who think about the teaching of emptiness *with doubt* are fortunate; simply having the curiosity to investigate emptiness from a position of skepticism—not yet convinced whether emptiness is true or not—is enough to cause samsara to begin to decompose.

The source of this interpretation is Asaṅga's *Compendium of Determinations,* which says:

> If someone asks: why are those worldly practices that destroy the craving for rebirth and generate the supermundane path leading in the opposite direction included within the truth of the cause?
>
> We reply: although essentially they are not on the side of rebirth in cyclic existence, they still are supportive of the positive activity of the body, speech, and mind, which is the cause of future happy rebirths. Therefore, you should understand that they are included within the truth of the cause.

The point being made here is that these contaminated virtuous actions are essentially very favorable attributes; their nature is to be an antidote to cyclic existence. Nonetheless, they do function as supporting causes that, in association with previously accumulated projecting karma, lead to future rebirths in the higher realms of cyclic existence. Because they have this samsara-producing aspect, they belong to the truth of the cause.

Tsongkhapa says that having carefully considered the faults of cyclic existence, you produce a mind that feels repugnance for samsaric life and is interested only in gaining freedom from it. Motivated by that thought of renunciation, you engage in the kinds of virtuous actions that will eventually produce the supermundane path. These virtuous practices are the true fulfillment of renunciation and the real cause of escaping samsaric life. Nevertheless, they are similar to and supportive of certain causes of rebirth in cyclic existence. Therefore, although they are not the *actual* cause of future rebirths, they are included within the truth of the cause.

This is the way the solution to this paradox has been taught. The most important thing is to understand that even though you have not yet obtained the ārya stage, you must apply your energy and effort to developing this thought of renunciation and the wisdom that realizes selflessness. These practices will lead you to the ārya stage, even though they are considered part of the truth of the cause of suffering.

Therefore, whatever meritorious Buddhist practice you engage in, you should keep certain principles in your mind. First, you should examine and come to recognize the faults of cyclic existence, and by this practice generate a sincere thought of renunciation. The true thought of renunciation involves generating a powerful aversion to the entirety of cyclic existence, from the most terrifying hell realms up to the most blissful abodes of the gods. When you clearly understand how all life within this samsaric cycle is produced by karma and afflictions and is subject to dissatisfaction and suffering, you will be inspired to focus all of your energy on the practices that lead to emancipation from this condition. All virtuous activities that are motivated by that thought of renunciation become part of the antidote that counteracts attachment to the wonders of samsara, and will ultimately lead to emancipation from cyclic existence.

The second principle that should guide your practice is the view of selflessness; you should direct your actions toward cutting the root of cyclic existence by attaining the wisdom that realizes the lack of an inherently existent self. The root of samsara is the so-called "egoistic view." This is the ignorance that grasps at a mistaken conception of self, that perceives an ultimately existent nature of the self and of all phenomena. This ignorance underlies all other obscuring afflictions and is the fundamental root of all the karma that creates cyclic existence.

The antidote to this process of karmic causality is to turn the mind in the opposite direction, and this is done by analyzing the meaning of selflessness. The direct realization of selflessness on the path of seeing will initiate the true antidote that cuts out ignorance from the root. But well before you achieve that level, just by hearing and thinking about the right view—by examining, analyzing, and meditating on selflessness—you can undermine the attachment that causes so much contaminated karma, and you can turn your actions into antidotes to cyclic existence.

The third principle that should guide your virtuous activities is bodhicitta, the altruistic intention to attain emancipation for the sake of others. You come to see that all other living beings are the same as you in being trapped in this deep ocean of misery. You should find it unbearable to see the inexhaustible nature of their suffering, and you should make the solemn determination that you will free them from this situation and lead them to the perfect life of buddhahood.

This bodhicitta motivation is based on cultivating great compassion and love. Even before you have become an ārya—even at the early stages of your practice—you can generate this kind of compassionate, loving attitude from the heart. As long as the thought of compassion lies behind your virtuous activities, they will become part of the antidote to samsaric existence, and they will ultimately lead to the perfection of bodhicitta.

Tsongkhapa places great emphasis on these three principal paths: renunciation, bodhicitta, and the view of emptiness. When all of your virtuous practices are aspects of these three paths, they become antidotes to cyclic existence and they lead toward emancipation. When virtuous actions lack these three principles as their motivation and purpose, they become ordinary causes for rebirth in cyclic existence—ordinary aspects of the truth of the cause of suffering.

There are some situations in which, even though your virtuous actions are *not* motivated by one of these higher principles, they still would not become ordinary causes of rebirth. This is mainly due to the power of the *object* of your virtuous practice. For example, when you make offerings or prostrations to the spiritual teacher, the buddhas, and bodhisattvas, these powerful objects of practice enable your actions to achieve a special level of merit, and cause them to become part of the antidotes to samsara.

Such cases, however, are exceptions to the rule. In general, virtuous actions taken without one of these three higher motivations become merely causes for higher rebirths and happy circumstances in future samsaric lives. As such, they are ordinary parts of the truth of the cause. You should reflect on this and make an effort to bring all of your practices under the power of the thought of renunciation, or under the power of bodhicitta, or under the power of the wisdom that realizes emptiness. These are the principal paths leading to the highest goals of sentient beings.

We are talking about the way karma is accumulated. In regards to whatever karma we sentient beings create, whether virtuous or nonvirtuous, we can say that all our actions are for the purpose of finding some kind of happiness. In some cases, as in the higher deva realms and the formless realms, we are trying to achieve a peaceful, neutral feeling. But in general we can say that all beings are acting in order to obtain some kind of mental happiness or physical pleasure. Nobody is trying to obtain suffering. Although we constantly create karma that becomes the cause of suffering, nobody is creating karma with the *intention* of producing suffering for themselves. Therefore, we can understand the process of accumulating karma in terms of two categories:

(a) Accumulating karma for pleasant feelings
(b) Accumulating karma for neutral feelings

(a) Accumulating karma for pleasant feelings

(i) Accumulating karma for the pleasure that comes from enjoying desirable objects: sights, sounds, and the like

Here we are mainly talking about sensual pleasure: the pleasurable experience of form, sound, taste, smell, or touch. Most of the pleasures of the desire realm—which includes the three lower realms, humans, and the desire realm devas—are sensual pleasures. In the desire realm, most karma is accumulated in the effort to achieve some type of sensual enjoyment.

There are two types of action intended to achieve sensual pleasure. If your object is to achieve pleasure only in this life, then you are mainly accumulating demeritorious karma. In contrast, if you are mainly seeking pleasure for a future life, you are accumulating meritorious karma. The actions you will have to take to achieve desire realm pleasures in your next life—such as a happy rebirth, long life, wealth, and beauty—will be meritorious, such as observing ethical conduct, giving charity, and practicing patience. When your only concern is this life, then even when you try to practice virtue—by meditating, making offerings, observing ethical conduct, and the like—there is actually no virtuous intent because you are only acting for the sake of immediate pleasure. Therefore, your actions are demeritorious karma. There is a Kadampa saying that goes, "If you circumambulate merely for the sake of this life, it will become the cause of birth in hell, the hungry ghosts, or the animals."

(ii) Accumulating karma for gaining bliss in meditative concentration, after you have rejected attachments to external sensual pleasures

Thus far we have been talking about pleasures we gain from external objects. This is actually a crude form of pleasure compared to the more subtle experience of the devas of the form and formless realms. Such beings are not attracted to sensual pleasure because, to them, sensual pleasure is such a rough type of experience that it seems like suffering. The pleasurable feeling they enjoy arises from meditative concentration; this is much deeper and more subtle than externally based pleasures.

Those who engage in such activities as focusing on a meditative object, mainly in order to experience the bliss that arises from meditative stabilization, accumulate immovable karma. The bliss being referred to here is the special kind of mental happiness that arises from meditative stabilization, and is experienced in the first three concentrations of the form realm. Achieving a particular level of meditative stabilization leads to rebirth in a corresponding level of the form realm. So when meditators reach one of these higher meditative states, they are accumulating immoveable karma, and that karma becomes the cause to be born into one of the first three levels of the form realm.

At each succeeding level of the form and formless realms, the body-mind continuum becomes more subtle and experience becomes more refined. At the level of the first concentration of the form realm, beings still experience physical pleasure. On the second and third concentrations, however, there is no more pleasure, but there is still mental happiness. On the fourth concentration there is neither pleasure nor mental happiness, and from there on through the formless absorptions there is only neutral feeling—the experience of deep, peaceful meditative absorption.

(b) Accumulating karma for neutral feelings

When you have turned away from attachment to sensual pleasure, and on top of that you have lost interest in the mental happiness of meditative bliss, you may engage in activities for the purpose of experiencing neutral feeling. Then you will be accumulating immoveable karma that will become the cause for rebirth in the fourth concentration up through the four formless absorptions and their highest level: the peak of existence.

At these levels the mind is extremely subtle and calm, deeply engaged in meditative absorption. From our current position here in the desire realm, we can hardly imagine the subtlety of these states and the nature of the neutral feeling they experience.

When we speak of the "activities" or "karma" you engage in to be born in these states, we are not talking about any kind of physical action. This karma is deep meditation. The more subtle the level of meditative stabilization you achieve, the higher the level among the four formless absorptions you will be born into. The highest level in the samsaric world is called the "peak of existence."

This explanation follows the thought of Vasubandhu according to his *Treasury of Knowledge* and its auto-commentary. The key to this system is understanding the following: those beings who accumulate karma for the sake of sensual pleasure are born in the desire realm; those beings who accumulate karma for the sake of the mental happiness from meditative bliss are born in the first three levels of the form realm; and those beings who accumulate karma for the sake of the neutral feeling of the deepest meditative absorptions are born from the fourth concentration up to the peak of existence.

Tsongkhapa then takes this approach to its logical conclusion. All these beings are creating a particular type of karma in their quest to experience some form of happiness and freedom from suffering. Because of their attachment to those gross and subtle forms of pleasure, their karma becomes the cause of further rebirth within cyclic existence. However, by the same logic, if you end that attachment and you feel nothing but revulsion for the whole of samsara—from the hell realms up to the peak of existence—and you engage in virtuous activities purely for the sake of achieving complete freedom from samsaric existence altogether, you will leave cyclic existence further and further behind and emancipation will grow nearer and nearer.

With this topic we have concluded the discussion of karma in the *Lamrim Chenmo.* We have learned about its divisions, how it operates, and how it is accumulated. It is very important to study the cause and effect of karma so that you can make it the basis of your own actions in the future. By studying, thinking about, and meditating on the details of karma, you can integrate your understanding with the way you live your life, and this will create a solid foundation for progress on the path.

c" The process of death and rebirth

We have been discussing the process that gives rise to cyclic existence. We have looked at how the obscuring afflictions arise and how they cause karma to be accumulated. Now we examine how these two causes, karma and affliction, give rise to the process of death and rebirth. This explanation has five parts:

1" Conditions of death
2" The mind at the time of death
3" Where heat gathers
4" How you reach the intermediate state after death
5" How you then take rebirth

1" Conditions of death

There are three conditions that cause death. The first is death due to the exhaustion of the life span. Obviously, when you die you have exhausted the span of your life, but that is not the meaning here. This means that whatever life span was originally projected by the projecting karma that produced that rebirth has been spent. It is like the expression you have in English: "His time had come." When there is no interruption to your natural longevity and you live out the length of life that was originally projected, that is death due to the exhaustion of life span.

This type of death can occur after a long life or after a short one; it depends on the karma that initially projected that life. Some karmic seeds will produce a very short life. If you have the karma to be a human for only a very short time, you might die immediately after birth; some infants even die in their mother's womb. On the other hand, some humans live more than ninety years. Either one of these could be death due to the exhaustion of the life span.

The second condition is death due to the exhaustion of merits. This takes the form of dying from a lack of the necessities that support life. The merits you have accumulated are the cause for the food, clothing, shelter and all the basic requirements that make life possible. When these merits are exhausted, those supporting conditions disappear, resulting in death from poverty, hunger, cold, or other conditions of deprivation.

The third condition is death due to the failure to avoid unfortunate circumstances. This refers to dying an untimely death due to carelessness, putting yourself in danger, and doing things you could have avoided. In the sutras we find nine examples of this cause of death:

1. Overeating.
2. Eating unsuitable, unhealthy, or poisonous things.
3. Eating before you have digested the previous meal.
4. Not fully eliminating undigested food that has accumulated in the stomach.
5. Obstructions that block the passage of digested food.
6. Not using medicines appropriately. This means that certain substances when taken individually may be beneficial, but when mixed together they can cause illness.
7. Not knowing what requires practice and what does not. This refers to trying to imitate people who have special skills and do dangerous things. An example of this would be trying to climb a difficult mountain or walk across a tightrope when you have not trained to do so.
8. Going somewhere at the wrong time. At certain times, certain places are dangerous, so if you go there at that time you may have a serious accident.
9. Certain types of sexual conduct can also cause untimely death.

Some of these causes, like overeating, are familiar to all of us, so we should be careful not to cause our own untimely death.

Of these three general causes of death, dying due to the exhaustion of life span is the one that you cannot do anything about. Once your life span is projected by previous karma, you cannot change it by your own efforts. For the others, you can accumulate more merits during your lifetime, and you certainly can avoid putting your life in danger in the ways we have just described.

2" The mind at the time of death

There are three states of mind at the time of death:

(a) Dying with a virtuous mind
(b) Dying with a nonvirtuous mind
(c) Dying with a neutral mind

(a) Dying with a virtuous mind

As you approach death, the grosser levels of consciousness dissolve and the more subtle levels come to the fore. The final *subtle dying mind* is always neutral, never virtuous or nonvirtuous. This level of consciousness rises in the last moments of the death process. The organs and sense faculties have already stopped functioning, breathing has stopped, and the mind is becoming more and more subtle with less and less control by the dying person. In the final moments at the end of this life, the subtle dying mind arises and, as stated, it is always neutral.

Prior to that very subtle level of mind, as long as the grosser levels of consciousness are still active, the mind can be virtuous, nonvirtuous, or neutral. It makes a great difference to your future rebirth whether you die with a virtuous mind or a nonvirtuous mind. When death comes with a virtuous mind you are born in a higher rebirth; when it comes with a nonvirtuous mind you will be going to a lower rebirth.

Obviously, the mental state when you are close to death is very important. The question then is: "What determines whether the mind goes in a virtuous or a nonvirtuous direction during that final period of life?" If you spent your life cultivating virtuous qualities—such as faith in the Three Jewels—as death approaches your mind will naturally return to those virtuous objects, because it is accustomed to those kinds of thoughts. On the other hand, if you spent your life absorbed in anger or hatred, your mind will go *that* way at the time of death. If you were obsessed with desire and attachment during life, *those* afflictions will once again possess your mind during death. It is the natural power of one's own habitual action that takes control of the mind.

What become extremely important at this stage of the death process are the secondary, supportive conditions that nourish the main karmic seeds and enable them to sprout. Just as a seed planted in the ground requires supportive conditions to sprout and yield fruit, the powerful karmic seeds in your mental continuum able to project a future rebirth require supportive conditions to nourish and activate them. At the time of death the most powerful karmic seed will act as the projecting karma, with the power to cast you into a particular kind of rebirth. Other seeds become the secondary supportive conditions that nourish and activate that projecting karma.

Actually, there are *three* particular supportive conditions that come together at the time of death to nourish and activate the previously planted projecting karma. There are two forms of attachment, which act as the moisture that nourishes the seed; when these two appear in the context of the twelve links of dependent origination (as explained in the next chapter), we call them "craving" and "grasping." The first, c*raving,* is a general attachment to cyclic existence, the desire for pleasure to continue and for discomfort to cease. When craving intensifies into the urge to reach out and grasp the object of desire, that is the second form of attachment: *grasping.*

There is also a third nourishing factor, which is like the warmth that is necessary for a seed to germinate. This third factor is another, secondary action, which is *a similar type of karma to the main projecting karma.* If the projecting karma is nonvirtuous, nonvirtuous thoughts—mental karmas—arise at the time of death and act as that third supportive condition. If the projecting karma is virtuous, then virtuous thoughts arise and nourish that main seed. Once these three conditions activate that seed, you take rebirth in your next life.

Therefore, the mental karma, or thoughts, of the dying person as he or she approaches death act as an essential condition, along with craving and grasping, nurturing and activating the main projecting karmic seed. That is why it is so important to guide the mind to the side of virtue as one approaches death.

Generally, whatever type of action—virtuous or nonvirtuous—you were accustomed to performing during your lifetime will be the most powerful type of seed in your continuum; it is this that will naturally come to mind at the time of death. Gradually other thoughts become weaker and weaker until they are forgotten. At that point the mind is completely absorbed in those most powerful, habitual actions and, with those actions propelling the mind, you take rebirth.

Of course, at the time of death the person does not have much control over his or her own mind, even at the gross level. Sensory awareness has disappeared and even conscious thinking has faded away, so the mind is essentially passive. Under those circumstances the influence of previous experience stored in the mind as karmic propensities becomes the dominant force determining what will come into the mind. If you were accustomed to doing nonvirtuous actions during your life—for example, if you were a slaughterer of animals or a fisherman—thoughts of killing will naturally push to the surface when your mind is in this passive state. If your life was spent practicing powerful virtues, those are the thoughts that will come to the mind most vividly.

There is a verse from Vasubandhu's *Treasury of Knowledge* that describes which types of karmic seeds ripen first at the time of death:

> In the round of karma that produces rebirth, karma will ripen in the following order: whichever karma is heaviest, whichever is nearest, whichever was most habitual, what was previously performed.[8]

This means that the dying mind will be influenced by whatever is the heaviest karma accumulated during that lifetime; that karma is what will project the next rebirth. If you have powerful negative *and* positive seeds in your continuum, and they are of equal weight, then whichever was performed closest to the time of death will ripen first. If the powerful karmas are also similar in terms of closeness, then whichever was more habitual during that lifetime will ripen first. When all of these criteria are equal, then some other karma that was performed earlier in this lifetime, or a strong karma from a previous lifetime, will ripen at the time of death.

According to this principle, the heaviest, or nearest, or most habitual action will naturally come to mind during the death process. If you have cultivated a strong Dharma practice, you can direct your mind to virtuous objects as your time to die approaches by intensifying your practice and eliminating all other concerns from your thoughts. It is also possible for someone else—someone who is sitting with you as you die—to influence the direction your mind will take. This kind of assistance, which leads the dying person's mind toward faith and other virtuous qualities, can be tremendously beneficial and can make a great difference in determining the next life.

For example, when a man who has engaged in a Dharma practice during his lifetime is dying, his friends and relatives may know what his daily practice consisted of. Then, as long as the dying one can still hear, someone can sit beside his bed and remind him of those practices, perhaps reading the prayers or mantras that he recited every day. The person providing this assistance may be a spiritual teacher, a relative, or a close friend. This person can gently guide the dying man's mind back to the virtuous practices he cultivated when he was still alive and healthy. This also keeps the mind focused on virtuous thoughts and pulls it away from wandering to unwholesome objects. This type of outside help leading the mind in a positive direction can be quite helpful.

On the other side, it is important to avoid disturbing the peaceful mind of the dying person. Sometimes people gather near the deathbed and indulge in all sorts of distracting conversation, with a lot of crying, or arguing, or expressions of fear. When the dying person hears this disturbing chatter, negative thoughts and emotions of anger, fear, or attachment can be churned up. That kind of distracting talk can cause real damage to a person who is about to die.

Knowing how to assist people through the dying process can be especially useful for those of you—such as doctors, nurses, and social workers—who work in the medical and helping professions. You need to do a little research to determine what kind of spiritual practice the dying patient was involved in, or what his or her belief system and values were. With that knowledge, you can discuss these things with the dying person in a way that guides his or her mind to the positive side. In general, we are helpless to change other people's karma, and when they are so close to death there is not very much we can do for them. But seeing to it that the external conditions are peaceful, and trying to guide their mind in the virtuous direction, can influence the way their death process proceeds and can be a very good and helpful thing to do.

The process of falling asleep offers an experience that is similar to the death process. The thoughts you are having as you fall asleep influence the entire sleep session. Even those who are intensively engaged in virtuous practices may get angry just before going to bed. If they dwell on their anger as they fall asleep, that powerful negative mind will determine the nature of their sleep, their dreams, and even how they feel when they wake up in the morning. Conversely, those who normally are enmeshed in unwholesome actions may have a virtuous thought enter their mind just as they are falling asleep. In that case, the mind enters sleep in a peaceful, virtuous way. This is analogous to the process that takes place at the time of dying.

Here we are with this precious human rebirth that can achieve so much. If you cannot achieve enlightenment in this lifetime, you should at least have confidence that your next life will be a high rebirth and you will not fall into a lower realm. In order to have this kind of confidence when the time of your death arrives, you must begin right now eliminating negative thoughts and actions and cultivating a mind that is naturally directed toward virtues. If you spend your healthy years accustoming your mind to Dharma practice and accumulating a storehouse of merits, this preparation will serve you very well when you arrive, as you inevitably will, at the process of death.

Finally we come to a description of the inner experience of those who are dying. The experience at the time of death is like being in a dream. Those who have practiced mostly virtuous actions during their life feel as though they are passing out of thick darkness into light, like walking toward a field of bright shining sunlight. They do not encounter terrifying or repulsive forms. As in a pleasant dream, they find themselves in an attractive place where they meet a variety of friendly, beneficial beings. They die peacefully, and at the point of death they do not suffer from severe pain or physical discomfort. Those who have practiced with an awareness of the cause and effect of karma pass smoothly and without great misery into their next life when the vital essence of this life is finally extinguished.

(b) Dying with a nonvirtuous mind

How does the process go for those who have engaged primarily in nonvirtuous actions? As long as the gross level of discrimination persists, their mind is filled with negative thoughts, which arise naturally as the result of their previous habits. In some cases they are reminded of previous harmful actions by external conditions or by other people. And at the time of death they experience severe pain in their bodies.

These beings have unpleasant experiences that foreshadow the results of the negative karma they have created. For example, they may have nightmares in which they meet terrifying creatures or undergo horrible torments. Such visions, which foretell the future awaiting them after they die, cause deep anguish and even physical pain, and often cause the dying person to scream, groan, cry, and shake. They have the experience of passing from a place of light into thick, impenetrable darkness.

When those who have committed great negative actions see these signs of their unwelcome future, they experience such physical pain and fear that their hair stands on end, their limbs flail, and they lose control of their bladder and bowels. They seem to be falling, and reach out to the sky as if they were trying to hold on to something. Their eyes roll back and bubbles gurgle from their mouth. Those who have committed the heaviest types of negative karma will meet this kind of experience at the time of death.

For those who have committed an intermediate amount of negative karma, the experience will be less severe; some of the things just described will occur and some will not. In general, when the vital essence of their life is finally extinguished, those who have practiced nonvirtuous karma pass with great difficulty and misery into their next life.

This kind of suffering at the time of death is experienced by the beings in all the types of rebirth except for the devas and the hell denizens. The devas of the form and formless realms experience no physical pain or mental anguish. For the hell beings, their existence has been such pure pain that the death process cannot be any worse than what they have already experienced.

All beings—whether dominated by virtue or nonvirtue, and as long as the gross level of consciousness is proceeding and until the last moment when discrimination becomes completely unclear—feel a strong attachment to the self. This is something they have been accustomed to for a very long time. Under the power of that attachment to the self, they feel as if they are headed toward nonexistence, that their self is being annihilated. From that fear a strong attachment to the body arises as they grasp at their physical embodiment. That attachment to the body becomes one of the main causes of birth into the intermediate state.

Of course, every samsaric birth—that is, each time you take a new body—requires both karma and affliction. First a strong projecting karma plants the seed of the next rebirth; then, at the time of dying, the supportive secondary conditions arise that nourish that seed so that it sprouts into a new birth. At the moment of death, attachment to the body acts as the affliction that brings about birth into the intermediate state.

When we discuss the twelve links of dependent origination in the next chapter, we will see that the eighth and ninth links are the two levels of attachment we mentioned earlier: craving and grasping. These two act as supportive secondary conditions that nourish and activate the main karmic seed, just as moisture nourishes a dry seed in the earth. At the moment of birth into the intermediate state, it is grasping at a body that acts as the affliction that activates the projecting karma and sends the dying person into that rebirth.

What happens to ārya beings at their time of death? When they reach their time to die, stream-enterers and once-returners still retain attachment to self. However, because of the power of their direct realization of selflessness, they do not willingly fall under the influence of this attachment. Viewing the self with the wisdom of analysis, rather than assenting to and grasping at a self, they reject it. As we mentioned earlier, their wisdom realizing selflessness overpowers self-grasping just as a strong man beats a weak one.

As for non-returners, they no longer possess attachment to self because they have abandoned all attachment to the desire realm.

(c) Dying with a neutral mind

Those whose actions have not been predominantly virtuous or nonvirtuous, but mostly of an ethically neutral nature, generally have neutral thoughts coming to mind as they proceed through the death process, and they do not have a strong experience of either pleasure or pain.

For all beings, the last moment of mind is always neutral. If you are dying with a virtuous mind, that virtuous mind sustains only as long as the gross levels of consciousness are active. It is the same for a being who is dying with a nonvirtuous mind. Gradually the five sense consciousnesses and the mental consciousness dissolve into more and more subtle levels. Once the gross levels of consciousness have ceased and the subtle levels have come to the fore, the virtuous or nonvirtuous states of mind stop and the mind becomes ethically neutral. At that point you can no longer access your previous virtue, even though you were accustomed to it for a long time. Others cannot turn your mind in that direction because you can no longer hear or cognize speech. A certain amount of cognitive clarity is necessary for a thought to be virtuous or nonvirtuous. The gross levels of mind that function while you are alive have thoughts that are clear and have virtuous or nonvirtuous intent. But the subtle mind at the time of dying does not have that kind of clarity simply because it is so subtle.

Once the consciousness has dissolved to that most subtle level of mind, all minds of death are neutral. An outsider looking at your body at that time would say that you are already dead, because your breathing has ceased, and your sense faculties and all internal organs have stopped functioning. Only the subtle mind is active at this stage, and it is on the verge of passing on to the intermediate state.

3" Where heat gathers

We have now finished the conditions that cause death, and the various states of mind that arise as one experiences death. Now we turn to another aspect of this process in which an external sign appears that helps indicate what type of rebirth a dying person can expect.

Those who have created predominantly nonvirtuous karma, and who will therefore be born in a lower rebirth, lose their heat from the upper part of their body first. The head of such a person will be the first part of the body to become cold, and gradually this cold feeling will make its way downward to the heart area. For those who have created predominantly virtuous karma, it is their feet that first lose heat, and the body cools progressively from the bottom up to heart. In both cases, the consciousness finally exits the body from the heart area. At the moment of conception consciousness enters the fertilized ovum—what is traditionally called the joined "semen and menstrual blood"—and the place where it enters the ovum eventually becomes the heart of that body. Then, at the end of that life, consciousness exits the body from the same place.

Although it is not explicitly stated in the commentaries that explain this process, it is understood that after the heat gathers in the heart from the upper or lower end of the body, the heat from the opposite end also gathers at the heart, so that all the heat is collected there when the consciousness departs.

4" How you reach the intermediate state after death

At the very final moment of death the consciousness transfers from the heart of the old body into the intermediate state. This movement from the old body to the new one is described as virtually simultaneous, like the movement of a balance scale: when one end goes down, the other end goes up.

Just as with all samsaric rebirth, the two causes of karma and affliction come together, like a father and mother, to produce birth in the intermediate state. The first cause—the particular affliction that causes rebirth into the intermediate state for most beings—is attachment to the body. (For some beings who have higher realizations, it is a joy over their previous virtuous activities.) The second cause is a virtuous or nonvirtuous karma.

In the intermediate state you take a body that resembles the form you will have in your next life. If you will be born as a human, you take a human-like body; if you will be an elephant, your intermediate-state form resembles that of an elephant. However, the intermediate-state body is much, much more subtle than the material body of the approaching life.

The sense faculties of an intermediate-state body are always complete and fully functional, but again, they are far more subtle than ordinary organs. For example, the eyes are like the so-called "divine eye," which can see a great distance without obstruction, right through solid objects such as walls. The whole body is so subtle that it too can pass through solid obstructions as if it possessed supernatural powers. The mind only needs to think that it wants to go to a certain place and it immediately arrives at that spot. This subtle body can travel into space, under water, or through fire without suffering any ill effects. The *Treasury of Knowledge* says:

> Because it is projected by the same karma,
> It has the form that it will have in the "previous-time existence,"
> That is, after the first moment of conception
> And prior to death in the next life.
>
> It is seen by beings of the same type and by beings with the divine eye.
> It has supernatural powers due to karma.
> Its faculties are complete and unobstructed.
> It cannot be reversed. It eats odors.

The term "previous-time existence" refers to the life of beings between the moment they are conceived up until the time of their death. The word "previous" here refers to the time *prior to death*. The *Treasury of Knowledge* says that there are four states of existence, and "existence" must be understood here as the coming together of the five aggregates. The "birth existence" is the very moment of conception, when the consciousness enters the mother's womb. From that moment onward until the moment of death—i.e., the entire lifetime—is called the "previous-time existence." The final moment of death is called the "death existence." After that comes the "intermediate-state existence."

Tsongkhapa takes pains to clear up certain misconceptions about the form that a being takes in the intermediate state. Some have mistakenly interpreted this term "previous-time existence" to mean that in the intermediate state one takes a body in the form of their *previous* life, but this is incorrect. It is equally wrong to interpret the canonical texts, as some do, to say that for three and one half days one takes a body like the one of the *previous* life, and that for the next three and one half days this body changes to one resembling the body of the *next* life. He says that these interpretations have no textual basis and should be considered pure fabrications. The form in the intermediate state looks like the body you will have when you are born in the next life.

The first line of this verse from the *Treasury of Knowledge* makes the point that the intermediate-state existence is projected by the same karmic seed as the lifetime that follows. Since one karma projects both the intermediate state and the rebirth that follows, it makes sense that one will have the same form in both those rebirths.

Furthermore, as the *Levels of Yogic Deeds* points out, consciousness does not remain in the previous body; it no longer has any relationship with that form nor any desire for that form. Therefore, it is a complete fabrication to claim, as some do, that the being of the intermediate state becomes distressed upon seeing its previous body.

Who can see an intermediate-state being? Intermediate-state humans can see others of the same type, but cannot see, for example, intermediate-state hungry ghosts. Also, meditators who have obtained the supernatural vision of the divine eye by means of attaining a high level of meditative equipoise will also be able to see intermediate-state beings. This of course includes buddhas, bodhisattvas, arhats and other āryas. Unlike those meditators, however, the supernatural powers that the intermediate-state being possesses are not achieved by means of meditative accomplishment, but are purely due to the power of karma.

As we have just discussed, prior to death it is possible to affect one's rebirth by using special practices and guiding the mind in a virtuous direction. According to the *Treasury of Knowledge,* once you are born into the intermediate state you can no longer "reverse" or affect the type of rebirth you are about to take in the next life. However, the *Compendium of Knowledge* by Asaṅga maintains that the coming rebirth can be changed even *after* taking birth in the intermediate state.

Based on this latter theory, people in some Buddhist countries like Tibet recite many prayers and perform special tantric rituals for seven weeks after a person dies. Forty-nine days is the longest a being will remain in the intermediate state before moving on to the next rebirth. These special practices are performed because it is believed that there is a chance for certain external conditions to affect the rebirth of the dead person. These external conditions include the invoked power of the buddhas and bodhisattvas as well as the power of the meditative equipoise and realizations of those performing the rituals.

The qualities of the intermediate state

Now we turn to a description of the intermediate states themselves. For those who have created powerful nonvirtuous karma, the intermediate state appears gloomy, as when rain clouds darken the sky; sometimes it is a darkness as deep as the night. For those who have accumulated virtuous karma, it appears light, like a white cotton cloth or the night sky when it is lit with moonlight.

The *Descent into the Womb Sutra* describes the colors of the intermediate state this way:

> For one who will be born in the hell realms the intermediate state appears like the scorched stump of a tree. For one to be born as an animal it looks like smoke. The intermediate state of the hungry ghosts is like seeing water. For beings to be born as desire realm devas and humans the intermediate state is like gold. The intermediate state of beings to be born in the form realm appears white.

When you die in the formless realm and are to be born in the desire realm or form realm, you do pass through an intermediate state existence. However, if you are going the other way, and are about to be born in the formless realm from the two lower realms, you do not pass through an intermediate state but proceed directly from the present life to your existence as a formless being. This is the only exception that can be found in authoritative texts where a being is not born in an intermediate state after death.

Therefore, it is incorrect to claim, as some do, that those who commit one of the automatic transgressions—such as killing one's father or mother or an arhat—go directly to a rebirth in the hells without passing through an intermediate-state existence. Because the Sanskrit and Tibetan terms for these five most powerful negative karmas literally mean "without any interval," some have mistakenly taken this to mean that there is no intervening birth in the intermediate state. But the term "without any interval" actually refers to the fact that those who commit these extremely novirtuous deeds will definitely be born in a hell realm after they die, and that no intervening birth in another realm is possible. These beings do take birth in the intermediate state before they are born in hell, but their stay in the intermediate state is extremely brief.

It says in the *Descent into the Womb Sutra* that in the intermediate state of the devas it seems as if the beings are moving uphill. In the human intermediate state, beings seem to moving straight ahead. Those who are going to be born in lower rebirths move with their heads lowered and eyes cast downward as if walking downhill. The *Treasury of Knowledge Auto-commentary* has a different description. It says, "Humans, hungry ghosts, and animals each move in their own manner." In other words, in the intermediate state these beings move in the same way they move in their own realms.

The life span of beings in the intermediate state depends on when they find suitable conditions for rebirth. Sometimes the necessary conditions for their next rebirth come together very quickly, in which case a being spends a brief time in the intermediate state. In such cases the intermediate state may last just a moment, a day, or a few days; there is no set length of time. In cases where the right conditions cannot be found, it is possible to remain in one body in the intermediate state for a maximum of seven full days. If you do not find a suitable rebirth in those seven days, you die and are born again in another body in the intermediate state, at which point another period of seven days begins. As soon as the right conditions are met you take rebirth into your next life. But if the conditions are not met, you can be reborn into the intermediate state up to seven times. That means the maximum stay in the intermediate state is seven rounds of seven days, or forty-nine days. The duration of a day in the intermediate state varies. For beings who are going to be born human, a day is the same length as our human day, but for most of the other types of beings it is much longer.

As we mentioned, according to the higher Abhidharma system found in Asaṅga's *Compendium of Knowledge,* the karma of a being can change even after taking birth in the intermediate state. In accordance with this view it is possible, for example, that a being who is born as a deva in the intermediate state dies after seven days and is then born back into the intermediate state as a human, or in some other form. This type of change is caused when a change in a being's karma changes the seeds that are projecting the rebirth.

5" How you then take rebirth

Following your stay in the intermediate state comes your next rebirth, and the moment of conception in that next life is called the "birth existence." There are four types of birth, or birth-sources: birth from an egg, birth from a womb, birth from moist heat, and miraculous birth.

We begin with a description of birth from a womb. While residing in the intermediate state, by the power of karma you observe other beings of the same type in the place where you are going to be reborn. For example, if you are going to be born as a human, you see other humans in the place you are about to be born. You are not actually seeing real people, but by the power of karma you have a kind of dreamlike vision of them.

You then want to have contact with them—to play with them and talk to them—and this desire inspires an urge to go to that place. There you see the joined semen and blood—that is, the fertilized ovum—of the father and mother and, as a result of distorted vision, you misperceive this as the father and mother lying together engaged in sexual intercourse. Asaṅga's *Levels of Yogic Deeds* says that such sexual contact is not actually happening at that time, but this is how you misperceive the fertilized ovum in an illusory vision. This perception causes attachment to arise. If you are going to be born as a female, you feel desire for the man and want to lie with him, and you want to stay away from the woman. If you are going to be born as a male, you desire the woman and want to join with her. Driven by that desire you approach closer and closer to the man and woman, but as you get closer the rest of their bodies disappear, leaving only a vision of their genitals. This makes you angry. At that moment you die from the intermediate state and you take rebirth in your next life.

What is the material locus where the consciousness enters? The father and mother are inspired by desire to engage in sexual activity. The desire becomes intense and at its culmination a gelatinous semen is emitted by the father. Then, within the mother's reproductive organ, drops of the father's semen mix with the ovum of the mother, traditionally referred to as the "drop of blood." When these two "drops" are joined together, they congeal into a substance that has the consistency of the skin that forms on boiled milk when it cools. This is the material cause of the body in the new life. Simultaneous with that, the intermediate state existence ceases and the consciousness enters this fertilized ovum: the united drops of semen and blood.

According to the Yogācāra system, this main consciousness that enters the new body is called the "foundation consciousness" (often translated as "storehouse consciousness"). Those who do not accept the existence of the foundation consciousness—the other three tenet systems of Buddhism: the Vaibhāṣika, Sautrāntika, and Madhyamaka—hold that it is the mental consciousness that carries the karmic seeds and takes rebirth in this new body.

Until the consciousness enters, the combination of blood and semen is an inert, unaware material liquid. By the power of that entering consciousness, the blood-and-semen combination is brought into contact with the four great elements[9] in their subtle aspect, giving rise to the subtle level of the five sense faculties. In this way a transformation is brought about in the previously inert, purely material blood-and-semen combination; it comes to life, so to speak. Awakened with consciousness and the sense faculties, it is now something other than the material substance that was there before the consciousness entered; it is now a sentient being.

If you boil milk, then you let it cool off a bit, and then you add a yoghurt culture, this combination of warm milk and culture brings about a transformation that we call "yoghurt." In a somewhat similar manner, consciousness—which is the mental faculty—brings with it the subtle aspect of the great elements, which are the material cause of the subtle sense faculties, and together they bring about a transformation of the inert liquid of the blood and semen into an aware, sentient being, enlivened by the mental faculty and the five sense faculties. Remember that in the intermediate state, although your body is so subtle it can pass through walls, you always have all five faculties fully functioning. This is a very subtle level of the physical faculties, brought into the new body with the consciousness. If you are born as a blind human, it is because something goes wrong with the gross faculty as it develops, but in the intermediate state the subtle level of that faculty was complete and fully functioning.

The moment at which the consciousness enters the fertilized ovum is what we call "birth." You should understand that "birth" or "rebirth" does not refer to the moment you come out of your mother's womb; it points specifically to that moment of conception, when the consciousness enters the mother's womb and joins with the combined blood and semen: the beginning of the new body.

As you proceed through this process you have various experiences, depending on the nature of your rebirth. If you have accumulated very little merit, then even though you are being born as a human you will be born into a low class, or a generally humble condition. As you die in the intermediate state and then enter the womb, you are disturbed by a howling, clamorous noise, and it appears as though you are entering a muddy swamp, or a dense, prickly thicket. Such experiences arise in a dreamlike fashion. Conversely, if you have been practicing virtue, you will begin life with a high birth. The experience of dying and entering the womb will be a peaceful one, as you hear sweet sounds, and feel as though you are entering a beautiful mansion or even a celestial palace.

After conception you remain in the mother's womb for thirty-eight weeks, during which the trunk of the body, the limbs, and all the organs grow to completion. Four days after that you are born. This, of course, is a general description of the process; some individuals are born sooner and some later. The *Descent into the Womb Sutra* deals with this birth process in detail, and you can study that text if you are interested in knowing more about the birth process. This sutra says:

> If the fetus remains there for nine months or longer, it will be fully developed. After eight months it is fairly complete but not fully developed. After six or seven months it will not be complete and the limbs will not be fully developed.

As I said earlier, samsaric rebirth requires karma and affliction joined together, like the father and mother. The main affliction, which acts like the glue that joins things together, is desire. If the intermediate-state being does not have the desire to go to a particular place of rebirth, it will not be born there. Then how is it that beings are born into the hell realms, which certainly is not a place they desire to go?

Take as an example someone who has created the karma to be born into hell by butchering sheep, poultry, or pigs throughout his or her entire life. The term for this kind of habitual, dedicated, negative action is "anti-vow" or "non-vow." It is similar to a vow in that it involves an intentional lifelong commitment to engage in a certain kind of action. The butcher who slaughters animals in order to support his family does this because his father and grandfather were butchers before him. It is a lineage that may go back many generations. They make a deep, lifetime commitment to this activity as their livelihood and way of life. It is as if they take a vow to slaughter animals for as long as they live. This anti-vow creates a powerful nonrevealing negative karma that is always with the butcher, so that even when he is not actively killing an animal, that commitment and intention to keep killing constantly produces negative karmic potential.

If we take that butcher of hogs as an example, he has created the cause to be born in hell. When he is in the intermediate state he sees the place he is going to be reborn, but what he sees, as if in a dream, is a lot of hogs. He has worked with hogs during his whole life, so he is very pleased to see them, and he is eager and excited to go there. However, when he arrives he does not find what he saw in his dreamlike vision. The hogs are not there, and instead he finds the kind of hell he is about to be born into. With that, desire is lost and anger arises. When the anger arises he dies from the intermediate state and is immediately born into that hell realm. Some hungry ghosts live in circumstances that are almost as bad as hell, and they take rebirth in a similar manner.

One feature of this explanation of rebirth into the hells is that the object of attraction is not necessarily similar in type to what you will become in your rebirth. For example, what attracted the butcher was the hogs that he used to kill. Still, it is an object that is pleasing and the being wants to get to it and have contact with it. Other beings who are destined for hell, but who do not possess such powerful negative karma as those with the anti-vow, go through a similar process of death and rebirth into the hell realms. This explanation is according to the *Levels of Yogic Deeds* by Asaṅga.

In general, intermediate state beings who are going to be born as animals, hungry ghosts, humans, desire realm devas, and devas of the form realm, go through a similar experience. They observe the place where they will be reborn, and there they see living beings who are similar to themselves. If they will be born as a dog they see dogs, and being delighted to see these similar beings they are attracted and have a strong desire to get to that spot.

You may have had an experience something like this in a dream. You see some attractive object and try to reach it, but when you go there you find nothing, or perhaps the attractive object has turned into something else. Even in a dream this can make you angry. For the beings of the intermediate state, when that anger arises they die, and they are directly born in the place they were attracted to. Remaining in the intermediate state is a delicate mental balance. You stay only as long as you have strong attachment to the experiences there. When your reaction reverses and becomes anger and strong aversion, you immediately die from that place and you are cast into whatever is your suitable next rebirth. All of this happens as the ripening of your karma.

In his explanation of this process in the *Treasury of Knowledge,* Vasubandhu says, "Others go out of a desire for odor or an abode."[10] This means that beings who are about to be born from heat and moisture are attracted by some distinctive smell, and going toward that they die from the intermediate state and are reborn. Those to be born from egg take birth in a process that is similar to those born from a womb.

Beings who will take miraculous birth—such as devas and most hell denizens—feel a strong attraction to a particular kind of place and are spontaneously born there. For example, a likely cause of taking birth in a hot hell is having killed others by burning them to death. Let's say you have committed such heavy negative karma and you have died and taken birth in the intermediate state. When it is time to die in the intermediate state and go to your next rebirth, you will have a dreamlike experience of feeling very cold. You will be shivering and thinking to yourself, "How nice it would be if I could be someplace really hot." That kind of craving for intense heat will bring you directly to a rebirth in a hot hell. If you are going to born in the cold hells, you will feel too hot and dream about being plunged into icy water. This is the process as it is explained in the *Treasury of Knowledge.* In general, Tsongkhapa says, he has explained the process of death and of taking rebirth in accordance with the presentation in the *Levels of Yogic Deeds* by Asaṅga.

This brings us to the conclusion of the section on contemplating suffering and the cause of suffering, which was the first of the two methods for producing the mind that strives for emancipation. In this section we have focused on the first two noble truths: the truth of suffering and the truth of the cause of suffering, which is karma and afflictions.

Now we turn to another approach the Buddha used to explain the cause and effect of cyclic existence: the analysis of the twelve links of dependent origination. This presents another method for discovering the true nature of the self and, thereby, for breaking out of the cycle of samsaric suffering.

9

The Twelve Links of Dependent Origination

b' Contemplating the twelve links of dependent origination
- 1' The division into twelve links
- 2' The condensed presentation of the links
- 3' How many lifetimes are required to complete the cycle
- 4' How to summarize their significance

b' Contemplating the twelve links of dependent origination

All the teachings of the Buddha are methods for obtaining liberation from cyclic existence. When we practice according to the presentation in the *Lamrim Chenmo* we are engaging in Mahayana practice, so we are not striving merely for our own salvation. Our ultimate goal is to benefit all sentient beings by leading them to liberation as well. In order to achieve that goal for others we must first develop the wish to achieve liberation for ourselves. This is why we are studying these practices, which are common to the beings of intermediate scope and which lead to individual liberation from cyclic existence.

In order to generate the powerful motivation required to follow this path to its ultimate conclusion, we need to begin with a clear realization of what is wrong with cyclic existence and why we should want to get out of it. After all, we ordinarily enjoy this existence. Since beginningless time we have been enjoying it, wanting to continue living within it, endlessly involving ourselves with it. The negative mind says, "What is wrong here? Why do you want to spend so much energy trying to get free of this pleasant place?" Of course, this attitude is rooted in not knowing the faults of cyclic existence and not understanding its true suffering nature. We crave birth in samsara because we do not realize what a thoroughly miserable situation it really is. That is one of the main causes of not being able to gain freedom from it.

For this reason we have been looking at various ways of understanding the faults of cyclic existence. We examined this in terms of the Buddha's teaching of the four noble truths, analyzing the truth of suffering and the truth of the cause of suffering. Now we look at the nature of cyclic existence from another angle, in terms of the Buddha's teaching of the twelve links of dependent origination. This is not an easy topic to understand, but by studying it, analyzing it, and then meditating on it, we can come to understand quite clearly how cyclic existence evolves, and this can lead us to a direct and clear understanding of selflessness.

When you understand how each link in this chain of causality gives rise to the next link, you also grasp the means by which you can interrupt this process of samsaric evolution by cutting the causal links at certain points. As the Buddha said, "When this is, that is. When this arises, that arises. When this is not, that is not. When this ceases, that ceases." By meditating on the links in this chain of causality, in both the serial and reverse orders, you come to realize the process that gives rise to cyclic existence as well as the means by which that process can be interrupted. This is the great benefit of familiarizing yourself with this teaching on the twelve links of dependent origination.

We are not talking about gaining just a theoretical understanding of this teaching, but a realization that leads to direct transformation of your daily life and the behavior of your body, speech, and mind. When you replace ignorance—the first link in this chain—with wisdom, you naturally bring about a revolution in your actions, your karma—the second link. Up until now all of your actions have been directed toward the samsaric side. But once you begin acting out of wisdom, everything turns around completely and whatever you do becomes the practice of purification, leading ultimately to emancipation.

Studying, thinking about, and meditating on this teaching of the Buddha has really only one purpose, and that is to bring about an inner transformation. It is not about intellectual understanding or some external show of knowledge. We have to deal with the root of the problem, beginning from ignorance and proceeding from there. We have to integrate our realization with our experience. Emancipation depends on this inner realization. That is the main goal of studying these twelve links of dependent origination.

It is not, as I said, an easy topic to understand, but you begin by hearing about and studying it, then thinking about and analyzing it. Then, by meditating on this topic, your mind becomes totally familiar with the causal nexus that gives rise to samsaric existence. By understanding this causal process you will come to a firm understanding of selflessness. If you apply your understanding to your daily life, putting it into practice with your body, speech, and mind, and you use your understanding to strive for emancipation from cyclic existence, then as you cultivate this realization you will be able to practice properly, and in time you will achieve your goal of liberation for yourself and others.

This topic—contemplating the twelve links of dependent origination—has four parts:

1' The division into twelve links
2' The condensed presentation of the links
3' How many lifetimes are required to complete the cycle
4' How to summarize their significance

1' The division into twelve links

The theory of the twelve links of dependent origination, or dependent arising, was taught by the Buddha to show the process of cause and effect by which the circumstances of cyclic existence arise. The multifarious effects that we experience as life in samsara arise from a conjunction of many, many different causes and conditions. There is nothing that arises without depending on causes and conditions. When something arises, it always depends on something else.

What we will be discussing here, in particular, is the *dependent arising of affliction.* This is a presentation of the way impure, samsaric phenomena arise based on causes and conditions having at their root the obscuring affliction of ignorance. In contrast, it is also possible to talk about the *dependent arising of purification,* in which you look at the causes and conditions that bring about liberation from cyclic existence. For now, we will be dealing with the afflicted, samsaric side of the twelve links of dependent origination. And the first of the twelve factors—the most fundamental root of samsara—is ignorance.

1. Ignorance

Ignorance is the root cause of everything in samsaric life, from rebirth to all the experiences you have in all your lifetimes. All these experiences are the ripening results of karma; karma depends on afflictions; and all the afflictions depend on ignorance.

What is ignorance? There are different systems of explanation regarding this term. The *Treasury of Knowledge* says, "Ignorance is like an enemy or a falsehood." To understand why Vasubandhu defines "ignorance" this way, let us first look at its etymology. The Sanskrit word for "ignorance" is *avidya,* with *a* meaning "not" and *vidya* meaning "knowing." Similarly, the Tibetan term is *ma rig pa,* with *ma* meaning "not" and *rig pa* meaning "knowing." The English word "ignorance" is composed of the very same elements; it comes from the Latin *ignārus,* in which the prefic *i* means "not" and *gnārus* means "knowing." However, the point that the *Treasury of Knowledge* is making is that ignorance is not a *mere absence* of knowing. It is more like an "enemy," someone who is not merely *not* a friend (such as a stranger), or *other than* a friend (such as a tree), but rather someone who is the very *opposite* of a friend—someone who is actively *un-friendly.* In the same way, a "falsehood," or "un-truth," is defined as the *opposite* of true words; it is a statement that *contradicts* the truth.

So the ignorance we are talking about does not imply the mere absence of knowing; after all, a piece of stone has an absence of knowing but we do not call it ignorant. Ignorance is something that is *contrary to* and *directly opposed to* knowing. Here, in the Buddhist context, "knowing" or "wisdom" refers specifically to the wisdom that knows the true nature of the self and the true nature of phenomena. The cause of cyclic existence is *not knowing* the true nature of the self, and as a result of that, grasping at a *false* conception of self. That is ignorance: not only does it not know the self, but it grasps at a conception of self that is contradictory and opposed to its true nature. Ignorance is not the mere absence of knowing wisdom, nor something other than that wisdom—it involves holding affirmatively to a conception that is contradictory and incompatible with knowing wisdom.

On this issue Tsongkhapa presents two points of view. First he quotes the great master Dharmakīrti who said in his *Commentary on the "Compendium of Valid Cognition":*

> Here, the antidote, knowledge, is understanding the truth, the meaning of the selflessness of persons. Its opposite is the view of the transitory collections, which grasps at a self of persons.

The antidote of ignorance is *knowledge,* which is seeing the truth, understanding the meaning of selflessness. The opposite of that is the *view of the transitory collections,* which regards the five aggregates and based upon that collection imputes a substantial self, which is then conceived of as real, independent, and substantially existent.

The great master Asaṅga and his brother Vasubandhu do not agree that ignorance is actually *grasping at* an incorrect conception of reality. They say that ignorance is merely *not knowing* the true nature of reality. This definition is more in tune with the common usage of the term "ignorance," as not knowing something clearly.

These are the two definitions of ignorance. The first sees it as a *wrong understanding* of reality. The second sees it as a mere *not knowing* the truth. Tsongkhapa says that regardless of this disagreement, all agree that the principle antidote of ignorance is the wisdom that realizes selflessness.

According to Asaṅga's *Compendium of Knowledge* there are two types of ignorance. The first type is not knowing about the cause and effect of karma and its results. This ignorance of the consequences of virtuous and nonvirtuous actions underlies nonvirtuous action, and it is this type of ignorance that gives rise to lower rebirths.

The second type of ignorance is not knowing the true nature of ultimate reality. It is this type of ignorance that leads to the actions that cause you to be born in higher rebirths within cyclic existence. To be born in higher rebirths you must accumulate virtuous karma, but those virtuous actions are still motivated by an interest in gratifying a self that does not exist. The root motivation of samsaric virtuous karma is ignorance of the true nature of the self. Even beings in the upper realms, who abide in the subtle bliss of meditative equipoise, act out of the ignorance that grasps at a mistaken conception of self. Although each individual act has its own immediate, proximate motivation, the fundamental motivation that underlies them *all* is this grasping at a false conception of self.

For both of these types of ignorance the antidote is knowledge, understanding, and realization; and the ultimate antidote to the fundamental misconception of self is the wisdom realizing selflessness.

2. *Formative activity*

Formative activity refers to the actions that arise because of ignorance, which become the causes and conditions that eventually bring all future results. In short, this refers to karma. Karma is action of body, speech, and mind, and there are two types: nonvirtuous or demeritorious karma, which produces unhappy rebirths, and virtuous karma, which produces happy rebirths. As we explained earlier, there are two types of virtuous karma: meritorious karma, which projects rebirth in the desire realm, and immovable karma, which projects rebirth in the form or formless realms. For *all* samsaric karma the underlying cause is ignorance.

3. *Consciousness*

The third link is consciousness. In general, the sutras speak of six consciousnesses: the five sense consciousnesses plus mental consciousness. For those who adhere to the Yogācāra system, where eight types of consciousness are described, the consciousness of this third link is what that system refers to as *foundation consciousness.* For those who do not accept the existence of a foundation consciousness, this link refers to the *mental consciousness.*

Motivated by the ignorance of self-grasping, you take actions of body, speech, and mind. Each action deposits a seed or impression on the consciousness, which carries that seed forward as a potential, which will eventually ripen and yield a result in the form of some type of future life experience.

In order to discuss this more clearly we can divide consciousness into two stages. First there is the consciousness that receives the impression deposited by a seeding action; this is referred to as the *causal consciousness.* For example, because of the ignorance of not knowing the cause and effect of karma, you perform negative actions. All negative actions, such as harming others by killing or by stealing, are done to benefit oneself; after all, beings act under the misapprehension that what they are doing will bring them happiness. This fundamental ignorance of cause and effect causes beings to perform harmful actions. As soon as a particular nonvirtuous action is completed, it deposits a seed on the consciousness, which is carried forward as a potential that will ripen in the form of suffering experience in the future. The consciousness that receives this seed, and carries it forward without interruption until the conditions are met for that seed to ripen, is called the causal consciousness. In general, it is this causal consciousness that we refer to as the third link of dependent origination.

When a nonvirtuous seed that was *previously* deposited on that causal consciousness ripens and gives rise to a new unpleasant birth, the first moment when that consciousness becomes conjoined with the new life is referred to as *resultant consciousness.* Thus, when we speak of the two stages of consciousness, we are referring, first of all, to consciousness during the time it is functioning as a cause, and second, to that consciousness at the first moment of its ripening as a result.

The process works in the same way when you perform virtuous karma, which has as its underlying motivation ignorance about the true nature of self. Because of the ignorance that grasps at an inherently existent self, you act in ways that you believe will make that self happy—you may make offerings, give charity, observe pure ethical conduct, and perform other virtuous actions. These actions deposit seeds on the consciousness, which are carried forward until they ripen into happy rebirths at some time in the future. This virtuous karma—which is "contaminated" because it is motivated by ignorance—becomes the cause of birth in the desire realm as a human or deva; in the case of immovable karma, it ripens as birth in the form or formless realms. The consciousness that receives and carries forward those karmic seeds is called the *causal consciousness.* The consciousness at the first moment when such a seed ripens as birth in one of these happy migrations is called the *resultant consciousness.*

4. Name and form

The fourth link is called "name and form" *(nāma-rūpa).* "Name" refers to the combination of the four nonphysical aggregates: feelings, discrimination, formative activity, and consciousness. For the Buddhist schools, these nonphysical parts of the mind-body continuum, which combine to create the mental life of an individual, are what we are really talking about when we talk about a "person," a "being," a "personality," or a "life."

"Form" refers to the physical aggregate, what we commonly call the "body." For all beings (except those in the formless realm) consciousness joins with the body, the form aggregate, at the moment of conception, and as the five aggregates come together and develop, life begins. That developmental period is called "name and form." If you are born in the formless realm you have only four aggregates; you have *name* but no *form.* All other beings have all five aggregates; they have both *name* (the four mental aggregates) and whatever *form* is appropriate to the realm in which they are born.

Actually, there are two different views on whether the beings of the formless realm have form or not. According to the Yogācāra system they have no form at all. Other schools, including the Madhyamaka, say that although there is no *gross* body, beings still have the "mere seed" of form, which means they have an extremely subtle body of form—and this is the view of tantra as well.

When the Buddha first taught the twelve links of dependent origination, he was speaking to human beings, so he laid out this evolutionary process in a manner that applies to *human* development. To better understand what name and form is actually talking about we can take a human life as an example. From the time that the consciousness first joins with the fertilized ovum—the mixed parental blood and semen—all five psycho-physical aggregates are already present. These five aggregates, during the period between conception and the stage when the six sense organs have developed, is given the designation "name and form." The body, consisting of the combined blood and semen before the six sense organs have developed, is called "form." The four mental aggregates as they exist in this developmental period are designated "name" because they form a basis or referent for naming.

Traditionally, we have a description of five stages of development in the womb. The first stage is when the consciousness joins the mixture of parental semen and blood, called *mer mer po* in Tibetan. Then this coagulates into a small soft mass called *nur nur po*. Then it grows longer, into an oval shape called *nar nar po*. This oval mass grows longer, and as it does it becomes harder and more substantial, called *trang gyur*. In the final stage the embryo begins to develop limbs and is described as "having five bumps"; this stage is called *kang lag gyu*.[1]

In brief, the period during which the fetus is developing through these five stages, up until the six sense organs are complete, is designated "name and form."

5. *The six sense bases*

Here we have the continuation of the development of the mind-body complex described in the name and form link. Again, we can take a human life as our example. At this stage of the gradual growth of the sense faculties, the body faculty has already been established, but the eye, ear, nose, and tongue faculties are still developing. "The six sense bases" refers to this developmental phase, during which the person develops the *capability* to experience an object through the coming together of sense faculty, object, and consciousness, although that *contact* has not yet taken place. In other words, with the completion of *name and form* you have an actual body; then, with the completion of the *six sense bases*, the specific physical properties of that embodiment are fully developed, and the sensory faculties thereby become utilizable instruments.

This process of gradual development takes place for beings born from a womb, from an egg, or from warmth and moisture. For those with miraculous birth—such as devas and beings in the intermediate state—the sense bases do not gradually evolve but are fully manifested at the moment of birth. This is explained in Asaṅga's *Levels of Yogic Deeds*.

6. *Contact*

Once the sense faculties are complete, they begin to operate. *Contact* is the moment when a faculty, an object of cognition, and a moment of consciousness meet. In dependence on this moment of contact, the object is distinguished as either attractive, unattractive, or neutral. There are six kinds of contact, corresponding to the six faculties and the six types of consciousness: tactile, visual, auditory, olfactory, gustatory, and mental.

7. *Feeling*

Depending on whether you have contact with an attractive, unattractive, or neutral object, you experience a pleasant, unpleasant, or neutral feeling. When contact and feeling are complete, the experience is complete.

Let us look again at this whole process of the evolution of a human being, thinking of the being as an *experiencer.* All samsaric life is experience, and whatever you experience within a particular life is due to causes and conditions; your physical form and your mental life are both the results of karmic seeds planted at an earlier time.

The human as experiencer has these two parts: the physical and the mental. The physical aspect coalesces in the mother's womb with the union of the parental semen and blood, and the consciousness joins at the moment of conception. As we said earlier, with the completion of name and form you have an actual body. At that stage of the fertilized ovum enlivened with consciousness, you have obtained the entity of a body, although the details of its shape have not yet fully manifested. By the power of karma, the body with its faculties continues to develop and, at the stage of the six sense bases, the sense faculties come to their full manifestation. At that point the entire physical instrument that enables the being to be an experiencer is complete; all the particular physical requirements and capacities to experience life—to be a *subject* who experiences an object—are in place. The faculty, consciousness, and object are now linked together.

Then comes contact—the point at which a faculty, consciousness, and object meet. This meeting creates experience as a consciousness grasping an object as attractive, unattractive, or neutral. In other words, from contact feeling arises. In dependence on whether you come in contact with an object you determine to be attractive, unattractive, or neutral, you experience a feeling that is pleasant, suffering, or neutral. This is the way you experience life; feeling is the experience of the ripening of your karmic seeds. Sometimes you have pleasant feelings, sometimes you have unpleasant feelings, sometimes they are kind of neutral. One feeling after another—this is the way you experience your life. Most of the effort of your life is directed at striving for pleasant feelings.

Each experience of feeling is the ripened fruit of karmic seeds you planted in the past, the results of causes you created by your previous actions. Beings in the form and formless realms experience only pleasant, peaceful feelings during their whole life. Inhabitants of the lower realms—hell beings, hungry ghosts, and many animals—experience mostly suffering feelings. For humans and some other beings in the desire realm, experience is mixed. But for *all* beings in cyclic existence, the feelings they experience are the ripening of their previous karma.

Contact is the point at which the subjective components of experience—the faculty and consciousness—meet and utilize the object; at that point the object's role in the experience is complete. From that contact, *feeling*—the subjective reaction—arises; this is the experience of the object as pleasant, unpleasant, or neutral. This feeling is the ripening of previous karmic seeds, and once that feeling has arisen, the entire experience is complete—the karmic seeds have yielded their fruit.

8. Craving

Craving is attachment. When an enjoyable feeling arises you become attached to it. You do not want to separate from it; on the contrary, you want more and better. Even when pain and discomfort arise there is a craving, but in this case the craving is to be free from that unpleasant feeling.

Tsongkhapa points out that the statement, "Craving arises as the result of feeling" needs to be qualified. Feeling itself is not the ultimate cause of craving; craving is caused when feeling is *accompanied by ignorance.* In the twelve links, ignorance is the root cause that sets the whole process in motion. When a particular feeling arises, it is rooted in ignorance and dominated by ignorance. Therefore, when a feeling of pleasure or aversion arises toward an object, that object is being perceived in a distorted way. Because of ignorance, the feeling arises based on this mistaken perception: when that feeling is pleasurable you desire the object and want to possess it; when the feeling is unpleasant you desire separation from the object. In either case the feeling gives rise to the craving only because it is dominated by ignorance.

Craving, of course, is another word for desire. We need to keep in mind that not all desire is nonvirtuous. There are certain kinds of virtuous, pure desires, such as the desire of a bodhisattva to liberate all sentient beings and free them from suffering. When a desire like that is free of ignorance or other afflictions, it does not operate to perpetuate entrapment in cyclic existence. Once ignorance is cut out from the root, feelings still arise but craving does not. For example, arhats experience pleasant feelings, and buddhas also have blissful feelings. But because these feelings are not dominated by ignorance, they will not give rise to craving or attachment.

This nexus between the seventh and eighth links provides a good illustration of how these twelve links operate as a chain of causation. A feeling is the culminating result of a previous set of causes—ignorance, karma, consciousness, etc.—and when that feeling arises that particular sequence of cause and result is complete. But at the same time, that feeling is giving rise to a new craving, which may take the form of attachment, aversion, or some other affliction. That new craving will motivate new karma, and a whole new cause-result sequence will be set in motion by the completion of the last one. In this way the chain of experience within one lifetime, and the chain of lifetimes within cyclic existence, perpetuate themselves. That self-perpetuating process is what the twelve links of dependent origination are really talking about.

There are three types of craving (and in this context we might prefer to use the term "attachment" to refer to them): there is attachment that belongs to the desire realm, attachment that belongs to the form realm, and attachment that belongs to the formless realm. Consider the following question: "How are phenomena that belong to the desire realm, to the form realm, or to the formless realm distinguished?" The distinction is based on the type of attachment that any particular phenomena give rise to; they become part of that realm of existence based on their capacity to generate attachment to that particular realm. Phenomena of the desire realm nourish attachment to *that* realm, and phenomena of the form realm nourish attachment to *that* realm. These points make it clear that this eighth link of craving, or attachment, plays a central role in perpetuating and structuring samsaric existence.

9. Grasping

In the eighth link we took a form of desire or attachment and we called it "craving." This craving then gives rise to a more intense, more powerful form of attachment, which we call "grasping." Craving is a general attachment to objects. Grasping augments craving in a way that strengthens and actualizes the ripening of karmic seeds into samsaric rebirth or other experiences. Grasping is divided into four categories based on four types of objects, as follows:

1. The first category is called "grasping out of desire," and refers to attachment to the sensory objects we enjoy in the desire realm: form, sound, smell, taste, and tangible objects, which are referred to as the "attributes of the desire realm." Here in the desire realm the mind is dominated by sense consciousness. Between mental objects and sensual objects, we ordinarily have a stronger attachment to sensual objects. In this realm beings spend their whole lives chasing after the attributes of the desire realm, such as attractive forms, delicious tastes, and fragrant smells. They feel happy when they find such pleasures and they suffer when they do not.

Higher up, in the form and formless realms, beings do not even use the tongue or the nose because they have no need to eat or smell. The beings of these upper realms survive by the very subtle food of samādhi, the nourishment of meditative stabilization.

2. The second type is "grasping for views." This refers to grasping at any of the various types of wrong view, with the exception of the view of the transitory collections. These four wrong views, which will be discussed at greater

length below, relate to certain misguided behaviors and religious practices that are based on mistaken dogmas, philosophies, and beliefs. Grasping for views arises when you have a strong attachment to these kinds of wrong views.

3. "Grasping for mistaken morality and asceticism" is the third type of grasping. This is a type of wrong view in which you hold that some distorted system of ethics or mode of religious behavior will lead to emancipation, such as sacrificing other beings, or burning your body with fire, or imitating dogs or pigs. You become attached to these beliefs and practices based on arguments you find convincing even though they are flawed, and based on these faulty convictions you grasp at mistaken morality and asceticism. Although you are convinced that you are on the right path, such perverted ethics and practices lead only to negative karma and future suffering.

4. The fourth type is "grasping for a self." This is a strong attachment to the self that comes from holding the mental and physical aggregates to be a real "I." This grasping at a false imputation of an absolute, substantially existent self—where there is, in fact, only a transitory aggregation of elements—leads you to hold onto this self with pride, egoism, and attachment.

This fourth type of grasping is equivalent to the view of the transitory collections. All of the other afflictions, such as attachment, pride, and jealousy, develop out of this fundamental misunderstanding: the wrong view that imputes an essential self upon the perishable aggregates. If you do not make this mistake—if you view the nature of the aggregates correctly and do not impute a real self where none exists—then all these other faults and wrong attitudes will not develop.

These are the four types of grasping that are taught in the sutras. The powerful form of attachment we call "grasping" acts as the moisture that awakens, stimulates, and nourishes the dormant karmic seeds you have deposited on your mental continuum by previous actions. The latent seeds of past actions are always present, but they require the moisture of attachment in order to ripen and bear fruit. Once the two levels of attachment, craving and grasping, actualize the potentiality of a karmic seed, it ripens quickly into a resultant experience.

For example, in the continuum of an arhat there are many latent karmic seeds deposited by actions taken in the innumerable lifetimes before attaining arhatship. But these remain as dry seeds because they will never be moistened and actualized by attachment. Why? Because without attachment these seeds will never yield their fruit. We can see how these two levels of attachment—called "craving" and "grasping" here in the context of the twelve links of dependent origination—are the critical factors in actualizing and ripening karmic seeds, and thereby bringing about rebirth and all the experiences of cyclic existence.

10. Existence

The tenth link is called "existence," which generally refers to the subsequent rebirth brought about by the ripening of the seed planted by the action of the second link. Specifically, this tenth link refers to the moment *just before* that next life happens, at the point when the karmic seed is fully actualized and ready to yield its fruit. So the name of this tenth link, "existence," is a case of giving the name of the result to the cause. The result is a new existence, and that name is given to the moment when the causes of that new existence have all come together and are about to produce that result.

Let's look again at how a samsaric rebirth is brought about. There are actually two distinct periods of causation: a period of seeding and a period of actualization, or germination. Both of these periods require an action, or karma, coupled with the supportive cause of an obscuring affliction. At the stage of planting the seed, the first link—ignorance—is the affliction, and the action of the second link—formative activity—is what actually plants the projecting karmic seed that will eventually ripen into the next rebirth.

That seed remains dormant until it is nourished and activated by the moisture of the afflictions of craving and grasping, the eighth and ninth links. The projecting karmic seed is thereby reactivated and ready to yield its fruit as a new rebirth. However, there is one more causal element necessary to complete the causes of this period of actualization, and that is a secondary karma, an action taken just at the time of death.

In other words, there are three supportive causes that actualize the main karmic seed. Craving and grasping are the afflictions that act as the moisture awakening and activating the seed, and then a final karma—which is usually a mental action, a thought at the time of death—acts as the third supportive cause. This final karma will be similar in its ethical tone—virtuous or nonvirtuous—to the main karmic seed. If the first two factors are like moisture, then we can say that this third nourishing factor is like the warmth necessary for a seed to germinate. If the projecting karma is nonvirtuous, at the time of death nonvirtuous thoughts—which are mental karma—arise and act as this third supportive condition; if the projecting karma is virtuous, then virtuous thoughts arise and nourish that main seed. In this way the thoughts of a person who is approaching death act as an essential condition that nurtures and activates the main projecting karmic seed. This is why it is important to guide the mind of a dying person to the side of virtue as he or she approaches death.

We can say that this tenth link, existence, is actually the potency that was established by the karma of the second link to bring forth the next rebirth, when it has been fully nourished and activated by craving, grasping, and a final, secondary karma. At that point it is fully empowered to produce the next life, and it is that fully empowered karmic potential that is called "existence." This is the last link in the previous life, the moment just before rebirth. The next existence has not yet come into being, but at the stage of the tenth link it is about to do so; that is why the name of that result, existence, is given to its fully potentiated cause.

11. Birth

The result of that fully potentiated cause is rebirth. The first moment of that new life, when the consciousness enters its new body, is the eleventh link, called "birth." Birth can take place by any of the four modes: birth from a womb, from an egg, from heat and moisture, or miraculous birth. Hell beings, devas, and intermediate state beings always have miraculous birth. Hungry ghosts usually experience this type of birth as well, but some are said to be womb-born. Humans and animals share all four types of birth.

12. Aging and death

The twelfth link, which combines aging and death, begins in the second moment after birth. If you are born into a mother's womb, the first moment when your mental and physical aggregates conjoin there is called birth. By the second moment you have already begun to age. From that moment on aging never stops; you are moving irrevocably toward death.

Aging is the maturation of the aggregates and the unceasing, unstoppable change they undergo in each moment. Although in every moment you are getting older, and the aggregates are never identical from moment to moment, there is a continuity and an identifiable similarity that distinguishes one being's aggregates from another's. Death is the cessation of the continuum of that seemingly identical set of aggregates. The continuity of the present aggregates comes to an end at the moment of death.

Aging and death are combined into one link because death can occur without the common signs of aging such as white hair, a bent body, and the loss of memory. In fact, death can occur immediately after birth, in which case there is hardly any aging at all.

It is traditional to mention, in connection with this link of aging and death, the sorrow, lamentation, and anguish of losing those you love, and the suffering of dying yourself; this is done in order to bring to mind the unsatisfactory nature of cyclic existence. The previous eleven causes and conditions function in their interdependent fashion to produce an experiencer, a being living a life. But regardless of the nature of that life, in the end it will undoubtedly culminate in the suffering of death. Although some practitioners who have maintained excellent ethical conduct die with their bodies and minds at ease, the death process in general is one of severe pain and sorrow. The chain of dependent origination by which beings continue to cycle in samsara inevitably ends with the pain and sorrow of its final link: death.

2' The condensed presentation of the links

Having identified each of the twelve links of dependent origination, we now analyze the meaning of this sequence from various points of view. Asaṅga's *Compendium of Knowledge* says that these twelve links can be subsumed under four categories:

> What do you get if you summarize the links? There are four types: projecting factors, projected factors, actualizing factors, and actualized factors. Which are the projecting factors? They are ignorance, formative activity, and consciousness. Which are the projected factors? They are name and form, the six sense bases, contact, and feeling. Which are the actualizing factors? They are craving, grasping, and existence. Which are the actualized factors? They are birth and aging and death.

From this explanation we see that there are two stages of this causal sequence. There are the projecting causes, which "plant" the projected effects; and then there are the actualizing causes, which bring about the actualized effects. The question is then raised, "Does this sequence represent one round of rebirth for a given individual, or is it a description of two cycles?"

If these twelve factors represent the cause and effect for only one life, then it seems incorrect to have the set of actualizing factors occurring *after* the projected factors. To put it another way, if this sequence represents one cycle of life, why would the projected effects, which are *effects,* come before the actualizing causes, which are *causes*? Such an order only makes sense if the sequence describes two rounds of rebirth.

However, if the twelve links represent two rounds of causality for two different lives, then the actualizing causes of the latter causal sequence appear inadequate to produce a rebirth, because this group lacks ignorance, formative activity, and causal consciousness. By the same token, the initial causal sequence of projecting causes lacks the actualizing causes of craving, grasping, and existence, so it is inadequate to produce rebirth in the first cycle.

To state the problem in the most concise form: if the sequence represents one life, all the projecting and actualizing causes should come before all the projected and actualized effects, and all those effects should occur together as one life. If the sequence represents two lives, then the first life will be lacking the actualizing causes and the second life will be lacking the projecting causes.

How do we resolve this apparent contradiction? In general, every life requires all six causes and includes all six results. Whatever is projected by a projecting cause has to be completed by an actualizing cause. Take my life as an example. At some time in the distant past the three projecting causes were initiated—ignorance, karma, and causal consciousness. In order to yield any result, these projecting causes must be activated by the three actualizing causes—craving, grasping, and existence. Nothing will be brought into existence without all six of these causes operating together. Name and form, the six sense bases, contact, and feeling were projected by the projecting causes of ignorance, karma, and causal consciousness. They were then brought to fruition by the actualizing causes of craving, grasping, and existence. Thus actualized, those very same projected factors are designated as the actualized effects and are called birth, aging, and death.

Therefore, for one person's single life, all the causes have carried out their function before birth. First the projecting cause projected name and form, the six sense bases, contact, and feeling; then later, when these are brought to fruition by the actualizing causes, those very same projected factors become the actualized factors of birth, aging, and death. In short, for one life, all the causes must operate before the fruition of the actualized effects.

If that is the case the question becomes: "What is the reason for explaining this in terms of two cycles of causality?"

The reason two sets of causality are shown is in order to point out the differences between the effects of projection and the effects of actualization in terms of their suffering natures. The projected effects actually remain in a state of dormancy, of potentiality, until such time as they meet the conditions to manifest in their actualized state. In other words, at the time they are projected they do not come into existence in their fully actualized nature of suffering. They have that potential—they are suitable to become factors of suffering—but that will only happen when they meet the actualizing conditions. We can say that, when they are projected, the projected factors are made suitable to manifest at some time in the future, when they meet the necessary actualizing conditions; at that time they will become factors of suffering. But at the time of projection, this has not yet occurred.

For example, in some previous lifetime, perhaps a long time ago, I projected the virtuous karma to be born a human, as Geshe Sopa. We can say it was virtuous karma because I am now living a human life. At that past time those karmic seeds were planted in this mental continuum [links 1, 2, and the causal aspect of 3]. What was planted by that action was the seed or potentiality of the projected effects: the factors of resultant consciousness, name and form, the six sense bases, contact, and feeling [the resultant aspect of 3, plus links 4–7]. Then, at the time of death in my previous life, just before I was born in this life, the actualizing causes [links 8–10] ripened this potentiality and brought about birth in this life [links 11–12].

When we say that the seeds were planted—that the projected effects were projected—it means that they were rendered suitable to manifest when they meet the necessary actualizing factors. Until they meet those necessary conditions, the projected effects remain dormant, in a state of potentiality. This is the meaning of projected effects. Calling them "effects" does not mean that these factors are already manifest and fully functioning; it does not mean that contact and feeling have already occurred.

This is the same as planting a seed in the garden. You can plant a seed in the fall and it will lie dormant right through the winter. Then in the spring, when the ground warms up and the rains fall, that seed sprouts. It is brought to germination by the actualizing causes of warmth and moisture. It was rendered suitable to be actualized by planting (projecting) it in the ground. If you hadn't put the seed there, then no matter how much moisture and warmth appeared in the spring, you would not have a sprout.

The actualized effects—birth, aging, and death—are factors that have already been actualized; they are fully manifest, fully functioning, and are therefore conditions of suffering in a current lifetime. Every causal relationship has these two stages, requiring both a primary *cause* and secondary actualizing *conditions.*

According to this method of explaining the twelve links, these two different sets of causes and effects were presented in order to illustrate this difference. The projected effects will only become suffering factors of life at some time in the future—possibly many lives after they are planted—because they remain in a dormant state of potential until they are awakened by actualizing causes. Once those seeds have been awakened by the actualizing causes, the actualized effects ripen immediately as the suffering factors of birth in the next life, without any other life intervening.

Another reason why two separate cycles of cause and effect were taught was to emphasize the point that two types of causes are necessary to produce the result of taking birth in cyclic existence. Presenting the twelve links in this manner enables us to distinguish projecting causes from actualizing causes, and to understand how both are necessary to produce that result. Asaṅga explains this in the *Levels of Yogic Deeds* this way:

> Since it is the case that the factors from consciousness up to feeling have the character of being intermingled with the factors of birth, aging, and death, why were they taught as two different types? They were taught that way in order to show the different characteristics of things that produce suffering, and in order to differentiate between projecting and actualizing.

The same text also says:

> Among these twelve factors, how many are included in the truth of suffering and will become sufferings in the current life? Two: birth and aging and death. How many are included within the truth of suffering but will only become suffering at a later time? Those that remain in a state of potential, from resultant consciousness up to feeling.

The first quotation states that the projected and actualized factors are "intermingled." This means that the factors come together; they are functioning at the same time, in the same lifetime. For example, the actualized factor of birth and the projected factor of name and form start at the same time. During the time that the six sense bases, contact, and feeling are operating, the actualized factor of aging is also operating. In this sense they are intermingled. Then why are they shown separately? It is in order to show the different kinds of causes that bring about the suffering factors of cyclic existence, and in order to help us differentiate these two distinct types of causes.

The twelve links as a presentation of two lifetimes

So far we have been discussing the purpose of showing two cause and effect cycles within the twelve links under the assumption that these twelve links all occurred within *one* lifetime. However, what becomes evident from the preceding discussion is that these twelve links are presented in a way that seems to fit *two* separate rounds of dependent origination. The *Rice Seedling Sutra (Śāli-stamba-sūtra),* one of the primary sources of the Buddha's presentation of the twelve links, teaches, on the face of it, a sequence that takes place over two lifetimes. The factors from ignorance up through feeling describe one round of dependent origination; the factors from craving through aging and death describe a second round.

Let's once again take my life as an example. The twelve links begin with the two and a half projecting causes—ignorance, karma, and the causal stage of consciousness. These projecting causes give rise to a series of projected effects, which constitute the experience of my life—from resultant consciousness up to feeling. Then, from the activity of feeling, craving arises, which increases into grasping, and finally, just before I die, I perform the actualizing karma of existence. These are the three actualizing causes, and they occur just before I die. But these three are not the actualizing causes that produced this present lifetime. They are not part of the round of dependent origination that I am experiencing now. What they are actualizing is the next lifetime—another birth, aging, and death.

The craving, grasping, and existence that occur just before I die cannot be part of the causality of my current life because the causes for this life cannot be happening at the *end* of my life. These actualizing causes are the causes of a *subsequent* life, and as such they are part of a separate round of dependent origination.

The way the Buddha has presented these twelve links of dependent origination is to first introduce the three projecting causes that produced this life—ignorance, karma, and causal consciousness. Then he shows some of the results of those causes, which constitute the experience of this life, from causal consciousness up to feeling. Then, near the end of this life, craving arises in dependence upon feeling, and this craving leads to grasping and then to existence. This second causal nexus gives rise to birth and aging and death, but that actualizing causal nexus and its actualized results are a separate sequence of dependent origination. They are the cause and effect of a separate lifetime.

What this means is that for each of the two lifetimes it is necessary to infer one of the causal sets. As a description of my current life, the twelve links include the projecting causes, but it is necessary to infer that in the previous life there were actualizing causes that brought my birth to fruition. Within that same set of twelve links we have the actualizing causes for my next rebirth, but it is necessary to infer that projecting causes were created at some previous time, which are actualized at the time of death and will bring into being my next life.

Why did the Buddha teach the twelve links in a manner that spreads them over two lifetimes? It was in order to demonstrate how this process is a perpetual chain. In this life you are experiencing the results of previous ignorance and karma. At the same time, during this very life, you are creating the causes of another rebirth in the future. The twelve links operate as an endless chain.

The projecting causes and projected effects

To clarify how these factors operate, Tsongkhapa says that projecting causes and projected effects should be understood by way of four points:

1. What has been projected? Four and a half factors: resultant consciousness, name and form, the six sense bases, contact, and feeling.

2. By what are they projected? They are projected by karma—called formative activity in the twelve links—which depends on ignorance. Ignorance is the root motivating factor leading to karma, the main projecting activity.

3. How are they projected? By means of instilling in the causal consciousness the subtle propensities or karmic seeds. Ignorance creates the formative activity of good and bad karma. That karma instills in the consciousness a subtle seed or propensity to ripen into a certain kind of result at some time in the future when it meets the necessary conditions. Before the karma was created, that potential was not there. Karma has left this new potential on the consciousness—that is how the factors are projected.

4. The meaning of "projected" is that those factors that are projected are rendered suitable to be actualized and to manifest when the actualizing causes are met.

The actualizing causes and actualizing effects

Now we turn to the actualizing causes and these can be understood by means of three points:

1. What does the actualizing? The main actualizing cause is grasping, which has craving as its own cause. Both of these are types of desire, but grasping is desire that is intensified to the point where it has the power to bring its result immediately. The craving form of desire arises over and over again, getting stronger and stronger, until it turns into grasping, with the power to bring forth the result.

The actualizing causes are described as three: craving, grasping, and existence. Earlier we discussed existence as a final, actualizing karma. Here, in the context of this explanation, existence is not treated as some new karma. The emphasis here is on the potential of the projected karmic seed. When it meets the moisture and warmth of craving and grasping, that potential is actualized and it becomes ready to bring forth its fruit. That very actualized seed—that empowered potential ready to ripen into its result—is itself called existence, the tenth factor.

There are these two modes of explaining this tenth factor. It is still true that at the time of death a virtuous or nonvirtuous action arises that combines with the grasping to actualize the seed. In our earlier explanation that karma was referred to as existence. But this explanation only mentions craving and grasping as the actualizing causes, and according to this mode of explanation existence is defined as that fully potentiated seed itself.

2. What is actualized? It is the two actualized effects: birth, and aging and death.

3. How are they actualized? By means of empowering the subtle karmic propensities that were instilled in the consciousness by the formative activity of karma. The second factor, karma, deposited the subtle propensities of the projected factors on the consciousness some time in the past. Now these propensities are empowered to ripen and bring forth their results by these actualizing causes. This is what "actualize" means—to render the potentiality of the seed powerful enough to bring its result immediately.

Another way of looking at this comes from Vasubandhu who wrote in his *Explanation of the Divisions of Dependent Arising* that the only actualized factor is birth itself, while aging and death demonstrate the faults of birth.

With all this information we can now put together examples of how the twelve links operate. The first example describes the process of dependent origination for someone who is headed toward a lower rebirth. Ignorance of the cause and effect of karma is the first cause. Motivated by that ignorance, nonvirtuous karma deposits on the consciousness the subtle propensity or seed of an unpleasant rebirth. This potentiates the four and a half projected factors—from resultant consciousness to feeling—and makes them suitable to ripen in one of the three lower realms when the necessary conditions are met. These dormant karmic propensities are revitalized and repeatedly nourished by craving. And with the complete nourishment of grasping, these seeds become empowered to manifest and ripen into birth in a lower realm, where aging and the various sufferings of bad rebirths will ensue.

The next example describes the sequence for someone who is going to a higher rebirth. Motivated by ignorance about the meaning of selflessness, karma deposits on the consciousness the subtle propensity of a pleasant rebirth. The good karma to be born in higher rebirths in the desire realm is called "meritorious karma" and consists of virtuous behaviors such as maintaining ethical conduct. The good karma to be born in the form and formless realms is called "immoveable karma" and includes such practices as cultivating single-pointed concentration. Depositing these karmic propensities on the consciousness renders the projected factors—from resultant consciousness up to feeling—suitable to be actualized and to ripen into the experience of either the higher rebirths of the desire realm or rebirth among the devas in the upper realms. Subsequently, craving and grasping revitalize those dormant seeds and repeatedly nourish them, and this empowers them to ripen into birth in those higher realms and the experiences that ensue.

You may have some confusion about how ignorance can be the motivation of virtuous karma. For ordinary individuals—until they reach the ārya stage where they directly realize the emptiness of self—all actions, whether virtuous or nonvirtuous, have as their most fundamental motivation the ignorance that does not know the true nature of the self. This ignorance not only does not know the nature of the self, it holds onto a conception of self that is utterly mistaken. For all rounds of dependent origination, first there is the "I," this deep misunderstanding and misperception of the nature of the self.

That grasping at a misconceived "I" creates other afflictions, such as desire, hostility, pride, and so forth. Attachment to the "I" can lead you to want some genuinely worthwhile things for the sake of the "I," such as a higher rebirth and pleasant experience in future lives. For this purpose you will naturally engage in virtuous, meritorious karma. Although you perform meritorious deeds, deep down there is always that subtle attitude, the egotistic view, which has at its root the ignorance of not knowing the true nature of the self. That ignorance always remains the underlying, basic motivation. It gives rise to attachment to the self, holding the self at the center of all other concerns, perceiving the self as the most important thing in the world. Of course that attitude can lead you to perform nonvirtuous actions; but even when you perform virtues those virtuous actions will be contaminated by that underlying thought. You can maintain pure ethical conduct, never breaking even the slightest moral precept, and that will become the cause of rebirth as a human or as a desire-realm deva. These are certainly happy rebirths, but they are still within cyclic existence; they are still within the cycle of suffering.

Until you attain the ārya stage, you will almost never perform any action—virtuous or nonvirtuous—without that egotistic motivation. That is called "contaminated action." Virtuous karma still brings merits, the accumulation of positive potential, which will ripen into happy results in the future. But that happiness will be *samsaric* happiness, happiness mixed with the sorrows of cyclic existence. It is still rooted in afflictions and therefore it is still impure.

You may even recognize how inferior life is in the desire realm and accumulate the merits to obtain a higher, more peaceful, more subtle, and longer life in the form or formless realms. To obtain rebirth in those peaceful realms you must first attain single-pointed concentration. Depending on the level of meditative stabilization you achieve, you can be born into one of the four concentrations of the form realm, or one of the four formless absorptions. If you achieve the level of meditative stabilization equal to one of these levels while you are a human, you deposit the karmic propensity to be born on that level at some time in the future; you render that seed suitable to be actualized and to ripen into the experience of that higher rebirth when the necessary conditions come together. This is called "immoveable karma," the good karma to be born in the form or formless realms. The necessary conditions arise when craving and grasping revitalize that seed and nourish it over and over again until it is fully empowered to bring forth its fruit as birth into one of those higher realms.

For example, in this human body, if you practice single-pointed concentration and you attain the level of meditative stabilization that belongs to the "actual stage" of the first concentration,[2] and you do not degenerate from that level, nor do you attain the direct realization of emptiness that comes on the path of seeing, then you have projected the karmic seed to be born in the first concentration, the first level of the form realm. Now you have the potential, the *possibility,* to be born there. But that potential must be actualized in order to ripen into that rebirth. Before the time of death in this life, the craving and grasping that belong to the first concentration must revitalize and nourish that projected seed. In other words, even while you are living in a human body, you have obtained the afflictions that belong to the first concentration by attaining that level of meditative stabilization. You have attained a level of consciousness that is beyond the desire realm, and abiding in that state brings with it the functioning of the afflictions of that level. It is the craving and grasping of that level that nourish the karmic seed to be born there and bring that birth to fruition.

You have to attain the "actual stage" of the first concentration because the afflictions of the first concentration are part of the actual stage, but not part of the "preparatory stage." Although this topic can get very technical and complicated, the main point is that the afflictions of craving and grasping are necessary to ripen any projected karmic seed into an actual rebirth. And the craving, grasping, and existence must be of the same level on which you are going to be born.

Other ways to categorize the twelve links

Nāgārjuna explains in the *Heart of Dependent Arising (Pratītya-samutpāda-hṛdaya-kārikā)* that these twelve links can be subsumed under three categories: afflictions, karma, and sufferings:

> The first, eighth, and ninth are afflictions.
> The second and tenth are karma.
> The remaining seven are sufferings.

Nāgārjuna calls these categories "paths," so he is saying that the factors of ignorance, craving, and grasping are the path of afflictions, karma and existence are the path of karma, and the other seven factors are all the path of suffering.

In the *Rice Seedling Sutra* the Buddha, holding up a green rice sprout as an example, taught the twelve links of dependent origination and presented them in terms of four causes leading to rebirth. The analogy he uses in this sutra is a little bit different from the usual one we encounter—that karma is the seed and consciousness is the field in which it is planted. Instead, in the *Rice Seedling Sutra* the Buddha likened ignorance to the planter, the agent who plants the seed; karma itself is like a field in which the seed is planted; and the seed that is planted is actually the seed of consciousness, specifically causal consciousness. When that seed is moistened by the water of grasping it becomes the sprout of name and form in the mother's womb. In this analysis it is the planter, the field, the seed, and the supporting condition of moisture [i.e., ignorance, karma, causal consciousness, and grasping] that together produce the birth of the being in the womb.

3' How many lifetimes are required to complete the cycle

How many lives does it take in order to complete all twelve of these factors?

Many eons can intervene between the projecting factors of ignorance and karma, and the projected factors from name and form down to feeling. On the other hand, it is also possible that the projected factors will be actualized and ripen into the very next life after they are projected, with no intervening lives at all. For example, we are born here as humans with so many wonderful conditions that our lives are almost incomparable in terms of the precious opportunity we have achieved. In a previous life we must have projected the virtuous karmic seeds that ripened into this life. The lifetime in which we performed that meritorious karma may have been the immediately preceding life, or it could have been some distant lifetime many eons ago.

When it comes to the actualizing factors of craving, grasping, and existence, there is never an intervening life before they yield the actualized factors of birth, aging, and death; these actualized factors always arise in the very next lifetime. (Remember that the intermediate state is not counted as a separate life although it does occur between this life and the next. The intermediate state is considered part of the life it precedes, because both of them are projected by the same karma.)

Given that the projecting factors *can* ripen in the very next life, and the actualizing factors *always* ripen in the very next life, the minimum number of lifetimes in which you can complete one round of the twelve links is two.

For example, let's say that during this life you create the karma to be born as a deva in your next life. This is done by the three projecting causes of ignorance, karma, and causal consciousness. Later in this life, before you die, you create the actualizing causes of craving, grasping, and existence, which revitalize and nourish those seeds and bring them to fruition. All six causes are then functioning in this present life, and at the time of death they give rise to the projected factors of resultant consciousness, name and form, the six sense bases, contact, and feeling, as well as the two actualized factors of birth and aging and death. Remember that the projected and actualized effects are "intermingled"—they come together in the same lifetime, functioning at the same time. As we explained earlier, they were taught separately in order to clarify and help to identify the two different types of causes that bring about suffering in cyclic existence. In this way, all twelve links of dependent origination are completed in a minimum of two lifetimes.

Now then, what is the maximum number of lives it takes to complete the twelve links? A thousand lives? More? Sorry, that is wrong. The maximum is only three.

Let's take my current life as an example. Let's say that I did not project the causes to be born in this form in my immediately preceding life—it could have been two lifetimes ago, or many eons before—but the first of the three lives will be the life in which I planted the projecting karma. Remember that the actualizing causes must occur in the life immediately preceding the projected and actualized effects. That would have been in my last life. Therefore, we have a maximum of three lifetimes to complete all twelve factors: the life in which the projecting causes are planted, the life in which the actualizing causes occur, and the very next life in which the effects of all these causes ripen. Even though there may be many, many lifetimes intervening between the lives in which the projecting and actualizing causes occur, these intervening lifetimes are not part of this particular sequence of dependent origination. The twelve factors that created and constitute this current life of mine took place over a maximum of three lives.

How dependent origination illuminates the emptiness of self

When you look at this process of cause and effect and how it gives rise to all experience in cyclic existence, you can see how there is no absolute self who is the creator of the karma, and no absolute self who is experiencing the result of karma. When we look for the "person" who creates the karma and the "person" who experiences the results, instead of discovering such an absolute self, we only find the numerous ever-changing factors of mind and body, the five impermanent aggregates. Upon those five aggregates we impute a self, an "I," an independent "person." That imputed self, what we think of as "I," is what we hold to be the creator of karma and the experiencer of the results of karma. But in reality there is no such independent or absolute self. There is merely an imputation of such a self upon a collection of impermanent phenomena.

The causal factors—the projecting and actualizing causes—are themselves merely impermanent phenomena. The resultant factors—all the projected and actualized effects—are also nothing more than impermanent phenomena that arise from the causal factors. There is no independent, absolute creator of karma or experiencer of its results. There is merely the imputation of such a self upon transitory phenomena having nothing more than a relative, nominal existence.

It is due to your ignorance of the true nature of things that you grasp at a false conception of self. You hold the "I" to be ultimately, substantially, independently real and you grasp at that "real thing" as being your true self. Once you start holding tightly to that false, misperceived self, you naturally want to make that self happy. In order to accomplish that you engage in all sorts of actions of body, speech, and mind—sometimes virtuous and sometimes not. All such action ripens into future experience and perpetuates the cycle of existence.

Once again we see how the two karmic factors, karma and existence [the second and tenth links], arise from the three afflictions [ignorance, craving, and grasping], and in turn give rise to the seven factors of suffering [consciousness, name and form, the six sense bases, contact, feeling, and aging and death]. As you experience the pleasure and discomfort of those resultant factors, other afflictions, such as attachment and hostility, emerge in response.

They in turn set in motion another round of actions—one set of results instigates yet another set of causes. Here again we see how the cause of all cyclic existence is karma and affliction. Again we see how the cycle—affliction causing karma, causing experience, causing affliction—perpetuates itself; cause and effect drives the wheel of life, turning it round and round in perpetual motion. As Nāgārjuna said in his *Heart of Dependent Arising:*

> From the three arise the two,
> From the two the seven arise,
> And from the seven three arise—
> That is the wheel of life, going around, and around, and around.

If you carefully contemplate how all sentient beings, including yourself, are helplessly wandering up and down through the miseries and disappointments of cyclic existence as a result of this very process of cause and effect, that will be the best means for you to recognize the faults of samsara and to generate disenchantment with it. This is extremely important because to the extent that you realize just how unsatisfactory cyclic existence is, to that extent your mental life will turn in the direction of renunciation. If you fail to see the faults of cyclic existence thoroughly and deeply, you will never become disenchanted with its attractions. You will continue to seek out samsaric pleasures, and this will only cause you to continue your helpless wandering through the sufferings of cyclic existence.

You have been born in samsara in various forms over and over again for countless eons. During every single one of those lives you performed uncountable thousands of actions, thereby planting new karmic seeds. Even during one day in one life, from early morning until you go to bed, you create so many actions, so many different karmas. Sometimes your actions are virtuous, sometimes they are nonvirtuous. When you think about your situation like this, you realize that you have created countless karmas since beginningless time. You have accumulated vast amounts of virtuous and nonvirtuous projecting karma that has not yet yielded its results. If those unripened seeds had physical form, they would make a huge mountain reaching far into the sky. If these seeds are not destroyed by the antidotes, they will remain dormant in your mental continuum, ready at any time to be reawakened and nourished by the actualizing factors of craving and grasping. Then they will yield their results, and you will continue to wander through higher and lower rebirths in cyclic existence.

Nevertheless, although you have mountains of karmic seeds ready to ripen, if they are never revitalized and nourished by afflictions they will never be able to yield their results. Arhats, for example, also accumulated masses of projecting karma in their previous lives. But because they have destroyed their afflictions, they will never again be born into cyclic existence as the result of karma. For their accumulated projecting karma to produce another rebirth it must be nourished by the afflictions, and since arhats are free of afflictions, they are liberated from cyclic existence.

Once you have a firm understanding of all this, you will regard the obscuring afflictions as your enemy. You will see that the true enemy, the source of all your problems, is not outside somewhere. It is the inner enemy, the afflictions, that produce all your disappointment, unhappiness, and suffering. As Śāntideva said, if you are able to destroy this one enemy, you will destroy all enemies. If you destroy the inner enemy of ignorance and the other afflictions from the root, then you will no longer be forced to wander in cyclic existence, because although you may still possess many seeds of projecting karma, without the afflictions to nourish them they will never be able to ripen.

The great Kadampa Geshe Puchungwa spent his whole life practicing the meditation of the three types of spiritual individuals—the beings of small, intermediate, and great scope—by rolling that system of teaching (which is presented here in the *Lamrim Chenmo*) into his method of meditating on the twelve links of dependent origination. He did this by making the stages of the path, the *lamrim*, a meditation on the way sentient beings involve themselves in these twelve factors creating cyclic existence, and on the way they can extricate themselves from cyclic existence by disengaging from these twelve factors.

His system of correspondence worked this way. Meditation on the twelve links of dependent origination as they apply to birth in the three lower realms constitutes the training for beings of small scope. At this stage the focus of practice is to recognize how the ten nonvirtuous actions lead to the terrible sufferings of the lower rebirths. You meditate on what the experience will be in those realms, and this engenders a powerful determination to avoid that fate. You realize that the best protection is to take refuge in the Three Jewels, and then to adhere to ethical conduct. By meditating on how engagement in the twelve links of dependent origination leads to lower rebirths, and how disengagement from that cycle frees you from them, all the practices of the being of small scope are integrated into the contemplation of the twelve links.

Meditation on the twelve links as they apply to birth in the upper realms constitutes the training for beings of intermediate scope. By contemplating the experience of humans and devas you come to realize that, no matter where you are born within cyclic existence, you are subject to the various forms of suffering—that even the highest rebirths are still conditioned by karma and afflictions, still in the nature of suffering. Recognizing that stable happiness can only come with freedom from *all* of cyclic existence, you determine to attain emancipation for yourself. These meditations are integrated into the contemplation of how engagement in and disengagement from the twelve links of dependent origination lead, respectively, to high rebirth within or emancipation from the whole of samsara.

Cyclic existence is brought into being by the twelve links of dependent origination, and the root of that chain of causality is ignorance. Ignorance is the root of samsara. Therefore, the being of intermediate scope must ask, "How do I get rid of ignorance?" The answer is to meditate on the four noble truths, culminating in the direct realization of the emptiness of self. This, too, is included in the practice of the being of intermediate scope as it is integrated with the twelve links of dependent origination.

Then, for the being of great scope who is engaged in the Mahayana practice, you apply the very same understanding to all other sentient beings. You see how all these other beings—who have been your close relations over many previous lifetimes—have been wandering in cyclic existence because of the six causal factors and have experienced all the miseries of the six results. Seeing this, you develop powerful love and compassion for all other living beings. You determine that you will quickly obtain buddhahood so that you will be able to benefit all these suffering beings. With this intention you train in the practice of bodhicitta, and you strive with great energy to vanquish the inner enemies: ignorance, craving, and grasping.

If you know how to practice this method of Geshe Puchungwa, you will be able to incorporate the practices of all three spiritual beings into your meditation on dependent origination. This brings the entire path into your meditation, including the trainings of both the Hinayana and Mahayana.

Some people believe that the Buddha taught the twelve links of dependent origination mainly for Hinayana practitioners, who are seeking emancipation only for themselves, and that this training is therefore mainly for them. It is true that it is important for them, but it is just as central for anyone who is pursuing the Mahayana way. In order to produce great love and compassion for other beings, it is essential to see clearly how they are suffering, how they are trapped in the endless cycle of samsaric misery. That realization comes by way of this meditation on dependent origination. Therefore, this is a practice that is extremely beneficial to all three types of spiritual practitioners, and when it is done by the Mahayana individual of great scope, it will be of great benefit to all sentient beings.

4' How to summarize their significance

Tsongkhapa now brings his discussion of the twelve links of dependent origination to a conclusion. By means of the preceding discussion you should come to a clear understanding of how cyclic existence, which is made up of the suffering aggregates, is brought into existence by karma and affliction. Among the four noble truths, this is the truth of the cause of suffering: how karma and the afflictions together produce samsaric life. In particular, you should clearly see how the wheel of samsara turns by means of these twelve links of dependent origination, and how this chain of causality compels you to wander perpetually around that wheel of unhappy existence.

Once you gain this comprehension, you must accustom your mind to the reality it reveals by meditating on it until it is completely integrated with your view of the world. Doing that will destroy the dark ignorance lying at the root of all misfortune. This is not only the ignorance that fails to recognize the cause and effect that creates cyclic existence, but also the ignorance that grasps at a mistaken conception of self. It will clear away all the wrong views about the way experience arises, including the view that our inner and outer world arises without a cause, or the view that it can arise from a completely incompatible cause.

What do we mean by an "incompatible" cause? In reality, all the causes that give rise to cyclic existence are *within* the individual; this is the very point that the twelve links of dependent origination bring to mind. Although this is the Buddhist view, many other tenet systems hold that the root cause of existence is an eternal, divine creator, such as Īśvara or Viṣṇu in the Vedic tradition. The Sāṃkhya school of Indian philosophy holds that some kind of permanent, pervasive, universal principle is the cause of everything. We consider such causes to be "incompatible" because we wonder how a permanent, essential, unitary cause can possibly give rise to an impermanent, ever-changing, dependently arisen world? When you hold that kind of wrong view you cannot possibly extricate yourself from cyclic existence because you are aiming at the wrong target. Although the cause of your suffering is over here, you are always busy looking over there.

The insight you gain from contemplating dependent origination eliminates this type of misunderstanding. The realization of the true nature of samsara, exactly as it is, leads to a powerful thought of renunciation, which will arouse and encourage you to pursue the path that leads to liberation. In this way, familiarizing your mind with dependent origination increases the precious, essential treasure of the Buddha's teaching.

We all have the capacity to realize emptiness. Learning about the twelve links of dependent origination, understanding them clearly, then meditating on them until your mind is completely familiar with them, is the best method to awaken your potential for direct realization of the truth. Seeing things as they truly are, you are able to steer your behavior and your practice onto the path that leads to emancipation.

As it says in the *Tantra Requested by Subāhu,* "The path of dependent origination destroys ignorance." Understanding dependent origination is the antidote to ignorance because ignorance lies at its root; when you fully comprehend the twelve links and how they operate, ignorance no longer has the power to delude your mind.

The *Rice Seedling Sutra* says that when you properly understand dependent origination, it clears away wrong views about the past, the future, and the present. What are those wrong views? "Wrong views about the past" refers to denying that existence has a cause, or imputing an incompatible cause; these are the kinds of view we were just discussing. "Wrong views about the future" refers to thinking that there is no future life after this life ends, that the causes you create in this life will have no results in the future. This is a kind of nihilism that leads to a "wrong view about the present." This is the belief that your present behavior does not matter because virtue and nonvirtue have no effect on future experience; you can do whatever you please because you will never suffer any consequences. All of these wrong views are dispelled by the correct view of dependent origination. Nāgārjuna said in his *Friendly Letter:*

> This teaching of dependent origination is the profound prize
> In the treasury of the Buddha's instructions.

We should also remember that Nāgārjuna opened his *Fundamental Treatise on the Middle Way* with the following dedication:

> I prostrate to the perfect Buddha,
> The best of teachers, who taught that
> Whatever is dependently arisen
> Is unceasing, unborn,
> Not annihilated, not permanent,
> Not coming, not going,
> Not diverse, not unitary,
> And free from conceptual elaboration.[3]

Tsongkhapa himself quoted this homage at the beginning of his poem *In Praise of Dependent Arising (rTen 'grel bstod pa)* and then added:

> I pay homage to the victorious Buddha,
> Who saw directly and taught to others dependent origination,
> Unsurpassed in insight and as teacher
> For this vision and this teaching.[4]

The *Bases of Discipline* tells of the "supreme pair," the Buddha's superior disciples Śāriputra (who was called "supreme in wisdom") and Maudgalyāyana (who was called "supreme in psychic powers"). Often when we see the Buddha's image in a painting or a statue, these two monks are standing on either side of him. With their supernatural powers they used to visit the various samsaric realms in order to help different types of beings. When they returned from these miraculous travels they would recount what they had seen and explain the miseries of each realm to the Buddha's four types of disciples: the monks, nuns, laymen, and laywomen.

Living among these people were various friends and relatives of the true disciples who had no regard for the practice of virtuous conduct. These people were taken to see Śāriputra and Maudgalyāyana and the great masters taught them the importance of ethical conduct, illustrating their talks with accounts of the horrible sufferings they had seen in other realms. Inspired by these teachings, many of them came to appreciate the practice of pure conduct and eventually obtained higher realizations.

In this manner Śāriputra and Maudgalyāyana taught many disciples and other interested people. Seeing these two so often in the company of large gatherings, the Buddha asked Ānanda what they were doing. Ānanda explained how Śāriputra and Maudgalyāyana were giving instruction to the public on the five realms, based on their own experience. He recounted how many people had gained great benefit from these teachings. To this the Buddha replied:

> Teachers like this supreme pair will not always be available. Therefore, make a painting in the vestibule that depicts the wheel of cyclic existence in five parts. At the outer rim draw the twelve links of dependent origination in both forward progression and in reverse.

These were instructions for the Wheel of Life, which many of you have probably seen on Tibetan scroll paintings, or *tangkas*. This wheel is a representation of all of cyclic existence, with pictures symbolizing the five (or sometimes six) realms, and along the outer circumference are scenes symbolizing the twelve links of dependent origination, beginning with ignorance—represented by a blind old man or woman. At the center you find the three root afflictions—ignorance, desire, and hostility—depicted as a pig, a pigeon or a rooster, and a snake forming a circle with each one grasping the tail of the next. The entire wheel is held in the mouth of Yama, the Lord of Death, in the form of a savage demon.

The Buddha himself instructed his disciples to devise this kind of representation of dependent origination because he knew that in the future teachers like Śāriputra and Maudgalyāyana would not be around to teach the nature of samsara. He told them to paint this picture in the vestibule or entryway of the monastery and later, at the time of the great monastic centers such as Nālandā and Vikramaśīla, this was most likely the custom.

At most monasteries in Tibet you would find the Wheel of Life painted on a wall in the vestibule of the main temple. The instructions for composing these paintings can be found in the *Sutra on the Discipline (Vinaya-sūtra)* of Guṇaprabha, one of the most authoritative works on the Vinaya of the Sarvāstivādins, the school that provides the canon for Tibetan monasticism.

Also in Tibet, there was a certain type of *yogi* who wore ragged robes and, in between retreats, wandered from village to village carrying an iron rod, a tangka of the Wheel of Life, a begging bowl, and a conch shell. When he arrived in a village he would blow his conch shell, "Oooooooh!" and anyone who was not busy working—especially the old people and children—would come out to sit and listen to the yogi's discourse. He would hang his tangka up and put out a little offering bowl for donations, and then he would teach about the Wheel of Life. Often his verses were composed in a simple and catchy way so they were easy for children to understand. The yogi would point at the different scenes on the tangka and tell the people about ignorance and karma, explaining, "If you do this you will end up here." Everyone enjoyed these entertaining teachings and in this way the general population learned the basics of karma and rebirth.

In the Vinaya commentary, the *Section on Nuns,*[5] we find another story in which the Buddha recommends creating an illustration of the twelve links of dependent origination. This is an account of King Bimbisāra of Magadha, who was a close supporter of the Buddha. Bimbisāra became concerned about the power of a distant kingdom ruled by King Udrāyaṇa, so he sent letters and established a friendly relationship with that king. Although they had never met, they established a cordial relationship by sending letters and gifts back and forth with traveling merchants. Then Udrāyaṇa sent to Bimbisāra a magnificent jewel-studded suit of armor. Bimbisāra summoned his appraisers who informed him that every single gem in this suit was itself priceless, so the whole suit of armor was beyond value. This put King Bimbisāra in a quandary. He thought, "Udrāyaṇa has sent me such a fabulous gift. How can

I repay this favor? If I do not send him something of equal value, he may become angry and this could cause trouble between our kingdoms. But what can I offer him that would compare with what he has given me?"

The king was discouraged until a minister reminded him that within his kingdom was the perfectly enlightened Buddha, something "more excellent than anything in the three worlds." Why not send King Udrāyaṇa a painting of the Buddha? The story tells how the Buddha consented to this saying, "Just as soon as King Udrāyaṇa sees it, he will come to experience faith and to perceive the truth." However, the royal painters found it impossible to capture an image of the Buddha with his extraordinary marks. After several failed efforts, the Buddha told them to bring some fabric. He cast his shadow on it and told them to fill in the shadow with their colors. He then instructed the king that underneath his likeness they should paint the wheel of life depicting the twelve links of dependent origination in forward and reverse order. Underneath he should write the two stanzas that generally appear beneath the Wheel of Life even to this day:

> Gather up and cast away.
> Engage in the Buddha's teaching.
> Like a great elephant in a house of mud,
> Conquer the Lord of Death's battalions.
>
> Whoever with great conscientiousness
> Practices this discipline of the Dharma,
> Abandoning the wheel of births,
> Will make an end to suffering.

When the Buddha suggested they create this combination of images and words, King Bimbisāra was extremely happy. He realized that this work of art, containing both an image of the Buddha and a presentation of his essential teaching, was truly something beyond value, even more precious than any suit of armor. King Bimbisāra sent a message to Udrāyaṇa saying, "I am bringing a very special present. You should come to meet me with a procession so that you may receive this gift with the appropriate welcoming ceremony."

Although Udrāyaṇa was not a Buddhist, the Buddha must have seen that he had strong propensities that were ready to ripen when he met the teachings. Perhaps Udrāyaṇa did not believe that Bimbisāra was bringing anything so precious, but he nevertheless agreed to meet him on the road. He was most pleased with the gift and he studied the verses until he memorized them. He then began to meditate on them through the whole night, sitting cross-legged with focused concentration, all extraneous thoughts pushed aside. He meditated on the cause and effect of dependent origination, seeing how samsaric life evolves as one link gives rise to another, and how emancipation from cyclic existence is achieved by interrupting this chain of causation. Meditating in this way on dependent origination, he realized the true nature of the self and attained the state of an ārya. This story points up how the teaching of dependent origination was already considered the heart of the Buddha's teaching, even at the time of the Buddha, because it has the power to lead those who practice it all the way to emancipation from cyclic existence.

You may think that this story took place a long time ago and is therefore not relevant to us. But we are the same kind of human being as King Udrāyaṇa, with the same kind of mind. We do not lack any attributes, physically or mentally, and we have the teachings right here before us. In fact, we have access to many more teachings, with commentaries and translations, than were ever available in the early history of Buddhism. We too can use our life and the strength of our minds to shine the light of understanding upon the darkness of ignorance. To do this you have to begin by studying, learning, examining, and understanding, until finally the light of wisdom will shine within you, and this will naturally banish the darkness of ignorance and harmful behavior. First you need to develop confidence in these teachings of dependent origination. You need to accept them, not out of blind faith, but with the conviction that arises from thorough understanding and experience.

This conviction comes from understanding the teachings, and then accustoming your mind to them through the continuous practice of meditation. In the beginning you practice this meditation quietly, on a cushion, with a single-pointed mind. But as your conviction strengthens and your wisdom grows, you don't need to be sitting quietly in your meditation room to see how the process of cause and effect brings about the samsaric world we inhabit. You can find this process unfolding everywhere you go—on the street, in a crowd, at a party, or sitting drinking tea with your friend. Wherever you go you are in samsara; wherever you go you can find pain, disappointment, sorrow, and agitation. Some beings are being born, some are aging, some are dying, some are gaining, some are losing. There isn't any limit to the kinds of problems sentient beings encounter in cyclic existence. Once wisdom's fire is kindled within you, all of this—whatever you see—becomes pure fuel feeding the powerful fire of wisdom.

Without some level of understanding, everything goes to the side of ignorance. Just by reading and thinking about these teachings right here, we are gaining a certain level of understanding. But too often we just leave it there. We don't accustom our minds to this view through meditation, and we don't apply our insights assiduously to transform our behavior. We plant some positive seeds, but we do not cultivate those seeds so that they are actualized and ripen into the wisdom of directly seeing the truth. We do gain some insight, but then we slide back to our earlier ways of thinking and acting. The seeds we have planted are still there, and may ripen at some time in the future—perhaps many eons in the future—but the opportunity we have right here and now to transform our view from ignorance to wisdom slips away for lack of effort.

We are talking here about building the most basic foundation of all future progress on the path—the thought of renunciation. This thought grows naturally out of seeing the faults of cyclic existence from many different points of view. We have approached this from two different angles: contemplating suffering and the causes of suffering, karma and afflictions; and contemplating the twelve links of dependent origination, the nexus of cause and effect that perpetually drives the cycle of suffering existence. Once you understand how thoroughly your life is enmeshed in suffering and dissatisfaction, the thought wishing to get free from this will spontaneously arise. This thought is the key to all of the Buddha's teachings. The Hinayana, the Mahayana, the Tantrayana—all are based on this thought of renunciation.

Without this thought you will never seek emancipation for yourself, which is the practice of the Hīnayana. Without this thought you can never generate the bodhisattva's sincere, compassionate determination to help other sentient beings become free of suffering, which is the practice of the Mahayana. Without this thought of renunciation whatever tantric practice you engage in will be only for your own selfish ends. You may hide in a cave for three years or even ten years reciting great mantras, visualizing splendid mandalas, propitiating powerful deities, but whatever you do, you are still attached to this world. Your mind and motivation are still oriented to worldly concerns; your practice remains on a selfish basis. You remain under the control of the ignorant self, which says, "If you do this you will become famous, or rich. You will be protected from your enemies. Demons will not harm you. You will become powerful and be able to control others." Without genuine renunciation these are the kinds of thoughts that will lurk in the back of the mind. The selfish, egotistic idea remains in control. Ignorance is telling you what to do.

Such people may call themselves "Mahayana practitioners" or "tantric practitioners," but they are practicing the Mahayana and Vajrayana in name only. Their mental attitude remains that of worldly beings, working only for their own temporary goals. Without the sincere thought of renunciation that kind of practice will not work—it will not pacify their own sufferings nor will it be of any benefit to others. The thought of renunciation is the foundation of all further progress on the path, and understanding dependent origination is the method to produce that thought.

In his poem, *In Praise of Dependent Arising,* Tsongkhapa praises the Buddha for his way of teaching dependent origination and emptiness as an integrated, unified view of the true nature of things. Over many stanzas he points out how exceptional this teaching is—how meaningful, how valuable, how profound—and how unique is the teacher who realized this true nature and presented it to the world:

> Among teachers, the teacher of dependent origination,
> Among wisdoms, that which realizes dependent origination—
> These are like the foremost conquerors of the world;
> There are no others who can match your glorious insight.
>
> Whatever you have taught
> Is penetrated by dependent origination,
> And since that leads to nirvana,
> There is nothing you do that does not bring peace.[6]

On one level dependent origination is a description of how beings exist in the world and the causal chain that perpetuates the life process. At the same time, it describes how beings can liberate themselves from the cycle of suffering by understanding this process, disengaging from these causes, and breaking the causal chain.

But the teaching of dependent origination goes even deeper than that. It demonstrates how everything that exists in the world is relative, depends on other parts, and arises from causes and conditions. It reveals how there is nothing that has independent existence. Most things appear to us to be independent—the inner self, external phenomena, all appear to have their own self-existence. They appear to be exactly the opposite of dependently arisen. On this level, in teaching dependent origination the Buddha is showing that everything is empty of this independent, absolute nature. In showing how everything arises in dependence on other causes and conditions, he is revealing the final nature of all things—the emptiness of all phenomena.

Most of the problems of sentient beings are due to ignorance—not knowing the true nature of the self and of things in the world. That ignorance creates all the other obscuring afflictions, such as desire and hostility. These afflictions motivate action, and that karma creates all of the many different kinds of life that sentient beings experience—all of which culminate in the sufferings of aging, sickness, and death. In this way, everything that happens during life is created by ignorance.

This ignorance is vanquished by the wisdom that realizes dependent origination, the emptiness of any absolute, independent mode of existence. This wisdom, as Tsongkhapa says in these stanzas, is the highest wisdom, the best weapon to destroy all the problems that constitute the sufferings of cyclic existence. The Buddha—the teacher who has revealed to us this most powerful insight—is the highest teacher, the perfect teacher, whose function is to help others by introducing them to their true nature. This teacher, equipped with this teaching, has power like that of the "foremost conquerors of the world." As long as this kind of teaching—coming from this kind of teacher and revealing this kind of wisdom—survives in the world, sentient beings will have the ability to gradually eliminate all of their problems from the root.

10

The Attitude of a Person of Intermediate Scope

b) The measure of having produced the attitude of a person of intermediate scope
c) Clarifying misconceptions

b) The measure of having produced the attitude of a person of intermediate scope

The previous chapters have described in detail the actual trainings of the being of intermediate scope. We now turn to the measurement of that thought: the qualities of mind that must be developed in order to say you are a being of intermediate scope. The essence of this attitude is the thought of renunciation, the determination to achieve complete emancipation from the suffering of cyclic existence. To achieve this thought of renunciation you need to gain a clear and detailed understanding of the truth of suffering and the truth of the cause of suffering, as well as the way beings cycle through samsara by means of the twelve links of dependent origination. Once you have that understanding, the desire will arise to cast away suffering along with its causes, together with the desire to obtain the peace that comes with emancipation. When that desire to abandon all of cyclic existence and to attain the highest peace arises, is that enough? Is that the final goal of this training? No, that still is not sufficient. The mere thought of renouncing samsara that arises once, or arises for a short time, is not enough.

As Candrakīrti says in his *Commentary on the "Sixty Stanzas of Reasoning" (Yukti-ṣaṣtikā-vṛtti):*

> By realizing how living in the blazing fires of the three levels of impermanent cyclic existence is just like being caught in a house that is engulfed in flame, you desire to escape it.

Once you see that the situation you are in is extremely dangerous, a powerful desire to escape as soon as possible spontaneously emerges. With that desire comes an urgent need to know what method will get you out of those circumstances without delay. That kind of spontaneous, effortless, and urgent desire to escape from cyclic existence is the genuine, uncontrived thought of renunciation. It is a pressing need that emerges naturally, instinctively out of the realization of just how desperate your circumstances are. That is the real goal of these practices, the true "measure of renunciation." Once that thought develops, all your energy and everything you do is turned toward getting out of cyclic existence. Before that thought develops, you must apply effort to generate an attitude of aversion toward cyclic existence, and you do that by practicing these meditations. But once that true thought of renunciation arises, your determination to get out of samsara will be effortless and spontaneous.

Here Tsongkhapa revisits a quotation he cited from Atiśa text, the *Concise Method of Achieving the Mahayana Path (Mahāyāna-patha-sādhana-varṇa-saṃgraha),* which says:

> When the chance suddenly turns up
> For a prisoner to escape from jail,
> He will consider the chance to flee that place
> As more valuable than any other prize.
> Just like that, when opportunities arise
> To pass beyond this great ocean of samsara,
> It is incomparable to any other attraction:
> You should escape from the house of cyclic existence.[1]

Like a person caught in a burning house, a prisoner in jail will escape whenever an opportunity arises. There is no inducement you could offer that would be more appealing than escape. That should be your attitude toward cyclic existence—it should appear to be the worst kind of prison, and you should feel an urgent, single-minded need to get out of there at the earliest opportunity.

The great Kadampa Geshe Sharawa used a very Tibetan image to describe the superficial thought of renunciation. He said it was like the barley powder sprinkled on top of a cup of beer—it will always float on the surface and never sink in. In Tibet, people generally did not drink plain water—most laypeople drank a form of beer called *chang,* and everyone drank tea. Many people drank beer all day long, and in order to make the beer more filling and more nutritious some of them would pour a little of bit of tsampa into their chang. *Tsampa* is roasted barley flour and this was the staple food of Tibet. People would have their favorite ways of mixing the tsampa into the chang—sometimes they would pour the chang over the tsampa, sometimes they would sprinkle the tsampa into the chang and then stir it together. And sometimes they would just sprinkle the tsampa onto the chang and drink it without stirring. When you sprinkle tsampa powder on top of chang it just sits there on the surface and does not penetrate into the drink.

Sharawa is comparing the thought of escaping cyclic existence to tsampa sprinkled on top of beer. You meditate on the sufferings of samsara or on dependent origination and for a short while you feel inspired to seek emancipation. But that attitude only lasts a short while, and it just floats on the surface of your mind, never penetrating deep down into your heart. If you cannot generate a realization that goes beyond this superficial level, then your interest in pursuing emancipation, which finally brings an end to all the sufferings of samsara, will also remain superficial and short-lived. If your motivation remains superficial, your actual practice of the path will become mere words, and it will never penetrate deep into your mind.

If your practice becomes mere words, with no real depth of feeling or understanding, then there will be no way to generate great compassion for other beings who are also suffering the miseries of cyclic existence. If compassion remains only on the surface and does not rise from the depths of your heart, then genuine bodhicitta, the real Mahayana attitude—the spontaneous, uncontrived determination to obtain buddhahood for the sake of other sentient beings—will not arise. In that case your Mahayana practice—the so-called "great" practice—will be nothing more than an intellectual understanding of mere words.

Therefore, you should recognize these trainings, which are common to the being of intermediate scope, as being fundamental and essential to the entire path leading to liberation and to buddhahood. Until you fully develop this quality of mind that seeks, night and day, to be free of the sufferings of cyclic existence, you should cherish these teachings and apply yourself to these trainings. You should not make the mistake of viewing these meditations as purely Hinayana practices and think, "I want higher teachings." Too often we are hungry for the "highest teachings," but we neglect those that can really transform our practice and put us squarely on the path to liberation.

Meditation on the sufferings of samsara and the twelve links of dependent origination lead to the genuine thought of renunciation. That thought is the cornerstone of the path to liberation. Once you have achieved that thought according the measure we have just described, we say that you have "entered the path." As soon as that spontaneous, uncontrived determination to be free of cyclic existence arises, you have passed through the gate and entered the path to liberation. From that point on, whatever you do that is virtuous becomes part of the path. Because all of your actions are dominated by this thought, so they naturally become causes of emancipation rather than causes of future cycling in samsara. Therefore, this thought is most important—it is the gateway to emancipation.

c) Clarifying misconceptions

Now we try to clear up certain misunderstandings that can arise regarding these practices. Some may say that cultivating disenchantment with cyclic existence is appropriate for the Hinayana practice of the śrāvakas and pratyekabuddhas because their goal is to selfishly obtain their own freedom from samsara. But, they say, it is not suitable for a Mahayana practitioner because if you generate a strong sense of disgust toward samsara you may fall into the *extreme of peace,* wanting to have no further involvement in any aspect of cyclic existence. Therefore, the bodhisattva should not engage in meditations that lead to a complete renunciation of cyclic existence. In support of this view we can cite the *Sutra of Showing the Tathāgata's Inconceivable Secret (Tathāgatācintya-guhya-nirdeśa-sūtra):*

> Bodhisattvas, who hold the ripening of sentient beings as the primary goal, view cyclic existence as beneficial, but not their own great nirvana.

Since the main concern of bodhisattvas is to ripen other beings, samsara is the very place where bodhisattvas work. Therefore, they should not become preoccupied by the faults of cyclic existence, but rather should view samsara as a beneficial circumstance for helping others. In fact, in order to continue to benefit other beings, bodhisattvas should strive to be born into samsara, rather than to escape from it. The same text says:

> If bodhisattvas were afraid of involvement in the activities of cyclic existence, they would fall to a place devoid of bodhisattva activity.

Cyclic existence is the field of activity where bodhisattvas carry out their work of leading sentient beings out of suffering. If bodhisattvas were afraid to enter such a place to undertake that work, they would fall to the extreme of peace, a place of quiescence for themselves, but a place where they could not do any benefit for other beings. That text also says:

> Bhagavan, śrāvakas fear involvement in the activities of cyclic existence, but bodhisattvas hold cyclic existence as a place to take rebirth innumerable times.

On the surface, these quotations seem to be saying that these meditations are only for Hinayana practitioners and not for those on the Mahayana path. This is a common misconception. Many people who have studied a little bit of Buddhism think that Mahayana practice means that you should *enjoy* samsara, and that seeing just its faults is only for those on a lower level of practice. However, this is a wrong understanding of the meaning of this sutra and of the purpose of these practices.

When the sutra says that "bodisattvas should not become disenchanted with cyclic existence," it is not saying that they should not feel disgust over the helpless condition of wandering in samsara under the power of karma and afflictions, and dismay over having to experience the sufferings of birth, aging, sickness, and death. The sutra is *not* teaching that the bodhisattva should avoid meditating on these sufferings. Bodhisattvas are utterly opposed to this miserable condition and they *do* meditate on this. In their meditation they *do* produce disenchantment, disgust, and dismay over this condition—in fact, to a greater degree than even Hinayana practitioners do. Seeing so vividly how miserable and powerless sentient beings are, bodhisattvas resolve not merely to liberate themselves but to lead *all* living beings out of this condition.

It is the work of guiding other beings out of cyclic existence for which bodhisattvas feel no disgust or dismay. Regardless of what adversity they must undergo themselves, bodhisattvas take great pleasure in working for the benefit of other sentient beings. As long as there is a benefit to others, they never turn away from any action, no matter where they have to go or what pain they must experience. Bodhisattvas take on the activities of samsara with joyous perseverance because they are doing it for the benefit of others. That is the meaning that this sutra is trying to express.

After bodhicitta arises, when you become a bodhisattva, your foremost objective is to help sentient beings by leading them to freedom from cyclic existence. You take the Mahayana vow never to give up sentient beings until the very end of cyclic existence—that you will never waver from that great bodhisattva activity. Taking this vow with a firm conviction is called "putting on armor." When an army goes out to fight its enemy, the troops put on whatever equipment is necessary—in the old days it was armor—and they carry the weapons they need to accomplish their task. These soldiers are not concerned with their own welfare and they enter the battlefield with courage—they feel that even if they have to face death or mutilation, they will carry on until they defeat the enemy. In the same way, bodhisattvas put on the armor of their vow, and they remain steadfast in their determination to help others, never deterred or disenchanted by the sufferings they see or the sufferings they themselves must undergo.

Even if all the misery of all sentient beings were gathered together and dropped upon the bodhisattvas every moment, still they would feel no fear or discouragement, because they are protected by the courage of their mental armor, their commitment to help other beings. They will only be more inspired to persevere with joy in the great undertaking in which they are engaged. That is the meaning of the teaching that "bodhisattvas should not become disenchanted with cyclic existence." That is the point of this sutra. This is confirmed by a quotation from Candrakīrti, which says:

> Even if all the sufferings of sentient beings brought injury to their body and mind every moment until the end of cyclic existence, the bodhisattvas would not be afraid. Taking on the sufferings of all sentient beings simultaneously until the end of cyclic existence, bodhisattvas carry on with joyous persevering effort. Every moment of that joyous perseverance becomes the cause that produces the boundless accumulation of the treasure of merits that will bring omniscient buddhahood to all beings. Understanding this, they are willing to take rebirth in cyclic existence hundreds of times.

To support his statement, Candrakīrti cites the same quotations that were just referred to as representing the contradictory view.

In fact, this same sutra, the *Sutra of Showing the Tathāgata's Inconceivable Secret,* says that the reason for viewing cyclic existence as a place of benefit is that bodhisattvas feel happiness to the extent they are able to work for the welfare of other beings. Again, this indicates that the meaning of not becoming disenchanted with cyclic existence is that bodhisattvas do not become disenchanted with acting for the benefit of suffering sentient beings, but actually enjoy that effort. This is how we should understand this sutra.

When you are forced to wander helplessly in cyclic existence, constantly assaulted by innumerable types of suffering, completely under the power of karma and afflictions, you cannot even do anything to help yourself, so how could you possibly do anything that would benefit others? This helpless entrapment is the door through which all the troubles of all beings arrive. Seeing this, the bodhisattva should actually develop a far more intense feeling of disenchantment toward cyclic existence than even a Hinayana practitioner does, and should resolve to bring an end to these conditions.

Bodhisattvas take rebirth in cyclic existence by the special of power of their compassion and the willed direction of their aspirational prayer. They take rebirth with the express purpose of helping those who are still cycling through suffering states without any control. There is a big difference between entering samsara in this way and wandering helplessly under the control of karma and afflictions. Bodhisattvas are *choosing* to take rebirth in order to benefit others, and it is that opportunity to assist beings who are trapped in samsara that they enjoy—that is what it means when the sutra says that they enjoy being reborn in cyclic existence. Bodhisattvas see all too clearly the sufferings of samsara, and they abhor what they see. But they have nothing to fear in taking rebirth because they are doing so with an altruistic purpose. It is important to understand this distinction.

If you have taken the bodhisattva vows but fail to make this distinction, and you hold the position that bodhisattvas should *not* see cyclic existence as a suffering condition, and should *not* cultivate the thought of renunciation, then you are committing an infraction of the bodhisattva vows. This point is fully explained in Asaṅga's *Bodhisattva Levels,* but Tsongkhapa says he will not go into it any further here.

Actually, it is marvelous and amazing that bodhisattvas, who see so vividly how miserable cyclic existence truly is—who produce such a powerful thought of renunciation—still do not abandon their willingness to reenter samsara. This is an indication of just how strong their love, compassion, and wish to help other sentient beings really are.

Some people claim, "I am a Mahayanist. I am a great helper to others. I must stay here in samsara because I am benefiting other sentient beings." But, instead of cultivating the thought of renunciation, they are indulging without hesitation in samsaric wonders like wealth, fame, and sensual pleasure. Though they proclaim that they are working for the benefit of other beings, in fact they cannot give up samsara because they are incurably attached to its illusory pleasures. That is the real reason they do not want to renounce samsara. Such people view cyclic existence as if it were a celestial mansion, and their attachment to it never diminishes even a little bit. That is the opposite of the courageous commitment of the bodhisattva, and wise people are not fooled by such hypocrisy.

Bhāvaviveka says in his *Heart of the Middle Way (Madhyamaka-hṛdaya):*

> Because they see its faults, they do not abide in cyclic existence.
> Because of compassion, they do not remain in nirvana.
> In order to accomplish the goals of others, they undertake the courageous conduct
> Of remaining in cyclic existence.

Bodhisattvas do not remain in samsara out of attachment because they see the disadvantages of cyclic existence with the eye of wisdom. Because they have great compassion for all suffering beings, they do not remain in the peace of nirvana, even though they have the power to stay in that blissful state. Even though they see its faults, bodhisattvas have the courage to remain in cyclic existence in order to help other suffering beings. It is their own wish to remain, born out of the power of their compassion and wisdom.

To say that bodhisattvas do not become disenchanted with cyclic existence is also contradictory to the very method they use to cultivate great compassion for all beings. They contemplate the measureless miseries of beings in terms of the one hundred and ten sufferings described in the *Bodhisattva Levels.* This generates an empathy for the pain of living beings that is almost unbearable, and gives rise to a powerful and enduring unwillingness to tolerate such wretched circumstances. Since this is the method they use to generate the altruistic thought to benefit others, it is absurd to suggest that they do not develop aversion toward cyclic existence in even the tiniest way.

In his text, *Four Hundred Stanzas,* Āryadeva points out that the path of the bodhisattva consists of developing a powerful attitude of aversion toward cyclic existence by looking into the innumerable sufferings of beings who are caught in its web. You then see how all these suffering beings are your dearest friends and closest relatives, and it is for their sake that you enter into the ocean of samsara. It is out of the determination to help those other beings that bodhisattvas are freely reborn many times, in many different forms, in that samsaric cycle. Candrakīrti made this clear in his commentary on the *Four Hundred Stanzas:*

> By explaining the faults of cyclic existence, beings become frightened and want to be freed from it. In order to lead such trainees to the Mahayana the Buddha said, "O monks, among sentient beings who have been cycling for a very long time in samsara, among all the many types of beings, there is not one being who has not been like a father, mother, son, daughter, relative, or some type of step-relation to you."

And he goes on:

> Understanding this teaching of the Bhagavan, bodhisattvas are able to jump into the ocean of cyclic existence in order to carry to freedom, on the great vessel of the Mahayana method, all those beings who have been wandering helplessly since beginningless time through cyclic

> existence without protection—beings they see as their mothers, fathers, friends, and so forth.

Just as a mother is able to bear any hardship in order to save her children when they are in danger, the bodhisattva sees all beings as close relatives, and is able to bear the hardship of repeatedly jumping back into the ocean of samsara in order to pull them up onto the vessel of freedom, the Mahayana path.

And it is not only the sutra path of the Mahayana that requires this way of thinking. Even in the highest Mahayana practice, the Vajrayāna method, it is necessary to develop this attitude. Āryadeva says in his *Lamp That Is a Compendium of Deeds (Caryā-melāpaka-pradīpa):*

> By these steps you should engage in these practices without elaboration. These steps are as follows. First of all, practitioners should recollect the beginningless sufferings of cyclic existence. Then, with a desire for the bliss of nirvana, they should completely abandon the distraction of worldly pleasure, and cultivate the understanding that even the ruler of empires is suffering.

For those who are going to engage in tantric practice, referred to here as "practices without elaboration," the instructions are the same: recollect the sufferings of cyclic existence and, based on that, generate an all-encompassing thought of renunciation, and a powerful determination to be free of the faults of samsara.

This final quotation of this section clears away the misconception that the tantric practitioner does not need to produce the thought of renunciation. As this entire section has made clear, the Mahayana practitioner must have an even sharper realization of the sufferings of cyclic existence than the Hinayana practitioner. This quotation makes clear that without the thought of renunciation there is no way to achieve the tantric path.

In fact, within tantric practice, when you think of the mandala (the representation of the abode of the meditational deity), its outer circle is visualized as a cemetery; this is a reminder of death and impermanence, a symbol of the thought of renunciation. The passage into the mandala starts there; you cannot enter the practice of the deity without passing through the cemetery reminding you of the true nature of cyclic existence. All the paths follow this same route.

Now we can see that there is no contradiction when these sutras say that bodhisattvas, the great Mahayana saints, find joy in entering cyclic existence. In fact, they realize better than anyone else just how adverse the conditions of samsara truly are. Their enthusiasm is directed purely at the endless opportunities they take to lead unhappy living beings out of that helpless condition and onto the path to liberation.

11

Ascertaining the Nature of the Path Leading to Liberation

d) Establishing the nature of the path that leads to liberation
- i) What kind of life can overcome cyclic existence
- ii) What kind of path you must cultivate to overcome cyclic existence
  - a' Specifying the number of trainings as three
    - 1' Specifying the number in terms of the stages of subduing the mind
    - 2' Specifying the number in terms of the results
    - 3' Specifying the number in terms of the objects to be abandoned
  - b' Ascertaining the order of the three trainings

d) Establishing the nature of the path that leads to liberation

THE FOURTH AND FINAL TOPIC in our discussion of the trainings of the being of intermediate scope concerns the nature of the path that leads to liberation from cyclic existence. This discussion begins with advice from Śrī Jagan-mitrānanda from his *Letter to King Candra (Candra-rāja-lekha)* in which he says:

> Although we have sunk into the vastness of cyclic existence,
> A fathomless ocean of unbounded suffering,
> We are full of excitement and joy, without a trace of fear or dismay.
> What is going on in our minds?
>
> We are constantly engulfed in the flames of blazing troubles:

> Poverty, the difficulty of finding resources, of protecting them, of losing them,
> The pain of separation, sickness, and aging.
> The pride we take in our pleasure appears to be that of a lunatic.

The same author continues:

> Alas! Though worldly beings have eyes, they are blind.
> Although you clearly see what is always evident,
> You pay no attention whatsoever.
> Is your mind as impenetrable as a vajra?

In these verses we are getting the perspective of the *yogi*, the true spiritual practitioner who has realized the disastrous nature of cyclic existence. Such practitioners see sentient beings sinking deeper and deeper into this endless ocean of suffering, and as they sink they are laughing with excitement over their illusory and short-lived pleasures. To the yogi, that is the behavior of a mad person. It is as if people do not see what is right before their eyes. Or if they do see it, they ignore it. Are their minds made of stone, so that nothing at all can affect them?

These stanzas give us some idea of how we ourselves should be thinking, how we should be exhorting ourselves to wake up to the true nature of cyclic existence, and to stop acting as if life were an endless round of pleasure. When you think clearly about this, and meditate on the faults of samsara, you will get the kind of results that are described by Guhyadatta in the *Edifying Tale of the Seven Maidens (Sapta-kumārikāvadāna).* This is the story of the daughter of King Kṛkin, an ancient king of Benares at the time of Buddha Kāśyapa. She had a strong thought of renunciation and wanted very much to become a nun, but to do that she needed her father's permission. In this passage she is explaining to her father why she wants to renounce the worldly life:

> We see worldly circumstances as unsteady, like the reflection of the moon in water.
> We see desirable objects as like the shadow of the head of an angry, coiled snake.
> When we see these beings completely engulfed in the fires of suffering,
> We take ourselves to charnel grounds, O King, delighting in the thought of renunciation.

All beings, all things arising in this samsaric world, are like the reflection of the moon in the water: unstable, constantly changing, ungraspable. Just as the image of the moon is formed by light and water, all beings in cyclic existence are formed by karma and afflictions—they are like the reflection of karma and afflictions. They are not firmly established, but are constantly changing, formed and conditioned by karma and afflictions. That is what the princess sees and explains to her father.

When you see how the inanimate universe and all the living beings within it are just like the moon observed in a lake stirred by the wind—never stable for even one moment, constantly transforming—then you see how all objects of desire are insignificant. All the exciting forms, sounds, smells, tastes, and textures that once looked so juicy now lose their appeal, like a dried-up old bone hanging in a butcher's shop. Still, as long as you remain attracted to them, they are as dangerous as the shadow of a poisonous snake. When you see how all the sentient beings within samsara are constantly tormented in the fires of the three types of sufferings, the attachments of cyclic existence bring you nothing but a deep-seated feeling of nausea.

This sense of nausea or disgust is illustrated by the story of a "nomad child of the north." Generally, Tibetans eat tsampa, roasted barley flour. But in the far north, where the nomads run their herds, barley is not easy to get. In this story a nomad child asks his mother for some tsampa. She doesn't have any tsampa, so instead she gives the child *nyungma,* a certain kind of turnip, which can be prepared in many different ways. First she offers him fresh turnip, but he says, "I don't want that. I want tsampa." Then she tries giving him dried turnip, but the child says, "No. I don't want that. I want tsampa." Then the mother tries cooked turnip, but the boy says, "I don't want that. I want tsampa." Finally she presents him with turnip that is cooked and dried and covered with a sweet sauce, and with this the boy says, "No, I don't want that either." And turning away with a feeling of nausea he exclaims, "All of these are just turnips!"

When you don't like turnips, it doesn't matter how your mother prepares them. It is the same way for the practitioner in cyclic existence. It doesn't matter where you are, or whether you are surrounded by blissful pleasures or hideous tortures, you should see it all equally in its faulty, suffering nature. You should respond to all forms of samsaric experience with the same feeling of nauseous aversion and the thought, "I want nothing to do with any of it. It is all just cyclic existence!"

In that way, by contemplating how you have been wandering in cyclic existence from beginningless time, you will produce a strong feeling of dismay and disenchantment. By contemplating how you still have to wander in the same circumstances with no end in sight, you will produce strong fear. When this combination of thoughts arise from deep in the heart, your thought of renunciation will no longer be mere words, but will emerge as an urgent determination to prevent all future birth in cyclic existence. As Nāgārjuna says in his *Friendly Letter:*

> Understand that cyclic existence is like this:
> Whether among the devas, humans, hell beings, hungry ghosts,
> Or animals, there is no good rebirth,
> It is only a vessel of numerous ills.

Once you have determined to prevent future birth in cyclic existence, the method you employ will have to destroy its two causes, karma and afflictions. There is no way to be free from samsara without destroying these two causes. We can say that the obscuring afflictions are the primary root of samsara, and it is most important to destroy these afflictions. This is because, if you do not have any obscuring afflictions, then no matter how many karmic causes you may have, you will not be born in samsara. Karma without affliction is like a dry seed; it will not germinate or yield the fruit of samsaric birth.

On the other hand, if you have obscuring afflictions, then even if you could somehow eliminate all previously produced karma, the afflictions—which are the root of karma—will only produce more. As long as the afflictions are present you will continue to accumulate karma. That is why we say that it is most important to destroy the afflictions. In order to do that you must meditate on an unmistaken and complete path. Your path of practice must contain all the stages that are necessary to completely remove the afflictions from the root. That kind of comprehensive path is the only one that will actually lead you to emancipation from the trap of cyclic existence. Now we turn to focus on the specific qualities of that path to liberation.

i) What kind of life can overcome cyclic existence

The actual training in the stages of the path to enlightenment, which we call *lamrim,* begins with realizing the tremendous value of this life endowed with eight leisures and ten endowments. We discussed this at length in the first volume of this series. You have obtained the eight leisures when you are free of the eight hindrances to engaging in a Dharma practice listed by Nāgārjuna in a passage from his *Friendly Letter.* Nāgārjuna describes the type of life that is best for halting rebirth in cyclic existence as follows:

> To be born with wrong views, as an animal,
> A hungry ghost, or in the hells,
> Taking rebirth in a place without the Buddha's teaching,
> Or as a barbarian in some remote land,
> As an imbecile, or mute, or a long-lived god—
> These are the eight faulty unfavorable conditions.
> Being free from them, you have found an opportunity,
> So strive now to put an end to rebirth.

If you are born in a lower realm the obstacles to pursuing a spiritual path are obvious. Among the hell denizens and hungry ghosts, life is so absorbed in physical pain or desperate hunger that they cannot even think of anything else. At the other end of the spectrum are the devas, who live a life absorbed in peaceful bliss for eons on end. Such beings remain blissfully ignorant of the faults of samsara and the pervasive nature of suffering, so they never think it is necessary to escape from cyclic existence. Also, because their lives are so long, they have no awareness that their happy state will not last forever—they have no way to realize the truth of impermanence. This is a real handicap, because one of the most powerful forces motivating beings to take up religion is their awareness of death and the impermanent nature of existence.

In general, the human rebirth is the most conducive to spiritual pursuits, but even within this human realm there are serious hindrances to practice. You can be born mentally handicapped, lacking the intelligence to understand the teachings. Or you may have physical disabilities that hinder your practice. Even if you are mentally and physically fully qualified, you may be born into a primitive culture, as a "barbarian," where there is little conception of right and wrong or the cause and effect of actions. Even if you are born in a civilized society, it may be a place where the Buddhist teachings are unknown, or a time when no buddha has appeared to teach a path to liberation.

Even if you are free from all these other hindrances, and you are born as a human with a sharp mind and you meet the Buddha's teachings, you may still reject them. Your mind may be inclined to reject the teachings of karma and rebirth, or you may not believe that liberation from samsara and buddhahood are possible. In this case, even though all the favorable conditions are in place for you to engage in a successful Dharma practice, you turn your back on such practice and live your life purely for worldly gratification.

Any being who is not free from all of these hindrances will not have the leisure to practice this path having the power to destroy all the obscuring afflictions and grant release from the bondage of cyclic existence. Therefore, now that you have obtained a human rebirth that *is* free of these obstructions, while you hold this precious path in your hands, you must make every effort to use this opportunity to put an end to samsaric rebirth. That is the advice that Nāgārjuna gave to his friend, the king.

When you think about it, the king that Nāgārjuna is writing to did not have anything that you do not have—you have the same leisures and endowments that he had. You are born human, with complete faculties, in a central land where you have access to the Buddhadharma. And, like the king, you have already developed some level of trust and faith in the teachings. Just like the king, you have all the necessary equipment to destroy the afflictions from the root and put an end to samsaric misery. Therefore, it is so important to make use of this opportunity while you have it.

The great practitioner Jangchub Rinchen said, "Now is the time to distinguish ourselves from cattle." And the great Kadampa teacher Potowa said:

> In the past we wandered endlessly in samsara and it did not stop by itself, so it is not going to stop by itself now either. Therefore, we must put an end to it, and the time to do this is now, while we have obtained the leisure and endowments.

No matter how much you may hope for it, cyclic existence is never going to go away by itself. If you want the suffering to end, you must make the effort to destroy the causes of suffering from the root. Now that you have in your hands the method to do this, and you have the mental and physical capacity to apply that method, you should get on with it. There will never be a better time, a more auspicious opportunity, to finally bring an end to suffering in cyclic existence.

If you do not use the special capacity of this wonderful life to destroy the root of suffering—but instead spend all your time and energy chasing after temporary comforts such as food, shelter, sensual pleasure, and the thrill of defeating your adversaries—then your life is no more meaningful than that of an animal. As Jangchub Rinchen says, now is the time to raise your aspirations above those of cattle.

This life, and the precious little time we have to spend here, is so important. Just gaining a full appreciation of its significance can be a tremendous aid to your practice. The Kadampa geshes often spoke of this life as the border; from here you can turn in one direction that will lead you out of cyclic existence, or you can turn back to where you came from and continue to wander for a long time to come. You stand at the border, and which direction you turn is entirely your choice.

In general, all sentient beings have the capacity to obtain emancipation or buddhahood. In order to fulfill this potential you need to eliminate the obscuring afflictions from the root. To accomplish that task requires a life with unusually favorable conditions; these are the special conditions we have described as the leisures and endowments of the precious human rebirth. Since Tsongkhapa is explaining in this section which type of life and livelihood is the best to practice the Dharma, he now goes on to explain the special virtues of living as an ordained monk or nun.

The advantages of the ordained life

Among humans who have all of the leisures and endowments there are many different lifestyles. Within the context of Buddhist practice and culture there are basically two ways of living: as a layperson, or as an ordained monk or nun. Those who remain in the household life usually encounter many more obstacles to practice, and this constitutes a significant disadvantage to life as a layperson. Therefore, the best kind of life for overcoming cyclic existence is the life of a renunciate, and wise people truly rejoice in taking ordination. [In Tibetan, the term for taking ordination is *rabjung*, which literally means: "rising out *(jung)* of the householder's life to a better *(rab)* kind of life."]

Whether you have found a way to become ordained or not, it is beneficial to recognize and contemplate the virtues of leading the life of a renunciate and the disadvantages of the householder's life. For those who have already been ordained, this practice will reinforce confidence in their choice. Those who have not yet ordained will establish positive predispositions to take ordination at some time in the future. For those who already have such predispositions, this practice will awaken that potential and inspire them to act on it. Because meditating on the virtues of ordination in comparison to the disadvantages of the householder's life has all these benefits, Tsongkhapa says that he will explain this practice in some detail.

When you study this section it is important to keep in mind that Tsongkhapa is *not* saying that ordained monastics are the only people who can attain liberation, and that laypeople do not have a chance. That is not the case. The point we are emphasizing here is that the ordained life has many advantages for those who are on the path, and it is useful to know what those advantages are so that you can make a wise choice at some appropriate time in the future.

The underlying principle here is that, in general, the best type of life for bringing an end to cyclic existence is the life of an ordained monastic. This is because those who live the life of a householder encounter so many hindrances and interruptions to their practice, and most of those hindrances are avoided by those who enter the monastic life. Householders have so many concerns, which are all forms of dissatisfaction and suffering. If they are poor, they exhaust themselves trying to acquire wealth. When they have wealth, they face the problem of how to protect it. So whether they are rich or poor there is no stable happiness. Out of ignorance they believe that finding riches and holding onto wealth will bring true happiness.

This delusion of grasping at material comforts as the ultimate source of happiness is itself the result of previous negative karma. Although right now you have the opportunity to completely escape all of these petty concerns, the predispositions you have created by habitually chasing after material comfort in previous lifetimes cause you to waste this precious opportunity by repeating that senseless behavior over and over again.

In fact, this practice of contemplating the benefits of ordination and the disadvantages of lay life is a way of creating positive predispositions, so that in the future you will find it easy to turn away from worldly concerns and pursue the path to liberation with all your energy. Though you may not be able to take ordination right now and take advantage of these benefits in this present life, by creating these predispositions you will reap the benefits at some later time. It may be later in this same lifetime, or it may be a future life. Once those causes are there, they only need to be reawakened. But if you do not plant these seeds, they will never ripen for you in the future. If you have the proper predispositions, in your next life you could be born as a child who has the interest in becoming a monk or nun from a very early age, and has the opportunity to do so. In this way you can create not only the causes to have that special inclination, but also the causes to be born into a situation where you meet pure religious teachings and excellent Mahayana teachers. If you use this life to create such conditions in the future, you have really accomplished a great deal.

The *Garland of Birth Stories* says:

> Never think of the householder's life as happiness;
> It is like a prison.
> Whether they are rich or poor,
> Those who remain as householders have a great disability.
> One is afflicted by having to protect wealth,
> The other is exhausted by seeking after it.
> Whether they are poor or rich,
> Neither one has happiness.
> The delusion that finds joy in that life
> Is the result of nonvirtuous action.[1]

Therefore, Tsongkhapa says, those who have taken ordination should not hold many worldly goods and strive for still more wealth; if they engage in that kind of activity they are no different than householders. For those who remain in the lay life it is difficult to practice the real Dharma because their circumstances require so many activities that are actually contrary to the Dharma.

In the same tale from the *Garland of Birth Stories* it says:

> When you do the work of a householder,
> It is impossible not to tell lies,
> And it is inappropriate not to punish
> Others who do you harm.
> If you try to practice Dharma, your lay work will suffer.
> If you stick to householders duties, what Dharma can you accomplish?
> The work of Dharma is completely peaceful;
> The goals of the householder are accomplished by forceful action.
> Since lay life has this fault of being contradictory to the Dharma,
> Who, wanting to benefit themselves, would remain a householder?

When you engage in the commerce of worldly life it is very difficult not to tell lies, or at least bend the truth to your own advantage. Since your primary goal is to advance the prosperity of your household, it is almost foolish *not* to say things that are untrue when it would be beneficial (in the worldly sense) to do so. For laypeople, it seems, sometimes you just have to lie.

When other people harm you, take advantage of you, or cheat you, you have to defend your interests and protect your family by punishing the offenders so that they will not do that again. When someone steals your family's property, you cannot merely meditate on patience and on cherishing others more than yourself as a monk or nun might do. It would almost be irresponsible not to defend your family by aggressively defending their economic interests.

Of course, once you have achieved a certain level of stability, it is possible to mix your Dharma practice with householder activity. For bodhisattvas and others with high levels of realization, every activity—regardless of how worldly it may appear—becomes meaningful Dharma action. But in the early stages of a practice it is extremely difficult to do justice to both of these endeavors at the same time, because the requirements of one often conflict with the responsibilities of the other.

Basically, the Dharma is about achieving peace, and it uses peaceful means. In order to succeed at the work of a layperson you have to use forceful, harsh, even fierce and ruthless means to achieve your goals. This kind of wrathful activity does not accord well with the peaceful attitude you are trying to cultivate in your Dharma practice. And if you try to remain completely peaceful and passive in your worldly pursuits, you will not succeed at what needs to be done.

The same text continues:

> Like a nest full of the vipers of arrogance, pride, and ignorance,
> The household life destroys the blissful happiness of peace.
> The householder lives with so many unbearable sufferings,
> Who would stay in such a snake-pit?

Over and over you should contemplate the faults of remaining in the household life as they are described in these examples, and you should aspire to enter the religious life of an ordained renunciate.

But merely becoming a monk or a nun is not sufficient. You should learn to be satisfied with the bare necessities of such a life: simple monastic robes, a plain begging bowl, and food given to you as alms as your sole source of sustenance. It is important to cultivate this kind of joyful contentment with whatever meager resources come your way, and to feel that whatever comes is enough.

Actually, one of the worst obstacles is insatiability, the lack of contentment. It is a state of mind that never knows how to be satisfied. No matter how much wealth you accumulate, you still crave more. We see this among very rich people, or very powerful rulers—no matter how much they have they always crave more and more. This is a state of mind that completely prevents you from recognizing the unsatisfactory nature of samsaric wonders. It is a tremendous obstacle to entering the spiritual path.

The opposite of insatiability is satisfaction, and renunciates who have achieved this quality of satisfaction repair to a place of solitude to purify their own inner afflictions. Then they pray and strive to be of benefit to others, and to become the means by which others are able to progress on the path. For example, the householders who offer them food as they go on their begging rounds gain merit. Making offerings to bodhisattvas and other serious spiritual practitioners is one of the most powerful means of accumulating great merit.

Earlier we mentioned the princess described in the *Edifying Tale of the Seven Maidens* by Guhyadatta. Her only aspiration was to become a nun and retire from the world to pursue the path to liberation. In her explanation to her father of why she wishes to leave the luxuries of the royal household, we find a beautiful description of the pure aims of a renunciate:

When will I be able to do as I wish,
To shave my hair,
Wear rags from the rubbish heap,
And retire to a solitary place?

When will I be able to beg for alms,
Blameless, wandering from house to house,
Looking no further ahead than the length of a yoke,
Carrying an earthen begging bowl?

Having cleansed the swamps where the thorns of the afflictions grow,
Without attachment to wealth or esteem,
When will I become the object of charity,
For those who live in the towns?

Renuciates have no need of fine clothes. They can pick out of the rubbish old clothes that others have worn and thrown away. They can patch them up and wear them to protect their body from the cold and from the sun. There is no reason to wear fine garments because they are not concerned with how they look—only with maintaining good health and a long life so that they can continue to practice.

If you are following the Vinaya rules for monks and nuns carefully, when you walk around you should keep your eyes focused just a short distance in front of you, rather than looking around at all the interesting sights. It is said in these stanzas that you should gaze ahead only a yard or so, the length of a yoke that is used to fasten oxen or yaks to a plow. This is because the sense faculties, especially the eye organs, are so powerful, and have such a capacity to stimulate the afflictions. You see something attractive and suddenly attachment rises. You see someone you don't like, and suddenly you are angry. The senses are constantly sending invitations to the afflictions, welcoming them into your mind. You need to use many different methods to control them.

The princess asks when she can go on begging rounds, carrying a modest clay alms bowl—there is no need to own some fancy vessel made of silver or gold. Also, householders are constantly accusing each other and attacking those they don't agree with, or people they don't like, but when you live in that kind of simplicity no one criticizes, blames, or attacks you. The mendicant, wearing tattered robes and carrying a simple bowl, is free of all that nonsense.

The afflictions are like thorns that constantly prick you with desire and hostility. They are thorn bushes that grow in the mud of ignorance, the swamp of cyclic existence. When you pull out the afflictions by cleaning away the mud in which they grow, you become a truly worthy object of generosity for the householders who live in the towns where you seek alms. You not only benefit yourself, but by becoming an extraordinary field of merit, you help all those who offer you alms. Why? Because, by virtue of your own good qualities, their act of generosity will produce greatly increased results.

The *Edifying Tale of the Seven Maidens* continues:

> When will I become unattached to my body,
> Rising from a bed of grass,
> My clothes laden with frost,
> Living on the most basic food and drink?
>
> When will I lie down beneath a tree,
> Wearing clothes of soft grass
> As green as a parrot,
> To enjoy this life's blissful feast?

These stanzas point out how satisfaction is the greatest wealth. When you are happy with whatever comes to you, the entire natural world becomes your mansion, and whatever simple food comes your way is like a feast. You can sleep in the forest on a bed of grass, and when you get up your clothes will be decorated with the morning frost. This is the wealth of the person who sincerely renounces all worldly concerns.

Compare that easy satisfaction with our usual obsessions with how we look, what we wear, and what we eat. For many people it seems as though their whole life is dedicated to serving their body—they spend all their time trying to look good, adorning their body with elaborate clothing. Wearing functional clothes to protect the body is not enough—they have to be beautiful, expensive, fancy, and up to date. And eating simple foods in order to survive is never enough—they want many different tastes and fancy dishes that are complicated to prepare. The princess asks when she will be able to leave such worldly concerns behind, and enter the gloriously simple life of the mendicant in the forest.

As humans, we don't easily experience the blissful states of meditative equipoise that are known to beings in the form and formless realms. But within this human life, you experience a deep sense of inner peace—a constant and abiding happiness that is itself a form of bliss—when you are satisfied with everything just as it is. As the princess says, though the mendicants in the forest owns nothing, whatever they encounter in this life is to them like a joyous feast.

You should contemplate these beautiful words of the princess again and again. If you are able to take ordination as a monk or a nun in this life, that is the best result. But even if you cannot ordain in your current life, this practice will turn your mind in that direction. Although it may be clear to you that you will not become ordained in this life, you can begin to aspire to it in the future. The powerful aspiration prayer of the princess awakens you to the marvelous attributes of the monastic life. It counteracts the common misconception that monasticism has no purpose, is outdated, or a waste of time. Cultivating this admiration for the monastic life, and the aspiration to enter that life in the future, will plant the seeds that will eventually ripen into the opportunity to enter this state. Planting seeds for the future is itself an essential Dharma practice.

Finally, the Princess describes the highest goal of the monastic life:

> When will I live in a meadow by a river,
> Observing over and over
> How the world of this life
> Is like the coming and going of the waves?
>
> When will I become
> Free of desire for samsara's pleasures,
> Uprooting the view of the transitory collections,
> The mother of all wrong views?
>
> When will I come to realize
> That the animate and inanimate worlds
> Are just like dreams, hallucinations, magic shows,
> Clouds, or a city of odor-eaters?

What better place is there to meditate on the truth of impermanence than sitting in a mountain pasture by the banks of river? In the summer the grass is green and thick and the wild flowers light up the field with their bright colors. But as the seasons change the grass grows brown, the leaves drop from the trees, and the flowers wilt and disappear. In fact, when you watch the natural world closely, you see how everything is changing in every moment. Then it is not so hard to see how your own body, mind, and life are constantly moving in the same way—how whole worlds of creation arise, and then fade away, just like the ripples on the passing river.

Nothing in the outer world of creation or the inner life of the mind remains as you wish it to be. All expectations are subject to disappointment and suffering. Although beautiful objects appear so real and so attractive, when you examine them closely you find that everything is as illusory and insubstantial as a dream or a magical illusion. Everything is impermanent, constantly changing, ultimately lacking in any substantial reality.

The root of cyclic existence, the producer of the many types of wrong views, is grasping at a misconceived notion of self. That self-grasping egotism is destroyed by the wisdom that analyzes and realizes the true nature of the self. According to Buddhist teachings, there is no unitary, absolute, inherently existent self within this body and mind. What there is is an aggregation of many physical parts and mental functions—what we call the five aggregates. And each of these parts is itself not partless or independent, but is made up of other parts, and arises in dependence on causes and conditions. And each thing that arises is transitory, changing in every moment, and finally perishable.

When we examine reality with analytical wisdom in this way, we find nothing that is real, substantially existent, or unitary. However, that is precisely the way we ignorantly conceive and grasp at the self: as a real, substantially existent, unitary self, which we call "I." That is our ordinary way of thinking, and based on that innate sense of I, we conceive of real objects around us that are "mine," over which we have dominion. The egotism that grasps at an absolute self or soul—that kind of wrong view—is the cause of attachment, hostility, and all the other afflictions. It is the fundamental root of cyclic existence; we call it the "view of the transitory collections."[2] That fundamental ignorance about the true nature of self is what must be removed from the root.

Living the life of an ordained nun and aspiring to these highest of realizations was the practice of this princess. By meditating on this, and admiring that type of practice, you too will eventually be able to follow that path. The Kadampa Geshe Potowa referred to this text by Guhyadatta and the attitude of satisfaction with the monastic life when he said:

> Tonight a heavy snow fell on my small hut. It was just like something that happened in the *Edifying Tale of the Seven Maidens,* and this made me very happy. My only desire is to practice in this way—nothing else concerns me.

Another great Kadampa, Geshe Chekawa said:

> If it happens that someone is living in an austere mountain valley, practicing like a sage, then truly that child was well bred by his father.

Place Stamp Here

WISDOM PUBLICATIONS

199 Elm Street • Somerville MA 02144 USA

A well-bred child is one who comes to master all the skills and good qualities of character that his father has to teach. Here, we should understand that Geshe Chekawa is referring to a child's spiritual father, or *guru.*

And another Kadampa, Geshe Sharawa, suggested to his monk disciples this clever method to generate virtuous thoughts among the laity:

> When the householders are overwhelmed with work, you should put on your finest dress and go to see them. They will think, "Ah! Isn't the ordained life marvelous!" and this will plant the predispositions to become ordained in the future.

You can imagine the farmers at a busy time, exhausted, covered in dust and sweat, and then a monk casually walks by in crisp, clean robes, looking like he has nothing important to do. Wouldn't the hard-working peasants think, "What a wonderful life that must be!"?

The *Questions of Householder Ugra Sutra (Gṛha-paty-ugra-paripṛcchā-sūtra)* says that bodhisattvas who are living as householders should have the following aspiration:

> When will I be able to take leave of this householder's life, which is a source of suffering, and practice as a renunciate? When will I be able to perform the ritual of ordination into the Sangha, the ritual of confession, the ritual of release from the summer retreat, and the ritual of veneration of the teacher? With these thoughts the bodhisattva who remains in the household should rejoice in the aspiration to take ordination.

In this passage the bodhisattva who has remained a layperson is being encouraged see the householder's life as a source of hindrances to practice, and to cultivate an aspiration to enter the monastic life.

At the time of the Buddha, the Sangha would assemble to perform various ritual activities—most of which are still observed today—and it is these duties of the Sangha that are being referred to here. The ritual of confession is performed by monks and nuns twice each month when they gather to confess to one another whatever vows they have broken in the preceding period. Through this process they restore those virtues that have degenerated, and purify the negative actions they have committed.

The custom in the Buddha's day was for the Sangha to gather at a monastic settlement, called a *vihāra,* and spend the three months of the summer rainy season in retreat. At the beginning of the retreat a formal ritual would mark the sealing up of the monastery, and from that day until the end of the retreat the monks or nuns were not supposed to go beyond the limits specified as the border of the retreat. There were special exceptions, such as parental illness, but the principle is that you stay within the borders during the entire retreat. The reason for entering retreat is to protect the practitioner from the many distractions and pitfalls of everyday life. Within that monastic setting you are much less likely to be distracted by other people and worldly activities; you won't be traveling around so you won't have to deal with so many insects, or wild animals, and you will have the solitude, peace, and quiet to engage more deeply in your meditative practice.

On the first day of the rainy season retreat—the sixteenth day of what is usually the sixth month on the lunar calendar—the borders of the retreat are sealed, everyone takes a vow not to transgress those limits except for some exceptional reason, and the retreat begins. During the retreat a special set of monastic rules applies, which is somewhat modified from the ordinary guidelines. Then, at the end of the retreat, another special ceremony is held, this time to open the gates and release the limits and restrictions that were established at the beginning. Then, everyone enjoys a special holiday for several weeks!

The main point is that all of these monastic activities are directed purely toward emancipation and buddhahood. Even if you are on the bodhisattva path, if you remain as a householder you inevitably get bogged down in problems ("How do we produce more grain from this field?") and disputes ("That property belongs to me, not you!"). All such worldly concerns are the opposite of Sangha activity and are antagonistic to the peaceful mind you are cultivating on the path. This is why even bodhisattvas who are living the householder's life should aspire to become ordained monastics.

There are several levels of ordination vows, but some of the activities that are mentioned in this list are only performed by fully ordained monks and nuns, so the implication of this passage is that bodhisattvas should aspire to taking the full ordination of a bhikṣu or bhikṣuṇī.

The *Ornament for the Mahayana Sutras* by Maitreya says:

> Those who have entered the religious order
> Possess immeasurable virtues.
> Therefore, bodhisattvas who take and observe vows,
> Are superior to those who are householders.

Therefore, Tsongkhapa says, the life of the ordained renunciate is praised as the best way of life for those who seek personal liberation from cyclic existence.

Not only that, the life of a renunciate is also the best for those who seek the omniscience of buddhahood by means of either the Mahayana perfection vehicle or the tantric vehicle. Mahayana practitioners are striving to obtain complete omniscience in order to save other sentient beings. Because they cannot bear to see the infinite sufferings of all the beings in cyclic existence, and they take responsibility for ending that suffering, they seek the quickest, most powerful methods to achieve this goal. The fastest, most sophisticated—and also most dangerous—method is tantric practice. But even for those who enter into that Vajrayana path, the renunciate's life is best.

For the Mahayana practitioner there are three levels of vows: the vow of individual liberation *(prātimokṣa),* the bodhisattva vow, and the tantric vow. Among these, the vow of the ordained renunciate referred to here as the best basis for all levels of practice is the vow of individual liberation. As its name suggests, the intention of this vow is to lead the individual to his or her own emancipation from cyclic existence. Living according to this vow, as a monk or nun, is the key to achieving that goal. In fact, some level of prātimokṣa vow is indispensable to attaining liberation from samsara.

But beyond that, the vow of individual liberation also empowers and increases the effectiveness of the other two vows by insuring the purity of the actions that underlie them. In this way, the vow of individual liberation is the foundation of all Mahayana practice; it is the root of the teaching. It is like the great earth, upon which all other structures are built; it is the basis of all development and growth. Therefore, you should never think that this vow is only for Hinayana practitioners. Whether you are Hinayana or Mahayana, you should always maintain the highest respect for the vow of individual liberation.

As we have said many times, the human life, with its many qualities of leisure and opportunity, is the best form of life for practicing the path to liberation. The section we are now concluding, with its many quotations from sutras and aspirational poetry, has been showing us the ways in which the life of an ordained monk or nun is the best among the many types of human life, because renunciates are able to fully dedicate their mind and body to attaining freedom from cyclic existence.

This does not mean that you cannot practice as a layperson, or that the householder's life is completely meaningless. But in general, lay life means living in the world, accumulating wealth, producing children, and concentrating on the innumerable activities necessary to survive and prosper amidst the challenges of the world. When you are so wrapped up in that worldly context, it is difficult to turn in the opposite direction and try to be free from samsara. Although you may aspire to emancipation, it is difficult to do what needs to be done in order to attain it.

When you become ordained you renounce all those worldly concerns and you leave behind the life focused on temporary happiness, sensual pleasure, wealth, fame, and praise. All of these are then seen to be like nothing, and all your energy goes toward freedom from cyclic existence. From the perspective of the renunciate, this fortunate, powerful human life is a vehicle, an instrument to be used to gain emancipation. In order to succeed in that journey it is necessary to protect this body and preserve this life. For that purpose you need adequate clothes to protect you from the weather, and sufficient food and drink to sustain a healthy body. You need nourishment, but simple food is sufficient. And once you have enough, what purpose is served by additional food and clothes? The essence of the life of the renunciate is to be satisfied with simple things, to use just what you need and to be satisfied with what you have, to find joy in the simple pleasure of having enough.

The real meaning of entering the religious order is not that I sit here with yellow or red robes and shave my head. It doesn't mean that I am sitting here as some kind of stupid monk with no particular purpose, telling you that the monk's life is the best and the lay life is the worst. Taking ordination means learning to be satisfied with simple things. It means learning to live with much less attachment, learning to be satisfied with whatever comes. All of the external signs—the robes and shaved head—are markers and reminders designed to reinforce that inner attitude; they set you apart from the world of samsaric concerns and remind you and others that your goals lie beyond the things of this world.

Once you have that calm sense of satisfaction, and that separation from worldly concerns, then you can fully turn your attention and your energy toward the training that leads to freedom. You can concentrate all the action of your body, speech, and mind on that single purpose. When you say, "I now renounce cyclic existence," every aspect of your life takes on a different meaning.

These are the benefits of taking ordination and the disadvantages of remaining in the householder's life. But we should be clear that just as the quality of monks or nuns is not measured by their robes or haircut, but by their mental attitude, for laypeople the quality of their lives is not measured by the clothes they wear or their long hair. If they apply their time and energy to the path of liberation, and actually control the actions of their body, speech, and mind so that they are constantly accumulating merit and refraining from nonvirtue, and if their inner mental attitude is one of peaceful satisfaction rather than constant craving, then there is no problem—such people are also on the road to liberation from cyclic existence.

The distinction that has been made here is that *in general* it is much more difficult to engage in a complete, wholehearted practice when you are involved in the worldly concerns of a layperson. This is especially true in the early stages of practice. Later on, when your motivation is more powerful and your concentration more stable, your practice will be able to stand on its own and will not be damaged by external conditions. This is the way the high bodhisattva lives in the world in order to help others without being distracted from the path by samsaric attractions. But until you have achieved that degree of stability, the advice here is that the life of a renunciate is the best for achieving the goal of liberation.

ii) What kind of path you must cultivate to overcome cyclic existence

We have established the kind of life that is required if you want to overcome cyclic existence. We now examine the nature of the path that will lead you to that goal. Nāgārjuna says in his *Friendly Letter:*

> If your head or your clothes suddenly caught fire,
> Rather than trying to put it out,
> You should strive to put an end to rebirth,
> Because there is no purpose more important than this.
>
> By means of ethical conduct, wisdom, and concentration,
> Attain nirvana—the undefiled, contained state of peace,
> Inexhaustible, beyond aging and death,
> Free of earth, water, fire, wind, sun, and moon.

In these stanzas Nāgārjuna is telling his friend the king that gaining freedom from the sufferings of cyclic existence is so urgent that even if your hair catches fire you should not take the time to put it out! Why? Because once you are born into a miserable rebirth under the power of karma and afflictions you will be subject to every imaginable form of suffering and you will have no control over your future. But if you succeed in attaining emancipation you will never need to worry about these gross forms of suffering again.

But how do you attain liberation? The essence of all the methods are summarized in three trainings: ethical conduct, concentration, and wisdom. *Wisdom* is the understanding that realizes the true nature of reality. In order for that wisdom to become effective, for it to be realized directly, the mind must be completely calm and stable; therefore you need *concentration,* which is a perfectly focused and stabilized mind. And *ethical conduct* is the indispensable basis upon which all good qualities, including wisdom and concentration, are built. When you combine these three you have all the necessary conditions that lead to nirvana, a state that is beyond suffering.

Certain non-Buddhists believe that nirvana is an actual earthly place, but it is not like that. It is a mental state of complete peace in which all suffering, with its causes, has completely ceased. It is "undefiled" because all of the inner stains, the obscuring afflictions, have been completely removed. Once you obtain that state of nirvana you no longer need to experience the sufferings of old age, sickness, and death. This is referring to *conditioned* death, death that occurs under the power of karma and afflictions. Though bodhisattvas still undergo death, it is under their own control, and it is done for the beneficial purpose of helping other sentient beings.

Once you attain that state it is "inexhaustible"—it remains forever. It is not a state that is produced out of the material elements of earth, water, fire, and wind. Some people worship the sun or the moon, but nirvana is not such a place. It is a state of being free of the afflictions and the suffering that they cause. Nāgārjuna tells the king *that* is the kind of nirvana you should obtain.

Since the entire path that leads to that goal is encompassed by the three trainings, the *Lamrim Chenmo* now proceeds to explain those three trainings in detail. But at this point we are still studying the practices of the being of intermediate scope. The trainings of concentration and wisdom will be explained later, when we look at the Mahayana path, the path of the being of great scope. At this stage of his explanation Tsongkhapa will only explain the training of ethical conduct.

a' Specifying the number of trainings as three

You don't need very many methods to attain liberation—three is enough. Only three—that sounds pretty easy, doesn't it? But first we need to understand why three is actually sufficient, and this is explained under the following three headings:

1' Specifying the number in terms of the stages of subduing the mind
2' Specifying the number in terms of the results
3' Specifying the number in terms of the objects to be abandoned

1' Specifying the number in terms of the stages of subduing the mind

Everything that a practitioner needs to do is included within these three trainings. First of all, the training in *ethical conduct* will enable you to subdue and take control of the mind. Ordinarily the mind is untamed, like a wild elephant. It runs wherever it wants to in a completely uncontrolled manner, and like a wild elephant, if you do not bring it under control it becomes very dangerous. The uncontrolled mind leads you to many harmful actions, which in turn lead to endless rebirths in bad migrations.

To control a wild elephant you have to contain it within a limited space, and you have to make sure it does not escape from that containment. Ethical conduct uses precepts and vows to contain the mind within the space of virtuous behavior, and thereby protects you from the damage that the wild elephant of the mind can do. The ordinary, distracted mind usually chases after sense objects—following uncontrollably whatever appears to the eyes, ears, nose and so forth. The first step in taking control of that unruly mind is to set boundaries beyond which you will not let the mind wander. This is the function of training in ethical conduct: it establishes limits and restricts the body, speech, and mind from straying into nonvirtuous areas. This becomes a powerful means of protection, and it works simply by making rules and keeping strictly within the boundaries of those rules.

Once you have begun to control the negative tendencies by restraining the distracted mind, you must institute the positive training of *concentration,* called *samādhi* in Sanskrit. This means settling down the fluctuating mind, stabilizing it in meditative equipoise. By training in concentration your mind becomes pliable; you are able to do with your mind just what you wish. Once you reach an advanced level of concentration you will be able to maintain your attention on whatever object you choose, focusing without distraction for as long as you wish.

The mind is not free from suffering because it is enmeshed in a web of obscuring afflictions, and the root of those afflictions is ignorance. It is the training of *wisdom* that is the direct antidote to the cause of suffering in cyclic existence. Wisdom cuts the root of ignorance by seeing reality as it truly is.

From this brief and simple analysis we can see that for any practitioner who desires emancipation, all that is required to achieve that goal is encompassed in these three trainings. The ultimate wish of such a practitioner will be fulfilled if he or she properly practices and completes these three stages of subduing the mind: ethical conduct, concentration, and wisdom. Thus, we can say that these three are sufficient, and no other methods are necessary.

2' Specifying the number in terms of the results

We have spoken previously of the two goals of sentient beings. The first is the temporary goal of a high rebirth within cyclic existence. The second is the ultimate goal, what we call the "definite good," which is emancipation from cyclic existence, and ultimately, the perfect enlightenment of buddhahood. These three trainings are all you need to accomplish these two desired results.

The temporary goal, higher rebirth, is divided into two: higher rebirth in the desire realm, and rebirth in the form and formless realms. To achieve these two goals requires, respectively, the two trainings of ethical conduct and concentration. Maintaining pure ethical conduct is the cause of taking rebirth among the humans or devas of the desire realm. This means practicing the ten virtuous actions of body, speech, and mind, and avoiding the ten nonvirtuous actions. If you do not maintain ethical conduct—if you perform many harmful actions—the result will be rebirth in the three lower realms.

The result of training in concentration is rebirth in the form or formless realms. After you attain single-pointed concentration you can develop various levels of meditative absorption. Depending on which level of meditative absorption you achieve in this lifetime you will be reborn in a corresponding upper realm in your next life. By obtaining one of the first four concentrations you will be born in the corresponding level of the form realm; by attaining one of the four formless absorptions you will be born in the corresponding level of the formless realm.

The result of the training in wisdom is the final goal of emancipation, the definite good. Thus, these three trainings are all that is necessary to achieve both the temporary and final goals of sentient beings. These first two ways of establishing the number of trainings as three are taught in Asaṅga's *Levels of Yogic Deeds.*

3' Specifying the number in terms of the objects to be abandoned

Some earlier teachers said that the number of trainings can also be established as three in terms of the afflictions to be abandoned. They explained ethical conduct as the training that disowns and prevents the afflictions. Ethical conduct directly blocks you from doing harmful actions, but it only works temporarily, in a present circumstance, and it does not eliminate the afflictions in any ultimate fashion.

The training of concentration can be a powerful tool for suppressing afflictions when they arise. In fact, the method of practice we call the "mundane path" is a technique for temporarily suppressing the afflictions that is common to both Buddhists and non-Buddhists, and it can lead to the highest levels of meditative absorption. It involves attaining progressively higher meditative states by concentrating on the virtues of the higher state, the one you are trying to achieve, in comparison to the faults of the lower state that you have already achieved. By this method you progressively suppress the afflictions of each level by meditating on its faults. Although this can be a very useful tool, it too does not eliminate the afflictions from the root. As an analogy, you can imagine how meditating on love will temporarily subdue hatred. It works similarly to that. By meditating on the impurities of a particular realm, attachment to *that* level is suppressed. In this way, nearly all of the obscuring afflictions of the three realms can be temporarily suppressed. However, it is only when such concentration is combined with the training of wisdom that the afflictions can be eliminated from the root.

To summarize, we can see that from three points of view the three trainings are sufficient to lead to the highest goals of emancipation and buddhahood. In many sutras and commentaries you will find the path described in terms of three trainings, so it is useful to understand how all the stages of practice are subsumed in these three.

b' Ascertaining the order of the three trainings

Does the order of the three trainings have any significance? Usually they are presented with ethical conduct first, then concentration, and finally wisdom. Asaṅga's *Levels of Yogic Deeds* quotes a passage from the *Sutra Requested by Brahma (Brahmā-paripṛcchā-sūtra)* in which the three trainings are presented in that order:

> Ethical conduct is a very firm foundation.
> The peaceful mind of concentration has a joyous quality.
> With wisdom you gain the view of the āryas, which you should have,
> And forsake the view of sinners, which you should abandon.

In his comments on this verse Tsongkhapa says that ethical conduct is the root or foundation because the other two arise from it, and without ethical conduct you will not achieve concentration or wisdom. Concentration depends on ethical conduct, and takes joy in placing the mind in meditative equipoise. Without taming the mind and restraining its habit to chase after desirable sense objects, you will not be able to meditate or attain concentration. Wisdom depends on concentration, and in order to see reality just as it is, it leads one to possess the view of an ārya being and to eschew the view of sinners. In order to realize that kind of wisdom, you must have the control and peace of concentration.

This stanza demonstrates that the three trainings are presented in this order because they depend on one another and build on one another. Without taming the mind through ethical conduct you will not gain concentration; without concentration you will not achieve wisdom. You must develop these trainings in this order, and that is why they are presented this way.

12

The Nature of the Three Trainings

c' The nature of the three trainings

The final section on the path of the being of intermediate scope describes the nature of the three trainings, beginning with ethical conduct. Once again the *Sutra Requested by Brahma,* as quoted in the *Levels of Yogic Deeds,* is a primary source for this topic:

> Ethical conduct has six branches.
> Concentration is the four blissful abodes.
> The four aspects of the four noble truths
> Are pure eternal wisdom.

Six branches

The sutra says that ethical conduct possesses *six branches* and these are explained as follows:

1. The first is *possessing ethical conduct,* which means refraining from the ten nonvirtues and practicing the ten virtuous actions.

2. The second is being *bound by the vows of individual liberation.* These first two aspects of ethical conduct are instrumental in attaining emancipation, and they definitely lead to full liberation. By possessing ethical conduct you refrain from harmful actions. In order to support that practice of self-control you take vows that commit you to that effort; you bind yourself by vows to virtuous action.

3. The third is *ritual,* which means correctly performing certain rituals that are taught in the Vinaya. Having bound yourself to virtuous practice by means of vows, there are many ritual activities that are prescribed in the

Vinaya. We have mentioned some of these before, such as the confession ceremony twice each month. There are also daily activities that are supposed to be done in certain formal ways, such as blessing food before you eat it, wearing clean, proper robes, or showing respect to your teacher in specific ways.

4. Fourth is the *range of activity,* which refers to keeping pure conduct by maintaining the kind of pure environment that supports virtuous practice. For example, you avoid going to certain places where you know you might be tempted into harmful actions, or you avoid associating with certain kinds of people. To really keep pure ethical conduct you have to attend to every detail of your life, so that ordinary activities like eating, walking, or looking around do not lead you in a wayward direction. For this to work you have to insure that your environment—the people and places that constitute the range of your activities—is supportive of your practice.

The third and the fourth branches represent ethical conduct that is unimpeachable and pure. When you are meticulous in performing the prescribed rites of the Vinaya, and careful about where you go and whom you associate with, your practice will be above reproach and your behavior will always be admirable.

5. Fifth is *viewing even small infractions with apprehension.* Even very small negative actions can give rise to very bad results. Therefore, you should regard even the most subtle misdeeds as dangerous. Of course the big, obvious actions are easy to recognize and so they may be easier to avoid. But sometimes you may think, "This little thing will not make any difference; it will be okay if I do this." But once you make friends with "okay," many unfortunate things can happen. When you guard your behavior in this meticulous way you are practicing ethical conduct that does not degenerate.

6. The sixth branch is *correctly studying and undertaking the basic trainings.* In order to actually carry out this meticulous practice you must have a very clear understanding of what is right and what is wrong, down to the smallest details. There are many situations in which you may commit nonvirtues simply because you do not know what the correct course of action should be. Therefore, it is important to study the teachings on ethical conduct and the detailed explanations of the vows and precepts that are found in the Vinaya. When it comes to difficult situations, you should always check with your teacher, or with those you trust who are knowledgeable and live up to those standards themselves. Studying the meaning of the vows, consulting your

teacher, and observing the precepts properly, creates a practice that is pure and unmistaken.

With these six qualities your practice of ethical conduct will become firm, stable, and deep, and it will form the ideal foundation for all further progress on the path. That explains the first line of this stanza, "Ethical conduct has six branches."

Four blissful abodes

The second line, "Concentration is the four blissful abodes," refers to the training in concentration. What are those four abodes of mind? They are the four *concentrations (dhyāna),* which are four levels of meditative equipoise, each one corresponding to a particular level of the upper realms. When you attain one of these concentrations through meditation, you achieve a special kind of mental bliss; even though your body remains in the human realm, your mind abides blissfully on a higher plane of existence. At the ordinary, grosser levels of consciousness, the mind is agitated, uneasy, and difficult to control. But when, as the result of entering meditative equipoise, this agitation is relieved, a feeling of bliss arises, and you settle into a more peaceful state, your mind becomes more pliable, and you are able to let it remain undisturbed wherever you want it to be.

When you attain the meditative equipoise of the first concentration, you experience both a physical feeling of pleasure and a blissful mental peace. In order to reach such a level you have to temporarily suppress all of the afflictions of the desire realm, as we were just discussing. This naturally produces a more subtle level of mental peace and bliss. As you achieve more subtle levels of absorption, you attain the higher levels of concentration, and at each level you experience a more subtle form of mental bliss. The attainment of these four concentrations is common to both Buddhists and non-Buddhists. If you do not attain at least one of these four, you cannot proceed to any of the higher realizations on the Buddhist path.

Sixteen aspects

The next line of the stanza reads, "The four aspects of the four noble truths." Each of the four noble truths has four aspects, which are as follows:

1. The truth of suffering has the aspects of being impermanent, suffering, empty, and selfless.
2. The truth of the cause of suffering has the aspects of being cause, origin, arising, and condition.

3. The truth of the cessation of suffering has the aspects of being cessation, pacification, excellence, and freedom.
4. Truth of the path has the aspects of being path, correctness, achievement, and deliverance.

The third training, that of wisdom, is the direct realization of the four noble truths, and each truth is realized with its four aspects. The direct realization of these sixteen aspects is the wisdom that cuts the root of cyclic existence. That is the nature of the training of wisdom.

Tsongkhapa says that if he were only teaching the path of the being of intermediate scope, he would provide a detailed presentation of all three trainings at this point, but instead he will limit himself to an explanation of the training of ethical conduct. The other two trainings will be discussed extensively in the remainder of the *Lamrim Chenmo,* which lays out the path of the being of great scope. This is a Mahayana text, organized for Mahayana practitioners, and for them the trainings of concentration and wisdom are better explained in the Mahayana context of striving for perfect buddhahood for the benefit of other sentient beings. Therefore, these two topics are presented in two large sections on single-pointed concentration and highest insight, which will appear in volumes 4 and 5, respectively.

The benefits of ethical conduct

The previous discussion has made it quite clear that whether you are ready to take ordination vows or not, if you want to make any progress on the spiritual path it is vitally important to maintain pure conduct. The kind of enthusiasm and constant effort this requires can only come from a deep appreciation of the benefits of such conduct. If you don't understand the benefits of behaving virtuously and the consequences of harmful behavior, you will never develop the inspiration to make ethical conduct the center of your practice. This is true of any difficult activity: if you don't see much benefit, you won't want to do it. Therefore, to begin this practice you must contemplate its benefits repeatedly and from many different points of view until a genuine enthusiasm for practicing virtue arises from deep in your heart.

What are the benefits of practicing ethical conduct? They are described this way in the *Great Final Nirvana Sutra:*

> Ethical conduct is the stairway to all virtues. It is the foundation, just as the earth is the foundation of all plants and so forth. It precedes all virtues just as the leader of the merchants goes first, before all the

> other merchants. It is the victory banner of all virtues, like the upraised victory banner of Indra. It decisively cuts the route to bad migrations and all nonvirtue. It is like the medicine tree, which cures the illness of nonvirtue. It is the stock of provisions for the dangerous road of cyclic existence. It is the armaments that defeat the enemies of the afflictions. It is the magical formula that counteracts the poisonous snakes of the afflictions. It is the bridge that crosses over the water of nonvirtue.

There are many steps on the stairway to emancipation, and ethical conduct is the very first one. It is like the threshold that marks the entrance to a house; you cannot enter the house of liberation without crossing the threshold of ethical conduct. A banner of victory symbolizes the conquest of a dangerous enemy; when you are able to conquer bodily negative actions, verbal negative actions, and mental negative actions—the root of all troubles—that is the real spiritual banner of victory.

The journey through cyclic existence is very long and filled with terrifying obstacles. It is a journey into the unknown, because after death you will go to a future life that is a complete mystery to you now. What kind of provisions will be useful for such a dangerous and unpredictable journey? The best provisions, the necessary provisions, are just this practice of ethical conduct. Because, as another line in this quotation says, by this practice you will cut off the route that leads to suffering rebirths, and you open up the bridge that leads across the water of samsara to the far shore of liberation.

Nāgārjuna says in his *Friendly Letter:*

> As the earth is the foundation for the animate and inanimate worlds,
> Ethical conduct is said to be the foundation of all good qualities.

And the *Tantra Requested by Subāhu* says:

> Just as all crops grow perfectly
> In dependence on the earth,
> All of the highest, positive results depend on ethical conduct
> Moistened by the water of compassion.

Human beings strive for many worldly positive results, such as long life, wealth, honor, fame, and to be reborn in a happy state in the future. The cause for all of these desirable ends is the meritorious action of pure ethical conduct. Of course the ultimate, highest goals of the Buddhist path are liberation from cyclic existence and the perfect enlightenment of buddhahood, and these two also depend on ethical conduct as their foundation. Even the ultimate purpose of the bodhisattva, to place all other beings in the bliss of buddhahood, grows from the ground of ethical conduct when one's actions are nourished with the water of compassion. When you plant your seeds of virtue in earth that has been prepared with vows, and you add the moisture of great compassion, you will reap the harvest of perfect enlightenment.

These are the benefits of taking vows and practicing ethical conduct as has been taught in the sutras. You should contemplate these examples to develop a firm understanding of these benefits.

It is also helpful to think about the disadvantages of *not* maintaining pure conduct. For example, if you take a vow but then break it, the consequences can be very serious. Even without taking a vow, if you habitually perform nonvirtuous activities, you will suffer many unhappy results. It is not enough to merely take religious vows; you must carry through your commitment and keep your vows purely. Because of this, for some the taking of vows is very beneficial, but for others it creates many problems. It says in the *Sutra Beloved of Monks (Bhikṣu-prareju-sūtra):*

> For some ethical conduct leads to happiness;
> For some ethical conduct leads to suffering.
> Those who maintain ethical conduct find happiness;
> Those who break ethical conduct find suffering.

If you take religious vows and keep them, the only result will be happiness. If you take vows, but instead of keeping them you constantly break them, they will become the cause of misery. It is much better not to take vows than to take them but not keep them, because taking a vow and then transgressing it creates a much heavier negative action than committing that same action without a vow. Therefore, it is quite important to investigate the faults of transgressing vows so that you will gain a full appreciation of their power and respect them.

Causes and remedies

The way to practice this is to understand what causes people to commit nonvirtuous actions, and to know how to apply the antidotes to those causes. In general, there are four causes that bring about infractions of ethical conduct: not knowing the precepts, carelessness, having no respect for the precepts, having various afflictions.

The antidote to not knowing the precepts—which explain what is right and what is wrong—is to listen to an explanation of ethical conduct from a qualified teacher. Then you must study and contemplate what you have learned until you clearly understand which actions are beneficial and which are harmful.

Carelessness is a state of mind which simply has no regard for virtuous behavior and does not care what other people think. The remedy for carelessness is to cultivate the following variety of mental factors, which will replace this heedlessness with a focused attention and a determination to act well. You should cultivate *mindfulness,* which is the quality of mind that does not forget which objects are suitable to engage in and which should be avoided. You should cultivate *introspective awareness,* which examines what is passing through the three doors of body, speech, and mind in each moment, and understands what is right to engage in and what is wrong. You should cultivate a sense of *shame,* which shuns faulty behavior with respect to oneself or the Dharma. You should cultivate *embarrassment,* which shuns behavior that is considered blameworthy by others.[1] You should cultivate *trepidation,* which fears the result that will be experienced when nonvirtuous actions ripen. And you should constantly be concerned with preventing your virtue from degenerating and your nonvirtue from increasing.

The antidote to having no respect for the precepts is to cultivate respect for the Buddha, who taught the importance of this system of ethics. Based on your respect for the teacher, you should cultivate respect for his system of ethics and the rules he prescribed. Furthermore, you should cultivate respect for those practitioners who observe those rules with great care.

The antidote to having various afflictions is to examine your own mental continuum to determine which afflictions predominate and have the most influence over your mind. Once you have identified them, you must make a concerted effort to apply the appropriate antidotes, cultivating the qualities that counteract those afflictions, and working hard to eliminate them from the root. If you don't make this kind of effort—if you take a lackadaisical attitude towards the precepts and think, "I can commit small infractions and it won't do much harm"—you are headed for nothing but trouble.

The *Exegesis of the Discipline* says:

> Those who take lightly and transgress in small ways
> What the compassionate Buddha taught
> Will earn from that suffering that is out of their control,
> Just as a mango orchard declines when its protective hedge is breached.

> Here in the world, some may violate the king's edicts a few times
> And never get punished,
> But those who improperly transgress the precepts of the Sage
> Will become animals, like the *nāga* Elapatra.

Some farmers plant a thick, thorny hedge, like a fence, around their orchards to protect their trees. If that hedge is damaged or deteriorates, animals or thieves can get through and the orchard may suffer. Although nothing has directly damaged the fruit, the orchard has become vulnerable and eventually the fruit will be lost. This metaphor is applied to the Buddha's precepts, and especially to the minor rules, which were established to build a fence around the central practice of ethical conduct.

We need to understand the distinction between two different kinds of nonvirtuous actions: *misdeeds by nature* and *misdeeds of disobedience.* Misdeeds by nature are actions that are intrinsically harmful and will always yield unpleasant results. Whether you have taken a vow or not, when you perform a misdeed by nature—such as killing someone—you are accumulating negative karmic potential. In contrast, misdeeds of disobedience are actions that are not intrinsically bad, but are negative karma because they violate rules prescribed by the Buddha. If you have never taken any vows, which commit you to uphold a set of rules prescribed by the Buddha, a misdeed of disobedience is not a negative action for you.

Killing or stealing are examples of misdeeds by nature. Examples of misdeeds of disobedience are drinking intoxicants or, for a monk, eating at improper times. Drinking, for example, is not intrinsically evil, and alcohol can be taken with a good motivation, for example as medicine. But drinking alcohol is forbidden for the sake of safeguarding the other precepts, because when you are intoxicated you are more likely to commit harmful actions. In this way, the minor precepts laid down by the Buddha are intended to act as a fence that guard against the weightier actions, which are intrinsically nonvirtuous.

The point of this stanza is that once that protective fence has been breached—once you begin to break the minor rules, which may seem harmless at first—you have opened the way to much heavier transgressions and these will eventually destroy your Dharma practice and your future. In worldly matters you can often get away with breaking minor laws. But it does not work that way when it comes to the cause and effect of karma. When you break the precepts that were prescribed by the Buddha, those negative actions will naturally ripen into very unfortunate results, such as being born as an animal like the nāga Elapatra.

The story of the nāga Elapatra is told in the Vinaya. One day the Buddha was teaching to a large crowd when a stranger, dressed in the fine clothes of a prince, arrived to listen to the teachings. This being was actually the nāga Elapatra, who had been transformed by the magical power of the Buddha so that he could attend these teachings. The Buddha told him to return the following day in his actual form.

The next day Elapatra arrived with a long serpent's body, many legs, and a tree growing out of his head. The crowd took one look at this strange creature and began to flee in horror. The Buddha reassured everyone and told them that this was the same being who had appeared the previous day in the form of a prince. He told them to sit down while he explained Elapatra's situation. Many millions of years before, at the time of Buddha Kāśyapa, this being was a young man who was ordained as a monk. He became a yogi and lived in a cave for a long time. Outside his cave grew a bush that was covered in sharp thorns, and as he passed by his robes would often get caught on these thorns and torn. This irritated him so much that one day he went out and chopped down the bush.

The Vinaya rules forbid monks and nuns from cutting trees, crops, grass, or any growing vegetation. This is not because the plants themselves are considered living beings, but because they contain and support so many different life forms. There are special circumstances in which cutting plants is permitted, but in general it is a transgression of the vows to do this.

Because it was such a minor infraction, this young monk thought it would not be a problem to cut down this bush. However, the actual karmic result was that he was born as this nāga, Elapatra, and a tree grew out of the side of his head. Whenever the wind blew it caused him great pain. This story demonstrates that once you have taken vows, even a small infraction of the precepts will result in serious karmic consequences. Although cutting a bush is not in itself negative karma, since it violates the vows of a monk it is a misdeed of disobedience; the negative karma comes from breaking the rules one has promised to uphold.

You should therefore always make a concerted effort to avoid even the smallest violations of vows you have taken. If something happens so that you cannot avoid breaking some rule, do not carelessly ignore your misdeed and do nothing about it. Whether your action was a misdeed by nature or a misdeed of disobedience, you should try to purify and repair the breach as best you can by means of confession, as the Buddha explained in the Vinaya.

If your action was a misdeed by nature, you can purify it by means of the *four opponent powers* of confession as we discussed in chapter 3 of this volume.

Of course, purifying a harmful action does not necessarily mean that you are completely freed of all consequences and that the root of the action has been cut. There are different levels of purification. But when you apply an effective antidote, at least you know that the weightiness of the result will be reduced. You are placing some limit on the negative consequences of that action.

Even if you can't fully apply the antidote of confession, it is beneficial simply to maintain a mental awareness that you have done wrong, and a lingering sense of regret about what you have done. Even when you could not help doing a negative action, you should reflect on the negative consequences of that action, and even generate fear of what will come in the future because of it; you are then at least applying a countervailing force against the negative karmic potential. If you do this, the result of the action will be mitigated because you are not participating in it with mental enthusiasm. In general, you should know that there are many different kinds of antidotes for negative actions, and by studying and listening to teachings you should learn how to apply the powers of purification.

Nuns and monks perform a purification ritual in which they recite the *Prātimokṣa Sutra* every two weeks. In this ritual the abbot or preceptor puts questions to the assembly and they directly confess their transgressions to each other. There are many detailed rules that indicate when and how you should confess various categories of infractions. For example, some infractions can be confessed to one other fully ordained monk; others require at least four to hear the confession. What Tsongkhapa is saying here is that anyone who has taken vows should confess his or her downfalls in accordance with the instructions found in the Buddha's teachings.

Keeping vows purely

The *Sutra Requested by Brahma,* quoted by Asaṅga in the *Levels of Yogic Deeds,* says:

> Rely upon the training in ethical conduct,
> Apply it assiduously from the heart,
> Do not give it up in the future,
> And do not break it, even for the sake of your life.
> Engage in the study and practice of the Vinaya,
> And abide in it always with perseverance.

This stanza stresses that you should engage in the training of ethical conduct from your heart, and once you make commitments and take vows, you should not give them up in the future. Don't fall into a discouraged state of mind and think, "I cannot do this any more; this vow is too difficult for me to sustain." Some people take a vow and then want to give it back as soon as it becomes inconvenient or difficult to keep. They discover that they do not like a vow they have taken, so they just want to go out and break it. You should not do that. Do not abandon the vows you have taken.

You should not break your vows even at the cost of your life. Here we are talking about the *vows of individual liberation,* the *prātimokṣa vows.* In the context of the Hinayana system, you take these vows for the purpose of attaining your own emancipation from cyclic existence. Based on that premise, you should never commit even a single nonvirtuous action, no matter what. There are exceptions made with regard to some of the minor precepts, but in general, the principle in the Vinaya is that you should not break a vow even if it costs you your life. When it comes to major negative actions such as killing another being, there are no exceptions. If you have the choice of killing another person or losing your own life, the Vinaya says that you should lose your life.

However, once you have taken the *bodhisattva vows* in the Mahayana system and you have developed the special Mahayana attitude, then the rules are a little bit different. At this level you are not working only for your own individual liberation but for the sake of all sentient beings. In certain circumstances, actions that are usually forbidden are permitted for the person on the bodhisattva path. With bodhicitta as their motivation and using discerning wisdom to determine the consequences of their deeds, Mahayana practitioners may use special means when they are sure they will be of benefit. They may even be allowed to kill if it will help many other beings. On the Hinayana path this is always forbidden but, in the context of the Mahayana, lying or killing can be permissible for a special purpose. As Nāgārjuna says in his *Precious Garland:*

> Sometimes what is thought harmful
> Is regarded as helpful by the wise.
> General rules and their exceptions
> Are commended in all treatises.
>
> Who with intelligence would deride
> The explanation in the Great Vehicle
> Of deeds motivated by compassion
> And of stainless wisdom![2]

The stanza quoted by Asaṅga concludes by saying that you need to both practice and study the Vinaya, because in order to maintain the precepts faithfully you must know what they are, and understand them.

In the *Sutra on Having Pure Ethical Discipline (Śīla-saṃyukta-sūtra)* the Buddha explains the reason why maintaining pure ethical conduct and protecting your vows are more important than giving up your life:

> O monks and nuns, dying and separating from your life is fine. But dying with broken and degenerated ethical conduct is not the same. Why is that? Because dying and separating from this life is only the exhaustion of this particular span of life. But when you die with broken and degenerated ethical conduct, you will experience a great downfall; you will give up happiness and be separated from the lineage of high rebirth for ten million lifetimes.

The Buddha says that dying is nothing more than the exhaustion of this temporary life. But if you die with broken vows and degenerated conduct, you may be separated from high rebirth for a very long time to come. You will experience the helpless states of animals, hungry ghosts, or even the horrors of the hells. Once you start moving in the downward direction there is always a tendency to continue spiraling down and down, so it can be many millions of lifetimes before you see a happy rebirth again.

If you maintain pure ethical conduct, when you die you will only be exchanging an old body for a young and fresh one. You may even obtain a better rebirth than the one you have right now. In this sense, dying with pure ethical conduct is not a terrible thing. But dying with broken vows and degenerated conduct is a very dangerous situation.

You should also think, "If keeping my vows was not as important as prolonging my life, then shaving off my hair and putting on these religious robes had no purpose." The purpose of making these external changes in your appearance is only to change your inner mental attitude, which will change the action of your body, speech, and mind. It represents the movement of mind from impure worldly concerns to the pure thought that is concerned only for liberation. The *King of Concentrations Sutra* says:

> For those who have gone forth through ordination into these teachings of the Buddha,
> But perform nonvirtuous actions,
> Who think that wealth and crops are the essence of life,
> Who hanker after horses, cows, and vehicles,
> Who have not earnestly applied themselves to any of the trainings,
> Why did they even bother to shave their heads?

If you want to escape from this cyclic existence, which was created by karma and afflictions, the vehicle that can take you to the city of emancipation is pure ethical conduct. Without that vehicle you cannot reach your destination, and instead of arriving at the city of emancipation you will return again to samsara where you will be hammered by various forms of misery. The Buddha gave the following example in the *King of Concentrations Sutra:*

> When a person is attacked by a band of thieves,
> Wishing to stay alive he will try his best to flee.
> If his feet are not capable of carrying him away quickly,
> The thieves will seize and overcome him.
>
> Like that, ignorant people whose ethical conduct has declined,
> Although they want to escape from conditioned existence,
> Cannot flee because their vehicle of ethical conduct is impaired,
> So they will be overcome by sickness, aging, and death.

Therefore, this sutra says:

> The trainings I prescribed
> For laypeople wearing ordinary clothes—
> At that degenerate time, even fully ordained monks
> Will not have those trainings.

In the passage just quoted, the Buddha is looking into the future and saying that a time will come when even ordained monastics will not be able to keep the five basic vows that he prescribed for lay disciples in his own time. During times when the practice of the Dharma has degenerated—such as the age we are living in now—it becomes very difficult to maintain precepts with perfect purity, and it is very rare to find someone who is doing it. A fully ordained monk has 253 rules to observe, and a fully ordained nun has 364, so of course it is rare to find someone who can keep them all with perfect purity. The Buddha is saying here that it will become rare to find someone who can keep even five!

When such a time comes—and we are living in such a time today—it becomes especially meritorious to train in ethical conduct and maintain pure precepts. Because it is so much more difficult, the merits of maintaining pure precepts will actually be greater than they were at the extremely auspicious time of the Buddha. Therefore, there is great benefit in striving to maintain pure ethics. As this sutra says, even keeping one precept purely for one day and night creates great merits:

For ten million eons, as many as sands in the Ganges,
With a pure mind I paid homage to infinite buddhas,
Offering food, drink, umbrellas,
Banners, lamps, and garlands.

Yet the merits are infinitely greater than that,
For anyone who practices just one ethical training day and night,
At a time when the holy Dharma is perishing,
And the teachings of the Sugata are disappearing.

If you make vast offerings, with deep faith, to the exalted field of the buddhas, the merits are virtually measureless. This is what the Buddha himself did. Nevertheless, the Buddha says in this sutra that at a time like our current age, when his teaching is degenerating—when inner spiritual practice is dying and materialistic concerns dominate people's minds—if you keep one precept of ethical conduct purely, all the time, day and night, the merits will actually be greater than those infinite offerings to the buddhas.

We may be living in a degenerate time, but we still have the opportunity to accumulate great merits by simply trying hard to maintain pure conduct. Even if you can't keep all the precepts strictly every day, all the time, you can at least apply yourself on special days. For example, on days when you are free from work and you have some spare time, you can take the one-day ordination vows with the motivation: "In order to benefit all sentient beings I will keep these vows purely for the next twenty-four hours."[3]

This is the kind of practice you can do, even in this so-called "degenerate time," and the benefits will be great. Controlling the actions of your body, speech, and mind is the heart of the Dharma, the foundation of all progress on the path to enlightenment. When you train in the precepts of ethical conduct, you free yourself from your ordinary, habitual behavior by setting boundaries beyond which you will not let your mind and body go. When you keep your vows purely for one whole day, you gain great confidence in your own capacity to change, and with this confidence you gain more and more control over your own behavior.

You may get the idea, "I can break this rule now and it won't make any difference because I can confess and purify it later." But this won't work, because you lack the resolve, "I will never do this again in the future." The essence of confession is the clear understanding, through wisdom and reason, of the consequences of the negative action you have done; growing from that comes a determination to avoid such actions in the future. If you genuinely, sincerely, and deeply feel both *regret* and *resolve,* your confession will be strong and the purification will be effective.

If these two are not in your heart, then no matter how much you confess you will not succeed in purifying the karma. If you harbor the attitude, "I can do this action now and then later I can confess," it is the same as eating poison with the thought, "I will eat poison today and then later I will take the antidote." This approach is a little like an elephant taking a bath. When an elephant gets hot it goes to the water hole and sprays itself with water. Then it feels too wet so it leaves the water and covers itself with dust. Now it is all dirty again, so it goes back to the water hole and takes another bath. This approach doesn't get you anywhere. The danger of this mistaken way of thinking is addressed in the *Lion's Roar of Maitreya Sutra (Maitreya-mahā-siṃha-nāda-sūtra):*

> Maitreya, in future times, during the last five hundred years of the teachings, some bodhisattvas who remain householders and some who have ordained will say this: "Nonvirtuous karma can be completely wiped out by confessing the fault." They will disclose the downfall with the attitude, "After I have performed the nonvirtuous act, I will confess it." They do not take on the resolve to refrain from the action in the future. I tell you that these people possess the karma of death. And what do I mean by death? For example, it is like someone who eats poison. Having created their own time of death, they fall into the wrong kind of rebirths.

And the same sutra goes on:

> Maitreya, what I call "poison" in the noble Dharma of the Vinaya is this: transgressing the basic trainings as I have explained them. Therefore, do not eat this poison.

In these two passages transgressing the ethical precepts that the Buddha has prescribed is compared to eating poison. The object of maintaining pure ethics is to progress to the state of liberation, which is a *deathless* state. When you violate these ethical standards you put yourself under the power of karma and afflictions; you make yourself subject to the destroyer: death. After you eat the poison of nonvirtuous behavior, you guarantee that you will experience the pain of death.

But the poison of transgressing the Buddha's ethics is not like ordinary poison, because ordinary poison can only end this single life, and that is something that will eventually happen anyway. But when you take the poison of breaking the precepts, you send yourself in a downward direction that can cause misery and pain for many lifetimes to come. The destroyer of the heart of the spiritual life is nonvirtuous action, breaking the precepts, negative karma. This is what poisons the spiritual life. Therefore, the Buddha says, you should not eat this very dangerous poison.

Ethical conduct in tantric practice

Protecting vows and ethical conduct in this way is certainly the obligation of those who have taken the vows of individual liberation. But even those who have entered the highest Mahayana practice of tantra are obliged to guard the vows of individual liberation in the same way. In fact, except for a few exceptions mentioned here in the *Tantra Requested by Subāhu*, tantric practitioners are supposed to be *even more careful* and strict in their observance of the ethical precepts:

> All of the Vinaya rules which I, the Conqueror, taught,
> All the precepts of ethical conduct of the vows of individual liberation,
> Should be observed by lay practitioners of tantra,
> With the exception of the external marks and rituals.

Even householders who have taken the tantric vows and practice the path of tantra are expected by the Buddha to observe the vows of individual liberation set forth in the Vinaya. Because they are not monks and nuns, they can set aside those rules that relate to the "external marks" of renunciates, such as shaving the head, wearing religious robes, and so forth. They are also not required to perform certain monastic rituals, such as accepting offered food in a special manner, and blessing that food in a special way.

Since all the rest of the Vinaya rules are to be followed by lay tantric practitioners, it goes without saying that those rules should be observed by ordained tantric practitioners as well. In order to enter tantric practice, you have to take the tantric vows, and in order to do that you first have to take the bodhisattva vows. Monks and nuns who do this have already taken the vows of individual liberation, and of course they have to keep *all* of those vows without any exceptions.

In fact, the root of accomplishing any of the spiritual attainments of the tantric vehicle is maintaining pure ethical conduct. As it says in the *Tantra Requested by Subāhu:*

> The root of the tantric vehicle is, first of all, ethical conduct,
> Followed by persevering effort, patience,
> Faith in the Conqueror, the mind of enlightenment,
> Tantra itself, and the absence of laziness.
>
> Just as a great ruler who holds the seven precious possessions
> Can subdue all beings without difficulty,
> So a tantric practitioner who possesses these seven things
> Tames nonvirtuous action.

The Cakravartin kings, the world-conquering emperors of ancient India, possessed seven treasures that enabled them to rule virtuously, harmoniously, and without challenge. These seven are: the precious wheel, the precious jewel, the precious queen, the precious minister, the precious elephant, the precious horse, the precious army general, and the great treasure vase. When we offer a mandala representing the entire universe to the buddhas and bodhisattvas, we include these seven treasures in the mandala because they are symbols of benevolent worldly power. When a king possesses them, he is able to rule without violence or coercion; instead he uses the wisdom of virtuous action. Under his righteous leadership, the subjects will follow the king onto the virtuous path.

In the same way, tantric practitioners have *seven treasures* enabling them to achieve the spiritual attainments that are the goal of tantric practice. The root of that practice is *ethical conduct,* and from that root grow the other qualities of *diligence, patience, faith,* and *freedom from laziness.* The motivation is *bodhicitta,* the mind of enlightenment, which undertakes this practice in order to benefit all sentient beings. With those qualities as the basis, you then require the *tantra* itself: the specific practices of secret mantra through which you enter into the practice of a specific meditational deity. Tantra has many marvelous methods for transforming and controlling both the inner mental life and the outer conditions of the practitioner. When you apply these tantric methods with the proper motivation, supported by these precious qualities of diligence, patience, and faith, you will be able to control nonvirtuous behavior, just as the Cakravartin king subdues his adversaries without difficulty.

The *Root Tantra of Mañjuśrī (Mañjuśrī-mūla-tantra)* says:

> Those who recite mantras but weaken their ethical conduct
> Will not achieve the highest spiritual attainments.
> They will not even achieve mediocre attainments,
> They won't even reach the lowest attainment.

The King of Sages did not teach that those
With corrupted discipline can achieve the tantric attainments.
They are not even going in the same direction
As those who are heading for the city of nirvana.

How can disobedient immature people like this
Achieve the attainments of tantra?
How can these beings with corrupted ethical conduct
Go to happy rebirths?

Since none of them will reach the higher realms,
Nor attain high states of bliss,
It goes without saying that they will not achieve
The attainments of the tantra taught by the Conqueror.

The *Root Tantra of Mañjuśrī* is describing the various benefits of tantric practice. Through the recitation of mantras many high spiritual attainments *(siddhis)* are possible; these include both mundane attainments and supermundane attainments. But no matter how many millions of mantras you recite, if you let your ethical conduct deteriorate and you do not keep the vows of individual liberation, the bodhisattva vows, and the tantric vows purely, you will not achieve even the lowest level of spiritual attainment. In other words, ethical conduct is the foundation of all tantric attainments. People who let their conduct degenerate in this way are like disobedient children. How could such immature people ever complete the tantric path? Since they will not even attain a happy rebirth in the future, how could they possibly attain the culmination of the tantric path?

We have already discussed how pure ethical conduct is the foundation of all positive results, from a higher rebirth in the next lifetime to emancipation from all of cyclic existence. The general point of these passages is to establish that keeping pure ethics and guarding vows is absolutely essential to any progress on the tantric path as well. In this regard, there is no difference between the sutra path and the tantric path: all good results, from worldly good fortune to the highest realization of buddhahood, begin with and depend on pure ethical conduct.

Advice from the Kadampa geshes

The great Tibetan Kadampa geshes, who were the direct disciples of Atiśa, emphasized the practice of ethical conduct. Many of them were great yogis who lived in caves and meditation huts in a place near Lhasa called Phenpo. They were famous not only as great practitioners, but they also had a special style of teaching the Dharma through pithy sayings. Many of these sayings were collected and form a treasury of instructions on the topics of the lamrim.

We have here a series of their statements on ethical conduct, and the first quotation is from Geshe Kamlungba, who lived mostly in caves. He was known as someone who would cry and cry and cry when he practiced bodhicitta meditation. Meditating on love and compassion, he would reflect on the sufferings of beings in samsara, and this would cause him to break down in tears of sympathy. He said this about ethical conduct:

> When famine arises, everything centers on barley. In the same way, all positive results depend on ethical conduct. Therefore, apply yourself to this. If you do not pay attention to the cause and effect of karma, pure ethics will not come. Therefore, it is advised to think about that.

In Tibet barley was the staple food. Other than barley there was not much else to eat. So in times of famine, getting some barley became the focus of everyone's attention. In a similar way, whatever good results you may desire—whether worldly happiness, higher rebirth, or emancipation—it all comes down to ethical conduct. And pure ethical conduct in turn depends on understanding and thinking about karma and its results, the way that good or bad actions bring happy or unpleasant results. If you are not aware of this natural causality, it is difficult to apply yourself earnestly to the practice of pure ethics. When you are aware, and you continue to think about the way good karma brings happy results, it becomes much easier to tolerate adverse circumstances or to resist dangerous temptations, because you know that in the future you will reap good results.

Another Kadampa, Geshe Sharawa said:

> In general, whether good or bad arises in your experience, you should rely on the Dharma. And within the Dharma, if you depend on the explanations in the Vinaya you will not need to keep starting over, your behavior will become naturally and consistently pure, you will be content, and you will be confident that the final outcome will be excellent.

Regardless of what happens in your life, if you rely on the rules of the Vinaya and its detailed guidance on how to behave, you will be rewarded with the following five benefits: (1) Your practice will be constant; you will not need to try many different things and keep starting over again. (2) Your behavior will naturally become pure and (3) consistently virtuous, rather than sometimes good and sometimes bad. A pure mind is a satisfied mind, so (4) your mental attitude will become one of joyous contentment. It often happens that people who have all the physical comforts they require still suffer, because of feelings of guilt, anger, or frustration, from deep mental anguish. But when your actions are pure, your mind is at peace because (5) you are confident of the result. This confidence in the eventual outcome of your actions is the fifth and final benefit, and it means you are able to make sacrifices and tolerate difficult conditions because you are sure of reaching your goal.

Geshe Dromtonpa said:

> Some groups, who rely on the Vinaya, disdain tantric practice. Others, who rely on tantra, disdain the Vinaya. The understanding that the Vinaya is the companion of the tantra, and the tantra is the companion of the Vinaya, is only found in the teaching lineage of my guru.

Here Dromtonpa is referring to the period in Tibetan history, not so many years before his own time, when many corrupt forms of tantric practice had become widespread. The first diffusion of Buddhism in Tibet ended around 838 C.E., when the anti-Buddhist king Langdarma attained the throne by assassinating his brother, the devout Dharma king Ralpachen. Although Langdarma was himself assassinated after only five years in power, the century following his reign was a dark period in Tibetan history, during which the political cohesion of the state disintegrated and most of the pure lineages of Buddhist practice were wiped out or forced underground.

Corrupt forms of Buddhist tantra, emphasizing magical elements and sexual practices, were propagated by lay people who had no real understanding of Buddhist tantric principles. At the same time, so-called tantric "masters" from India taught practices based on Hindu tantric lineages, which were quite different from the Buddhist system. One method was called "union and release," which referred to sexual union and release from cyclic existence by means of animal or even human sacrifice. In the absence of living Buddhist lineages, this kind of corrupt and harmful conduct, masquerading as Buddhist tantra, came to dominate the religious landscape of Tibet. This scene, in which pure Buddhist practice had been supplanted by wrong view and wrong practice, was the context in which Atiśa was invited to visit Tibet.

It was Atiśa who reestablished the Vinaya and the monastic lineage in Tibet. It was Atiśa who reestablished the basic Buddhist view that Vinaya and tantra are entirely complementary and mutually supportive, that they are in no way contradictory. It was this teaching of Atiśa that the Kadampa lineage carried on and established as the authentic Buddhist view throughout Tibetan Buddhism. And Atiśa himself described the preeminent place of the Vinaya this way:

> When I was in India, when important matters or unexpected events arose, we would assemble the scholars of the scriptures to determine whether there was any objection to be found in the Tripiṭaka to a proposed solution, or whether it contradicted anything in the Tripiṭaka. Based on that determination we would proceed with our decision.
>
> In addition to this, we at Vikramaśīla would also determine whether there was any objection to the proposed actions in the conduct permitted for a bodhisattva or whether it was contradictory to the bodhisattva's conduct. In any case, the final decision was made by the masters of the Vinaya.

Atiśa is talking about the way important decisions were made at the great monasteries of North India such as Nālandā, Odantapuri, and Vikramaśīla. He says that the greatest scholars would assemble and investigate whether a particular plan of action was in any way contradictory to the *three baskets (tripiṭaka)* of the Buddhist canon: the Sutra-piṭaka, Vinaya-piṭaka, and Abhidharma-piṭaka. At his own monastery of Vikramaśīla, they would also inquire to see if the plan contradicted the bodhisattva vows. In the end, it was the scholars of the Vinaya that would make the final decision, based on whether the actions were contradictory to anything in the Vinaya.

The great teacher Neusurpa had this to say about how to keep ethical conduct purely:

> For now, this battle against the inner afflictions is the only thing that is important. If you do not fight against the afflictions, pure ethical conduct will not come. In that case, you will not succeed in the trainings of concentration and wisdom, which, respectively, suppress the afflictions and eliminate them from the root. Then, as the Buddha has said, you will have to wander continually in cyclic existence.
>
> Therefore, as I have said before, you must identify the obscuring afflictions, contemplate their faults and the benefits of eliminating them, and plant the mental spies of mindfulness and introspective alertness. Then, you must regularly puncture whichever affliction sticks its head out.

> Furthermore, as soon as any affliction arises in your mind, you should see it as your enemy and attack it. Otherwise, if you tolerate the affliction when it first arises, you will nurture it with unwholesome thinking until you have no means to fight against it and you fall under its power.

Neusurpa is saying that, in your present situation, there is no point in blaming everybody else for your problems; the only enemies you should be fighting against are your own afflictions. The fight is inside, against the inner enemies, because they are the source of all impure action.

Combatting the afflictions

To succeed in this struggle you first have to identify the enemy. This means you must know the six rudimentary afflictions, which are listed by Vasubandhu in the *Treasury of Knowledge* as attachment, hostility, ignorance, pride, doubt, and wrong views. These, says Vasubandhu, are the roots of cyclic existence. They are the roots from which nonvirtuous karma grows. From these, many other subsidiary afflictions branch off and arise in different forms. You need to recognize them not merely as some terms in a book, but you need to be able to spot them immediately when they arise in your mind. When the enemy comes knocking at your door, you need to know it is the enemy so you can close the door tight.

Once you know what the afflictions look like, you need to think about the great harm they can do to you and also realize what great benefits you will get when they are permanently removed. Then you protect yourself from these enemies by establishing the spies of mindfulness and introspective alertness at the door of the mind. Mindfulness is like a tether that restrains the mind, keeping it from wandering away from its object of attention. Introspective alertness is the spy that is constantly checking what is coming in and going out, what the mind and body are doing. Then, whenever an affliction dares to stick its head out, it is spotted by these mental spies; you immediately strike it with the spear of wisdom and destroy it with the inner antidotes. This is the way great practitioners guard their minds.

You have to fight this battle against the inner enemies constantly, with vigilance. Once you see the enemy, you have to ask yourself, "How can I get rid of this? What kind of antidote should I use?" There are many different types of antidotes for the different types of afflictions. When hatred or anger arises, for example, you might meditate on love. When desire arises, you might meditate on impermanence, or the impure nature of the object. You have to be knowledgeable as well as creative in finding the right method that works to temporarily suppress the affliction disturbing you at any particular moment. Ultimately, it is through meditation on emptiness that you will get rid of this affliction from the root. The point here is to recognize the affliction as an enemy and be ready to defend against it.

Without that constant vigilance, the afflictions will sneak up on you. When one arises you will not pay it much attention, you will be okay with it, and then it will begin to do its work. If you give the enemy this kind of opportunity, it will only get stronger and stronger, because your own misperceptions and mistaken imputations will feed it, and lead you to surrender to its power.

Think of what happens, for example, if an attractive person appears and you feel desire for him or her. If you do not counteract that afflictive desire, you will start to think how beautiful, how nice, how wonderful that person is. You begin imputing qualities that the object does not actually have. Fundamentally, you impute a pure nature on something that is impure; you impute a pleasant nature on something whose nature is suffering; and you impute a permanent nature on something that is impermanent. This process of imputation feeds the attachment so that it grows sharper and stronger. In the end, the affliction wins the battle and you are totally under its power. This is what will happen if you do not constantly battle the obscuring afflictions. If you sincerely make this effort, but are still not able to prevent a strong affliction from entering your mind, you should at least strive to shorten and reduce its effect. Never let an affliction persist without trying to counteract it. If you consistently apply the countermeasures, eventually you will be able to reduce the effect of any affliction and turn it away.

In Nāgārjuna's *Friendly Letter* we find the image of three types of drawing: a drawing on the water, which dissolves as soon as it is created; a drawing in the dust, which will stay for a while, but eventually is blown away; and a drawing in stone, which remains for a very long time. An affliction should be like a drawing on the water; although it may appear, it should be dispersed almost immediately. If you can't fully achieve that, your affliction should be like a drawing in dust; though it persists for a while, eventually it will be wiped out. When it comes to the virtuous qualities, the cultivation of the antidotes, they should be like drawings in stone; although they take some time to create, once they are established they remain solid and stable for as long as you need to rely on them.

> Understand the mind can be like a drawing
> On water, in earth, or in stone.
> For those with afflictions it is best if it is the first;
> For those who seek the Dharma it should be the last.

For serious practitioners who spend their whole life trying to train the mind, at the beginning their virtuous thoughts may be like drawings on water—they don't last very long. Then, as their practice becomes stronger, the virtuous qualities remain longer and longer, until finally they are as firmly established as a carving in stone. Conversely, the negative attitudes get weaker and weaker, more and more unstable, and they end up as drawings on water. Once you reach that level, where the afflictions arise but are immediately dispersed, it becomes easy to eliminate them from the root.

Śāntideva says in *Engaging in the Bodhisattva Deeds:*

> This shall be my obsession:
> Despising the afflictions, I shall meet them in battle,
> Making an exception those afflictions
> That destroy other afflictions.[3]
>
> Let me be burned to death,
> Let me have my head chopped off,
> But I will never submit in any way
> To the enemy of the obscuring afflictions.

Sometimes our approach to the afflictions takes the form of hatred. We resent them because they cause all of our problems. We focus on the way wrong view, attachment, and the other afflictions damage our life and steal our happiness. Seeing that, we grow to despise them as our worst enemies. Then we resolve to destroy that enemy. This is the way Dharma practitioners should direct their anger.

Ordinarily, people do the opposite. They consider the afflictions to be their friends and they try to make them happy. They believe that the enemy is external, someone who is interfering with their attempts to satisfy their desires. The Dharma practitioner knows that the enemy is inside, and they determine to do battle with that enemy.

This kind of hatred, which is directed towards the afflictions, is not itself an affliction. It is the destroyer of afflictions. It is the thought, "What can I do to get rid of this enemy? How can I destroy the enemy that is trying to destroy me?" As the stanza above says, this should even become your obsession—concentrating on what you can do to injure, harm, and destroy these afflictions. This attitude takes on the form of hatred, but it is *not* hatred, because it *destroys* hatred. This is the way practitioners should think.

Whatever happens, you should never bow down and submit to the afflictions. It doesn't matter if you are burned to death or have your head chopped off. The worst that your external enemies can do is kill you. You are going to die anyway, so that is not too serious. But when someone comes to kill you, if you obey your ignorance and turn your mind over to powerful anger and hatred, and if you die with that state of mind, then you will suffer a double injury. Physically, your killer has taken away this life. But by surrendering to your inner enemy you have destroyed your own chances of finding good rebirths in the future. So, not only have you lost this physical body, but your spiritual life is also destroyed.

When others come to attack you, they are operating under the power of their own inner afflictions of ignorance and hatred. So who is the enemy? Is it those people attacking you or is it their afflictions? The enemy of those attackers is compelling them to perform all kinds of harmful actions that will cause them a great deal of suffering in the future. But if you get angry in response, then the attackers' afflictions have also taken control of you! Now your mind is doing the same thing that their mind is doing.

This stanza is therefore saying in essence, "I will never bow down to anger and the other afflictions. It does not matter if they burn me and kill me. I will never surrender for even a moment to powerful hatred towards the people who harm me." This is the practice of the true bodhisattva practitioner.

Geshe Puchungwa said, "Although I am powerfully oppressed by the afflictions, from underneath I can still snarl with gritted teeth." When Potowa heard that he said, "If you do that, you will immediately turn away from the afflictions."

In the following verses Śāntideva goes on to say that in one way the afflictions are easier to conquer than an ordinary enemy, such as an invading army. Although you may defeat an enemy army and drive it out of your country, there is always the chance that its troops will regroup, regain their strength, and return to attack you again. The afflictions are not like that. If you are able to drive them out of your mental continuum by eliminating them from the root, there is no place else for them to go. There is no way for them to regroup and return to cause you more trouble. Once you have eliminated them from the root they will never come back. The only reason you are not able to eliminate them from the root is that you do not make the kind of determined, persevering effort that is required.

> Even when ordinary enemies are expelled from the country,
> They may settle in another place and take control.
> Having recovered their strength they will return.
> The enemy of the afflictions does not work that way.

> The various afflictions are cast out by the eye of wisdom.
> Once cleared out of my mind, where will they go?
> Where can they rest, in order to return and do me harm?
> But with a weak mind, I totally lack persevering effort.

Therefore, says Nyugrumpa, you should not be lazy. As soon as you detect an affliction arising in your mind, you should take action to defend against it:

> When an affliction appears, do not be lazy, but fend it off by applying the antidote. If you cannot prevent it, get up and arrange a mandala and other offerings. Present them to your guru and meditational deities, and request inspiration to overcome the affliction. Focusing on the affliction, recite the mantras of wrathful deities. As a result of these practices the affliction will subside.

Langri Tangpa has this simple advice: "Even changing your sitting position or turning your head will cause the afflictions to dissipate." And Gonpawa also said that when it comes to protecting yourself from the obscuring afflictions, "What is better than keeping a watch over your mind day and night?"

As for the Great Lord Atiśa, the teacher of this lamrim tradition, whenever he met someone he would greet them with the question, "Have you had a good mind?" He didn't say "How are you?" or "Have a nice day!" He asked, "Have you had a good mind?" What did he mean by that?

First of all, the key is to have a very kind, loving attitude towards other sentient beings, cultivating the bodhicitta motivation to work for the benefit of others. The second essential aspect is to guard your mind so that it is not dominated by the afflictions. You must be prepared to apply an antidote whenever a harmful thought begins to rise; that is the meaning of a "good mind." In this way Atiśa was always concerned with the other person's mental attitude: was it good, straight, warm, and kind? It is difficult to find all those qualities in a person, but when that happens it is wonderful to see and so enjoyable to experience the company of that person.

How to eliminate the individual afflictions

Since all negative actions begin from one of the inner afflictions, you need to guard your mind against them and fight them when they appear. What, then, is the best method for defeating each type of affliction? Ultimately, you must eliminate them from the root by perfecting the two trainings of concentration and wisdom. But until you reach that level, you need methods of temporarily combating the afflictions so that they do not take control of your mind. As Geshe Gonpawa said, there is basically no better method than keeping a close watch on your own mind at all times. In order to do that, you have to be able to recognize the afflictions when they arise. This requires studying and learning the nature of the enemy so you can spot it whenever it appears. Once you clearly understand what is and is not an affliction, you need to apply the methods that can remove each of them. Here we will discuss methods for eliminating some of the obscuring afflictions,[4] beginning with the three poisons: the three basic afflictions from which all other subsidiary afflictions branch off.

Ignorance

We begin with *ignorance.* This affliction acts as the basis for all the others, has the most far-reaching consequences, and is the most difficult to remove. Ignorance is like the root of a poison tree. It is much easier to cut off the leaves, branches, and even the trunk of the tree than to pull out the root. But until you have pulled that root out of the ground, you have not permanently eradicated the danger of that tree. We therefore need to know how we can eliminate ignorance, the root of all other afflictions.

The antidote for ignorance is to study, contemplate, and meditate on the various aspects of dependent origination. You need to concentrate on the cause and effect relationship whereby virtue creates happiness and nonvirtue produces suffering. You need to master the process of the twelve links of dependent origination by which beings enter into cyclic existence, and through which they can gain freedom from it. If you have familiarized your mind with this process of dependent origination—first by studying it and then by integrating it with your mind in meditation—you will not be troubled by any of the five wrong views, which are the fundamental creators of all negative thoughts and actions.

Hostility

The second of the three poisons is *hostility.* When you give your mind over to anger and hatred, the results are sure to be suffering in this life and in the future. Hostile thoughts lead to harmful actions, which not only result in future pain, but also destroy the meritorious roots of virtue that have accumulated by past virtuous actions. Just as a powerful forest fire indiscriminately destroys the most beautiful flowers, trees, and wildlife, just a few minutes of uncontrolled anger can completely wipe out the roots of virtue accumulated over many previous lifetimes. As Candrakīrti says in his *Commentary on the "Middle Way":*

Anger directed towards a son of the conquerors
Destroys, in an instant, the merit from generosity and ethical conduct
Accumulated over hundreds of eons.
Therefore, there is no nonvirtue greater than impatience.[5]

In an instant of anger many lifetimes of positive potential can be wiped out. Merits are created when you cherish others and you act in ways intended to help them. The basic meaning of pure ethical conduct is to not harm others, to protect others from injury.

Patience and all other virtuous actions are positive by virtue of the way in which they affect other beings. In precisely the same way, hostility is negative by virtue of its damaging effects on others. Anger and hatred are the desire to hurt others, the wish to make them suffer. The actions unleashed by such a motivation are the opposite of merits. To the extent that this negative attitude becomes strong, the positive ones become weak. To say that the positive potential of merits is destroyed by hostility does not mean it is physically burned up as in a fire. "To be destroyed" here means that those virtuous seeds—those propensities for happy future experiences—become less able to bring about their results. The power of the hostile mind damages the capacity of positive potentials to yield their fruit. This is why we say that hostility is the enemy that destroys past virtues.

Śāntideva says in *Engaging in the Bodhisattva Deeds:* "There is no nonvirtue like hatred." It is the most powerful of all the negative attitudes. When hatred arises, it is not simply the enemy of the person you hate, it is *your own* worst enemy. Therefore, you should never allow it an opening. Never think that you can get friendly with it for a little while, because once you let it in the door, it will grow stronger and stronger until it has you under its power. You close the door to hostility by recognizing it as your own worst enemy and by cultivating the powerful antidote of patience. Use your wisdom to understand the situation, and instead of opening the way to anger, be wide open to patience. As Śāntideva says, patience will bring peace to your mind, calm to your surroundings, and it will pacify the hostility of others:

Whoever assiduously overcomes anger
Finds happiness in this and other lives.

Making a concerted effort to develop and strengthen patience is the best way to fight the enemy of hostility. When we explain the *perfection of patience* in a subsequent volume of this series, we will get into this topic in more detail. Right now, at this stage of your practice, it is very difficult to eliminate hostility from the root. In fact, the root is ignorance, and the wisdom that eliminates ignorance comes only at a higher stage of realization. But right now it is entirely possible to overcome hostility by shutting it out, suppressing it, not letting it rise.

You may think that this is only a temporary solution, and that the seeds still lie dormant in your mental continuum. Nevertheless, shutting out hostility, even temporarily, is a great victory in the battle against negative karma. If hostile feelings are not in your mind, you will not take actions that harm others. When mental action is subdued, bodily action is naturally controlled. You no longer feel the need to use harsh speech or deceitful words. In this way, the person who wins the battle with the inner enemy of hostility also defeats the destructive power of nonvirtuous karma. That person will be safe, happy, and content in this life and in lives to come.

Attachment

The third of the three poisons is *attachment.* What do we mean by attachment? Attachment is the affliction that empowers and actualizes previously accumulated virtuous and nonvirtuous karmic seeds so that they have the power to ripen into happy or suffering forms of rebirth.

In this life, and in all previous lives, you have performed innumerable actions and each action planted a seed, a certain type of propensity, in your mind-stream. When the necessary conditions are met, a particular seed will ripen into experience in your current life. The seeds of the most powerful karmas, so-called "projecting karmas," have the potential to ripen into new rebirths. Each seed remains dormant until it is nourished and activated by the moisture of the affliction of attachment.

Within the twelve links of dependent origination, the afflictions that actualize dormant seeds are craving and grasping, the eighth and ninth links. At that point the projecting karmic seed is reactivated and ready to yield its fruit in a new rebirth. Just as seeds we plant in the ground require moisture to germinate and bring forth a sprout, attachment is the moisture that actualizes the already planted karmic seeds so they can ripen into the results of experience. We discussed this earlier in the presentation of craving, grasping, and existence—the eighth, ninth, and tenth links of dependent origination.

When it comes to virtuous karmic seeds or "merits," if they are not nourished by attachment, the result will be emancipation and buddhahood. But while you are enmeshed in cyclic existence your actions are habitually dominated by attachment—especially attachment to a mistaken notion of self. This is why you are constantly experiencing the unpleasantness of samsaric results. When you cultivate pure states of mind such as love, compassion, and bodhicitta—which are free of attachment—the results initially will be higher rebirth, and eventually you will transcend samsaric results completely.

Human beings live in the desire realm, where the predominant form of attachment is attachment to sense objects: beautiful forms, sweet fragrances, luscious tastes, and especially exciting touch, as in sexual contact. Life in the desire realm is dominated by the desire for the experience of contact with these sense objects. Most people spend their whole lives chasing after that contact. Then, depending on whether a particular object provides pleasant or unpleasant experience, attachment to one and hostility to the other emerges. Life in the desire realm has this quality of fluctuating between pleasure and pain, happiness and sorrow. We almost never get a chance to experience the constant bliss of the upper realms, where beings abide in the peace of meditative equipoise for eons on end. Our desire is more physical. It is a craving for the feelings that arise when the conditions for a sensory experience come together; when a sense object, sense faculty, and consciousness meet, the experience dawns. When the object is attractive we experience pleasure, and attachment arises as the craving for more of that feeling. When the object is unattractive, hostility arises in the form of a desire to make that object go away. This is the perpetual cycle of existence, in which contact with an object generates a pleasant, unpleasant, or neutral feeling, which generates the afflictions of attachment or hostility, which generates karmic action, which produces birth in a body that will have more contact with more sense objects.

To counteract that attachment serious practitioners meditate on the undesirable nature of inner and outer objects, and on the faults of becoming attached to seemingly desirable objects. For example, a common antidote to the attachment of sexual desire is to mentally open up the skin of the body you desire and look at what is really in there. This is the technique of investigating the true, impure nature of apparently attractive objects, and it is a very effective method to pacify attachment.

You should also meditate on the unhappy consequences of letting yourself get attached to sensual pleasures. Although an object may appear very attractive, and experiencing it may provide some degree of pleasure for a short time, you have to analyze the long-range results of indulging in that desire. You need to consider how brief moments of pleasure can lead to very long-term suffering. If you examine and meditate on the consequences of attachment, you will be able to turn down the fires of desire, and eventually you will overcome this affliction.

The great master Vasubandhu said:

> The five animals—deer, elephant, butterfly, fish, and bee—
> Are overcome by five different types of objects.
> If one single object can overwhelm them,
> Why wouldn't all five overcome those who constantly resort to them.

The metaphor used in this verse draws on a cultural notion that may not be literally true, but it makes a point about human beings. It is said that each one of these animals is absorbed in a single sense object. Deer are attached to beautiful sounds; so, it is said, they follow sounds into the range of the hunter and there lose their lives. Butterflies or, more precisely, moths are attached to light, so they fly into the fire of lamps and die. The point is that their attachment to a single sense object destroys them in the end. As for the other animals, I am not sure how their attachments destroy them, but the tradition is that elephants are attached to touch, bees are attached to smell, and fish are attached to taste. Vasubandhu asks, "If these animals can be destroyed by their attachment to only one type of sense object, what will happen to us humans, who are constantly attached to all five!" We have many different ways of destroying ourselves, many different desires that can damage our future lives.

Therefore, those who are real practitioners—who are seeking not merely temporary enjoyment but the everlasting happiness of emancipation—fight this affliction of attachment to sensual pleasures with all their energy. They do not allow an opening for desire to enter and overwhelm their minds. And when the enemy does manage to get in, they immediately try to cast it out by applying effective countermeasures. They never let the enemy of attachment infiltrate and gather strength in their minds.

As Nāgārjuna said, when afflictions appear in your mind, they should be like drawings on water, which disperse as soon as they are created. If you cannot erase them immediately, they should be like drawings in sand, which sit for a little while but are soon blown away. You should never allow attachment to establish itself in your mind like a carving in stone, because its consequences will stay with you for a very long time.

The eight wordly concerns

We humans have a special problem with what are called the "eight worldly concerns." These eight occur easily but are difficult to get away from. They are divided into two groups: the four positive goals and the four negative ones. The four positive worldly goals are wealth, fame, praise, and pleasure. Most people are attached to wealth in some way, and many sacrifice their whole life chasing after it. Fame is one of the most seductive attachments.

Even great spiritual practitioners, who have transcended any craving for wealth, still have an attachment to fame lingering in the back of their minds. People do extreme and dangerous things to acquire fame; some even give up their lives for it. Often people think that after they die their fame will live on. But it doesn't always happen that way, and many people who were once world-famous are now totally forgotten.

Praise is similar to fame but it is more direct and immediate. The pleasure comes from actually hearing the praise, not from what will happen after you die. Everybody enjoys being praised with sweet words such as, "You are wonderful, you are beautiful, you are great." Such sounds make almost anyone feel happy. In fact, when someone is praising you and gets interrupted, you may become mad, or feel disappointed that the praise has stopped.

Finally there is pleasure, and of course everyone wants pleasure, enjoyment, a feeling of happiness. When we speak of the eight worldly concerns, we are not talking about the bliss of enlightenment, the ultimate state of "pleasure." The problem is that we are attached to *temporary* pleasure, which generally takes the form of sensual enjoyment here in the desire realm. This brings some short-lived experience of comfort and release, but our attachment to that experience leads to compulsive behavior and all kinds of nonvirtuous actions.

The second four of the eight worldly concerns are the opposites of these four positive worldly goals: poverty, disgrace, blame, and pain. No one wants to experience these states and everyone tries to avoid them. These eight are the worldly goals that absorb the attention and time of most human lives. They have no higher, spiritual value. They do not lead to any everlasting, stable form of happiness. Therefore, spiritual practitioners should strive to avoid falling under their influence by cultivating the antidotes to these forms of attachment.

As Nāgārjuna says in the *Friendly Letter,* "A wise person has no interest in the eight worldly concerns." Wise people apply their time and energy in the opposite direction; they try to avoid becoming attached to these worldly goals. They apply methods that lead them away from samsaric attachment and towards freedom from that attachment. What are those methods? How do you counteract attachment to the eight worldly concerns? You should meditate on the faults of cyclic existence in general and, in particular, you should cultivate mindfulness of death. Realizing the actual suffering nature of this samsaric existence—that life is short and is soon coming to an end—will undermine compulsive attachment to these worldly attractions. We have already discussed the *general sufferings of cyclic existence* and *the suffering of death* earlier in this volume.

Although you may not die today, you can never be sure. You should always keep death in mind and ask yourself, "If I die today, then what?" You should cultivate a deep-seated awareness that death is certain, its time is uncertain, and because death is always looming, you must prepare yourself for what will come afterward. It is this awareness that redirects your energy from the common concerns of surviving and prospering in just this current life, and turns your attention to higher goals.

If you don't remember death, your only concerns are the gratifications of this temporary life. Since you have no higher purpose, you apply all your talent, time, and energy to acquiring those four positive goals; you spend your entire life chasing after them. But at the end, as you approach your hour of death, what do you have that can protect you after you leave this life?

The state of mind of a true practitioner is to think of this life as merely a brief rest stop on a long journey. When you are traveling on a long trip and you stop somewhere for a meal, or perhaps to sleep overnight, you do not become attached to that rest stop. You don't spend all your time preparing to stay in that place, because it is clear that you are only passing through, and that you still have a long way to go in your journey. Similarly, when we set out with the goal of reaching liberation from cyclic existence, we are embarking on a very long spiritual journey. This present life is nothing more than a temporary way station where we have a chance to make preparations for the rest of the trip. That is the work of a practitioner: to use this peaceful life with its many opportunities to prepare for the rest of the journey to enlightenment.

Pride

So far, from among the six rudimentary afflictions, we have discussed the three poisons: the three fundamental afflictions of ignorance, hostility, and attachment. The next affliction we need to consider is *pride.* Pride is one of the biggest obstacles to entering and progressing on the spiritual path. The path we are following here leads to emancipation and ultimate enlightenment. It is difficult to even meet this path, but if you are obscured by pride, then even when you get a chance to practice such a path, you will not be able to take advantage of it. Your pride won't let you even listen to the teachers who can show you the path. You don't want to learn from others because you think that you already know everything.

We say that this conceited attitude is like a balloon: you are all puffed up, but inside you are completely empty. You think you know everything, but inside you have no understanding and no true realization. When a balloon is filled up with air, nothing else can go inside. In the same way, pride prevents these teachings from penetrating your heart and mind, and it thereby prevents you from engaging in the path in this life.

When you consider yourself superior, you naturally look down on everyone else. You think that you are the highest and best, so you treat everyone else as inferior to you. This karma causes precisely the opposite result in future rebirths: you will be born as the most menial kind of servant, looked down upon by everyone else in society. In other words, you will experience just exactly what you did to others in this lifetime. When you are born as a lowly servant you are compelled to follow the commands of others. You have no control over your own life or how you spend your time, so even if you wanted to pursue a spiritual path you would not be permitted to do so. In this way, pride obstructs the path both in this lifetime and in future rebirths. Understanding that pride leads to all of these problems, you should do your best to abandon this affliction.

How do you eliminate pride? Nāgārjuna explains the method this way in his *Friendly Letter:*

> If you consider over and over again,
> "Because of my own actions I have not transcended
> Sickness, aging, death, or separation from the desirable,"
> By means of that antidote you will not become puffed up with pride.

He is saying that the antidote to pride is to realize that you are still completely enmeshed in the web of cyclic existence; you are still subject to all of its sufferings, and who do you have to blame for your condition? No one but yourself, because your sufferings are nothing but the results of your own previous actions. You have to meditate on this again and again because often the tendency is to blame others, to look outside for the cause of your difficulties. What you need to do is to face the truth: "It is all my fault."

That is the antidote to pride. You are admitting to yourself that you are not so great, that you have not come very far in freeing yourself from the miseries that all other beings have to face. And the cause of those miseries is nothing other than your own ignorant actions. When you constantly think about that, there will be no room to get puffed up with pride. Understanding the cause and effect of karma will actually make you more humble. It will make you more accepting of the adversity that you encounter in your life. And instead of trying to blame others for your difficulties, it will inspire you to correct your harmful behavior, and to redirect your energy to the methods that will bring better conditions in the future.

When you accept responsibility for your own circumstances, you open yourself up for all the good qualities of the path and the instruction of the teachers to come in. You are like a balloon in which all of the stale air of arrogance has been squeezed out, so that now it is ready for the fresh air of wisdom to come in.

Doubt and wrong views

The next in our list of six rudimentary afflictions is doubt. This does not refer to just any kind of doubt, but to instances of doubt that interfere with spiritual practice. When you hold onto doubt about the teachings or the teacher, you are limited by reservations about engaging the path with full enthusiasm. This hesitation, based on doubt, can be a serious obstruction to entering and making progress on the path.

For example, in your study of the four noble truths you learn about the truth of suffering, its cause, the cessation of suffering, and the path to that cessation. When you first learn about these four, it is proper to examine and analyze whether they are true or not. But if you conclude, "This is probably *not* the way things are. This doesn't seem to have any value and I don't think I should get involved with this," then you have created a major mental block that will prevent any serious practice.

Similarly, when you get involved with Buddhism you will hear about the Three Jewels of Refuge. The Buddha is said to be the perfect teacher, who has attained the perfection of enlightenment and is able to lead us to that same goal. Is this true or not? The Dharma Jewel is the supreme method, taught by the Buddha, which is supposed to lead us to buddhahood. Does this method work or not? The Sangha Jewel consists of those individuals who are seriously pursuing that method and who are people you can trust to assist you on the path. Is the Sangha a trustworthy refuge or not? For Buddhists, their whole practice is based on these Three Jewels of Refuge. If you don't believe that this teacher, and the method he taught, and the path he described, are actually reliable and have the capacity to lead you to the cessation of suffering, how can you enter that path? If you don't trust the Three Jewels, how can you turn to them for refuge?

We are not talking about replacing doubt with blind faith. Stable trust and faith arise from studying the scriptures, listening to knowledgeable teachers, applying logical analysis, and meditation. You have to build faith on a foundation of reason and understanding. When you do that, all doubts are dispelled with confidence, and your practice becomes resolute; it rests on a firm foundation of irreversible faith.

The teaching on karma and its results is the place where doubt can be most destructive, and where faith must be relied on in the beginning. According to

Buddhism, virtuous action brings only happy results and harmful action brings only suffering. This is the general law of karma. In the scriptures the Buddha taught the details of karma by recounting particular cases in which a person performed a certain action in one lifetime and reaped a concordant result in a later lifetime. It takes a very high level of realization to see previous or future lives, so ordinary people like us cannot see this process of cause and effect operating over several lives. Nor can we access this field of knowledge through logical thinking.

But sometimes we can see the cause and effect of karma operating within one lifetime. We often see people experiencing the results of their own actions. We can learn more of the details of how karma operates by studying the scriptures and commentaries and listening to teachings. But when it comes to eliminating doubt—when you try to make a judgment of the validity of this description of how karma operates over numerous lifetimes—there is really no substitute for faith. This faith is built upon learning, trust in your teachers, analysis, and meditation, but because you cannot know directly, or by logical inference, the detailed operations of karmic cause and effect, you have to develop a level of faith that these teachings of the Buddha are true.

If you develop strong faith in the cause and effect of karma, based on trust in the word of the Buddha and the eminent teachers of the lineage, your practice will become strong. On the other hand, if you reject this possibility based on a superficial understanding—or even worse, if you slip into wrong view with the thought, "This cannot be true; these things are nothing but someone's stupid imagination"—then you face a huge obstacle to entering the path, and a great danger of disregarding the karmic consequences of your deeds.

Therefore, you must be very careful about how you handle doubt in your mind, especially doubt about karmic cause and effect. It is not uncommon for doubt to arise in the mind, but you need to observe which way your mind is tilting. It is one thing to think, "I am not sure about karma and rebirth. I am not completely convinced this is absolutely true. But this is the teaching of the Buddha, and of my teachers, so I will continue to think about it, and take it as a serious possibility." This is a balanced approach, which does not close down your mind but opens you up to a deeper understanding. It is a different matter if you find yourself leaning towards the wrong view that cause and effect definitely do not operate through the agency of karma. The attitude that thinks, "There is no proof for this; I cannot see it, therefore I doubt it can be true"—that is the dangerous area to fall into. That is the attitude you need to watch out for and you need to fight against.

In general, the method to counteract doubt is to build wisdom based on knowledge, reason, and the experience of meditation. You need to build up a firm foundation of understanding the four noble truths, the Three Jewels, and the cause and effect of karma. Then, through your practice of study, analysis, and meditation, wisdom will dawn, and unshakable confidence will replace your wavering doubt.

The subsidiary afflictions

Growing out of those six rudimentary afflictions, like branches growing out of a root and trunk, are many subsidiary afflictions. These afflictions are very common, they arise easily, and when they do they interrupt your practice and obstruct your pursuit of virtue. The subsidiary afflictions that are discussed here are excitement, lethargy, sleep, laziness, carelessness, immodesty, forgetfulness, and inattention. It is important to be able to recognize these afflictions and understand the problems they produce. It is only when you understand their faults and see that they are your enemies that you will be able to apply effective antidotes. Then, as soon as one appears, you determine that you will defeat it and drive it out of your mind. Even if you can't completely destroy it, you can weaken its power and shorten its duration so it will do less harm.

We have a series of quotations which describe the disadvantages of various afflictions. The first is from the *Friendly Letter* of Nāgārjuna:

> Excitement and regret, malice, lethargy and sleep,
> Desire for pleasure, and doubt—
> Understand these five afflictions
> As thieves that steal the treasure of virtue.

Excitement is a distracted mind that wants to wander away from the object of focus and go towards desired objects. When you are sitting in meditation and trying to concentrate, excitement is the part of the mind that says, "I don't want to sit here; I want to think about that over there." It is the mind being distracted by pleasurable past experiences; it wants to enjoy that memory by returning to it and thinking about it.

As for *regret,* there is a kind of sorrow that you *should* have when you have done something wrong. When you have committed nonvirtuous actions and subsequently understood the faults of those actions, regret is a very positive step towards purifying those misdeeds. But regret towards virtuous actions is a problem. For example, if others abuse you verbally, you may decide that instead of responding with anger and harsh words, you will be patient and try to calm them down by being friendly in return. But later, when you think back on the incident, your anger rises and you think, "Why did I do that? I let them get away with their insults when I should have attacked them and made them feel as bad as they made me feel." This is regret towards virtuous action and it directly undermines your virtuous practice.

Lethargy causes the mind to become dark, listless, and insensitive, so you cannot discern the object of attention clearly. It makes the mind and body feel heavy, and it leads to sleepiness.

The faults associated with some of these subsidiary afflictions are elaborated in the *Exhortation to Wholehearted Resolve (Adhyāśaya-saṃcodana-sūtra):*

> Phlegm, wind, and bile
> Occur predominantly in the bodies
> Of those who take pleasure in sleep and lethargy.
> Their elements are completely out of balance.
>
> For those who take pleasure in lethargy and sleep,
> Their stomachs are not clean due to impure food.
> Their bodies feel heavy, their complexions are unhealthy,
> And even the words they speak are unclear.

And it continues:

> Those who take pleasure in lethargy and sleep
> Become confused and their interest in Dharma declines.
> They degenerate from even the virtues of immature beings,
> Their positive qualities decline and they head towards darkness.

Concerning *laziness,* the *Mindfulness of the Excellent Teaching* says:

> The single foundation of the afflictions
> Is laziness. Whoever has it—
> Whoever has a single instance of laziness—
> Is a person completely without the Dharma.

Laziness is a state of mind that hinders you from applying yourself to virtuous action—even to obtain a worldly goal—because of a lack of energy or sleepiness. Even when you *want* to take positive action, because of your laziness you lack the will, and you are seduced by the pleasure of lying down, doing nothing, and falling asleep. Laziness undermines enthusiastic perseverance, causes previously acquired virtuous qualities to degenerate, and prevents future virtues from developing.

About *carelessness,* the *Collection of Indicative Verses* says:

Those who indulge in careless behavior
Are immature people who waste their minds.
Wise people take great care,
The way a merchant protects his precious goods.

Concerning the affliction of *immodesty,* the *Garland of Birth Stories* says:

It would be better to wear rags and carry a beggar's bowl,
While watching the opulence of your enemy's mansion,
Than to cast aside shame, violating the Dharma in your mind,
Even if it brought you dominion over the gods.

On *forgetfulness,* Nāgārjuna says in his *Friendly Letter:*

Lord, mindfulness of the body is taught
As the only road for those traveling to the state of the Sugatas.
Attend to mindfulness and guard it well,
For when it degenerates all virtues will be destroyed.

And Śāntideva has this to say about *inattention* in *Engaging in the Bodhisattva Deeds:*

Even those who are learned, possess faith,
And apply themselves with diligent perseverance,
Will become defiled by downfalls
Because of the fault of inattention.

The affliction of inattention is a lack of introspective alertness. It is not knowing what is going on in your body and mind, and it is due to a lack of interest and lack of awareness. As we have discussed, introspective alertness is a mental spy that constantly observes what is coming in and what is going out of the mind-body continuum. If you want to maintain pure ethical conduct, mindfulness and introspective alertness must constantly be working together, standing guard at the door of the senses. The affliction of inattention—the lack of introspective alertness—is like being without protection. When there is no guard at the door, there is no telling what negative thoughts and actions may take hold of your body and mind.

Therefore, Śāntideva says, even a highly qualified person who has studied the teachings and understands the difference between good and bad must pay attention to what is going on in his or her mind. Even for those who have faith in the Dharma and are working hard on the path, if they fail to pay attention to what is happening in their mind and what they are doing with their body, their ethics will become corrupted.

The highest spiritual attainment

These stanzas provide a concise presentation of the dangers you face if you fall under the influence of these rudimentary and subsidiary afflictions. Tsongkhapa offers this advice: even if you are not able to completely prevent these afflictions from arising, it is absolutely essential that you understand that they are true enemies. You must not befriend them and take their side, so that when they say, "Do this," you respond, "Yes, my lord." That is the indispensable message of this teaching right now: you must see these afflictions as enemies, take the side of the antidotes, and strive to eliminate them. Whatever level of vows you have taken, whatever system of ethical conduct you have committed to, whether you are a layperson or a fully ordained renunciate, you should protect the purity of those commitments. Even though you cannot achieve everything you hope for right now, if you pursue this endeavor with perseverance you will eventually succeed. This was the heart of the practice of the great Kadampa practitioners, who were the direct students of Atiśa.

The glorious Gonpawa, a disciple of Atiśa, said to Neusurpa:

> If tomorrow or the day after, someone were to ask all of your virtuous practitioners, "What is the very pith of the special instructions?" the answer might come: "It is to obtain supernatural knowledge," or "To achieve a direct vision of one's meditational deity." However, the answer should be: "It is making my understanding of the cause and effect of karma more and more certain, so that I can protect the purity of whatever vows I have taken."

Gonpawa was not satisfied by the idea that high tantric achievements, like a direct experience of the deity, was the essence of the practice. To him a person who said, "I saw my deity," was nothing too great. The real practitioner would say that understanding karma is the heart of the matter. It is based on that understanding that you will be able to keep whatever vows you have taken, whether they are vows of individual liberation, bodhisattva vows, or tantric vows. In his view, that is the best form of practice. If you maintain pure ethical conduct, you have established a foundation upon which you can build all the other practices of the Hinayana, Mahayana, and Vajrayana systems. All inner development must begin with this foundation. The person who recognizes that is the true practitioner.

Many Buddhist teachings make this point: the purpose of Buddhist practice is to subdue the obscuring afflictions. The afflictions are the cause of negative actions, and negative actions are the cause of all future suffering. By eliminating the afflictions and preventing nonvirtuous actions, you place yourself on the path to freedom. All levels of practice—from personal emancipation up to perfect buddhahood in order to liberate other sentient beings—grow from that fundamental discipline of maintaining pure ethical conduct.

Therefore, when we speak of the spiritual attainments that result from prolonged meditation practice, the "common" or "lower" attainments are the seemingly miraculous powers, such as directly communicating with your meditational deity, or such powers as accumulating wealth, living a long life, or reading minds. The "highest" spiritual attainment is actually diminishing the power of the afflictions, and eventually eliminating them from the root. When your meditation starts producing that kind of result, then you know you are on the right track.

When people in the world get into a bitter disagreement, they turn all their attention and energy toward actions intended to damage their enemy. Of course, the main result of those actions will be suffering for themselves in this and future lives. Nevertheless, there is no limit to the discomfort, pain, and injury that people will endure in order to defeat and destroy an enemy. Some are even willing to sacrifice their lives for no other purpose than to harm those they dislike. Then, when the fight is over, people proudly display their battle scars to show off their heroism and say, "Here is the wound I received when I helped to crush the foe."

If people are willing to bear such burdens and go to such extremes to accomplish worldly, nonvirtuous goals, which will only bring them disastrous consequences in the future, how much more sensible and appropriate it is to bear the difficulties you may encounter in the effort to destroy the obscuring afflictions. Since the afflictions are the real enemy, the true source of all your difficulties, you should be willing to endure any hardship to accomplish the ultimate goal of bringing an end to them.

When you destroy an external enemy, nothing good comes of it. You only bring suffering upon them and upon yourself, and there is a good chance that their supporters will return for revenge. But when you destroy the inner enemy of the afflictions, they can never return, and the consequences will be nothing but peace, happiness, and freedom from suffering. Then, if you return from the hardships of years spent meditating in a cave and you show off the sores on your legs, or the pain in your back, you will be justified in saying, "This is the wound I received while battling the inner afflictions in my cave." There is no comparison between this kind of heroism and the other.

This is exactly what the great Śāntideva says in *Engaging in the Bodhisattva Deeds:*

> If even scars inflicted by meaningless enemies
> Are displayed on the body like ornaments,
> Why should suffering be a hardship for me,
> Who unfailingly strives to achieve the great purpose?

The "great purpose" is to attain enlightenment for the sake of other sentient beings. A practitioner who sincerely wants to achieve that goal must be willing to put up with many types of discomfort and even physical pain. But if you are enduring suffering for the sake of ultimate emancipation, why would you consider that to be a hardship? In that case, the hardship itself becomes the antidote, the cause of emancipation. In this verse by Śāntideva, the practitioner is asking himself this question: "Why can't I happily endure the troubles I will face on this path when the goal is such a great and ultimate purpose?"

Those who struggle against the inner enemy of the afflictions will ultimately achieve victory. That is why the Buddha is often called the "Victorious One" or the "Conqueror" in the scriptures. The person who realizes *that* victory is the one who is properly called a "hero." Ordinary heroes, renowned in battle and famous for killing many enemies, have not really accomplished very much because the people they killed were going to die anyway. What is heroic about that? You might as well kill a corpse. When you kill your human enemies the only thing you accomplish is to bring suffering on yourself, because only you will experience the results of that karma. Your enemy only gets death, which is their fate in any case. But you heap terrible new sufferings upon yourself, which is, after all, just what your enemy would wish. As Śāntideva puts it:

> Those who utterly disregard all sufferings
> To destroy enemies such as hatred—
> They are the conquering heroes,
> The others merely kill corpses.

Therefore, Śāntideva says a little later, you should remain fearless and unperturbed by the afflictions, because you have the power to conquer them:

> When I find myself encircled by a crowd of afflictions,
> I shall stand up to them in a thousand ways;
> Just as lions are not bothered by foxes and such,
> I will not be harmed by the host of afflictions.

You live with the afflictions constantly threatening you; one minute desire is arising, the next minute jealousy, and then comes hatred. You must understand clearly that these are your most dangerous enemies, and you must stand up to them with courage. Standing up to them means always resisting the urge to yield to their temptations. In order to do that you may face many discomforts, hardships, and pain, but whatever difficulties you may face, you must bear them with the enthusiasm of knowing that you are on the path that will finally vanquish these enemies.

Śāntideva says that you should be like the lion, who is the king of the beasts. A lion may be surrounded by foxes, or jackals, or other animals who might like to kill and eat him, but it does not bother him, and he rests with utter confidence, because he knows that he has the power to subdue all of his enemies. Like the lion, your mind should rest with the confidence that, through the cultivation of wisdom and virtuous practice, you cannot be defeated by any afflictions, and that ultimately you have the power to subdue them.

In this way, says Tsongkhapa, you should not let any of the factors that are contradictory to the path harm or disturb you. Instead, you should conquer them all. As a practitioner, wherever you stay—whether it is in a solitary cave or in the swirl of busy crowds—you should never allow yourself to be wounded by the afflictions. You should rest comfortably in the safety of compassion, loving-kindness, and virtuous thought. Regardless of what conditions you encounter, what adversity may seem to block your way, you should rest securely under the indestructible protection of pure ethical conduct, the compassionate motivation, and the wisdom that sees the true nature of things.

That is the real victory over the afflictions. When you practice with that approach you will be able to maintain pure ethical conduct, and with that you will build a solid foundation for all future progress on the spiritual path. When you plant seeds in pure, good earth, healthy and abundant fruit will grow. Building a foundation of pure ethical conduct is just like the good earth, and all of the abundant fruit of the spiritual path will grow out of that pure ground.

Appendix: Outline of the Text

THE OUTLINE USED in the commentary was created by Tsongkhapa to organize his massive text. We have used the same outline so that readers of this commentary can refer to the relevant sections of the original Tibetan and the English translation of the *Lamrim Chenmo.* To make it as easy as possible for readers to use this commentary along with the English translation of the *Lamrim Chenmo,* The Lamrim Chenmo Translation Committee and Snow Lion Publications graciously gave us permission to use their format of the outline headings. We also follow their practice of including the outline for each chapter's content at the beginning of the chapter. While our translation of the outline differs in some cases from the one that appears in the English translation of the *Lamrim Chenmo,* these differences are minimal and should not cause any confusion.

In this appendix, two sets of numbers follow each outline topic. The first number refers the reader to the page on which this topic is discussed in this commentary. The second number refers the reader to the page in the edition of the Tibetan text published by the People's Press, mTsho sngon, Xining, 1985, and reprinted in Dharamsala, 1991. To find the page number in the English translation of the *Lamrim Chenmo, The Great Treatise on the Stages of the Path to Enlightenment,* the reader should refer to Appendix 1 of that work.

- 3" If an action is not performed, its results will not be met [31, 162]
- 4" Actions that are done do not perish [33, 162]

Chapter 2
The Varieties of Karma [35, 162]

- b" Contemplating specific categories of karma [36, 162]
  - 1" The principal teaching of the ten karmic paths [36, 163]
  - 2" Establishing karma and its results [45, 165]
    - (a) Nonvirtuous karma and its results [45, 165]
      - (i) The actual nonvirtuous karmic paths [45, 165]
      - (ii) Distinguishing heavy and light karma [72, 174]
        - (a') The heaviness and lightness of the ten karmic paths [72, 174]
        - (b') An ancillary presentation of a selection of some of the heaviest karmas [81, 177]
          - (1') Powerful in terms of the field [82, 177]
          - (2') Powerful in terms of the actor [86,179]
          - (3') Powerful in terms of the substance [91, 181]
          - (4') Powerful in terms of the attitude [92, 181]
      - (iii) A presentation of the results [96, 182]
        - (a') Fruitional results [97, 182]
        - (b') Results corresponding to the cause [97, 182]
        - (c') Environmental results [100, 183]
    - (b) Virtuous karma and its results [104, 184]
      - (i) Virtuous karma [104, 184]
      - (ii) The results of virtuous karma [105, 185]

(c) A presentation of other classifications of karma [109, 185]
(i) The distinction between projecting and completing karma [109, 185]
(ii) Karma whose result will definitely or not definitely be experienced [113, 186]

2' Contemplating karma and its results in detail [119, 188]
a" The qualities of the eight fruitions [120, 189]
b" The effects of the eight fruitions [123, 189]
c" The causes of the eight fruitions [126, 190]

Chapter 3
Cultivating Ethical Behavior [135, 192]

3' Having contemplated the principles of karma, how to engage in virtue and desist from nonvirtue [135, 192]
a" A general presentation [135, 192]
b" In particular, how to purify by means of the four opponent powers [148, 195]
1" The first power: remorse [150, 196]
2" The second power: applying antidotes [153, 196]
3" The third power: turning away from faults [159, 197]
4" The fourth power: reliance [160, 197]

Chapter 4
The Attitude of a Person of Small Scope [175, 203]

b) The measure of the attitude of a person of small spiritual scope [175, 203]
c) Clearing up misconceptions concerning the attitude of a person of small spiritual scope [177, 203]

Chapter 5
The Eight Types of Suffering [183, 206]

2) Training the mind in the stages of the path shared with persons of intermediate capacity [186, 206]
   a) The actual training to develop the attitude of the person of intermediate spiritual scope [190, 207]
      i) Identifying the mind that strives for emancipation [190, 207]
      ii) The method for producing the mind that strives for emancipation [191, 208]
         a' Contemplating suffering and the cause of suffering [192, 208]
            1' Contemplating the truth of suffering: the faults of cyclic existence [193, 209]
               a" Explaining the significance of the Buddha's having taught the truth of suffering first among the four noble truths [193, 209]
               b" The actual meditation on suffering [198, 211]
                  1" Contemplating the general sufferings of cyclic existence [198, 211]
                     (a) Contemplating the eight types of suffering [199, 211]
                        (i) The suffering of birth [202, 212]
                        (ii) The suffering of aging [208, 216]
                        (iii) The suffering of sickness [212, 217]
                        (iv) The suffering of death [214, 218]
                        (v) The suffering of encountering the unpleasant [217, 219]
                        (vi) The suffering of separating from the pleasant [218, 219]
                        (vii) The suffering of not getting what you want [219, 219]
                        (viii) The suffering of the appropriating aggregates [219, 219]

Chapter 6
The Six Types of Suffering [225, 221]

(b) Contemplating the six types of suffering [225, 221]

(i) The fault of uncertainty [225, 221]
(ii) The fault of insatiability [228, 221]
(iii) The fault of repeatedly losing one's life [232, 223]
(iv) The fault of having to take rebirth repeatedly [233, 224]
(v) The fault of constantly fluctuating from high to low states [235, 224]
(vi) The fault of having no companions [239, 226]

Chapter 7
Further Meditations on Suffering [243, 226]

(c) Contemplating the three types of suffering [243, 226]
(i) The suffering of change [243, 227]
(ii) The suffering of suffering [244, 227]
(iii) The suffering of conditionality [245, 227]
2" Contemplating specific sufferings [252, 229]
(a) The suffering of human beings [252, 229]
(b) The suffering of the demigods [253, 230]
(c) The suffering of the devas [254, 230]
(i) The suffering of the devas of the desire realm [254, 230]
(a') The suffering of dying and falling [254, 230]
(1') The suffering of dying [254, 230]
(2') The suffering of falling to a lower state [257, 231]
(b') The suffering of being frightened [258, 231]
(c') The sufferings of being cut, gashed, killed, and banished [258, 231]
(ii) The suffering of the gods of the form and formless realms [260, 232]

Chapter 8
The Origin of Suffering [265, 232]

2' Contemplating the process of cyclic existence in terms of its origin [266, 232]
- a" How the obscuring afflictions arise [266, 232]
  - 1" Identifying the obscuring afflictions [267, 233]
  - 2" The process of their production [275, 235]
  - 3" The causes of the obscuring afflictions [278, 235]
  - 4" The faults of the obscuring afflictions [281, 236]
- b" How that causes karma to be accumulated [287, 237]
  - 1" Identifying the karma that is accumulated [287, 237]
    - (a) Karma that is intention [288, 237]
    - (b) Karma that is intended action [289, 237]
  - 2" How karma is accumulated [292, 238]
    - (a) Accumulating karma for pleasant feelings [301, 240]
      - (i) Accumulating karma for the pleasure that comes from enjoying desirable objects: sights, sounds, and the like [301, 241]
      - (ii) Accumulating karma for gaining bliss in meditative concentration, after you have rejected attachments to external sensual pleasures [302, 241]
    - (b) Accumulating karma for neutral feelings [302, 241]
- c" The process of death and rebirth [304, 241]
  - 1" Conditions of death [304, 241]
  - 2" The mind at the time of death [305, 242]
    - (a) Dying with a virtuous mind [305, 242]
    - (b) Dying with a nonvirtuous mind [309, 242]
    - (c) Dying with a neutral mind [311, 243]
  - 3" Where heat gathers [312, 244]
  - 4" How you reach the intermediate state after death [312, 244]
  - 5" How you then take rebirth [316, 246]

Chapter 9
The Twelve Links of Dependent Origination [323, 248]

- b' Contemplating the twelve links of dependent origination [323, 248]
  - 1' The division into twelve links [325, 249]
  - 2' The condensed presentation of the links [337, 252]
  - 3' How many lifetimes are required to complete the cycle [346, 254]
  - 4' How to summarize their significance [352, 256]

Chapter 10
The Attitude of a Person of Intermediate Scope [361, 257]

- b) The measure of having produced the attitude of a person of intermediate scope [361, 257]
- c) Clarifying misconceptions [364, 258]

Chapter 11
Ascertaining the Nature of the Path Leading to Liberation [371, 261]

- d) Establishing the nature of the path that leads to liberation [371, 261]
  - i) What kind of life can overcome cyclic existence [374, 263]
  - ii) What kind of path you must cultivate to overcome cyclic existence [389, 267]
    - a' Specifying the number of trainings as three [389, 267]
      - 1' Specifying the number in terms of the stages of subduing the mind [390, 267]
      - 2' Specifying the number in terms of the results [391, 268]
      - 3' Specifying the number in terms of the objects to be abandoned [392, 268]
    - b' Ascertaining the order of the three trainings [393, 268]

Chapter 12
The Nature of the Three Trainings [395, 268]

- c' The nature of the three trainings [395, 268]

Glossary

Abhidharma *(chos mngon pa)*. The Abhidharma, one of three major sections of the Buddhist canon, contains texts that systemize and classify the essence of the Buddha's teachings found in the sutras. This body of commentarial texts is encyclopedic in that it deals with Buddhist ontology, psychology, cosmology, the operation of karma and affliction, the path to liberation, and the nature of its stages and attainments. *See* Tripiṭaka.

absorption of cessation *('gog pa'i snyoms 'jug)*. A level of meditative absorption, similar to but higher than the absorption of nondiscrimination, that arrests the mind and mental factors. By cultivating this absorption one will be reborn in the Peak of Existence, the highest level of the formless realm. It can only be attained by ārya beings because it is only by means of the supermundane path that it can be reached. Beings enter this absorption with a virtuous motivation, wishing to abide in a peaceful state where desires and afflictions are pacified.

absorption of nondiscrimination *('du shes med pa'i snyoms 'jug)*. A level of meditative absorption that arrests the mind and mental factors from the moment of one's entering this absorption until arising from it. The karmic result is to be born in one's next life among the beings of nondiscrimination on the level of the fourth concentration. Ordinary individuals can mistake this state for liberation, but ārya beings avoid it as a pitfall.

actualizing karma *(grub byed kyi las)*. *See* completing karma.

afflictions *(nyon mongs; Skt: kleśa)*. Obscuring afflictions, such as desire, hostility, and ignorance, are the obstacles to emancipation. They are nonvirtuous mental states that obscure the mind from seeing reality in its true nature and motivate actions (karma) that cause one to continue to be born in cyclic existence.

appropriating aggregates *(nyer len gyi phung po)*. The five aggregates in their aspect of grasping at the desires of samsara. Grasping (or appropriating) out of attachment is the cause for perpetually taking rebirth in samsara (i.e., taking aggregates). Because the five appropriating aggregates are inextricably bound up with karma and afflictions, their nature is suffering.

arhat *(dgra bcom pa)*. A person who has attained nirvana, the final goal of the Hinayana path.

ārya *('phags pa)*. A person who has achieved a direct realization of emptiness *(śūnyatā)*, the true nature of all phenomena. Literally, *ārya* means "noble" or "superior" being. *See also* ordinary individual.

automatic transgressions *(mtshams med lnga)*. These are the five heinous actions that lead to a bad rebirth without any intervening lifetime: killing your father, your mother, or an arhat, deliberately drawing blood from a buddha with the intent to do harm, and causing a schism in the Sangha.

Avīci *(mnar med pa)*. The lowest and most suffering level of the eight great hot hells.

bhikṣu *(dge slong)*. Fully ordained monk.

bhikṣuṇī *(dge slong ma)*. Fully ordained nun.

bhūmi *(sa)*. Bodhisattva stages.

bodhicitta *(byang chub kyi sems)*. The altruistic mind of enlightenment. The motivation to become a buddha in order to benefit other sentient beings caught in the misery of samsara.

bodhisattva *(byang chub sems dpa')*. A person who has entered the Mahayana path. Such beings have a continuous, spontaneous wish to attain enlightenment in order to benefit other sentient beings.

body-mind continuum. *See* five aggregates.

Bön *(bon)*. The shamanistic religion that dominated Tibet before the advent of Buddhism.

completing karma *(rdzogs byed kyi las)*. The supporting causes and conditions that actualize and bring to fruition a seed of projecting karma. *See also* projecting karma.

contaminated phenomena *(zag bcas kyi chos)*. Phenomena are called contaminated if they increase afflicted states of mind that lead to suffering. All phenomena are contaminated except for those in the following four categories: the three uncompounded phenomena (space and the two types of cessation) and phenomena included in the truth of the path.

desire realm *('dod khams)*. All beings in the samsaric world live in one of three realms: the desire, form, or formless realms. Each realm is dominated by particular types of afflictions; the predominant affliction in the desire realm is desire or attachment—in particular the craving for the sensual pleasures of sex and food.

deva *(lha)*. Deities or gods. In Buddhism, those beings called gods have extremely pleasurable and long lives, but they are still caught in samsara. Their lives are not permanent, and they do not have the power to end their own or others' cycle of misery.

Dharma *(chos).* The teachings of the Buddha and his followers.

dharmakāya *(chos sku).* In the Mahayana system there is a discussion of the three *kāyas,* or bodies, of a buddha: the dharmakāya, saṃbhogakāya, and nirmāṇakāya. The dharmakāya—the wisdom body—is ultimate and immaculate wisdom; it is the mind that has been transformed beyond all states of impurity. The latter two bodies—the saṃbhogakāya and the nirmāṇakāya—are together called the form body *(rūpakāya)* of a buddha and are manifestations, in various forms, of the perfect wisdom of dharmakāya.

downfall *(ltung ba).* An action that would not necessarily be negative if performed by a layperson who has not taken any vows but is negative because it involves breaking a vow one has taken. *See also* misdeed.

eight worldly concerns *('jig rten chos brgyad).* The eight worldly concerns, or dharmas, are preoccupation with the following four pairs: gain and loss, pleasure and pain, praise and scorn, and fame and ill repute. These four pairs encapsulate an ordinary person's concerns. People desire the first member of each pair and wish to avoid the second.

embarrassment *(khrel yod pa).* An attitude that turns away from nonvirtuous actions out of concern for what others might think, or concern that your spiritual friends will be displeased.

emptiness *(stong nyid).* Emptiness, suchness, or śūnyatā, is the final nature of all phenomena: their absence of inherent existence.

environmental results *(bdag po'i 'bras bu).* Karmic results that manifest as one's external surrounding environment, possessions, and material circumstances.

extremely hidden phenomena *(shin tu lkog tu gyur pa).* One of the three types of objects of knowledge. The first two are phenomena that can be known directly through the senses and those that can be inferred through the use of logic. Extremely hidden phenomena are those that are too subtle for ordinary beings to know directly by these two means. To know these phenomena one must put trust in the word of the Buddha until one attains the realizations that bring direct knowledge.

five aggregates *(phung po lnga).* Form, feeling, discrimination, formative activity, and consciousness. Ignorance causes us to grasp at these impermanent collections as a unitary, inherently existent self. This self-grasping is a fundamental cause of our perpetual suffering in cyclic existence. *See also* appropriating aggregates.

five paths *(lam lnga).* The five consecutive paths leading to or culminating in enlightenment. These consist of: (1) the path of accumulation *(tshogs lam),* during which one begins to amass the accumulation of merit and wisdom that will ripen in enlightenment; (2) the path of preparation *(sbyor lam),* so named because (apart from Hinayana ārya beings or arhats who later enter into the Mahayana paths) practitioners are preparing for a direct realization of emptiness, during which they progress through four levels—heat, peak, patience, and supreme dharma—as their conceptual understanding of emptiness becomes more and more subtle; (3) the path of seeing *(mthong lam),* during which one sees emptiness directly and nonconceptually for the first time and ceases to be an ordinary individual, becoming an ārya being (Note: This description does not apply to practitioners who become āryas or arhats on the Hinayana paths and later enter into the Mahayana paths. Such practitioners already realized emptiness directly on the Hinayana paths; from the first bodhisattva ground up to and including the seventh, those arhats are engaged in fulfilling the accumulation of merit and thereafter in removing the knowledge obstacles.); (4) the path of meditation *(sgom lam),* during which one continuously familiarizes oneself with the emptiness that was initially and directly cognized on the path of seeing, thereby gradually eliminating the obstacles connected with each stage of development; and (5) the path of no further training *(mi slob lam),* in which there is no longer any need to abandon further obstacles or develop new realizations. At this point the final fruit of their respective spiritual journeys is achieved: those who followed the Mahayana path of the bodhisattva attain perfectly complete buddhahood, while those who followed the Hinayana path attain arhatship.

form body *(gzugs sku).* The saṃbhogakāya and the nirmāṇakāya; together these two are referred to as the form body *(rūpakāya)* of the Buddha. They are manifestations of perfect wisdom in various forms. *See also* saṃbhogakāya; nirmāṇakāya.

formless realm *(gzugs med khams).* When an individual attains a meditative absorption of the formless realm and then passes away, his or her four mental aggregates are born into one of the four levels of the formless realm, called the *four formless absorptions.* Because the beings in this realm do not possess obstructive form, the formless realm is without a physical dimension.

form realm *(gzugs khams).* Along with the desire realm and the formless realm, this is one of the three realms of samsaric existence. Its basic divisions are the *four concentrations.* Each of the first three concentrations has three levels, and the fourth concentration has eight levels; a particular type of "form-realm god" resides on each of these seventeen levels.

foundation consciousness *(kun gzhi rnam par shes pa; Skt: ālaya-vijñāna).* The Yogācāra school of Buddhism holds that there are eight types of consciousness. The eighth type, foundation consciousness, is the principal consciousness underlying the remaining minds and all of experience. It is the level of mind upon which karmic seeds are planted; it carries those seeds through time until they ripen into experience. Because of its function as the repository of karmic seeds, it is often translated as the "storehouse consciousness."

four concentrations *(bsam gtan bzhi).* The four levels of existence in the form realm. From the first up to the fourth concentration, beings abide in increasingly subtle levels of meditative absorption.

four formless absorptions. *See* formless realm.

four great elements *('byung ba chen po).* The indivisible building blocks of material existence: earth, water, fire, and wind. Each performs its particular function: earth provides support, water brings cohesion, fire ripens, wind increases and expands.

four noble truths *('phags pa'i bden pa bzhi).* The principal subject matter of Buddha's first discourse: (1) the truth of suffering, (2) the truth of the cause of suffering, (3) the truth of the cessation of suffering, and (4) the truth of the path to cessation.

fruitional result *(rnam smin gyi 'bras bu).* The main results of the ripening of a karmic seed. The fruitional result is the type of rebirth you take and is distinguished from *environmental results* and *results corresponding to the cause,* which together determine the variety of experiences one meets while in that particular type of rebirth.

garuḍa *(khyung).* The mythic king of birds who destroys poisonous snakes, which are symbolic of anger.

Gelug *(dge lugs).* The school of Tibetan Buddhism founded by Tsongkhapa and his disciples.

geshe *(dge bshes).* A contraction of *geyway sheynyen (dge ba'i bshes gnyen),* which means virtuous friend, spiritual friend, or guru. In the Gelug school of Tibetan Buddhism it is the title bestowed on those scholars who complete the course of study at one of the three great monasteries.

guru *(bla ma).* Spiritual teacher.

Hinayana (*theg dman; Skt: hīnayāna).* The Vehicle of Smaller Scope, leading to the attainment of nirvana, personal liberation from suffering.

ignorance *(ma rig pa).* A lack of realization of the final nature of all phenomena; the innate belief that things exist as substantial, independent, self-sufficient entities.

intermediate state *(bar do).* The state a being enters after death and before one's next rebirth.

introspective awareness *(shes bzhin).* A mental factor that, like a spy, constantly observes what is happening within one's mind-body continuum.

Jambudvīpa *('dzam bu gling).* According to Buddhist cosmology, there are four continents surrounding Mount Meru, the *axis mundi,* and the human world is located on Jambudvīpa, the southern continent.

Jātaka tales *(skyes rabs).* Edifying stories about the previous lives of the Buddha when he was a bodhisattva on the path to full enlightenment.

Kadam *(bka' gdams).* The school of Tibetan Buddhism established by followers of Atiśa.

kalpa *(bskal pa).* A kalpa is 4,320 million years, commonly referred to as one eon.

karma *(las). Karma* means action. There is the contaminated action of sentient beings and the uncontaminated action of buddhas. Every contaminated action of body, speech, and mind plants a seed of potential on the mental continuum that will eventually ripen into experience. Virtuous action (i.e., virtuous karma) ripens into pleasant experience, and nonvirtuous action ripens into unpleasant experience.

lama *(bla ma).* Spiritual teacher, guru.

lamrim *(lam rim).* The term *lamrim* literally means the "stages of the path." The lamrim method is a progressive system of teachings and meditations organized to lead the practitioner from the very beginning of the spiritual path, through the middle phase, and ultimately all the way to buddhahood.

Madhyamaka *(dbu ma).* A Mahayana school of philosophy based on the writings of Nāgārjuna. It is called the "Middle Way" school because it teaches the doctrine of emptiness *(śunyatā)* as a middle position between the extremes of nihilism and inherent existence.

Mahayana path *(theg chen gyi lam; Skt: mahāyāna).* The Mahayana path is an outline of the essential methods leading to the goal of perfect buddhahood. The Mahayana disciple wishes to become a buddha so that he or she can help free all other beings from suffering. In contrast, the goal for the followers of the Hinayana path is liberation from suffering for themselves alone.

mandala *(dkyil khor; Skt: maṇḍala).* In the tantric context *mandala* refers to the pure abode of a meditational deity. The term is also used to denote the traditional Buddhist representation of the physical universe as a circle of four continents surrounding Mount Meru. *See also* Mount Meru.

māras *(bdud).* Māras are demonic forces. According to the *Ornament for Clear Knowledge (Abhisamayālaṃkāra)*, the four māras are (1) the contaminated aggregates, (2) the obscuring afflictions, (3) death, and (4) the Divine-Youth demon, which represents the obstacles preventing one from overcoming the other three.

meditational deity *(yi dam).* A tantric form of a buddha that a practitioner worships as well as strives to become. The deity, or yidam, guides the practitioner along the path to enlightenment; the practitioner's subsequent enlightenment will be experienced in the form and nature of that yidam.

mental afflictions. *See* afflictions.

mindfulness *(dran pa).* A mental factor that functions to hold the mind to its object, not letting the mind forget about or move away from its object. It is the quality of mind that does not forget which objects are suitable to engage in and which should be avoided.

misdeed *(sdig pa).* A nonvirtuous action that is negative karma regardless of whether the person committing it has taken a vow against performing it or not. *See also* downfall.

Mount Meru *(ri rab).* The central four-sided mountain which is the *axis mundi* of the universe. Its upper regions are the abodes of the gods. Surrounding it are rings of oceans and mountains and the four continents. The world of humans is located on the southern continent, Jambudvīpa.

mundane path *('jig rten pa'i lam).* A method of temporarily subduing the afflictions through the practice of single-pointed concentration and meditating on the faults of the level of existence one is trying to transcend. This method is common to both Buddhists and non-Buddhists and can lead to the highest levels of meditative absorption and rebirth in higher realms, but it does not eliminate afflictions from the root.

nāga *(klu).* Nāgas are demigods with the head of a human and the body of a snake who generally live underground or in lakes and rivers. They are sometimes considered to be part of the animal realm.

negative tendencies *(gnas ngan len).* The potential, carried within every being in cyclic existence in the form of karma and afflictions, to experience undesirable circumstances. Because birth in samsara is inextricably bound up with these negative tendencies, it inevitably contains the potential to manifest pain and suffering.

neutral action *(lung ma bstan).* An action that is neither virtuous nor nonvirtuous.

nirvana *(mya ngan las 'das pa; Skt: nirvāṇa).* Liberation from samsara; freedom from all suffering; the attainment of an arhat.

nonrevealing karma *(rnam par rig byed ma yin pa'i las).* A karma (an action) is revealing if it enables others to understand your motivation. When you act physically, with either body or speech, you provide information to others concerning the intention that drives that physical act. Nonrevealing karma is the ongoing potentiality that is set in motion by that physical, revealing action of body or speech. It is the form in which the karma persists in the psycho-physical continuum. But it remains entirely inaccessible to our senses; it reveals nothing.

obscuring afflictions. *See* afflictions.

obstructions to liberation *(nyon sgrib).* There are two types of obscurations that must be removed in order to obtain buddhahood. The obstructions to liberation are the obscuring afflictions preventing one from attaining liberation from cyclic existence; when they are removed one attains arhatship. However, as the result of previous habitual engagement in the ignorance of cyclic existence, one still possesses subtle obscurations. In order to obtain complete buddhahood, one must remove these subtle obstructions to omniscience *(shes sgrib)* as well. Once these are removed one obtains omniscience or buddhahood.

obstructions to omniscience *(shes sgrib). See* obstructions to liberation.

one-day ordination vows *(bsnyen gnas).* A set of vows that can be taken by laypeople in which one commits to observing eight precepts for one full day. The first five of these precepts are the same as the five vows of a lay person *(dge bsnyen):* not to kill, not to steal, not to lie, not to take intoxicants, and to refrain from sexual misconduct (which is here extended to include all sexual activity). The three additional vows are (1) not to eat after the midday meal; (2) not to sing, dance, or play music, and not to wear rosaries as ornaments, jewelry, or perfumes; and (3) not to use a high or grand seat or bed. The vows are taken before dawn, and they last for twenty-four hours.

ordinary being/ordinary individual *(so so'i skye bo).* A being who has not reached the state of an ārya, or superior being.

parinirvāṇa *(yongs su mya ngan las 'das pa).* Final nirvana; the state entered when an arhat or buddha "passes away" at the end of his or her life.

path of accumulation *(tshogs lam). See* five paths.

path of meditation *(sgom lam). See* five paths.

path of no more learning *(mi slob lam). See* five paths.

path of preparation *(sbyor lam). See* five paths.

path of seeing *(mthong lam). See* five paths.

perfections *(phar phyin). See* six perfections.

perfection vehicle *(phar phyin theg pa; Skt: pāramitāyāna).* The vehicle of the bodhisattva, emphasizing the practice of the perfections over a long period of time as the path to enlightenment.

prātimokṣa *(so so thar pa).* The "vows of individual liberation" laid out in the Vinaya and forming the basis of Buddhist ethics. There are eight types of prātimokṣa vows: lay vows for men and women, novice vows for monks and nuns, vows for probationary nuns, full ordination vows for monks and nuns, and one-day ordination vows for laypeople.

pratyekabuddha *(rang sangs rgyas).* Solitary realizers, so called because in their last lifetime prior to attaining liberation they stay alone—they do not interact with a teacher. Prior study and practice over many lives enable them to be silent and solitary during their last life, in which they attain the state of a Hinayana arhat.

preceptor *(mkhan po).* A senior monk or learned teacher who gives vows to junior students.

projecting karma *('phen byed kyi las).* The strong karma that projects or throws one into a particular type of rebirth. *See also* completing karma

psycho-physical complex. *See* five aggregates.

pure land *(zhing khams).* A buddhafield; an environment of unimaginably excellent qualities, far beyond our ordinary conception, attained as the result of the accumulation of merit.

renunciation *(nges 'byung).* Intense interest in attaining freedom from suffering.

results corresponding to the cause *(rgyu mthun gyi 'bras bu).* A karmic result that is similar to the cause that produced it. For example, the result that corresponds to killing is a shortened life.

revealing karma. *See* nonrevealing karma.

śamatha *(zhi gnas).* Single-pointed concentration; calm-abiding.

saṃbhogakāya *(longs sku).* The enjoyment body of a buddha. This is the perfected form in which a buddha attains enlightenment, the ultimate physical body, completely absorbed in enjoyment of the Mahayana Dharma. It is always present but is only perceptible to advanced-level bodhisattvas.

samsara *('khor ba; Skt: saṃsāra).* The uncontrolled taking of rebirth under the force of karma and the afflictions. The six realms of samsaric existence consist of three lower realms—the hells, hungry ghosts, and animals—and three higher realms—humans, demigods, and gods.

Sangha *(dge 'dun).* Assembly, community. Conventionally this refers to a group of at least four fully ordained monks or nuns. Ideally, this refers to anyone, lay or ordained, who has attained a direct realization of the ultimate nature of reality.

śāstras *(bstan bcos).* Independent works explaining religious topics and treatises on the sutras.

Sautrāntika *(mdo sde pa).* One of the four schools of Buddhist tenets.

Sera Je Monastery *(se ra byes grwa tshang).* A division of Sera Monastery, one of the three great Gelug monasteries in the vicinity of Lhasa, Tibet.

shame *(ngo tsha shes pa).* A mental factor that shuns faulty behavior with respect to oneself or the Dharma. It is defined in terms of its opposite, shamelessness: not having respect for virtue or people who have virtuous qualities.

siddhi *(dngos grub).* Spiritual attainments.

śīla *(tshul khrims).* Pure ethical conduct.

six perfections *(phar phyin drug; Skt: ṣaṭpāramitā).* The activities of practitioners on the Mahayana path after they have developed bodhicitta. The six perfections are giving, ethical conduct, patience, persevering effort, meditative concentration, and wisdom.

śrāvaka *(nyan thos).* Hearers; practitioners striving for their own liberation from samsara. They receive this name because—unlike pratyekabuddhas—they rely on listening to their teachers' instructions through the course of their spiritual practice.

stupa *(mchod rten; skt: stūpa).* Reliquary monument representative of the enlightened mind of a buddha.

subtle propensity *(bag chags).* This term refers to the obscuring afflictions in their latent status. Whether or not an affliction is active and present in the mind at a particular moment, it continuously abides at an unconscious level as a potentiality, a seed, or a subtle predisposition.

sugata *(bde bar gshegs pa).* An epithet of a buddha meaning "one who has reached the highest bliss" or "one who has gone well."

Sukhāvatī *(bde ba can).* The pure land of Amitabha.

śūnyatā *(stong nyid).* Suchness or emptiness; the final nature of all phenomena; the absence of inherent existence.

supermundane path *('jig rten las 'das pa'i lam).* The method of practice, unique to the Buddhadharma, leading to the direct realization of emptiness, which destroys karmic seeds from the root.

Sutra *(mdo; Skt: sūtra).* One of three major sections of the Buddhist canon, containing the general discourses (sutras) of the Buddha, largely dealing with topics of meditation. *See also* Tripiṭaka.

Sutrayana *(mdo'i theg pa; Skt: sūtrayāna).* The general Mahayana path, whose doctrines and practices are held in common by practitioners of the Tantrayana. *See also* perfection vehicle.

tantra *(rgyud).* The Tantrayana, or tantric path, is included in the Mahayana. In addition to the practices of the Sutrayana, the Tantrayana includes advanced meditation techniques to speed up progress to buddhahood. The texts containing these instructions are the tantras.

Tathāgata *(de bzhin gshegs pa).* The term the Buddha used to speak of himself after his enlightenment. It means "He who has gone thus on the path of all the buddhas."

thangka *(thang ga).* Tibetan religious painting, which can be rolled up for storage, usually done on canvas or cloth and framed by a border of brocade.

thirty-two major and eighty minor marks of a buddha *(mtshan dang dpe byad bzang po).* These are distinctive features of the form body of a buddha indicative of his supreme attainment. One common source of this list is Maitreya's *Ornament for Clear Knowledge.*

three poisons *(dug gsum).* The three root afflictions: desire, hostility, and ignorance.

three trainings *(bslab pa gsum).* Ethical conduct, meditative stabilization, and wisdom; these three together constitute the truth of the path.

Tripiṭaka *(sde snod gsum).* The Buddhist canon, consisting of the three "baskets" *(piṭaka)* of Sutra, Vinaya, and Abhidharma.

tsampa *(rtsam pa).* Roasted barley flour; one of the staple foods of Tibet.

tsa-tsa *(tsha tsha).* A small image of a holy being, produced from a mold and usually cast in clay.

Vaibhāṣika *(bye brag smra ba).* One of the four schools of Indian Buddhist tenets.

vajra *(rdo rje).* A ritual implement (fashioned after Indra's scepter) symbolic of the indestructible or adamantine nature of enlightened mind, or of emptiness. Paired with the bell, it is central to tantric practice, with the vajra representing method and the bell representing wisdom: the two aspects of the enlightened mind.

Vajrasattva *(rdo rje sems dpa').* A tantric buddha of purification.

Vajrayana *(rdo rje theg pa; Skt: vajrayāna).* Tantric vehicle. *See* tantra.

Vikramaśīla. One of several great Buddhist universities in north India.

Vinaya *('dul ba).* One of three major sections of the Buddhist canon, containing the scriptures dealing with ethical conduct. *See* Tripiṭaka.

vipaśyanā *(lhag mthong).* Superior wisdom; highest insight.

vows of individual liberation *(so sor thar pa'i sdom pa). See* prātimokṣa.

wisdom *(shes rab).* Perfect wisdom is realization of the final nature of all phenomena; it is direct comprehension of emptiness *(śunyatā),* the lack of inherent existence of self and phenomena.

yakṣa *(gnod sbyin).* A class of spirits generally considered harmful to human beings.

Yama *('chi bdag gshin rje).* Lord of Death.

yoga *(rnal 'byor).* Spiritual discipline, control.

Yogācāra *(rnal 'byor spyod pa)*. One of the four schools of Indian Buddhist tenets; a Mahayana school whose name means "the ones who practice yoga."

yogi *(rnal 'byor pa)*. An assiduous Dharma practitioner. Because they put the various teachings into strict daily practice, yogis (and their female counterparts, *yoginīs*) often adopt an ascetic lifestyle.

Notes

References are given for passages cited by Geshe Sopa that are not found in the *Lamrim Chenmo.* No references are provided for works quoted by Tsongkhapa in the *Lamrim Chenmo.* Readers interested in tracking particular quotations should refer to the translation of the *Lamrim Chenmo,* the *Great Treatise on the Stages of the Path to Enlightenment.*

Following is an example of a citation with an explanation of each element.

A B C D
Bodhisattva-caryāvatāra 1.4; P5272: 245.1.4–5.

A. Works are referenced according to the language in which they were composed.
B. If applicable, the chapter and verse of the cited work follows the title.
C. The abbreviation "P" followed by a number indicates the reference number of the text in the *Tibetan Tripiṭaka, Peking Edition* edited by D.T. Suzuki. The number of the volume in which the text is located can be found in the bibliography.
D. The numbers following the colon indicate the page, folio, and line numbers for the citation in the *Tibetan Tripiṭaka, Peking Edition.* If quotations continue over a number of lines or onto another folio, a hyphen is followed by a number indicating the termination point.

Notes to the Introduction

1 *Bodhisattva-caryāvatāra* 1:28; P5272:245.4.1–2.

2 Atiśa is the great Indian scholar who traveled to Tibet at the end of the tenth century to reconstitute the monastic lineage and reform the practice of Buddhism after it had passed through a period of degeneration. While in Tibet he composed a short text that summarizes the complete path called the *Lamp for the Path to Enlightenment.* Tsongkhapa wrote the *Lamrim Chenmo* as an extensive commentary on the teachings found in Atiśa's *Lamp for the Path.* At the very beginning of the *Lamrim Chenmo,* where he discusses "the greatness of the author in order to establish the authentic source of the teachings," Tsongkhapa presents a spiritual biography of Atiśa—essentially establishing Atiśa as the author of the lamrim tradition. (See the prologue and chapter 1 of volume 1 of this series.)

3 On Tsongkhapa's explanation of why the path is divided into three levels and why the disciple is led progressively through all three levels, see volume 1, 276ff.

4 *Bodhisattva-caryāvatāra* 4:13; P5272: 247.5.5.

5 rJe Gung thang pa dKon mchog bstan pa'i sgron me: v.25; Pabongka Rinpoche 1994: 133.

6 *Madhyamakāvatāra-nāma* 2.7; P5262: 100.5.1–2.

7 *Suhṛl-lekha* 7; P5682: 235.3.7.

8 *Bodhisattva-caryāvatāra* 4.23–27; P5272: 248.1.3–7.

Notes to Chapter 1

1 Adapted from Hopkins 1998: 96.

2 The full version of this story is told in volume 1, p. 452.

3. There are two types of obscurations, and they both must be removed in order to obtain buddhahood. The *obscuration of the afflictions (kleshāvaraṇa; nyon sgrib)* is the coarser of the two and constitutes the obstructions to liberation from cyclic existence. When they are removed by attaining the path of seeing, one attains *arhatship,* liberation from rebirth in samsara. However, one still has subtle obscurations due to previous habitual engagement in the ignorance of cyclic existence. In order to obtain complete buddhahood one must still remove these subtle *obscurations to knowledge (jñeyāvaraṇa; shes sgrib).* Once they are removed one obtains omniscience or buddhahood.

4. *mDzangs blun zhes bya ba'i mdo,* ch. 8. According to Engle: 1994, 237 n.36, in that sutra the former Buddha is identified as Kanakumuni, not Kāśyapa. For an English translation see Fry 1981.

5. Those who enter the Mahayana path do not enter the lower, Hinayana attainment of nirvana; they bypass that state on their way to perfect buddhahood.

6. This topic will be covered in chapter 3 under the heading: "In particular, how to purify by means of the four opponent powers."

7. See Engle: 1994, 208 for the story of this author.

8. See Engle: 1994, 241 n. 53.

Notes to Chapter 2

1. See volume 1, chapter 2, 409–27.

2. "Pratyekabuddhas who will definitely become self-realized" has a specific technical meaning here. It means that they will achieve their spiritual goal by accumulating merits for 100 eons, and in their last life they will practice in solitude, "like

a rhinoceros," without the aid of a teacher. In contrast, śrāvakas attain their goal in an *indefinite* period of time, and in their last life they do listen to teachings. For both of these beings the attainment they achieve is the elimination of the "obscurations of the afflictions" *(nyon sgrib),* which liberates them from cyclic existence. They do not achieve the elimination of the "obscurations to knowledge" *(shes sgrib),* which only comes with the attainment of perfect buddhahood.

The phrase, "sons of the buddhas" translates the Tibetan *rgyal sras,* which literally means "sons of the conquerors" and is an epithet for bodhisattvas. The sense of the term is that the son of a great king is not a king now but is definitely destined to become a king eventually. In the same way, a bodhisattva is not a buddha now but is born of the buddhas' lineage and is destined to become a buddha.

3. In the Vinaya the definition of complete karma for some of these actions is somewhat different. We will get into some of these distinctions later. In general, the difference is that the Vinaya stresses the heaviest type of karma when it describes complete karma. The Vinaya says that the basis or victim of the action of killing must be "human or almost human," which means either a human being or an unborn human being in the mother's womb.

4. Patt: I.89:

> All phenomena are subsumed in two categories: they are either contaminated *(zag bcas; sāsrava)* or uncontaminated *(zag med; anāsrava).* Only four types of phenomena are uncontaminated: the three uncompounded phenomena *(asaṃskṛta dharma),* and those included in the "truth of the path." All other compound phenomena *(saṃskṛta dharma)* are contaminated. Contamination means that they nourish or increase contaminated or afflicted or deluded states of mind—states of mind which lead to suffering and do not lead to liberation—either by being objects of, or by being concomitant with, other states of mind.
>
> For an ordinary individual, one who has not attained the level of an ārya by seeing the truths on the path of seeing and thereby transforming contaminated states into uncontaminated states, a mental factor such as memory is contaminated because it nourishes contamination by means of concomitants: As a man remembers a beautiful woman, contamination increases as concomitant mental factors such as attachment arise together with the memory.
>
> But even the eye faculty of an arhat is contaminated, because it is capable of nourishing the afflictions of someone else who takes it as an object; for example, someone who sees the arhat's eye and feels jealousy and attachment toward it.
>
> The soteriological intent of dividing all phenomena into these two categories is implicit. As the First Dalai Lama dGe 'dun grub says: "By teaching the afflicted *(kun nas nyon mongs; saṃkleśa)* and purified phenomena *(rnam byang; vyavadānika),* he wished beings to attain the ultimate good *(nges legs; niḥśreyas)* by virtue of taking up or abandoning these."

5. Once again the Vinaya has a slightly different interpretation of the basis of stealing. It says that stealing occurs only when an object has a certain value. But here we are explaining the ten nonvirtues in general. In this context, if you take any object—regardless of how small or insignificant—that belongs to someone else and was not given to you, it is stealing.

6. The one-day ordination vows are a set of vows *(upavāsa; bsnyen gnas)* taken by laypeople; one essentially takes ordination and commits to observing eight precepts for one full day. The first five of these precepts are the same as the five vows of a lay person *(upāsaka; dge bsnyen):* not to kill, not to steal, not to lie, not to take intoxicants, and to refrain from sexual misconduct (which is here extended to include all sexual activity). The three additional vows are: (1) not to eat after the midday meal; (2) not to sing, dance, or play music, and not to wear rosaries as ornaments, jewelry, or perfumes; and (3) not to use a high or grand seat or bed. The vows are taken before dawn and they last for twenty-four hours.

7. This discussion takes place in the commentary to verse 4.67, a discussion of which nonvirtuous karmic paths are revealing *(vijñapti)* or nonrevealing *(avijñapti)* karma. Vasubandhu says:

   > Sexual misconduct is always both revealing and nonrevealing karma because the actual action must be done by oneself. If one induces another to perform it, one does not get the same pleasure. (P5591: 209.1.3–4)

   The First Dalai Lama dGe 'dun grub says of this passage:

   > If one asks: Which virtuous and nonvirtuous karmic paths of body and speech have revealing and nonrevealing karmas?
   >
   > Six nonvirtuous karmic paths definitely have nonrevealing karma but do not definitely have revealing karma; because they can also be accomplished by having another person perform them. The six are: killing, stealing, lying, slander, harmful speech, and idle chatter. When one person has another person commit them they are only nonrevealing, because the one who orders another to do them commits no revealing karma.
   >
   > One, sexual misconduct, is always of both types, revealing and nonrevealing. Because it definitely has to be done by oneself without depending on another.
   >
   > And those six, when they are done by oneself, are both types, revealing and nonrevealing. (Patt: II.806)

8. The fourfold retinue *('khor rnam bzhi)* of the Buddha includes fully ordained monks and nuns, and male and female laypeople.

9. This is the highest of the six classes of desire realm gods. These gods are able to control for their own enjoyment things that have been manifested by others.

10. The Abhidharma describes three birth-sources *(skye gnas; yoni)* for sentient beings: birth from an egg, birth from a womb, birth from moist heat, and miraculous birth. Intermediate existence beings are miraculously born, which means they appear instantaneously in that realm in their full form (*Abhidharma-kośa-kārikā:* iii.9). The intermediate existence is defined as "that continuum of aggregates that arises between the existence at death and the birth existence." (Patt: II.600)

11. A probationary nun is a woman who has taken a level of ordination that comes after she has taken novice vows but before she takes full ordination; it involves keeping the novice vows plus eight additional precepts for about two years.

12. In his discussion of the five automatic transgressions (*Abhidharma-kośa-kārikā:* 4.98) the First Dalai Lama dGe 'dun grub says:

    > The first three, killing mother, father, or an arhat, are karma of body, because they are killing; and the fifth, wounding a tathāgata, is karma of body, because it is preparation for killing. The fourth, causing a schism in the saṅgha, is lying, so it is karma of speech.... The disgraceful karma *(kha na ma tho ba'i las)* that is the cause of the schism in the saṅgha is a lie which causes the division in the saṅgha, and it is that which is the automatic transgression; and it is that which is possessed by those who cause division in the saṅgha, such as Devadatta *(lHas byin)* and so forth. The fruition of the karma of causing a schism in the saṅgha is that for an intermediate eon the one who caused it will experience the fruition in the sufferings of Avīci hell. (Patt: II.837)

    And a little later (*Abhidharma-kośa-kārikā:* 4.103):

    > Telling a lie in order to divide the saṅgha in two is held to be the very greatest disgrace among the automatic transgressions. Because it injures the dharma-body *(chos kyi sku; dharma-śarīra)* of the tathāgatas; and until the divided saṅgha is once again reconciled, in the world there will be an obstacle to entry into the path *(nges pa; niyama),* to the obtainment of fruits, to being freed from attachment, and to the extinction of contamination. Also, people will not engage in the concentrations, in reading, reciting prayers, or virtuous mental karma; and so it obstructs the attainment of higher states and emancipation *(byang grol; apavarga).* And the world of the gods becomes disturbed, is mentally unhappy, without freedom, and their memories deteriorate. (Patt: II.846)

13. The "great hells of sentient beings" refers to the four hot hells in which the primary suffering is from extreme heat and fire. The "surrounding hells" are encountered after being freed from the great hells—they are surrounding, adjacent, or minor hells; each of the hot hells has four levels of surrounding hells. Then there are cold hells and, finally, occasional or sporadic hells. These are the four divisions or types of hell that exist according to Buddhism.

14. The bodhisattva trains in the ten perfections and passes through ten bodhisattva levels on the way to perfect buddhahood. The ten perfections are: giving, ethics, patience, effort, concentration, wisdom, skillful means, aspiration, power, and transcendental gnosis. The ten bodhisattva levels are named (1) Extremely Joyous, (2) Stainless, (3) Light Maker, (4) Radiant, (5) Very Difficult to Conquer, (6) Manifest, (7) Gone Far, (8) Unwavering, (9) Good Intelligence, and (10) Cloud of Dharma.

15. The First Dalai Lama Dge 'dun grub elaborates on this as follows (Patt: II.796):

    By doing benefit or harm to those who have just arisen from the absorption of cessation, the fruit is experienced immediately, because it is as if they have returned from nirvāṇa.

    By doing benefit or harm to those who have just arisen from the meditative stabilizations called Measureless Love *(byams pa; maitrī)* and Free of Afflictions *(nyon mongs med pa; araṇā),* the fruit is experienced immediately, because they are endowed with the superior intention, respectively, to benefit all sentient beings, and that all beings should be free of afflictions; and they are permeated by measureless sharp and clear merits.

    By doing benefit or harm to those who have just arisen from the Path of Seeing, the fruit is experienced immediately, because they attain the stainless newly transformed state *(gnas yongs su gyur ba gsar pa; pratyagra-āśraya-parivṛtti)* where all objects to be abandoned by seeing, without exception, have been eliminated.

    By doing benefit or harm to those who have just arisen from the fruit of arhatship, the fruit is experienced immediately, because they attain the stainless newly transformed state where all objects to be abandoned by meditation without exception have been eliminated.

16. This is actually a paraphrase of a passage from the end of the ninth chapter of the *Treasury of Knowledge Auto-commentary (Abhidharma-kośa-bhāṣya).* Pruden IV.1353 translates it:

    For example, when the mind at death is "associated with attachment," it possesses the capacity of producing a new existence. This mind has for its antecedents many actions of all types; nevertheless, it is the efficacy projected by a weighty action that informs (or qualifies) the last thought; in the absence of heavy action, the efficacy is projected by near action; in its absence by habitual action; and in its absence by the action of a previous life. There is a stanza by Rāhula which says, "Weighty action, near action, habitual action, old action: these four die in this order."

17. *Sa skya'i Legs bshad* by Sa skya pan-di ta kun dga' rgyal mtshan (1182–1251). A translation is published in Davenport 2000.

18. *rTogs brjod mdun legs ma.* In *Zhal 'dun nyer mTho phyogs bsdebs (Collection of Essential Recitations),* (Waa' na [Varanasi]: mtho slob dge ldan spyi las khang, 1975) 51.

19. *Subhāṣita-ratna-karaṇḍaka-kathā* 16–18b; P5424: 235.4.3–5.

Notes to Chapter 3

1. Kadampa *(bka' gdams pa)* was the sect of Tibetan Buddhism established by the followers of Atiśa. Geshe Potowa was one of the most famous of these scholar-practitioners. These geshes were known for their unique way of formulating pithy expressions about the main points of the path. These expressions are found in the collection known as the *Sayings of the Holy Kadampas (bKa' gdams kyi skyes bu dam pa rnams kyi gsungs bgros thor bu).*

2. The story of Prince Sutasoma from the *Jataka Tales,* or *Garland of Birth Stories,* is summarized in volume 1, where it is referred to several times. It can also be found at Speyer: 291.

3. The eight types of vows of individual liberation are (1–2) vows of a layman and laywoman, (3–4) vows of a novice monk and novice nun, (5) vows of a probationary nun, (6–7) vows of a fully ordained monk and nun, and (8) one-day ordination vows.

4. See the above section entitled: "Karma whose result will definitely or not definitely be experienced."

5. The source of this quotation is unknown. It appears in *Meditation on Emptiness,* p. 33 and n. 5, and also in mChan 376.5, but the original source is not given.

6. *Bodhisattva-caryāvatāra* 1.14; P5272: 245.2.8.

7. In the sutras, when the Buddha explained the results of the most powerful negative karma, he specified five heinous actions that, if left unpurified, bring their results immediately in your next life. These are called the *five automatic transgressions* because if you commit one in this life, after death you will automatically go straight to a hell realm without interruption by rebirth in any other place. The first two are to kill either your father or mother with deliberate concentrated intent. The third is to kill an arhat. The fourth is to wound or draw blood from the Buddha with the intent to do harm. This particular transgression cannot occur in our time since it specifically refers to harming Buddha Śākyamuni when he was alive. The fifth transgression is to cause a schism in the spiritual community, or Sangha. Technically speaking, in order to form a Sangha there must be four fully ordained monks or nuns. So in order to divide the Sangha into two separate groups, there must be at least eight monks or nuns to start with. The transgressor must interfere in a way that causes ill will between the Sangha members, thus causing them to completely split into two groups.

8. For a full elaboration of this argument, see Jackson 1993: 132–389.

9. The complete path to enlightenment is composed of five consecutive paths: accumulation, preparation, seeing, meditation, and no further training. At the time of the path of accumulation and the path of preparation you should generate a thorough understanding of the type of realization appropriate to your type of practice. Then, through meditation on the path of seeing, you directly realize that wisdom with a nonconceptual understanding. On the path of meditation, you fill out the understanding you have already produced by eliminating what is to be abandoned—the mental afflictions—and by cultivating and bringing to completion the realizations. In this way we have a three-stage accomplishment: developing understanding during the paths of accumulation and preparation, direct realization during the path of seeing, and fulfilling that realization during the path of meditation. The fifth path, that of no more learning, is the final result: full enlightenment.

Notes to Chapter 4

1. See volume 1, chapter 9, of this series.

2. The explanation of this training began in volume 1 of this series, chapter 9, page 309.

3. When you attain perfect buddhahood your body will no longer be an ordinary body; all your physical impurities will be cleared away. In the Mahayana system there is a discussion of the three *kāyas,* or *bodies,* of a buddha: the *dharmakāya, saṃbhogakāya,* and *nirmāṇakāya.* The dharmakāya—the *wisdom body*—is ultimate and immaculate wisdom; it is the mind that has been transformed beyond all states of impurity. The latter two bodies—the saṃbhogakāya and nirmāṇakāya—are together called the *form body (rūpakāya)* of a buddha. These are manifestations of perfect wisdom in various forms. The saṃbhogakāya—the *enjoyment body*—is the perfected form in which a buddha attains enlightenment. It is the ultimate physical body, completely absorbed in enjoyment of the Mahayana Dharma. It is always present, but is only perceptible to advanced-level bodhisattvas and does not transform into any other form. The nirmāṇakāya—the *emanation body*—on the other hand, takes various forms that can be perceived by our limited senses. It is the emanation body that we see as the Buddha in our world. This form also possesses special qualities; for example, various qualities of enlightenment manifest as thirty-two major marks and eighty minor marks adorning the body of the Buddha. The rūpakāya also encompasses the wealth and other glorious qualities of the pure land in which the Buddha abides, as well as the retinue of other nirmāṇakāya buddhas and bodhisattvas who surround him. All of these extraordinary qualities that come with buddhahood are included in what is referred to here as "high status."

Notes to Chapter 5

1. *Yon tan gzhir gyur ma;* P6003: 153.
2. See below, chapter 7: "Contemplating the three types of suffering."
3. There are four types of birth or "birth-sources": birth from an egg, birth from a womb, birth from moist heat, and miraculous birth. Hell beings, devas, and intermediate state beings always have miraculous birth. Hungry ghosts are usually miraculously born, but some are said be womb born. Humans and animals share all four types of birth. There is further discussion of this subject below, in chapter 8.
4. See volume 1, chapter 10, of this series.
5. These two types of meditation are discussed in volume 1 of this series, chapter 5, page 210.
6. *Bodhisattva-caryāvatāra* 5.16; P5272: 248.5.4.
7. "Negative tendencies" translates the Sanskrit *dauṣṭhulya* (Tib. *gnas ngan len*).
8. The stages of development in the womb are discussed below in chapter 9, in the section dealing with "the division into twelve links" under the outline heading: "Name and form."
9. Adapted from Chang 1989: I.138.
10. *Bodhisattva-caryāvatāra* 2.34; P5272: 246.3.4.
11. *Bodhisattva-caryāvatāra* 2.41; P5272: 246.4.1–2.

Notes to Chapter 6

1. Tsongkhapa mentions here that in the text called *Clear Words: Explanation of the "Friendly Letter"* by Mahāmati, it says that there are *seven* types of suffering. However, because the seventh merely gives a detailed explanation of the other six, he will explain six types of suffering, and that is the way you should do this meditation.
2. Here Chenngawa is addressing his teacher, the great Dromtonpa *('Brom ston pa),* who had three principal disciples: Chenngawa *(Spyan snga ba),* Potowa *(Po to ba),* and Puchungwa *(Phu chung ba).*
3. The great hells are discussed in volume 1 of this series, chapter 10, pp. 369–74.
4. This is another subsidiary hell called the Grove of Sword-leaves *(asipattravana; ral gri lo ma'i nags tshal),* where the leaves are swords, and when these are blown about by the wind they cut up one's body.

5. This is another subsidiary hell consisting of an extremely hot river of ashes, difficult to cross.

Notes to Chapter 7

1. See chapter 5: "Birth is suffering because it possesses the negative tendencies."
2. See chapter 5: "The suffering of the appropriating aggregates."
3. The length of a day for the devas is quite a bit longer than a human day. For the lowest gods of the desire realm, the group of the four great kings, fifty human years is equal to one deva day and night. Thirty of these days equals one month; twelve of those makes one year, and their life span is five hundred of those years. This is equivalent to 9,000,000 human years. For each higher level of devas, the length of their life span doubles.
4. *Lam gtso rnam gsum*, in Tsongkhapa 1978–83, 194a2–3.

Notes to Chapter 8

1. *Catuḥ-śataka* 6.10; P5246: 135.2.8–3.1.
2. For a detailed discussion of the mind and mental factors, see Rabten 1981; and Guenther and Kawamura 1975.
3. The four great elements *(mahābhūta; 'byung ba chen po)*—earth, water, fire, and wind—are the indivisible building blocks of material existence. Everything material, everything in the aggregate of form, is based upon these fundamental material units. These are not to be taken literally as atoms of those particular substances, but as material atoms that perform their respective functions: earth supports without letting fall down; water makes cohesion; fire ripens; wind increases and expands. These are their functions; their natures are, respectively: solidity, moisture, heat, and movement. Alfonso Verdu (1985; p. 21) says:

   > The four *mahābhūtas (great elements)* should be considered as simple primordial dharmas of materiality, each one carrying its own specific kind of activity or energy and thus establishing the basis for each one of the fundamental states which can characterize or affect any of the appearing things in the material world.

   In practice, these four elements always arise together, and the particular quality of the resultant complex matter *(bhautika; 'byung gyur)* that is manifested is dependent on the predominance of one or the other. These molecules of complex matter then combine into *collections of subtle atoms (saṃghāta-paramāṇu; rdul phra rab bsags pa)*. It is massive conglomerations of these collections of subtle atoms that we actually experience as matter in the world.

4. For an ordinary individual, one who has not reached the level of an ārya by attaining the path of seeing and thereby transforming contaminated states into uncontaminated states, a mental factor—such as memory—is contaminated because it nourishes contamination by means of concomitants. For example, when a man remembers a beautiful woman, contamination increases as concomitant mental factors—such as attachment—arise together with the memory. Even the eye faculty of an arhat is contaminated, because it is capable of nourishing the afflictions of someone else who takes it as an object; for example, someone who sees the arhat's eye and feels jealousy and attachment toward it.

5. See chapter 1, note 3, for an explanation of the obstacles to knowledge.

6. These nine levels are: the desire realm, four levels of the form realm, and four levels of the formless realm.

7. For a full discussion of completing or actualizing karma, see chapter 2: "The distinction between projecting and completing karma."

8. *Abhidharma-kośa-kārikā* 9; P5591: 283.4.1–3.

9. See above, note 3.

10. *Abhidharma-kośa-kārikā* 3.15c; P5590: 119.2.5.

Notes to Chapter 9

1. These are the five stages of gestation. They are difficult to translate, but their Sanskrit terms are: *arbuda (mer mer po), kalala (nur nur po), peśin (nar nar po), ghana (mkhrang 'gyur),* and *praśākhā (rkang lag 'gyus).*

2. Each of the four concentrations of the form realm has a *preparatory stage* and an *actual stage.* Here, to create the cause to be born in one of the concentrations, you must attain the level of concentration equal to the actual stage, the reasons for which follow in the text.

3. *Prajña-nāma-mūla-madhyamaka-kārikā;* P5224. Translation adapted from Garfield 1995: 2.

4. P6016: 37.2.6. The full title of this text is *Sangs rgyas bcom ldan 'das la zab mo rten cing 'grel bar 'byung ba gsung ba'i sgo nas bstod pa legs par bshad pa'i snying po.* It is translated in Thurman 1982: 99; and Wangyal 1973: 175.

5. The *Bhikṣunī-vibhaṅga* and the *Bhikṣu-vibhaṅga* make up the *vibhaṅga* division, the second of the four main works of the Sarvāstivāda Vinaya. These two works are commentaries on the Prātimokṣa sutras, and they elaborate the details of the vows for nuns and monks respectively. They contain numerous stories of Śākyamuni as he traveled the kingdoms of North India.

6. P6016: 37.2.6.

Notes to Chapter 10

1. *Mahāyāna-patha-sādhana-varṇa-saṃgraha,* P5351: 50.3.3–5. This quotation first appears in volume 1, chapter 8, pp. 296–97, in the discussion of why the teacher guides the disciple through these steps on the path to enlightenment.

Notes to Chapter 11

1. The full story from which this and the following quotations from the *Garland of Birth Stories* are drawn can be found in Speyer 1982: 151ff.

2. The view of the transitory collections is discussed in chapter 8 under the heading: "Identifying the obscuring afflictions."

Notes to Chapter 12

1. There is a subtle distinction made between the mental factors of *shame* and *embarrassment,* which are generally defined in terms of their opposites. Not having respect for virtue or people who have virtuous qualities is shamelessness. Immodesty, the opposite of embarrassment, is an attitude that does not regard disgraceful conduct with fear. Some commentators define them slightly differently. They say that not refraining from nonvirtue in regard to oneself is shamelessness, while not refraining from nonvirtue in regard to others is immodesty.

2. Hopkins 1998: 144.

3. See chapter 2, note 6.

4. In the presentation of six obscuring afflictions, the sixth one is wrong view. In this section, only the first five are discussed. In the presentation of ten obscuring afflictions, wrong view is subdivided into five distinct erroneous views. This is discussed in chapter 8 under the heading "Identifying the obscuring afflictions."

5. *Madhyamakāvatāra* 3.6: P5262: 101.1.1–2. English translation: Huntington and Wangyal, 153.

Bibliography

Sutras and Śāstras

Alleviating Sorrow
Śoka-vinodana
Mya ngan bsal ba
author: Aśvaghoṣa
P5677, vol. 129

Array of Stalks Sutra
Gaṇḍa-vyūha-sūtra
sDong pos brgyan pa / sDong po bkod pa'i mdo
P761, vol. 26

Bases of Discipline
Vinaya-vastu
'Dul ba gzhi
P1030, vol. 41

Blaze of Reasons
Tarka-jvālā: Madhyamaka-hṛdaya-vṛtti-tarka-jvālā
dBu ma'i snying po'i 'grel pa rtog ge 'bar ba
author: Bhāvaviveka
P5256, vol. 96

Bodhisattva Levels
Bodhisattva-bhūmi: Yoga-caryā-bhūmau-bodhisattva-bhūmi
rNal 'byor spyod pa'i sa las byang chub sems dpa'i sa
author: Asaṅga
P5537, vol. 110

Chapter of the Truth Speaker
Satyaka-parivarta
bDen pa po'i le'u
P813, vol. 32

Clear Words: Explanation of the "Friendly Letter"
Vyakta-padā-suhṛl-lekha-ṭīkā
bShes pa'i spring yig gi rgya cher bshad pa tshig gsal ba
author: Mahāmati
P5690, vol. 129

Collection of Indicative Verses
Udāna-varga
Ched du brjod pa'i tshoms
P992, vol. 39

Commentary on the "Compendium of Valid Cognition"
Pramāṇa-vārttika-kārikā
Tshad ma rnam 'grel gyi tshig le'ur byas pa
author: Dharmakīrti
P5709, vol. 130

Commentary on the "Middle Way"
Madhyamakāvatāra
dBu ma la 'jug pa
author: Candrakīrti
P5262, vol. 98

Commentary on the "Sixty Stanzas of Reasoning"
Yukti-ṣaṣṭikā-vṛtti
Rigs pa drug cu pa'i 'grel pa
author: Candrakīrti
P5265, vol. 98

Compendium of Determinations
Yoga-caryā-bhūmi-nirṇaya-saṃgraha (Viniścaya-saṃgrahaṇī)
rNal 'byor spyod pa'i sa rnam par gtan la dbab pa bsdu ba
author: Asaṅga
P5539, vol. 110

Compendium of Knowledge
Abhidharma-samuccaya
Chos mngon pa kun las btus pa
author: Asaṅga
P5550, vol. 112

Compendium of the Perfections
Pāramitā-samāsa
Pha rol tu phyin pa bsdus pa
author: Āryaśūra
P5340, vol. 103

Compendium of Trainings
Śikṣā-samuccaya
bSlab pa kun las bTus pa
author: Śāntideva
P5336, vol. 102

Concise Method of Achieving the Mahayana Path
Mahāyāna-patha-sādhana-varṇa-saṃgraha
Theg pa chen po'i lam gyi sgrub thabs yi ger bsdus pa
author: Atiśa
P5351, vol. 103

Confession to the Thirty-five Buddhas
cf. Sutra of the Three Aggregates

Descent into the Womb Sutra
Garbhāvakrānti-sūtra: Ārya-nanda-garbhāvakrānti-nirdeśa [-nāma-mahāyāna-sūtra]
'Phags pa dga' bo mngal na gnas pa bstan pa shes bya ba theg pa chen po'i mdo
P760, vol. 23

Discussion of the Requisite Collections
Sambhāra-parikathā
Tshogs kyi gtam
author: Vasubandhu
P5422, vol. 103

Edifying Tale of the Seven Maidens
Sapta-kumārikāvadāna
gZhon nu ma bdun gyi rtogs pa brjod pa
author: Guhyadatta
P5419, vol. 103

Engaging in the Bodhisattva Deeds
Bodhisattva-caryāvatāra
Byang chub sems dpa'i spyod la 'jug pa
author: Śāntideva
P5272, vol. 99

Exegesis of the Discipline
Vinaya-vibhaṅga
'Dul ba rnam par 'byed pa
P1032, vol. 42-43

Exhortation to Wholehearted Resolve
Ārya-Adhyāśaya-saṃcodana-nāma-mahāyāna-sūtra

'Phags pa lhag pa'i bsam pa bskul pa shes bya ba theg pa chen po'i mdo
P760, vol. 22–24

Explanation of the Five Aggregates
Pañca-skandha-prakaraṇa
Phung po lnga'i rab tu byed pa
author: Vasubandhu
P5560, vol. 113

Explanation of the Ten Virtuous Paths of Action
Daśākuśala-karma-patha-nirdeśa
Mi dge ba bcu'i las kyi lam bstan pa
author: Aśvaghoṣa
P5416, vol. 103; P5678, vol. 129

Extensive Sport Sutra
Lalita-vistara-sūtra: Ārya-lalita-vistara-nāma-mahāyāna-sūtra
Phags pa rgya cher rol pa shes bya ba theg pa chen po'i mdo
P763, vol. 27

Four Hundred Stanzas
Catuḥ-śataka-śāstra-kārikā
bsTan bcos bzhi brgya pa zhes bya ba'i tshig le'ur byas pa
author: Āryadeva
P5246, vol. 95

Friendly Letter
Suhṛl-lekha
bShes pa'i spring yig
author: Nāgārjuna
P5682, vol. 129

Fundamental Verses of the Middle Way
Mūla-madhyamaka-kārikā
dBu ma rtsa ba'i tshig le'ur byas pa shes rab
author: Nāgārjuna
P5224, vol. 95

Garland of Birth Stories
Jātaka-mālā
sKyes pa'i rabs kyi rgyud
Āryaśūra or Aśvaghoṣa
P5650, vol. 128

Great Final Nirvāṇa Sutra
Mahā-parinirvāṇa-sūtra: Ārya-mahā-parinirvāṇa-sūtra
'Phags pa yongs su mya ngan las 'das pa chen po'i mdo
P787, vol. 31

Heap of Jewels Sutra
Ratna-rāśi-sūtra: Ārya-ratna-rāśi-nāma-mahāyāna-sūtra
'Phags pa rin po che'i phung pO shes bya ba theg pa chen po'i mdo
P760, vol. 24

Heart of Dependent Arising
Pratītya-samutpāda-hṛdaya-kārikā
rTen cing 'brel par 'byung ba'i snying po'i tshig le'ur byas pa
author: Nāgārjuna
P5467, vol. 103

Heart of the Middle Way
Madhyamaka-hṛdaya-kārikā
dBu ma'i snying po'i tshig le'ur byas pa
author: Bhāvaviveka
P5255, vol. 96

Hundred Actions Sutra
Karma-śataka-sūtra
Las brgya tham pa'
P1007, vol. 39

Hundred Bodhisattva Stories
Bodhisattvāvadāna-kalpalatā
Byang chub sems dpa'i rtogs pa brjod pa'i dpag bsam Gyi 'khri shing
Kṣemendra
P5655, vol. 129

King of Concentrations Sutra
Samādhi-rāja-sūtra: Sarva-dharma-svabhāva-samatā-vipañcita-samādhi-rāja-sūtra
Chos tham cad kyi rang bzhin mnyam pa nyid rnam par spros pa ting nge 'dzin gyi rgyal po'i mdo
P795, vol. 31

Lamp That Is a Compendium of Deeds
Caryā-melāpaka-pradīpa
sPyod pa bsdus pa'i sgron ma
author: Āryadeva
P2668, vol. 61

Letter to a Student
Śiṣya-lekha
Slob ma la springs pa'i spring yig
author: Candragomin
P5683, vol. 129; P5410, vol. 103

Letter to King Candra
Candra-rāja-lekha
rGyal po zla ba la springs pa'i phrin yig
author: Śri Jagan-mitrānanda
P5689, vol. 129

Levels of Yogic Deeds
Yoga-caryā-bhūmi
rNal 'byor spyod pa'i sa
author: Asaṅga
P5536, vol. 110

Lion's Roar of Maitreya Sutra
Maitreya-mahā-siṃha-nāda-sūtra: Ārya-maitreya-mahā-siṃha-nāda-nāma-mahāyāna-sūtra
'Phags pa byams pa seng ge'i sgra chen po shes bya ba theg pa chen po'i mdo
P760, vol. 24

Long Explanation of the Perfection of Wisdom Sutra in Eight Thousand Lines
Abhisamayālaṃkārāloka: Āryāṣṭa-sāhasrikā-prajñāpāramitā-vyākhyāna Abhisamayālaṃkārāloka-nāma
'Phags pa shes rab kyi pha rol tu phyin pa brgyad stong pa'i bshad pa mngon par rtogs pa'i rgyan gyi snang ba shes bya ba
author: Haribhadra
P5189, vol. 90

Mindfulness of the Excellent Teaching
Sad-dharmānusmṛty-upasthāna
Dam pa'i chos dran pa nye bar gzhag pa
P953, vol. 37–38

Ornament for Clear Knowledge
Abhisamayālaṃkāra: Abhisamayālaṃkāra-nāma-prajñāpāramitopadeśa-śāstra-kārikā
Shes rab kyi pha rol tu phyin pa'i man ngag gi bstan bcos mngon par rtogs pa'i rgyan zhes bya ba'i tshig le'ur byas pa
author: Maitreya
P5184, vol. 88

Ornament for the Mahayana Sutras
Mahāyāna-sūtrālaṃkāra-kārikā
Theg pa chen po'i mdo sde'i rgyan gyi tshig le'ur byas pa
author: Maitreya
P5521, vol. 108

Praise of the Exalted One
Viśeṣa-stava
Khyad par du 'phags pa'i bstod pa
author: Udbhaṭasiddhasvāmin
P2001, vol. 46

Prayer of Samantabhadra
Samantabhadra-caryā-praṇidhāna
bZang po spyod pa'i smon lam
P761, vol. 26

Precious Garland
Ratnāvalī: Rāja-parikathā-ratnāvalī
rGyal po la gtam bya ba rin po che'i phreng ba
author: Nāgārjuna
P5658, vol. 129

Questions of Householder Ugra Sutra
Gṛha-paty-ugra-paripṛcchā-sūtra: Ārya-gṛha-paty-ugra-paripṛcchā-nāma-mahāyāna-sūtra
'Phags pa khyim bdag drag shul can gyis zhus pa shes bya ba theg pa chen po'imdo
P760, vol. 23

Questions of the Nāga Kings of the Ocean
Sāgara-nāga-rāja-paripṛcchā: Ārya-sāgara-nāga-rāja-paripṛcchā-nāma-mahāyāna-sūtra
'Phags pa klu'i rgyal po rgya mtshos zhus pa shes bya ba theg pa chen po'i mdo
P820, vol. 33

Rice Seedling Sutra
Śāli-stamba-sūtra: Ārya-śālistamba-nāma-mahāyāna-sūtra
'Phags pa sa lu'i ljang ba shes bya ba theg pa chen po'i mdo
P876, vol. 34

Root Tantra of Mañjuśrī
Mañjuśrī-mūla-tantra: Ārya-mañjuśrī-mūla-tantra
'Phags pa 'jam dpal gyi rtsa ba'i rgyud
P162, vol. 6

Seal of Engaging in Certain and Uncertain Destinies Sutra
Niyatāniyata-gati-mudrāvatāra-sūtra: Ārya-niyatāniyata-gati-mudrāvatāra-nāma-mahāyāna-sūtra
'Phags pa nges pa dang mi nges par 'gro ba'i phyag rgya la 'jug pa shes bya ba theg pa chen po'i mdo
P868, vol. 34

Seal of Engaging in Developing the Power of Faith Sutra
Śraddhā-balādhānāvatāra-mudrā-sūtra: Ārya-śraddhā-balādhānāvatāra-mudrā-nāma-mahāyāna-sūtra
Dad pa'i stobs bskyed pa la 'jug pa'i phyag rgya shes bya ba theg pa chen po'i mdo
P867, vol. 34

Sublime Continuum
Uttara-tantra: Mahāyānottara-tantra-śāstra
Theg pa chen po'i rgyud bla ma'i bstan bcos
author: Maitreya
P5525, vol. 108

Sun Essence Sutra
Sūrya-garbha-sūtra: Ārya-sūrya-garbha-nāma-vaipulya-sūtra
'Phags pa shin tu rgyas pa chen po sde nyi ma'i snying po shes bya ba'i mdo
P923, vol. 36

Sutra Beloved of Monks
Bhikṣu-prareju-sūtra-nāma
dGe slong la rab tu gces pa'i mdo shes bya ba
P968, vol. 39

Sutra Gathering All the Threads
Sarva-vaidalya-saṃgraha-sūtra: Ārya-sarva-vaidalya-saṃgraha-nāma-mahāyāna-sūtra
'Phags pa rnam par 'thag pa thams cad bsdus pa shes bya ba theg pa chen po'i mdo
P893, vol. 35

Sutra Giving the Four Teachings
Catur-dharma-nirdeśa-sūtra: Ārya-catur-dharma-nirdeśa-nāma-mahāyāna-sūtra
'Phags pa chos bzhi bstan pa shes bya ba theg pa chen po'i mdo
P915, vol. 36

Sutra of Cultivating Faith in the Mahayana
Mahāyāna-prasāda-prabhāvanā-sūtra: Ārya-mahāyāna-prasāda-prabhāvanā-nāma-mahāyāna-sūtra
'Phags pa theg pa chen po la dad pa rab tu sgom pa shes bya ba theg pa chen po'i mdo
P812, vol. 32

Sutra of Kṣitigarbha
Kṣitigarbha-sūtra: Daśa-cakra-kṣitigarbha-nāma-mahāyāna-sūtra
'Dus pa chen po las sa'i snying po'i 'khor lo bcu pa'i mdo
P905, vol. 36

Sutra of Showing the Tathāgata's Inconceivable Secret
Tathāgatācintya-guhya-nirdeśa-sūtra: Ārya-tathāgatācintya-guhya-nirdeśa-nāma-mahāyāna-sūtra
'Phags pa de bzhin gshegs pa'i gsang ba bsam gyis mi khyab pa bstan pa shes bya ba'i theg pa chen po'i mdo
P760, ch. 3, vol. 22

Sutra of the Golden Light
Suvarṇa-prabhāsa-sūtra: Ārya-suvarṇa-prabhāsottama-sūtrendra-rāja-nāma-mahāyāna-sūtra
'Phags pa gser 'od dam pa mdo sde'i dbang po'i rgyal po shes bya ba theg pa chen po'i mdo
P176, vol. 7

Sutra of the Three Aggregates
Ārya-tri-skandha-nāma-mahāyāna-sūtra
'Phags pa phung po gsum pa shes bya ba theg pa chen po'i mdo
P950, vol. 37

Sutra of the Wise and the Foolish
Dama-mūko-nāma-sūtra
mDzangs blun zhe bya ba'i mdo
P1008, vol. 40

Sutra on Having Pure Ethical Discipline
Śīla-saṃyukta-sūtra
Tshul khrims yang dag par ldan pa'i mdo
P969, vol. 39

Sutra on Overcoming Faulty Ethical Discipline
Duḥśīla-nigraha-sūtra: Buddha-piṭaka-duḥśīla-nigraha-nāma-mahāyāna-sūtra
Sangs rgyas kyi sde snod tshul khrims 'chal ba tshar gcod pa shes bya ba theg pa chen po'i mdo
P886, vol. 35

Sutra on the Discipline
Vinaya-sūtra
'Dul ba'i mdo
author: Guṇaprabha
P5619, vol. 123

Sutra on the Magic of Final Peace
Praśānta-viniścaya-prātihārya-sūtra: Ārya-praśānta-viniścaya-prātihārya-samādhi-nāma-mahāyāna-sūtra
Rab tu zhi ba rnam par nges pa'i cho 'phrul gyi ting nge 'dzin ces bya ba theg pa chen po'i mdo
P797, vol. 32

Sutra on the Ten Levels
Daśa-bhūmika-sūtra
Sa bcu pa'i mdo
P761, vol. 26

Sutra Requested by Brahma
Brahmā-paripṛcchā-sūtra
Tshang pas zhus pa'i mdo
P825, vol. 33

Sutra Unraveling the Intended Meaning
Saṃdhi-nirmocana-sūtra: Ārya-saṃdhi-nirmocana-nāma-mahāyāna-sūtra
'Phags pa dgongs pa nges par 'grel pa shes bya ba theg pa chen po'i mdo
P774, vol. 29

Talk That is Like a Jeweled Receptacle of Good Explanations
Subhāṣita-ratna-karaṇḍaka-kathā
Legs par bshad pa rin po che za ma tog lta bu'i gtam
author: Āryaśūra or Aśvaghoṣa
P5668, vol. 129

Tantra Requested by Subāhu
Subāhu-paripṛcchā-tantra: Ārya-subāhu-paripṛcchā-nāma-tantra
'Phags pa dpung bzang gis zhus pa shes bya ba'i rgyud
P428, vol. 9

Treasury of Knowledge
Abhidharma-kośa-kārikā
Chos mngon pa'i mdzod kyi tshig le'ur byas pa
author: Vasubandhu
P5590, vol. 115

Treasury of Knowledge Auto-commentary
Abhidharma-kośa-bhāṣya
Chos mngon pa'i mdzod kyi bshad pa
author: Vasubandhu
P5591, vol. 115

Verse Summary of the "Perfection of Wisdom in Eight Thousand Lines"
Ratna-guṇa-sañcaya-gāthā: Ārya-prajñāpāramitā-ratna-guṇa-sañcaya-gāthā
'Phags pa shes rab kyi pha rol tu phyin pa sdud pa tshigs su bcad pa
P735, vol. 21

Other Works

Ba so chos kyi rgyal mtshan, sDe drug mkhan chen kha rog ngag dbang rab brtan, 'Jam dbyangs bzhad pa ngag dbang brtson 'grus, and Bra sti dge bshes rin chen don grub. 1972. *mNyam med rje btsun tsong kha pa chen pos mdzad pa'i byang chub lam rim chen mo'i dka' ba'i gnad rnams mchan bu bzhi'i sgo nas legs par bshad pa theg chen lam gyi gsal sgron (Lamp Illuminating the Mahayana Path: an Explanation of the Difficult Points in the Lam Rim Chenmo of the Incomparable Tsongkhapa by Means of Four Interwoven Commentaries).* 2 vols. New Delhi: Chos 'phel legs ldan.

Beyer, Stephan. 1974. *The Buddhist Experience.* Belmont, CA: Wadsworth Publishing Company.

Chang, Garma C. C., trans. and ann. 1989. *The Hundred Thousand Songs of Milarepa.* 2 vols. Boston: Shambhala Publications.

Chattopadhyaya, Alaka. 1981. *Atīśa and Tibet.* Delhi: Motilal Banarsidass.

Cleary, Thomas. 1985–87. *The Flower Ornament Scripture: A Translation of the Avatamsaka Sutra.* 3 vols. Boston: Shambhala Publications.

Dalai Lama, Tenzin Gyatso. 1991. *Path to Bliss.* Geshe Thubten Jinpa, trans. Ithaca: Snow Lion Publications.

Das, Sarat Chandra. 1983. *Tibetan-English Dictionary.* Kyoto: Rinsen Book Company.

Davenport, John. T., trans. 2000. *Ordinary Wisdom: Sakya Pandita's Treasury of Good Advice.* With a commentary by Sakya Khenpo Sangyay Tenzin. Boston: Wisdom Publications.

dGe 'dun grub. 1982. *mDzod tik thar lam gsal byed.* 2nd ed. Varanasi: Gelugpa Students Welfare Committee, Central Institute of Higher Tibetan Studies.

Dhargyey, Geshe Ngawang. 1975. *A Short Biography and Letter of Je Tzong K'a Pa.* Khamlung Tulku and Sharpa Tulku, trans. Dharamsala: Library of Tibetan Works and Archives.

Edgerton, Franklin. 1953. *Buddhist Hybrid Sanskrit.* New Haven: Yale University Press. Reprint, 1985. Delhi: Motilal Banarsidass.

Garfield, Jay L., trans. 1995. *The Fundamental Wisdom of the Middle Way: Nāgārjuna's Mūlamadhyamakakārikā.* Oxford: Oxford University Press.

Goldstein, Melvyn C. 1975. *Tibetan-English Dictionary of Modern Tibetan.* 3rd edition. Reprint, 1983. Kathmandu: Ratna Pustak Bandhar.

Guenther, Herbert V., and Leslie S. Kawamura. 1975. *Mind in Buddhist Psychology.* Emeryville, CA: Dharma Publishing.

Gung thang pa dkon mchog bstan pa'i sgron me. 1972–79. *Advice for Meditating on Impermanence (Mi rtag bsgom tshul gyi bslab bya),* in *Collected Works of Gung thang dkon-mchog-bstan-pa'i sgron-me,* vol. 5 (nga), pp. 117–21. New Delhi: Ngawang Gelek Demo.

Gyatso, Lobsang. 1994. *The Four Noble Truths.* Sherab Gyatso, trans. Ithaca: Snow Lion Publications.

Harvey, Peter. 1991. *An Introduction to Buddhism.* Cambridge: Cambridge University Press.

Hirakawa, Akira, ed. 1973. *Index to the Abhidharmakoshabhásya.* Tokyo: Daizo Shuppan Kabushikikaisha.

Hopkins, Jeffrey. 1980. *Compassion in Tibetan Buddhism.* London: Ryder and Co.

———. 1983. *Meditation on Emptiness.* London: Wisdom Publications.

———. 1998. *Buddhist Advice for Living and Liberation.* Ithaca: Snow Lion Publications.

Huntington, C. W., with Geshe Namgyal Wangchen. 1989. *The Emptiness of Emptiness.* Honolulu: University of Hawai'i Press.

Jackson, Roger R. 1993. *Is Enlightenment Possible? Dharmakīrti and rGyal tshab rje on Knowledge, Rebirth, No-Self and Liberation.* Ithaca: Snow Lion Publications.

Kawamura, Leslie. 1975. *Golden Zephyr.* Emeryville, CA: Dharma Publishing.

Kilty, Gavin, trans. and ed. 2001. *The Splendor of an Autumn Moon: The Devotional Verse of Tsongkhapa.* Boston: Wisdom Publications.

Kloetzli, Randy. 1983. *Buddhist Cosmology.* Delhi: Motilal Banarsidass.

Lati Rinbochay. 1980. *Mind in Tibetan Buddhism.* Translated by Elizabeth Napper. Ithaca: Snow Lion Publications.

Lati Rinbochay and Jeffrey Hopkins. 1979. *Death, Intermediate State and Rebirth in Tibetan Buddhism.* London: Ryder and Company.

Lindtner, Christian. 1987. *Nagarjuniana.* Delhi: Motilal Banarsidass.

Loden, Geshe Acharya Thubten. 1996. *Meditations on the Path to Enlightenment in Tibetan Buddhism.* Melbourne: Tushita Publications.

Maitreya. 1991. *The Uttaratantra of Maitreya: Containing Introduction by H.S. Prasad, E.H. Johnston's Sanskrit Text and E. Obermiller's English Translation.* Delhi: Sri Satguru Publications.

Monier-Williams, Sir Monier. 1899. *A Sanskrit-English Dictionary.* Oxford University Press. Reprint, 1984. Delhi: Motilal Banarsidass.

Mullin, Glenn H., ed. and trans. 1985. *Selected Works of the Dalai Lama I.* Ithaca: Snow Lion Publications.

Nakamura, Hajime. 1987. *Indian Buddhism: A Survey with Bibliographical Notes.* Delhi: Motilal Banarsidass.

Napper, Elizabeth. 1989. *Dependent Arising and Emptiness.* Boston: Wisdom Publications.

Obermiller, E., trans. 1984. *Uttaratantra or Ratnagotravibhaga: The Sublime Science of the Great Vehicle to Salvation.* Talent, OR: Canon Publications.

Pabongka Rinpoche. 1990–94. *Liberation in Our Hands.* 2 vols. Geshe Lobsang Tharchin and Artemus Engle, trans. Howell, N.J.: Mahayana Sutra and Tantra Press.

———. 1991. *Liberation in the Palm of Your Hands.* Michael Richards, trans. Boston: Wisdom Publications.

Patt, David. 1993. *Elucidating The Path to Liberation: A Study of The Commentary on The "Abhidharmakośa" by The First Dalai Lama.* Ph.D. Thesis, University of Wisconsin.

People's Publishing House. 1984. *Bod rgya tshig mdzod chen mo (Tibetan-Chinese Dictionary).* 3 vols. Beijing.

Powers, John. 1995. *Introduction to Tibetan Buddhism.* Ithaca: Snow Lion Publications.

Pruden, Leo M., trans. 1988. *Abhidharmakośabhāṣyam by Louis de La Vallée Poussin.* 4 vols. Berkeley: Asian Humanities Press.

Rabten, Geshe. 1981. *The Mind and Its Functions.* Stephen Batchelor, trans. and ed. Mt. Pelerin, Switzerland: Tharpa Choeling.

Rigzin, Tsepak. 1986. *Tibetan-English Dictionary of Buddhist Terminology.* Dharamsala: Library of Tibetan Works & Archives.

Rinchen, Geshe Sonam. 1994. *Yogic Deeds of the Bodhisattvas.* Ruth Sonam, trans. and ed. Ithaca: Snow Lion Publications.

———. 1997. *Atisha's "Lamp for the Path."* Ruth Sonam, trans. and ed. Ithaca: Snow Lion Publications.

Rockhill, W. Woodville, tr. 1982. *Udanavarga: A Collection of Verses from the Buddhist Canon.* New Delhi: D.K. Publisher's Distributors.

Sadakata, Akira. 1997. *Buddhist Cosmology: Philosophy and Origins.* Gaynor Sekimori, trans. Tokyo: Kosei Publishing Co.

Śāntideva. 1960. *Bodhicaryāvatāra.* Vidhushekhara Bhattacharya, ed. Calcutta: Asiatic Society

———. 1995. *The Bodhicaryāvatāra.* Kate Crosby and Andrew Skilton, trans. Oxford: Oxford University Press.

———. 1979. *A Guide to the Bodhisattva's Way of Life.* Stephen Batchelor, trans. Dharamsala: Library of Tibetan Works and Archives.

———. 1997. *A Guide to the Bodhisattva Way of Life.* Vesna A. Wallace and B. Allan Wallace, trans. Ithaca: Snow Lion Publications.

Sa skya Pandita Kun dga' rgyal mtshan. 1968. *Treasury of Good Advice (Sa skya'i legs bshad).* Delhi: Tenzin Chagdor.

Sherburne, Richard, trans. 2000. *The Complete Works of Atiśa.* New Delhi: Aditya Prakashan.

Sopa, Geshe Lhundub. 1986. "The Special Theory of Pratītyasamutpāda: The Cycle of Dependent Origination." *Journal of the International Association of Buddhist Studies* 9, no. 1: 105–18.

Sopa, Geshe Lhundub, and Jeffrey Hopkins. 1976. *Practice and Theory of Tibetan Buddhism.* New York: Grove Press.

Sparham, Gareth, trans. 1983. *The Tibetan Dhammapada compiled by Dharmatrāta.* London: Wisdom Publications.

Speyer, J.S., trans. 1982. *The Jātakamālā or Garland of Birth-Stories of Āryaśūra.* Delhi: Motilal Banarsidass.

Stcherbatsky, Theodore. 1976. *The Soul Theory of the Buddhists.* Delhi: Bharatiya Vidya Prakashan.

———. 1988. *The Central Conception of Buddhism.* Delhi: Motilal Banarsidass.

Takasaki, Jikido. 1966. *A Study of the Ratnagotravibhāga (Uttaratantra).* Serie Orientale Roma 33. Rome: Istituto Italiano per il Medio ed Estremo Oriente.

Tharchin, Geshe Lobsang. 1979. *The Logic and Debate Tradition of India, Tibet, and Mongolia.* Howell, N.J.: Rashi Gempil Ling First Kalmuk Buddhist Temple.

Thurman, Robert A.F., ed. 1982. *Life and Teachings of Tsong Khapa.* Dharamsala: Library of Tibetan Works and Archives.

Tsongkhapa. *Foundations of All Good Qualities (Yon tan gzhir gyur ma* in *Byang chub lam gyi rim pa'i brgyud pa rnams la gsol ba 'debs pa'i rim pa "Lam mchog sgo 'byed" shes bya ba).* P6003, vol. 153.

———. *In Praise of Dependent Arising (Sangs rgyas bcom ldan 'das la zab mo rten cing 'grel bar 'byung ba gsung ba'i sgo nas bstod pa legs par bshad pa'i snying po),* P6016, vol. 153.

———. *Spiritual Biography: My Destiny Fulfilled (Rang gi rtogs pa brjod pa mdo tsam du bshad pa)*, P6060, vol. 153.

———. 1985. *Mnyam med tshong kha pa chen pos mdzad pa'i Byang chub lam rim che ba.* Zi-ling (Xining): mTsho sngon Mi rigs dPe skrun khang (Kokonor People's Press). P6001, vol. 152.

———. 1988. *The Principal Teachings of Buddhism.* Geshe Lobsang Tharchin with Michael Roach, trans. Howell, NJ: Mahayana Sutra and Tantra Press.

———. 2000. *The Great Treatise on the Stages of the Path to Enlightenment.* vol. 1. The Lamrim Chenmo Translation Committee, Joshua W.C. Cutler, Editor-in-Chief, trans. Ithaca: Snow Lion Publications.

———. 1978–83. *Three Principal Aspects of the Path (Lam gyi gtso bo rnam gsum)*, in *The collected works (gsuṅ 'bum) of the incomparable Lord Tsoṅ-kha-pa Blo-bzaṅ-grags-pa*, vol. 2 (kha). New Delhi: Mongolian Lama Gurudeva.

Vasubandhu (sLob dpon dByig gnyen). 1969. *Chos mngon pa mdzod kyi bshad pa.* Dharamsala: Council of Cultural & Religious Affairs of His Holiness the Dalai Lama.

———. 1978. *Chos mngon pa'i mdzod kyi tshig le'ur byas pa.* 3rd ed. Sarnath: Sarnath Legs bshad gter mdzod par khang.

———. 1981. *Abhidharmakośa and Bhāṣya of Ācārya Vasubandhu with Sphuṭārthā Commentary of Ācārya Yaśomitra.* 2nd ed. Swāmi Dwārikādās Śastri, ed. Varanasi: Bauddha Bharati.

Waldron, William S. 1990. "The Alayavijñana in the Context of Indian Buddhist Thought: The Yogacara Conception of an Unconscious." Ph.D. Thesis, University of Wisconsin.

Wangyal, Geshe. 1978. *The Door of Liberation.* New York: Lotsawa.

Warren, Henry Clarke. 1977. *Buddhism in Translations.* New York: Atheneum.

Whitney, William Dwight. 1983. *Sanskrit Grammar.* Delhi: Motilal Banarsidass.

Zahler, Leah, Jeffrey Hopkins, Lati Rinbochay, and Denma Locho Rinbochay. 1983. *Meditative States in Tibetan Buddhism.* London: Wisdom Publications.

Index

About Wisdom

Wisdom Publications, a nonprofit publisher, is dedicated to making available authentic Buddhist works for the benefit of all. We publish translations of the sutras and tantras, commentaries and teachings of past and contemporary Buddhist masters, and original works by the world's leading Buddhist scholars. We publish our titles with the appreciation of Buddhism as a living philosophy and with the special commitment to preserve and transmit important works from all the major Buddhist traditions.

To learn more about Wisdom, or to browse books online, visit our website at www.wisdompubs.org. You may request a copy of our mail-order catalog online or by writing to:

Wisdom Publications
199 Elm Street
Somerville, Massachusetts 02144 USA
Telephone: (617) 776-7416
Fax: (617) 776-7841
Email: info@wisdompubs.org
www.wisdompubs.org

The Wisdom Trust

As a nonprofit publisher, Wisdom is dedicated to the publication of fine Dharma books for the benefit of all sentient beings and dependent upon the kindness and generosity of sponsors in order to do so. If you would like to make a donation to Wisdom, please do so through our Somerville office. If you would like to sponsor the publication of a book, please write or email us at the address above.

Thank you.

Wisdom is a nonprofit, charitable 501(c)(3) organization affiliated with the Foundation for the Preservation of the Mahayana Tradition (FPMT).